8 Real SATs

8 Real SATs

College Entrance Examination Board, New York

The College Board is a national nonprofit association that champions educational excellence for all students through the ongoing collaboration of more than 3,000 member schools, colleges, universities, education systems, and associations. The Board promotes—by means of responsive forums, research, programs, and policy development—universal access to high standards of learning, equity of opportunity, and sufficient financial support so that every student is prepared for success in college and work.

Copies of this book are available from your bookseller or may be ordered from College Board Publications, Box 886, New York, New York, 10101-0886. The price is $16.95.

Editorial inquiries concerning this book should be addressed to the College Board, 45 Columbus Avenue, New York, New York 10023-6992.

International Standard Book Number: 0-87447-550-3

Library of Congress Card Catalog Number: 96-085401

Contents

Preface...vii

Part One: Introducing the SAT I 1
Chapter 1: What's in the Test? 3
   About the SAT I...4
   Preparing for the Test.................................5
   Understanding Your Scores 6
   Using Your Scores 7
   Student Services...8
   The PSAT/NMSQT.....................................8
Chapter 2: Test-Taking Strategies.....................11
   The Golden Rules of Test Taking 12
   Pacing 16
   Guessing 18
Chapter 3: Psyching Yourself Up 23
   Relaxation Techniques 24

Part Two: SAT I: Verbal Reasoning 27
Chapter 4: Sample Verbal Questions
and Answers 29
   Introduction 30
   Analogy Questions 33
   Sentence Completion Questions...................42
   Critical Reading Questions...........................53
Chapter 5: Practice Questions 73
   Independent Practice.................................74
   Answer Key...80

**Part Three: SAT I: Mathematical
Reasoning 81**
Chapter 6: Mathematics Review........................83
   Introduction to the Mathematics Sections 84
   Concepts You Need to Know 84
   Math Reference Material...............................86
   Types of Questions 86
   Calculators Are Recommended......................93
   Some General Tips 95
   Arithmetic Concepts You Should Know........95
Chapter 7: Sample Mathematics Questions
and Answers 133
   Introduction 134
   Five-Choice Multiple-Choice Questions.........135
   Quantitative Comparison Questions 159
   Grid-in Questions 170

**Part Four: Ten Complete Practice Tests
With Answer Keys.......................................185**

Preface

The SAT I: Reasoning Test was introduced in March of 1994. This book is intended first and foremost to explain clearly what the SAT I is and to give students an opportunity to become familiar with the different types of questions they will encounter. It also offers a variety of strategies for test takers both for approaching the SAT I as a whole and for tackling specific types of questions. Our intention was not to present a hard-and-fast method for taking the test, but to give students the tools with which to approach the SAT I in a positive frame of mind. While every effort has been made to ensure that the contents of this book are as up-to-date as possible, students are urged to consult the free publication, *Taking the SAT I*, for the most current information on the test.

How This Book Is Organized

This book is divided into four parts. The first offers a general introduction to the SAT I: Reasoning Test as well as valuable test-taking strategies. It is not intended to help students "psych out" the test. Instead, the information is meant to help students develop sound techniques that will enable them to do their best in what, for some, can be a stressful situation. The section should also enable students to approach the SAT I with realistic expectations. We recommend that students try out the different techniques using either the practice verbal and mathematical questions given in Parts Two and Three or other SAT I test-preparation materials.

Parts Two and Three deal specifically with the Verbal and Mathematical sections of the SAT I. They contain an in-depth discussion of each type of question a student will encounter on the test, as well as hints and strategies for answering them. Students should use these sections to become familiar with the questions, the test instructions, and the kind of answers required. Particular attention should be paid to the Student-Produced Response (Grid-in) questions in the mathematical section. This type of question requires that the answers be given in specific formats. Students should also become familiar with the paired Reading Passage format, which requires them to answer questions comparing and contrasting two related passages.

The sections dealing with the Verbal and Mathematical questions are arranged somewhat differently. Part Two, which deals with the verbal questions, contains two sets of practice questions in Chapters 4 and 5. Those in Chapter 4 are accompanied not only by answers, but by explanations and hints as well. Students can use the explanations and hints to hone their skills and develop their test-taking strategies. The questions in Chapter 5 are intended for students to use independently to check their progress and identify areas where further review is needed. After completing the practice questions, students may want to review specific material in Chapter 4 before taking the practice test.

Part Three contains two chapters. The first, Mathematics Review, describes the concepts and operations that will appear on the SAT I. It is not intended to replace a solid high school mathematics program, but should help the reader identify strengths and areas where further review is needed. Chapter 7 contains practice questions arranged by type of question—Multiple Choice, Quantitative Comparison, and Grid-in—followed by complete solutions to each one. While the solutions given reflect current classroom practice, we realize there is more than one way to find the right answer. Students should use the techniques they are most comfortable with to solve the problems and shouldn't be concerned if their methods are different from the ones given. On the other hand, if a student has difficulty with particular types of problems, studying the sample solutions should help him or her develop the skills needed to solve similar problems in the future.

The final section contains practice tests: two editions of the PSAT/NMSQT and eight editions of the SAT I. We recommend taking them under timed conditions and using the results along with Part One of this book to set realistic goals for the actual test-taking experience.

How to Use This Book

8 Real SATs provides readers with ample opportunity for practicing with the different types of questions that will appear on the SAT I. While the best preparation for the test is still a solid course of study in high school, the practice questions should help students—and their teachers, parents, and counselors—identify strengths and areas that will require additional work. In this sense, it should help readers with long-term preparation for the SAT I and beyond. On the other hand, the hint boxes and marginal notes will allow readers to quickly find and review important information shortly before taking the test. Each chapter also includes a table of contents, so that needed material is easily accessible. The staff of the College Board hopes that you will find this book both easy to use and helpful. If you have specific comments or questions, please write to us at: College Board SAT Program, P.O. Box 6200, Princeton, NJ 08541-6200, or e-mail us at: sat@ets.org.

PART ONE

Introducing the SAT I

▲ ▼ ▲ **Chapter 1**
What's in the Test?

▲ ▼ ▲ **Chapter 2**
Test-Taking Strategies

▲ ▼ ▲ **Chapter 3**
Psyching Yourself Up

CHAPTER ONE

What's in the Test?

About the SAT I 4

Preparing for the Test 5
Short-Term Preparation............................5
Long-Term Preparation 5
Gaining Points..6

Understanding Your Scores 6
The SAT I Scoring System 6
Score Range 7
Percentiles 7

Using Your Scores 7

Student Services 8
Question and Answer Service 8
Student Answer Service............................8

The PSAT/NMSQT 8
Practice for the SAT I................................9
Preparing for the PSAT/NMSQT 9
Scholarships 9
Student Search Service 10

About the SAT I

The SAT I is designed to help predict your freshman grades in college, so that admission officers can make appropriate decisions about your chances of succeeding in the courses you will take at their colleges.

The SAT I includes both verbal and math sections, with a total of six types of questions.

Types of Questions

Verbal	#	Math	#
Analogies	19	Five-choice	35
Sentence Completions	19	Quantitative Comparisons	15
Critical Reading	40	Grid-ins*	10
Total	78	Total	60

*(Student-produced responses)

Timing

The SAT I is three hours long and consists of seven test sections:

3 Verbal Sections	3 Math Sections
30 minutes	30 minutes
30 minutes	30 minutes
15 minutes	15 minutes

1 More Verbal or Math
Equating Section**
30 minutes

**The equating section will not count toward your final score. It is used to try out new questions for future editions of the SAT I and to help make sure that your test scores are comparable to scores on other editions of the SAT I. You won't be able to tell which section this is.

Preparing for the Test

Test preparation can be divided into two broad categories: short-term and long-term.

- Short-term preparation gets the quickest results.
- Long-term preparation has the biggest potential payoff.

Short-Term Preparation

Short-term preparation focuses on the test itself. It includes specific test-taking tips and techniques, including:

- Knowing what to expect from the test: what types of questions, how many questions, in what order.
- Knowing the test directions.
- Learning how to pace yourself.
- Learning when and how to guess.
- Knowing how to identify the easiest questions.
- Learning specific approaches for each of the six types of test questions.

These are the types of tips and hints you'll find in Chapter 2.

Short-term preparation is designed to make sure that you correctly answer every question that you currently have the ability to answer.

Short-term preparation can gain you some points on the test. But alone it doesn't help you become a more able student.

Long-Term Preparation

Long-term preparation focuses on your overall academic performance. It's designed to improve your abilities—to help you gain the skills necessary to answer more difficult questions. Long-term preparation includes things you can and should be doing all year, such as:

- Reading effectively: gives you the ability to figure out what the author means as well as merely what the author says.
- Improving your vocabulary: gives you tools to figure out new words from the context in which they are used.
- Developing your problem-solving abilities: helps you figure out what to do and how to do it, and helps you get started on challenging problems when you seem to be stumped.

Remember, short-term preparation helps you correctly answer all the questions you already can. Long-term preparation, on the other hand, can actually help you improve your abilities so that you can answer even more questions correctly. Ultimately, long-term preparation can have the greatest effect both on your scores and on how well you'll do in college.

Gaining Points

Based on statistical findings of the Educational Testing Service (ETS) and the College Board, your SAT I scores will probably go up a little if you take the test more than once. But a gain is not guaranteed. The higher your first test score, the less likely you are to improve and the smaller the improvement is likely to be. Also, taking the test more than a couple of times will probably not bring about continued score gains.

Improving your overall abilities through long-term preparation can result in higher scores.

 HINTS

THINGS YOU SHOULD DO

1. Make sure you're familiar with the test.
2. Make sure you're familiar with the tips and techniques in this book.
3. Practice.
4. Limit your test-specific preparation to 12 to 20 hours, at most. This can be done reasonably close to the time you take the test— within a month or two.
5. Work on your long-term preparation. Use the strategies in this book throughout your high school career.
6. Continue to work hard in school.

Understanding Your Scores

This chapter is designed to clear up a lot of mysteries surrounding the SAT—how the test is scored, what the scores mean, and how the scores should be used.

The SAT I Scoring System

The SAT I is scored in the following way: first, the number of questions answered right minus a fraction of the multiple-choice questions answered wrong is computed. (No points are earned or subtracted for unanswered questions, and nothing is subtracted from your score for incorrect answers to grid-in questions.) If the resulting score includes a fraction, the score is rounded to the nearest whole number—1/2 or more is rounded up, less than 1/2 is rounded down.

Your score is then converted into a 200 (lowest) to 800 (highest) scaled score using a statistical process called equating. Tests are equated to adjust for minor differences between test editions. Equating assures test takers and colleges that a score of, say, 450, on one edition of a test indicates the same level of ability as a score of 450 on another edition. The equating process also ensures that your score doesn't depend on how well others did on the same test. The tests are not marked on a curve, so you won't be marked down if other students do very well on the test.

Score Range

No test can ever measure your skills precisely, but it can provide good estimates. If you took many editions of the test within a short time, your scores would tend to vary, but not too far above or below your actual abilities. The score range is an estimate of how your scores might vary if you were tested many times. The SAT I score range is usually about 32 points above and below your specific numerical score, and it indicates the range in which your true abilities probably fall.

Percentiles

In addition to the scaled SAT I score, you'll also get a percentile score. This compares your scores to the scores of other students who took the test. The comparison is given as a number between 1 and 99 that tells what percentage of students earned a score lower than yours. For example, if your percentile is 53, it means that out of every 100 test takers in the comparison group, you performed better than 53 of them.

Your percentile changes depending on the group with which you are being compared. For the SAT I, your national percentile (all recently graduated college-bound seniors from across the nation who took the test) is often higher than your state percentile (all recently graduated college-bound seniors from your state who took the test). That's mainly because the national group contains a larger, more diverse group of test takers.

Using Your Scores

Along with your score, your score range, and percentile score, the SAT I score report gives you raw score information (the number you got right, wrong, or omitted) for different types of verbal and math questions. This information can help you analyze your performance.

Your score report will also provide the profiles of up to four colleges or universities to which you asked that your scores be sent. These profiles include institutional characteristics, what high school preparation is required, freshman admission policies, and cost/financial aid information. If you fill out the Student Descriptive Questionnaire, that information will also be included.

Guides such as *The College Handbook* often provide information about SAT I scores of enrolled freshmen. (Your score report will also contain this information.) If your scores are in the range of the scores at a campus you are interested in, you will probably be able to handle the academic challenge there. If your scores fall far below, you may be in for a struggle. If your scores are much higher, you may not be academically challenged at that campus.

You should not, however, select a college simply because your scores match the profile of students already enrolled there. Perhaps you perform best under pressure and need the challenge of a tough academic environment. Or, a particular college may offer a unique program or social environment that makes it right for you.

Student Services

You can order these services when you register for the SAT I, or you can use the order form that is sent with your score report.

Question and Answer Service

For the disclosed administrations (specified in the *Registration Bulletin*) this service provides you with a computer-generated report that lists the question number, the correct answer, your answer, the type of question, and the difficulty level of that question. You will also receive the actual questions from the edition of the test you took, so you can review your work on that test.

Student Answer Service

This service is available if the Question and Answer Service is not offered. The Student Answer Service provides your answer, the correct answer, the type of question, and difficulty level of that question. This service does not provide the test questions but can help you identify types of questions on which you performed well or poorly.

The PSAT/NMSQT

The PSAT/NMSQT serves three main purposes:

- Provides one of the best ways to practice for the SAT I.
- Is the first step in qualifying for scholarships sponsored by the National Merit Scholarship Corporation and other scholarship programs.
- Gives you the opportunity to participate in the Student Search Service (SSS).

Practice for the SAT I

Because the PSAT/NMSQT is composed of test questions that have been used previously on the SAT I, it is one of the best ways to practice. The main difference in the tests is that the PSAT/NMSQT is shorter than the SAT I, with about 108 questions instead of 138 questions.

Preparing for the PSAT/NMSQT

The six types of questions on the PSAT/NMSQT are the same as on the SAT I, so here's what you'll need to do to prepare:

1. Familiarize yourself with each type of SAT question.
2. Practice applying the hints and tips in this book.
3. Go through the math review section carefully. If it's close to exam time, concentrate on the math skills and concepts that you've studied but may need to review. If you have time before the test, start learning some of the unfamiliar skills and concepts.
4. Make sure you're familiar with the basic test-taking tips in Chapter 2—Test-Taking Strategies.
5. Recognize the differences in how the PSAT/NMSQT and the SAT are organized.

Scholarships

The National Merit Scholarship Corporation uses PSAT/NMSQT scores to help select students who wish to enter its scholarship programs. Many corporations and other scholarship programs also use the test scores as part of their criteria for selecting students for scholarships.

The two primary sources of information about these programs are the PSAT/NMSQT *Student Bulletin* and the counseling office in your high school. The *Bulletin* is available, free, from your high school counseling office. It contains test information as well as information on many of the scholarship programs that use the test scores.

Check with your counselor and with specific scholarship programs to find out what scores you need in order to qualify. Most students are not taking the PSAT/NMSQT to compete for scholarships. For the majority of test takers, the PSAT/NMSQT is practice for the SAT I.

Student Search Service

The Student Search Service helps colleges find prospective students. When you take the PSAT/NMSQT, you can ask to be included in this free Search. Here's how it works.

When you indicate on the answer sheet that you want to be part of the Search, your name is put in a data base along with other information you provide: address, high school grade-point average, social security number, intended college major, and projected career.

Colleges and scholarship programs then use the Search to help them locate and recruit students with characteristics they are interested in.

Things to keep in mind about the Student Search Service:

- Your participation is voluntary. You may take the test without participating in the Search.
- Colleges participating in the search do not receive your PSAT/NMSQT scores. They can ask for the names of students within certain score ranges, but your exact score is not reported.
- Being contacted by a college is not the same as being admitted. You can be admitted only after you apply. The Student Search Service is a means by which colleges reach prospective students, that's all.
- You may also participate in the Student Search Service when you take the SAT I, SAT II, or Advanced Placement (AP) Examinations.

CHAPTER TWO

Test-Taking Strategies

The Golden Rules of Test Taking........12
1. Know the Directions...........................12
2. Keep Moving 12
3. Check Your Answer Sheet.................13
4. Don't Panic 13
5. Don't Throw Away Points..................14
6. Use Your Test Booklet 14
7. Eliminate Choices.............................15

Pacing 16
Strategies for Pacing 16
Critical Reading...................................17
Don't Lose Work You've Done 17
Rushing Loses You Time.......................18
Keep a Steady Pace.............................18

Guessing..18
Some Good Advice About Guessing.......19
Guessing Experiment...........................20

The Golden Rules of Test Taking

The following Golden Rules are designed to help you make sure that you don't lose points unnecessarily.

⚡ THE GOLDEN RULES

1. **Know the Directions**
   Make sure you're thoroughly familiar with the directions for every type of question on the SAT I before you actually take it.

2. **Keep Moving**
   Never spend lots of time on any one question until you have tried all of the other questions in the section.

3. **Check Your Answer Sheet**
   Always check the number of the question and the number on the answer sheet to be sure you're putting the answer in the right place. Check your sheet every few questions.

4. **Don't Panic**
   Don't worry over questions that you can't answer. Feel good about each question you can answer.

5. **Don't Throw Away Points to Carelessness**
   Never go so fast that you lose points on easy questions through careless errors.

6. **Use Your Test Booklet As Scratch Paper**
   Make a mess of your test booklet if it helps you—marking, noting, and drawing as needed. But don't waste too much time; you get credit only for answers marked on your answer sheet.

7. **Eliminate Choices**
   If you are unsure of the correct answer, try eliminating one or more choices before giving up on any question.

---

1. Know the Directions

Take some time to read the directions carefully for different types of questions. (The practice questions in Parts 2 and 3 are a good place to begin.) That way, you won't lose time reading the directions on the day you take the SAT. You'll feel more confident and be less likely to make careless errors because you will understand the instructions. This strategy is particularly important in the math sections for the quantitative comparisons and the student-produced responses ("grid-ins").

2. Keep Moving

The single biggest time waster (and therefore the single biggest point stealer) is getting hung up on a question.

If you can't answer a question without spending a long time figuring it out, go on to the next one. If you aren't sure about how to answer a question, or you don't know where to begin, stop working on that question. You may have time to come back to it later.

Put a mark in *your test booklet (not on your answer sheet)* next to any question that you don't answer. That way, you'll be able to find it easily when you go back.

A two-way marking system works well for many students:

1. Put a question mark (?) in the margin next to any question you didn't answer but that you have a reasonable chance of answering with some more time.
2. Put an X next to any question that you don't think you have much chance of answering correctly.

A system like this one takes very little time, thought, or effort, and can save lots of time when you go back through the test.

? 1.

X 2.

3. Check Your Answer Sheet

Losing your place on the answer sheet can be a major problem that affects your score. But it's easy to prevent this from happening. Here's how you might lose your place.

- You're moving through the test. You get stuck on a couple of questions, so you jump ahead. (A good use of your testing time.)
- You're concentrating on the next question. (And you're congratulating yourself for being able to find questions you can answer instead of wasting time on ones that you can't.)
- Then you get to the last question of the section, and realize you're off on the answer sheet. *When you skipped the questions, you forgot to skip ahead on your answer sheet!*

Protect yourself by checking the number of the question and the number on the answer sheet every few questions. Check them carefully every time you skip a question.

4. Don't Panic

Getting panicky or depressed can be a subtle but very serious problem when you're taking the SAT. If you find that there are lots of questions you can't answer, you have to work hard to keep your focus on the ones that you can. If you aren't concentrating on the question you're working on, you are less likely to answer it correctly.

Avoiding Test Panic

1. Remember that some questions are harder than many on the classroom tests you take. It's all right to find questions you can't answer.
2. Remember that you don't have to answer every question. You can miss a lot of questions and still get an average score.

3. If you get that sweaty-palm, I'm-getting-a-headache feeling:

- Take a few deep breaths.
- Tell yourself that you're taking one question at a time.
- Tell yourself that every question you get right is worth points and you're not going to let any of those points get away.
- Then go on with the test.

4. Each time you find a question you can answer, congratulate yourself and start looking for the next one.

Some of this advice may seem pretty simple, but it's very important. There's more like it in the chapter on "Psyching Yourself Up."

5. Don't Throw Away Points to Carelessness

Don't rush! Be sure to consider all of the choices in each question. You could lose points on easy questions through careless errors. Work quickly but accurately. No matter how frustrated you are, don't pass over questions without, at least, reading through them. Take each question as it comes.

Here are a few things you can do to keep from losing points through carelessness:

1. Make sure you are answering the question asked. For example, if you are asked to find the area of a shaded region, you do not want to answer with the unshaded area.
2. Always read all the answers to a verbal question before choosing the one you think is correct.
3. For math questions, especially word problems, check to see whether your answer makes sense. Is a discount bigger than the original price? Is someone making $150 an hour selling Girl Scout cookies? Is the average age of the students in a high school class 56 years old?
4. Again for math, when you check your work, start from the beginning. If you can, use a *different* method than the one you used to get the answer. If you use the same method, you may make the same mistake twice.
5. Try to work at an even, steady pace. It's important to keep moving and to avoid wasting time, but it's never a good idea to work so quickly that you make careless mistakes.

6. Use Your Test Booklet As Scratch Paper

While you have to keep your *answer sheet* neat and free of stray marks, you can mark up your test booklet. You can write whatever you want, wherever you want, in the section of the booklet you're working on. You will not receive credit for anything written in the booklet.

How should you use your test booklet?

1. You know one suggestion already—mark each question using the **?**, **X** system described on page 13.
2. When you're working on a question, put a line through each choice as you eliminate it.
3. Feel free to use your pencil to mark sections, sentences, or words in reading passages.
4. In math, make drawings to help you figure out word problems. Mark key information on graphs. Add information to drawings and diagrams as you figure.

Mark your booklet in any way that will help you work efficiently, find information, or figure out the answers.

7. Eliminate Choices

Don't give up right away if you can't answer a question. Take a shot at eliminating choices.

It's sometimes easier to eliminate the wrong choices than it is to find the one correct answer.

- On some questions, you can eliminate all the choices until you have only the one correct answer left.
- In some cases, eliminating some choices helps you think your way through to the correct answer.
- If you can eliminate any choice as definitely wrong, it will pay over the long run to guess an answer from among the other choices.

Developing a good strategy for guessing is covered in detail beginning on page 18.

RECAP: GOLDEN RULES

The Golden Rules are principles you should keep in mind throughout the test. Once again, they are:

1. **Know the Directions**
   Don't lose time on test day reading the directions for the first time.
2. **Keep Moving**
   Don't get hung up on any one question.
3. **Check Your Answer Sheet**
   Don't mark answers in the wrong place.
4. **Don't Panic**
   Focus on what you can do, not on what seems difficult.
5. **Don't Throw Away Points to Carelessness**
   Keep moving but don't rush.
6. **Use Your Test Booklet As Scratch Paper**
   Write or mark anything that will help you.
7. **Eliminate Choices**
   If you can't answer the question, try to identify wrong answers.

Pacing

Pacing is based on the idea that each question on the test takes a certain amount of time to read and answer. If you had unlimited time, or very few questions to answer, pacing would not be a problem.

Strategies for Pacing

Following are some basic principles of pacing—strategies that will help ensure that you don't waste time on the SAT I and that you'll have time to consider all the questions you have the ability to answer.

Keep Moving

One of the Golden Rules of test taking is that you should always keep moving. Don't spend so much time puzzling out hard questions that you lose the time to find and answer the easier ones. Work on less time-consuming questions before moving on to time-consuming ones. You get the same credit for every correct answer, no matter how long it took you to figure it out.

SOME REMINDERS:
- Mark the questions as you work on them, especially the ones you want to go back to, so you can find them later.
- If you can eliminate any choices on the way, cross out those you have eliminated. This will also save time when you come back to the question.

Easy to Hard

The SAT I is designed so that most test takers have time to consider most of the questions. But the more time-consuming questions tend to be at the end of each section, so a student halfway through a section with one-half of the time already used is not likely to reach all of the questions. You can get a good score without finishing every question on the test. But by pacing yourself and working on the easier questions first, you'll be optimizing your testing time.

VERBAL: In general, it's best to work from easy to hard. Analogy and Sentence Completion questions are arranged in order of difficulty. The easier questions come first, followed by the more difficult ones. If you find that the Sentence Completions are getting too hard, look through the rest of the questions quickly, then jump ahead to the beginning of the Analogy questions to pick up the easy ones.

The Critical Reading questions are *not* necessarily arranged in easy-to-hard order. More hints on pacing your way through the Reading Passages are given in "Critical Reading Questions" in Part Two of this book and in the sample Critical Reading passages in Chapter 4.

MATH: Math questions generally go from easy to hard, but there's a little more variety in their arrangement. Look for the easiest math questions at the beginning of each section and answer these first, then move to the questions that take longer.

Going After the Math You Know

Unless you're a math whiz, you'll probably find that some types of math questions are easier for you than others. Here's a tip for handling the math sections more efficiently:

- First, work on the questions that you're sure you know how to answer.
- Second, work on the questions that have familiar concepts and procedures.
- Save the really tough ones for last.

Critical Reading

Because Critical Reading questions are based on the passage, once you make the investment in reading the passage, don't throw away the time and effort you've put into it.

1. Try to answer all the questions you can about one reading passage before you move on to another passage or go back to the analogies and sentence completions.
2. Keep moving. If one question slows you down, move on to the other questions on that passage. But, go back to the tough questions and give them a second try before moving to another passage.

   There are two reasons for this strategy. First, you don't want to have to reread the passage to figure out the tough questions later. Second, you may pick up extra information from the passage that will help you answer one question when you are searching for the answers to others.
3. The fastest reading questions to answer are usually the vocabulary-in-context questions. They ask the meaning of a word as it is used in the passage.

Don't Lose Work You've Done

You don't want to have to start over when you come back to a question.

1. Make sure you mark (in the test booklet) all questions you want to come back to.
2. Cross out in the test booklet any choices you have been able to eliminate.

> *REMEMBER:*
> Always check that the question number in your test book and on your answer sheet agree every time you skip a question.

Rushing Loses You Time

- If you try to go too fast, you won't think clearly and you'll take extra time settling down to work on the more challenging questions.
- Rushing promotes carelessness. Correcting careless errors takes time; not correcting them is even worse. Both situations could lower your score significantly.
- Rushing makes you concentrate on going fast instead of on answering questions. You should keep an even pace so you can concentrate on each question as you face it.

Keep a Steady Pace

If you remember only one thing, it's this: Work steadily. Don't rush. Don't stop.

RECAP: PACING

Keep moving.
Work from easier to harder questions (when possible).
Work on familiar types of math problems first.
Answer all the questions you can on one reading passage before
    moving on to the next.
Know when and how to move on.
Keep a steady pace.

Guessing

There's a lot of misunderstanding about guessing on the SAT. The fact is, the scoring system for all the multiple-choice questions is set up so that you will get one point for each correct answer and lose a fraction of a point for each wrong answer. Questions that you omit will neither gain nor lose points.

The deduction for a wrong answer is designed to offset exactly the chance of getting the answer right by wild guessing. Does that mean you should never guess? No! Sometimes guessing is a good idea.

SOME GOOD ADVICE ABOUT GUESSING

If you can eliminate one or more choices as definitely wrong, then it is to your advantage to guess among the choices that are left.

The more choices you can eliminate as definitely wrong, the better your odds of getting the correct answer.

There is one type of question on which there is no deduction for a wrong answer: the grid-in math questions, for which you have to write in your own answer instead of choosing. If you worked out an answer but are not certain it is correct, go ahead and grid it in—you won't lose any points.

If you can eliminate some choices on multiple-choice questions, you can make an educated guess. The following question, though not at all like an SAT question, provides a simple example of how educated guessing works.

Which of the following is true of Hydra, the monster of Greek legend?

(A) It lured sailors with music.
(B) It had many heads.
(C) It shopped at the mall.
(D) It wrote Beethoven's 5th symphony.
(E) It is the lead singer for a punk-rock group.

You might not know exactly who/what Hydra is, but you should be able to eliminate some of the choices using common sense. Generally speaking, monsters—especially if they're legendary—don't shop at malls. Odds are, Beethoven wrote his own symphony. And, to fit the description, the punk rocker would have to be both Greek and a legend—not to mention a monster. So that leaves you with choices A and B.

If you guess from among the two remaining choices, your chance of getting the question right is better than the penalty for getting it wrong. You should guess.

To see the difference between wild guessing and making an educated guess (where you can eliminate some answers), try the exercise at the end of this chapter.

The more choices you can eliminate, the better your odds. But even if you can eliminate only one choice, your odds of guessing correctly improve.

Guessing Experiment
Wild guessing

The answer grid below represents a set of wild guessing questions. To make sure that you're making wild guesses, you're not even going to get to see the questions!

Fill in the answer grid below to see how you do in a wild guessing situation:

Wild guessing score:

Number of
right answers _____

Minus 1/4 point
for each wrong
answer _____

Total _____

1. Ⓐ Ⓑ Ⓒ Ⓓ Ⓔ
2. Ⓐ Ⓑ Ⓒ Ⓓ Ⓔ
3. Ⓐ Ⓑ Ⓒ Ⓓ Ⓔ
4. Ⓐ Ⓑ Ⓒ Ⓓ Ⓔ
5. Ⓐ Ⓑ Ⓒ Ⓓ Ⓔ
6. Ⓐ Ⓑ Ⓒ Ⓓ Ⓔ
7. Ⓐ Ⓑ Ⓒ Ⓓ Ⓔ
8. Ⓐ Ⓑ Ⓒ Ⓓ Ⓔ
9. Ⓐ Ⓑ Ⓒ Ⓓ Ⓔ
10. Ⓐ Ⓑ Ⓒ Ⓓ Ⓔ
11. Ⓐ Ⓑ Ⓒ Ⓓ Ⓔ
12. Ⓐ Ⓑ Ⓒ Ⓓ Ⓔ
13. Ⓐ Ⓑ Ⓒ Ⓓ Ⓔ
14. Ⓐ Ⓑ Ⓒ Ⓓ Ⓔ
15. Ⓐ Ⓑ Ⓒ Ⓓ Ⓔ
16. Ⓐ Ⓑ Ⓒ Ⓓ Ⓔ
17. Ⓐ Ⓑ Ⓒ Ⓓ Ⓔ
18. Ⓐ Ⓑ Ⓒ Ⓓ Ⓔ
19. Ⓐ Ⓑ Ⓒ Ⓓ Ⓔ
20. Ⓐ Ⓑ Ⓒ Ⓓ Ⓔ

Now score your wild guessing test. The answers are on page 22.
Give yourself 1 point for each correct answer.
Most people will come out pretty close to zero.
If you don't . . . well, remember, wild guessing is about odds.

Educated guessing

To test educated guessing, two choices on each question have been eliminated, just as you would eliminate any choices that you decided were definitely wrong. Remember, even when you're making educated guesses, you're choosing randomly among the choices that remain.

Fill in the answer grid below. Then check how you did against the answer key on page 22. Unless you are very unlucky (and some of you may be), you should end up with a positive score.

Educated guessing score:

Number of
right answers   _____

Minus 1/4 point
for each wrong
answer   _____

Total   _____

1. (B) (C)   (E)
2. (B) (C)   (E)
3. (B) (C)   (E)
4. (B) (C)   (E)
5. (B) (C)   (E)
6. (B) (C)   (E)
7. (B) (C)   (E)
8. (B) (C)   (E)
9. (B) (C)   (E)
10. (B) (C)   (E)
11. (B) (C)   (E)
12. (B) (C)   (E)
13. (B) (C)   (E)
14. (B) (C)   (E)
15. (B) (C)   (E)
16. (B) (C)   (E)
17. (B) (C)   (E)
18. (B) (C)   (E)
19. (B) (C)   (E)
20. (B) (C)   (E)

RECAP: GUESSING

If you can eliminate even one answer as definitely wrong, it will probably pay to guess among the rest of the choices.

Answers for the Guessing Experiment

Wild Guessing	Answers	Educated Guessing	Answers
1	D	1	C
2	B	2	B
3	E	3	E
4	C	4	E
5	A	5	B
6	C	6	C
7	D	7	B
8	D	8	E
9	A	9	C
10	C	10	C
11	E	11	B
12	B	12	E
13	A	13	C
14	E	14	B
15	D	15	B
16	B	16	B
17	E	17	C
18	A	18	E
19	C	19	C
20	B	20	E

CHAPTER THREE

Psyching Yourself Up

Relaxation Techniques.................24
Before the Test 24
Think Positively 24
Keep Yourself Focused....................25
Concentrate on Your Own Work 25
Put the Test in Perspective 25
Remember You're in Control 25

Your SAT I results depend on how much you know and on how well you can put what you know to work. But your results can also reflect how you feel. Nerves, distractions, poor concentration, or a negative attitude can pull down your performance.

Relaxation Techniques

Being nervous is natural. Being nervous, by itself, isn't really a problem. A bit of a nervous edge can keep you sharp and focused. Too much nervousness, however, can keep you from concentrating and working effectively.

Here are some techniques you can use to keep your nerves in check.

Before the Test

You can start your psychological preparation the day before the test:

- Get a good night's sleep.
- Have everything that you need for the test ready the night before:
  - The appropriate ID, which must include your photo, or a brief description of you. The description must be on school stationery or a school ID form, and you must sign it in front of your principal or guidance counselor, who must also sign it.
  - Admission Ticket
  - #2 pencils
  - Calculator with fresh batteries
- Make sure you know the way to the test center and any special instructions for finding the entrance on Saturday or Sunday.
- Leave yourself plenty of time for mishaps and emergencies.
- If you're not there when the test starts, you can't take the test.

Think Positively

Getting down on yourself during the test does more than make you feel bad. It can rob you of the confidence you need to solve problems. It can distract you. If you're thinking that you aren't doing well, you aren't thinking about the question in front of you. Think positive thoughts that will help you keep up your confidence and focus on each question. Try telling yourself things like:

- "This test is going to seem harder than tests I usually take, so it's okay if I can't answer as many questions as usual. What's important is to do well on the questions that I can do."
- "I've already answered some questions right, and there are other easy questions that I have yet to find."

Keep Yourself Focused

- Try not to think about anything except the question in front of you.
- If you catch yourself thinking about something else, bring your focus back to the test, but congratulate yourself. You have just demonstrated that you are in control.

Concentrate on Your Own Work

The first thing some students do when they get stuck on a question or find themselves running into a batch of tough questions is to look around to see how everyone else is doing. What they usually see is that others are filling in their answer sheets.

"Look at how well everyone else is doing . . . What's wrong with me?" If you start thinking this way, try to remember:

- Everyone works at a different pace. Your neighbors may not be working on the exact question that has puzzled you.
- Thinking about what someone else is doing doesn't help you answer even a single question. In fact, it takes away time you should be using on your test.

Put the Test in Perspective

The SAT I is important, but how you do on one test will not determine whether you get into college.

- The test is only one factor in the college admission decision.
- High school grades are considered more important than the SAT by most college admission officers.
- Nonacademic admission criteria are important, too. These include things like extracurricular activities and personal recommendations. College admission officers at individual colleges will usually be glad to discuss the admission policies at their institutions with you.
- If you don't do as well as you wanted to, you can take the test again.

Remember You're in Control

If you create a good plan for taking the test—practice each type of question, know where and how to find all the questions you can answer, and remember how to pace yourself and guess wisely—you'll stay in control as you take the SAT I. And if you're in control, you'll have a good chance of getting all the points you deserve.

PART TWO

SAT I: Verbal Reasoning

▲ ▼ ▲ **Chapter 4**
Sample Verbal Questions and Answers

▲ ▼ ▲ **Chapter 5**
Practice Questions

CHAPTER FOUR

Sample Verbal Questions and Answers

Introduction **30**
Strategies for Tackling the Questions . . 30
Building Vocabulary Skills 31

Analogy Questions **33**
Hints 34
Sample Questions 36
Answers and Explanations 37

Sentence Completion Questions . . . **42**
Hints 45
Sample Questions 48
Answers and Explanations 49

Critical Reading Questions **53**
Hints 54
Questions Involving Two Passages 55
Vocabulary-in-Context Questions 56
Sample Passages 56
Answers and Explanations 59
A Final Note on Critical Reading
Questions 71

Introduction

The verbal sections of SAT I contain three types of questions:

• Analogies
• Sentence Completions
• Critical Reading

Analogies focus on the relationships between pairs of words; they measure your reasoning ability as well as the depth and breadth of your vocabulary. Sentence Completions are fill-in questions that test your vocabulary and your ability to understand fairly complex sentences. Critical Reading questions are based on passages 400 to 850 words long. The content of the passages is drawn from the Humanities, the Social Sciences, and the Natural Sciences. Narrative passages (prose fiction or nonfiction) also are used in the test.

The three types of verbal questions are designed to test how well you understand the written word. Your ability to read carefully and to think about what you read is crucial to your success in college. In college, you will have to learn a great deal on your own from your assigned reading. And that's just as true in mathematics and science and technical courses as it is in "reading" courses like literature, philosophy, and history. Verbal skills are fundamental building blocks of academic success.

Strategies for Tackling the Questions

About half of the Verbal questions are Analogies and Sentence Completions. Work on these first in any section that includes all three types of Verbal questions. But don't spend half your time on them, because the Critical Reading passages take a lot more time. As you work on one of the 30-minute Verbal sections, you may want to use the following strategy:

Get your quick points first

• Begin with the first set of Sentence Completions. Answer as many as you can. Mark the others with a question mark (?) or an X. You'll recall from Chapter 2 that a question mark means you have a good chance of answering the question with a little more time. An X means you don't think you'll have much chance of answering the question correctly.

Take a look at all the sentence completions and analogies

• Move on next to the Analogy questions and work through them the same way you worked through the Sentence Completions.
• Go back and take a second, quick look at the questions you marked with a question mark. Answer the ones you can without spending lots of time.
• Then move on to the Critical Reading passages and questions.
• **Important:** One 15-minute Verbal section includes *only* Critical Reading questions.

Even when questions of one type become difficult to answer, give the rest of them a quick read before you skip ahead to the next type. All of these questions are based in part on your knowledge of vocabulary, and you never can tell when you might hit on a word that you know. It doesn't take long to read these questions and you may pick up a correct answer or two.

If you have time to go back to some of the more difficult questions that you skipped, try eliminating choices. Sometimes you can get to the correct answer that way. If not, eliminating choices will at least allow you to make educated guesses.

Consider related words, familiar sayings and phrases, roots, prefixes, and suffixes. If you don't know what a word means right away, stop for a moment to think about whether you have heard or seen a word that might be related to it.

You might get help from common sayings and phrases. If you don't know a word but are familiar with a phrase that uses it, you might be able to figure the word out.

For instance, you might not immediately remember what the words *ovation* and *annul* mean. But you probably would recognize them in the phrases *a standing ovation* and *annul a marriage*. If you can recall a phrase or saying in which a word is used, you may be able to figure out what it means in another context.

Eliminate Choices on Tough Questions

If You Don't Know a Word . . . Attack!

Building Vocabulary Skills

Building vocabulary takes time, but it doesn't take magic. The single most effective thing you can do to build your vocabulary, over time, is to read a lot. Your teachers and librarians will be more than happy to recommend a variety of helpful and enjoyable reading materials for you.

In addition to reading, there are many other things you can do to improve your vocabulary. The suggestions offered here are presented in outline form, but vocabulary building is a long-term effort. If you succeed, the results will go a long way toward helping you reach your academic goals, including and beyond getting good SAT I verbal scores.

- When you read to improve your vocabulary, have a dictionary and a pencil handy. Each time you encounter a word you don't know, stop. Try to figure out what it means from the context. If you can't figure the word out, look it up and make a note of it.
- When you look up a word in the dictionary, pay attention to the different definitions and the contexts in which each is appropriate.
- Practice your expanding vocabulary by using the new words you have learned in your reading with your friends and in your school writing assignments.
- Pay close attention to roots, prefixes, and suffixes.

Target some of your reading toward vocabulary building

Knowing foreign languages can help—even if you're just a beginner

Play word games

- Check your school or local library and/or bookstore for vocabulary-building books. Almost all of them include lists of common roots, prefixes, and suffixes.
- Memorizing the meanings of roots, prefixes, and suffixes will be more helpful than memorizing individual words.
- Apply your knowledge of foreign languages, especially those related to Latin, such as Spanish, French, and Italian. English has many cognates, or words with similar meanings, from these languages.
- Work crossword puzzles.
- Play Scrabble or Boggle.
- Play word-find games.

 HINT

If you take the time to do vocabulary-building work every time you read, you may not get much reading done or enjoy your reading as fully as you should. So set aside a reasonable amount of time, perhaps half an hour, for vocabulary building two or three times a week. If you keep it up week-in and week-out, month after month, you'll be surprised at how much you will add to your vocabulary in a year's time.

Analogy Questions

Analogies are vocabulary questions, but they require more than just knowing the definitions of words. Analogies ask you to figure out the relationships between pairs of words. They challenge you to think about why it makes sense to put two words together. So, you have to know the definitions of words, but you also have to know how the words are used.

In the box below is an example of the kind of question you'll encounter, and the directions for Analogies.

Each question below consists of a related pair of words or phrases, followed by five pairs of words or phrases labeled A through E. Select the pair that <u>best</u> expresses a relationship similar to that expressed in the original pair.

Example:

CRUMB:BREAD::
(A) ounce:unit
(B) splinter:wood
(C) water:bucket
(D) twine:rope
(E) cream:butter

The correct answer is (B).

Explanation:

   To answer Analogy questions, you must first figure out the relationship between the two words in CAPITAL LETTERS. Then look for the pair of words among the answers that has the same relationship.

   In the sample, the words in capital letters are CRUMB and BREAD. What is the relationship between these two words? *A CRUMB is a very small piece that falls off or breaks off of a piece of BREAD.*

   What makes (B) splinter:wood the right answer? *A splinter is a very small piece that breaks off or splits away from a piece of wood.* You can use almost the very same words to describe the relationships between CRUMB and BREAD, on the one hand, and *splinter* and *wood*, on the other. That is what makes the relationships *analogous,* what makes them similar.

None of the relationships between the two words in the other choices is similar to the relationship between CRUMB and BREAD:

- An **ounce** is a type of **unit**; it is not a small piece of a **unit**.
- **Water** can be carried in a **bucket**; it is not a piece of a **bucket**.
- **Twine** is thinner and less strong than **rope**, but it is not a small piece that breaks off of a **rope**.
- **Cream** is what **butter** is made from, but **cream** is not a small piece of **butter**.

Hints

With analogies, you are looking for similar *relationships*, not similar *meanings*. Analogy questions do not ask you to look for words that have the same meaning as the word in capital letters.

In the preceding example, (B) is the correct answer because the relationship between **splinter** and **wood** is similar to the relationship between CRUMB and BREAD. The word CRUMB does not mean the same thing as the word **splinter**, and the word BREAD does not have the same meaning as the word **wood**.

The explanation of the preceding example gives you two clues: first, you can express the relationship between the two words in capital letters in a sentence that explains how they are related. Second, you can express the relationship between the two words in the correct answer by using almost the *same sentence* and substituting the words in the answer for the words in capitals.

To answer Analogy questions, start by making up a "test sentence" that explains how the two words in capital letters are related. Then try the words from each answer in your test sentence to see which pair makes the most sense.

Here's a question to practice on.

ALBUM:PHOTOGRAPHS::
(A) trial:briefs
(B) board:directors
(C) meeting:agendas
(D) scrapbook:clippings
(E) checkbook:money

Make up a sentence that expresses the relationship between the two words in capital letters. That sentence will become your test sentence for the answers.

> An ALBUM is a place for saving PHOTOGRAPHS.
> A _____ is a place for saving _____.

Look for similar *relationships*, not similar *meanings*

Learn the basic strategy

Try the words in each choice in your test sentence and eliminate any choices that don't make sense. The pair that makes the most sense in the test sentence is the correct answer.

(A) A **trial** is a place for saving **briefs**.

(B) A **board** is a place for saving **directors**.

(C) A **meeting** is a place for saving **agendas**.

(D) A **scrapbook** is a place for saving **clippings**.

(E) A **checkbook** is a place for saving **money**.

Only choice (D) makes sense. It's analogous to the words in capital letters.

Be Flexible

If you don't get a single correct answer right away, you'll have to revise your test sentence. Many English words have more than one meaning. And pairs of words can have more than one relationship. So you may have to try a couple of test sentences before you find one that gives you a single correct answer. Some test sentences will state a relationship that is so broad or general that more than one answer makes sense. Other test sentences may be so narrow or specific that none of the choices fit.

Practice is the key here. You may have to try several test sentences before you find one that gives you a single correct answer. Don't worry about writing style when making up your test sentences. You're just trying to state the relationship between the pair of words in a way that will help you choose the correct answer. And you don't get any points for making up grammatically correct test sentences. You get points for choosing correct answers. The sentences are only a technique. Once you make up a test sentence, you still have to think about how the choices work in it.

If you can't tell how a word in capital letters is being used (if it is a word that can represent more than one part of speech), look at the answers. The words in the answer can sometimes help you make sense of the two words in capital letters.

Don't be distracted by the relationships between individual words in the answers and individual words in capital letters. Remember that you are looking for analogous relationships between *pairs* of words.

It's okay to reverse the order of the words in capital letters when you make up your test sentence. But if you do, remember to reverse the order of the words in the answers, too, when you try them in your test sentence.

Although abstract words may be more challenging than concrete words, the same strategies are applicable to answering both kinds of analogy questions. Identify the relationship between the two words, then express that relationship in a test sentence. Finally, use the test sentence to identify the correct answer.

Analogy questions use words consistently

Comparing individual words

Reversing word order

Handling abstract questions

Sample Questions

1 ACT:PLAY::
    (A) song:music
    (B) rhyme:poem
    (C) page:novel
    (D) chapter:book
    (E) scenery:performance

Your test sentence:

Your answer:

2 BOLD:FOOLHARDY::
    (A) lively:enthusiastic
    (B) natural:synthetic
    (C) generous:spendthrift
    (D) wise:thoughtful
    (E) creative:childlike

Your test sentence:

Your answer:

3 CHILL:COLD::
    (A) parch:dry
    (B) crush:soft
    (C) freeze:white
    (D) feed:hungry
    (E) scrub:hard

Your test sentence:

Your answer:

4 LAWYER:CLIENT::
    (A) doctor:surgeon
    (B) admiral:sailor
    (C) judge:defendant
    (D) musician:audience
    (E) tutor:student

Your test sentence:

Your answer:

5 IRON:BLACKSMITH::
    (A) gold:miser
    (B) clay:potter
    (C) food:gourmet
    (D) steel:industrialist
    (E) silver:miner

Your test sentence:

Your answer:

6 ILLOGICAL:CONFUSION::
    (A) profound:laughter
    (B) revolting:sympathy
    (C) astounding:amazement
    (D) obscure:contrast
    (E) deliberate:vitality

Your test sentence:

Your answer:

Answers and Explanations

1 ACT:PLAY::
  (A) song:music
  (B) rhyme:poem
  (C) page:novel
  (D) chapter:book
  (E) scenery:performance

The correct answer is (D).
Test sentence:

> An ACT is a large section of a PLAY.
> A _____ is a large section of a _____.

Explanation:
  Your first test sentence may have stated a more general relationship, such as an ACT is a *part of* a PLAY. But this test sentence works for several answers because *part of* is too broad. It can refer to elements of some larger entity—like chapters and pages. It can also refer to anything that is related to something else—like scenery in a performance. But an ACT is the way the content of a play is divided up, just as a *chapter* is the way the content of a book is divided up. However you may word your test sentence, it must be precise and detailed enough to yield only one correct answer.

 HINT

If more than one answer makes sense in your test sentence, revise your sentence so it states a more specific relationship.

---

2 BOLD:FOOLHARDY::
  (A) lively:enthusiastic
  (B) natural:synthetic
  (C) generous:spendthrift
  (D) wise:thoughtful
  (E) creative:childlike

The correct answer is (C).
Test sentence:

> To be overly BOLD is to be FOOLHARDY.
> To be overly _____ is to be _____ .

Explanation:

The relationship between BOLD and FOOLHARDY expresses a positive quality turning into a negative quality. Even though these terms are abstract, the basic approach is still the same: establish the relationship between the capitalized words in a test sentence and then try each of the choices in the test sentence until you figure out which choice fits best.

 HINT

Whether the words are hard or easy, abstract or concrete, solve analogies by establishing the relationship between the words in capitals first and then looking for a similar or parallel relationship in the answers.

3 CHILL:COLD::
  (A) parch:dry
  (B) crush:soft
  (C) freeze:white
  (D) feed:hungry
  (E) scrub:hard

The correct answer is (A).
Test sentence:

> To CHILL something is to make it COLD.
> To _____ something is to make it _____.

Explanation:

The word CHILL can be used as several different parts of speech. It can be used as a verb (as it is in the test sentence), as an adjective (a CHILL wind), or as a noun (I caught a CHILL).

In this question, if you used the word CHILL as anything but a verb, your test sentence wouldn't work for any of the answer choices. If you're unsure of how to state the relationship between the words in capital letters, try working your way through the answers to establish relationships.

 HINT

Pay attention to the way you are using the words in capital letters in your test sentence. They should be used the same way (be the same parts of speech) as the words in the answers.

4 LAWYER:CLIENT::
   (A) doctor:surgeon
   (B) admiral:sailor
   (C) judge:defendant
   (D) musician:audience
   (E) tutor:student

The correct answer is (E).
Test sentence:

> A LAWYER is hired to help a CLIENT.
> A _____ is hired to help a _____.

Explanation:
   Some students get distracted by the relationships between the individual words in the answers and the individual words in capital letters. There is a close relationship between a *judge* and a LAWYER, but the relationship between a *judge* and a *defendant* is not similar to the relationship between a LAWYER and a CLIENT.
   Of course, tutors mostly teach (which lawyers do only rarely) and lawyers represent their clients in courtrooms (which tutors never do). Every analogy has some dissimilarities as well as similarities. The correct answer is the one that "best expresses" a similar relationship with the pair in capital letters.

 HINT

Remember that you are looking for analogous relationships between pairs of words. Don't be distracted by individual words in the answers that have relationships to individual words in capital letters.

---

5 IRON:BLACKSMITH::
   (A) gold:miser
   (B) clay:potter
   (C) food:gourmet
   (D) steel:industrialist
   (E) silver:miner

The correct answer is (B).

Test sentence:

> A BLACKSMITH shapes things out of IRON.
> A _____ shapes things out of _____.

Explanation:

You may initially have expressed the relationship with the test sentence a BLACKSMITH *deals with* IRON, but *deals with* is a very general statement and would not have eliminated many choices. The phrase *shapes things out of* is more precise because it specifies what the BLACKSMITH does with IRON.

You might also have thought of the sentence a BLACKSMITH *hammers* IRON. But *hammers* is too specific. It is only one of the things that the BLACKSMITH does while working with IRON. None of the choices would have worked using *hammers* as the key to the relationship.

 HINT

Be flexible when establishing relationships. If your first test sentence yields no possible answers, try a different or more general approach. If it yields several possible answers, try a more specific approach. And remember: it's okay to switch the order of the words in capitals when you make up your test sentence, but make sure that you also switch the order of the words in the answer choices when you test them.

---

6 ILLOGICAL:CONFUSION::
- (A) profound:laughter
- (B) revolting:sympathy
- (C) astounding:amazement
- (D) obscure:contrast
- (E) deliberate:vitality

The correct answer is (C).
Test sentence:

If something is ILLOGICAL, it leads to CONFUSION.
If something is _____ , it leads to _____ .

Explanation:

CONFUSION is usually thought of as negative or undesirable, and amazement is more positive. But the dissimilarity between these words doesn't matter as long as the *relationship* between the words in capitals is parallel to the *relationship* between the words in the correct answer.

 HINT

In Analogy questions, always look for similar *relationships* between words, NOT for similar meanings or similar connotations of words.

RECAP: HINTS ON ANALOGY QUESTIONS

1. Look for *analogous relationships* between pairs of words, *not* for words that have *similar meanings*.

2. Learn the basic approach to Analogy questions. First state the relationship between the pair of words in capital letters as a sentence. Then try the pair of words in each answer in your test sentence, one at a time. Eliminate choices that don't make sense. If necessary, revise your test sentence until you can identify a single correct answer. Very general statements of the relationship often need to be made more specific. Overly specific relationships may need to be broadened.

3. Be flexible. Words can have more than one meaning, and pairs of words different relationships. So you may have to try a few test sentences before you come up with the right relationship.

4. Analogy questions use parts of speech consistently. If you can't tell how a word in capital letters is being used (if it is a word that can represent more than one part of speech), check the answers. The words in capital letters will be used in the same way as the words in the answers are used.

5. Remember that you are looking for analogous relationships between pairs of words. Don't compare individual words in the answers to one of the words in capital letters.

6. You can reverse the order of the words in capital letters when you make up your test sentence. But if you do, remember to reverse the order of the words in the answers, too, when you try them in your test sentence.

7. You should use the same strategy for answering abstract questions that you use for concrete questions.

Sentence Completion
questions challenge
both reasoning and
vocabulary skills

Sentence Completion Questions

Sentence Completion questions require a broad vocabulary plus the ability to understand the logic of sentences that are sometimes quite complex. There is no short, simple approach to Sentence Completions. But there are a number of strategies that will help you through even the toughest questions.

The box below gives an example of the kind of questions that will appear in the test, and the directions for Sentence Completions.

Each sentence below has one or two blanks, each blank indicating that something has been omitted. Beneath the sentence are five words or sets of words labeled A through E. Choose the word or set of words that, when inserted in the sentence, <u>best</u> fits the meaning of the sentence as a whole.

Example:

Medieval kingdoms did not become constitutional republics overnight; on the contrary, the change was - - - -.

(A) unpopular
(B) unexpected
(C) advantageous
(D) sufficient
(E) gradual

The correct answer is (E).

Explanation:

The first part of the sentence says that the kingdoms did not change *overnight.* The second part begins with *on the contrary* and explains the change. So the correct answer will be a word that describes a change that is *contrary* to an *overnight* change. *Gradual* change is contrary to *overnight* change.

- Sentence Completion questions can have one or two blanks, but each sentence, as a whole, still counts as only **one** question.
- Some of the questions with one blank are straightforward vocabulary questions. Others require that you know more than just the meanings of the words involved. They also require that you understand the logic of fairly complicated sentences.
- Most Sentence Completions involve compound or complex sentences, that is, sentences made up of several clauses. In many cases, to answer the question correctly you have to figure out how the parts of the sentence—the different clauses—relate to each other.

Here are some examples of the different types of Sentence Completion questions you will see:

Example 1: A one-blank vocabulary-based question

This type of question depends more on your knowledge of vocabulary than on your ability to follow the logic of a complicated sentence. You still need to know how the words are used in the context of the sentence, but if you know the definitions of the words involved, you almost certainly will be able to select the correct answer.

These one-blank vocabulary-based questions tend to be relatively short, usually not more than 20 words.

Ravens appear to behave - - - -, actively
helping one another to find food.

(A) mysteriously
(B) warily
(C) aggressively
(D) cooperatively
(E) defensively

The correct answer is (D).

Explanation:

This sentence asks you to look for a word that describes how the ravens behave. The information after the comma restates and defines the meaning of the missing word. You are told that the ravens *actively help one another.* There is only one word among the choices that accurately describes this behavior—*cooperatively.*

Example 2: A two-blank vocabulary-based question

You will also find some two-blank sentences with rather straightforward logic but challenging vocabulary.

Both - - - - and - - - -, Wilson seldom spoke
and never spent money.

(A) vociferous..generous
(B) garrulous..stingy
(C) effusive..frugal
(D) taciturn..miserly
(E) reticent..munificent

The correct answer is (D).

Explanation:

In this sentence, the logic is not difficult. You are looking for two words that describe Wilson. One of the words has to mean that he *seldom spoke* and the other that he *never spent money*. The correct answer is *taciturn..miserly*. *Taciturn* means "shy, unwilling to talk." *Miserly* means "like a miser, extremely stingy."

Example 3: A one-blank logic-based question

Success in answering these questions depends as much on your ability to reason out the logic of the sentence as it does on your knowledge of vocabulary.

After observing several vicious territorial fights, Jane Goodall had to revise her earlier opinion that these particular primates were always - - - - animals.

(A) ignorant
(B) inquisitive
(C) responsive
(D) cruel
(E) peaceful

The correct answer is (E).

Explanation:

To answer this question, you have to follow the logical flow of the ideas in the sentence. A few key words reveal that logic:

- First, the introductory word **After** tells you that the information at the beginning of the sentence is going to affect what comes later. The word **After** also gives an order to the events in the sentence.
- Second, the word **revise** tells you that something is going to change. It is going to change **after** the events described at the beginning of the sentence. So the events at the beginning really cause the change.
- Finally, the end of the sentence—**her earlier opinion that these particular primates were always - - - - animals**—tells you what is changing. The word filling the blank should convey a meaning you would have to revise after seeing the animals fight. **Peaceful** is the only such word among the five choices.

Example 4: A two-blank logic-based question

The following question requires you to know the meanings of the words, know how the words are used in context, and understand the logic of a rather complicated sentence.

Although its publicity has been - - - -, the
film itself is intelligent, well-acted,
handsomely produced, and altogether - - - -.

(A) tasteless..respectable
(B) extensive..moderate
(C) sophisticated..amateur
(D) risqué..crude
(E) perfect..spectacular

The correct answer is (A).

Explanation:
 The first thing to notice about this sentence is that it has two
parts or clauses. The first clause begins with *Although,* the second
clause begins with *the film.*
 The logic of the sentence is determined by the way the two
clauses relate to each other. The two parts have contrasting or
conflicting meanings. Why? Because one of the clauses begins
with *Although.* The word *Although* is used to introduce an idea
that conflicts with something else in the sentence: *Although* something is true, something else that you would expect to be true is
not.
 The answer is *tasteless..respectable.* You would not expect a film
with *tasteless publicity* to be *altogether respectable.* But the introductory word *Although* tells you that you should expect the unexpected.

Hints

Start out by reading the entire sentence saying *blank* for the blank(s).
This gives you an overall sense of the meaning of the sentence and
helps you figure out how the parts of the sentence relate to each other.

 Always begin by trying to pin down the standard dictionary definitions of the words in the sentence and the answers. To answer Sentence Completion questions, you usually don't have to know a non-
standard meaning of a word.

 Introductory and transitional words are extremely important. They
can be the key to figuring out the logic of a sentence. They tell you
how the parts of the sentence relate to each other. Consider the following common introductory and transitional words: *but, although,
however, yet, even though.* These words indicate that the two parts of
the sentence will contradict or be in contrast with each other. There
are many other introductory and transitional words that you should
watch for when working on Sentence Completion questions. *Always*
read the sentences carefully and don't ignore any of the details.

Read the entire sentence

Know your vocabulary

**Small words make a big
difference**

Watch out for negatives

Some of the most difficult Sentence Completion questions contain negatives, which can make it hard to follow the logic of the sentences. Negatives in two clauses of a sentence can be even more of a challenge:

> According to Burgess, a novelist **should not** preach, for sermonizing **has no place** in good fiction.

Try answering the question without looking at the choices

A negative appears in each clause of this sentence. The transitional word "for" indicates that the second part of the sentence will explain the first.

Figure out what sort of word(s) should fill the blank(s) before looking at the choices, then look for a choice that is similar to the one(s) you thought up. For many one-blank questions, especially the easier ones, you'll find the word you thought of among the choices. Other times, a close synonym for your word will be one of the choices.

Try answering the following Sentence Completion question without looking at the choices.

> Once Murphy left home for good, he wrote no letters to his worried mother; he did not, therefore, live up to her picture of him as her - - - - son.

The transitional word **therefore** indicates that the information in the second part of the sentence is a direct, logical result of the information in the first part. What words might fit in the blank?

_____   _____

_____   _____

The second part of the sentence includes a negative **(he did not...live up to her picture...)**, so the blank must be a positive term. Words like **perfect, sweet, respectful, favorite**—all could fit in the blank. Now, look at the actual choices:

(A) misunderstood
(B) elusive
(C) destructive
(D) persuasive
(E) dutiful

(E) **dutiful** is the only choice that is even close to the ones suggested. (E) is the correct answer.

You can also try this technique with two-blank questions. You are less likely to come up with as close a word match, but it will help you get a feel for the meaning and logic of the sentence.

With two-blank questions, try eliminating some answers based on just one blank. If one word in an answer doesn't make sense in the sentence, then you can reject the entire choice.

Try approaching two-blank questions like this:

Try answering two-blank questions one blank at a time

- Work on the first blank, alone. Eliminate any choices for which the first word doesn't make sense.
- Work on the second blank, alone. Eliminate any choices for which the second word doesn't make sense. If there is only one choice left, that choice is the correct answer. If more than one choice remains, go on to the next step.
- Work on both blanks together only for those choices that are left. Always read the complete sentence with both words in place to make sure your choice makes sense.

Example 4, discussed previously, shows how this approach works. The first words in all the choices could make sense:

Work on the first blank

> its publicity has been **tasteless**
> its publicity has been **extensive**
> its publicity has been **sophisticated**
> its publicity has been **risqué**
> its publicity has been **perfect**

The second blank is part of a list that includes **intelligent, well-acted, handsomely produced,** and _____. The word **and** indicates that the last word in the list (the blank) should be a positive word, in general agreement with the others. With that in mind, examine the second words in the choices:

Work on the second blank

> intelligent, well-acted...and altogether **respectable**
> intelligent, well-acted...and altogether **moderate**
> ~~intelligent, well-acted...and altogether amateur~~
> ~~intelligent, well-acted...and altogether crude~~
> intelligent, well-acted...and altogether **spectacular**

Amateur and **crude** are definitely not complimentary. No matter what the rest of the sentence says, neither of these words makes sense in the second blank. So you can eliminate the answers that contain **amateur** and **crude**. With two choices eliminated, the question becomes much easier to deal with.

Remember that the instructions for all the verbal questions ask you to choose the *best* answer. One choice may seem to make sense, but it still might not be the *best* of the five choices. Unless you read all the choices, you may select only the *second best* and thus lose points.

Always check all of the choices

Check your choice by reading the entire sentence with the answer you have selected in place to make sure the sentence makes sense. This step is extremely important, especially if you have used shortcuts to eliminate choices.

Check your choice

Sample Questions

1 A judgment made before all the facts are known must be called - - - -.

(A) harsh
(B) deliberate
(C) sensible
(D) premature
(E) fair

2 Despite their - - - - proportions, the murals of Diego Rivera give his Mexican compatriots the sense that their history is - - - - and human in scale, not remote and larger than life.

(A) monumental..accessible
(B) focused..prolonged
(C) vast..ancient
(D) realistic..extraneous
(E) narrow..overwhelming

3 The research is so - - - - that it leaves no part of the issue unexamined.

(A) comprehensive
(B) rewarding
(C) sporadic
(D) economical
(E) problematical

4 A dictatorship - - - - its citizens to be docile and finds it expedient to make outcasts of those who do not - - - -.

(A) forces..rebel
(B) expects..disobey
(C) requires..conform
(D) allows..withdraw
(E) forbids..agree

5 Alice Walker's prize-winning novel exemplifies the strength of first-person narratives; the protagonist tells her own story so effectively that any additional commentary would be - - - -.

(A) subjective
(B) eloquent
(C) superfluous
(D) incontrovertible
(E) impervious

6 The Supreme Court's reversal of its previous ruling on the issue of states' rights - - - - its reputation for - - - -.

(A) sustained..infallibility
(B) compromised..consistency
(C) bolstered..doggedness
(D) aggravated..inflexibility
(E) dispelled..vacillation

Answers and Explanations

1 A judgment made before all the facts are known must be called
- - - -.

    (A) harsh
    (B) deliberate
    (C) sensible
    (D) premature
    (E) fair

The correct answer is (D).

Explanation:
   Getting the correct answer to this question depends almost entirely on your knowing the definitions of the five words you must choose from. Which of the choices describes a judgment made before *all the facts are known*? Such a judgment, by definition, is not deliberate, and the sentence doesn't tell us whether the judgment was *harsh* or lenient, *sensible* or dumb, *fair* or unfair. *Premature* means hasty or early. It fits the blank perfectly.

 HINT

Know your vocabulary. Think carefully about the meanings of the words in the answer choices.

---

2 Despite their - - - - proportions, the murals of Diego Rivera give his Mexican compatriots the sense that their history is - - - - and human in scale, not remote and larger than life.

    (A) monumental..accessible
    (B) focused..prolonged
    (C) vast..ancient
    (D) realistic..extraneous
    (E) narrow..overwhelming

The correct answer is (A).

Explanation:
   The keys to this sentence are the word *Despite*, the words *human in scale*, and the words *not remote and larger than life*. The word filling the first blank has to be one that would relate closely to something that seems *larger than life*. The word filling the second blank has to fit with *human in scale*. If you focus on just one of the two blanks, you will be able to eliminate several choices before you even think about the other blank.

HINT

Watch for key introductory and transitional words that determine how the parts of the sentence relate to each other. Then try answering two-blank questions one blank at a time. If you can eliminate one word in a choice, the entire choice can be ruled out.

3 The research is so - - - - that it leaves no part of the issue unexamined.

    (A) comprehensive
    (B) rewarding
    (C) sporadic
    (D) economical
    (E) problematical

The correct answer is (A).

Explanation:
Try filling in the blank without reading the answer choices. What kind of words would fit? Words like *complete, thorough,* or *extensive* could all fit. Now look at the answer choices. *Comprehensive* is very similar to the words suggested, and none of the other choices fits at all.

 HINT

Try thinking about the logic of the sentence without looking at the choices. Then look for the choice that has a similar meaning to the words you thought up.

4 A dictatorship - - - - its citizens to be docile and finds it expedient to make outcasts of those who do not - - - -.

    (A) forces..rebel
    (B) expects..disobey
    (C) requires..conform
    (D) allows..withdraw
    (E) forbids..agree

The correct answer is (C).

Explanation:

Answering this question depends in part on your knowledge of vocabulary. You have to know what the words *dictatorship, docile,* and *expedient* mean. You also have to watch out for key words such as *not.* If you leave out the word *not,* then answer choices like (A) and (B) make sense.

⚙ HINT

Think carefully about the standard dictionary definitions of the important words in the sentence. And remember that small words such as *not* can make a big difference. When you pick your answer, read the entire sentence with the blank(s) filled in to be sure that it makes sense.

---

5 Alice Walker's prize-winning novel exemplifies the strength of first-person narratives; the protagonist tells her own story so effectively that any additional commentary would be - - - -.

(A) subjective
(B) eloquent
(C) superfluous
(D) incontrovertible
(E) impervious

The correct answer is (C).

Explanation:

Words like *prize-winning, strength,* and *effectively* tell you that the writer thinks Alice Walker's novel is well written. So would *additional commentary* be necessary or unnecessary? Once you've figured out that it is unnecessary, you can look for an answer with a similar meaning. That way, you may be able to answer the question more quickly, since you won't have to plug in each choice one by one to see if it makes any sense.

⚙ HINT

Think about the meaning of the sentence before you look at the choices. Get a sense of what you're looking for *before* you start looking.

---

6 The Supreme Court's reversal of its previous ruling on the issue of states' rights - - - - its reputation for - - - -.

(A) sustained..infallibility
(B) compromised..consistency
(C) bolstered..doggedness
(D) aggravated..inflexibility
(E) dispelled..vacillation

The correct answer is (B).

Explanation:
Getting the correct answer to this question depends in large part on your knowledge of the meanings of the words offered as choices. You have to know the definitions of the words before you can try the choices one by one to arrive at the correct pair.

You also need to think about the central idea in the sentence: the court's *reversal* blank *its reputation for* blank. The logic is complicated and the vocabulary in the choices is hard: but, if you stick with it, you'll figure out that only (B) makes sense.

 HINT

When you read the sentence to yourself, substitute the word *blank* for each blank. Try to figure out what the sentence is saying before you start plugging in the choices.

RECAP: HINTS ON SENTENCE
COMPLETION QUESTIONS

1. Read the sentence, substituting the word *blank* for each blank. This helps you figure out the meaning of the sentence and how the parts of the sentence relate to each other.

2. Know your vocabulary. Always begin by trying to pin down the dictionary definitions of the key words in the sentence and the answer choices.

3. Small words make a big difference. Watch for the key introductory and transitional words. These determine how the parts of the sentence relate to each other. Also watch carefully for negatives.

4. Try figuring out words to fill in the blank or blanks without looking at the answers. Then look for the choice that is similar to the one you thought up.

5. Try answering two-blank questions one blank at a time. If you can eliminate one word in an answer, the entire choice can be eliminated.

6. Always check all of the answer choices before making a final decision. A choice may seem okay, but still not be the best answer. Make sure that the answer you select is the best one.

7. Check your answer to make sure it makes sense by reading the entire sentence with your choice in place.

Critical Reading Questions

Of the three types of verbal questions, the Critical Reading questions give you the best shot at getting the right answers. Why? Because all the information you need to answer the questions is in the passages.

Success in answering Critical Reading questions depends less on knowledge you already have and more on your ability to understand and make sense of the information given to you in the passages. The passages are drawn from a wide variety of subject areas. You may find that you are familiar with the topics of some of the passages, but you will probably not be familiar with most of them. The passages are selected so that you can answer the questions without any prior study or in-depth knowledge of the subjects.

Answering most of the Critical Reading questions will take more than just looking back at the passage to see what it says. You'll also have to *think* about the content of each passage, analyze and evaluate the ideas and opinions in it, figure out the underlying assumptions, and follow the author's argument. You'll have to make inferences, which means drawing conclusions from what the author says so you can figure out what the author really *means*. You'll also have to relate parts of the passage to each other, compare and contrast different theories and viewpoints, understand cause and effect, and pay attention to the author's attitude, tone, and overall purpose.

Like a lot of college-level reading, the passages will be thoughtful and sophisticated discussions of important issues, ideas, and events. A few questions in each test will ask you to demonstrate that you have understood what the author is saying at some point in the passage. And a few other questions will ask you to figure out the meaning of a word as it is used in the passage. But the great majority of the Critical Reading questions will require "extended reasoning." You'll have to do more than just absorb information and then recognize a restatement of it. You'll have to be an *active* reader and think carefully about what you're reading.

Hints

Details in a passage are there because they mean something. And those details determine the answers to some of the Critical Reading questions.

The answers come from the passage

Every single answer to the Critical Reading questions can be found in or directly inferred from the passage. So be sure to read the passages carefully. If the author mentions that it's a rainy day, he or she has probably done so for a reason. The author did not have to talk about the weather at all. Rainy days suggest a certain mood, or reflect certain feelings, or set up certain situations—slippery roads, for instance—that the author wants you to know about or feel.

Every word counts

The same goes for words describing people, events, and things. If someone's face is described as *handsome* or *scarred*, if an event is *surprising*, or a word is *whispered* or *shouted* or *spoken with a smile*, pay attention. Details like these are mentioned to give you an understanding of what the author wants you to feel or think.

When you are faced with a question about the mood or tone of a passage, or when you are asked about the author's attitude or intent or whether the author might agree or disagree with a statement, you have to think about the details the author has provided.

Mark the passages or make short notes

It may help you to mark important sections or words or sentences. But be careful that you don't mark too much. The idea of marking the passage is to help you find information quickly. If you have underlined or marked three-quarters of it, your marks won't help.

Some students jot a short note—a few words at most—on the margin that summarizes what a paragraph or key sentence is about. Just be careful not to spend more time marking the passage than you will save. And remember, you get points for answering the questions, not for marking your test booklet.

Read the questions and answers carefully

Most Critical Reading questions require three things: You have to think about what the question is asking. You have to look back at the passage for information that will help you with the question. Then you have to think again about how you can use the information to answer the question correctly. Unless you read the question carefully, you won't know what to think about, and you won't know where to look in the passage.

The correct choice is the one that best answers the question, not any choice that makes a true statement. An answer may express something that is perfectly true and still be the wrong choice. The only way you're going to keep from being caught by a choice that is true but wrong is to make sure you read the passage, the questions, and the answer choices carefully.

There should always be information or details in the passage that provide support for your answer—specific words, phrases, and/or sentences that help to prove your choice is correct. Remember that Critical Reading questions depend on the information in the passage and your ability to *interpret* it correctly. Even with the inference, tone, and attitude questions—the ones in which you have to do some reading between the lines to figure out the answers—you can find evidence in the passage supporting the correct choice.

Compare each choice to the passage and you'll find that some choices can be eliminated as definitely wrong. Then it should be easier to choose the correct answer from the remaining choices.

When you have made your choice, read quickly (again) through the other choices to make sure there isn't a better one.

You will spend a lot of time reading a passage before you're ready to answer even one question. So take the time to answer as many questions as you can about each passage before you move on to another.

- Jump around within a set of questions to find the ones you can answer quickly, but don't jump from passage to passage.
- Don't leave a reading passage until you are sure you have answered all the questions you can. If you return to the passage later, you'll probably have to reread it.

When you've gone through all the questions on a passage, go back and review any you left out or weren't sure of. Sometimes information you picked up while thinking about one question will help you answer another.

Some verbal sections contain more than one reading passage. Students often find it easier to read about familiar topics or topics that they find interesting. So if you have a choice, you may want to look for a passage that deals with a familiar or especially interesting subject to work on first. If you skip a passage and set of questions, be sure that you don't lose your place on the answer sheet.

Questions Involving Two Passages

One of the reading selections will involve a *pair* of passages. The two passages will have a common theme or subject. One of the passages will oppose, support, or in some way relate to the other. If one of the paired passages seems easier or more interesting than the other, you may want to start with that one and answer the questions specific to it first. Then go back and wrestle with the questions specific to the other passage and with the questions that refer to both passages.

Sidebar notes:

An answer can be true and still be wrong

The passage must support your answer

Try eliminating choices

Double-check the other choices

Pace yourself

Go back to any questions you skipped

Pick your topic

In most cases, you'll find that the questions are grouped: first, questions about Passage 1, then questions about Passage 2, finally questions comparing the two passages.

When a question asks you to compare two passages, don't try to remember everything from both passages. Take each choice one at a time. Review the relevant parts of each passage before you select your answer.

If a question asks you to identify something that is true in *both* passages, it is often easiest to start by eliminating choices that are *not* true for one of the passages.

Don't be fooled by a choice that is true for one passage but not for the other.

Vocabulary-in-Context Questions

Some Critical Reading questions will ask about the meaning of a word as it is used in the passage. When a word has several meanings, a vocabulary-in-context question won't necessarily use the most common meaning.

Even if you don't know the word, you can sometimes figure it out from the passage and the answers. This is why the questions are called *vocabulary-in-context*. The context in which the word is used determines the meaning of the word. You can also use the context to figure out the meaning of words you're not sure of.

Vocabulary-in-context questions usually take less time to answer than other types of Critical Reading questions. Sometimes, but *not* always, you can answer them by reading only a sentence or two around the word, without reading the entire passage.

If you can't answer a vocabulary-in-context question right away, or if you don't know the meaning of the word, pretend that the word is a blank. Read the sentence substituting *blank* for the word. Look for an answer that makes sense with the rest of the sentence.

Sample Passages

Sample directions and a sample pair of passages and questions are followed by discussions of the correct answers and some hints.

The two passages below are followed by questions based on their content and the relationship between the two passages. Answer the questions on the basis of what is *stated* or *implied* in the passages and in any introductory material that may be provided.

In Passage 1, the author presents his view of the early years of the silent film industry. In Passage 2, the author draws on her experiences as a mime to generalize about her art. (A mime is a performer who, without speaking, entertains through gesture, facial expression, and movement.)

Passage 1

Talk to those people who first saw films when they were silent, and they will tell you the experience was magic. The silent film had extraordinary powers to draw members of an audience into the story, and an equally
(5) potent capacity to make their imaginations work. It required the audience to become engaged—to supply voices and sound effects. The audience was the final, creative contributor to the process of making a film.

The finest films of the silent era depended on two
(10) elements that we can seldom provide today—a large and receptive audience and a well-orchestrated score. For the audience, the fusion of picture and live music added up to more than the sum of the respective parts.

The one word that sums up the attitude of the silent
(15) filmmakers is *enthusiasm*, conveyed most strongly before formulas took shape and when there was more room for experimentation. This enthusiastic uncertainty often resulted in such accidental discoveries as new camera or editing techniques. Some films experimented
(20) with players; the 1915 film *Regeneration*, for example, by using real gangsters and streetwalkers, provided startling local color. Other films, particularly those of Thomas Ince, provided tragic endings as often as films by other companies supplied happy ones.

(25) Unfortunately, the vast majority of silent films survive today in inferior prints that no longer reflect the care that the original technicians put into them. The modern versions of silent films may appear jerky and flickery, but the vast picture palaces did not attract four to six
(30) thousand people a night by giving them eyestrain. A silent film depended on its visuals; as soon as you degrade those, you lose elements that go far beyond the image on the surface. The acting in silents was often very subtle, very restrained, despite legends to the contrary.

Passage 2

(35) Mime opens up a new world to the beholder, but it does so insidiously, not by purposely injecting points of interest in the manner of a tour guide. Audiences are not unlike visitors to a foreign land who discover that the modes, manners, and thoughts of its inhabitants are not
(40) meaningless oddities, but are sensible in context.

I remember once when an audience seemed perplexed at what I was doing. At first, I tried to gain a more immediate response by using slight exaggerations. I soon realized that these actions had nothing to do with the
(45) audience's understanding of the character. What I had believed to be a failure of the audience to respond in the manner I expected was, in fact, only their concentration on what I was doing; they were enjoying a gradual awakening—a slow transference of their understanding
(50) from their own time and place to one that appeared so unexpectedly before their eyes. This was evidenced by their growing response to succeeding numbers.

Mime is an elusive art, as its expression is entirely dependent on the ability of the performer to imagine a
(55) character and to re-create that character for each performance. As a mime, I am a physical medium, the instrument upon which the figures of my imagination play their dance of life. The individuals in my audience also have responsibilities—they must be alert
(60) collaborators. They cannot sit back, mindlessly complacent, and wait to have their emotions titillated by mesmeric musical sounds or visual rhythms or acrobatic feats, or by words that tell them what to think. Mime is an art that, paradoxically, appeals both to those who
(65) respond instinctively to entertainment and to those whose appreciation is more analytical and complex. Between these extremes lie those audiences conditioned to resist any collaboration with what is played before them, and these the mime must seduce despite
(70) themselves. There is only one way to attack those reluctant minds—take them unaware! They will be delighted at an unexpected pleasure.

1 The author of Passage 1 uses the phrase "enthusiastic uncertainty" in line 17 to suggest that the filmmakers were

(A) excited to be experimenting in a new field
(B) delighted at the opportunity to study new technology
(C) optimistic in spite of the obstacles that faced them
(D) eager to challenge existing conventions
(E) eager to please but unsure of what the public wanted

2 In context, the reference to "eyestrain" (line 30) conveys a sense of

(A) irony regarding the incompetence of silent film technicians
(B) regret that modern viewers are unable to see high quality prints of silent films
(C) resentment that the popularity of picture palaces has waned in recent years
(D) pleasure in remembering a grandeur that has passed
(E) amazement at the superior quality of modern film technology

3 In lines 19-24, *Regeneration* and the films of Thomas Ince are presented as examples of

(A) formulaic and uninspired silent films
(B) profitable successes of a flourishing industry
(C) suspenseful action films drawing large audiences
(D) daring applications of an artistic philosophy
(E) unusual products of a readiness to experiment

4 In line 34, "legends" most nearly means

(A) ancient folklore
(B) obscure symbols
(C) history lessons
(D) famous people
(E) common misconceptions

5 The author of Passage 2 most likely considers the contrast of mime artist and tour guide appropriate because both

(A) are concerned with conveying factual information
(B) employ artistic techniques to communicate their knowledge
(C) determine whether others enter a strange place
(D) shape the way others perceive a new situation
(E) explore new means of self-expression

6 In lines 41-52, the author most likely describes a specific experience in order to

(A) dispel some misconceptions about what a mime is like
(B) show how challenging the career of a mime can be
(C) portray the intensity required to see the audience's point of view
(D) explain how unpredictable mime performances can be
(E) indicate the adjustments an audience must make in watching mime

7 In lines 60-63, the author's description of techniques used in the types of performances is

(A) disparaging
(B) astonished
(C) sorrowful
(D) indulgent
(E) sentimental

8 Both passages are primarily concerned with the subject of

(A) shocking special effects
(B) varied dramatic styles
(C) visual elements in dramatic performances
(D) audience resistance to theatrical performances
(E) nostalgia for earlier forms of entertainment

9 The incident described in lines 41-52 shows the author of Passage 2 to be similar to the silent filmmakers of Passage 1 in the way she

(A) required very few props
(B) used subtle technical skills to convey universal truths
(C) learned through trial and error
(D) combined narration with visual effects
(E) earned a loyal audience of followers

10 What additional information would reduce the apparent similarity between these two art forms?

(A) Silent film audiences were also accustomed to vaudeville and theatrical presentations.
(B) Silent films could show newsworthy events as well as dramatic entertainment.
(C) Dialogue in the form of captions was integrated into silent films.
(D) Theaters running silent films gave many musicians steady jobs.
(E) Individual characters created for silent films became famous in their own right.

11 Both passages mention which of the following as being important to the artistic success of the dramatic forms they describe?

(A) Effective fusion of disparate dramatic elements
(B) Slightly exaggerated characterization
(C) Incorporation of realistic details
(D) Large audiences
(E) Audience involvement

Answers and Explanations

1 The author of Passage 1 uses the phrase "enthusiastic uncertainty" in line 17 to suggest that the filmmakers were

(A) excited to be experimenting in a new field
(B) delighted at the opportunity to study new technology
(C) optimistic in spite of the obstacles that faced them
(D) eager to challenge existing conventions
(E) eager to please but unsure of what the public wanted

The correct answer is (A).

Explanation:
Look at the beginning of the third paragraph of Passage 1. The filmmakers were *enthusiastic* about a new kind of art form in which they could experiment. And experimentation led to *accidental discoveries* (line 18), which suggests *uncertainty*.

The other choices

Choice (B) is wrong because the filmmakers were delighted to use the new technology rather than to study it.

Choice (C) can be eliminated because the passage does not talk about **obstacles** faced by the filmmakers.

Choice (D) is specifically contradicted by the words in line 16 that refer to the fact that these filmmakers were working **before formulas took shape**. The word **formulas** in this context means the same thing as **conventions**.

Choice (E) is not correct because the **uncertainty** of the filmmakers was related to the new technology and how to use it, not to **what the public wanted**.

 HINT

Read each choice carefully and compare what it says to the information in the passage.

2 In context, the reference to "eyestrain" (line 30) conveys a sense of

(A) irony regarding the incompetence of silent film technicians
(B) regret that modern viewers are unable to see high quality prints of silent films
(C) resentment that the popularity of picture palaces has waned in recent years
(D) pleasure in remembering a grandeur that has passed
(E) amazement at the superior quality of modern film technology

The correct answer is (B).

Explanation:
The author draws a distinction between the way silent films look when viewed today—*jerky and flickery* (line 28)—and the way they looked when they were originally shown. He implies that thousands of people would not have come to the movie houses if the pictures had given them *eyestrain*. The author indicates that the perception of silent films today is unfortunate. This feeling can be described as regret.

The other choices

Choice (A) can be eliminated because there is no indication in the passage that silent film technicians were **incompetent**. The author even mentions **the care** taken by **the original technicians** (lines 26-27).

Both choices (C) and (D) are wrong because they do not answer this question. Remember, the question refers to the statement about **eyestrain**. The remark about eyestrain concerns the technical quality of the films, not the **popularity of picture palaces** or **a grandeur that has passed**.

Choice (E) is incorrect for two reasons. First, no sense of **amazement** is conveyed in the statement about eyestrain. Second, the author does not say that modern films are **superior** to silent films, only that the **prints** of silent films are **inferior** to what they once were (lines 25-26).

 ⊘ HINT

Try eliminating choices that you know are wrong. Rule out choices that don't answer the question being asked or that are contradicted by the information in the passage.

---

3 In lines 19-24, *Regeneration* and the films of Thomas Ince are presented as examples of

(A) formulaic and uninspired silent films
(B) profitable successes of a flourishing industry
(C) suspenseful action films drawing large audiences
(D) daring applications of an artistic philosophy
(E) unusual products of a readiness to experiment

The correct answer is (E).

Explanation:
The author's argument in the third paragraph is that there was lots of *room for experimentation* (line 17) in the silent film industry. Both *Regeneration* and Ince's films are specifically mentioned as examples of that readiness to experiment.

Choice (A) is directly contradicted in two ways by the information in the passage. First, line 16 says that the filmmakers worked **before formulas took shape**, so their work could not be **formulaic**. Second, the author refers to *Regeneration* as having some **startling** effects and indicates that the endings of Ince's films were different from other films of the time. So it would not be correct to describe these films as **uninspired**.

Choices (B), (C), and (D) are wrong because the author does not argue that these films were **profitable, suspenseful,** or **applications of an artistic philosophy**. He argues that they are examples of a willingness to **experiment**.

The other choices

 HINT

As you consider the choices, think of the words, phrases, and sentences in the passage that relate to the question you are answering. Be aware of how the ideas in the passage are presented. What is the author's point? How does the author explain and support important points?

4 In line 34, "legends" most nearly means

    (A) ancient folklore
    (B) obscure symbols
    (C) history lessons
    (D) famous people
    (E) common misconceptions

The correct answer is (E).

Explanation:
    A *legend* is an idea or story that has come down from the past. A secondary meaning of *legend* is anything made up rather than based on fact. Throughout the final paragraph of Passage 1, the author emphasizes that people today have the wrong idea about the visual quality of silent films. In the last sentence, the author states that the acting was *often very subtle* and *very restrained*, and then he adds, *despite legends to the contrary*. So, according to the author, silent film acting is today thought of as unsubtle and unrestrained, but that is a misconception, an idea not based on fact, a *legend.*

The other choices

    Choice (A) is the most common meaning of **legend**, but it doesn't make any sense here. There is no reference to or suggestion about **ancient folklore**.
    Choice (B) has no support at all in the passage.
    Choice (C) can be eliminated because the author does not refer to **history lessons** in this sentence, but to mistaken notions about the performances in silent films.
    Choice (D) simply doesn't make sense. In line 34, the word **legends** refers to acting, not to **people**.

 HINT

    This is a vocabulary-in-context question. Even if you don't know the meaning of the word, try to figure it out from the passage and the choices. Examine the context in which the word is used.
    Think of some word(s) that would make sense in the sentence, then look at the answers to see if any choice is similar to the word(s) you thought of.

5 The author of Passage 2 most likely considers the contrast of mime artist and tour guide appropriate because both

    (A) are concerned with conveying factual information
    (B) employ artistic techniques to communicate their knowledge
    (C) determine whether others enter a strange place
    (D) shape the way others perceive a new situation
    (E) explore new means of self-expression

The correct answer is (D).

Explanation:
   To answer this question, you have to find a choice that describes a similarity between the performances of a mime and the work of a tour guide. The author begins Passage 2 by saying that a mime *opens up a new world to the beholder,* but in a *manner* (or way) different from that of a tour guide. Thus the author assumes that contrasting the mime and the tour guide is appropriate because both of them *shape the way others perceive a new situation.*

Choice (A) may correctly describe a tour guide, but it doesn't fit the mime. Nowhere in the passage does the author say the mime conveys **factual information**.

Choice (B) is true for the mime but not for the tour guide.

Choice (C) is wrong because the author of Passage 2 contrasts how mimes and tour guides introduce others to **a new world**, not how they **determine** entrance to **a strange place**.

Choice (E) is incorrect because the author does not discuss **self-expression** as a tour guide's work, and because she indicates that, as a mime, she expresses a particular character, not her own personality.

The other choices

 HINT

Pay close attention when authors make connections, comparisons, or contrasts. These parts of passages help you identify the authors' points of view and assumptions.

---

6 In lines 41-52, the author most likely describes a specific experience in order to

(A) dispel some misconceptions about what a mime is like
(B) show how challenging the career of a mime can be
(C) portray the intensity required to see the audience's point of view
(D) explain how unpredictable mime performances can be
(E) indicate the adjustments an audience must make in watching mime

The correct answer is (E).

Explanation:
The correct answer must explain why the author described a particular experience in lines 41-52. The author's point is that she learned the audience was *enjoying a gradual awakening*. Only choice (E) indicates that the story shows the *adjustments* the audience had to make to appreciate her performance.

The other choices

Choice (A) can be eliminated because the only **misconception** that is dispelled is the author's **misconception** about the audience.

Choice (B) is wrong because, while the story might suggest that mime is a **challenging career**, that is not the author's point in describing the experience.

Choice (C) can't be correct because there is no reference to **intensity** on the part of the mime.

Choice (D) is wrong because the emphasis of lines 41-52 is not on how **unpredictable** mime performance is but on what the author learned from her failure to understand the audience's initial reaction.

 HINT

Every word counts. When you're asked about the author's intent in describing something, you have to pay close attention to how the author uses details to explain, support, or challenge the point being made.

7 In lines 60-63, the author's description of techniques used in the types of performances is

(A) disparaging
(B) astonished
(C) sorrowful
(D) indulgent
(E) sentimental

The correct answer is (A).

Explanation:
The sentence beginning in line 60 says that when viewing mime, the audience *cannot sit back, mindlessly complacent.* The author then says that other types of performances *titillate* audience emotions by *mesmeric musical sounds* or *acrobatic feats.* The author uses these kinds of words to belittle other techniques—her tone is *disparaging.*

Choices (B), (C), and (E) can be eliminated because no **astonishment**, **sorrow**, or **sentimentalism** is suggested in lines 60-63.

The other choices

Choice (D) is almost the opposite of what the author means. She is not at all **indulgent** toward these other types of performance.

 HINT

To figure out the author's attitude or tone, or how the author feels about something, think about how the author uses language in the passage.

---

8 Both passages are primarily concerned with the subject of

(A) shocking special effects
(B) varied dramatic styles
(C) visual elements in dramatic performances
(D) audience resistance to theatrical performances
(E) nostalgia for earlier forms of entertainment

The correct answer is (C).

Explanation:
This question asks you to think about *both* passages. Notice that the question asks you to look for the main subject or focus of the pair of passages, not simply to recognize that one passage is about silent film and the other about mime.

The discussion in Passage 1 is most concerned with the effectiveness of silent films for audiences of that era. The discussion in Passage 2 is most concerned with what makes a mime performance effective for the audience. The main subject for *both* passages is ways that a silent, visual form of entertainment affects an audience. Choice (C) is correct because it refers to performance in a visual art form.

The other choices

Choice (A) can be eliminated because **shocking special effects** is not a main subject of either passage.

Choice (B) is wrong because, although **varied dramatic styles** (used by film performers and in mime) is briefly touched on in both passages, it is not the main subject of the *pair* of passages.

In Choice (D), **audience resistance to theatrical performances** is too specific: both authors are making points about the overall role of audiences in the performance. Choice (D) is also incorrect because that topic is primarily addressed only in Passage 2.

Choice (E) can be eliminated because a tone of nostalgia appears only in Passage 1.

 HINT

This question involves a comparison of two reading passages. Review the relevant parts of *each* passage as you make your way through the choices.

---

9 The incident described in lines 41-52 shows the author of Passage 2 to be similar to the silent filmmakers of Passage 1 in the way she

(A) required very few props
(B) used subtle technical skills to convey universal truths
(C) learned through trial and error
(D) combined narration with visual effects
(E) earned a loyal audience of followers

The correct answer is (C).

Explanation:

The question focuses on the story related in lines 41-52 and already examined in question 6. This question asks you to explain how that story shows that the mime is similar to silent film-makers. So the correct answer has to express a point made about the mime in lines 41-52 that is also true for the filmmakers described in Passage 1. Lines 41-52 show the mime changing her performance when she found something that did not work. Passage 1 says that filmmakers learned through *experimentation* and *accidental discoveries*. So all of these people *learned through trial and error*.

Choices (A), (B), (D), and (E) are not correct answers because they don't include traits both *described in lines 41-52* and *shared with the film-makers*.

The other choices

Choice (A) is wrong because **props** aren't mentioned in either passage.

Choice (B) is wrong because **conveying universal truths** is not discussed in Passage 1.

Choice (D) is wrong because a mime performs without speaking or **narration**.

Choice (E) is wrong because Passage 1 describes loyal audiences but lines 41-52 do not.

 HINT

When a question following a pair of passages asks you to identify something that is common to both passages or true for both passages, eliminate any answer that is true for only one of the two passages.

---

10 What additional information would reduce the apparent similarity between these two art forms?

(A) Silent film audiences were also accustomed to vaudeville and theatrical presentations.

(B) Silent films could show newsworthy events as well as dramatic entertainment.

(C) Dialogue in the form of captions was integrated into silent films.

(D) Theaters running silent films gave many musicians steady jobs.

(E) Individual characters created for silent films became famous in their own right.

The correct answer is (C).

Explanation:

This question asks you to do two things: first, figure out a similarity between silent films and mime; second, choose an answer with information that isn't found in either passage but would make mime performance and silent films seem *less* similar.

If you think about the art forms discussed in the two passages, you should realize that neither uses *speech*. And this is an important similarity. Silent films include music but not spoken words. As stated in the Introduction to the two passages, a mime entertains *without speaking*. Choice (C) adds the information that *dialogue* between characters was part of silent films. Characters "spoke" to each other even though audiences read captions instead of hearing spoken words. So silent film indirectly used speech and was different from mime, which relies on *gesture, facial expression, and movement*.

The other choices

Choices (A), (B), (D) and (E) are wrong because they don't deal with the fundamental **similarity** between the two art forms—the absence of words. These may all be interesting things to know about silent film, but **vaudeville** performances, **newsworthy events**, **steady jobs** for musicians, and fame of **individual characters** have nothing to do with mime. None of these things is related to an apparent similarity between mime and silent films.

 HINT

This question asks you to think about the two reading passages together. Remember that you should also consider the information in the introduction when you compare passages.

---

11 Both passages mention which of the following as being important to the artistic success of the dramatic forms they describe?

(A) Effective fusion of disparate dramatic elements
(B) Slightly exaggerated characterization
(C) Incorporation of realistic details
(D) Large audiences
(E) Audience involvement

The correct answer is (E).

Explanation:

Passage 1 very clearly states in lines 5-8 that audience involvement was important to the success of silent films. In lines 58-60 of Passage 2, the author makes a similarly strong statement about how important it is for the audience to be involved in mime performance.

Choices (A)-(D) are wrong because they don't refer to ideas mentioned in *both* passages as **important to the artistic success of the dramatic forms**. Choice (A) can be eliminated because Passage 1 talks about the **fusion** of pictures and music, but Passage 2 is not concerned at all with **disparate dramatic elements**.

Choice (B) refers to something mentioned in Passage 2 (line 43), but it is *not* something important to the success of a mime performance. And Passage 1 says that the **acting in silents was often very subtle, very restrained** (lines 33-34), which is the opposite of **exaggerated**.

Choice (C) is mentioned only in Passage 1 (lines 20-22), and not as an element **important to the artistic success** of silent films in general.

Choice (D) is not correct because the author of Passage 1 says that silent films did enjoy **large audiences**, but he doesn't say that **large audiences** were critical to the **artistic success** of the films. Passage 2 doesn't mention the size of the audiences at all.

The other choices

 HINT

When comparing two passages, focus on the specific subject of the question. Don't try to remember everything from both passages. Refer to the passages as you work your way through the five choices.

RECAP: HINTS ON CRITICAL READING QUESTIONS

1. The information you need to answer each question is *in the passage(s)*. All questions ask you to base your answer on what you read in the passages, introductions, and (sometimes) footnotes.

2. Every word counts. Details in a passage help you understand how the author wants you to feel or think.

3. Try marking up the passages or making short notes in the sample test and practice questions in this book. Find out whether this strategy saves you time and helps you answer more questions correctly.

4. Reading the questions and answers carefully is as important as reading the passage carefully.

5. An answer can be true and still be the wrong answer to a particular question.

6. There should always be information in the passage(s) that supports your choice—specific words, phrases, and/or sentences that help to prove your choice is correct.

7. If you're not sure of the correct answer, try eliminating choices.

8. When you have made your choice, double-check the other choices to make sure there isn't a better one.

9. For some passages, you might want to read the questions before you read the passage so you get a sense of what to look for. If the content of the passage is familiar, looking at the questions before you read the passage might be a waste of time. So try both methods when you take the sample test and do the practice questions in this book to see if one approach is more helpful than the other.

10. Don't get bogged down on difficult questions. You might want to skim a set of questions and start by answering those you feel sure of. Then concentrate on the harder questions. Don't skip between sets of reading questions, because when you return to a passage you'll probably have to read it again.

11. When you have gone through all the questions associated with a passage, go back and review any you left out or weren't sure about.

12. If a verbal section contains more than one reading passage, you may want to look for one that deals with a familiar or especially interesting topic to work on first. If you skip a set of questions, however, be sure to fill in your answer sheet correctly.

A Final Note on Critical Reading Questions

There's no shortcut to doing well on Critical Reading questions. The best way to improve your reading skills is to practice—not just with specific passages and multiple-choice test questions but with books, magazines, essays, and newspapers that include complex ideas, challenging vocabulary, and subjects that make you think.

There are some things to keep in mind as you tackle the actual test questions. The most important is always to go back to the passages and look for the specific words, phrases, sentences, and ideas that either support or contradict each choice.

You may not have time to go back to the passage for every answer to every question. If you remember enough from what you have read to answer a question quickly and confidently, you should do so, and then go on to the next question. But the source for the answers is the passages. And when you're practicing for the test, it's a good idea to go back to the passage after answering a question and prove to yourself that your choice is right and the other choices are wrong. This will help you sharpen your reading and reasoning skills and give you practice in using the information in the passages to figure out the correct answers.

CHAPTER FIVE

Practice Questions

Independent Practice **74**
Analogies 74
Sentence Completions 76
Critical Reading 78

Answer Key **80**

Independent Practice

The following questions are meant to give you a chance to practice the test-taking skills and strategies you've developed so far. Use them to try out different hints and ways of approaching questions before you take the practice tests in the last section of this book. If you have trouble with any of the questions, be sure to review the material in Chapter 4. Keep in mind that this chapter is intended to give you practice with the different types of questions, so it isn't arranged the way the questions will actually appear on the SAT.

Analogies

Each question below consists of a related pair of words or phrases, followed by five pairs of words or phrases labeled A through E. Select the pair that best expresses a relationship similar to that expressed in the original pair.

Example:

CRUMB:BREAD::
(A) ounce:unit
(B) splinter:wood
(C) water:bucket
(D) twine:rope
(E) cream:butter

1 NEEDLE:KNITTING::

(A) finger:sewing
(B) sign:painting
(C) throat:singing
(D) hurdle:running
(E) chisel:carving

2 SUBMERGE:WATER::

(A) parch:soil
(B) bury:earth
(C) suffocate:air
(D) disperse:gas
(E) extinguish:fire

3 TALON:HAWK::

(A) horn:bull
(B) fang:snake
(C) claw:tiger
(D) tail:monkey
(E) shell:tortoise

4 ACRE:LAND::

(A) distance:space
(B) speed:movement
(C) gallon:liquid
(D) degree:thermometer
(E) year:birthday

5 COMPATRIOTS:COUNTRY::

(A) transients:home
(B) kinsfolk:family
(C) competitors:team
(D) performers:audience
(E) figureheads:government

6 INFURIATE:DISPLEASE::

(A) release:drop
(B) oppress:swelter
(C) drench:moisten
(D) stir:respond
(E) conceive:imagine

7 STRATAGEM:OUTWIT::

(A) prototype:design
(B) variation:change
(C) decoy:lure
(D) riddle:solve
(E) charade:guess

8 WANDERLUST:TRAVEL::

(A) fantasy:indulge
(B) innocence:confess
(C) ignorance:know
(D) digression:speak
(E) avarice:acquire

9 DEFECTOR:CAUSE::

(A) counterfeiter:money
(B) deserter:army
(C) critic:book
(D) advertiser:sale
(E) intruder:meeting

10 TACIT:WORDS::

(A) visible:scenes
(B) inevitable:facts
(C) colorful:hues
(D) suspicious:clues
(E) unanimous:disagreements

Sentence Completions

Each sentence below has one or two blanks, each blank indicating that something has been omitted. Beneath the sentence are five lettered words or sets of words labeled A through E. Choose the word or set of words that, when inserted in the sentence, best fits the meaning of the sentence as a whole.

Example:

Medieval kingdoms did not become constitutional republics overnight; on the contrary, the change was - - - -.

    (A) unpopular
    (B) unexpected
    (C) advantageous
    (D) sufficient
    (E) gradual   

1 Investigation of the epidemic involved determining what was - - - - about the people who were affected, what made them differ from those who remained well.

    (A) chronic
    (B) unique
    (C) fortunate
    (D) misunderstood
    (E) historical

2 Because management - - - - the fact that employees find it difficult to work alertly at repetitive tasks, it sponsors numerous projects to - - - - enthusiasm for the job.

    (A) recognizes..generate
    (B) disproves..create
    (C) respects..quench
    (D) controls..regulate
    (E) surmises..suspend

3 They did their best to avoid getting embroiled in the quarrel, preferring to maintain their - - - - as long as possible.

    (A) consciousness
    (B) suspense
    (C) interest
    (D) decisiveness
    (E) neutrality

4 The strong affinity of these wild sheep for mountains is not - - - -: mountain slopes represent - - - - because they effectively limit the ability of less agile predators to pursue the sheep.

    (A) useful..peril
    (B) accidental..security
    (C) instinctive..attainment
    (D) restrained..nourishment
    (E) surprising..inferiority

5 Even those who do not - - - - Robinson's views - - - - him as a candidate who has courageously refused to compromise his convictions.

    (A) shrink from..condemn
    (B) profit from..dismiss
    (C) concur with..recognize
    (D) disagree with..envision
    (E) dissent from..remember

6 The alarm voiced by the committee investigating the accident had a - - - - effect, for its dire predictions motivated people to take precautions that - - - - an ecological disaster.

    (A) trivial..prompted
    (B) salutary..averted
    (C) conciliatory..supported
    (D) beneficial..exacerbated
    (E) perverse..vanquished

7 At the age of forty-five, with a worldwide reputation and an as yet unbroken string of notable successes to her credit, Carson was at the - - - - of her career.

(A) paradigm
(B) zenith
(C) fiasco
(D) periphery
(E) inception

8 The fact that they cherished religious objects more than most of their other possessions - - - - the - - - - role of religion in their lives.

(A) demonstrates..crucial
(B) obliterates..vital
(C) limits..daily
(D) concerns..informal
(E) denotes..varying

9 Mary Cassatt, an Impressionist painter, was the epitome of the - - - - American: a native of Philadelphia who lived most of her life in Paris.

(A) conservative
(B) provincial
(C) benevolent
(D) prophetic
(E) expatriate

10 In the nineteenth century many literary critics saw themselves as stern, authoritarian figures defending society against the - - - - of those - - - - beings called authors.

(A) depravities..wayward
(B) atrocities..exemplary
(C) merits..ineffectual
(D) kudos..antagonistic
(E) indictments..secretive

Critical Reading

Each passage below is followed by questions based on its content. Answer the questions following the passage on the basis of what is *stated* or *implied* in that passage and in any introductory material that may be provided.

Fear of communism swept through the United States in the years following the Russian Revolution of 1917.
Line *Several states passed espionage acts that restricted political discussion, and radicals of all descriptions were*
(5) *rounded up in so-called Red Raids conducted by the attorney general's office. Some were convicted and imprisoned; others were deported. This was the background of a trial in Chicago involving twenty men charged under Illinois's espionage statute with*
(10) *advocating the violent overthrow of the government. The charge rested on the fact that all the defendants were members of the newly formed Communist Labor party.*
The accused in the case were represented by Clarence Darrow, one of the foremost defense attorneys in the
(15) *country. Throughout his career, Darrow had defended the poor and the despised against exploitation and prejudice. He defended the rights of labor unions, for example, at a time when many sought to outlaw the strike, and he was resolute in defending constitutional*
(20) *freedoms. The following are excerpts from Darrow's summation to the jury.*

Members of the Jury . . . . If you want to convict these twenty men, then do it. I ask no consideration on behalf of any one of them. They are no better than any other
(25) twenty men or women; they are no better than the millions down through the ages who have been prosecuted and convicted in cases like this. And if it is necessary for my clients to show that America is like all the rest, if it is necessary that my clients shall go to prison to show it,
(30) then let them go. They can afford it if you members of the jury can; make no mistake about that. . . .
The State says my clients "dare to criticize the Constitution." Yet this police officer (who the State says is a fine, right-living person) twice violated the federal Con-
(35) stitution while a prosecuting attorney was standing by. They entered Mr. Owen's home without a search warrant. They overhauled his papers. They found a flag, a red one, which he had the same right to have in his house that you have to keep a green one, or a yellow one, or any
(40) other color, and the officer impudently rolled it up and put another flag on the wall, nailed it there. By what right was that done? What about this kind of patriotism that violates the Constitution? Has it come to pass in this country that officers of the law can trample on constitu-
(45) tional rights and then excuse it in a court of justice? . . .
Most of what has been presented to this jury to stir up feeling in your souls has not the slightest bearing on proving conspiracy in this case. Take Mr. Lloyd's speech in Milwaukee. It had nothing to do with conspiracy.
(50) Whether the speech was a joke or was serious, I will not

attempt to discuss. But I will say that if it was serious it was as mild as a summer's shower compared with many of the statements of those who are responsible for working conditions in this country. We have heard from people
(55) in high places that those individuals who express sympathy with labor should be stood up against a wall and shot. We have heard people of position declare that individuals who criticize the actions of those who are getting rich should be put in a cement ship with leaden sails and sent
(60) out to sea. Every violent appeal that could be conceived by the brain has been used by the powerful and the strong. I repeat, Mr. Lloyd's speech was gentle in comparison. . . .
My clients are condemned because they say in their platform that, while they vote, they believe the ballot is
(65) secondary to education and organization. Counsel suggests that those who get something they did not vote for are sinners, but I suspect you the jury know full well that my clients are right. Most of you have an eight-hour day. Did you get it by any vote you ever cast? No. It came
(70) about because workers laid down their tools and said we will no longer work until we get an eight-hour day. That is how they got the twelve-hour day, the ten-hour day, and the eight-hour day—not by voting but by laying down their tools. Then when it was over and the victory won
(75) . . . then the politicians, in order to get the labor vote, passed legislation creating an eight-hour day. That is how things changed; victory preceded law. . . .
You have been told that if you acquit these defendants you will be despised because you will endorse everything
(80) they believe. But I am not here to defend my clients' opinions. I am here to defend their right to express their opinions. I ask you, then, to decide this case upon the facts as you have heard them, in light of the law as you understand it, in light of the history of our country, whose institutions you and I are bound to protect.

1 Which best captures the meaning of the word "consideration" in line 23?

(A) Leniency
(B) Contemplation
(C) Due respect
(D) Reasoned judgment
(E) Legal rights

2 By "They can afford it if you members of the jury can" (lines 30-31), Darrow means that

(A) no harm will come to the defendants if they are convicted in this case
(B) the jurors will be severely criticized by the press if they convict the defendants
(C) the defendants are indifferent about the outcome of the trial
(D) the verdict of the jury has financial implications for all of the people involved in the trial
(E) a verdict of guilty would be a potential threat to everyone's rights

3 Lines 32-45 suggest that the case against Owen would have been dismissed if the judge had interpreted the constitution in which of the following ways?

(A) Defendants must have their rights read to them when they are arrested.
(B) Giving false testimony in court is a crime.
(C) Evidence gained by illegal means is not admissible in court.
(D) No one can be tried twice for the same crime.
(E) Defendants cannot be forced to give incriminating evidence against themselves.

4 In line 47, the word "bearing" most nearly means

(A) connection
(B) posture
(C) endurance
(D) location
(E) resemblance

5 In lines 46-62, Darrow's defense rests mainly on convincing the jury that

(A) a double standard is being employed
(B) the prosecution's evidence is untrustworthy
(C) the defendants share mainstream American values
(D) labor unions have the right to strike
(E) the defendants should be tried by a federal rather than a state court

6 The information in lines 46-62 suggests that the prosecution treated Mr. Lloyd's speech primarily as

(A) sarcasm to be resented
(B) propaganda to be ridiculed
(C) criticism to be answered
(D) a threat to be feared
(E) a bad joke to be dismissed

7 Darrow accuses "people in high places" (lines 54-55) of

(A) conspiring to murder members of the Communist party
(B) encouraging violence against critics of wealthy business owners
(C) pressuring members of the jury to convict the defendants
(D) advocating cruel and unusual punishment for criminals
(E) insulting the public's intelligence by making foolish suggestions

8 The word "education" (line 65) is a reference to the need for

(A) establishing schools to teach the philosophy of the Communist Labor party
(B) making workers aware of their economic and political rights
(C) teaching factory owners about the needs of laborers
(D) creating opportunities for on-the-job training in business
(E) helping workers to continue their schooling

9 The statement "victory preceded law" (line 77) refers to the fact that

(A) social reform took place only after labor unions organized support for their political candidates
(B) politicians need to win the support of labor unions if they are to be elected
(C) politicians can introduce legislative reform only if they are elected to office
(D) politicians did not initiate improved working conditions but legalized them after they were in place
(E) politicians have shown that they are more interested in winning elections than in legislative reform

10 Judging from lines 78-80, the jury had apparently been told that finding the defendants innocent would be the same as

(A) denying the importance of the Constitution
(B) giving people the right to strike
(C) encouraging passive resistance
(D) inhibiting free speech
(E) supporting communist doctrine

11 In order for Darrow to win the case, it would be most crucial that the jurors possess

(A) a thorough understanding of legal procedures and terminology
(B) a thorough understanding of the principles and beliefs of the Communist Labor party
(C) sympathy for labor's rights to safe and comfortable working conditions
(D) the ability to separate the views of the defendants from the rights of the defendants
(E) the courage to act in the best interests of the nation's economy

Answer Key

	ANALOGIES		SENTENCE COMPLETIONS		CRITICAL READING
1.	E	1.	B	1.	A
2.	B	2.	A	2.	E
3.	C	3.	E	3.	C
4.	C	4.	B	4.	A
5.	B	5.	C	5.	A
6.	C	6.	B	6.	D
7.	C	7.	B	7.	B
8.	E	8.	A	8.	B
9.	B	9.	E	9.	D
10.	E	10.	A	10.	E
				11.	D

PART THREE

SAT I: Mathematical Reasoning

▲ ▼ ▲ **Chapter 6**
Mathematics Review

▲ ▼ ▲ **Chapter 7**
Sample Mathematics Questions and Answers

PART THREE

Mathematical Reasoning

CHAPTER SIX

Mathematics Review

Introduction to the Mathematics Sections 84

Concepts You Need to Know 84

Math Reference Material 86

Types of Questions 86
Five-Choice Multiple-Choice Questions...86
Quantitative Comparison Questions 87
Grid-in Questions 89

Calculators Are Recommended 93
Bring Your Own Calculator....................93

Some General Tips 95

Arithmetic Concepts You Should Know 95
Properties of Integers 95
Number Lines...97
Squares and Square Roots......................98
Fractions 99
Factors, Multiples, and Remainders 100
Sample Questions 100
Averages 101
Sample Question...................................104
Ratio and Proportion 104
Sample Question...................................105
Sample Question...................................106

Algebra...107
Factoring..107
Exponents 108
Solving Equations 108
Direct Translations of Math Terms.........109
Inequalities...110
Number Sequences 111

Word Problems 111
Hints on Solving Word Problems 111
Sample Questions 112

Geometry 115
Triangles...115
Quadrilaterals, Lines, and Angles..........118
Areas and Perimeters 119
Other Polygons 121
Circles...123

Miscellaneous Math Questions........125
Data Interpretation...............................126
Sample Questions 127
Counting and Ordering Problems.........129
Special Symbols....................................130
Logical Analysis....................................131

Introduction to the Mathematics Sections

These sections of the SAT emphasize mathematical reasoning. They evaluate how well you can think through mathematics problems.

The test requires that you know some specific math concepts and have learned some math skills, but it's intended to evaluate how well you can use what you know to solve problems.

This chapter presents many of the skills and concepts that will appear on the test and shows you how to use them.

Concepts You Need to Know

There are four broad categories of problems in the math test: Arithmetic, Algebra, Geometry, and Miscellaneous.

The following table lists the basic skills and concepts with which you need to be familiar in each of the four categories. Remember, *be familiar with* means that you understand them and can apply them to a variety of math problems.

Arithmetic
• Problem solving that involves simple addition, subtraction, multiplication, and division • Conceptual understanding of arithmetic operations with fractions • Averages (arithmetic mean), median, and mode • Properties of integers: odd and even numbers, prime numbers, positive and negative integers, factors, divisibility, and multiples • Word problems involving such concepts as rate/time/ distance, percents, averages • Number line: order, betweenness, and consecutive numbers • Ratio and proportion **Not included** • Tedious or long computations

---

Algebra

- Operations involving signed numbers
- Word problems: translating verbal statements into algebraic expressions
- Substitution
- Simplifying algebraic expressions
- Elementary factoring
- Solving algebraic equations and inequalities
- Manipulation of positive integer exponents and roots
- Simple quadratic equations

Not included
- Complicated manipulations with radicals and roots
- Solving quadratic equations that require the use of the quadratic formula
- Exponents that are NOT whole numbers.

Geometry

- Properties of parallel and perpendicular lines
- Angle relationships—vertical angles and angles in geometric figures
- Properties of triangles: right, isosceles, and equilateral; 30°-60°-90° and other "special" right triangles; total of interior angles; Pythagorean theorem; similarity
- Properties of polygons: perimeter, area, angle measures
- Properties of circles: circumference, area, radius, diameter
- Solids: volume, surface area
- Simple coordinate geometry, including slope, coordinates of points

Not included
- Formal geometric proofs
- Volumes other than rectangular solids and those given in the reference material or in individual questions

Miscellaneous

- Probability
- Data interpretation
- Counting and ordering problems
- Special symbols
- Logical analysis

Math Reference Material

Reference material is included in the math test. You may find these facts and formulas helpful in answering some of the questions on the test. To get an idea of what's included, take a look at the practice tests in Part Four of this book.

Don't let the Reference Material give you a false sense of security. It isn't going to tell you how to solve math problems. To do well on the math test, you have to be comfortable working with these facts and formulas. If you haven't had practice using them before the test, you will have a hard time using them efficiently during the test.

For instance, if you forgot that the ratio of the sides of a 45°-45°-90° triangle is 1:1:$\sqrt{2}$, then the Reference Material will help you. If you don't know that there is a specific ratio for sides of a 45°-45°-90° triangle, or you don't know how to look for and recognize a 45°-45°-90° triangle, then the Reference Material isn't likely to help very much.

Doing well on the math test depends on being able to apply your math skills and knowledge to many different situations. Simply knowing formulas will not be enough.

Types of Questions

There are three types of questions on the math test: Five-Choice Multiple-Choice questions, Quantitative Comparison questions, and Student-Produced Responses ("Grid-in" questions).

Five-Choice Multiple-Choice Questions

Here's an example of a Multiple-Choice question with five choices:

If $2x + 2x + 2x = 12$, what is the value of $2x - 1$?

(A) 2
(B) 3
(C) 4
(D) 5
(E) 6

We'll return to this example later in the section; for now, we'll just tell you the correct answer is (B). Hints for answering specific kinds of Five-Choice Multiple-Choice questions are presented in Chapter 7.

Quantitative Comparison Questions

Quantitative Comparison questions are quite different from regular Five-Choice Multiple-Choice questions. Instead of presenting a problem and asking you to figure out the answer, Quantitative Comparison questions give you two quantities and ask you to compare them.

You'll be given one quantity on the left in Column A, and one quantity on the right in Column B. You have to figure out whether:

- The quantity in Column A is greater.
- The quantity in Column B is greater.
- The quantities are equal.
- You cannot determine which is greater from the information given.

Here are the directions you'll see on the test.

Directions for Quantitative Comparison Questions

<u>Questions 1-15</u> each consist of two quantities in boxes, one in Column A and one in Column B. You are to compare the two quantities and on the answer sheet fill in oval

A   if the quantity in Column A is greater;
B   if the quantity in Column B is greater;
C   if the two quantities are equal;
D   if the relationship cannot be determined from the information given.

AN E RESPONSE WILL NOT BE SCORED.

<u>Notes:</u>
1. In some questions, information is given about one or both of the quantities to be compared. In such cases, the given information is centered above the two columns and is not boxed.
2. In a given question, a symbol that appears in both columns represents the same thing in Column A as it does in Column B.
3. Letters such as x, n, and k stand for real numbers.

EXAMPLES

	Column A	Column B	Answers
E1	5^2	20	● Ⓑ Ⓒ Ⓓ Ⓔ

$150° \diagup x°$

E2	x	30	Ⓐ Ⓑ ● Ⓓ Ⓔ

r and s are integers

E3	$r + 1$	$s - 1$	Ⓐ Ⓑ Ⓒ ● Ⓔ

Specific hints on Quantitative Comparison questions are presented in Chapter 7.

All you are asked to do is make a comparison between two quantities. Frequently, you don't have to finish your calculations or determine an exact answer. You just have to know enough about the quantities to determine which one is greater.

The four answer choices are printed at the top of each page of every Quantitative Comparison section, but you can save some time if you memorize them:

- (A) if the column A quantity is greater;
- (B) if the column B quantity is greater;
- (C) if they are equal;
- (D) if you cannot tell from the information given.

If any two of the relationships (A), (B), or (C) can be true for a particular Quantitative Comparison question, then the answer to that question is (D).

Think of the columns as a balanced scale. You are trying to figure out which side of the scale is heavier. Before you make your measurement, you can eliminate any quantities that are the same on both sides of the scale. In other words, look for ways to simplify expressions and remove equal quantities from both columns before you make your comparison. For example:

Column A	Column B
34 + 43 + 58	36 + 43 + 58

You don't have to add up all the numbers to compare these two quantities. You can eliminate numbers 43 and 58, which appear in both columns. Now your comparison is much easier to make.

If you have a question in which quantities containing variables must be compared, try substituting values for the variables. Make sure you check above the columns for any information about what the values can be.

When substituting values to answer a Quantitative Comparison question, make sure you check the special cases: 0, 1, at least one number between 0 and 1, a number or numbers greater than 1, and a few negative numbers.

Grid-in Questions

In contrast to the Multiple-Choice question format, the student-produced response format requires you to figure out the correct answer and grid it on the answer sheet rather than just be able to recognize the correct answer among the choices.

Grid-in questions emphasize the importance of active problem solving and critical thinking in mathematics. Grid-in questions are solved just like any other math problems, but you have to figure out the correct answer exactly and fill it in on the grid. Here's the same question presented in the discussion of Five-Choice Multiple-Choice questions, but as a Grid-in question.

If $2x + 2x + 2x = 12$, what is the value of $2x - 1$?

The answer is still 3, but instead of filling in Choice (A), (B), (C), (D), or (E), you have to write 3 at the top of the grid and fill in 3 below.

Note: No question in this format has a negative answer since there is no way to indicate a negative sign in the grid.

One of the most important rules to remember about Grid-in questions is that **only answers entered on the grid are scored. Your handwritten answer at the top of the grid is not scored.** However, writing your answer at the top of the grid may help you avoid gridding errors.

In many cases, the Grid-in format allows you to provide your answer in more than one form. Here is an example of how you can use the grid to express the same answer as either a decimal or a fraction.

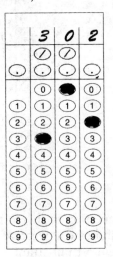

Here is an example of how you can enter the same answer in different ways on the grid. (Both are correct.)

Mixed numbers can't be entered due to grid limitations. An answer of 2 1/4 can't be gridded in that form.

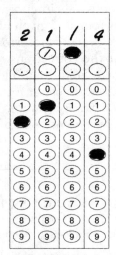

Wrong! Grid error!

The grid scoring system cannot distinguish between 2 1/4 and 21/4, so this answer would have to be entered as 2.25 or 9/4.

I M P O R T A N T ! ! !

Remember that only the answer entered on the grid, and not the answer handwritten at the top of the grid, is scored. You must decide whether to first write your answer in at the top of the grid and then transfer it to the grid, or to transfer your answer directly from notes in your test book, or in your head, to the grid. You might practice both approaches and see which one works best for you. You want to make sure you enter your answer correctly. While it might be more time-consuming to first write your answer in at the top of the grid, you may find this approach helps you avoid errors.

Grid-in Scoring

Answers to Grid-in questions are either completely correct and given full credit or completely wrong and given no credit. No partial credit is given, and *no* points are deducted for wrong answers.

You have to figure out the correct answer (or one of the correct answers on questions where more than one answer is possible), and correctly grid that answer to get credit for the question. **Remember**, you *won't* be penalized for a wrong answer in a Grid-in question. So it's better to put in an answer you're not sure of than to leave it blank.

 HINTS

GRID-IN QUESTIONS

The slash mark (/) is used to indicate a fraction bar.

You do not have to reduce fractions to their lowest terms, unless your answer will not fit in the grid.

You may express an answer as a fraction or a decimal. You can grid 1/2 as 1/2 or .5.

Mixed numbers must be expressed as improper fractions or decimals: You **must** express 1 3/5 as 8/5 or 1.6.

You don't have to grid in a zero in front of a decimal less than 1. 1/2 can be gridded as .5 or 0.5.

Grid as much of a repeating decimal as will fit in the grid. You may need to round a repeating decimal, but round only the last digit: grid 2/3 as 2/3, or as .666, or as .667. Do not grid the value 2/3 as .66 or .67 because these decimals don't fill the grid and aren't as accurate as .666 or .667.

Since you don't have choices provided to help avoid careless errors on Grid-in questions:

• Check your calculations carefully.

• Always double-check your answers. Make sure the answer you enter makes sense.

Make sure you have gridded your answer accurately and according to all the Grid-in rules.

Important: If you change your answer, erase your old gridded answer completely.

Practice a few Grid-in questions with a variety of answer types—whole numbers, fractions, and decimals. Get familiar with the mechanics of gridding.

Some Grid-in questions have more than one correct answer. You can grid any one of the correct answers and get full credit for the question.

Calculators Are Recommended

It is recommended that you bring a calculator to use on the math sections of the test. Although no question will require a calculator, field trials of the SAT I have shown that, on average, students who used calculators did slightly better on the test than students who did not.

While a number of factors influence your performance on the math sections, students with solid math preparation who use calculators on a regular basis are likely to do better on the test than students without this preparation.

Although math scores may improve on average with the use of calculators, there is no way of generalizing about the effect of calculator use on an individual student's score. It is likely that different students' scores will be affected in different ways.

Bring Your Own Calculator

You are expected to provide your own calculator, which can be any basic four-function, scientific, or graphing model (programmable or nonprogrammable).

You won't be permitted to use pocket organizers, handheld mini-computers, laptop computers, calculators with a typewriter type of keypad, calculators with paper tape, calculators that make noise, or calculators that require an external power source like an outlet. In addition, calculators can't be shared.

HINTS

CALCULATORS

Bring a calculator with you when you take the test, whether you think you will use it or not.

Only bring a calculator that you're comfortable using. Don't rush out to buy a sophisticated new calculator just for the test.

Don't try to use your calculator on every question.

First decide how you will solve each problem—then decide whether to use the calculator. The best way to learn which types of questions can be solved with a calculator is to practice on a variety of problems with and without the calculator. You'll learn when to turn to the calculator, and you'll be much more comfortable using your calculator during the actual test.

The calculations you are likely to do will usually involve simple arithmetic. If the arithmetic of a question gets so complicated or difficult that you need a calculator to figure it out, you are probably doing something wrong.

Make sure your calculator is in good working order and has fresh batteries. If it breaks down during the test, you'll have to go on without it.

Enter numbers very carefully. The calculator doesn't leave any notes, so if you enter the wrong numbers, you may not realize it.

Some General Tips

- Don't rush.
- Make notes in your test book.
- Draw figures to help you think through problems that involve geometric shapes, segment lengths, distances, proportions, sizes, etc.
- Write out calculations so that you can check them later.
- When a question contains a figure, note any measurements or values you calculate right on the figure.
- If you have time to check your work, try to redo your calculations in a different way from the way you did them the first time. This may take a bit more time, but it may help you catch an error.
- Use the choices to your advantage:
- If you can't figure out how to approach a problem, the form of the choices may give you a hint.
- You may find that you can eliminate some choices so you can make an educated guess, even if you aren't sure of the correct answer.
- If you decide to try all the choices, start with choice (C). *This is not because (C) is more likely to be the correct answer.*

    Start with (C) because, if the choices are numbers, they are usually listed in ascending order, from lowest to highest value. Then, if (C) turns out to be too high, you don't have to worry about (D) or (E). If (C) is too low, you don't have to worry about (A) or (B).
- Even though the questions generally run from easy to hard, always take a quick look at all of them. You never know when one of the "hard" ones just happens to involve a concept that you have recently learned or reviewed.

Arithmetic Concepts You Should Know

Properties of Integers

You will need to know the following information for a number of questions on the math test:

- Integers include positive whole numbers, their negatives, and zero (0).

$$-3, -2, -1, 0, 1, 2, 3, 4$$

- Integers extend indefinitely in both negative and positive directions.
- Integers *do not* include fractions or decimals.

    The following are negative integers:
    $$-4, -3, -2, -1$$

The following are positive integers:
$$1, 2, 3, 4$$

The integer zero (0) is neither positive nor negative.

Odd Numbers

$$-5, -3, -1, 1, 3, 5$$

Even Numbers

$$-4, -2, 0, 2, 4$$

The integer zero (0) is an even number.

Consecutive Integers

Integers that follow in sequence, where the positive difference between two successive integers is 1, are consecutive integers.

$$-1, 0, 1, 2, 3$$
$$1001, 1002, 1003, 1004$$
$$-14, -13, -12, -11$$

The following is a general mathematical notation for representing consecutive integers:

$$n, n + 1, n + 2, n + 3 \ldots, \text{where } n \text{ is any integer.}$$

Prime Numbers

A prime number is any number that has exactly two whole number factors—itself and the number 1. The number 1 itself *is not* prime.
　　Prime numbers include:

$$2, 3, 5, 7, 11, 13, 17, 19$$

Addition of Integers

$$\text{even} + \text{even} = \text{even}$$
$$\text{odd} + \text{odd} = \text{even}$$
$$\text{odd} + \text{even} = \text{odd}$$

Multiplication of Integers

$$\text{even} \times \text{even} = \text{even}$$
$$\text{odd} \times \text{odd} = \text{odd}$$
$$\text{odd} \times \text{even} = \text{even}$$

Number Lines

A number line is used to geometrically represent the relationships between numbers: integers, fractions, and/or decimals.

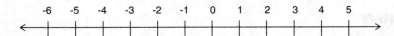

- Numbers on a number line always increase as you move to the right.
- Negative numbers are always shown with a negative sign (–). The plus sign (+) is usually not shown.
- Number lines are drawn to scale. You will be expected to make reasonable approximations of positions between labeled points on the line.

Number-line questions generally require you to figure out the relationships among numbers placed on the line. Number-line questions may ask:

- Where a number should be placed in relation to other numbers;
- The differences between two numbers;
- The lengths and the ratios of the lengths of line segments represented on the number line.

Sample Question

Here is a sample number-line question:

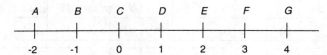

On the number line above, the ratio of the length of *AC* to the length of *AG* is equal to the ratio of the length of *CD* to the length of which of the following?

(A) *AD*
(B) *BD*
(C) *CG*
(D) *DF*
(E) *EG*

In this question, the number line is used to determine lengths: $AC = 2$, $AG = 6$, $CD = 1$. Once you have these lengths, the question becomes a ratio and proportion problem.

- The ratio of *AC* to *AG* is 2 to 6.
- *AC* is to *AG* as *CD* is to what?
- $\frac{2}{6} = \frac{1}{x}$
- $x = 3$

Now you have to go back to the number line to find the segment that has the length of 3. The answer is (A).

⚡ HINT

The distances between tick marks on a number line *do not* have to be measured in whole units.

The number line shown above is from a question that appeared on the SAT. The question requires that you figure out the coordinate of point *P*.

The units of measure are *thousandths*. (The distance between adjacent tick marks is .001.) Point *P* is at 0.428 on this number line.

Squares and Square Roots

Squares of Integers

Although you can always figure them out with paper and pencil or with your calculator, it's helpful if you know or at least can recognize the squares of integers between −12 and 12. Here they are:

x	1	2	3	4	5	6	7	8	9	10	11	12
x^2	1	4	9	16	25	36	49	64	81	100	121	144

x	−1	−2	−3	−4	−5	−6	−7	−8	−9	−10	−11	−12
x^2	1	4	9	16	25	36	49	64	81	100	121	144

Your knowledge of common squares and square roots may speed up your solution to some math problems. The most common types of problems for which this knowledge will help you will be those involving:

- Factoring and/or simplifying expressions;
- Problems involving the Pythagorean theorem ($a^2 + b^2 = c^2$);
- Areas of circles or squares.

Squares of Fractions

Remember that if a positive fraction whose value is less than 1 is squared, the result is always *smaller* than the original fraction:

If $0 < n < 1$
Then $n^2 < n$.

Try it.
What are the values of the following fractions?

$$\left(\frac{2}{3}\right)^2$$

$$\left(\frac{1}{8}\right)^2$$

The answers are 4/9 and 1/64, respectively. Each of these is less in value than the original fraction. For example, 4/9 < 2/3.

Fractions

You should know how to do basic operations with fractions:

- Adding, subtracting, multiplying, and dividing fractions;
- Reducing to lowest terms;
- Finding the least common denominator;
- Expressing a value as a mixed number (2 1/3) and as an improper fraction (7/3);
- Working with complex fractions—ones that have fractions in their numerators or denominators.

Decimal Fraction Equivalents

You may have to work with decimal/fraction equivalents. That is, you may have to be able to recognize common fractions as decimals and vice versa.

To change any fraction to a decimal, divide the denominator into the numerator.

Although you can figure out the decimal equivalent of any fraction (a calculator will help here), you'll be doing yourself a favor if you know the following:

Fraction	$\frac{1}{4}$	$\frac{1}{3}$	$\frac{1}{2}$	$\frac{2}{3}$	$\frac{3}{4}$
Decimal	0.25	0.3333*	0.5	0.6666*	0.75

*These fractions don't convert to terminating decimals—the 3 and 6 repeat indefinitely.

Factors, Multiples, and Remainders

In most math tests, you'll find several questions that require you to understand and work with these three related concepts.

Factors

The factors of a number are integers that can be divided into the number without any remainders.

For instance, consider the number 24:

> The numbers 24, 12, 8, 6, 4, 3, 2, and 1 are all factors of the number 24.

Common Factors—Common factors are factors that two numbers have in common. For instance, 3 is a common factor of 6 and 15.

Prime Factors—Prime factors are the factors of a number that are prime numbers. That is, the prime factors of a number cannot be further divided into factors.

> The prime factors of the number 24 are:
> 2 and 3.

The term "divisible by" means divisible by *without any remainder* or *with a remainder of zero*. For instance, 12 is divisible by 4 because 12 divided by 4 is 3 with a remainder of 0. Twelve is not divisible by 5 because 12 divided by 5 is 2 with a remainder of 2.

Multiples

The multiples of any given number are those numbers that can be divided by that given number *without a remainder*.

For instance: 16, 24, 32, 40, and 48 are all multiples of 8. They are also multiples of 2 and 4. Remember: The multiples of any number will always be multiples of all the factors of that number.

For instance:

- 30, 45, 60, and 75 are all multiples of the number 15.
- Two factors of 15 are the numbers 3 and 5.
- That means that 30, 45, 60, and 75 are all multiples of 3 and 5.

Sample Questions

Example 1:

What is the *least* positive integer divisible by the numbers 2, 3, 4, and 5?

- To find *any* number that is divisible by several other numbers, multiply those numbers together. You could multiply $2 \times 3 \times 4 \times 5$ and the result would be divisible by all those factors.

- But the question asks for the *least* positive number divisible by all four. To find that, you have to eliminate any extra factors.

- Any number divisible by 4 will also be divisible by 2. So you can eliminate 2 from your initial multiplication. If you multiply $3 \times 4 \times 5$, you will get a smaller number than if you multiply $2 \times 3 \times 4 \times 5$. And the number will still be divisible by 2.

- Because the remaining factors (3, 4, and 5) have no common factor, the result of $3 \times 4 \times 5$ will give you the answer.

Example 2:

Which of the following could be the remainders when four consecutive positive integers are each divided by 3?

(A) 1,2,3,1
(B) 1,2,3,4
(C) 0,1,2,3
(D) 0,1,2,0
(E) 0,2,3,0

Remember, the question asks only for the remainders.

- When you divide *any* positive integer by 3, the remainder must be less than or equal to 2.
- All the choices except (D) include remainders greater than 2. So (D) is the correct answer.

Averages

The word "average" can refer to several different measures.

- Arithmetic mean
- Median
- Mode

Arithmetic Mean

Arithmetic mean is what is usually thought of when talking about averages. If you want to know the arithmetic mean of a set of values, the formula is:

$$\frac{\text{The sum of a set of values}}{\text{The number of values in the set}}$$

For example, if there are three children, aged 6, 7, and 11, the arithmetic mean of their ages is:

$$\frac{6 + 7 + 11}{3}$$

or 8 years.

Median

The median is the middle value of a set. To find the median, place the values in ascending (or descending) order and select the middle value.

> **For instance:**
> What is the median of the following values?

$$1, 2, 667, 4, 19, 309, 44, 6, 200$$

- Place the values in ascending order:

$$1, 2, 4, 6, 19, 44, 200, 309, 667$$

- Select the value in the middle.
- There are nine values listed. The middle value is the fifth.
- The median of these values is 19.

The Median of a Set With an Even Number of Values

When you have an even list of values, the median is the average (arithmetic mean) of the two middle values. For example, the median of 3, 7, 10, 20 is $\dfrac{7 + 10}{2} = 8.5$

Mode

The mode of a set of values is the value or values that appears the greatest number of times.

In the list used to illustrate the median, there was no mode, because all the values appeared just once. But consider the following list:

$$1, 5, 5, 7, 276, 4, 100, 276, 89, 4, 276, 1, 8$$

- The number 276 appears three times, which is more times than any other number appears.
- The **mode** of this list is 276.

Multiple Modes

It is possible to have more than one mode in a set of numbers:

$$1, 5, 5, 7, 276, 4, 10004, 89, 4, 276, 1, 8$$

In the set above, there are four modes: 1, 4, 5, and 276.

Weighted Average

A weighted average is the average of two or more groups in which there are more members in one group than there are in another. For instance:

15 members of a class had an average (arithmetic mean) SAT I: Math score of 500. The remaining 10 members of the class had an average of 550. What is the average score of the entire class?

You can't simply take the average of 500 and 550 because there are more students with 500s than with 550s. The correct average has to be weighted toward the group with the greater number.

To find a weighted average, multiply each individual average by its weighting factor. The weighting factor is the number of values that correspond to a particular average. In this problem, you multiply each average by the number of students that corresponds to that average. Then you divide by the total number of students involved:

$$\frac{(500 \times 15) + (550 \times 10)}{25} = 520$$

So the average score for the entire class is 520.

⚡ CALCULATOR HINT

You might find that a calculator will help you find the answer to this question more quickly.

Average of Algebraic Expressions

Algebraic expressions can be averaged in the same way as any other values:

What is the average (arithmetic mean) of $3x + 1$ and $x - 3$?

There are two expressions, $3x + 1$ and $x - 3$, to be averaged. Take the sum of the values and divide by the number of values:

$$\frac{1}{2}\left[(3x + 1) + (x - 3)\right]$$

$$= \frac{(4x - 2)}{2}$$

$$= 2x - 1$$

Using Averages to Find Missing Numbers

You can use simple algebra in the basic average formula to find missing values when the average is given:

- The basic average formula is:

$$\frac{\textit{The sum of a set of values}}{\textit{The number of values in the set}}$$

- If you have the average and the number of values, you can figure out the sum of the values:

$$(\text{average})(\text{number of values}) = \text{sum of values}$$

Sample Question

Try putting this knowledge to work with a typical question on averages:

The average (arithmetic mean) of a set of 10 numbers is 15. If one of the numbers is removed, the average of the remaining numbers is 14. What is the value of the number that was removed?

- You know the average and the number of values in the set, so you can figure out the sum of all values in the set.
- The difference between the sum before you remove the number and after you remove the number will give you the value of the number you removed.
- The sum of all the values when you start out is the average times the number of values: $10 \times 15 = 150$.
- The sum of the values after you remove a number is $9 \times 14 = 126$.
- The difference between the sums is $150 - 126 = 24$.
- You only removed one number, so the value of that number is 24.

Ratio and Proportion

Ratio

A ratio expresses a mathematical relationship between two quantities. Specifically, a ratio is a quotient of those quantities. The following are all relationships that can be expressed as ratios:

- My serving of pizza is 1/4 of the whole pie.
- There are twice as many chocolate cookies as vanilla cookies in the cookie jar.
- My brother earns $5 for each $6 I earn.

These ratios can be expressed in several different ways. They can be stated in words:

- The ratio of my serving of pizza to the whole pie is one to four.
- The ratio of chocolate to vanilla cookies is two to one.
- The ratio of my brother's earnings to mine is five to six.

They can be expressed as fractions:

- $\dfrac{1}{4}$

- $\dfrac{2}{1}$

- $\dfrac{5}{6}$

Or they can be expressed with a colon (:) as follows:

- 1:4
- 2:1
- 5:6

Sample Question

The weight of the tea in a box of 100 identical tea bags is 8 ounces. What is the weight, in ounces, of the tea in 3 tea bags?

Start by setting up two ratios. A proportion is two ratios set equal to each other.

- The ratio of 3 tea bags to all of the tea bags is 3 to 100 (3/100).
- Let x equal the weight, in ounces, of the tea in 3 tea bags.
- The ratio of the weight of 3 tea bags to the total weight of the tea is x ounces to 8 ounces (x/8).

The relationship between x ounces and 8 ounces is equal to the relationship between 3 and 100:

$$\frac{x}{8} = \frac{3}{100}$$
$$100x = 24$$
$$x = 24/100 \text{ or } .24$$

Sample Question

You may find questions that involve ratios in any of the following situations:

- Lengths of line segments;
- Sizes of angles;
- Areas and perimeters;
- Rate/time/distance;
- Numbers on a number line.

You may be asked to combine ratios with other mathematical concepts. For instance:

The ratio of the length of a rectangular floor to its width is 3:2. If the length of the floor is 12 meters, what is the perimeter of the floor, in meters?

The ratio of the length to the width of the rectangle is 3:2, so set that ratio equal to the ratio of the actual measures of the sides of the rectangle:

$$\frac{3}{2} = \frac{length}{width}$$
$$\frac{3}{2} = \frac{12}{x}$$
$$3x = 24$$
$$x = 8 = the\ width$$

Now that you have the width of the rectangle, it is easy to find the perimeter: 2(length + width). The perimeter is 40 meters.

Algebra

Many math questions require a knowledge of algebra, so the basics of algebra should be second nature to you. You have to be able to manipulate and solve a simple equation for an unknown, simplify and evaluate algebraic expressions, and use algebraic concepts in problem-solving situations.

Factoring

The types of factoring included on the math test are:

• Difference of two squares:

$$a^2 - b^2 = (a + b)(a - b)$$

• Finding common factors, as in:

$$x^2 + 2x = x(x + 2)$$
$$2x + 4y = 2(x + 2y)$$

• Factoring quadratics:

$$x^2 - 3x - 4 = (x - 4)(x + 1)$$
$$x^2 + 2x + 1 = (x + 1)(x + 1) = (x + 1)^2$$

You are not likely to find a question instructing you to "factor the following expression." You may see questions that ask you to evaluate or compare expressions that require factoring. For instance, here is a Quantitative Comparison question:

<u>**Column A**</u>   <u>**Column B**</u>

$$x \neq -1$$

$$\dfrac{x^2 - 1}{x + 1}$$ $$x - 1$$

The numerator of the expression in Column A can be factored:

$$x^2 - 1$$
$$= (x + 1)(x - 1)$$

The $(x + 1)(x - 1)$ cancels with the $(x + 1)$ in the denominator, leaving the factor $(x - 1)$. So the two quantities—the one in Column A and the one in Column B—are equal.

Exponents

Three Points to Remember

1. When multiplying expressions with the same base, *add* the exponents:

$$a^2 \cdot a^5$$
$$= (a \cdot a)(a \cdot a \cdot a \cdot a \cdot a)$$
$$= a^7$$

2. When dividing expressions with the same base, subtract exponents:

$$\frac{r^5}{r^3} = \frac{r \cdot r \cdot \cancel{r} \cdot \cancel{r} \cdot \cancel{r}}{\cancel{r} \cdot \cancel{r} \cdot \cancel{r}} = r^2$$

3. When raising one power to another power, *multiply* the exponents:

$$(n^3)^6 = n^{18}$$

Solving Equations

Most of the equations that you will need to solve are linear equations. Equations that are not linear can usually be solved by factoring or by inspection.

Working With "Unsolvable" Equations

At first, some equations may look like they can't be solved. You will find that although you can't solve the equation, you can answer the question. For instance:

If $a + b = 5$, what is the value of $2a + 2b$?

You can't solve the equation $a + b = 5$ for either a or b. But you can answer the question:

- The question doesn't ask for the value of a or b. It asks for the value of the entire quantity ($2a + 2b$).
- $2a + 2b$ can be factored:
  $2a + 2b = 2(a + b)$
- $a + b = 5$

You are asked what 2 times $a + b$ is. That's 2 times 5, or 10.

Solving for One Variable in Terms of Another

You may be asked to solve for one variable in terms of another. Again, you're not going to be able to find a specific, numerical value for all of the variables.

For example:

If $3x + y = z$, what is x in terms of y and z?

You aren't asked what x equals. You are asked to manipulate the expression so that you can isolate x (put it by itself) on one side of the equation. That equation will tell you what x is in terms of the other variables:

- $3x + y = z$
- Subtract y from each side of the equation.
  $3x = z - y$
- Divide both sides by 3 to get the value of x.
  $x = \dfrac{(z-y)}{3}$

The value of x in terms of y and z is $\dfrac{(z-y)}{3}$.

Direct Translations of Mathematical Terms

Many word problems require that you translate the description of a mathematical fact or relationship into mathematical terms.

Always read the word problem carefully and double-check that you have translated it exactly.

A number is 3 times the quantity (4x + 6) translates to $3(4x + 6)$

A number y decreased by 60 translates to $y - 60$

5 less than a number k translates to $k - 5$

A number that is x less than 5 translates to $5 - x$

20 divided by n is $\dfrac{20}{n}$

20 divided into a number y is $\dfrac{y}{20}$

See the Word Problem tips in this chapter.

> **⚡ HINT**
>
> Be especially careful with subtraction and division because the order of these operations is important.
>
> 5 – 3 is not the same as 3 – 5.

Inequalities

An inequality is a statement that two values are *not* equal, or that one value is greater than or equal to or less than or equal to another. Inequalities are shown by four signs:

- Greater than: >
- Greater than or equal to: ≥
- Less than: <
- Less than or equal to: ≤

Most of the time, you can work with simple inequalities in exactly the same way you work with equalities.

Consider the following:

$$2x + 1 > 11$$

If this were an equation, it would be pretty easy to solve:

$$2x + 1 = 11$$
$$2x = 11 - 1$$
$$2x = 10$$
$$x = 5$$

You can use a similar process to solve inequalities:

$$2x + 1 > 11$$
$$2x > 11 - 1$$
$$2x > 10$$
$$x > 5$$

> **⚡ HINT**
>
> Remember that multiplying or dividing both sides of an inequality by a negative number reverses the direction of the inequality:
>
> If –x < 3, then x > –3.

Number Sequences

A number sequence is a sequence of numbers that follows a specific pattern. For instance, the sequence

$$3, 7, 11, 15, \ldots$$

follows the pattern, **add 4**. That is, each term in the sequence is **4** more than the one before it. The three dots (. . .) indicate that this sequence goes on forever.

Not all sequences go on indefinitely. The sequence

$$1, 3, 5, \ldots, 21, 23$$

contains odd numbers only up to 23, where the sequence ends. The three dots in the middle indicate that the sequence continues according to the pattern as shown, but it ends with the number 23.

The math test *does not* usually ask you to figure out the rule for determining the numbers in a sequence. When a number sequence is used in a question, you will usually be told what the rule is.

Number sequence questions might ask you for:

- The sum of certain numbers in the sequence;
- The average of certain numbers in the sequence;
- The value of a specific number in the sequence.

Word Problems

Some math questions are presented as word problems. They require you to apply math skills to everyday situations. With word problems you have to:

- Read and interpret what is being asked.
- Determine what information you are given.
- Determine what information you need to know.
- Decide what mathematical skills or formulas you need to apply to find the answer.
- Work out the answer.
- Double-check to make sure the answer makes sense.

Hints on Solving Word Problems

Translate as You Read
As you read word problems, translate the words into mathematical expressions:

- When you read **Jane has three dollars more than Tom**, translate $J = T + 3$.
- When you read **the average (arithmetic mean) of the weights of three children is 80 pounds**, translate to $(a + b + c)/3 = 80$.

- When you read **Jane buys one clown fish and two guppies for $3.00**, translate $c + 2g = \$3.00$.

When you've finished reading the problem, you will have already translated it into mathematical expressions. The following table will help you with some of the more common phrases and mathematical translations:

Words	Operation	Translation
Is, was, has: Jane's son is as old as Tom's daughter.	= =	$S = D$ or $J = T$
More than, older than, farther than, greater than, sum of: Jane has 2 more dollars than Tom. Tom ran 10 miles farther than Jane. The sum of two integers is 36.	+ +	Addition $J = 2 + T$ or $J = T + 2$ $T = 10 + J$ or $T = J + 10$ $x + y = 36$
Less than, difference, younger than, fewer: Tom has 5 fewer marbles than twice the number Jane has. The difference between Tom's height and Jane's height is 22 centimeters.	– –	Subtraction $T = 2J - 5$ (Don't make the "$5 - 2J$" mistake!) $T - J = 22$ (or maybe $J - T = 22$)
Of: 20% of Tom's socks are red. Jane ate 3/4 of the candy.	× %	Multiplication $R = .2 \times T$ $J = 3/4 \times C$
For, per: Jane won 3 games for every 2 that Tom won. 50 miles per hour 2 bleeps per revolution	ratio ÷	Division $J/T = 3/2$ 50 miles/hour 2 bleeps/revolution

Sample Questions

Figuring out these problems takes more than just knowing a bunch of math formulas. You have to think about what math skills and tools you will apply to the questions in order to reason your way through to the correct answer.

1. The price of a sweater went up 20% since last year. If last year's price was x, what is this year's price in terms of x?

- Last year's price = 100% of x
- This year's price is 100% of x plus 20% of x. $(100/100)x + (20/100)x = 1.2x$

2. One year ago an average restaurant meal cost $12.00. Today, the average restaurant meal costs $15.00. By what percent has the cost of the meal increased?

You can figure percent increase by taking the difference in prices first and then expressing it as a percentage of the original price:

$15 – $12 = $3 difference.
What percentage of the original price is $3?

$$\left(\frac{x}{100}\right)12 = 3$$

$$\frac{x}{100} = \frac{3}{12}$$

$$12x = 300$$

$$x = 25\%$$

Or you can figure what percent the new price is of the old price:

15 is what percent of 12?

$$15 = \left(\frac{x}{100}\right)12$$

$$\frac{15}{12} = \frac{x}{100}$$

$$x = 125\%$$

This tells you what percent the current price ($15) is of the old price ($12). But the question asks for the percent increase. So you have to subtract 100 percent from 125 percent.

$$125 - 100 = 25\% \text{ increase}$$

3. The average height of four members of a six-person volleyball team is 175 cm. What does the average height in centimeters of the other 2 players have to be if the average height of the entire team equals 180 cm?

Start with the formula for the average:

$$\frac{sum\ of\ values}{number\ of\ values} = average$$

Use what you know to find out the sum of the heights of the 4 members whose average is 175 cm.

$$\frac{sum}{4} = 175$$

$$sum = 4(175) = 700$$

The average of all 6 players is 180 cm.

$$\text{Average of 6} = \frac{(sum\ of\ 4 + sum\ of\ 2)}{6}$$

$$180 = \frac{(700 + sum\ of\ 2)}{6}$$

$$1080 = 700 + sum\ of\ 2$$
$$1080 - 700 = sum\ of\ 2$$
$$380 = sum\ of\ 2$$

What is the average of the heights of the 2 players?
Average = sum/number of players
Average = 380/2 = 190 cm.

4. A car traveling at an average rate of 55 kilometers per hour made a trip in 6 hours. If it had traveled at an average rate of 50 kilometers per hour, the trip would have taken how many <u>minutes</u> longer?

• How long was the trip?
Distance = rate × time
Distance = 55 kph × 6 hours
Distance = 330 km.

• How long does the 330-kilometer trip take if the car is traveling at 50 kilometers per hour?

$$\text{Time} = \frac{distance}{rate}$$

$$\text{Time} = \frac{330}{50}$$

$$\text{Time} = 6\frac{3}{5}\ \text{hours}$$

• What does the question ask?
The difference <u>in minutes</u> between the two trips.

$$\text{Difference} = \frac{3}{5}\ \text{hour}$$

Difference = ? minutes
$$\frac{3}{5} = \frac{x}{60}$$
$$5x = 180$$
$$x = 36\ \text{minutes}$$

Geometry

The geometry questions focus on your ability to recognize and use the special properties of many geometric figures. You will find questions requiring you to know about:

- Triangles, in general;
- Special triangles—right triangles, isosceles, and equilateral triangles;
- Rectangles, squares, and other polygons;
- Areas and perimeters of simple figures;
- The angles formed by intersecting lines and angles involving parallel and perpendicular lines;
- Area, circumference, and arc degrees in a circle.

Triangles

Equilateral Triangles

The three sides of an equilateral triangle (a, b, c) are equal in length. The three angles (x, y, z) are also equal and they each measure 60 degrees ($x = y = z = 60$).

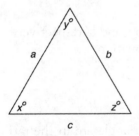

Isosceles Triangles

An isosceles triangle is a triangle with two sides of equal length ($m = n$). The angles opposite the equal sides are also equal ($x = y$).

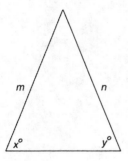

Right Triangles and the Pythagorean Theorem

You can get a lot of information out of figures that contain right triangles. And this information frequently involves the Pythagorean theorem:

> The square of the hypotenuse of a right triangle is equal to the sum of the squares of the other two sides.

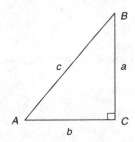

The hypotenuse is the longest side of the triangle and is opposite the right angle. The other two sides are usually referred to as legs. In the figure above:

- AB is the hypotenuse with length c.
- BC and AC are the two legs with lengths a and b, respectively.
- The Pythagorean theorem leads to the equation:

$$a^2 + b^2 = c^2$$

30°-60°-90° Right Triangles

The lengths of the sides of a 30°-60°-90° triangle are in the ratio of $1:\sqrt{3}:2$, as shown in the figure:

- Short leg = x
- Long leg = $x\sqrt{3}$
- Hypotenuse = $2x$

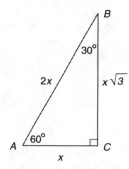

If you know the lengths of any two sides, the Pythagorean theorem will help you to find the length of the third.

For instance, if you know the length of the short leg is 1 and the length of the hypotenuse is 2, then the theorem gives you the length of the longer leg:

$$c^2 = a^2 + b^2$$
$$c = 2, b = 1$$
$$2^2 = a^2 + 1$$
$$4 = a^2 + 1$$
$$3 = a^2$$
$$\sqrt{3} = a$$

45°-45°-90° Triangle

The lengths of the sides of a 45°-45°-90° triangle are in the ratio of 1:1:$\sqrt{2}$, as shown in the figure below. If the equal sides are of length 1, apply the Pythagorean theorem to find the length of the hypotenuse:

$$c^2 = a^2 + b^2$$
$$a = 1, b = 1$$
$$c^2 = 1^2 + 1^2$$
$$c^2 = 1 + 1$$
$$c^2 = 2$$
$$c = \sqrt{2}$$

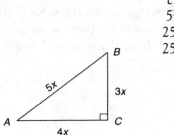

3-4-5 Triangle

The sides of a 3-4-5 right triangle are in the ratio of 3:4:5. In the figure below, if $x = 1$, then:

$$c^2 = a^2 + b^2$$
$$5^2 = 3^2 + 4^2$$
$$25 = 9 + 16$$
$$25 = 25$$

Quadrilaterals, Lines, and Angles

As with some triangles, you can figure out some things about the sides of quadrilaterals from their angles and some things about their angles from the lengths of their sides. In some special quadrilaterals—parallelograms, rectangles, and squares—there are relationships among the angles and sides that can help you solve geometry problems.

Parallelograms

In a parallelogram, the opposite angles are equal and the opposite sides are of equal length.

Angles *BAD* and *BCD* are equal; and angles *ABC* and *ADC* are equal. *AB* = *CD* and *AD* = *BC*.

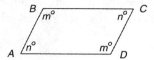

Rectangles

A rectangle is a special case of a parallelogram. In rectangles, all the angles are right angles.

Squares

A square is a special case of a rectangle in which all the sides are equal.

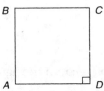

Notice that if you know the length of any side of a square, you also know the length of the diagonal.

The diagonal makes two 45°-45°-90° triangles with the sides of the square. So you can figure out the length of the sides from the length of the diagonal or the length of the diagonal from the length of a side.

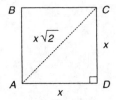

REMEMBER THE
REFERENCE INFORMATION

Formulas for areas of common figures are given in the reference material that is printed in the test booklet.

Areas and Perimeters

Rectangles and Squares

The formula for the area of any rectangle is:

$$\text{Area} = \text{length} \times \text{width}$$

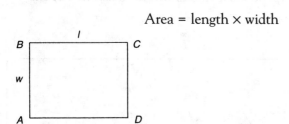

Because all sides of the square are equal, the length and width are often both referred to as the length of a side, s. So the area of a square can be written as:

$$\text{Area} = s^2$$

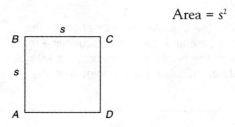

Perimeters of Rectangles and Squares—The perimeter of a simple closed figure is the length all the way around the figure. Because the opposite sides of rectangles are equal, the formula for the perimeter of a rectangle is:

$$\text{Perimeter of rectangle} = 2(\text{length} + \text{width}) = 2(l + w)$$

The same is true for any parallelogram. For a square, it's even easier. Because all four sides of a square are equal, the perimeter of a square is:

$$\text{Perimeter of a square} = 4(\text{length of any side}) = 4s$$

Area of Triangles

The area of a triangle is:

$$A = \left(\frac{1}{2}\right) bh$$

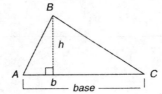

- b is the base
- h is the height, a perpendicular line drawn from a vertex of the triangle to the base.

HINT

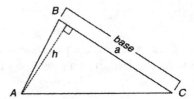

You can start with any vertex of the triangle. The side opposite the vertex you choose becomes the base and the perpendicular line from that vertex to the base becomes the height. For instance, the area of the triangle in the figure could be calculated using point A as the vertex instead of point B.

Area of Parallelograms

To find the area of a parallelogram, you "square up" the slanted side of the parallelogram by dropping a perpendicular—line BE in the figure shown below. This makes a right triangle ABE.

If you take this triangle away from the parallelogram and add it to the other side (triangle DCF) you have a rectangle with the same area as the original parallelogram.

The area of the rectangle is length × width.

The width of this rectangle is the same as the height of the parallelogram. So the formula for the area of a parallelogram is:

$$Area = length \times height$$

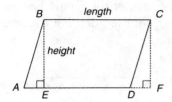

Other Polygons

Occasionally, a math question will ask you to work with polygons other than triangles and quadrilaterals. Here are a few things to remember about other polygons.

Angles in a Polygon

You can figure out the total number of degrees in the interior angles of most polygons by dividing the polygon into triangles:

- From any vertex, divide the polygon into as many nonoverlapping triangles as possible. Use only straight lines. Make sure that all the space inside the polygon is divided into triangles.
- Count the triangles. In this figure, there are four triangles.
- There is a total of 180° in the angles of each triangle, so multiply the number of triangles by 180. The product will be the sum of the angles in the polygon (720° in the hexagon shown below).

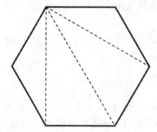

Sample Question

In the figure shown below, lengths AB, BD, and DC are all $3\sqrt{2}$ units long. Angles BAD and BCD are both 45°. What is the perimeter of $ABCD$? What is the area of $ABCD$?

You are asked for the perimeter and the area of the figure. For the perimeter you will need to know the lengths of the sides. For the area you will need to know the length and height.

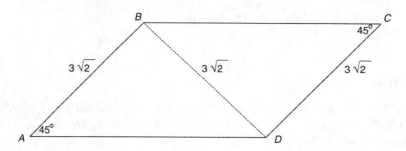

Perimeter

- You are given the lengths of 3 line segments, all of which are the same: $3\sqrt{2}$.
- You are given two angles, both of which are the same: 45°.
- $\sqrt{2}$ and 45° are both characteristics of a special right triangle: 45°-45°-90°.
- ABD is a triangle with two equal sides.
- BCD is a triangle with two equal sides.
- So, they are both isosceles triangles.
- Angle BCD is 45°, so angle CBD has to equal 45°.
- The same is true for angles ADB and DAB, which both equal 45°.
- Both triangles are 45°-45°-90° triangles.
- You can figure out the lengths of AD and BC by the Pythagorean theorem:

$$AD^2 = (3\sqrt{2})^2 + (3\sqrt{2})^2 = 36, \text{ so } AD = 6$$

- Do the same for the length of BC to find that $BC = 6$.
- You can now add up the lengths of the sides to get the perimeter:

$$2(6+3\sqrt{2}) = 12 + 6\sqrt{2}.$$

Area

- $ABCD$ is a parallelogram. You know this because both sets of opposite sides are equal: $AB = CD$ and $AD = BC$.
- That means that you can use the formula for the area of a parallelogram: area = length × height.
- To find the height, drop a perpendicular from B.
- That creates another 45°-45°-90° triangle whose hypotenuse is AB.
- The ratio of the sides of a 45°-45°-90° triangle is $1:1:\sqrt{2}$.
- From that ratio, you know the height of the figure is 3.
- With the height, you can then calculate the area: $3 \times 6 = 18$.

If you label everything you figure out as you go along, you will end up with a figure that looks like the one below.

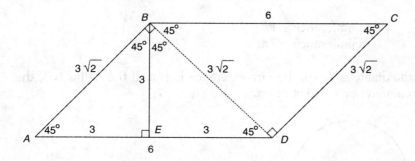

Circles

Diameter

The diameter of a circle is a line segment that passes through the center and has its endpoints on the circle. All diameters of the same circle have equal lengths.

Radius

The radius of a circle is a line segment extending from the center of the circle to a point on the circle. In the figure shown below, OB and OA are radii.

All radii of the same circle have equal lengths, and the radius is half the diameter. In the figure, the length of OB equals the length of OA.

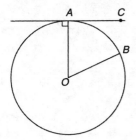

Arc

An arc is a part of a circle. In the figure above, AB is an arc. An arc can be measured in degrees or in units of length.

If you form an angle by drawing radii from the ends of the arc to the center of the circle, the number of degrees in the arc (arc AB in the figure) equals the number of degrees in the angle formed by the two radii at the center of the circle (∠AOB).

Tangent to a Circle

A tangent to a circle is a line that touches the circle at only one point. In the figure, line AC is a tangent.

Circumference

The circumference is the distance around a circle, and it is equal to π times the diameter d (or π times twice the radius r).

$$\text{Circumference} = \pi d$$
$$\text{Circumference} = 2\pi r$$

If the diameter is 16, the circumference is 16π. If the radius is 3, the circumference is $2(3)\pi$ or 6π.

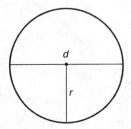

Area

The area of a circle is equal to π times the square of the radius.

$$\text{Area} = \pi r^2$$

Sample Question

In the figure shown below, A is the center of a circle whose area is 25π. B and C are points on the circle. Angle ACB is $45°$. What is the length of line segment BC?

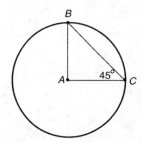

- Point A is the center of the circle.
- That makes both line segments AB and AC radii, which means that they are of equal length.
- Because AB and BC are equal, ΔABC is an isosceles triangle, and one angle opposite one of the equal sides is $45°$.
- That means the angle opposite the other equal side is also $45°$.
- The remaining angle is $90°$.
- The area of the circle is 25π.

- The formula for the area of a circle is πr^2. You can use that formula to figure out the length of the radius, r.
- That length, r, is also the length of the legs of the triangle whose hypotenuse (BC) is the length you are trying to figure out.

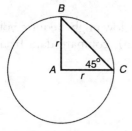

What is the value of r?

$$\text{Area} = \pi r^2$$
$$\text{Area} = 25\pi$$
$$r^2 = 25$$
$$r = 5$$

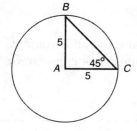

Figuring out the final answer to the problem is a simple matter of working through the Pythagorean theorem or remembering that the ratio of the sides of 45°-45°-90° triangles is $1:1:\sqrt{2}$. The answer is $5\sqrt{2}$.

Miscellaneous Math Questions

Most math questions fall into the three broad areas of arithmetic, algebra, and geometry. Some questions, however, do not fall neatly into one of these areas. Miscellaneous questions on the math test cover areas such as:

- Data interpretation;
- Counting and ordering problems;
- Special symbols;
- Logical analysis;
- Probability.

Data Interpretation

Your primary task in these questions is to interpret information in graphs, tables, or charts, and then compare quantities, recognize trends and changes in the data, or perform calculations based on the information you have found.

A question on a graph like the one shown below might require you to identify specific pieces of information (data), compare data from different parts of the graph, and manipulate the data.

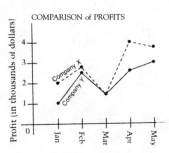

When working with data interpretation questions, you have to:

- Look at the graph, table, or chart to make sure you understand it. Make sure you know what type of information is being displayed.
- Read the question carefully.

🟢 HINT

With data interpretation questions—graphs, charts, and tables—always make sure you understand the information being presented:
- Read the labels.
- Make sure you know the units.
- Make sure you understand what is happening to the data as you move through the table, graph, or chart.

The graph below shows profits over time. The higher the point on the vertical axis, the greater the profits. (Each tick mark on the vertical axis is another $1,000.) As you move to the right along the horizontal axis, months are passing.

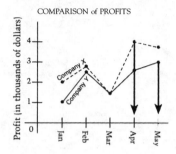

COMPARISON of PROFITS

Sample Questions

1. In what month or months did each company make the greatest profit?

Follow the line labeled Company X to its highest point. Then check the month at the bottom of the graph. Follow the same procedure for Company Y.

For Company X, the greatest profit was made in April.
For Company Y, the greatest profit was made in May.

2. Between which two consecutive months did each company show the greatest increase in profit?

The increase (or decrease) in profit is shown by the steepness or "slope" of the graph.

For Company X, it's easy to see that the biggest jump occurred between March and April.

For Company Y, you have to be a little more careful. The biggest increase in profits occurred between January and February. You know this because the slope of the line connecting January and February is the steepest.

The increase between January and February is about $1,500, which is greater than the increase for any other pair of consecutive months.

3. In what month did the profits of the two companies show the greatest difference?

To figure this out, you have to compare one company to the other, month by month. The month in which the dots are farthest apart is the one in which there is the greatest difference between the two companies. The distance between the two graph points is greatest in April.

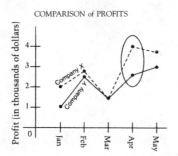

4. If the rate of increase or decrease for each company continues for the next six months at the same rate shown between April and May, which company would have higher profits at the end of that time?

This question is asking you to look at the graph and project changes in the future. To project changes, extend the lines between April and May for each company. The lines cross pretty quickly—well before six more months have passed. So the answer is that Company Y would be doing better in six months if the rates of change from month to month stay the same as they were between April and May.

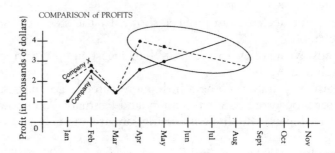

From Graph to Table—The same information presented in the profit chart could be presented in a profit table, which might look something like this:

	Profit (in dollars)				
	Jan.	Feb.	Mar.	Apr.	May
Company X	2,000	2,750	1,500	4,000	3,750
Company Y	1,000	2,500	1,500	2,500	3,000

With a table it's a little harder to make the comparisons and see the trends. But the table is much more precise. The graph does not show the exact numbers the way the table does.

Counting and Ordering Problems

Counting and ordering problems involve figuring out how many ways you can select or arrange members of groups, such as letters of the alphabet, numbers, or menu selections.

Fundamental Counting Principle

The fundamental counting principle is the principle by which you figure out how many possibilities there are for selecting members of a group:

If one event can happen in n ways, and a second event can happen in m ways, the total ways in which the two events can happen is n times m.

For example:

On a restaurant menu, there are three appetizers and four main courses. How many different dinners can be ordered if each dinner consists of one appetizer and one main course?

- The first event is the choice of appetizer, and there are three choices available.
- The second event is the choice of main course, and there are four main courses.
- The total number of different dinners is therefore, $3 \times 4 = 12$.

This idea can be extended to more than two events:

If you had two choices for beverage added to your choices for appetizer and main course, you would multiply the total by 2: $2 \times 3 \times 4 = 24$.

If you also had three choices for dessert, you would multiply by 3: $3 \times 2 \times 3 \times 4 = 72$.

For example:

A security system uses a four-letter password, but no letter can be used more than once. How many possible passwords are there?

- For the first letter, there are 26 possible choices—one for each letter of the alphabet.
- Because you cannot reuse any letters, there are only 25 choices for the second letter (26 minus the letter used in the first letter of the password).
- There are only 24 choices for the third letter, and only 23 choices for the fourth.

The total number of passwords will be $26 \times 25 \times 24 \times 23$.

Special Symbols

To test your ability to learn and apply mathematical concepts, a special symbol is sometimes introduced and defined.

These symbols generally have unusual looking signs (★, *, §) so you won't confuse them with real mathematical symbols.

The key to these questions is to make sure that you read the definition carefully.

A typical special symbol question might look something like this:

Let $= ce - df,$

where c, d, e, and f are integers.

What is the value of ?

To answer this question, substitute the numbers according to the definition:

- Substitute 2 for c, 3 for d, 4 for f, and 1 for e.

- $= (2)(1) - (3)(4) = -10$

Some questions will ask you to apply the definition of the symbol to more complicated situations. For instance:

- You may be asked to compare two values, each of which requires the use of the symbol.

- You may be asked to evaluate an expression that involves multiplying, dividing, adding, squaring, or subtracting terms that involve the symbol.
- You could be asked to solve an equation that involves the use of the symbol.
- You may find a special symbol as part of a Quantitative Comparison question.

Logical Analysis

Some math questions emphasize logical thinking. You have to figure out how to draw conclusions from a set of facts.

Here's an example:

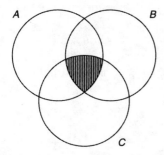

In the figure above, circular region A represents the set of all numbers of the form $2m$, circular region B represents the set of all numbers of the form n^2, and circular region C represents the set of all numbers of the form 10^k, where m, n, and k are positive integers. Which of the following numbers belongs in the set represented by the shaded region?

(A)   2
(B)   4
(C)   10
(D)   25
(E)   100

Answering this question correctly depends on understanding the logic of the figure:

- The question is asking about the shaded region.
- The shaded region is part of *all* of the circles.
- Therefore, any numbers in the shaded region have to obey the rules for *all* the circles:

The rule for A: The numbers must be of the form $2m$, which means that they must all be even numbers.

And the rule for B: the numbers must be of the form n^2, which means that they must all be perfect squares.

And the rule for C: the numbers must also be of the form 10^k, which means they have to be some whole-number power of 10 (10, 100, 1000, 10000, etc.).

- When you realize that the numbers in the shaded area must obey *all* the individual rules, you have figured out the logic of the question, and the answer is easy. The only choice that obeys *all* the rules is (E).

CHAPTER SEVEN

Sample Mathematics Questions and Answers

Introduction **134**
Question Difficulty................................134
Grid-in Questions 134
Alternate Methods 134

**Five-Choice Multiple-Choice
Questions** **135**
Practice Questions.................................135
Answers and Explanations...................140
Recap: Hints for Five-Choice
Multiple-Choice Questions 159

**Quantitative Comparison
Questions** **159**
Practice Questions.................................159
Answers and Explanations...................162
Recap: Hints on Quantitative
Comparison Questions 169

Grid-in Questions **170**
Practice Questions.................................170
Answers and Explanations...................174
Recap: Hints on Grid-in Questions........183
Recap: General Hints on
Mathematical Questions.......................184

Introduction

On the math test, the questions are grouped by question type: Five-Choice Multiple-Choice questions, Quantitative Comparison questions, and Grid-in questions (called "Student-Produced Response" on the SAT). But the content areas tested will change from question to question. You may have a geometry question, followed by an arithmetic question, followed by an algebra question.

This makes the mathematics section of the test different from most of your classroom math tests. To do well on the math portion, you must be flexible. You have to be able to shift quickly from one type of math content to another. To help you get used to these shifts, the sample math questions are presented the way they appear on the test, in mixed order in terms of the kinds of skills and concepts required to answer them.

Question Difficulty

The difficulty of every question is determined before that question is used in a test. The sample questions are labeled easy, medium, or hard.

Grid-in Questions

It's very important for you to get used to the Grid-in questions. The special rules for expressing and entering the answers to the Grid-in questions on the answer sheet were presented in Chapter 6. For many of the Grid-in questions, the answers that are acceptable and the different ways the answer can be entered are shown in this chapter.

Alternate Methods

As you work with the math questions, you'll find that many of them can be solved in more than one way. There is often a direct method that depends on your remembering and applying some specific pieces of information. Other methods may take longer, relying on your ability to reason out the problem step-by-step from the facts given. Still others will depend on some special insight.

The questions in this chapter are meant to give you practice with the different types of problems you'll meet on the SAT and to help you identify both your strengths and the areas where you need to do more work. In addition to the correct answers, solutions to the problems are also given. If you're able to answer a question correctly but used a different solution from the one given, don't worry. There are often several ways to solve a problem. However, if you *don't* know how to solve a problem, study the solution in the answer section. It could help you answer a similar question on the SAT.

HINT

The best method for approaching the math questions is the method that you can work with most comfortably, confidently, efficiently, and accurately. However, if you aren't familiar with one of the methods shown, it might be a good idea to study it carefully so you can increase your efficiency if you meet a similar type of problem later. You might also want to refresh your math skills by studying the concepts discussed in Chapter 6, Mathematics Review.

Five-Choice Multiple-Choice Questions

Practice Questions

Chapter 6, Mathematics Review, discusses the five-choice format of multiple-choice math questions and suggests some approaches to solving the kinds of problems you'll find in that section of the SAT. Remember that while the questions are presented in the familiar five-choice (A) to (E) format, the content areas tested will vary from question to question.

If you find you're having trouble figuring out the solutions to the following 14 problems, turn to the Answers and Explanations, which start on page 140.

In this section solve each problem, using any available space on the page for scratchwork. Then decide which is the best of the choices given and fill in the corresponding oval on the answer sheet.

Notes:

(1) The use of a calculator is permitted. All numbers used are real numbers.

(2) Figures that accompany problems in this test are intended to provide information useful in solving the problems. They are drawn as accurately as possible EXCEPT when it is stated in a specific problem that the figure is not drawn to scale. All figures lie in a plane unless otherwise indicated.

Reference Information:

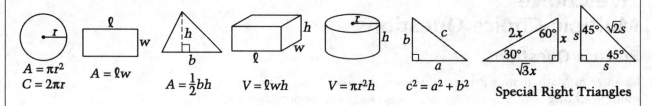

$$A = \pi r^2$$
$$C = 2\pi r$$
$$A = \ell w$$
$$A = \tfrac{1}{2}bh$$
$$V = \ell w h$$
$$V = \pi r^2 h$$
$$c^2 = a^2 + b^2$$

Special Right Triangles

The number of degrees of arc in a circle is 360.
The measure in degrees of a straight angle is 180.
The sum of the measures in degrees of the angles of a triangle is 180.

1 $\dfrac{1}{2} \cdot \dfrac{2}{3} \cdot \dfrac{3}{4} \cdot \dfrac{4}{5} \cdot \dfrac{5}{6} \cdot \dfrac{6}{7} =$

(A) $\dfrac{1}{7}$

(B) $\dfrac{3}{7}$

(C) $\dfrac{21}{27}$

(D) $\dfrac{6}{7}$

(E) $\dfrac{7}{8}$

2 If $\dfrac{x}{3} = x^2$, the value of x can be which of the following?

I. $-\dfrac{1}{3}$

II. 0

III. $\dfrac{1}{3}$

(A) I only
(B) II only
(C) III only
(D) II and III only
(E) I, II, and III

3 All numbers divisible by both 4 and 15 are also divisible by which of the following?

(A) 6
(B) 8
(C) 18
(D) 24
(E) 45

5

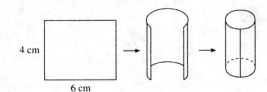

The figure above shows how a rectangular piece of paper is rolled to form a cylindrical tube. If it is assumed that the 4-centimeter sides of the rectangle meet with no overlap, what is the area, in square centimeters, of the base of the cylindrical tube?

(A) 16π
(B) 9π
(C) 4π
(D) $\dfrac{9}{\pi}$
(E) $\dfrac{4}{\pi}$

4 If United States imports increased 20 percent and exports decreased 10 percent during a certain year, the ratio of imports to exports at the end of the year was how many times the ratio at the beginning of the year?

(A) $\dfrac{12}{11}$

(B) $\dfrac{4}{3}$

(C) $\dfrac{11}{8}$

(D) $\dfrac{3}{2}$

(E) 2

6 The odometer of a new automobile functions improperly and registers only 2 miles for every 3 miles driven. If the odometer indicates 48 miles, how many miles has the automobile actually been driven?

(A) 144
(B) 72
(C) 64
(D) 32
(E) 24

7

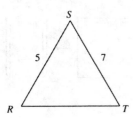

Note: Figure not drawn to scale.

If the perimeter of $\triangle RST$ above is 3 times the length of RS, then $RT =$

(A) 3
(B) 5
(C) 8
(D) 9
(E) 10

9

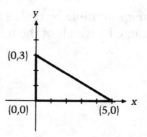

What is the area of the triangle in the figure above?

(A) 4.0
(B) 7.5
(C) 8.0
(D) 8.5
(E) 15.0

8 A, B, C, and D are points on a line, with D the midpoint of segment BC. The lengths of segments AB, AC, and BC are 10, 2, and 12, respectively. What is the length of segment AD?

(A) 2
(B) 4
(C) 6
(D) 10
(E) 12

10

A = {3,6,9}
B = {5,7,9}
C = {7,8,9}

If three <u>different</u> numbers are selected, one from each of the sets shown above, what is the greatest sum that these three numbers could have?

(A) 22
(B) 23
(C) 24
(D) 25
(E) 27

11 Let the symbol ⓧ represent the number of different pairs of positive integers whose product is x. For example, ⑯ = 3, since there are 3 different pairs of positive integers whose product is 16:

$$16 \times 1, \ 8 \times 2, \text{ and } 4 \times 4$$

What does ㊱ equal?

(A) 5
(B) 6
(C) 8
(D) 10
(E) 12

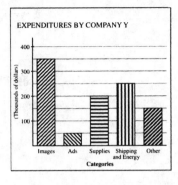

13 In the graph above, if the total expenditures by Company Y were \$1,000,000, the shaded areas of which of the following pie charts best represents the expenditures other than shipping and energy?

(A)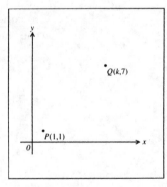
(B)
(C)
(D)
(E)

12 Several people are standing in a straight line. Starting at one end of the line Bill is counted as the 5th person, and starting at the other end he is counted as the 12th person. How many people are in the line?

(A) 15
(B) 16
(C) 17
(D) 18
(E) 19

14 In the figure above, the slope of the line through points P and Q is $\frac{3}{2}$. What is the value of k?

(A) 4
(B) 5
(C) 6
(D) 7
(E) 8

Answers and Explanations

 HINT

If it seems like you have a lot of calculating to do, look for a shortcut.

QUESTION 1
Arithmetic shortcuts

1. $\dfrac{1}{2} \cdot \dfrac{2}{3} \cdot \dfrac{3}{4} \cdot \dfrac{4}{5} \cdot \dfrac{5}{6} \cdot \dfrac{6}{7} =$

(A) $\dfrac{1}{7}$

(B) $\dfrac{3}{7}$

(C) $\dfrac{21}{27}$

(D) $\dfrac{6}{7}$

(E) $\dfrac{7}{8}$

Difficulty: Easy
The correct answer is (A).

If a question looks like it requires a lot of calculating, that's often a tip-off that something else is going on. There's usually a quick way to find the answer. In this question, all the fractions are being multiplied, so canceling is a possibility. The denominators cancel diagonally with the numerators that follow.

- The 2 from $\dfrac{1}{2}$ cancels with the 2 from $\dfrac{2}{3}$.

- The 3 from $\dfrac{2}{3}$ cancels with the 3 from $\dfrac{3}{4}$.

- And so on, right down to the equal sign.

$$\dfrac{1}{\cancel{2}} \cdot \dfrac{\cancel{2}}{\cancel{3}} \cdot \dfrac{\cancel{3}}{\cancel{4}} \cdot \dfrac{\cancel{4}}{\cancel{5}} \cdot \dfrac{\cancel{5}}{\cancel{6}} \cdot \dfrac{\cancel{6}}{7}$$

After you have canceled everything that can be canceled, you are left with the fraction $\dfrac{1}{7}$.

2. If $\frac{x}{3} = x^2$, the value of x can be which of the following?

   I. $-\frac{1}{3}$

  II. 0

 III. $\frac{1}{3}$

(A) I only
(B) II only
(C) III only
(D) II and III only
(E) I, II, and III

Difficulty: Hard
The correct answer is (D).

 HINT

When checking the values of expressions, remember the rules for multiplying positive and negative numbers:

$(+)(+) = (+)$
$(-)(+) = (-)$
$(-)(-) = (+)$

This means that the square of any nonzero number will be positive.

Question 2 uses what is referred to as the Roman numeral answer format. This format is used in both math and Reading Passage questions. The way to approach these is to work on each Roman numeral as a separate true/false question. Once you have decided (and marked) each Roman numeral as true or false, it's easy to find the correct answer.

Roman Numeral I: Can the Value of x Be $-\frac{1}{3}$?

You could test this answer by substituting $-\frac{1}{3}$ for x in the equation and seeing whether the result is true. But you can also reason this question out without substituting numbers:

- x^2 has to be a positive number, because any nonzero number squared is positive.

- If x were negative, $\frac{x}{3}$ would be negative.

- So $\frac{x}{3}$ is negative and x^2 is positive.

- Therefore, x cannot be $-\frac{1}{3}$.

Mark Roman numeral I with an "F" for false.

Roman Numeral II: Can the Value of x Be 0?

This is a very easy substitution to make:

$$\frac{x}{3} = x^2$$

$$\frac{0}{3} = 0^2 = 0$$

Roman numeral II is true, so mark it with a "T" for true.

Roman Numeral III: Can the Value of x Be $\frac{1}{3}$?

Substitute $\frac{1}{3}$ for x:

If $x = \frac{1}{3}$, $\frac{x}{3} = \frac{1}{9}$.

Also, $x^2 = \left(\frac{1}{3}\right)^2 = \frac{1}{9}$.

Roman numeral III is true, so mark it with a "T" for true.

Check the Answers:

You now know whether each of the Roman numeral statements is true or false:

I is false.

II is true.

III is true.

Find the answer that says only II and III are true, choice (D).

⚡ HINT

Remember the approach to Roman numeral format answers:

- Take each Roman numeral statement as a separate true/false question.
- Mark each Roman numeral with a "T" for True or an "F" for False as you evaluate it.
- Look for the answer that matches your "T"s and "F"s.

---

3. All numbers divisible by both 4 and 15 are also divisible by which of the following?

(A) 6
(B) 8
(C) 18
(D) 24
(E) 45

Difficulty: Medium
The correct answer is (A).

 HINT

"Divisible by" means that the remainder is zero after the division. For example, 8 is divisible by 4, but it is not divisible by 3.

First find a number that is divisible by both 4 and 15. One such number is 60. Now check each choice to see if 60 is divisible by that choice. 60 is divisible by choice (A) but is not divisible by any of the other choices. The answer must be (A).

 HINT

When the arithmetic is simple and you understand what the question is asking, it's okay to find the answer by:

• checking each choice
• eliminating choices

In more complicated problems, this can take more time than finding a solution through mathematical reasoning.

QUESTION 4
Percent increase and decrease

4. If United States imports increased 20 percent and exports decreased 10 percent during a certain year, the ratio of imports to exports at the end of the year was how many times the ratio at the beginning of the year?

(A) $\frac{12}{11}$

(B) $\frac{4}{3}$

(C) $\frac{11}{8}$

(D) $\frac{3}{2}$

(E) 2

Difficulty: Hard
The correct answer is (B).

Express What You Know in Mathematical Terms

• State the ratio of imports to exports as $\frac{I}{E}$.

• At the end of the year, imports were up by 20%. So the change in imports can be expressed as 100% of beginning year imports *plus* 20%:

$$100\% + 20\% = 120\%$$

• At the end of the year, exports were down by 10%. So the change in exports can be expressed as 100% of beginning year exports *minus* 10%:

$$100\% - 10\% = 90\%$$

• Express the ratio of imports to exports at the end of the year:

$$\frac{I}{E} = \frac{120\%}{90\%}$$

Cancel the %s and reduce the fraction.

$$\frac{120\%}{90\%}$$
$$= \frac{12}{9}$$
$$= \frac{4}{3}$$

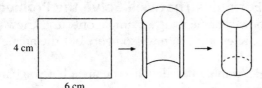

5. The figure above shows how a rectangular piece of paper is rolled to form a
cylindrical tube. If it is assumed that
the 4-centimeter sides of the rectangle
meet with no overlap, what is the area,
in square centimeters, of the base of
the cylindrical tube?

(A) 16π
(B) 9π
(C) 4π
(D) $\dfrac{9}{\pi}$
(E) $\dfrac{4}{\pi}$

Difficulty: Hard
The correct answer is (D).

QUESTION 5
Two- and three-
dimensional figures

 HINT

Label diagrams and figures with the information you have. This often
reveals key information that you need to answer the question.

What Do You Know?
• You know the *circumference* of the circle.
• Label the middle and right-hand figures in the diagram.

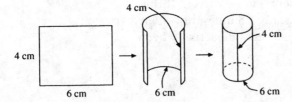

Notice that the 4-centimeter sides meet to form the seam in the
cylinder and the 6-centimeter sides curl around to become the top and
bottom of the cylinder.

• So the circumference of the circle is 6 centimeters.

Are There Any Formulas That Will Solve the Problem?

The question has now become a rather simple one. You know the circumference of the circle, and you have to figure out the area.

- There is no single formula to calculate the area, but you can get there in two steps:
  Relate the radius to the circumference by the formula:

$$\text{Circumference} = 2\pi r$$

  Relate the area to the radius by the formula:

$$\text{Area} = \pi r^2$$

- You know the circumference, so start there and work toward the area. The radius (r) is the common term in the two formulas so start by solving for r.

Apply the Formula to Get the Answer

$$\text{Circumference} = 2\pi r$$
$$6 = 2\pi r$$
$$\pi r = 3$$
$$r = \frac{3}{\pi}$$

- Now use the value for r in the formula for the area.

$$A = \pi r^2$$

$$r = \frac{3}{\pi}$$

$$A = \pi \left(\frac{3}{\pi}\right)^2$$

$$A = \pi \left(\frac{9}{\pi^2}\right)$$

$$A = \frac{9}{\pi}$$

QUESTION 6
Proportions

6. The odometer of a new automobile functions improperly and registers only 2 miles for every 3 miles driven. If the odometer indicates 48 miles, how many miles has the automobile actually been driven?

(A) 144
(B) 72
(C) 64
(D) 32
(E) 24

Difficulty: Medium
The correct answer is (B).

In this problem you are told that the odometer registers only 2 miles for every 3 miles driven. So the ratio of miles registered to miles driven is 2 to 3 or $\frac{2}{3}$. This can be expressed as

$$\frac{\text{odometer reading}}{\text{actual miles}} = \frac{2}{3}$$

If the odometer indicates 48 miles, the actual miles can be found using the above relationship as follows:

$$\frac{48}{x} = \frac{2}{3}$$
$$2x = 144$$
$$x = 72$$

So if the odometer indicates 48 miles, the actual number of miles driven is 72.

How to Avoid Errors When Working With Proportions

The most important thing with proportions is to be consistent in the way you set them up. If you mix up the terms, you won't get the correct answer. For instance, if you put the registered mileage in the numerator of one ratio but the actual mileage in the numerator of the other ratio, you will come up with a wrong answer:

$$\frac{3}{2} = \frac{48}{x}$$
$$3x = 96$$
$$x = \frac{96}{3} = 32 \text{ miles} \quad \text{Wrong!}$$

Make a "Does-It-Make-Sense?" Check

When you arrive at an answer to a word problem, check to see whether it makes sense. The question states that the actual mileage is greater than the registered mileage. So the actual mileage has to be a number *larger* than 48.

Your check should warn you not to choose the incorrect answer (D) 32 that was obtained by setting up the wrong proportion.

 HINT

A quick "make-sense" check before you start working on a question can help you eliminate some of the answers right away. If you realize that the actual mileage has to be greater than the registered mileage, you can eliminate answers D and E immediately.

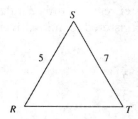

Note: Figure not drawn to scale.

QUESTION 7
Figures not drawn to scale

7. If the perimeter of ΔRST above is 3 times the length of RS, then RT =

(A) 3
(B) 5
(C) 8
(D) 9
(E) 10

Difficulty: Easy
The correct answer is (A).

"Note: Figure not drawn to scale" means that the points and angles are in their relative positions, but the lengths of the sides and the sizes of the angles may not be as pictured.

What Do You Know?
- The perimeter of the triangle is the sum of the lengths of the three sides.
- The question states that the perimeter is 3 times the length of RS.
- RS is 5 units long.
- ST is 7 units long.

Express the Problem Using an Equation
- The perimeter is equal to three times the length of RS.
- That means that the perimeter is 3 times 5 or 15.
- So 5 + 7 + RT = 15
    RT = 3

⚡ **HINT**

It's always a good idea to draw the lines and figures that are described in a question if a figure is not given.

Make sure that what you draw fits the information in the question.

Don't worry about how pretty the figure is. It only has to be neat enough for you to work with it.

---

8. *A*, *B*, *C*, and *D* are points on a line, with *D* the midpoint of segment *BC*. The lengths of segments *AB*, *AC*, and *BC* are 10, 2, and 12 respectively. What is the length of segment *AD*?

(A) 2
(B) 4
(C) 6
(D) 10
(E) 12

QUESTION 8
Draw your own figure . . .
carefully

Difficulty: Medium
The correct answer is (B).

The key to this question lies in *not* jumping to incorrect conclusions. The question names the points on a line. It gives you a variety of information about the points. The one thing it *does not* do is tell you the order in which the points fall.

Many students assume that the order of the points is *A*, then *B*, then *C*, then *D*. As you will see, if you try to locate the points in this order, you will be unable to answer the question.

What Is the Question Asking?
The question asks for the length of line segment *AD*. In order to find this length, you have to establish the relative positions of the four points on the line.

What Do You Know?
Try to draw the figure. You might be tempted to locate point *A* first. Unfortunately, you don't have enough information about *A*, yet, to place it.

• You can place *B*, *C*, and *D* because *D* is the midpoint of *BC*.

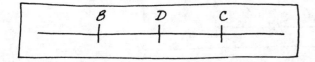

• You know the lengths of three of the line segments:

$$AB = 10$$
$$AC = 2$$
$$BC = 12$$

149

- Because you know where BC is, you can label the length of BC.

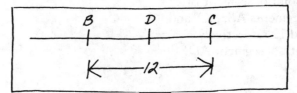

Build the Figure, Adding What You Know and What You Can Figure Out

Because *D* is the midpoint of *BC*, you know that *BD* and *DC* are each 6 units long.

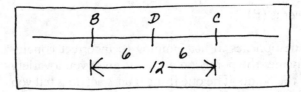

Where can you place point A?
It has to be 2 units from C, because AC = 2.
It also has to be 10 units from B, because AB = 10.
So the only location for A is between B and C, but closer to C.

- Place point A and mark the distances.

It is now an easy matter to figure out the answer to the question:

- *DC* is 6 units.
- A is 2 units closer to *D* than C, so *AD* is 4 units.

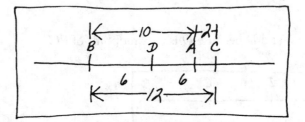

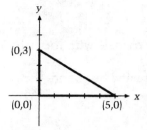

9. What is the area of the triangle in the figure above?

    (A)   4.0
    (B)   7.5
    (C)   8.0
    (D)   8.5
    (E)   15.0

    Difficulty: Medium
    The correct answer is (B).

QUESTION 9
Figures on a coordinate plane

> ### ⚙ HINT
>
> The coordinate system provides essential information for solving this problem.
>
> Your knowledge of the coordinate system can give you information about lengths and angles, such as:
>
> - Whether lines are parallel, perpendicular, or neither;
> - Whether figures are squares, special triangles, etc.;
> - How long line segments are;
> - Whether angles are right angles or other special angles.

The figure provides all the information you need to answer the question.

What Is the Question Asking?
You are asked to figure out the area of a triangle that is defined by three points on a coordinate plane.

What Do You Know?

- The triangle in the figure is a right triangle with the right angle at the lower left.
- Because it is a right triangle, its base and height are the two sides that form the right angle.
- The area of a triangle is $\frac{1}{2}\,bh$.
- The base of the triangle extends from point (0,0) to point (5,0). So it is 5 units long.
- The height of the triangle extends from point (0,0) to point (0,3). So it is 3 units long.

$$\begin{aligned}
\text{Area} &= \tfrac{1}{2}\,bh \\
&= \tfrac{1}{2}\,(3)(5) \\
&= \tfrac{1}{2}\,(15) \\
&= 7.5
\end{aligned}$$

⚡ HINT

If you are presented with a math question that shows the grid lines of a graph, you may rely on the accuracy of those lines.

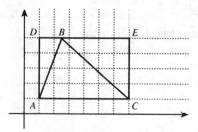

You can use the grid on the graph above to determine the following information:

- *AC* is 6 units long.
- *ADEC* is a rectangle.
- Side *AD* is 4 units long.
- The height of the triangle *ABC* is the same as the width of the rectangle (*ADEC*). So the height of the triangle is 4 units.

- The area of the triangle is $\frac{1}{2}$ the area of the rectangle.

- The area of a rectangle = width × length = $AD \times AC$ = 4 × 6 = 24 units.

- The area of the triangle = $\frac{1}{2}$ (base × height) = $\frac{1}{2}$ ($AC \times AD$) = $\frac{1}{2}$ (6 × 4) = 12 units.

QUESTION 10
Logical analysis

10. A = {3,6,9}
B = {5,7,9}
C = {7,8,9}

If three different numbers are selected, one from each of the sets shown above, what is the greatest sum that these three numbers could have?

(A) 22
(B) 23
(C) 24
(D) 25
(E) 27

Difficulty: Medium
The correct answer is (C).

This question challenges your ability to reason with numbers. In other words, it is more a question of logic than of arithmetic.

What Is the Question Asking?

The question asks what is the largest sum you can get if you choose one number from each set and add those numbers together. There's a catch, however. Each number you select must be different. So you *cannot* take the largest number, 9, from each set, add the nines together, and come up with choice (E) 27.

What Do You Know?

- 9 is the largest number in each set.
- You can only take one number 9. This means that you will have to take the second largest number from two of the sets.

Make Your Selections

- The second largest number in set A is 6, which is smaller than the second largest number in sets B and C. So select 9 from set A.
- The other two choices are now easy. Take the largest numbers available from sets B and C.
- The greatest sum is 9 + 7 + 8 = 24.

QUESTION 11
Working with special symbols

11. Let the symbol ⓧ represent the number of different pairs of positive integers whose product is x. For example, ⑯ = 3, since there are 3 different pairs of positive integers whose product is 16:

$$16 \times 1, 8 \times 2, \text{ and } 4 \times 4$$

What does ㊱ equal?

(A)   5
(B)   6
(C)   8
(D)   10
(E)   12

Difficulty: Easy
The correct answer is (A).

Most SAT math tests have at least one question involving a newly defined symbol. Sometimes there will be an easy question, like this one, followed by a more difficult one in which you might have to use the new symbol in an equation.

To answer these questions, you have to read the definition of the special symbol carefully and follow the instructions. *It is not expected that you have ever seen the new symbol before.*

The question asks you to figure out how many pairs of positive integers can be multiplied together to give you the number in the circle.

Put the Special Symbol to Work

- To figure out ㊱, list the pairs of positive integers whose product is 36:

$$1 \times 36$$
$$2 \times 18$$
$$3 \times 12$$
$$4 \times 9$$
$$6 \times 6$$

- Count up the pairs. The answer is 5.

 HINT

When you're faced with a special symbol, read the definition carefully and use it as your instruction for working out the answer.

---

12. Several people are standing in a straight line. Starting at one end of the line Bill is counted as the 5th person, and starting at the other end he is counted as the 12th person. How many people are in the line?

(A) 15
(B) 16
(C) 17
(D) 18
(E) 19

Difficulty: Easy
The correct answer is (B).

You can answer this question by careful reasoning, or you can draw it out and count. Either way, be careful that you don't leave Bill out or count him twice.

What Do You Know?
- Bill is the 5th person from one end of the line.
- Bill is the 12th person from the other end.

Using Logic to Solve the Problem
- If Bill is the 5th person from one end of the line, there are 4 people (not counting Bill) between him and that end of the line.
- If Bill is the 12th person from the other end of the line, there are 11 people (not counting Bill) between him and that end of the line.
- 4 people between Bill and one end, plus 11 people between Bill and the other end, add up to 15 people. Then you have to add Bill. So there are 16 people in line.

 HINT

Problems like this one focus on your ability to reason logically.

There's nothing wrong with drawing a figure using dots to represent the people in line. Just make sure that you follow the instructions carefully when you draw your figure.

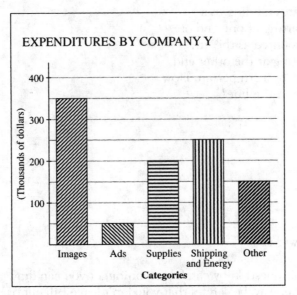

EXPENDITURES BY COMPANY Y

(Thousands of dollars)

Categories: Images, Ads, Supplies, Shipping and Energy, Other

QUESTION 13
Working with data from a graph

13. In the graph above, if the total expenditures by Company Y were $1,000,000, the shaded area of which of the following pie charts best represents the expenditures other than shipping and energy?

(A)

(B)

(C)

(D)

(E)

Difficulty: Medium
The correct answer is (D).

In this question you have to interpret information from one type of graph (bar graph) and translate that information into another type of graph (pie chart).

Questions that involve interpreting data presented on graphs or in tables will be common on the SAT.

What Is the Question Asking?
The question asks you to identify the pie chart that shows all of Company Y's expenses *other than* shipping and energy. That *other than* is important. It's easy to overlook.

What Do You Know?

All you need to know to answer the question is the amount of money spent on Shipping and Energy and the total expenses for the company.

- You are given the total expenses: $1,000,000. (You also could have figured that total out from the graph by adding all the expenses from the individual categories.)
- The graph will show you that the expenditures for Shipping and Energy amount to $250,000.

Translating the Information

- The question really asks you to identify approximately what fraction of the total costs *did not* go for Shipping and Energy. Although the question does not ask this specifically, the pie charts in the answer choices show fractions of the whole. So that's the way you will have to express the information you have.

- Shipping and Energy expenses amount to $250,000 of the $1,000,000 of total expenses.

- Shipping and Energy cost $\dfrac{\$250,000}{\$1,000,000}$ or $\dfrac{1}{4}$ of the total.

- That means that the answer is (B) because the pie chart in (B) shows about $\dfrac{1}{4}$ of the total, right? . . . WRONG!!!!

- Remember, the question asks which pie chart "best represents expenditures *other than* shipping and energy?"

- If $\dfrac{1}{4}$ goes for shipping and energy, that leaves $\dfrac{3}{4}$ for other things.

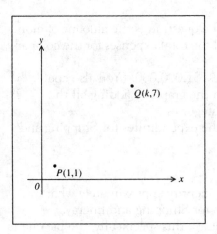

QUESTION 14
Slope of a line in a graph

14. In the figure above, the slope of the line through points P and Q is 3/2. What is the value of k?

(A) 4
(B) 5
(C) 6
(D) 7
(E) 8

Difficulty: This question was written for this book. We do not know the difficulty.

The correct answer is (B).

Your ability to answer this question depends on your knowing and being able to apply the definition of "slope."

The **slope** of a line in the xy-coordinate plane is:

$$\frac{\text{the change in } y \text{ between any two points on the line}}{\text{the change in } x \text{ between the same points on the line}}$$

The question asks for the value of k, which is the x coordinate of point Q.

What Do You Know?
- The slope of the line that goes between P and Q is $\frac{3}{2}$.
- That means for every 3 units that y changes, x will change 2.
- The coordinates of P are $(1,1)$.
- The coordinates of Q are $(k,7)$.
- The change in the value of y between P and Q is 6 units $(7 - 1 = 6)$.

Apply What You Know
- *y* changes 6 units between the two points.
- That means that *x* will change 4 units, since for every 3 units that *y* changes, *x* changes 2 units.
- The *x* coordinate of point *P* is 1.
- The *x* coordinate of point *Q* will be 1 + 4 = 5.

R E C A P :
H I N T S   F O R   F I V E - C H O I C E
M U L T I P L E - C H O I C E   Q U E S T I O N S

Remember the approach to Roman numeral format questions: Consider each Roman numeral statement as a separate true-false question.

A quick "make-sense" check before you start working on multiple-choice questions can help to eliminate some of the choices.

Quantitative Comparison Questions

Practice Questions

The next six questions are Quantitative Comparison problems. They do not require that you figure out a specific value or answer. Rather, you must determine which of two quantities has the greater value.
Here's how they work:

- Each Quantitative Comparison question shows two quantities to be compared—one in the left column (Column A) and one in the right column (Column B). Some may also have additional information that you'll find centered above the quantities to be compared.
- Your job is to determine which quantity, if either, has the greater value.

You choose the letter that indicates the correct relationship between the two quantities being compared.
If you find you're having trouble figuring out the solutions to these questions, turn to the Answers and Explanations that follow the questions.

Directions for Quantitative Comparison Questions

Questions 15-20 each consist of two quantities in boxes, one in Column A and one in Column B. You are to compare the two quantities and on the answer sheet fill in oval

A   if the quantity in Column A is greater;
B   if the quantity in Column B is greater;
C   if the two quantities are equal;
D   if the relationship cannot be determined from the information given.

AN E RESPONSE WILL NOT BE SCORED.

Notes:

1. In some questions, information is given about one or both of the quantities to be compared. In such cases, the given information is centered above the two columns and is not boxed.
2. In a given question, a symbol that appears in both columns represents the same thing in Column A as it does in Column B.
3. Letters such as x, n, and k stand for real numbers.

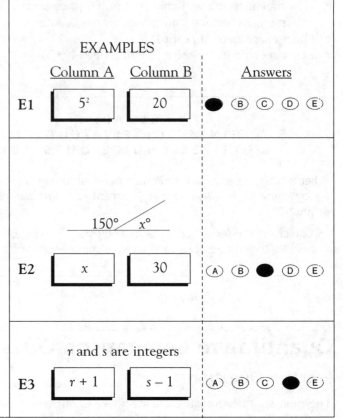

Special note: On the actual test, directions to Quantitative Comparison questions are summarized at the top of every page containing Quantitative Comparisons.

Column A	Column B		Column A	Column B

$$23 + 16 + 57 + x = 108$$
$$23 + 16 + 27 + y = 108$$

$$y^2 = x$$
$$y > 0$$

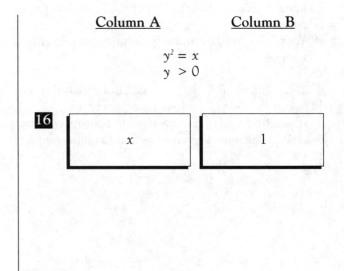

	Column A	Column B
15	x	y
16	x	1

SUMMARY DIRECTIONS FOR COMPARISON QUESTIONS

<u>Answer</u>: A if the quantity in Column A is greater;
B if the quantity in Column B is greater;
C if the two quantities are equal;
D if the relationship cannot be determined from the information given.

<u>Column A</u>	<u>Column B</u>	<u>Column A</u>	<u>Column B</u>

A fair six-sided die with faces numbered 1 through 6 is to be rolled twice.

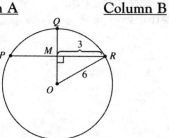

17

The probability of obtaining a 6 on the top face on the first roll and 5 on the top face of the second roll	The probability of obtaining a 5 on the top face on both the first and second rolls

<u>Note</u>: Figure not drawn to scale.
P, Q, and R are points on the circle with center O. PR and OQ are line segments.

19

The length of OM	The length of MQ

In ΔABC, side AB has length 6 and side BC has length 4.

18

The length of side AC	8

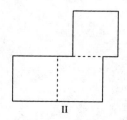

Six squares of equal size form the figures above.

20

The perimeter of I	The perimeter of II

Answers and Explanations

<u>Column A</u>   <u>Column B</u>

$$23 + 16 + 57 + x = 108$$
$$23 + 16 + 27 + y = 108$$

QUESTION 15
Don't waste time doing
calculations.

15.

x	y

Difficulty: Easy
The correct answer is (B).

What Do You Know?

- The two equations contain some common terms. The only differences are in the two terms just before the equal sign.
- In both equations, the expressions on the left side of the equal sign add up to the same number.
- The numbers that are common to the two expressions will have no effect on which variable has the greater value, so you can eliminate 23 and 16.

$$57 + x = 27 + y$$

- Which has to be greater, x or y, in order for this equation to be true?
- Because y is added to a smaller number, y has to be greater.

🗲 **HINT**

By estimating and comparing, you can frequently establish which quantity is greater without figuring out the value of either quantity.

<u>Column A</u>   <u>Column B</u>

$$y^2 = x$$
$$y > 0$$

16.

x	1

Difficulty: Medium
The correct answer is (D).

To answer this question, you can sample a few values for y, but you must make sure that you sample a variety of values.

 HINT

When you are substituting values to answer a Quantitative Comparison question, make sure you check the special cases:

- 0
- 1
- at least one number between 0 and 1
- a number or numbers greater than 1
- negative numbers

Substituting Values

Because y is greater than 0, you don't have to worry about 0 or negative values. But when you raise numbers to powers, fractions and the number 1 act differently than numbers greater than 1.

 HINT

If any two of the answers (A), (B), or (C) can be true for particular values in a Quantitative Comparison question, then the answer to that question is (D).

So you need to sample:

The number 1;
A number between 0 and 1;
A number greater than 1.

Try $y = 1$.

$$y^2 = x$$
$$1^2 = x$$
$$1 = x$$

Try a value of y between 0 and 1, such as $\frac{1}{2}$.

$$y^2 = x$$
$$\left(\frac{1}{2}\right)^2 = x$$
$$\frac{1}{4} = x$$

We've found two possible values of x (1 and $\frac{1}{4}$). In the first case, the quantity in column A ($x = 1$) is equal to the quantity in Column B. In the second case, the quantity in column A ($x = \frac{1}{4}$) is less than the quantity in column B. So you cannot tell and the answer is (D).

Column A	Column B

A fair six-sided die with faces numbered 1 through 6 is to be rolled twice.

QUESTION 17
Probability

17.

The probability of obtaining a 6 on the top face on the first roll and 5 on the top face of the second roll	The probability of obtaining a 5 on the top face on both the first and second rolls

Answer: C
Difficulty: Medium

You are given that a fair die is to be rolled twice. This means that on each roll each of the six numbered faces is equally likely to be the top face. For example, the face numbered 3 is just as likely to be the top face as the face numbered 4. The probability that any specific number will appear on the top die is $\frac{1}{6}$.

- In Column A, the probability of obtaining a 6 on the first roll and a 5 on the second roll is $\frac{1}{6} \times \frac{1}{6} = \frac{1}{36}$.

- In Column B, the probability of obtaining a 5 on the first roll and another 5 on the second roll is also $\frac{1}{6} \times \frac{1}{6} = \frac{1}{36}$.

Therefore, the two quantities are equal.

Caution: In this question, you are given the order in which the numbered faces appear. If in Column A you had been asked for "The probability of obtaining a 6 on the top face of one roll and a 5 on the top face of the other roll," the answer would be different. Why? Because there are *two* equally likely ways to succeed: a 6 on the first roll and a 5 on the second, or a 5 on the first roll and a 6 on the second. Each of these two outcomes has a probability of $\frac{1}{36}$. Therefore, in this case, the quantity in Column A would equal $\frac{2}{36}$.

<u>**Column A**</u>   <u>**Column B**</u>

In $\triangle ABC$, side AB has length 6 and side BC has length 4.

18.

The length of side AC

8

QUESTION 18
Ask yourself: Is there more than one way to draw the figure?

The correct answer is (D).

 HINT

The sum of the lengths of any two sides of a triangle is always greater than the length of the third side.

There are two related properties of triangles that you should remember. The length of any one side must be less than the sum of the lengths of the other two sides. And the length of any one side must be greater than the difference between the lengths of the other two sides.

If you remember these properties, the answer to this question is easy:

- The sum of lengths *AB* and *BC* is 6 + 4 or 10. So side *AC* has to be less than 10.
- The difference between lengths *AB* and *BC* is 6 – 4 or 2. So *AC* must be greater than 2.
- The length of *AC* can be greater than 8, equal to 8, or less than 8. In other words, you cannot tell which quantity (Column A or Column B) is greater.

<u>Column A</u>   <u>Column B</u>

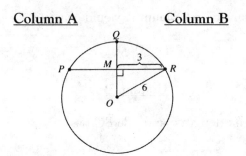

Note: Figure not drawn to scale.
P, *Q*, and *R* are points on the circle with center *O*. *PR* and *OQ* are line segments.

QUESTION 19
Use all the information

19.

| The length of OM | The length of MQ |

Difficulty: Hard
The correct answer is (A).

What Do You Know?

- O is the center of the circle. Therefore, OR is a radius of the circle with a length of 6.
- OQ is a line segment that starts from the center and extends to the edge of the circle. So it is also a radius with a length of 6.
- Angle OMR is a right angle. Therefore, triangle OMR is a right triangle.

What Lengths Do You Need to Find?
- OQ has a length of 6.
- OM is a side of right triangle (OMR). And you know the length of the other side and of the hypotenuse.
- Therefore, you can find the length of OM by using the Pythagorean theorem.

Apply the Theorem
The Pythagorean theorem:

$$a^2 + b^2 = c^2$$

Where:

a and b are the lengths of the two perpendicular sides (the legs) of a right triangle.
c is the length of the hypotenuse.

In the triangle in Question 19

The two legs are OM and MR
$MR = 3$
The hypotenuse OR is 6.

Substitute these numbers into the Pythagorean theorem:

$$a^2 + b^2 = c^2$$
$$3^2 + (OM)^2 = 6^2$$
$$9 + (OM)^2 = 36$$
$$(OM)^2 = 27$$
$$OM = \sqrt{27}$$

Compare the Lengths
- $OM = \sqrt{27}$, which is a little more than 5.
- $MQ = 6 - OM$
- $MQ = 6 - \sqrt{27}$
- You don't have to figure out the exact lengths. If OM is more than 5, MQ has to be less than 1. So OM is longer than MQ.

> **HINT**
>
> The Reference section of the math test book gives the properties of some special triangles. Because the hypotenuse (6) is twice the shorter leg (3) you know the ratio of the sides of the right triangle in this question is 1: $\sqrt{3}$: 2. Then you can figure out that $OM = 3\sqrt{3}$, so $OM > MQ$.
>
> You will probably find that if you are not familiar with most of the information in the Reference section before you take the test, you will have a hard time using it efficiently during the test.

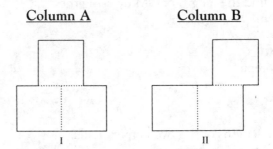

Six squares of equal size form the figures above.

QUESTION 20
Visualizing

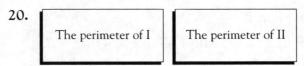

20.

Difficulty: Medium
The correct answer is (B).

Explanation:
   If you know the definition of perimeter, you should be able to figure out the answer to this question just by looking at the figures.

What Do You Know?
- Three squares make up each figure, and all the squares are of equal size.
- The perimeter of a figure is equal to the sum of the lengths of its sides, not the sides of the individual squares that make up the figure. The perimeters *do not* include any of the dotted lines.
- The lengths of the bottoms of both figures are equal. So your focus should be on what's happening where the top square and the top of the bottom squares meet.
- Look at the top square of I. Its entire bottom side overlaps with the upper sides of the lower squares, so its bottom side *does not* add to the perimeter. The tops of the bottom squares in I add a length equal to one side of a square to the perimeter.

- Now look at the top of square II. Some of its bottom side—the part that sticks out—does add to the perimeter. The tops of the bottom squares in II add a length greater than one side of a square to the perimeter.
- Therefore, the perimeter of II is greater.

RECAP:
HINTS ON QUANTITATIVE
COMPARISON QUESTIONS

With Quantitative Comparison questions, frequently you don't have to finish your calculations or determine an exact answer. You just have to know enough about the quantities to determine which one is greater.

Memorize the four answer choices for Quantitative Comparison questions.

If any two of the answers (A), (B), or (C) can be true for a particular Quantitative Comparison question, then the answer to that question is (D).

Think of the columns as a balanced scale. You are trying to figure out which side of the scale is heavier, so eliminate any quantities that are the same on both sides of the scale.

Try evaluating the quantities by substituting values for variables. Just remember:

- Make sure you check above the columns for any information about what the values can be.
- When substituting values to answer a Quantitative Comparison question, make sure you check the special cases: 0, 1, at least one number between 0 and 1, a number or numbers greater than 1, and negative numbers.

Grid-in Questions

Practice Questions

The math skills and reasoning abilities required for Grid-in questions are much the same as those required for the other two types of math questions. In fact, many Grid-in questions are similar to regular Multiple-Choice questions except that no answers are provided.

There are, of course, some differences:

- Because no answers are given, you'll always have to work out the solutions yourself.
- If you have no idea of the correct answer, random guessing on Grid-in questions isn't very useful. Even though no points are deducted for wrong answers, your chances of guessing correctly are usually not good. But if you have worked out an answer and you think it might be correct, go ahead and grid it in. You won't lose any points for trying.
- You can enter your answers on the grid in several forms. When appropriate, you may use fractions or decimals. Fractions do not have to be reduced to lowest terms—e.g., $\frac{3}{12}$ is acceptable.
- The details of the gridding procedure are discussed in Chapter 6. There are strict rules for rounding and for expressing repeating decimals. Make sure you understand the grid-in procedure very well.

Use the sample grids on page 173 to practice gridding techniques. If you find you're having trouble figuring out the solutions to these eight problems, turn to the Answers and Explanations that follow the questions.

21 In a restaurant where the sales tax on a $4.00 lunch is $0.24, what will be the sales tax due, in dollars, on a $15.00 dinner? (Disregard the $ sign when gridding your answer. For example, if the answer is $1.37, grid 1.37)

23 If n is a two-digit number that can be expressed as the product of two consecutive <u>even</u> integers, what is one possible value of n?

22 A team has won 60 percent of the 20 games it has played so far this season. If the team plays a total of 50 games all season and wins 80 percent of the remaining games, how many games will the team win for the entire season?

24 If the ratio of a to b is $\dfrac{7}{3}$, what is the value of the ratio of $2a$ to b?

25 If the population of a town doubles every 10 years, the population in the year X + 100 will be how many times the population in the year X?

27 If $\frac{x}{2} = y$ and $2y = y$, what is the value of x?

26

Number of Donuts	Total Price
1	$ 0.40
Box of 6	$ 1.89
Box of 12	$ 3.59

According to the information in the table above, what would be the <u>least</u> amount of money needed, in dollars, to purchase exactly 21 donuts? (Disregard the $ sign when gridding your answer. For example, if the answer is $1.37, grid 1.37)

28

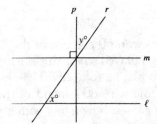

<u>Note</u>: Figure not drawn to scale.
In the figure above, line m is parallel to line ℓ and is perpendicular to line p. If $x = y$, what is the value of x?

21.

22.

23.

24.

25.

26.

27.

28.

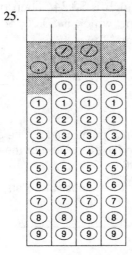

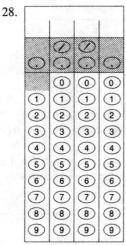

QUESTION 21
Gridding dollar amounts

Answers and Explanations

21. In a restaurant where the sales tax on a $4.00 lunch is $0.24, what will be the sales tax due, in dollars, on a $15.00 dinner? (Disregard the $ sign when gridding your answer. For example, if the answer is $1.37, grid 1.37)

Difficulty: Easy
The correct answer is .90 or .9.

One way to solve this problem is to determine the tax on each $1.00 and then multiply this amount by 15 to get the tax on $15.00. The tax on a $4.00 lunch is $0.24. Then the tax on $1.00 would be one-fourth this amount, which is $0.06. So the tax on $15.00 would be $15 \times .06 = .90$ dollars.

⊘ HINT

Zeros before the decimal point need not be gridded. (There isn't even a zero available in the far-left column of the grid.) So, don't try to grid 0.90; just grid .90 or .9.

The question asks for the number of dollars, so 90 for 90 cents would be wrong.

⊘ HINT

Some seemingly difficult questions are really just a series of easy questions.

- Take the question one step at a time.
- Think about what you need to know in order to answer the question.
- Use what you know to figure out what you need to know.
- Make sure your *final* answer answers the question that has been asked.

22. A team has won 60 percent of the 20 games it has played so far this season. If the team plays a total of 50 games all season and wins 80 percent of the remaining games, how many games will the team win for the entire season?

QUESTION 22
Work through a problem one step at a time

Difficulty: Medium
The correct answer is 36.

Express the Information in Mathematical Terms:
How many games has the team won so far?

60% of 20 games =
$$\frac{60}{100} \times 20 = .6 \times 20 = 12 \text{ games}$$

How many games will the team win the rest of the season? The total number of games left is $50 - 20 = 30$.

The team will win 80% of 30 games during the rest of the season.
$$\frac{80}{100} \times 30 = .8 \times 30 = 24 \text{ games}$$

The total number of wins is: $12 + 24 = 36$.
Grid in 36.

23. If n is a two-digit number that can be expressed as the product of two consecutive <u>even</u> integers, what is one possible value of n?

QUESTION 23
Properties of numbers: a question with multiple answers

Difficulty: Medium
There are three acceptable correct answers: 24, 48, and 80. You only have to find one.

Explanation:
Although there are several values for n that will work, you only have to find one.

Follow the Instructions

- *n* is the product of two consecutive even integers. In other words, the question tells you to multiply consecutive even integers.
- *n* is also a two-digit number.

Try Some Values

Start with two small consecutive even integers, 2 and 4.

- 2 × 4 = 8
- 8 is not a two-digit number, so *n* cannot be 8.

Try the next two consecutive even integers, 4 and 6.

- 4 × 6 = 24
- 24 is a two-digit number.
- 24 is the product of two consecutive even integers.

24 is an acceptable value for *n*. Grid in 24.

Other Correct Answers

The other possible values are 48 (6 × 8) and 80 (8 × 10). You can grid in *any one* of these three values and get credit for answering the question correctly.

 HINT

Some questions have more than one correct answer.

You can grid any *one* of the correct answers and you will get full credit.

---

24. If the ratio of a to b is $\frac{7}{3}$, what is the value of the ratio of $2a$ to b?

Difficulty: Easy
The correct answer is $\frac{14}{3}$.

The question is easy as long as you know the definition of ratio. It is included in the sample section to show you how to grid the answer.

Express the Ratio

The ratio of a to b can be written as $\frac{a}{b}$.

The ratio of a to b is $\frac{7}{3}$, which can be expressed as $\frac{a}{b} = \frac{7}{3}$.

If $\frac{a}{b} = \frac{7}{3}$

then $\frac{2a}{b} = 2\left(\frac{a}{b}\right) = 2\left(\frac{7}{3}\right) = \frac{14}{3}$.

Grid in the answer $\frac{14}{3}$.

H I N T   O N   G R I D D I N G

$\frac{14}{3}$ cannot be gridded as $4\frac{2}{3}$. The grid-reading system cannot tell the difference between $4\frac{2}{3}$ and $\frac{42}{3}$. Also, if you change $\frac{14}{3}$ to a decimal, either 4.66 or 4.67 is an acceptable answer.

QUESTION 24
Ratios; gridding improper fractions

QUESTION 25
Working with powers

25. If the population of a town doubles every 10 years, the population in the year $X + 100$ will be how many times the population in the year X?

Difficulty: Hard
The correct answer is 1024.

Express the Population Growth in Mathematical Terms

Each time the population doubles, multiply it by 2. Let p represent the population in year X.

- In 10 years the population increases from p to $2p$.
- In 10 more years it increases to $2(2p)$
- In 10 more years it increases to $2[2(2p)]$ and so on for 100 years.

This repeated doubling can be expressed by using powers of 2:

- Another way to express $2(2)$ is 2^2.
- So a population of $2(2p) = (2^2)p$.
- In 10 more years the population is $2(2^2)p$ or $(2^3)p$.
- In 10 more years the population is $2(2^3)p$ or $(2^4)p$, etc.

How Many Growth Cycles Are There?

- The population doubles (is raised to another power of 2) every 10 years.
- This goes on for 100 years.
- So there are $100/10 = 10$ cycles.
- The population increases 2^{10} times what it was in year X.

Figure Out the Answer

You can multiple ten 2s, but this invites error. You may want to use your calculator to find 2^{10}. Some calculators have an exponent key that allows you to find y^x directly. If your calculator does not have this feature, you can still quickly get the value of 2^{10} on your calculator as follows.

$$2^5 = 2 \times 2 \times 2 \times 2 \times 2 = 32$$
$$2^{10} = 2^5 \times 2^5 = 32 \times 32 = 1024.$$

Grid in the answer, 1024.

 HINT

On some questions a calculator can help speed up your answer.

26.

Number of Donuts	Total Price
1	$ 0.40
Box of 6	$ 1.89
Box of 12	$ 3.59

According to the information in the table above, what would be the *least* amount of money needed, in dollars, to purchase exactly 21 donuts? (Disregard the $ sign when gridding your answer. For example, if the answer is $1.37, grid 1.37)

Difficulty: Medium
The correct answer is $6.68.

What Do You Know?
- You can save money by purchasing donuts by the box. A box of 6 donuts costs $1.89, but 6 individual donuts cost $2.40.
- You can save more money by purchasing the larger box. A box of 12 donuts costs $3.59, but 2 boxes of 6 donuts cost 2($1.89) = $3.78.
- The question says you have to buy exactly 21 donuts.

Use Your Head
You want to buy as few individual donuts as you can.

You want to buy as many donuts in large boxes as you can. You cannot buy 2 boxes of 12, because that would put you over the 21-donut limit. So start with 1 box of 12 donuts.

- Mark down 12 donuts, so you can keep track as you add more donuts.
- Mark down $3.59, so you can keep track as you spend more money.

You have 12 donuts, so there are 9 left to buy. You can save money by buying a box of 6 donuts.

- Add 6 to your donut total.
- Add $1.89 to your money total.

You now have 18 donuts, which means you will have to buy 3 individual donuts.

- Add 3 to your donut total. You now have exactly 21 donuts.
- Add 3 × $.40 = $1.20 to your money total.
- Add up the dollar figures: $3.59 + $1.89 + $1.20 = $6.68

Grid in 6.68. Remember to disregard the $ sign.

<u>Note</u>: Do not grid 668 without the decimal mark—it will be interpreted as $668!

⚡ HINT

When you're working out an answer, jot down your calculations in the space provided in your test book.

QUESTION 27
Watch out for zero

27. If $\frac{x}{2} = y$ and $2y = y$, what is the value of x?

Difficulty: Medium
The correct answer is 0.

This is another question that takes some reasoning rather than simple mathematical manipulation.

Look at the Equations
The second equation may look a little unusual to you:

$$2y = y$$

If $2y = y$ then $y = 0$. Therefore:

$$\frac{x}{2} = 0$$
$$x = 0$$

Grid in the answer, 0.

HINT ON GRIDDING

To grid zero, just enter 0 in a single column (*any* column where 0 appears). Leave the other three columns blank.

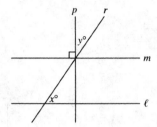

Note: Figure not drawn to scale.

28. In the figure above, line *m* is parallel to line *ℓ* and is perpendicular to line *p*. If *x* = *y*, what is the value of *x*?

Difficulty: Medium
The correct answer is 45.

QUESTION 28
Lines and angles

 HINT

Look for special properties that may help you answer the question. If it is about angles, look for special properties of angles. If it is about areas, look for special properties of areas.

Special properties that help you translate between different kinds of measurements can be especially useful.

For instance:
- If you know two sides of a triangle are of equal length, then you know that the measures of the angles opposite those two sides are equal.
- If you know two segments are radii of the same circle, you know that they are of equal length.

This question requires that you use your knowledge of lines, angles, and triangles to calculate values for parts of the figure that are not labeled. As you work on the question, remember:

- It's helpful to label parts of the figure as you work.
- Use your knowledge of special properties such as parallel lines, vertical angles, and special types of triangles.

What Do You Know?
- Lines ℓ and m are parallel.
- Line p is perpendicular to line m.
- $x = y$.

⚡ HINT

Write relevant facts (angles, lengths of sides) on the figure as you pick up more information.

What Can You Figure Out From the Figure?
You can use the parallel lines in the figure to label another angle that is equal to $x°$, since corresponding angles are congruent.

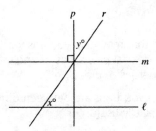

Since line p is perpendicular to line m, $x° + y° = 90°$. You are told that $x = y$. Therefore,

$$x° + x° = 90°$$
$$2x = 90$$
$$x = 45$$

Grid the answer, 45. Disregard the degree sign (°).

R E C A P :
H I N T S O N G R I D - I N Q U E S T I O N S

The slash mark (/) is used to indicate a fraction bar.

You don't have to reduce fractions to their lowest terms unless your answer will not fit in the grid.

You may express an answer as a fraction or a decimal: You can grid $\frac{1}{2}$ as 1/2 or .5.

Mixed numbers **must** be expressed as improper fractions: You must express $1\frac{3}{5}$ as 8/5. The grid-reading system cannot distinguish between 1 3/5 and 13/5.

Grid as much of a repeating decimal as will fit in the grid. You may need to round a repeating decimal, but round only the last digit: grid $\frac{2}{3}$ as 2/3 or .666 or .667. Do not grid the value $\frac{2}{3}$ as .67 or .66.

Since you don't have choices provided to help avoid careless errors on Grid-in questions:

• Carefully check your calculations.

• Always double-check your answers. Make sure the answer you enter makes sense.

Make sure you have gridded your answer accurately and according to all the Grid-in rules.

Practice a few Grid-in questions with a variety of answer types—whole numbers, fractions, and decimals. Get familiar with the mechanics of gridding.

Some Grid-in questions have more than one correct answer. You can grid any one of the correct answers and get full credit for the question.

To grid zero, just enter 0 in a single column (any column where 0 appears).

RECAP:
GENERAL HINTS ON MATHEMATICAL REASONING QUESTIONS

Be thoroughly familiar with the Reference materials provided in the test booklet, so you can refer to them quickly if you need to.

Refresh your math knowledge by studying the skills and concepts discussed in Chapter 6, Mathematics Review.

Make notes in your test book:

- Draw figures to help you think through problems that relate to geometric shapes, distances, proportions, sizes, and the like.

- Write out calculations so that you can check them later.

- When a question contains a figure, note any measurements or values you calculate right on the figure in the test book.

If you have time to check your work, try to redo your calculations in a different way from the way you did them the first time.

Use the choices to your advantage:

- If you can't figure out how to approach a problem, the form of the choices may give you a hint.

- You may find that you can eliminate some choices so you can make an educated guess, even if you aren't sure of the correct answer.

If you decide to try all the choices, start with choice (C). This is *not* because (C) is more likely to be the correct answer, but because the choices are usually listed in ascending order, from smallest to greatest value or greatest to smallest.

With data interpretation questions—graphs, charts, and tables—always make sure you understand the information being presented.

If it seems like you have a lot of calculating to do, there may be a shortcut.

With relatively simple questions, it's okay to substitute and/or eliminate choices. With more complicated problems, this approach may take more time than using mathematical reasoning.

If you're told that a figure is not drawn to scale, lengths and angles may not be shown accurately.

Number lines and graphs are generally accurately drawn.

When you are faced with special symbols, don't panic. Read the definition carefully and use it as your instruction for working out the answer.

Some seemingly difficult questions are really just a series of easy questions. Take the solution one step at a time.

PART FOUR

Ten Complete Practice Tests With Answer Keys

▲ ▼ ▲ **Taking the Practice Tests**

▲ ▼ ▲ **Two PSAT/NMSQT Practice Tests**

▲ ▼ ▲ **Eight SAT I Practice Tests**

Taking the Practice Tests

The practice tests that follow include two real editions of the PSAT/NMSQT and eight real editions of the SAT I. Both of the PSAT/NMSQTs are complete. Each edition of the SAT I, however, includes only six of the seven sections that the test contains. The equating sections have been omitted because they contain questions that may be used in future editions of the SAT I and do not count toward the scores. You'll get the most out of the practice tests by taking them under conditions as close as possible to those of the real tests.

- If you are taking one of the PSAT/NMSQTs, set aside two hours of uninterrupted time, so that you can complete the entire test at once.
- If you are taking one of the sample SATs, you'll need two-and-one-half hours to complete the test.
- Sit at a desk or table cleared of any other papers or books. You should have the calculator on hand that you plan to take with you to the test. Other items such as dictionaries, books, or notes will not be allowed.
- Have a kitchen timer or clock in front of you for timing yourself on the sections.
- Tear out the practice answer sheet located just before each practice test and fill it in just as you will on the day of the test.
- Once you finish a practice test, use the answer key, scoring instructions, and worksheet following it to calculate your scores.

Recentering

You may have heard that SAT scores are now reported on a recentered scale. What this means for you is that all the practice tests in this book will give you recentered verbal and math scores. Keep that in mind as you look through college guides or look at scores you may have received before April 1995. For more information on recentering, please see your guidance counselor.

Preliminary SAT/National Merit Scholarship Qualifying Test

Tuesday, October 12, 1993

Preliminary SAT/ National Merit Scholarship Qualifying Test

TUESDAY, OCTOBER 12, 1993

Time: The *new* PSAT/NMSQT has four sections. You will have 30 minutes to work on each section and a 5-minute break between Sections 2 and 3.

Scoring: For each correct answer you will receive one point (whether the question is easy or hard). For questions you omit, you will receive no points. For wrong answers to multiple-choice questions, you will lose only a fraction of a point.

Guessing: An educated guess may improve your score. That is, if you can eliminate one or more choices as wrong, you increase your chances of choosing the correct answer and earning one point. On the other hand, if you can't eliminate any choices, omit the question and move on.

Answers: You may write in the test book, but mark all answers on your answer sheet to receive credit. Make each mark a dark mark that completely fills the oval and is as dark as all your other marks. If you erase, do so completely.

Do your best.

DO NOT OPEN THE TEST BOOK UNTIL YOU ARE TOLD TO DO SO!

3PPT1

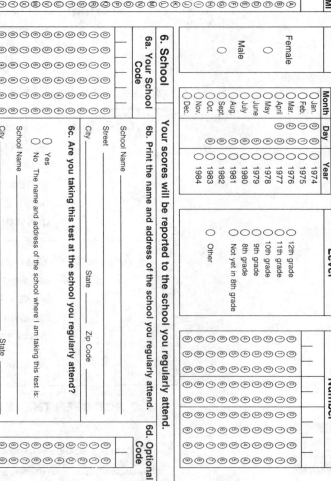

PSAT
NMSQT

Form S

1) Use a soft-lead No. 2 pencil only. Print the requested information in the boxes for each item.
2) Fill in the corresponding oval for each letter or number you enter. Completely erase any errors or stray marks.
Make each mark a dark mark that completely fills the intended oval and is as dark as all your other marks.

1. Name

Enter your full name, including your middle initial if you have one.
Omit hyphens, apostrophes, Jr., or III.

Last Name (Family Name) - first 15 letters

First Name - first 12 letters

MI

2. Sex

○ Male
○ Female

3. Date of Birth

Month	Day	Year
○ Jan.		○ 1974
○ Feb.		○ 1975
○ Mar.		○ 1976
○ April		○ 1977
○ May		○ 1978
○ June		○ 1979
○ July		○ 1980
○ Aug.		○ 1981
○ Sept.		○ 1982
○ Oct.		○ 1983
○ Nov.		○ 1984
○ Dec.		

4. Current Grade Level

○ 12th grade
○ 11th grade
○ 10th grade
○ 9th grade
○ 8th grade
○ Not yet in 8th grade
○ Other

5. Social Security Number

6. School

6a. Your School Code

6b. Print the name and address of the school you regularly attend.

School Name _____
Street _____
City _____ State _____ Zip Code _____

6c. Are you taking this test at the school you regularly attend?

○ Yes
○ No   The name and address of the school where I am taking this test is:

School Name _____
City _____ State _____

6d. Optional Code

Your scores will be reported to the school you regularly attend.

7. Ethnic Group

○ American Indian or Alaskan Native
○ Asian, Asian American, or Pacific Islander
○ Black or African American

Hispanic or Latino background
○ Mexican or Mexican American
○ Puerto Rican
○ South American, Latin American, Central American, or other Hispanic or Latino
○ White
○ Other

8. Grade Average

Cumulative high school average for all academic subjects.

○ A+ (97-100)
○ A (93-96)
○ A- (90-92)
○ B+ (87-89)
○ B (83-86)
○ B- (80-82)
○ C+ (77-79)
○ C (73-76)
○ C- (70-72)
○ D+ (67-69)
○ D (65-66)
○ E or F (below 65)

9. Language Background

What language did you learn to speak *first*?
○ English only
○ English and another language
○ Another language

What language do you know best?
○ English
○ English and another language about the same
○ Another language

10. Student Search Service®

The College Board would like to help you plan for college. Would you like information about you sent to colleges, universities, and certain scholarship programs?

○ Yes, I want the College Board to send information about me to colleges, universities, and certain scholarship programs interested in students like me.

○ No, I do not want the College Board to send information about me to colleges, universities, and certain scholarship programs.

11. College Major and Career

Select a code number from the lists of college majors and careers on the back of your test book.

Major   Career

For ETS Use Only

Your answers in Sections 7 and 8 will be used by the College Board to produce reports about groups of students, assure that tests are fair for all groups, and conduct research, but only in ways that protect your privacy.

Your answers in Section 9 will be used only for research purposes and will not be included on score reports.

CHW94146   Q2689-06   17012 • 01382 • TF54P925   I.N.203187
1   2   3   4

Make each mark a dark mark that completely fills the oval and is as dark as all your other marks. If you erase, do so completely. Incomplete erasures may be read as intended responses.

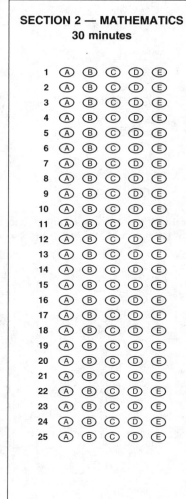

SECTION 1 — VERBAL
30 minutes

1 Ⓐ Ⓑ Ⓒ Ⓓ Ⓔ
2 Ⓐ Ⓑ Ⓒ Ⓓ Ⓔ
3 Ⓐ Ⓑ Ⓒ Ⓓ Ⓔ
4 Ⓐ Ⓑ Ⓒ Ⓓ Ⓔ
5 Ⓐ Ⓑ Ⓒ Ⓓ Ⓔ
6 Ⓐ Ⓑ Ⓒ Ⓓ Ⓔ
7 Ⓐ Ⓑ Ⓒ Ⓓ Ⓔ
8 Ⓐ Ⓑ Ⓒ Ⓓ Ⓔ
9 Ⓐ Ⓑ Ⓒ Ⓓ Ⓔ
10 Ⓐ Ⓑ Ⓒ Ⓓ Ⓔ
11 Ⓐ Ⓑ Ⓒ Ⓓ Ⓔ
12 Ⓐ Ⓑ Ⓒ Ⓓ Ⓔ
13 Ⓐ Ⓑ Ⓒ Ⓓ Ⓔ
14 Ⓐ Ⓑ Ⓒ Ⓓ Ⓔ
15 Ⓐ Ⓑ Ⓒ Ⓓ Ⓔ
16 Ⓐ Ⓑ Ⓒ Ⓓ Ⓔ
17 Ⓐ Ⓑ Ⓒ Ⓓ Ⓔ
18 Ⓐ Ⓑ Ⓒ Ⓓ Ⓔ
19 Ⓐ Ⓑ Ⓒ Ⓓ Ⓔ
20 Ⓐ Ⓑ Ⓒ Ⓓ Ⓔ
21 Ⓐ Ⓑ Ⓒ Ⓓ Ⓔ
22 Ⓐ Ⓑ Ⓒ Ⓓ Ⓔ
23 Ⓐ Ⓑ Ⓒ Ⓓ Ⓔ
24 Ⓐ Ⓑ Ⓒ Ⓓ Ⓔ
25 Ⓐ Ⓑ Ⓒ Ⓓ Ⓔ
26 Ⓐ Ⓑ Ⓒ Ⓓ Ⓔ
27 Ⓐ Ⓑ Ⓒ Ⓓ Ⓔ
28 Ⓐ Ⓑ Ⓒ Ⓓ Ⓔ
29 Ⓐ Ⓑ Ⓒ Ⓓ Ⓔ

SECTION 2 — MATHEMATICS
30 minutes

1 Ⓐ Ⓑ Ⓒ Ⓓ Ⓔ
2 Ⓐ Ⓑ Ⓒ Ⓓ Ⓔ
3 Ⓐ Ⓑ Ⓒ Ⓓ Ⓔ
4 Ⓐ Ⓑ Ⓒ Ⓓ Ⓔ
5 Ⓐ Ⓑ Ⓒ Ⓓ Ⓔ
6 Ⓐ Ⓑ Ⓒ Ⓓ Ⓔ
7 Ⓐ Ⓑ Ⓒ Ⓓ Ⓔ
8 Ⓐ Ⓑ Ⓒ Ⓓ Ⓔ
9 Ⓐ Ⓑ Ⓒ Ⓓ Ⓔ
10 Ⓐ Ⓑ Ⓒ Ⓓ Ⓔ
11 Ⓐ Ⓑ Ⓒ Ⓓ Ⓔ
12 Ⓐ Ⓑ Ⓒ Ⓓ Ⓔ
13 Ⓐ Ⓑ Ⓒ Ⓓ Ⓔ
14 Ⓐ Ⓑ Ⓒ Ⓓ Ⓔ
15 Ⓐ Ⓑ Ⓒ Ⓓ Ⓔ
16 Ⓐ Ⓑ Ⓒ Ⓓ Ⓔ
17 Ⓐ Ⓑ Ⓒ Ⓓ Ⓔ
18 Ⓐ Ⓑ Ⓒ Ⓓ Ⓔ
19 Ⓐ Ⓑ Ⓒ Ⓓ Ⓔ
20 Ⓐ Ⓑ Ⓒ Ⓓ Ⓔ
21 Ⓐ Ⓑ Ⓒ Ⓓ Ⓔ
22 Ⓐ Ⓑ Ⓒ Ⓓ Ⓔ
23 Ⓐ Ⓑ Ⓒ Ⓓ Ⓔ
24 Ⓐ Ⓑ Ⓒ Ⓓ Ⓔ
25 Ⓐ Ⓑ Ⓒ Ⓓ Ⓔ

SECTION 3 — VERBAL
30 minutes

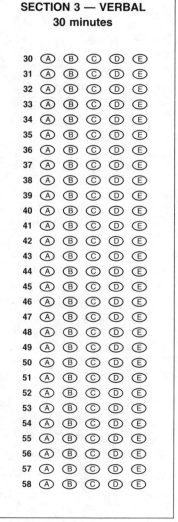

30 Ⓐ Ⓑ Ⓒ Ⓓ Ⓔ
31 Ⓐ Ⓑ Ⓒ Ⓓ Ⓔ
32 Ⓐ Ⓑ Ⓒ Ⓓ Ⓔ
33 Ⓐ Ⓑ Ⓒ Ⓓ Ⓔ
34 Ⓐ Ⓑ Ⓒ Ⓓ Ⓔ
35 Ⓐ Ⓑ Ⓒ Ⓓ Ⓔ
36 Ⓐ Ⓑ Ⓒ Ⓓ Ⓔ
37 Ⓐ Ⓑ Ⓒ Ⓓ Ⓔ
38 Ⓐ Ⓑ Ⓒ Ⓓ Ⓔ
39 Ⓐ Ⓑ Ⓒ Ⓓ Ⓔ
40 Ⓐ Ⓑ Ⓒ Ⓓ Ⓔ
41 Ⓐ Ⓑ Ⓒ Ⓓ Ⓔ
42 Ⓐ Ⓑ Ⓒ Ⓓ Ⓔ
43 Ⓐ Ⓑ Ⓒ Ⓓ Ⓔ
44 Ⓐ Ⓑ Ⓒ Ⓓ Ⓔ
45 Ⓐ Ⓑ Ⓒ Ⓓ Ⓔ
46 Ⓐ Ⓑ Ⓒ Ⓓ Ⓔ
47 Ⓐ Ⓑ Ⓒ Ⓓ Ⓔ
48 Ⓐ Ⓑ Ⓒ Ⓓ Ⓔ
49 Ⓐ Ⓑ Ⓒ Ⓓ Ⓔ
50 Ⓐ Ⓑ Ⓒ Ⓓ Ⓔ
51 Ⓐ Ⓑ Ⓒ Ⓓ Ⓔ
52 Ⓐ Ⓑ Ⓒ Ⓓ Ⓔ
53 Ⓐ Ⓑ Ⓒ Ⓓ Ⓔ
54 Ⓐ Ⓑ Ⓒ Ⓓ Ⓔ
55 Ⓐ Ⓑ Ⓒ Ⓓ Ⓔ
56 Ⓐ Ⓑ Ⓒ Ⓓ Ⓔ
57 Ⓐ Ⓑ Ⓒ Ⓓ Ⓔ
58 Ⓐ Ⓑ Ⓒ Ⓓ Ⓔ

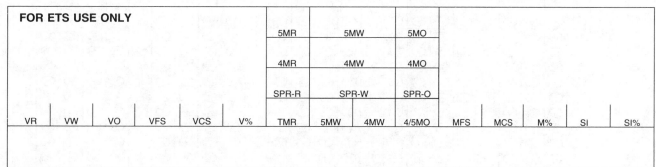

DO NOT WRITE IN THIS AREA.

3   0   0   0   0   0   0

SECTION 4 — MATHEMATICS
30 minutes

26 (A) (B) (C) (D)
27 (A) (B) (C) (D)
28 (A) (B) (C) (D)
29 (A) (B) (C) (D)
30 (A) (B) (C) (D)
31 (A) (B) (C) (D)
32 (A) (B) (C) (D)
33 (A) (B) (C) (D)
34 (A) (B) (C) (D)
35 (A) (B) (C) (D)
36 (A) (B) (C) (D)
37 (A) (B) (C) (D)
38 (A) (B) (C) (D)
39 (A) (B) (C) (D)
40 (A) (B) (C) (D)

Only answers entered in the ovals in each grid area will be scored.
You will not receive credit for anything written in the boxes above the ovals.

41   42   43   44   45

46   47   48   49   50

DO NOT WRITE IN THIS AREA.

3   0   0   0   0   0   0

192

Time—30 Minutes
29 Questions
(1-29)

For each question in this section, select the best answer from among the choices given and fill in the corresponding oval on the answer sheet.

Each sentence below has one or two blanks, each blank indicating that something has been omitted. Beneath the sentence are five words or sets of words labeled A through E. Choose the word or set of words that, when inserted in the sentence, best fits the meaning of the sentence as a whole.

Example:

Medieval kingdoms did not become constitutional republics overnight; on the contrary, the change was ----.

(A) unpopular
(B) unexpected
(C) advantageous
(D) sufficient
(E) gradual

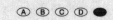

1 Unlike his brother, who sought solitude, Kahil was extremely ----.

(A) gregarious
(B) amenable
(C) terse
(D) avaricious
(E) cantankerous

2 In many cases, the formerly ---- origins of diseases have now been identified through modern scientific techniques.

(A) insightful
(B) mysterious
(C) cruel
(D) notable
(E) useful

3 Freeing embedded fossils from rock has become less ---- for paleontologists, who now have tiny vibrating drills capable of working with great speed and delicacy.

(A) exploratory
(B) conclusive
(C) tedious
(D) respected
(E) demeaning

4 Many people find Stanley Jordan's music not only entertaining but also ----; listening to it helps them to relax and to ---- the tensions they feel at the end of a trying day.

(A) soothing. .heighten
(B) therapeutic. .alleviate
(C) sweet. .underscore
(D) exhausting. .relieve
(E) interesting. .activate

5 Marine biologist Sylvia Earle makes a career of expanding the limits of deep-sea mobility, making hitherto-impossible tasks ---- through the new technology designed by her company.

(A) famous
(B) feasible
(C) fantastic
(D) controversial
(E) captivating

6 Two anomalies regarding her character are apparent: she is unfailingly ---- yet bursting with ambition, and she is truly ---- but unable to evoke reciprocal warmth in those with whom she works.

(A) aspiring. .generous
(B) mercenary. .impartial
(C) impulsive. .resolute
(D) persistent. .reserved
(E) humble. .compassionate

7 In many parts of East Africa at that time, wild animals were so ---- that it was almost impossible for a photographer to approach close enough to film them.

(A) rare
(B) large
(C) wary
(D) numerous
(E) unsightly

GO ON TO THE NEXT PAGE

8 The unflattering reviews that his latest recording received were ---- by his fans, who believe that everything he performs is a triumph of artistic ----.

(A) dismissed. .creativity
(B) hailed. .responsibility
(C) suppressed. .self-promotion
(D) accepted. .genius
(E) regretted. .pretension

9 The board members, accustomed to the luxury of being chauffeured to corporate meetings in company limousines, were predictably ---- when they learned that this service had been ----.

(A) satisfied. .annulled
(B) stymied. .extended
(C) displeased. .upheld
(D) disgruntled. .suspended
(E) concerned. .provided

10 Misrepresentative graphs and drawings ---- the real data and encourage readers to accept ---- arguments.

(A) obscure. .legitimate
(B) distort. .spurious
(C) illustrate. .controversial
(D) complement. .unresolved
(E) replace. .esteemed

11 Conservative historians who represent a traditional account as ---- because of its age may be guilty of taking on trust what they should have ---- in a conscientious fashion.

(A) ancient. .established
(B) false. .reiterated
(C) mythical. .fabricated
(D) accurate. .examined
(E) suspicious. .challenged

12 The art of Milet Andrejevic often presents us with an idyllic vision that is subtly --- by more sinister elements, as if suggesting the --- beauty of our surroundings.

(A) enhanced. .pristine
(B) invaded. .flawed
(C) altered. .unmarred
(D) redeemed. .hallowed
(E) devastated. .bland

13 State commissioner Ming Hsu expected that her Commission on International Trade would not merely ---- the future effects of foreign competition on local businesses but would also offer practical strategies for successfully resisting such competition.

(A) counteract
(B) intensify
(C) imagine
(D) forecast
(E) excuse

14 Since many teachers today draw on material from a variety of sources, disciplines, and ideologies for their lessons, their approach could best be called ----.

(A) eclectic
(B) simplistic
(C) invidious
(D) impromptu
(E) dogmatic

15 Unprecedented turmoil in the usually thriving nation has made the formerly ---- investors leery of any further involvement.

(A) pessimistic
(B) cautious
(C) clandestine
(D) reticent
(E) sanguine

16 Despite its apparent ----, much of early Greek philosophical thought was actually marked by a kind of unconscious dogmatism that led to ---- assertions.

(A) liberality. .doctrinaire
(B) independence. .autonomous
(C) intransigence. .authoritative
(D) fundamentalism. .arrogant
(E) legitimacy. .ambiguous

GO ON TO THE NEXT PAGE

The passages below are followed by questions based on their content; questions following a pair of related passages may also be based on the relationship between the paired passages. Answer the questions on the basis of what is <u>stated</u> or <u>implied</u> in the passages and in any introductory material that may be provided.

Questions 17-22 are based on the following passage.

The following passage is an excerpt from a book written by two female historians about professional women who began their careers in science in the late nineteenth and early twentieth centuries.

The strong efforts to gain equality for women in the scientific workplace began to show results in the last quarter of the twentieth century; women
Line have secured positions as research scientists and
(5) won recognition and promotion within their fields. Though the modern struggle for equality in scientific fields is the same in many ways as it was in the early part of the century, it is also different. The women who first began undertaking careers in
(10) science had little support from any part of the society in which they lived. This vanguard had to struggle alone against the social conditioning they had received as women members of that society and against the male-dominated scientific commu-
(15) nity.

Women scientific researchers made a seemingly auspicious beginning. In the first quarter of the twentieth century, some women scientists who engaged in research worked at the most prestigious
(20) institutes of the period and enjoyed more career mobility than women researchers would experience again for several decades. Florence Sabin, an anatomist at the Rockefeller Institute of Medical Research noted for her research on the lymphatic
(25) system, is one important example. This encouraging beginning, however, was not to be followed by other successes for many decades. To have maintained an active role in research institutions, women would have had to share some of the
(30) decision-making power: they needed to be part of hiring, promotion, and funding decisions. Unfortunately, these early women scientists were excluded from the power structure of scientific research. As a result, they found it almost impossible to
(35) provide opportunities for a younger set of female colleagues seeking employment in a research setting, to foster their productivity and facilitate their career mobility, and eventually to allow them access to the top ranks.
(40) Even those with very high professional aspirations accepted subordinate status as assistants if doing so seemed necessary to gain access to

research positions—and too often these were the only positions offered them in their chosen
(45) careers. Time and again they pulled back from offering any real resistance or challenge to the organizational structure that barred their advancement. But we must remember that these women scientists were few in number, their participation
(50) in decision-making positions was virtually nil, and their political clout was minimal. Thus they could easily become highly visible targets for elimination from the staff, especially if their behavior was judged in the least imprudent.
(55) Women's awareness that they were unequal colleagues, included in professional settings only on the sufferance of male colleagues, who held the positions of power, conflicted with their belief in meritocracy. They wanted to believe that achiev-
(60) ing persons would be welcomed for their abilities and contributions. Yet they were surrounded by evidence to the contrary. An assistant professor of zoology observed that the men who were heads of departments were insistent on having other men
(65) in the department; they told her that women ought to be satisfied teaching high school. She relates that, during her ten years in the department, men were given at least six positions that she was qualified for and wanted desperately, but
(70) for which she was not even considered because she was a woman.

17 The primary purpose of the passage is to

(A) explain a situation
(B) refute an argument
(C) propose a change
(D) predict an outcome
(E) honor an achievement

GO ON TO THE NEXT PAGE

18 The passage as a whole suggests that "career mobility" (lines 20-21 and 38) means the

(A) freedom to work on projects that one is most interested in
(B) freedom to publish research findings no matter how controversial they are
(C) ability to obtain funding to travel to important professional meetings
(D) ability to find a job in any part of the country
(E) ability to advance in one's chosen field

19 The statement that women could be eliminated from their jobs if their behavior was "the least imprudent" (line 54) suggests primarily that they

(A) were more likely than their male colleagues to be rebellious
(B) participated in the creation of the standards by which the performance of researchers was judged
(C) could gain advancement if they avoided political confrontations about their rights as women
(D) were judged by a standard different from the one used to judge their male colleagues
(E) were as critical of their colleagues as their colleagues were of them

20 The last paragraph of the passage suggests that for the majority of women scientists, the "belief in meritocracy" (lines 58-59) was

(A) justified, considering the opportunities available to them
(B) fortunate because it provided them with attainable goals
(C) inconsistent with the fact that they were discriminated against on the job
(D) understandable in that the concept had worked for the previous generation of women scientists
(E) trend-setting in that their views soon received universal acceptance

21 The example of the assistant professor of zoology (lines 62-71) serves primarily to indicate the

(A) extent of male bias against women in scientific fields at a particular time
(B) results of a woman's challenging male dominance in the early part of this century
(C) reasons for women's right to equal treatment
(D) inability of men and women to work together in an academic setting
(E) early attempts of women to achieve a share of scientific awards

22 All of the following questions can be explicitly answered on the basis of the passage EXCEPT:

(A) What conditions did women scientists find it necessary to struggle against in the first quarter of the twentieth century?
(B) What specific steps were taken in the early part of the twentieth century to help women gain equality in the scientific workplace?
(C) What changes in the organization of the scientific community would have enhanced the position of women scientists as the twentieth century advanced?
(D) What were the views of some women scientific researchers on the subject of meritocracy?
(E) What degree of success was attained by the generation of women scientists who followed those who came into prominence earlier in the twentieth century?

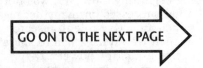

GO ON TO THE NEXT PAGE

Questions 23-29 are based on the following passages.

Both of the following passages are excerpts from books about the history of religion in early American public life.

Passage 1

The constitutional guarantee of religious freedom was intended to protect individuals from government interference in their religious lives. It
Line
(5) allowed for an exercise of religion free from the coercive power of the state. For Jefferson, Madison, and others influenced by the Enlightenment*, religion was essentially a matter of opinion. And to arrive at opinions individuals must be able to participate in a free and open arena of enquiry.
(10) Differences of religious opinion were not a concern of the state. The government was not concerned with deciding what might be orthodox or heretical religious beliefs. The notion of heresy, from the Greek word *hairesis*, meaning "to choose," was
(15) beyond the reach of law. In fact, the affirmation of religious freedom involved what has been called a heretical imperative. Individuals could choose to believe in anything they wished, or not to believe at all. To create an atmosphere of informed choice,
(20) the free exercise of reason and persuasion must be allowed to flourish and, as Jefferson insisted, "to make way for these, free enquiry must be indulged." Religious belief was not an issue in which the state had any interest; and it was certainly beyond
(25) the boundaries of legislation. No religious belief could be a crime. "It does me no injury," Jefferson observed, "for my neighbor to say there are twenty gods, or no god. It neither picks my pocket nor breaks my leg." The protection of religious belief,
(30) therefore, allowed for a variety of religious opinions to be held and to be expressed without any intervention on the part of the government.

Passage 2

At the time of the writing of the Constitution, the North American colonies were considered
(35) pluralistic because of their unusual religious diversity, but the colonies seemed diverse only by comparison with the tightly controlled religious culture of Europe. Protestant groups were the clear, and dominant, majority in the colonies,
(40) though there were Catholic and Jewish congregations in some urban areas. Many colonies had resisted tolerating much diversity, and in such Puritan strongholds as New Hampshire, Connecticut, and Massachusetts, hope for the political
(45) establishment of a state-sanctioned Protestant church was persistent. The early history of the colonies reflects a great deal of intolerance toward groups that strayed from the mainstream: Rhode Island was founded by groups who had been denied
(50) freedom of worship in Massachusetts.

Religious pluralism, the coexistence of different religious groups, emerged not so much because of the high-minded intentions of the early religious leaders as because of political necessity. Though
(55) many early settlers sought religious freedom, religious pluralism was not necessarily their goal. It was typical for Protestant groups to perceive themselves as the only true established church until they became a religious minority; they would then
(60) argue strongly for religious freedom for all. From the political perspective, the framers of the Constitution were committed primarily to a legal system that would ensure democracy in the new republic. The First Amendment, which states the "Congress
(65) shall make no law respecting an establishment of religion, or prohibiting the free exercise thereof," resulted from concerns that an established church would inhibit particular freedoms. The majority of both civic and ecclesiastical leaders rejected any
(70) one established religion; therefore it was only logical for them to support the tolerant approach.

While tolerance and religious pluralism were ideals, only the Constitution's legal power could put them into effect, and of course the First
(75) Amendment was unable to change attitudes. Thus the new republic did not have a unified approach to religious tolerance. For some, tolerance meant a grudging acceptance of the necessity of supporting religious diversity; for others, tolerance was not
(80) only necessary, but was something good in itself, one of the highest values of the republic. To the extent that tolerance was a necessity rather than an ideal in the republic, it contained the seeds of conflict—its very name, "tolerance," implied that
(85) a stronger group would put up with the wishes of weaker ones: that the stronger group would graciously accept what it deemed potentially intolerable.

*The Enlightenment was an eighteenth-century philosophical movement that focused on the use of reason to answer philosophical questions.

GO ON TO THE NEXT PAGE

23 As used in line 22, the word "indulged" most nearly means

(A) spoiled   (B) permitted   (C) humored
(D) luxuriated   (E) pampered

24 As used in line 39, the word "clear" most nearly means

(A) transparent   (B) pronounced
(C) innocent   (D) untroubled   (E) logical

25 According to Passage 2, what is the main reason that religious groups advocated religious freedom?

(A) They wanted to attract followers who had been influenced by the ideals of the Constitution.
(B) They wanted to prevent any other group from becoming the state-sponsored church.
(C) They wanted to remain above the rough world of politics.
(D) They were forced by law to accept the idea.
(E) They were swayed by the persuasive arguments of political leaders.

26 As used in line 62, the word "committed" most nearly means

(A) incarcerated   (B) confided   (C) entrusted
(D) perpetrated   (E) pledged

27 The passages differ in the analysis of the establishment of religious freedom in that Passage 1 emphasizes that

(A) the leaders cared most about it, while Passage 2 implies that the citizenry were most concerned
(B) free individuals were naturally religious, while Passage 2 assumes that only the oppressed felt strongly about religion
(C) the state posed the greatest threat to religious freedom, while Passage 2 implies that individual religions were the greatest potential threat
(D) religious freedom was an eighteenth-century innovation, while Passage 2 regards it as an ancient concept
(E) clear religious policies were crucial to a working government, while Passage 2 argues that religion was separate from politics

28 Which statement best expresses the objection that Passage 2's author would be most likely to make about Passage 1's analysis of religious tolerance?

(A) It is incomplete because it fails to place the debate about religious tolerance in its full social context.
(B) It is misguided because it uses quotations out of context and distorts their meaning.
(C) It is weak because it uses present-day attitudes about pluralism to explain an eighteenth-century idea.
(D) It is not useful because it fails to explain how Jefferson, Madison, and others came to their conclusions about religious freedom.
(E) It is incorrect because it misinterprets the ideas of Jefferson, Madison, and others about religion.

29 Which statement best explains the primary difference between the views of religious pluralism expressed in the two passages?

(A) Passage 1 presents it as a philosophical ideal, whereas Passage 2 argues that it grew out of political necessity.
(B) Passage 1 argues that it was a logical extension of the European tradition, whereas Passage 2 argues that it was an innovation.
(C) Passage 1 argues that it helped to hold the colonies together, whereas Passage 2 argues that it was an ideal but not a reality in early America.
(D) Passage 1 presents it as crucial to the political development of the republic, whereas Passage 2 implies that it was not a political issue.
(E) Passage 1 argues that it was the colonists' main goal for the republic, whereas Passage 2 implies that the colonists just assumed it would be the norm.

IF YOU FINISH BEFORE TIME IS CALLED, YOU MAY CHECK YOUR WORK ON THIS SECTION ONLY. DO NOT TURN TO ANY OTHER SECTION IN THE TEST.

Time—30 Minutes
25 Questions
(1-25)

In this section solve each problem, using any available space on the page for scratchwork. Then decide which is the best of the choices given and fill in the corresponding oval on the answer sheet.

Notes:

1. The use of a calculator is permitted. All numbers used are real numbers.

2. Figures that accompany problems in this test are intended to provide information useful in solving the problems. They are drawn as accurately as possible EXCEPT when it is stated in a specific problem that the figure is not drawn to scale. All figures lie in a plane unless otherwise indicated.

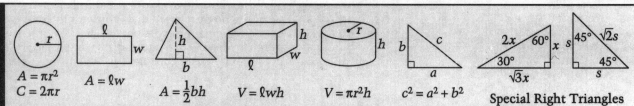

$A = \pi r^2$
$C = 2\pi r$

$A = \ell w$

$A = \frac{1}{2}bh$

$V = \ell wh$

$V = \pi r^2 h$

$c^2 = a^2 + b^2$

Special Right Triangles

The number of degrees of arc in a circle is 360.
The measure in degrees of a straight angle is 180.
The sum of the measures in degrees of the angles of a triangle is 180.

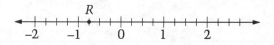

1 On the number line above, what number is the coordinate of point R?

(A) $-1\frac{3}{4}$

(B) $-1\frac{1}{4}$

(C) $-\frac{3}{4}$

(D) $-\frac{1}{3}$

(E) $-\frac{1}{4}$

2 If $\frac{w}{2} = 75$, then $3w =$

(A) 450
(B) 300
(C) 225
(D) 150
(E) 112

3 If a certain number is doubled and the result is increased by 7, the number obtained is 19. What is the original number?

(A) 2.5
(B) 6
(C) 13
(D) 16.5
(E) 24

GO ON TO THE NEXT PAGE

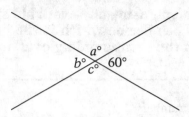

4 For the two intersecting lines above, which of the following must be true?

    I. $a > c$
   II. $a = 2b$
  III. $a + 60 = b + c$

(A) I only
(B) II only
(C) I and II only
(D) II and III only
(E) I, II, and III

5 Three consecutive integers are listed in increasing order. If their sum is 102, what is the second integer in the list?

(A) 28
(B) 29
(C) 33
(D) 34
(E) 35

ICE CREAM PURCHASES BY FLAVOR

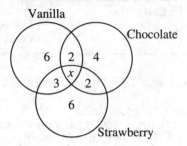

6 The diagram above shows the number of people who purchased one, two, or all three of the ice cream flavors shown. If 15 people purchased strawberry ice cream, how many people purchased chocolate ice cream?

(A) 8
(B) 12
(C) 14
(D) 15
(E) 18

Note: Figure not drawn to scale.

7 In the figure above, if $y = 60$, what is the value of x ?

(A) 30
(B) 45
(C) 60
(D) 75
(E) 90

GO ON TO THE NEXT PAGE

CALORIES NEEDED TO MAINTAIN WEIGHT

Activity Level	Number of Calories Needed
Basically inactive	Person's weight × 12
Moderately active	Person's weight × 15
Very active	(Person's weight × 15) + 900

8 According to the table above, the number of calories needed to maintain the weight of a very active 100-pound person is how many times the number of calories needed by a basically inactive 100-pound person?

(A) 6
(B) 5
(C) 3
(D) 2
(E) 1.5

9 If $x^2 + y^2 = 0$, what is the value of $3x + 5y$?

(A) 0
(B) 2
(C) 3
(D) 5
(E) 8

10 If 10,000 microns = 1 centimeter and 100,000,000 angstrom units = 1 centimeter, how many angstrom units equal 1 micron?

(A) 0.000000000001
(B) 0.0001
(C) 10,000
(D) 100,000
(E) 1,000,000,000,000

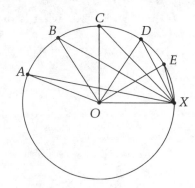

11 In the figure above, OX is a radius of the circle with center O. Which of the following triangles has the <u>least</u> area?

(A) $\triangle AOX$
(B) $\triangle BOX$
(C) $\triangle COX$
(D) $\triangle DOX$
(E) $\triangle EOX$

12 If the product of five integers is negative, then, at most, how many of the five integers could be negative?

(A) One
(B) Two
(C) Three
(D) Four
(E) Five

GO ON TO THE NEXT PAGE

13 If $x - 7 = 2y$ and $x = 5 + 3y$, what is the value of y?

(A) −5
(B) −2
(C) 2
(D) 5
(E) 12

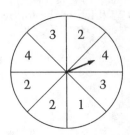

14 The circular region above has 8 nonoverlapping sectors of equal size. If the spinner shown is equally likely to stop on each sector, what is the probability that the spinner will stop on a sector labeled 2 ?

(A) $\dfrac{1}{8}$

(B) $\dfrac{1}{4}$

(C) $\dfrac{3}{8}$

(D) $\dfrac{1}{2}$

(E) $\dfrac{5}{8}$

15 If the area of one face of a cube is 25, what is the volume of the cube?

(A) 5
(B) 15
(C) 75
(D) 125
(E) 150

16 Wire, packaged in 80-foot coils, must be cut into 12-foot pieces for a certain job. If 28 such pieces of wire are required for the job, how many coils of wire are needed? (Assume that pieces less than 12 feet in length may <u>not</u> be joined to form a 12-foot piece.)

(A) Four
(B) Five
(C) Six
(D) Seven
(E) Eight

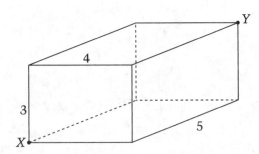

17 In the rectangular box above, there are how many different paths of total length 12 from X to Y along the edges?

(A) Three
(B) Four
(C) Five
(D) Six
(E) Eight

GO ON TO THE NEXT PAGE

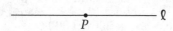

$$\ell$$
$$P$$

18 In the figure above, if two points S and T are to be placed on line ℓ on opposite sides of point P so that $2SP = PT$, what will be the value of $\frac{ST}{PT}$?

(A) $\frac{2}{1}$

(B) $\frac{3}{2}$

(C) $\frac{2}{3}$

(D) $\frac{1}{2}$

(E) $\frac{1}{3}$

19 There are g gallons of paint available to paint a house. After n gallons have been used, then in terms of g and n, what percent of the paint has <u>not</u> been used?

(A) $\frac{100n}{g}\%$

(B) $\frac{g}{100n}\%$

(C) $\frac{100g}{n}\%$

(D) $\frac{g}{100\,(g-n)}\%$

(E) $\frac{100\,(g-n)}{g}\%$

20 If x is an integer and $2 < x < 7$, how many different triangles are there with sides of lengths 2, 7, and x ?

(A) One
(B) Two
(C) Three
(D) Four
(E) Five

21 If $a > b$ and $a(b-a) = 0$, which of the following must be true?

    I. $a = 0$
    II. $b < 0$
    III. $a - b > 0$

(A) I only
(B) II only
(C) III only
(D) I and II only
(E) I, II, and III

GO ON TO THE NEXT PAGE

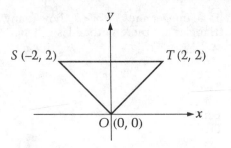

S (–2, 2)　　　T (2, 2)

y

O (0, 0)

x

22 In the figure above, what is the perimeter of $\triangle OST$?

(A) 8

(B) $8 + \sqrt{2}$

(C) $8 + 2\sqrt{2}$

(D) $4 + 2\sqrt{2}$

(E) $4 + 4\sqrt{2}$

23 Pat and Lee are removing cartons from a truck. If Pat removes $\frac{1}{8}$ of the number of cartons from the truck and Lee removes $\frac{1}{4}$ of the number of cartons, there are 40 cartons left. How many cartons were originally in the truck?

(A)　55

(B)　60

(C)　64

(D)　65

(E) 106

24 For how many integer values of x will the value of the expression $3x + 5$ be an integer greater than 1 and less than 300 ?

(A)　96

(B)　97

(C)　98

(D)　99

(E) 100

25 The enrollment at Lincoln High School this year is 25 percent greater than last year's enrollment. If this year's enrollment is k students, what was last year's enrollment in terms of k ?

(A) $1.50k$

(B) $1.25k$

(C) $1.20k$

(D) $0.80k$

(E) $0.75k$

IF YOU FINISH BEFORE TIME IS CALLED, YOU MAY CHECK YOUR WORK ON THIS SECTION ONLY. DO NOT TURN TO ANY OTHER SECTION IN THE TEST. **STOP**

Time — 30 Minutes
29 Questions
(30-58)

For each question in this section, select the best answer from among the choices given and fill in the corresponding oval on the answer sheet.

Each question below consists of a related pair of words or phrases, followed by five pairs of words or phrases labeled A through E. Select the pair that best expresses a relationship similar to that expressed in the original pair.

Example:

CRUMB : BREAD ::

(A) ounce : unit
(B) splinter : wood
(C) water : bucket
(D) twine : rope
(E) cream : butter

30 RIB CAGE : LUNGS ::
(A) skull : brain
(B) appendix : organ
(C) sock : foot
(D) skeleton : body
(E) hair : scalp

31 SELF-PORTRAIT : PAINTER ::
(A) soliloquy : actor
(B) interpretation : reader
(C) autobiography : writer
(D) manuscript : editor
(E) philosophy : thinker

32 BRITTLE : FRACTURE ::
(A) transparent : see
(B) fluid : melt
(C) perpetual : stop
(D) flammable : burn
(E) immobile : move

33 GYMNASIUM : EXERCISE ::
(A) birthday : celebrate
(B) building : construct
(C) store : shop
(D) disease : diagnose
(E) army : discharge

34 COMPASS : NAVIGATION ::
(A) physician : disease
(B) pilot : flight
(C) clock : dial
(D) camera : photography
(E) map : area

35 DAPPLED : SPOTS ::
(A) delicious : spices
(B) bleached : colors
(C) striped : lines
(D) rhymed : words
(E) squeaky : sounds

36 QUIBBLE : CRITICISM ::
(A) sermon : duty
(B) jeer : respect
(C) source : information
(D) tiff : quarrel
(E) scandal : disgrace

37 ETHICS : MORALITY ::
(A) premise : induction
(B) jurisprudence : law
(C) logic : error
(D) taboo : custom
(E) proof : generalization

38 GLOWER : ANGER ::
(A) sneer : contempt
(B) grin : expression
(C) fidget : movement
(D) console : grief
(E) slander : accusation

39 MELODIOUS : HEARD ::
(A) actual : witnessed
(B) legible : read
(C) mislaid : recovered
(D) pictorial : illustrated
(E) savory : eaten

40 EQUALIZE : PARITY ::
(A) coalesce : unity
(B) vary : frequency
(C) forestall : convenience
(D) synchronize : permanence
(E) normalize : individuality

41 ABERRATION : STANDARD ::
(A) censorship : news
(B) statement : policy
(C) detour : route
(D) rumor : gossip
(E) encore : performance

GO ON TO THE NEXT PAGE

Each passage below is followed by questions based on its content. Answer the questions on the basis of what is <u>stated</u> or <u>implied</u> in each passage and in any introductory material that may be provided.

Questions 42-52 are based on the following passage.

Charles Darwin theorized that all species face a struggle for survival. Those individuals that possess characteristics that enable them to
Line *survive in their environment have a greater likeli-*
(5) *hood of reproducing, thus passing these character-istics on to their offspring. In the essay from which the passage below is taken, the author examines two hypotheses about what would happen when two competing animal species occu-*
(10) *pied the same habitat. Both hypotheses are based on Darwin's theory. The first hypothesis predicted an unending struggle for dominance that would result in equilibrium. The second predicted that one species would emerge victorious and the other*
(15) *would die out.*

In this passage, the author explains how biolo-gist G. F. Gause experimented with different species of paramecia (one-celled animals) in order to see which hypothesis was correct, and to
(20) *explore how different animal populations coexist.*

Gause kept his paramecia in the glass tubes of a centrifuge,* which let him spin them in the machine each day to force the animals to the bottom while he poured off the exhausted food
(25) solution in which they lived, without losing any animals. He could then top up the tubes with fresh nutrient broth. From the eight individuals Gause put in at first, a thriving population of thousands would grow and this final number
(30) would remain constant for as long as he cared to spin them out daily in his centrifuge and replace their food supply. Eventually, Gause had several species at hand that he knew could live well in his tubes, that demonstrably thrived on the same food,
(35) and that were so similar that it was hard to tell them apart. If two species were placed together in the same tube and allowed to crowd, they must willy-nilly compete for that daily finite dose of nutrient broth. Thus he would see which hypothe-
(40) sis was right: whether the two species engaged in unending struggle or whether one scored total victory with the extinction of the other. The results were absolutely conclusive. There was total victory.
(45) No matter how many times Gause tested two chosen kinds of paramecia against each other the outcome was always the same: complete extermi-nation of one species, and always the same one of the two species in the tube. Both populations
(50) would do well in the early days when there was

plenty of room for all, but, as soon as they began to crowd, the losing species would go into a long decline that eventually left the winning population in sole possession of the tube.
(55) There are two obvious gut reactions to these results: one is amazement that what common sense would expect to be a permanent struggling balance in fact became an annihilation, and the other is wonder at how the losing species can exist
(60) at all. This second thought holds the key to the whole affair: it leads us to know that Darwinian competition in the real world means neither endless fighting nor deadly massacre, but a muted struggle.
(65) The various kinds of paramecia live together in nature; thus there must be circumstances in which the outcome of one of Gause's set-piece battles would be reversed. Gause knew enough about paramecia to guess at some of the ways in which
(70) this could happen. Like other protozoa, paramecia are known to secrete chemicals into the water that are toxic to other animals; they are inclined to live by chemical warfare. But when Gause changed the water each day, he removed any such toxins. So he
(75) tried leaving most of the water in and topping up with nutrient concentrate instead of changing the whole broth daily. In one of his series of experi-ments, this was enough to reverse the outcome; the animal that had before always been the winner
(80) was now always the loser.
Then Gause stumbled across an even more revealing situation, for when he tried yet another pair of species of paramecia against each other, neither became extinct; both went on living
(85) together in the tubes. When Gause looked at the tubes closely, he found that one species of parame-cium was living in the top halves while the other species lived in the bottoms. These kinds of paramecia had found unconflicting ways of life
(90) possible in even those simple glass tubes of broth; they avoided competition by dividing the space between them.
There have now been numerous experiments like those of Gause. They all result in either total
(95) annihilation or in a sharing of the habitat in ways

GO ON TO THE NEXT PAGE

that prevent competition. This at once leads to a splendid comprehension. Animals and plants in nature are not after all engaged in endless debilitating struggle, as a loose reading of Darwin might
(100) suggest. Nature is arranged so that competitive struggles are avoided; natural selection designs different kinds of animals and plants so that they avoid competition. A fit animal is not one that fights well, but one that avoids fighting altogether.

*A machine that spins test tubes rapidly in order to separate heavier from lighter substances

42 What factor in Gause's first experiment (lines 36-54) continually resulted in the extermination of one species and the success of the other?

(A) Gause did not supply the right food for one species.
(B) Gause removed most of the toxins by changing the water each day.
(C) Gause failed to provide enough oxygen in the water supply.
(D) Gause carefully balanced the nutrients in the broth.
(E) Gause spun the tubes in a centrifuge daily.

43 In what way was Gause's first experiment a success?

(A) It disproved two hypotheses at once.
(B) It yielded new information about metabolism in paramecia.
(C) It confirmed the viability of paramecia in laboratory conditions.
(D) It demonstrated the accuracy of Gause's assumptions about paramecia.
(E) It fully supported one hypothesis over another.

44 In line 63, "muted" most nearly means

(A) silenced
(B) overlooked
(C) subdued
(D) stagnant
(E) deadly

45 Which of the following led Gause to conduct his second experiment (lines 70-77)?

(A) Reinterpretation of Darwinian theory
(B) Variations in data obtained from different trials
(C) Consideration of conditions that exist in nature
(D) Discovery of a previously undocumented animal behavior
(E) Revision of the research goal

46 What contribution did Gause's second experiment make to the overall investigation?

(A) A test of the logic of basic premises
(B) An attempt to duplicate earlier results
(C) Exploration of an alternative situation
(D) Elimination of one of the original hypotheses
(E) Formulation of the final conclusion

47 During Gause's second experiment the paramecia that previously had been subordinate became dominant because

(A) they were better able to survive with less food
(B) they were no longer deprived of their natural defenses
(C) they learned to reach the available food before the other species did
(D) a new species of paramecium was introduced to the test tubes
(E) the conditions of the second experiment bore less resemblance to their natural environment

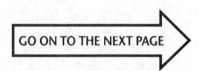
GO ON TO THE NEXT PAGE

48 Gause probably performed his third experiment (lines 81-92) as part of an effort to

(A) obtain more information about nutrient concentrates
(B) identify the different species with greater precision
(C) correct the errors made in the second experiment
(D) observe more closely the behavior of the paramecia in the second experiment
(E) test whether all species competed in the same way

49 In line 97, "splendid comprehension" conveys the author's opinion that the

(A) research had been ingenious
(B) results were easy to understand
(C) experiments revealed a profound truth
(D) experiments worked better than expected
(E) discovery was extremely subtle

50 The author concludes that one species can most effectively survive in an environment that it shares with a similar species by

(A) being more aggressive in defending its territory
(B) avoiding competition with the other species
(C) migrating often so that it is unnoticed by predators
(D) consuming the same food as the other species
(E) having strong defenses against the other species

51 The function of the final paragraph (lines 93-104) is to

(A) derive a general rule from particular instances
(B) show why both hypotheses have merit
(C) account for the difference between the laboratory and nature
(D) compare two different interpretations of Gause's data
(E) explain the need for intuitive reasoning in science

52 The sentence beginning "Nature is arranged so that competitive struggles are avoided" (lines 100-101) suggests that which of Gause's experiments reflected natural conditions?

(A) The first only (lines 36-54)
(B) The second only (lines 70-77)
(C) The third only (lines 81-92)
(D) The first and second only
(E) The second and third only

GO ON TO THE NEXT PAGE

Questions 53-58 are based on the following passage.

The following description of a small town is from a novel by an African American which was published in 1973.

In that place, where they tore the nightshade and blackberry patches from their roots to make room for the Medallion City Golf Course, there
Line was once a neighborhood. It stood in the hills
(5) above the valley town of Medallion and spread all the way to the river. It is called the suburbs now, but when Black people lived there it was called the Bottom. One road, shaded by beeches, oaks, maples, and chestnuts, connected it to the valley.
(10) The beeches are gone now, and so are the pear trees where children sat and yelled down through the blossoms to passersby. Generous funds have been allotted to level the stripped and faded buildings that clutter the road from Medallion up to the
(15) golf course. They are going to raze the Time and a Half Pool Hall, where feet in long tan shoes once pointed down from chair rungs. A steel ball will knock to dust Irene's Palace of Cosmetology, where women used to lean their heads back on
(20) sink trays and doze while Irene lathered Nu Nile into their hair. Men in khaki work clothes will pry loose the slats of Reba's Grill, where the owner cooked in her hat because she claimed she couldn't remember the ingredients without it.
(25)   There will be nothing left of the Bottom (the footbridge that crossed the river is already gone), but perhaps it is just as well, since it wasn't a town anyway: just a neighborhood where on quiet days people in valley houses could hear singing
(30) sometimes, banjoes sometimes, and, if a valley man happened to have business up in those hills— collecting rent or insurance payments—he might see a dark woman in a flowered dress doing a bit of cakewalk to the lively notes of a mouth organ.
(35) Her bare feet would raise the saffron dust that floated down on the coveralls and bunion-split shoes of the man breathing music in and out of his harmonica. The Black people watching her would laugh and rub their knees, and it would be easy for
(40) the valley man to hear the laughter and not notice the adult pain that rested somewhere under the eyelids, somewhere under their head rags and soft felt caps, somewhere in the palm of the hand, somewhere behind the frayed lapels, somewhere in
(45) the sinew's curve. He'd have to stand in the back of Greater Saint Matthew's Church and let the tenor's voice dress him in silk, or touch the hands of the spoon carvers (who had not worked in eight years) and let the fingers that danced on wood kiss
(50) his skin. Otherwise the pain would escape him even though the laughter was part of the pain.

53 The author's perspective on the Bottom is that of

(A) an unsympathetic outsider
(B) an adult recalling early dreams
(C) a participant defending a course of action
(D) an angry protestor trying to prevent an undesirable event
(E) a sad observer of a transformation

54 The name "the Bottom" is incongruous because the neighborhood

(A) contains only demolished buildings
(B) has become more prosperous since it was named
(C) is a fertile piece of land
(D) has only recently been established
(E) is located in hills above a valley

55 "Generous" as used to describe "funds" (line 12) is intended to seem

(A) ironic, because the funds are being used to destroy something
(B) progressive, because the narrator is showing how times change
(C) objective, because the narrator knows the amount
(D) humorous, because the cleanup is not truly expensive
(E) equivocal, because the funds are inadequate

56 In the second paragraph, the author conveys a feeling of tension by juxtaposing which two of the following elements?

(A) The assertion that the neighborhood's destruction is insignificant *versus* the carefully drawn richness of its life
(B) The author's expression of affection for the neighborhood *versus* frustration at its reluctance to change
(C) Nostalgia about the way the town used to be *versus* a sense of excitement about its future
(D) Appreciation for the town's natural beauty *versus* disapproval of its ramshackle state
(E) Sadness about the town's fate *versus* sympathy for the reasons for it

GO ON TO THE NEXT PAGE

57 The author's statement that the valley man might not perceive the pain underlying the laughter of the Bottom's residents (lines 38-45) emphasizes that the Bottom's residents

(A) had frequent contact with other residents of the valley
(B) understood the valley man well, even though they did not see him often
(C) were not the carefree people they might appear to be
(D) concealed their real feelings from outsiders
(E) were concerned about the destruction of their neighborhood

58 The author portrays the Bottom as a place

(A) that lacked economic prosperity but had a rich emotional life
(B) that was too filled with sadness to be able to survive
(C) that needed to become more up-to-date in order to prosper
(D) whose effect on its residents was difficult for them to understand
(E) in which people paid more attention to the way things seemed to others than to the way things really were

IF YOU FINISH BEFORE TIME IS CALLED, YOU MAY CHECK YOUR WORK ON THIS SECTION ONLY. DO NOT TURN TO ANY OTHER SECTION IN THE TEST.  STOP

Section 4

4 4 4 4

This section contains two types of questions. You have 30 minutes to complete both types. You may use any available space for scratchwork.

Notes:

1. The use of a calculator is permitted. All numbers used are real numbers.

2. Figures that accompany problems in this test are intended to provide information useful in solving the problems. They are drawn as accurately as possible EXCEPT when it is stated in a specific problem that the figure is not drawn to scale. All figures lie in a plane unless otherwise indicated.

Reference Information

$A = \pi r^2$
$C = 2\pi r$

$A = \ell w$

$A = \frac{1}{2}bh$

$V = \ell w h$

$V = \pi r^2 h$

$c^2 = a^2 + b^2$

Special Right Triangles

The number of degrees of arc in a circle is 360.
The measure in degrees of a straight angle is 180.
The sum of the measures in degrees of the angles of a triangle is 180.

Directions for Quantitative Comparison Questions

Questions 26-40 each consist of two quantities in boxes, one in Column A and one in Column B. You are to compare the two quantities and on the answer sheet fill in oval

    A if the quantity in Column A is greater;
    B if the quantity in Column B is greater;
    C if the two quantities are equal;
    D if the relationship cannot be determined
       from the information given.

Notes:

1. In some questions, information is given about one or both of the quantities to be compared. In such cases, the given information is centered above the two columns and is not boxed.
2. In a given question, a symbol that appears in both columns represents the same thing in Column A as it does in Column B.
3. Letters such as x, n, and k stand for real numbers.

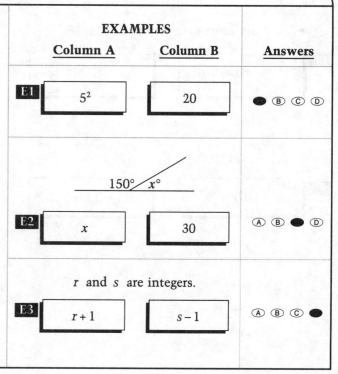

EXAMPLES

Column A	Column B	Answers
E1 5^2	20	● Ⓑ Ⓒ Ⓓ

150° $x°$

| E2 x | 30 | Ⓐ Ⓑ ● Ⓓ |

r and s are integers.

| E3 $r+1$ | $s-1$ | Ⓐ Ⓑ Ⓒ ● |

GO ON TO THE NEXT PAGE

Column A	Column B

26

| The total wages for working 40 hours at $5 per hour | The total wages for working 20 hours at $10 per hour |

A, B, C, and D are four points, in that order, on line ℓ.

27

| The length of AC | The length of BD |

Six more than a number n is 18.

28

| 5 more than n | 8 more than $\dfrac{n}{2}$ |

$x > 1$

29

| $-0.09x$ | $-0.11x$ |

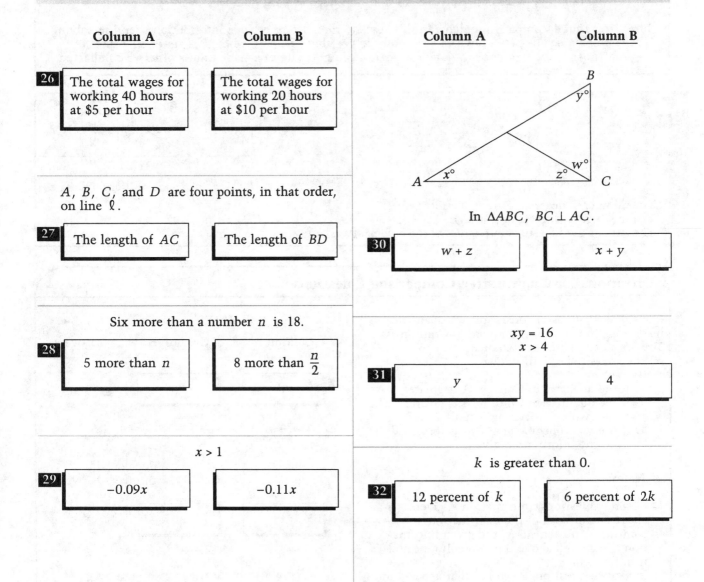

In $\triangle ABC$, $BC \perp AC$.

30

| $w + z$ | $x + y$ |

$xy = 16$
$x > 4$

31

| y | 4 |

k is greater than 0.

32

| 12 percent of k | 6 percent of $2k$ |

GO ON TO THE NEXT PAGE

SUMMARY DIRECTIONS FOR COMPARISON QUESTIONS

Answer: A if the quantity in Column A is greater;
B if the quantity in Column B is greater;
C if the two quantities are equal;
D if the relationship cannot be determined from the information given.

Column A	Column B

A circle intersects a square in exactly two points.

33

The area of the square	The area of the circle

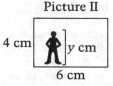

Picture I

Picture II

x cm $\quad \frac{9}{8}$ cm $\qquad$ 4 cm $\quad y$ cm

3 cm $\qquad\qquad$ 6 cm

Note: Figure not drawn to scale.

Picture II was enlarged from picture I so that each dimension of picture II is twice the corresponding dimension of picture I.

34

x	y

$x > 0$

35

$3\sqrt{x}$	$\sqrt{5x}$

$2x + 3 = 6 - x$

36

$2x$	$x + 2$

$$AB$$
$$+\ BA$$
$$\overline{88}$$

Digits A and B are even numbers.

37

A	B

38

The length of a diagonal of a square of side 2	The length of a leg of an isosceles right triangle with hypotenuse 2

Let a "dodeka" number be defined as a positive integer whose digits, when added together, equal 12.

39

The number of dodeka <u>even</u> numbers between 10 and 100	The number of dodeka <u>odd</u> numbers between 10 and 100

a and b are nonzero integers.

40

$(a + b)^2$	$(a^2 + b^2)$

GO ON TO THE NEXT PAGE

Directions for Student-Produced Response Questions

Each of the remaining 10 questions (41-50) requires you to solve the problem and enter your answer by marking the ovals in the special grid, as shown in the examples below.

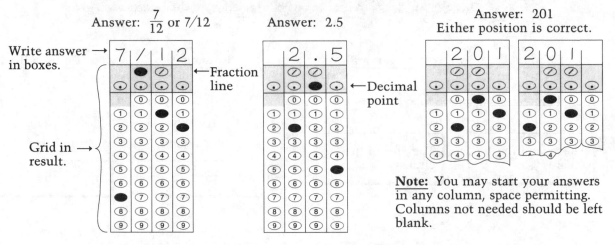

- Mark no more than one oval in any column.

- Because the answer sheet will be machine-scored, **you will receive credit only if the ovals are filled in correctly.**

- Although not required, it is suggested that you write your answer in the boxes at the top of the columns to help you fill in the ovals accurately.

- Some problems may have more than one correct answer. In such cases, grid only one answer.

- No question has a negative answer.

- **Mixed numbers** such as $2\frac{1}{2}$ must be gridded as 2.5 or 5/2. (If [2 1 / 2] is gridded, it will be interpreted as $\frac{21}{2}$, not $2\frac{1}{2}$.)

- **Decimal Accuracy**: If you obtain a decimal answer, **enter the most accurate value the grid will accommodate.** For example, if you obtain an answer such as 0.6666 . . . , you should record the result as .666 or .667. **Less accurate values such as .66 or .67 are not acceptable.**

Acceptable ways to grid $\frac{2}{3}$ = .6666 . . .

---

41 In 2 weeks, 550 cartons of juice were sold in the school cafeteria. At this rate, how many cartons of juice would one expect to be sold in 5 weeks?

42 For what integer value of x is $3x + 5 > 11$ and $x - 3 < 1$?

GO ON TO THE NEXT PAGE

43 The number 0.008 is equivalent to the ratio of 8 to what number?

45 The average (arithmetic mean) of 4 numbers is greater than 7 and less than 11. What is one possible number that could be the sum of these 4 numbers?

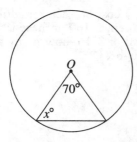

44 In the figure above, if O is the center of the circle, what is the value of x ?

46 A line ℓ with a slope of $\frac{1}{4}$ passes through the points $(0, \frac{1}{2})$ and $(4, y)$. What is the value of y ?

GO ON TO THE NEXT PAGE

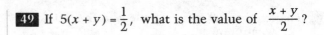
47 In an election for class president, Maria finished first, Kevin second, Carlos third, and Diane fourth. Maria received 91 votes and Diane received 32 votes. If a total of 224 votes were cast for these four candidates, what is the <u>minimum</u> number of votes that Kevin could have received?

49 If $5(x + y) = \frac{1}{2}$, what is the value of $\frac{x + y}{2}$?

48 Two squares, each composed of 16 small squares, overlap as shown in the figure above. If the area of each small square is 1, what is the area of the shaded region?

50 Tickets for a play cost $6 each for adults and $3 each for children. If 160 of these tickets were bought for a total of $816, how many adults' tickets were bought?

IF YOU FINISH BEFORE TIME IS CALLED, YOU MAY CHECK YOUR WORK ON THIS SECTION ONLY. DO NOT TURN TO ANY OTHER SECTION IN THE TEST. **STOP**

216

HOW TO SCORE THE PRACTICE TEST

When you take the PSAT/NMSQT, a computer performs these scoring steps for you and prints out a score report. Perform these steps now, to understand how guessing and omitting questions affect your scores. You can compare your scores on the practice test with those you earn later when you take the PSAT/NMSQT. You will probably find that your scores on the PSAT/NMSQT will not be exactly the same as your scores on the practice test. Scores vary because of slight differences between tests and the way you take tests on different occasions.

STEP 1: Correct your verbal answers

The correct answer and the difficulty level (E = easy question, M = medium question, H = hard question) for each verbal question on the practice test is given. There are boxes for your answers.

- For each question you got correct, put + in the "Your Answer" box.

- For any question you got incorrect, write the letter of the response you chose in the "Your Answer" box.

- For any question you omitted, put O in the "Your Answer" box.

- Count the number of correct (+), incorrect (A, B, C, D, E), and omitted responses. Enter the totals where indicated.

Questions 1-58   No. Correct _____   No. Incorrect _____   No. Omitted _____

STEP 2: Correct your math answers

The correct answer and the difficulty level (E = easy question, M = medium question, H = hard question) for each mathematics question on the practice test is given. There are boxes for your answers.

- For each question you got correct, put + in the "Your Answer" box.

- For any Standard Multiple-Choice question (1-25) or Quantitative Comparison question (26-40) you got incorrect, write the letter of the response you chose in the "Your Answer" box. For incorrect answers to a question that required a student-produced response (41-50), write the answer you gridded on the answer sheet in the "Your Answer" box.

- For any question you omitted, put O in the "Your Answer" box.

- Count the number of correct (+), incorrect (A, B, C, D, E, or the answer you gridded), and omitted responses. Enter the totals where indicated.

Questions 1-25 No. Correct _____   No. Incorrect _____   No. Omitted _____

Questions 26-40 No. Correct _____   No. Incorrect _____   No. Omitted _____

Questions 41-50 No. Correct _____   No. Incorrect _____   No. Omitted _____

STEP 3: Calculate your points

Verbal points—Refer to Step 1 above.

- Enter number of correct and incorrect answers to verbal questions 1-58. Divide number of incorrect answers by 4. Subtract result from the number of verbal questions answered correctly; record result (Subtotal A). Round Subtotal A; .5 or more, round up; less than .5, round down. The number you get is your total verbal points. Enter this number on line B.

Mathematics points—Refer to Step 2 above.

- Enter number of correct and incorrect answers to math questions 1-25. Divide number of incorrect answers by 4. Subtract result from the number of questions answered correctly; record result (Subtotal A).

- Enter number of correct and incorrect answers to math questions 26-40. Divide number of incorrect answers by 3. Subtract result from the number of questions answered correctly; record result (Subtotal B).

- Enter number of correct answers to math questions 41-50 (Subtotal C).

- Add Subtotals A, B, and C to get D. Round Subtotal D; .5 or more, round up; less than .5, round down. The number you get is your total mathematics points. Enter this number on line E.

Verbal

A   Questions 1-58   _____ − (_____ ÷ 4) =   _____
                     No. correct   No. incorrect   Subtotal A

B   Total rounded verbal points (Round off decimals;   _____
    .5 or more, round up; less than .5, round down.)   B

Mathematics

A   Questions 1-25   _____ − (_____ ÷ 4) =   _____
                     No. correct   No. incorrect   Subtotal A

B   Questions 26-40   _____ − (_____ ÷ 3) =   _____
                      No. correct   No. incorrect   Subtotal B

C   Questions 41-50   _____   =   _____
                      No. correct   Subtotal C

D   Total unrounded math points (A + B + C)   _____
                                                          Subtotal D

E   Total rounded math points (Round decimals;   _____
    .5 or more, round up; less than .5, round down.)   E

Score Conversion Table
PSAT/NMSQT
Recentered Scale

PSAT/NMSQT					
FORM T					
Tuesday, October 1993					
	Scores			Scores	
Points	Verbal	Math	Points	Verbal	Math
58	80		27	51	53
57	80		26	50	52
56	80		25	49	51
55	80		24	48	50
54	80		23	47	49
53	77		22	47	48
52	75		21	46	48
51	74		20	45	47
50	72	80	19	44	46
49	71	77	18	43	45
48	70	75	17	42	44
47	68	73	16	42	43
46	67	71	15	41	42
45	66	70	14	40	41
44	65	69	13	39	40
43	64	68	12	38	39
42	63	67	11	37	39
41	62	66	10	36	38
40	61	65	9	35	37
39	60	64	8	34	35
38	60	63	7	33	34
37	59	62	6	32	33
36	58	61	5	30	32
35	57	60	4	29	30
34	56	59	3	27	29
33	55	58	2	26	27
32	55	57	1	24	25
31	54	56	0	21	24
30	53	56	−1	20	22
29	52	55	−2	20	20
28	51	54	or below		

Preliminary SAT/National Merit Scholarship Qualifying Test

Tuesday, October 11, 1994

Name _____

Last   First   Middle Initial

Preliminary SAT/ National Merit Scholarship Qualifying Test

TUESDAY, OCTOBER 11, 1994

Time: The PSAT/NMSQT has four sections. You will have 30 minutes to work on each section and a 5-minute break between Sections 2 and 3.

Scoring: For each correct answer you will receive one point (whether the question is easy or hard). For questions you omit, you will receive no points. For a wrong answer to a multiple-choice question, you will lose only a fraction of a point.

Guessing: An educated guess may improve your score. That is, if you can eliminate one or more choices as wrong, you increase your chances of choosing the correct answer and earning one point. On the other hand, if you can't eliminate any choices, omit the question and move on.

Answers: You may write in the test book, but mark all answers on your answer sheet to receive credit. Make each mark a dark mark that completely fills the oval and is as dark as all your other marks. If you erase, do so completely.

Do your best.

DO NOT OPEN THE TEST BOOK UNTIL YOU ARE TOLD TO DO SO!

3QPT1

1) Use a soft-lead No. 2 pencil only. Print the requested information in the boxes for each item.
2) Fill in the corresponding oval for each letter or number you enter. Completely erase any errors or stray marks.
Make each mark a dark mark that completely fills the intended oval and is as dark as all your other marks.

1. Name

Enter your full name, including your middle initial if you have one.
Omit hyphens, apostrophes, Jr., or III.

Last Name (Family Name) - first 15 letters

First Name - first 12 letters

MI

2. Sex

- Female
- Male

3. Date of Birth

Month	Day	Year
Jan.		1974
Feb.		1975
Mar.		1976
April		1977
May		1978
June		1979
July		1980
Aug.		1981
Sept.		1982
Oct.		1983
Nov.		1984
Dec.		

4. Current Grade Level

- 12th grade
- 11th grade
- 10th grade
- 9th grade
- 8th grade
- Not yet in 8th grade
- Other

5. Social Security Number

6. School

6a. Your School Code

School Name

City

6b. Print the name and address of the school you regularly attend.

School Name

Street

City _____ State _____ Zip Code

6c. Are you taking this test at the school you regularly attend?

- Yes
- No The name and address of the school where I am taking this test is:

City _____ State

Your scores will be reported to the school you regularly attend.

6d. Optional Code

7. Ethnic Group

- American Indian or Alaskan Native
- Asian, Asian American, or Pacific Islander
- Black or African American

Hispanic or Latino background

- Mexican or Mexican American
- Puerto Rican
- South American, Latin American, Central American, or other Hispanic or Latino
- White
- Other

8. Grade Average

Cumulative high school average for all academic subjects.

- A+ (97-100)
- A   (93-96)
- A- (90-92)
- B+ (87-89)
- B   (83-86)
- B- (80-82)
- C+ (77-79)
- C   (73-76)
- C- (70-72)
- D+ (67-69)
- D   (65-66)
- E or F (below 65)

9. Language Background

What language did you learn to speak first?

- English only
- English and another language
- Another language

What language do you know best?

- English
- English and another language about the same
- Another language

Your answers in Section 9 will be used only for research purposes and will not be included on score reports.

10. Student Search Service®

The College Board would like to help you plan for college. Would you like information about you sent to colleges, universities, and certain scholarship programs?

- Yes, I want the College Board to send information about me to colleges, universities, and certain scholarship programs interested in students like me.
- No, I do not want the College Board to send information about me to colleges, universities, and certain scholarship programs.

11. College Major and Career

Select a code number from the lists of college majors and careers on the back of your test book.

Major

Career

For ETS Use Only

Your answers in Sections 7 and 8 will be used by the College Board to produce reports about groups of students, assure that tests are fair for all groups, and conduct research, but only in ways that protect your privacy.

CHW94146   Q2689-06   17012   • TF54P925   I.N.203187
1   2   3   4   • 01382

Make each mark a dark mark that completely fills the oval and is as dark as all your other marks. If you erase, do so completely. Incomplete erasures may be read as intended responses.

SECTION 1 — VERBAL
30 minutes

1 Ⓐ Ⓑ Ⓒ Ⓓ Ⓔ
2 Ⓐ Ⓑ Ⓒ Ⓓ Ⓔ
3 Ⓐ Ⓑ Ⓒ Ⓓ Ⓔ
4 Ⓐ Ⓑ Ⓒ Ⓓ Ⓔ
5 Ⓐ Ⓑ Ⓒ Ⓓ Ⓔ
6 Ⓐ Ⓑ Ⓒ Ⓓ Ⓔ
7 Ⓐ Ⓑ Ⓒ Ⓓ Ⓔ
8 Ⓐ Ⓑ Ⓒ Ⓓ Ⓔ
9 Ⓐ Ⓑ Ⓒ Ⓓ Ⓔ
10 Ⓐ Ⓑ Ⓒ Ⓓ Ⓔ
11 Ⓐ Ⓑ Ⓒ Ⓓ Ⓔ
12 Ⓐ Ⓑ Ⓒ Ⓓ Ⓔ
13 Ⓐ Ⓑ Ⓒ Ⓓ Ⓔ
14 Ⓐ Ⓑ Ⓒ Ⓓ Ⓔ
15 Ⓐ Ⓑ Ⓒ Ⓓ Ⓔ
16 Ⓐ Ⓑ Ⓒ Ⓓ Ⓔ
17 Ⓐ Ⓑ Ⓒ Ⓓ Ⓔ
18 Ⓐ Ⓑ Ⓒ Ⓓ Ⓔ
19 Ⓐ Ⓑ Ⓒ Ⓓ Ⓔ
20 Ⓐ Ⓑ Ⓒ Ⓓ Ⓔ
21 Ⓐ Ⓑ Ⓒ Ⓓ Ⓔ
22 Ⓐ Ⓑ Ⓒ Ⓓ Ⓔ
23 Ⓐ Ⓑ Ⓒ Ⓓ Ⓔ
24 Ⓐ Ⓑ Ⓒ Ⓓ Ⓔ
25 Ⓐ Ⓑ Ⓒ Ⓓ Ⓔ
26 Ⓐ Ⓑ Ⓒ Ⓓ Ⓔ
27 Ⓐ Ⓑ Ⓒ Ⓓ Ⓔ
28 Ⓐ Ⓑ Ⓒ Ⓓ Ⓔ
29 Ⓐ Ⓑ Ⓒ Ⓓ Ⓔ

SECTION 2 — MATHEMATICS
30 minutes

1 Ⓐ Ⓑ Ⓒ Ⓓ Ⓔ
2 Ⓐ Ⓑ Ⓒ Ⓓ Ⓔ
3 Ⓐ Ⓑ Ⓒ Ⓓ Ⓔ
4 Ⓐ Ⓑ Ⓒ Ⓓ Ⓔ
5 Ⓐ Ⓑ Ⓒ Ⓓ Ⓔ
6 Ⓐ Ⓑ Ⓒ Ⓓ Ⓔ
7 Ⓐ Ⓑ Ⓒ Ⓓ Ⓔ
8 Ⓐ Ⓑ Ⓒ Ⓓ Ⓔ
9 Ⓐ Ⓑ Ⓒ Ⓓ Ⓔ
10 Ⓐ Ⓑ Ⓒ Ⓓ Ⓔ
11 Ⓐ Ⓑ Ⓒ Ⓓ Ⓔ
12 Ⓐ Ⓑ Ⓒ Ⓓ Ⓔ
13 Ⓐ Ⓑ Ⓒ Ⓓ Ⓔ
14 Ⓐ Ⓑ Ⓒ Ⓓ Ⓔ
15 Ⓐ Ⓑ Ⓒ Ⓓ Ⓔ
16 Ⓐ Ⓑ Ⓒ Ⓓ Ⓔ
17 Ⓐ Ⓑ Ⓒ Ⓓ Ⓔ
18 Ⓐ Ⓑ Ⓒ Ⓓ Ⓔ
19 Ⓐ Ⓑ Ⓒ Ⓓ Ⓔ
20 Ⓐ Ⓑ Ⓒ Ⓓ Ⓔ
21 Ⓐ Ⓑ Ⓒ Ⓓ Ⓔ
22 Ⓐ Ⓑ Ⓒ Ⓓ Ⓔ
23 Ⓐ Ⓑ Ⓒ Ⓓ Ⓔ
24 Ⓐ Ⓑ Ⓒ Ⓓ Ⓔ
25 Ⓐ Ⓑ Ⓒ Ⓓ Ⓔ

SECTION 3 — VERBAL
30 minutes

30 Ⓐ Ⓑ Ⓒ Ⓓ Ⓔ
31 Ⓐ Ⓑ Ⓒ Ⓓ Ⓔ
32 Ⓐ Ⓑ Ⓒ Ⓓ Ⓔ
33 Ⓐ Ⓑ Ⓒ Ⓓ Ⓔ
34 Ⓐ Ⓑ Ⓒ Ⓓ Ⓔ
35 Ⓐ Ⓑ Ⓒ Ⓓ Ⓔ
36 Ⓐ Ⓑ Ⓒ Ⓓ Ⓔ
37 Ⓐ Ⓑ Ⓒ Ⓓ Ⓔ
38 Ⓐ Ⓑ Ⓒ Ⓓ Ⓔ
39 Ⓐ Ⓑ Ⓒ Ⓓ Ⓔ
40 Ⓐ Ⓑ Ⓒ Ⓓ Ⓔ
41 Ⓐ Ⓑ Ⓒ Ⓓ Ⓔ
42 Ⓐ Ⓑ Ⓒ Ⓓ Ⓔ
43 Ⓐ Ⓑ Ⓒ Ⓓ Ⓔ
44 Ⓐ Ⓑ Ⓒ Ⓓ Ⓔ
45 Ⓐ Ⓑ Ⓒ Ⓓ Ⓔ
46 Ⓐ Ⓑ Ⓒ Ⓓ Ⓔ
47 Ⓐ Ⓑ Ⓒ Ⓓ Ⓔ
48 Ⓐ Ⓑ Ⓒ Ⓓ Ⓔ
49 Ⓐ Ⓑ Ⓒ Ⓓ Ⓔ
50 Ⓐ Ⓑ Ⓒ Ⓓ Ⓔ
51 Ⓐ Ⓑ Ⓒ Ⓓ Ⓔ
52 Ⓐ Ⓑ Ⓒ Ⓓ Ⓔ
53 Ⓐ Ⓑ Ⓒ Ⓓ Ⓔ
54 Ⓐ Ⓑ Ⓒ Ⓓ Ⓔ
55 Ⓐ Ⓑ Ⓒ Ⓓ Ⓔ
56 Ⓐ Ⓑ Ⓒ Ⓓ Ⓔ
57 Ⓐ Ⓑ Ⓒ Ⓓ Ⓔ
58 Ⓐ Ⓑ Ⓒ Ⓓ Ⓔ

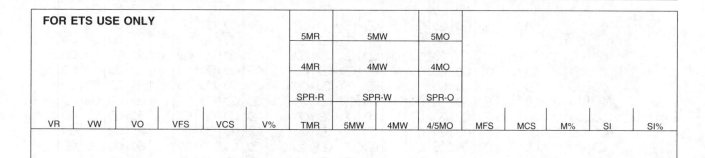

FOR ETS USE ONLY

						5MR	5MW	5MO					
						4MR	4MW	4MO					
						SPR-R	SPR-W	SPR-O					
VR	VW	VO	VFS	VCS	V%	TMR	5MW	4MW	4/5MO	MFS	MCS	M%	SI	SI%

DO NOT WRITE IN THIS AREA.

3   0   0   0   0   0   0

26 (A) (B) (C) (D)
27 (A) (B) (C) (D)
28 (A) (B) (C) (D)
29 (A) (B) (C) (D)
30 (A) (B) (C) (D)
31 (A) (B) (C) (D)
32 (A) (B) (C) (D)
33 (A) (B) (C) (D)
34 (A) (B) (C) (D)
35 (A) (B) (C) (D)
36 (A) (B) (C) (D)
37 (A) (B) (C) (D)
38 (A) (B) (C) (D)
39 (A) (B) (C) (D)
40 (A) (B) (C) (D)

Reminder: If you erase, do so completely.

Only answers entered in the ovals in each grid area will be scored.
You will not receive credit for anything written in the boxes above the ovals.

41 42 43 44 45

46 47 48 49 50

228

Section 1

1

Time — 30 Minutes
29 Questions
(1-29)

For each question in this section, select the best answer from among the choices given and fill in the corresponding oval on the answer sheet.

Each sentence below has one or two blanks, each blank indicating that something has been omitted. Beneath the sentence are five words or sets of words labeled A through E. Choose the word or set of words that, when inserted in the sentence, best fits the meaning of the sentence as a whole.

Example:

Medieval kingdoms did not become constitutional republics overnight; on the contrary, the change was ----.

(A) unpopular
(B) unexpected
(C) advantageous
(D) sufficient
(E) gradual

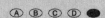

1 Consumers refused to purchase the beverage because it was rumored that the bottling plant's water supply was ---- and that all of the soft drink manufactured there was ----.

(A) purified. .effervescent
(B) medicated. .healthy
(C) contaminated. .tainted
(D) polluted. .distilled
(E) counterfeit. .fabricated

2 It is ---- to emulate the overall style of so effective a leader, but foolish to try to ---- those techniques that only she could employ successfully.

(A) wise. .imitate
(B) prudent. .abandon
(C) easy. .praise
(D) entertaining. .recall
(E) silly. .shun

·3 We are surrounded by their creations, but few, if any, automobile designers are as ---- as the most famous architects and clothing designers.

(A) insistent
(B) prominent
(C) inept
(D) decisive
(E) complacent

4 Professor Rivera argues that, rather than being ---- issue, homelessness is ---- aspect of the nation's economic problems that needs to be addressed.

(A) an irrelevant. .an inappropriate
(B) a moral. .an unimportant
(C) a typical. .a common
(D) a marginal. .a significant
(E) a practical. .a useful

5 Her voice, ---- but mellow, ample but controlled, and her ---- stage presence mark Kiri Te Kanawa as one of the finest operatic sopranos of our age.

(A) untutored. .soporific
(B) vibrant. .mesmerizing
(C) polished. .parochial
(D) thin. .compelling
(E) commanding. .belabored

6 In some universities, the effects of departmental politics can be ----: many academic careers are ruined by petty infighting.

(A) harmless
(B) flattering
(C) stimulating
(D) devastating
(E) futile

7 The ---- nature of their proposal ---- their belief that the problem has already reached crisis proportions.

(A) radical. .contradicts
(B) sweeping. .disguises
(C) drastic. .reflects
(D) earnest. .conceals
(E) tentative. .reveals

GO ON TO THE NEXT PAGE

8 In the past I have forgiven your minor offenses, but this crime you have now committed is so ---- that I have neither mercy in my heart nor ---- on my lips for you.

(A) outrageous. .contempt
(B) excusable. .solace
(C) justifiable. .indulgence
(D) accidental. .scorn
(E) monstrous. .pardon

9 The danger is not ----; it threatens within the next few days.

(A) universal
(B) plausible
(C) hazardous
(D) remote
(E) temporary

10 Despite the essay's tangled and convoluted language, the author's underlying message is surprisingly ----.

(A) pervasive
(B) opaque
(C) lucid
(D) obsolete
(E) despondent

11 He always proceeded ---- when developing new business contacts because he felt that those who act ---- are perceived as being too eager to take unfair advantage of others.

(A) injudiciously. .cautiously
(B) honestly. .properly
(C) gingerly. .precipitously
(D) basely. .gregariously
(E) immodestly. .vainly

12 Far from being the ---- area advertised in the brochure, the valley was frequently polluted by malodorous fumes.

(A) unsullied
(B) differential
(C) environmental
(D) extensive
(E) cohesive

13 Most ancient thinkers rejected the theory that knowledge is ---- and insisted that it can be acquired only by generalization from experience.

(A) innate
(B) sacrosanct
(C) definitive
(D) abstruse
(E) perceptible

14 Because most of the geologic changes in the Earth's surface occur so slowly that we cannot perceive them, we see the Earth as virtually ----.

(A) immutable
(B) impenetrable
(C) immeasurable
(D) interminable
(E) inaccessible

15 In her fiction, Ivy Compton-Burnett specialized in the exposure of that false morality that uses a ---- of altruism and public-spiritedness to ---- malicious manipulation of other people.

(A) philosophy. .combat
(B) pretense. .subvert
(C) pose. .cloak
(D) code. .forbid
(E) dread. .excuse

16 The defendants ---- that the victim died long before the time of the alleged murder, when they had what they considered an airtight alibi, but the prosecutor declared that their defense was based on ---- evidence.

(A) insisted. .specious
(B) avowed. .precise
(C) denied. .circumstantial
(D) swore. .unimpeachable
(E) protested. .incontrovertible

GO ON TO THE NEXT PAGE

The passages below are followed by questions based on their content; questions following a pair of related passages may also be based on the relationship between the paired passages. Answer the questions on the basis of what is <u>stated</u> or <u>implied</u> in the passages and in any introductory material that may be provided.

Questions 17-22 are based on the following passage.

This passage is adapted from a short story published in 1983.

The basement kitchen of the brownstone house where my family lived was the usual gathering place. Once inside the warm safety of its walls,
Line the women threw off their drab coats and hats,
(5) seated themselves at the large center table, drank their cups of tea or cocoa, and talked. While my sister and I sat at a smaller table over in a corner doing our homework, they talked—endlessly, passionately, poetically, and with impressive range.
(10) No subject was beyond them. True, they would indulge in the usual gossip. But they also tackled the great issues of the time. They were always, for example, discussing the state of the economy in their newly adopted country. It was the mid-and-
(15) late 1930's then, and the aftershock of the Depression, with its soup lines and suicides on Wall Street, was still being felt.

There was no way for me to understand it at the time, but the talk that filled the kitchen those
(20) afternoons was highly functional. It served as therapy, the cheapest kind available to my mother and her friends. It restored them to a sense of themselves and reaffirmed their self-worth. Through language they were able to overcome the humilia-
(25) tions of the workday.

But more than therapy, that freewheeling, wide-ranging, exuberant talk functioned as an outlet for the tremendous creative energy they possessed. They were women in whom the need for self-
(30) expression was strong, and since language was the only vehicle readily available to them, they made of it an art form that—in keeping with the African tradition in which art and life are one—was an integral part of their lives.
(35) And their talk was a refuge. They never really ceased being baffled and overwhelmed by America —its vastness, complexity, and power. Its strange customs and laws. At a level beyond words they remained fearful and in awe. Their uneasiness
(40) and fear were even reflected in their attitude toward the children they had given birth to in this country. They referred to those like myself, the little Brooklyn-born Bajans (Barbadians), as "these New York children."
(45) Confronted therefore by a world they could not encompass and at the same time finding themselves permanently separated from the world they had known, they took refuge in language. "Language is the only homeland," Czeslaw Milosz, the émigré
(50) Polish writer and Nobel laureate, has said. This is what it became for the women at the kitchen table.

It served another purpose also, I suspect. My mother and her friends were, after all, the female
(55) counterpart of Ralph Ellison's invisible man.* Indeed, you might say they suffered a triple invisibility, being black, female, and foreigners. But given the kind of women they were, they could not tolerate the fact of their invisibility, their
(60) powerlessness. And they fought back, using the only weapon at their command: the spoken word.

*Ralph Ellison, a Black American author, wrote a widely read novel entitled *Invisible Man*.

17 The main focus of the passage is on the

(A) situation encountered by immigrants in a new country
(B) isolation felt by a particular group of women
(C) difference between the author's generation and that of her mother
(D) benefits of language for a group of women
(E) contrast between New York and Barbados

18 The author implies that the African tradition of connecting art and life was

(A) evident in her mother's conversations
(B) familiar to most women writers
(C) a well-known theory that was difficult to apply
(D) a practice shared by several other cultures
(E) something her mother's friends did not follow

GO ON TO THE NEXT PAGE

19 The quotation from Czeslaw Milosz (lines 48-49) is included to emphasize the point that

(A) thoughts are easily translated from one language to another
(B) language is a way of finding and retaining identity
(C) translators must know many languages well
(D) spoken language differs from written language
(E) once learned, languages are seldom forgotten

20 The author mentions all of the following as ways in which her mother and her mother's friends used language EXCEPT to

(A) make their environment less alien
(B) regain self-esteem
(C) alleviate the difficulty of their lives
(D) comprehend their experience
(E) publicize their working conditions

21 The author's tone in describing the women is

(A) formal and argumentative
(B) quiet and somber
(C) celebratory and reflective
(D) both laudatory and critical
(E) alternately bewildered and knowing

22 In developing the passage, the author uses all of the following EXCEPT

(A) prophecies of the future
(B) a recollection of conversation
(C) references to her own background
(D) description and reminiscence
(E) comparison with a famous novel

GO ON TO THE NEXT PAGE

Questions 23-29 are based on the following passages.

The following passages are excerpts from two different sources that discuss particular approaches to history.

Passage 1

As authors, we should warn the professional historian that our presentation will appear Whiggish. For the benefit of the uninitiated, this term is
Line commonly used to describe the interpretation of
(5) history favored by the great Whig historians of the nineteenth century. These scholars believed that the history of humanity was a record of slow but continual progress. For them, such progress had directed their society inexorably toward a political
(10) system dear to their hearts: liberal democracy. The Whig historians thus analyzed the past from the point of view of the present rather than by trying to understand the people of the past on their own terms.
(15) Modern historians generally differ from the Whig historians in two ways: first, modern historians seldom discern any overall purpose in history. Second, modern historians try to approach history from the point of view of the actors rather than by
(20) judging the validity of archaic world views from our own Olympian heights.* Many professional historians believe it is wrong to pass moral judgments on the actions of those who lived in the past. A charge of Whiggery—analyzing and judging
(25) the past from our own point of view—has become one of the worst charges that one historian can level at another.

But in one sense we shall have to be a bit Whiggish: we shall try to interpret certain ideas of the
(30) past in terms a modern scientist can understand. There is more that explains the persistent hints of a Whiggish flavor to our history: we do want to pass judgments on the work of the scientists and philosophers of the past. Our purpose in doing so
(35) is not to demonstrate our superiority over our predecessors, but to learn from their mistakes and successes. Plus, there are recurring themes present in history; we are only reporting them. We refuse to distort history to fit the current fad of historical
(40) writing.

*The ancient Greeks believed that their gods and goddesses observed the activities of humans from Mount Olympus.

Passage 2

One can lie outright about the past. Or one can omit facts that might lead to unacceptable conclusions. In his historical works, Samuel Eliot Morison does neither. He refuses to lie about Columbus
(45) and other European explorers who followed him. He does not omit the story of mass murder; indeed he describes it with the harshest word one can use: genocide. But he mentions the truth quickly and then goes on to other things more important
(50) to him.

The treatment of such figures and their victims —the quiet acceptance of conquest and murder in the name of progress—is only one aspect of a certain approach to history, in which the past is
(55) told from the point of view of governments, conquerors, diplomats, leaders. It is as if they, like Columbus, deserve universal acceptance, as if they actually represent some all-encompassing, larger collective.
(60) "History is the memory of states," wrote Henry Kissinger in *A World Restored*, a book recounting the "restored peace" in nineteenth-century Europe from the viewpoint of the leaders of Austria and England. But for the factory workers in England,
(65) farmers in France, ordinary people in Asia and Africa, women and children everywhere except in the upper classes, it was a world of conquest, violence, hunger, exploitation—a world not restored but disintegrated.
(70) My viewpoint for telling history is different. Nations are not homogeneous, integrated social communities and never have been, so we must not accept the memory of political states as our own. But neither do I want to invent victories for
(75) people's movements. If history is to be creative, to anticipate a possible future without denying the past, it should, I believe, emphasize the new possibilities by disclosing those hidden episodes of the past when, even if in brief flashes, people showed
(80) their ability to resist, unite, occasionally to win. I am supposing, or perhaps only hoping, that our future may be found in the past's fugitive moments of compassion rather than in its solid centuries of warfare.
(85) That, being as blunt as I can, is my approach to the history of the United States.

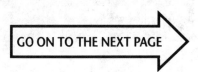
GO ON TO THE NEXT PAGE

23 Who are the "uninitiated" referred to in line 3 ?

(A) People who are unfamiliar with the Whig approach to history
(B) Readers who judge scientists only within original social contexts
(C) People who judge the past with reference to the present
(D) Historians who have rejected the Whig approach to history
(E) People who do not believe in social progress

24 The authors of Passage 1 assert that one of the basic beliefs of Whig historians is that

(A) scholars should rely on reason rather than emotion when dealing with controversial issues
(B) scholarly debate is about ideas, not the people who express them
(C) people are likely to develop their best ideas if encouraged, not criticized
(D) each generation builds on the advances of the preceding one
(E) the philosophy of ordinary people is more important than the philosophy of leaders

25 The author of Passage 2 is critical of both Morison and Kissinger chiefly for

(A) taking a populist approach to history
(B) concentrating only on the history of the Western world
(C) emphasizing the superiority of Western society
(D) being dishonest in their accounts of warfare
(E) telling history only from the point of view of a powerful elite

26 In line 82, "fugitive" most nearly means

(A) fleeting
(B) hunted
(C) lawless
(D) shamefaced
(E) skulking

27 The end of Passage 2 suggests that the author's history of the United States will emphasize the

(A) principles on which the nation was founded
(B) events that marked social, political, or economic collaboration among the common people
(C) real reasons for the wars in which the nation has been involved
(D) political institutions that have safeguarded the freedoms enjoyed by citizens of the United States
(E) lives of the elected leaders who have shaped the nation's destiny

28 The authors of both passages would most probably agree that

(A) the best way to study history is to analyze systematically recurring themes and patterns
(B) the Whig approach to history should be adopted by modern historians
(C) it is important to understand the particular bias of a historian
(D) historical writing cannot be creative
(E) historians should focus mostly on political events

29 If it can be assumed that Morison has been accurately represented in Passage 2, what would the authors of Passage 1 conclude about his work?

(A) It does not record humanity's progress toward a better society.
(B) It deals with the same topics as their work does.
(C) Its approach to history can be described as Whiggish.
(D) It is not sufficiently researched.
(E) It represents the best of its kind in historical writing.

IF YOU FINISH BEFORE TIME IS CALLED, YOU MAY CHECK YOUR WORK ON THIS SECTION ONLY. DO NOT TURN TO ANY OTHER SECTION IN THE TEST. STOP

Time—30 Minutes
25 Questions
(1-25)

In this section solve each problem, using any available space on the page for scratchwork. Then decide which is the best of the choices given and fill in the corresponding oval on the answer sheet.

Notes:

1. The use of a calculator is permitted. All numbers used are real numbers.

2. Figures that accompany problems in this test are intended to provide information useful in solving the problems. They are drawn as accurately as possible EXCEPT when it is stated in a specific problem that the figure is not drawn to scale. All figures lie in a plane unless otherwise indicated.

$A = \pi r^2$
$C = 2\pi r$

$A = \ell w$

$A = \frac{1}{2}bh$

$V = \ell wh$

$V = \pi r^2 h$

$c^2 = a^2 + b^2$

Special Right Triangles

The number of degrees of arc in a circle is 360.
The measure in degrees of a straight angle is 180.
The sum of the measures in degrees of the angles of a triangle is 180.

---

1 What is 453,719 rounded to the nearest thousand?

(A) 460,000
(B) 454,000
(C) 453,800
(D) 453,700
(E) 453,000

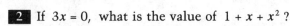

2 If $3x = 0$, what is the value of $1 + x + x^2$?

(A) $\frac{7}{9}$

(B) 1

(C) $\frac{13}{9}$

(D) 3

(E) 7

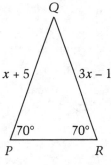

3 In $\triangle PQR$ above, what is the value of x ?

(A) 11
(B) 5
(C) 4
(D) 3
(E) 2

GO ON TO THE NEXT PAGE

4 At noon the temperature outside a weather station is 26° F. If the temperature drops 9 degrees by 4:00 p.m. and then drops 3 times as much as that by midnight, what would be the temperature at midnight?

(A) −62° F
(B) −18° F
(C) −10° F
(D)   0° F
(E)   14° F

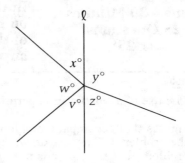

Note: Figure not drawn to scale.

6 In the figure above, ℓ is a line, $x + y = 130$, and $z + v = 80$. What is the value of x?

(A)   50
(B) 100
(C) 150
(D) 210
(E) It cannot be determined from the information given.

5 For all values of a, b, s, and t, let the expression equal $at − bs$. For what value of a will equal 0 ?

(A)   0

(B) $\frac{8}{5}$

(C) $\frac{5}{2}$

(D)   8

(E) 10

7 If Jim travels at an average speed of m miles per hour, how many hours would it take him to travel 400 miles?

(A) $400 − m$

(B) $400 + m$

(C) $\frac{m}{400}$

(D) $\frac{400}{m}$

(E) $400m$

GO ON TO THE NEXT PAGE

8 The area of Square I is $(2k - 7)^2$ square units and the area of Square II is 81 square units. If the areas of the two squares are equal, which of the following could be the value of k ?

(A) 8
(B) 9
(C) 18
(D) 22
(E) 44

$$x + y = 7$$
$$x^2 + y^2 = 29$$

9 In the equations above, if x and y are positive integers, then x could equal which of the following?

(A) 1
(B) 2
(C) 3
(D) 4
(E) 6

AFTER-SCHOOL ACTIVITIES OF
STUDENTS AT NORTH HIGH SCHOOL

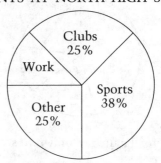

10 If each of the 1,800 students at North High School is included in exactly one of the categories in the circle graph shown above, what is the total number of students who either participate in sports or work?

(A) 50
(B) 380
(C) 450
(D) 684
(E) 900

11 Of the following, which number is the greatest?

(A) 0.03
(B) 0.29
(C) 0.293
(D) 0.2093
(E) 0.2893

GO ON TO THE NEXT PAGE

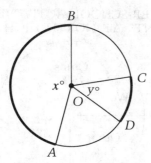

Note: Figure not drawn to scale.

12 In the circle with center O shown above, the ratio of the length of darkened arc AB to the length of darkened arc CD is 2 to 1. What is the ratio of x to y ?

(A) 1 to 4
(B) 1 to 2
(C) 1 to 1
(D) 2 to 1
(E) 4 to 1

13 If n is an integer and $n^2 + 3$ is even, which of the following must be odd?

(A) n
(B) $n + 1$
(C) $n + 3$
(D) $n^2 + 1$
(E) $2n^2$

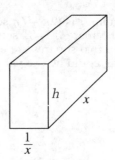

14 If the volume of the rectangular box in the figure above is 1, what does h equal?

(A) 1

(B) 2

(C) $\dfrac{1}{x^2}$

(D) $\dfrac{1}{x}$

(E) x

15 Grass seed is to be spread on a rectangular lawn that measures x feet by y feet. If one pound of grass seed is required for each 300 square feet of lawn, which of the following is an expression for the number of pounds of grass seed required for this lawn?

(A) $300(x + y)$

(B) $\dfrac{xy}{300}$

(C) $300xy$

(D) $\dfrac{300y}{x}$

(E) $\dfrac{300x}{y}$

GO ON TO THE NEXT PAGE

$$A = \{1, 2, 3\}$$
$$B = \{2, 3, 4\}$$

16 If x can be any number in set A above and y can be any number in set B, how many <u>different</u> values of xy are possible?

(A) Three
(B) Four
(C) Five
(D) Six
(E) Seven

17 The coordinates of the midpoint of line segment AB are $(2, 1)$. If the coordinates of point A are $(-1, -1)$, what are the coordinates of point B ?

(A) $(-4, -3)$

(B) $\left(\dfrac{1}{2}, 0\right)$

(C) $(4, 4)$

(D) $(5, 3)$

(E) $(5, -3)$

18 If $-4 < x < -2$, which of the following could be the value of $3x$?

(A) -2.5
(B) -3.5
(C) -4.5
(D) -7.5
(E) -14.5

19 An aerobics instructor burns 3,000 calories per day for 4 days. How many calories must she burn during the next day so that the average (arithmetic mean) number of calories burned for the 5 days is 3,500 calories per day?

(A) 6,000
(B) 5,500
(C) 5,000
(D) 4,500
(E) 4,000

20 If n is a nonzero integer, which of the following must be an integer?

I. $\dfrac{16}{n}$

II. $\dfrac{n^2 + 1}{n}$

III. n^2

(A) None
(B) II only
(C) III only
(D) I and II
(E) II and III

GO ON TO THE NEXT PAGE

21 If the expression $360(n-2)$ is equal to $720k$, which of the following gives the value of k in terms of n?

(A) $2n - 4$

(B) $2n - 2$

(C) $n - 1$

(D) $\dfrac{n}{2} - 2$

(E) $\dfrac{n}{2} - 1$

22 If $3 \le x \le 5$ and $7 \le y \le 9$, what is the greatest possible value of $\dfrac{2}{y-x}$?

(A) $\dfrac{1}{3}$

(B) $\dfrac{1}{2}$

(C) 1

(D) $\dfrac{3}{2}$

(E) 2

23 If $a^6 = 5$ and $a^5 = \dfrac{4}{x}$, which of the following is an expression for a in terms of x?

(A) $\dfrac{x}{20}$

(B) $\dfrac{20}{x}$

(C) $\dfrac{5}{4x}$

(D) $\dfrac{4x}{5}$

(E) $\dfrac{5x}{4}$

24 If the number of points of intersection of a set of 10 lines lying in a plane is denoted by n, what will be the greatest possible number of points of intersection when an eleventh line is added to the set?

(A) $n + 10$
(B) $n + 11$
(C) $2n$
(D) $10n$
(E) n^2

25 At City High School, H students study history and G students study geometry. Of these students, B students study both history and geometry. What fraction of these students study both subjects?

(A) $\dfrac{B}{H+G}$

(B) $\dfrac{B}{H-G}$

(C) $\dfrac{B}{H+G+B}$

(D) $\dfrac{B}{H+G-B}$

(E) $\dfrac{B}{H+G-2B}$

IF YOU FINISH BEFORE TIME IS CALLED, YOU MAY CHECK YOUR WORK ON THIS SECTION ONLY. DO NOT TURN TO ANY OTHER SECTION IN THE TEST. **STOP**

Time — 30 Minutes
29 Questions
(30-58)

For each question in this section, select the best answer from among the choices given and fill in the corresponding oval on the answer sheet.

Each question below consists of a related pair of words or phrases, followed by five pairs of words or phrases labeled A through E. Select the pair that best expresses a relationship similar to that expressed in the original pair.

Example:

CRUMB : BREAD ::

(A) ounce : unit
(B) splinter : wood
(C) water : bucket
(D) twine : rope
(E) cream : butter

30 WOOL : SHEEP ::
(A) tint : coat
(B) bell : cow
(C) silk : silkworm
(D) cotton : loom
(E) asbestos : fire

31 PRINCIPAL : SCHOOL ::
(A) mascot : team
(B) mayor : election
(C) guest : hotel
(D) physician : hospital
(E) captain : ship

32 ORCHARD : APPLES ::
(A) hill : trees
(B) swamp : weeds
(C) mirror : light
(D) grocery : meat
(E) field : corn

33 REQUEST : DEMAND ::
(A) converse : discuss
(B) suggest : order
(C) experiment : confirm
(D) ask : answer
(E) act : entertain

34 CUSHION : CHAIR ::
(A) pillow : bed
(B) drawer : desk
(C) quilt : blanket
(D) leg : table
(E) sheet : cloth

35 PAINT : PORTRAIT ::
(A) realize : idea
(B) remember : description
(C) converse : monologue
(D) write : biography
(E) laugh : comedy

36 AMOROUSNESS : LOVER ::
(A) government : tyrant
(B) model : paragon
(C) humanity : misanthrope
(D) gratitude : ingrate
(E) fear : coward

37 ALLEVIATE : SEVERE ::
(A) streamline : efficient
(B) bolster : supportive
(C) avoid : required
(D) alter : variable
(E) specify : vague

38 VERTIGO : DIZZINESS ::
(A) neurosis : emotion
(B) squalor : cleanliness
(C) dejection : sadness
(D) indigestion : gluttony
(E) laryngitis : voice

39 BRACKISH : WATER ::
(A) rancid : butter
(B) homogenized : milk
(C) tanned : leather
(D) tart : vinegar
(E) windy : air

40 ATROPHY : MUSCLE ::
(A) infest : parasite
(B) swell : injury
(C) contaminate : fungus
(D) wither : leaf
(E) stretch : ligament

41 REPRIEVE : PUNISHMENT ::
(A) pardon : kindness
(B) grant : assistance
(C) moratorium : activity
(D) prognosis : recovery
(E) incarceration : sentence

GO ON TO THE NEXT PAGE

Each passage below is followed by questions based on its content. Answer the questions on the basis of what is <u>stated</u> or <u>implied</u> in each passage and in any introductory material that may be provided.

Questions 42-47 are based on the following passage.

This passage has been adapted from a discussion of meteorites.

During the last half of the eighteenth century, European scientists had been pestered by reports of stones falling from the sky. Their reaction to
Line stories of meteorites falling to Earth is not a proud
(5) chapter in the history of science. Scientists tenaciously and repeatedly denied the possibility that stones could drop out of the blue. Astronomers, geologists, chemists, and physicists adopted an intellectual arrogance toward a phenomenon that
(10) ran contrary to their logic and their learning: there are no rocks in the sky, therefore none can fall. Consequently, eyewitness reports were dismissed as unreliable and unworthy of scientific attention.
(15) In defense of scientific obduracy, this was the Age of Reason in Europe, and scientists were anxious to distance themselves from a past they considered to be tainted by ignorance and superstition. Accounts of sky-stones were abhorred as
(20) shameful remnants of a past when people readily accepted strange stories as magical or supernatural.
Furthermore, a developing branch of science called astrogeology decreed that any genuine meteorite must appear quite unlike any terrestrial spec-
(25) imen. Iron meteorite specimens seemed unlike terrestrial rocks; however, practically all irons submitted as sky-stones had been found lying on the ground rather than observed dropping from heaven. Stone meteorite specimens compounded
(30) the quandary. Although many were supposedly observed to land, they looked like ordinary field rocks, much to the discredit of the witnesses. This conflicting evidence, along with the superstitious associations with the notion of stones from the
(35) sky, perhaps accounts for the scientific disdain that caused some museums to junk valuable collections of meteorites.
One young German physicist, Ernst Chladni, was fiercely dedicated to finding the truth about
(40) sky-stones. Ignoring popular superstition and scientific scorn alike, Chladni started his investigation by digging out from musty libraries and archives centuries-old accounts of "fallen masses." He studied numerous specimens of curiously
(45) heavy rocks gathered from all over the globe.

These led him to the unorthodox conclusion that meteorites are extraterrestrial objects. His theory was bolstered by an English chemist, Edward Charles Howard, who used new techniques to
(50) discover the link between iron and stone meteorites: the metal nickel, an element common to both, in a form unknown in any terrestrial rocks.
In 1794 a storm of abuse and vilification from the scientific establishment greeted Chladni's
(55) published findings, but Chladni remained undeterred. Some of Chladni's colleagues sided with him, mustering additional evidence that stones fall from space.
Vindication finally came in 1803, when even
(60) the vaunted French Academy of Sciences caved in, no doubt prompted by a thundering load of meteorites that landed in Normandy that year, virtually in the academy's backyard. As one twentieth-century scientist wryly noted, "It then became
(65) possible for a meteorite to land in France without fear of embarrassment."

42 The author mentions all of the following as reasons that late-eighteenth-century European scientists denied the existence of meteorites EXCEPT:

(A) The idea of rocks in the sky seemed illogical.
(B) Few iron meteorites were witnessed actually falling from the sky.
(C) Scientists had limited access to meteorite specimens from around the world.
(D) Stone meteorites offered for analysis closely resembled terrestrial field stones.
(E) Eyewitness reports were held to be unreliable.

GO ON TO THE NEXT PAGE →

43 In lines 40-43, the author implies which of the following?

(A) Recorded reports of "falling rocks" conclusively proved the extraterrestrial origin of meteorites.
(B) Historical accounts of meteorite falls had been previously neglected by most scientists.
(C) Meteorite showers occurred less frequently in Chladni's time than in previous centuries.
(D) Chladni recognized the link between superstition and scientific inquiry.
(E) Chladni placed more emphasis on eyewitness accounts than on chemical analysis.

44 It can be inferred that most scientists initially rejected Chladni's findings because he

(A) took credit for ideas that were first promoted by other scientists
(B) employed unorthodox methods of scientific investigation
(C) refused to allow members of the scientific establishment to participate in his study
(D) did not analyze any fresh samples of iron or stone meteorites
(E) challenged widely accepted tenets of the scientific community

45 According to the passage, Edward Charles Howard's findings were significant because they

(A) established that the metal nickel was found in many forms throughout the universe
(B) confirmed that meteorite specimens were extraterrestrial by establishing their unique properties
(C) determined that meteorite specimens were denser than terrestrial rocks
(D) proved that iron specimens were extraterrestrial but stone specimens were actually terrestrial field stones
(E) revealed that meteorite specimens were chemically indistinguishable from terrestrial stones

46 In the last paragraph, the author implies that members of the French Academy

(A) were not equipped to perform chemical analysis on the meteorites that fell on Normandy
(B) were not familiar with the published findings of Ernst Chladni
(C) might not have accepted Chladni's ideas without the overwhelming physical evidence in Normandy
(D) continued to place too much emphasis on general theorizing rather than on analyzing physical evidence
(E) received unfair credit for the discovery of extraterrestrial rocks on Earth

47 In the last paragraph, the author's attitude toward the French Academy is one of

(A) outrage
(B) mockery
(C) skepticism
(D) sympathy
(E) awe

GO ON TO THE NEXT PAGE

based on the following

...ge discusses the condition of women artists during the Renaissance (roughly 1350-1650). OPINION

In Italy during the Renaissance, a revolutionary change occurred in artists' images of themselves.
Artists, most of whom were from less privileged
Line social classes, struggled to give the status and
(5) rewards of an intellectual profession to what had hitherto been classified as a craft. A seven-year apprenticeship in a master's shop no longer sufficed.
Artists were expected to have a liberal arts education, with special emphasis on mathematics, and
(10) to have considerable knowledge of ancient art, derived both from literary texts and from the objects themselves. It became accepted that the training of every serious artist would include the study of the human body—at first from clothed
(15) models but increasingly from the nude male model—as well as travel to major art centers to study the achievements of other artists. These changes would seem to have made it even more difficult for women to become artists than it had
(20) been in earlier times. For such a level of education and freedom of movement was hardly possible for women when the Renaissance began.

Before the Renaissance, women led what would in modern times be considered highly circum-
(25) scribed lives. Except for a few women in the wealthiest class, women were expected to participate actively in the endless labor required to provide the food and the cloth their families would need.
The demands of childbearing and child-rearing also
(30) restricted their activities. The new emphasis on artistic "genius" in the Renaissance would seem to have excluded women from artistic endeavors even more. There was a widespread belief that women did not have the potential for artistic
(35) genius. When the Renaissance began, few women other than the daughters of artists had any access to artistic training. Only a few women of the aristocracy were educated, and their education was meant to enhance their chances of making
(40) marriages advantageous to their families rather than to develop any potential artistic or intellectual talent they may have shown.

In fact, there were more women artists during the Renaissance than during previous periods.
(45) While artists were winning new status in Renaissance society, there was also an important shift in attitudes toward the education of women. Early in the 1500's, at the Italian court of the duke of Urbino, Baldassare Castiglione wrote a handbook
(50) on court life that contained an entire chapter describing the ideal female member of an aristocratic household. Almost all the attributes and accomplishments necessary to the male courtier were also declared appropriate to the female,
(55) including a high level of educational attainment and the ability to paint, play musical instruments, sing, and write poetry. These ideas can be found earlier in medieval treatises on courtly behavior, but the invention of printing in the meantime
(60) meant that a far wider audience had access to Castiglione's ideas of ideal courtly behavior than could ever have learned about these customs in the Middle Ages. Castiglione's handbook was enormously popular; its influence on social behavior
(65) and educational theory extended far beyond the Renaissance courts, where it originated, to all lesser noble families and to all successful merchants wealthy enough to emulate the aristocratic way of life. Women were emancipated from the
(70) bondage of illiteracy and minimal education; the privileges and opportunities of a few women were extended to women of a much wider stratum of society. It became proper, even praiseworthy, for women of the upper classes to engage in a wide
(75) range of artistic, musical, and literary pursuits.
Although most of these women only dabbled as amateurs and formal education for women remained poor, after 1550 there are many references to women who were regarded as exception-
(80) ally fine artists, musicians, and writers.

The influence of these new ideas on women who became painters can be found in the ways in which women painters were presented to the world by themselves and their biographers. Sofo-
(85) nisba Anguissola (1532-1625) was one of many daughters of minor Italian aristocrats whose educational horizons were expanded by the new ideas.
Having been provided with an education and an opportunity to study with local artists, she became
(90) a celebrated portrait painter. Her portraits of herself playing a keyboard instrument changed the portrait tradition; former images of women holding prayer books or with their gazes modestly averted gave way in her works to a variety of indi-
(95) vidual portrayals of assertive female subjects.
Anguissola's success was an important precedent for the many gifted women who followed her.

Anguissola's noble origins and the high fees she was paid by court patrons were seen by male
(100) artists of her time as elevating the status of the profession. But for the next few centuries, the training and careers of most women artists were

GO ON TO THE NEXT PAGE

confined to the less remunerative specialties of portraiture and still life. By and large, women did (105) not compete with men for the more prestigious and higher-paying public commissions. Although there is little evidence of opposition to women artists from men artists before the eighteenth century, the few recorded examples of men artists' (110) resentment concern women who made sculpture or religious works for public sites.

48 The primary purpose of the passage is to

(A) explore causes of change in the roles of women artists
(B) explain the existence of women artists before the Renaissance
(C) establish a link between the growing number of artists and economic prosperity during the Renaissance
(D) criticize society for failing to support artists
(E) contrast conditions in Italy with those in the rest of Europe during the Renaissance

49 In the second paragraph (lines 23-42), the author presents evidence to show that

(A) traditional family roles did not have to be incompatible with artistic development
(B) the general population was beginning to reject the ideals of an earlier period
(C) women indirectly had a major effect on artistic developments during the Renaissance
(D) wealthy merchants were eager to emulate the life-styles of artists
(E) major social changes were required to remove the obstacles to women becoming artists

50 It can be inferred from the passage that few Renaissance women received artistic training equal to that of men because of

(A) the higher status of male artists
(B) the influence of numerous monarchs
(C) women's reluctance to pursue artistic education
(D) the influence of Castiglione's work
(E) limitations on women's social roles

51 Castiglione's book probably appealed to certain merchants because of their

(A) belief in the inherent value of education
(B) desire to assume courtly ways
(C) fascination with antiquity
(D) wish to increase the size of their markets
(E) urge to maintain the status quo

52 The third paragraph (lines 43-80) suggests that one reason for the great influence of Castiglione's book was the

(A) higher level of education of its audience compared to medieval audiences
(B) high political rank and power of the duke of Urbino
(C) accessibility of its language
(D) increased availability of books
(E) greater prevalence of women at royal courts than in earlier times

53 The author most likely includes the example of Sofonisba Anguissola (lines 84-101) in order to

(A) show the effect of Castiglione's ideas on one woman's career
(B) show the typical educational attainments of women during the Renaissance
(C) demonstrate the difficulty of a woman's becoming an artist
(D) show that conditions for women had not changed since the medieval period
(E) refute the belief that women were hindered in their efforts to pursue artistic careers

54 The change in portrait style mentioned in lines 90-95 suggests that there was also a change in

(A) the status of artists
(B) society's perception of women
(C) men's attitudes toward women artists
(D) the financial condition of artists
(E) the amount of training required of artists

GO ON TO THE NEXT PAGE

55 The author suggests that other artists viewed Sofonisba Anguissola's success favorably because

(A) Anguissola's success enhanced reputations and economic opportunities for all artists
(B) Castiglione's work had made artists advocates of the inherent equality of the sexes
(C) Anguissola's innovative style expanded the audience willing to support artists
(D) Anguissola's political influence on the aristocracy was significant
(E) Anguissola's work covered a wide variety of genres

56 The author would most likely agree with which of the following statements about women artists living before the Renaissance?

(A) Although there were many women artists, their works have not been studied until recently.
(B) It was more difficult for women to become recognized artists before the Renaissance than during the Renaissance.
(C) Placed on a pedestal, women artists living before the Renaissance found their works accepted uncritically.
(D) There is no evidence that women tried to pursue artistic careers.
(E) Women were major determiners of artistic trends.

57 The last paragraph suggests that men artists' welcoming reception of women artists like Anguissola was

(A) a result of the equal education women were then receiving
(B) reversed when men artists perceived women's success as an economic threat
(C) a forecast of increasingly open attitudes toward women's participation in the arts
(D) more enthusiastic than that of men in other professions
(E) strongly influential on women's decisions to pursue artistic careers

58 Which of the following Renaissance influences does the passage see as counterbalancing the forces that kept women subordinate?

(A) The rising popularity of the idea of artistic "genius"
(B) Greater public roles for artists
(C) The dissipation of class distinctions
(D) The spread of Castiglione's ideas
(E) A change in artistic styles

IF YOU FINISH BEFORE TIME IS CALLED, YOU MAY CHECK YOUR WORK ON THIS SECTION ONLY. DO NOT TURN TO ANY OTHER SECTION IN THE TEST. STOP

Time—30 Minutes
25 Questions
(26-50)

This section contains two types of questions. You have 30 minutes to complete both types. You may use any available space for scratchwork.

Notes:

1. The use of a calculator is permitted. All numbers used are real numbers.

2. Figures that accompany problems in this test are intended to provide information useful in solving the problems. They are drawn as accurately as possible EXCEPT when it is stated in a specific problem that the figure is not drawn to scale. All figures lie in a plane unless otherwise indicated.

Reference Information

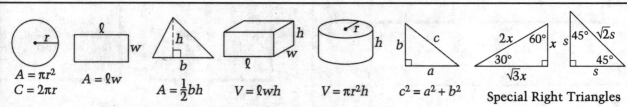

$$A = \pi r^2$$
$$C = 2\pi r$$
$$A = \ell w$$
$$A = \frac{1}{2}bh$$
$$V = \ell w h$$
$$V = \pi r^2 h$$
$$c^2 = a^2 + b^2$$

Special Right Triangles

The number of degrees of arc in a circle is 360.
The measure in degrees of a straight angle is 180.
The sum of the measures in degrees of the angles of a triangle is 180.

Directions for Quantitative Comparison Questions

Questions 26-40 each consist of two quantities in boxes, one in Column A and one in Column B. You are to compare the two quantities and on the answer sheet fill in oval

A if the quantity in Column A is greater;
B if the quantity in Column B is greater;
C if the two quantities are equal;
D if the relationship cannot be determined from the information given.

Notes:

1. In some questions, information is given about one or both of the quantities to be compared. In such cases, the given information is centered above the two columns and is not boxed.
2. In a given question, a symbol that appears in both columns represents the same thing in Column A as it does in Column B.
3. Letters such as x, n, and k stand for real numbers.

EXAMPLES

Column A	Column B	Answers
E1 5^2	20	● Ⓑ Ⓒ Ⓓ

150° / x°

| E2 x | 30 | Ⓐ Ⓑ ● Ⓓ |

r and s are integers.

| E3 $r + 1$ | $s - 1$ | Ⓐ Ⓑ Ⓒ ● |

GO ON TO THE NEXT PAGE

SUMMARY DIRECTIONS FOR COMPARISON QUESTIONS

<u>Answer:</u> A if the quantity in Column A is greater;
B if the quantity in Column B is greater;
C if the two quantities are equal;
D if the relationship cannot be determined from the information given.

<u>Column A</u>	<u>Column B</u>

$$2y - 1 = 9$$

26

$y - 1$	5

```
X X        1st Row
X X X      2nd Row
X X X X    3rd Row
X X X X X  4th Row
```

The first four rows in an arrangement of X's are shown. Each row has one more X than the row immediately above it. The arrangement continues indefinitely.

27

The total number of X's in the 1st, 3rd, 5th, and 7th rows	16

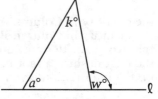

The figure is a rectangular solid.

28

The length of AD	The length of BC

<u>Column A</u>	<u>Column B</u>

Carlos tests 20 television sets per hour and Janice tests 30 radios per hour.

29

The number of hours needed by Carlos to test 100 television sets	The number of hours needed by Janice to test 120 radios

$2c$ is a negative integer.

30

$2c + 2$	0

<u>Note:</u> Figure not drawn to scale.

$$k = 40$$
$$w = 110$$

31

a	70

32

$2x^2 + 1$	$(2x)^2$

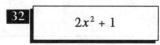
GO ON TO THE NEXT PAGE

SUMMARY DIRECTIONS FOR COMPARISON QUESTIONS

Answer: A if the quantity in Column A is greater;
B if the quantity in Column B is greater;
C if the two quantities are equal;
D if the relationship cannot be determined from the information given.

Column A	Column B

$x > 4$

33

$x^2 - 4$	$x + 2$

34

The length of the hypotenuse of a right triangle whose legs are 2 and 11	The length of the hypotenuse of a right triangle whose legs are 6 and 9

$x < y < 0$

35

$x + y$	x

$x \neq -3$

36

$\dfrac{2 + x}{3 + x}$	$\dfrac{2}{3} + x$

The average (arithmetic mean) of s and t is 20.

37

The average of s and t	The average of s, t, and 21

Column A	Column B

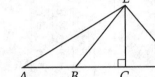

Note: Figure not drawn to scale.
$EC \perp AD$

38

The area of $\triangle ACE$	The area of $\triangle BDE$

Julie and Sara were each hired at a salary of $20,000 per year. Since their employment, Julie has received two separate salary increases of 6 percent each and Sara has received one salary increase of 12 percent.

39

Julie's present annual salary	Sara's present annual salary

n is a positive integer greater than 1.

40

The sum of $2n + 1$ consecutive integers if the middle integer is 0 when the integers are listed in increasing order	The sum of $2n - 1$ consecutive integers if the middle integer is 0 when the integers are listed in increasing order

GO ON TO THE NEXT PAGE

Directions for Student-Produced Response Questions

Each of the remaining 10 questions (41-50) requires you to solve the problem and enter your answer by marking the ovals in the special grid, as shown in the examples below.

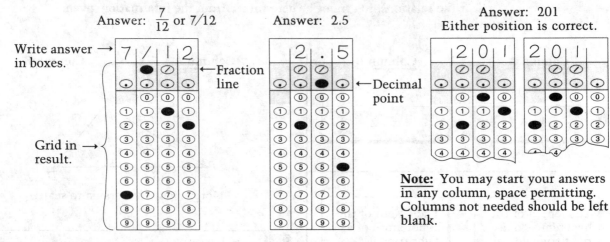

Answer: $\frac{7}{12}$ or 7/12

Write answer in boxes. ← Fraction line

Grid in result. →

Answer: 2.5

← Decimal point

Answer: 201
Either position is correct.

Note: You may start your answers in any column, space permitting. Columns not needed should be left blank.

- Mark no more than one oval in any column.

- Because the answer sheet will be machine-scored, **you will receive credit only if the ovals are filled in correctly.**

- Although not required, it is suggested that you write your answer in the boxes at the top of the columns to help you fill in the ovals accurately.

- Some problems may have more than one correct answer. In such cases, grid only one answer.

- No question has a negative answer.

- **Mixed numbers** such as $2\frac{1}{2}$ must be gridded as 2.5 or 5/2. (If [2 1 / 2] is gridded, it will be interpreted as $\frac{21}{2}$, not $2\frac{1}{2}$.)

- **Decimal Accuracy**: If you obtain a decimal answer, **enter the most accurate value the grid will accommodate.** For example, if you obtain an answer such as 0.6666 . . . , you should record the result as .666 or .667. **Less accurate values such as .66 or .67 are not acceptable.**

Acceptable ways to grid $\frac{2}{3}$ = .6666 . . .

---

41 If $k = 2$ and $n = 10$ in the formula $k = \dfrac{3n^2}{w}$, what is the value of w?

42 The scale on a certain world map indicates that a $\frac{1}{4}$-inch line segment along the equator represents 300 miles. How many miles apart are two locations on the equator if they are $2\frac{1}{4}$ inches apart on the map?

GO ON TO THE NEXT PAGE →

43 For what integer value of x is

$$\frac{2}{x+2} + \frac{x+2}{2} = \frac{2}{7} + \frac{7}{2} ?$$

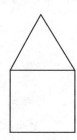

44 In the figure above, the triangle is equilateral and the area of the square is 36. What is the perimeter of the triangle?

45 Three children of different heights are to be randomly placed in a straight line. If it turns out that the tallest child is placed first in line, what is the probability that the shortest child is placed second in line?

46 Let s be the number of positive integers less than 431 that are divisible by 5, and let t be the number of positive integers less than 431 that are divisible by 30. What is the value of $s + t$?

GO ON TO THE NEXT PAGE

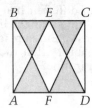

47 Square *ABCD* shown above has sides of length 5. If *E* and *F* are the midpoints of sides *BC* and *AD*, respectively, what is the total area of the shaded regions?

48 In a marching band, exactly $\frac{1}{3}$ of the musicians play trombone and, of these, $\frac{1}{6}$ also play trumpet. If at least 2 of the musicians play both instruments, what is the LEAST number of musicians that could be in the band?

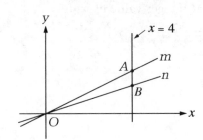

49 Points *A* and *B* lie on the line *x* = 4, as shown above. The slope of line *m* is $\frac{1}{2}$ and the slope of line *n* is $\frac{1}{3}$. If point *C* (not shown) lies on the line *x* = 4 between points *A* and *B*, what is one possible *y*-coordinate of point *C* ?

50 If the average (arithmetic mean) of *a*, *b*, and *c* is 10 and the average of *a*, *b*, and 2*c* is 14, what is the average of *a* and *b* ?

HOW TO SCORE THE PRACTICE TEST

When you take the PSAT/NMSQT, a computer performs these scoring steps for you and prints out a score report. Perform these steps now, to understand how guessing and omitting questions affect your scores. You can compare your scores on the practice test with those you earn later when you take the PSAT/NMSQT. You will probably find that your scores on the PSAT/NMSQT will not be exactly the same as your scores on the practice test. Scores vary because of slight differences between tests and the way you take tests on different occasions.

STEP 1: Correct your verbal answers

The correct answer and the difficulty level (E = easy question, M = medium question, H = hard question) for each verbal question on the practice test is given. There are boxes for your answers.

- For each question you got correct, put + in the "Your Answer" box.

- For any question you got incorrect, write the letter of the response you chose in the "Your Answer" box.

- For any question you omitted, put O in the "Your Answer" box.

- Count the number of correct (+), incorrect (A, B, C, D, E), and omitted responses. Enter the totals where indicated.

Questions 1-58   No. Correct _____   No. Incorrect _____   No. Omitted _____

STEP 2: Correct your math answers

The correct answer and the difficulty level (E = easy question, M = medium question, H = hard question) for each mathematics question on the practice test is given. There are boxes for your answers.

- For each question you got correct, put + in the "Your Answer" box.

- For any Standard Multiple-Choice question (1-25) or Quantitative Comparison question (26-40) you got incorrect, write the letter of the response you chose in the "Your Answer" box. For incorrect answers to a question that required a student-produced response (41-50), write the answer you gridded on the answer sheet in the "Your Answer" box.

- For any question you omitted, put O in the "Your Answer" box.

- Count the number of correct (+), incorrect (A, B, C, D, E, or the answer you gridded), and omitted responses. Enter the totals where indicated.

Questions 1-25 No. Correct _____   No. Incorrect _____   No. Omitted _____

Questions 26-40 No. Correct _____   No. Incorrect _____   No. Omitted _____

Questions 41-50 No. Correct _____   No. Incorrect _____   No. Omitted _____

STEP 3: Calculate your points

Verbal points—Refer to Step 1 above.

- Enter number of correct and incorrect answers to verbal questions 1-58. Divide number of incorrect answers by 4. Subtract result from the number of verbal questions answered correctly; record result (Subtotal A). Round Subtotal A; .5 or more, round up; less than .5, round down. The number you get is your total verbal points. Enter this number on line B.

Mathematics points—Refer to Step 2 above.

- Enter number of correct and incorrect answers to math questions 1-25. Divide number of incorrect answers by 4. Subtract result from the number of questions answered correctly; record result (Subtotal A).

- Enter number of correct and incorrect answers to math questions 26-40. Divide number of incorrect answers by 3. Subtract result from the number of questions answered correctly; record result (Subtotal B).

- Enter number of correct answers to math questions 41-50 (Subtotal C).

- Add Subtotals A, B, and C to get D. Round Subtotal D; .5 or more, round up; less than .5, round down. The number you get is your total mathematics points. Enter this number on line E.

Verbal

A   Questions 1-58   _____ – (_____ ÷ 4) =   _____
                       No. correct   No. incorrect   Subtotal A

B   Total rounded verbal points (Round off decimals;   _____
     .5 or more, round up; less than .5, round down.)   B

Mathematics

A   Questions 1-25   _____ – (_____ ÷ 4) =   _____
                       No. correct   No. incorrect   Subtotal A

B   Questions 26-40   _____ – (_____ ÷ 3) =   _____
                       No. correct   No. incorrect   Subtotal B

C   Questions 41-50   _____   =   _____
                       No. correct   Subtotal C

D   Total unrounded math points (A + B + C)   _____
                                                                     Subtotal D

E   Total rounded math points (Round decimals;   _____
     .5 or more, round up; less than .5, round down.)   E

Score Conversion Table
PSAT/NMSQT
Recentered Scale

<table>
<tr><td colspan="6" align="center">PSAT/NMSQT
FORM T
Tuesday, October 11, 1994</td></tr>
<tr><td></td><td colspan="2" align="center">Scores</td><td></td><td colspan="2" align="center">Scores</td></tr>
<tr><td>Points</td><td>Verbal</td><td>Math</td><td>Points</td><td>Verbal</td><td>Math</td></tr>
<tr><td>58</td><td>80</td><td></td><td>20</td><td>45</td><td>45</td></tr>
<tr><td>57</td><td>80</td><td></td><td>19</td><td>44</td><td>44</td></tr>
<tr><td>56</td><td>80</td><td></td><td>18</td><td>43</td><td>44</td></tr>
<tr><td>55</td><td>79</td><td></td><td>17</td><td>42</td><td>43</td></tr>
<tr><td>54</td><td>78</td><td></td><td>16</td><td>42</td><td>42</td></tr>
<tr><td>53</td><td>76</td><td></td><td>15</td><td>41</td><td>41</td></tr>
<tr><td>52</td><td>74</td><td></td><td>14</td><td>40</td><td>40</td></tr>
<tr><td>51</td><td>72</td><td></td><td>13</td><td>39</td><td>40</td></tr>
<tr><td>50</td><td>71</td><td>80</td><td>12</td><td>38</td><td>39</td></tr>
<tr><td>49</td><td>70</td><td>80</td><td>11</td><td>37</td><td>38</td></tr>
<tr><td>48</td><td>68</td><td>77</td><td>10</td><td>36</td><td>37</td></tr>
<tr><td>47</td><td>67</td><td>74</td><td>9</td><td>35</td><td>36</td></tr>
<tr><td>46</td><td>66</td><td>72</td><td>8</td><td>34</td><td>36</td></tr>
<tr><td>45</td><td>65</td><td>70</td><td>7</td><td>33</td><td>35</td></tr>
<tr><td>44</td><td>64</td><td>69</td><td>6</td><td>31</td><td>34</td></tr>
<tr><td>43</td><td>63</td><td>68</td><td>5</td><td>30</td><td>33</td></tr>
<tr><td>42</td><td>62</td><td>66</td><td>4</td><td>29</td><td>32</td></tr>
<tr><td>41</td><td>61</td><td>65</td><td>3</td><td>27</td><td>31</td></tr>
<tr><td>40</td><td>61</td><td>64</td><td>2</td><td>25</td><td>30</td></tr>
<tr><td>39</td><td>60</td><td>63</td><td>1</td><td>24</td><td>29</td></tr>
<tr><td>38</td><td>59</td><td>62</td><td>0</td><td>22</td><td>28</td></tr>
<tr><td>37</td><td>58</td><td>61</td><td>−1</td><td>20</td><td>26</td></tr>
<tr><td>36</td><td>57</td><td>60</td><td>−2</td><td>20</td><td>25</td></tr>
<tr><td>35</td><td>57</td><td>59</td><td>−3</td><td>20</td><td>24</td></tr>
<tr><td>34</td><td>56</td><td>58</td><td>−4</td><td>20</td><td>23</td></tr>
<tr><td>33</td><td>55</td><td>57</td><td>−5
or below</td><td>20</td><td>20</td></tr>
<tr><td>32</td><td>54</td><td>56</td><td></td><td></td><td></td></tr>
<tr><td>31</td><td>53</td><td>55</td><td></td><td></td><td></td></tr>
<tr><td>30</td><td>53</td><td>54</td><td></td><td></td><td></td></tr>
<tr><td>29</td><td>52</td><td>53</td><td></td><td></td><td></td></tr>
<tr><td>28</td><td>51</td><td>52</td><td></td><td></td><td></td></tr>
<tr><td>27</td><td>50</td><td>51</td><td></td><td></td><td></td></tr>
<tr><td>26</td><td>49</td><td>50</td><td></td><td></td><td></td></tr>
<tr><td>25</td><td>49</td><td>49</td><td></td><td></td><td></td></tr>
<tr><td>24</td><td>48</td><td>48</td><td></td><td></td><td></td></tr>
<tr><td>23</td><td>47</td><td>48</td><td></td><td></td><td></td></tr>
<tr><td>22</td><td>46</td><td>47</td><td></td><td></td><td></td></tr>
<tr><td>21</td><td>46</td><td>46</td><td></td><td></td><td></td></tr>
</table>

SAT I: Reasoning Test

SAT® I: Reasoning Test

Calculator use is permitted on the mathematics sections only.

You will have three hours to work on the questions in this test book. There are **five 30-minute sections and two 15-minute sections**. The supervisor will tell you when to begin and end each section. If you finish before time is called, you may check your work on that section, but you may <u>not work on any other section</u>.

Do not worry if you are unable to finish a section or if there are some questions you cannot answer. Do not waste time puzzling over a question that seems too difficult for you. Work as rapidly as you can without sacrificing accuracy.

Students often ask whether they should guess when they are uncertain about the answer to a question. Scores on the multiple-choice questions on this test are based on the number of questions answered correctly minus a fraction of the number answered incorrectly. Therefore, it is unlikely that random or haphazard guessing will change your scores significantly. If you have some knowledge of a question, you may be able to eliminate one or more of the answer choices as wrong. It is generally a good idea to guess which of the remaining choices is correct.

Some mathematics questions have no answer choices. Instead, you must solve the problem and record your answer in a special grid on your answer sheet. For these questions, you will receive credit for correct answers, but there will be no deduction for incorrect answers.

Mark all your answers on the separate answer sheet. Mark only one answer for each question. Since the answer sheet will be machine scored, be sure that each mark is dark and that it completely fills the oval. In each section of the answer sheet, there are spaces to answer 40 questions. When there are fewer than 40 questions in a section of your test, use only the spaces that correspond to the question numbers. Do not make stray marks on the answer sheet. If you erase, do so completely, because an incomplete erasure may be scored as an intended response.

You may use the test book for scratchwork, but you will not receive credit for anything written there.

(The passages for this test have been adapted from published material. The ideas contained in them do not necessarily represent the opinions of the College Board or Educational Testing Service.)

DO NOT OPEN THIS BOOK UNTIL THE SUPERVISOR TELLS YOU TO DO SO.

Use a No. 2 pencil only. Be sure each mark is dark and completely fills the intended oval. Completely erase any errors or stray marks.

1. Your Name

First 4 letters of Last Name | First init. | Mid. init.

(A) (B) (C) (D) (E) (F) (G) (H) (I) (J) (K) (L) (M) (N) (O) (P) (Q) (R) (S) (T) (U) (V) (W) (X) (Y) (Z)

2.

Your Name: (Print) _____ Last _____ First _____ M.I.

Signature: _____ **Date:** __/__/__

Home Address: (Print) _____ Number and Street

_____ City _____ State _____ Zip Code

Center: (Print) _____ City _____ State _____ Center Number

IMPORTANT: Please fill in items 8 and 9 exactly as shown on the back cover of your test book.

8. Form Code

(Copy and grid as on back of test book.)

(A) (B) (C) (D) (E) (F) (G) (H) (I) (J) (K) (L) (M) (N) (O) (P) (Q) (R) (S) (T) (U) (V) (W) (X) (Y) (Z)

0 1 2 3 4 5 6 7 8 9

3. Date Of Birth

Month	Day	Year
Jan. ○		
Feb. ○		
Mar. ○	0 0	0 0
Apr. ○	1 1	1 1
May ○	2 2	2 2
June ○	3 3	3 3
July ○	4 4	4 4
Aug. ○	5 5	5 5
Sept. ○	6 6	6 6
Oct. ○	7 7	7 7
Nov. ○	8 8	8 8
Dec. ○	9	9

4. Social Security Number

0 0 0 0 0 0 0 0 0
1 1 1 1 1 1 1 1 1
2 2 2 2 2 2 2 2 2
3 3 3 3 3 3 3 3 3
4 4 4 4 4 4 4 4 4
5 5 5 5 5 5 5 5 5
6 6 6 6 6 6 6 6 6
7 7 7 7 7 7 7 7 7
8 8 8 8 8 8 8 8 8
9 9 9 9 9 9 9 9 9

5. Sex

Female ○   Male ○

7. Test Book Serial Number

(Copy from front of test book.)

6. Registration Number

(Copy from your Admission Ticket.)

0 0 0 0 0 0 0
1 1 1 1 1 1 1
2 2 2 2 2 2 2
3 3 3 3 3 3 3
4 4 4 4 4 4 4
5 5 5 5 5 5 5
6 6 6 6 6 6 6
7 7 7 7 7 7 7
8 8 8 8 8 8 8
9 9 9 9 9 9 9

FOR ETS USE ONLY

9. Test Form

(Copy from back cover of test book.)

DO NOT WRITE IN THIS AREA.

Start with number 1 for each new section. If a section has fewer questions than answer spaces, leave the extra answer spaces blank.

SECTION 1

1 (A) (B) (C) (D) (E)   11 (A) (B) (C) (D) (E)   21 (A) (B) (C) (D) (E)   31 (A) (B) (C) (D) (E)
2 (A) (B) (C) (D) (E)   12 (A) (B) (C) (D) (E)   22 (A) (B) (C) (D) (E)   32 (A) (B) (C) (D) (E)
3 (A) (B) (C) (D) (E)   13 (A) (B) (C) (D) (E)   23 (A) (B) (C) (D) (E)   33 (A) (B) (C) (D) (E)
4 (A) (B) (C) (D) (E)   14 (A) (B) (C) (D) (E)   24 (A) (B) (C) (D) (E)   34 (A) (B) (C) (D) (E)
5 (A) (B) (C) (D) (E)   15 (A) (B) (C) (D) (E)   25 (A) (B) (C) (D) (E)   35 (A) (B) (C) (D) (E)
6 (A) (B) (C) (D) (E)   16 (A) (B) (C) (D) (E)   26 (A) (B) (C) (D) (E)   36 (A) (B) (C) (D) (E)
7 (A) (B) (C) (D) (E)   17 (A) (B) (C) (D) (E)   27 (A) (B) (C) (D) (E)   37 (A) (B) (C) (D) (E)
8 (A) (B) (C) (D) (E)   18 (A) (B) (C) (D) (E)   28 (A) (B) (C) (D) (E)   38 (A) (B) (C) (D) (E)
9 (A) (B) (C) (D) (E)   19 (A) (B) (C) (D) (E)   29 (A) (B) (C) (D) (E)   39 (A) (B) (C) (D) (E)
10 (A) (B) (C) (D) (E)   20 (A) (B) (C) (D) (E)   30 (A) (B) (C) (D) (E)   40 (A) (B) (C) (D) (E)

SECTION 2

1 (A) (B) (C) (D) (E)   11 (A) (B) (C) (D) (E)   21 (A) (B) (C) (D) (E)   31 (A) (B) (C) (D) (E)
2 (A) (B) (C) (D) (E)   12 (A) (B) (C) (D) (E)   22 (A) (B) (C) (D) (E)   32 (A) (B) (C) (D) (E)
3 (A) (B) (C) (D) (E)   13 (A) (B) (C) (D) (E)   23 (A) (B) (C) (D) (E)   33 (A) (B) (C) (D) (E)
4 (A) (B) (C) (D) (E)   14 (A) (B) (C) (D) (E)   24 (A) (B) (C) (D) (E)   34 (A) (B) (C) (D) (E)
5 (A) (B) (C) (D) (E)   15 (A) (B) (C) (D) (E)   25 (A) (B) (C) (D) (E)   35 (A) (B) (C) (D) (E)
6 (A) (B) (C) (D) (E)   16 (A) (B) (C) (D) (E)   26 (A) (B) (C) (D) (E)   36 (A) (B) (C) (D) (E)
7 (A) (B) (C) (D) (E)   17 (A) (B) (C) (D) (E)   27 (A) (B) (C) (D) (E)   37 (A) (B) (C) (D) (E)
8 (A) (B) (C) (D) (E)   18 (A) (B) (C) (D) (E)   28 (A) (B) (C) (D) (E)   38 (A) (B) (C) (D) (E)
9 (A) (B) (C) (D) (E)   19 (A) (B) (C) (D) (E)   29 (A) (B) (C) (D) (E)   39 (A) (B) (C) (D) (E)
10 (A) (B) (C) (D) (E)   20 (A) (B) (C) (D) (E)   30 (A) (B) (C) (D) (E)   40 (A) (B) (C) (D) (E)

261

Start with number 1 for each new section. If a section has fewer questions than answer spaces, leave the extra answer spaces blank.

SECTION 3

1 Ⓐ Ⓑ Ⓒ Ⓓ Ⓔ
2 Ⓐ Ⓑ Ⓒ Ⓓ Ⓔ
3 Ⓐ Ⓑ Ⓒ Ⓓ Ⓔ
4 Ⓐ Ⓑ Ⓒ Ⓓ Ⓔ
5 Ⓐ Ⓑ Ⓒ Ⓓ Ⓔ
6 Ⓐ Ⓑ Ⓒ Ⓓ Ⓔ
7 Ⓐ Ⓑ Ⓒ Ⓓ Ⓔ
8 Ⓐ Ⓑ Ⓒ Ⓓ Ⓔ
9 Ⓐ Ⓑ Ⓒ Ⓓ Ⓔ
10 Ⓐ Ⓑ Ⓒ Ⓓ Ⓔ
11 Ⓐ Ⓑ Ⓒ Ⓓ Ⓔ
12 Ⓐ Ⓑ Ⓒ Ⓓ Ⓔ
13 Ⓐ Ⓑ Ⓒ Ⓓ Ⓔ
14 Ⓐ Ⓑ Ⓒ Ⓓ Ⓔ
15 Ⓐ Ⓑ Ⓒ Ⓓ Ⓔ

16 Ⓐ Ⓑ Ⓒ Ⓓ Ⓔ
17 Ⓐ Ⓑ Ⓒ Ⓓ Ⓔ
18 Ⓐ Ⓑ Ⓒ Ⓓ Ⓔ
19 Ⓐ Ⓑ Ⓒ Ⓓ Ⓔ
20 Ⓐ Ⓑ Ⓒ Ⓓ Ⓔ
21 Ⓐ Ⓑ Ⓒ Ⓓ Ⓔ
22 Ⓐ Ⓑ Ⓒ Ⓓ Ⓔ
23 Ⓐ Ⓑ Ⓒ Ⓓ Ⓔ
24 Ⓐ Ⓑ Ⓒ Ⓓ Ⓔ
25 Ⓐ Ⓑ Ⓒ Ⓓ Ⓔ
26 Ⓐ Ⓑ Ⓒ Ⓓ Ⓔ
27 Ⓐ Ⓑ Ⓒ Ⓓ Ⓔ
28 Ⓐ Ⓑ Ⓒ Ⓓ Ⓔ
29 Ⓐ Ⓑ Ⓒ Ⓓ Ⓔ
30 Ⓐ Ⓑ Ⓒ Ⓓ Ⓔ

31 Ⓐ Ⓑ Ⓒ Ⓓ Ⓔ
32 Ⓐ Ⓑ Ⓒ Ⓓ Ⓔ
33 Ⓐ Ⓑ Ⓒ Ⓓ Ⓔ
34 Ⓐ Ⓑ Ⓒ Ⓓ Ⓔ
35 Ⓐ Ⓑ Ⓒ Ⓓ Ⓔ
36 Ⓐ Ⓑ Ⓒ Ⓓ Ⓔ
37 Ⓐ Ⓑ Ⓒ Ⓓ Ⓔ
38 Ⓐ Ⓑ Ⓒ Ⓓ Ⓔ
39 Ⓐ Ⓑ Ⓒ Ⓓ Ⓔ
40 Ⓐ Ⓑ Ⓒ Ⓓ Ⓔ

If section 3 of your test book contains math questions that are not multiple-choice, continue to item 16 below. Otherwise, continue to item 16 above.

ONLY ANSWERS ENTERED IN THE OVALS IN EACH GRID AREA WILL BE SCORED. YOU WILL NOT RECEIVE CREDIT FOR ANYTHING WRITTEN IN THE BOXES ABOVE THE OVALS.

16   17   18   19   20

21   22   23   24   25

BE SURE TO ERASE ANY ERRORS OR STRAY MARKS COMPLETELY.

PLEASE PRINT YOUR INITIALS

First   Middle   Last

Use a No. 2 pencil only. Be sure each mark is dark and completely fills the intended oval. Completely erase any errors or stray marks.

Start with number 1 for each new section. If a section has fewer questions than answer spaces, leave the extra answer spaces blank.

SECTION 4

1 Ⓐ Ⓑ Ⓒ Ⓓ Ⓔ
2 Ⓐ Ⓑ Ⓒ Ⓓ Ⓔ
3 Ⓐ Ⓑ Ⓒ Ⓓ Ⓔ
4 Ⓐ Ⓑ Ⓒ Ⓓ Ⓔ
5 Ⓐ Ⓑ Ⓒ Ⓓ Ⓔ
6 Ⓐ Ⓑ Ⓒ Ⓓ Ⓔ
7 Ⓐ Ⓑ Ⓒ Ⓓ Ⓔ
8 Ⓐ Ⓑ Ⓒ Ⓓ Ⓔ
9 Ⓐ Ⓑ Ⓒ Ⓓ Ⓔ
10 Ⓐ Ⓑ Ⓒ Ⓓ Ⓔ
11 Ⓐ Ⓑ Ⓒ Ⓓ Ⓔ
12 Ⓐ Ⓑ Ⓒ Ⓓ Ⓔ
13 Ⓐ Ⓑ Ⓒ Ⓓ Ⓔ
14 Ⓐ Ⓑ Ⓒ Ⓓ Ⓔ
15 Ⓐ Ⓑ Ⓒ Ⓓ Ⓔ

16 Ⓐ Ⓑ Ⓒ Ⓓ Ⓔ
17 Ⓐ Ⓑ Ⓒ Ⓓ Ⓔ
18 Ⓐ Ⓑ Ⓒ Ⓓ Ⓔ
19 Ⓐ Ⓑ Ⓒ Ⓓ Ⓔ
20 Ⓐ Ⓑ Ⓒ Ⓓ Ⓔ
21 Ⓐ Ⓑ Ⓒ Ⓓ Ⓔ
22 Ⓐ Ⓑ Ⓒ Ⓓ Ⓔ
23 Ⓐ Ⓑ Ⓒ Ⓓ Ⓔ
24 Ⓐ Ⓑ Ⓒ Ⓓ Ⓔ
25 Ⓐ Ⓑ Ⓒ Ⓓ Ⓔ
26 Ⓐ Ⓑ Ⓒ Ⓓ Ⓔ
27 Ⓐ Ⓑ Ⓒ Ⓓ Ⓔ
28 Ⓐ Ⓑ Ⓒ Ⓓ Ⓔ
29 Ⓐ Ⓑ Ⓒ Ⓓ Ⓔ
30 Ⓐ Ⓑ Ⓒ Ⓓ Ⓔ

31 Ⓐ Ⓑ Ⓒ Ⓓ Ⓔ
32 Ⓐ Ⓑ Ⓒ Ⓓ Ⓔ
33 Ⓐ Ⓑ Ⓒ Ⓓ Ⓔ
34 Ⓐ Ⓑ Ⓒ Ⓓ Ⓔ
35 Ⓐ Ⓑ Ⓒ Ⓓ Ⓔ
36 Ⓐ Ⓑ Ⓒ Ⓓ Ⓔ
37 Ⓐ Ⓑ Ⓒ Ⓓ Ⓔ
38 Ⓐ Ⓑ Ⓒ Ⓓ Ⓔ
39 Ⓐ Ⓑ Ⓒ Ⓓ Ⓔ
40 Ⓐ Ⓑ Ⓒ Ⓓ Ⓔ

If section 4 of your test book contains math questions that are not multiple-choice, continue to item 16 below. Otherwise, continue to item 16 above.

ONLY ANSWERS ENTERED IN THE OVALS IN EACH GRID AREA WILL BE SCORED.
YOU WILL NOT RECEIVE CREDIT FOR ANYTHING WRITTEN IN THE BOXES ABOVE THE OVALS.

16 17 18 19 20

21 22 23 24 25

BE SURE TO ERASE ANY ERRORS OR STRAY MARKS COMPLETELY.

PLEASE PRINT
YOUR INITIALS

First   Middle   Last

263

Use a No. 2 pencil only. Be sure each mark is dark and completely fills the intended oval. Completely erase any errors or stray marks.

Start with number 1 for each new section. If a section has fewer questions than answer spaces, leave the extra answer spaces blank.

SECTION 5

1 Ⓐ Ⓑ Ⓒ Ⓓ Ⓔ	11 Ⓐ Ⓑ Ⓒ Ⓓ Ⓔ	21 Ⓐ Ⓑ Ⓒ Ⓓ Ⓔ	31 Ⓐ Ⓑ Ⓒ Ⓓ Ⓔ
2 Ⓐ Ⓑ Ⓒ Ⓓ Ⓔ	12 Ⓐ Ⓑ Ⓒ Ⓓ Ⓔ	22 Ⓐ Ⓑ Ⓒ Ⓓ Ⓔ	32 Ⓐ Ⓑ Ⓒ Ⓓ Ⓔ
3 Ⓐ Ⓑ Ⓒ Ⓓ Ⓔ	13 Ⓐ Ⓑ Ⓒ Ⓓ Ⓔ	23 Ⓐ Ⓑ Ⓒ Ⓓ Ⓔ	33 Ⓐ Ⓑ Ⓒ Ⓓ Ⓔ
4 Ⓐ Ⓑ Ⓒ Ⓓ Ⓔ	14 Ⓐ Ⓑ Ⓒ Ⓓ Ⓔ	24 Ⓐ Ⓑ Ⓒ Ⓓ Ⓔ	34 Ⓐ Ⓑ Ⓒ Ⓓ Ⓔ
5 Ⓐ Ⓑ Ⓒ Ⓓ Ⓔ	15 Ⓐ Ⓑ Ⓒ Ⓓ Ⓔ	25 Ⓐ Ⓑ Ⓒ Ⓓ Ⓔ	35 Ⓐ Ⓑ Ⓒ Ⓓ Ⓔ
6 Ⓐ Ⓑ Ⓒ Ⓓ Ⓔ	16 Ⓐ Ⓑ Ⓒ Ⓓ Ⓔ	26 Ⓐ Ⓑ Ⓒ Ⓓ Ⓔ	36 Ⓐ Ⓑ Ⓒ Ⓓ Ⓔ
7 Ⓐ Ⓑ Ⓒ Ⓓ Ⓔ	17 Ⓐ Ⓑ Ⓒ Ⓓ Ⓔ	27 Ⓐ Ⓑ Ⓒ Ⓓ Ⓔ	37 Ⓐ Ⓑ Ⓒ Ⓓ Ⓔ
8 Ⓐ Ⓑ Ⓒ Ⓓ Ⓔ	18 Ⓐ Ⓑ Ⓒ Ⓓ Ⓔ	28 Ⓐ Ⓑ Ⓒ Ⓓ Ⓔ	38 Ⓐ Ⓑ Ⓒ Ⓓ Ⓔ
9 Ⓐ Ⓑ Ⓒ Ⓓ Ⓔ	19 Ⓐ Ⓑ Ⓒ Ⓓ Ⓔ	29 Ⓐ Ⓑ Ⓒ Ⓓ Ⓔ	39 Ⓐ Ⓑ Ⓒ Ⓓ Ⓔ
10 Ⓐ Ⓑ Ⓒ Ⓓ Ⓔ	20 Ⓐ Ⓑ Ⓒ Ⓓ Ⓔ	30 Ⓐ Ⓑ Ⓒ Ⓓ Ⓔ	40 Ⓐ Ⓑ Ⓒ Ⓓ Ⓔ

SECTION 6

1 Ⓐ Ⓑ Ⓒ Ⓓ Ⓔ	11 Ⓐ Ⓑ Ⓒ Ⓓ Ⓔ	21 Ⓐ Ⓑ Ⓒ Ⓓ Ⓔ	31 Ⓐ Ⓑ Ⓒ Ⓓ Ⓔ
2 Ⓐ Ⓑ Ⓒ Ⓓ Ⓔ	12 Ⓐ Ⓑ Ⓒ Ⓓ Ⓔ	22 Ⓐ Ⓑ Ⓒ Ⓓ Ⓔ	32 Ⓐ Ⓑ Ⓒ Ⓓ Ⓔ
3 Ⓐ Ⓑ Ⓒ Ⓓ Ⓔ	13 Ⓐ Ⓑ Ⓒ Ⓓ Ⓔ	23 Ⓐ Ⓑ Ⓒ Ⓓ Ⓔ	33 Ⓐ Ⓑ Ⓒ Ⓓ Ⓔ
4 Ⓐ Ⓑ Ⓒ Ⓓ Ⓔ	14 Ⓐ Ⓑ Ⓒ Ⓓ Ⓔ	24 Ⓐ Ⓑ Ⓒ Ⓓ Ⓔ	34 Ⓐ Ⓑ Ⓒ Ⓓ Ⓔ
5 Ⓐ Ⓑ Ⓒ Ⓓ Ⓔ	15 Ⓐ Ⓑ Ⓒ Ⓓ Ⓔ	25 Ⓐ Ⓑ Ⓒ Ⓓ Ⓔ	35 Ⓐ Ⓑ Ⓒ Ⓓ Ⓔ
6 Ⓐ Ⓑ Ⓒ Ⓓ Ⓔ	16 Ⓐ Ⓑ Ⓒ Ⓓ Ⓔ	26 Ⓐ Ⓑ Ⓒ Ⓓ Ⓔ	36 Ⓐ Ⓑ Ⓒ Ⓓ Ⓔ
7 Ⓐ Ⓑ Ⓒ Ⓓ Ⓔ	17 Ⓐ Ⓑ Ⓒ Ⓓ Ⓔ	27 Ⓐ Ⓑ Ⓒ Ⓓ Ⓔ	37 Ⓐ Ⓑ Ⓒ Ⓓ Ⓔ
8 Ⓐ Ⓑ Ⓒ Ⓓ Ⓔ	18 Ⓐ Ⓑ Ⓒ Ⓓ Ⓔ	28 Ⓐ Ⓑ Ⓒ Ⓓ Ⓔ	38 Ⓐ Ⓑ Ⓒ Ⓓ Ⓔ
9 Ⓐ Ⓑ Ⓒ Ⓓ Ⓔ	19 Ⓐ Ⓑ Ⓒ Ⓓ Ⓔ	29 Ⓐ Ⓑ Ⓒ Ⓓ Ⓔ	39 Ⓐ Ⓑ Ⓒ Ⓓ Ⓔ
10 Ⓐ Ⓑ Ⓒ Ⓓ Ⓔ	20 Ⓐ Ⓑ Ⓒ Ⓓ Ⓔ	30 Ⓐ Ⓑ Ⓒ Ⓓ Ⓔ	40 Ⓐ Ⓑ Ⓒ Ⓓ Ⓔ

SECTION 7

1 Ⓐ Ⓑ Ⓒ Ⓓ Ⓔ	11 Ⓐ Ⓑ Ⓒ Ⓓ Ⓔ	21 Ⓐ Ⓑ Ⓒ Ⓓ Ⓔ	31 Ⓐ Ⓑ Ⓒ Ⓓ Ⓔ
2 Ⓐ Ⓑ Ⓒ Ⓓ Ⓔ	12 Ⓐ Ⓑ Ⓒ Ⓓ Ⓔ	22 Ⓐ Ⓑ Ⓒ Ⓓ Ⓔ	32 Ⓐ Ⓑ Ⓒ Ⓓ Ⓔ
3 Ⓐ Ⓑ Ⓒ Ⓓ Ⓔ	13 Ⓐ Ⓑ Ⓒ Ⓓ Ⓔ	23 Ⓐ Ⓑ Ⓒ Ⓓ Ⓔ	33 Ⓐ Ⓑ Ⓒ Ⓓ Ⓔ
4 Ⓐ Ⓑ Ⓒ Ⓓ Ⓔ	14 Ⓐ Ⓑ Ⓒ Ⓓ Ⓔ	24 Ⓐ Ⓑ Ⓒ Ⓓ Ⓔ	34 Ⓐ Ⓑ Ⓒ Ⓓ Ⓔ
5 Ⓐ Ⓑ Ⓒ Ⓓ Ⓔ	15 Ⓐ Ⓑ Ⓒ Ⓓ Ⓔ	25 Ⓐ Ⓑ Ⓒ Ⓓ Ⓔ	35 Ⓐ Ⓑ Ⓒ Ⓓ Ⓔ
6 Ⓐ Ⓑ Ⓒ Ⓓ Ⓔ	16 Ⓐ Ⓑ Ⓒ Ⓓ Ⓔ	26 Ⓐ Ⓑ Ⓒ Ⓓ Ⓔ	36 Ⓐ Ⓑ Ⓒ Ⓓ Ⓔ
7 Ⓐ Ⓑ Ⓒ Ⓓ Ⓔ	17 Ⓐ Ⓑ Ⓒ Ⓓ Ⓔ	27 Ⓐ Ⓑ Ⓒ Ⓓ Ⓔ	37 Ⓐ Ⓑ Ⓒ Ⓓ Ⓔ
8 Ⓐ Ⓑ Ⓒ Ⓓ Ⓔ	18 Ⓐ Ⓑ Ⓒ Ⓓ Ⓔ	28 Ⓐ Ⓑ Ⓒ Ⓓ Ⓔ	38 Ⓐ Ⓑ Ⓒ Ⓓ Ⓔ
9 Ⓐ Ⓑ Ⓒ Ⓓ Ⓔ	19 Ⓐ Ⓑ Ⓒ Ⓓ Ⓔ	29 Ⓐ Ⓑ Ⓒ Ⓓ Ⓔ	39 Ⓐ Ⓑ Ⓒ Ⓓ Ⓔ
10 Ⓐ Ⓑ Ⓒ Ⓓ Ⓔ	20 Ⓐ Ⓑ Ⓒ Ⓓ Ⓔ	30 Ⓐ Ⓑ Ⓒ Ⓓ Ⓔ	40 Ⓐ Ⓑ Ⓒ Ⓓ Ⓔ

CERTIFICATION STATEMENT

Copy in longhand the statement below and sign your name as you would an official document. **DO NOT PRINT.**

I hereby agree to the conditions set forth in the *Registration Bulletin* and certify that I am the person whose name and address appear on this answer sheet.

_____

_____

_____

SIGNATURE: _____ DATE: _____

Time-30 Minutes — For each question in this section, select the best answer from among the choices given and
30 Questions   fill in the corresponding oval on the answer sheet.

Each sentence below has one or two blanks, each
blank indicating that something has been omitted.
Beneath the sentence are five lettered words or
sets of words labeled A through E. Choose the
word or set of words that, when inserted in the
sentence, <u>best</u> fits the meaning of the sentence as
a whole.

Example:

Medieval kingdoms did not become
constitutional republics overnight; on the
contrary, the change was ----.

(A) unpopular
(B) unexpected
(C) advantageous
(D) sufficient
(E) gradual

1 When Harvard astronomer Cecilia Payne was ----
professor in 1956, it marked an important step in
the reduction of ---- practices within the scientific
establishment.

(A) accepted for..disciplinary
(B) promoted to..discriminatory
(C) honored as..unbiased
(D) denounced as..critical
(E) considered for..hierarchical

2 Like a parasitic organism, the most detested
character in the play depended on others for ----
and ---- nothing.

(A) ideas..required
(B) diversion..spared
(C) assistance..destroyed
(D) survival..consumed
(E) sustenance..returned

3 Although refuse and ashes may seem ---- to some
individuals, archaeologists can use such materials
to draw conclusions about the daily lives of
ancient people.

(A) undetectable
(B) fabricated
(C) insignificant
(D) historical
(E) abundant

4 Ryan was neither brusque nor cunning but was
as ---- and as ---- a man as I have ever met.

(A) cordial..arrogant
(B) gentle..candid
(C) suave..wily
(D) insolent..tolerant
(E) treacherous..straightforward

5 The reporters' behavior was certainly ----, but they
believed that such infringement on personal
privacy was necessary to their work.

(A) dependable
(B) inconsequential
(C) predestined
(D) scintillating
(E) invasive

6 During the Middle Ages, plague and other ----
decimated the populations of entire towns.

(A) pestilences
(B) immunizations
(C) proclivities
(D) indispositions
(E) demises

7 Unlike most of their solitary relatives, arctic hares
are ----, clumping into herds that can include as
many as several thousand individuals.

(A) reserved
(B) cantankerous
(C) exclusive
(D) meritorious
(E) gregarious

8 Carolyn Bennett, a maker of kaleidoscopes,
attributes the current ---- of intact nineteenth-
century kaleidoscopes to the normal human desire
to ---- a mysterious object in order to discover how
it works.

(A) complexity..study
(B) uniqueness..acquire
(C) exorbitance..distribute
(D) paucity..disassemble
(E) fragility..discontinue

9 By nature he was ----, usually confining his
remarks to ---- expression.

(A) acerbic..friendly
(B) laconic..concise
(C) garrulous..voluminous
(D) shrill..complimentary
(E) vague..emphatic

GO ON TO THE NEXT PAGE

Each question below consists of a related pair of words or phrases, followed by five pairs of words or phrases labeled A through E. Select the pair that best expresses a relationship similar to that expressed in the original pair.

Example:

CRUMB:BREAD::
(A) ounce:unit
(B) splinter:wood
(C) water:bucket
(D) twine:rope
(E) cream:butter

10 LUMBERYARD:LUMBER::

(A) supermarket:food
(B) jungle:vines
(C) drugstore:druggist
(D) wood:plank
(E) bakery:ovens

11 UNBUCKLE:BELT::

(A) unravel:yarn
(B) unlock:key
(C) unfold:napkin
(D) undress:coat
(E) untie:shoelace

12 PSEUDONYM:WRITER::

(A) alias:criminal
(B) alibi:defendant
(C) rank:officer
(D) disclaimer:producer
(E) dissertation:scholar

13 OFFICIATE:GAME::

(A) review:movie
(B) compete:contest
(C) preside:convention
(D) adjourn:meeting
(E) participate:rally

14 RIFT:ROCK::

(A) gale:wind
(B) constellation:star
(C) fracture:bone
(D) rust:iron
(E) tremor:earthquake

15 EXPOSITION:CLARIFY::

(A) rebuttal:humiliate
(B) refutation:disprove
(C) illumination:darken
(D) allegation:verify
(E) summary:end

GO ON TO THE NEXT PAGE

Each passage below is followed by questions based on its content. Answer the questions following each passage on the basis of what is <u>stated</u> or <u>implied</u> in that passage and in any introductory material that may be provided.

Questions 16-21 are based on the following passage.

The following passage is an adaptation of an excerpt from a memoir written by Elizabeth Bishop about the poet Marianne Moore. Bishop herself became a well-known poet.

I became a devoted reader of Marianne Moore's poetry while attending college in the early 1930's. A school friend and her mother, both better read and more
Line sophisticated in their literary tastes than I was, were the
(5) first to mention her poetry, and soon I had read every poem of Moore's I could find.

I had not known poetry could be like that: her treatment of topics as diverse as glaciers and marriage struck me, as it still does, as a miracle of language and
(10) construction. Why had no one ever written about these things in this clear and dazzling way before?

As luck had it, when I first began searching for a copy of her volume entitled *Observations*, I found that the college library didn't own one. Eventually, though, I did
(15) borrow a copy, but from one of the librarians, Fanny Borden, not from the library. And I received an invitation to meet Marianne Moore in the process.

In retrospect, Fanny Borden seems like a most appropriate person to have suggested I might meet
(20) Marianne Moore. Borden was extremely shy and reserved and spoke in such a soft voice it was hard to hear her at all. The campus rumor was that her personality had been permanently subdued by her family history: the notorious Lizzie Borden* of Fall River was
(25) her aunt.

Contact with Fanny Borden was rare. Occasionally, in search of a book, students would be sent to her office, shadowy and cavelike, with books piled everywhere. She weighed down the papers on her desk with smooth,
(30) round stones, quite big stones, brought from the seashore. My roommate once commented on one in particular, and Borden responded in her almost inaudible voice, "Do you like it? You may <u>have</u> it," and handed it over.

*Lizzie Borden, the defendant in a highly publicized trial, was accused of murdering her parents.

(35) One day I was sent to her office about a book. During our talk, I finally got up my courage to ask her why there was not a copy of *Observations* by that wonderful poet Marianne Moore in the library. She looked ever so gently taken aback and inquired, "Do you <u>like</u>
(40) Marianne Moore's poems?" I said I certainly did, the few I had been able to find. She then said calmly, "I've known her since she was a girl," and followed that with the question that was possibly to influence the whole course of my life: "Would you like to meet her?"
(45) I was painfully—no, excruciatingly—shy and I had run away many times rather than face being introduced to adults of much less distinction than Marianne Moore. Yet I immediately said, "Yes."

16 To the author, Marianne Moore's poetry was

(A) reminiscent of poems by other great poets
(B) subtly satirical
(C) too scholarly for most readers
(D) inspiring and well crafted
(E) difficult but rewarding

17 The major purpose of the passage is to

(A) describe the events that led to a milestone in the author's life
(B) reveal the character of a college librarian
(C) relate the significant events of the author's college years
(D) analyze the impact of Marianne Moore's poetry on the author
(E) show the unexpected surprises that can happen in an ordinary life

GO ON TO THE NEXT PAGE

18 The reference to Lizzie Borden in line 24 provides all of the following EXCEPT

(A) one possible reason for the librarian's unusually quiet manner
(B) a piece of information about the librarian's family history
(C) a suggestion that the librarian might be deliberately hiding her true nature
(D) an indication that the students were curious about the shy librarian
(E) a fact that might be interesting to some readers

19 By mentioning the extent of her shyness (lines 45-48), the author primarily emphasizes

(A) her reasons for not asking Borden to introduce her to Marianne Moore
(B) her awareness of her own weakness
(C) how important meeting Marianne Moore was to her
(D) how hard it was for her to talk to people, even Borden
(E) how different her encounter with Borden was from her roommate's

20 The author most likely remembers Fanny Borden primarily with feelings of

(A) regret
(B) curiosity
(C) amusement
(D) gratitude
(E) loyalty

21 The passage suggests that the author's interest in meeting Marianne Moore was

(A) ultimately secondary to her interest in locating a copy of *Observations*
(B) prompted by a desire to have the poet explain a difficult poem
(C) motivated by the idea of writing a biography of the poet
(D) a secret dream she had cherished for many years
(E) sufficiently strong to make her behave uncharacteristically

GO ON TO THE NEXT PAGE

Questions 22-30 are based on the following passage.

There has been a great deal of scientific debate about the nature of the object that exploded above Tunguska in 1908. The following passage presents one theory of what happened.

opinion

The thought came and went in a flash: there was not a chance in a billion years that an extraterrestrial object as large as Halley's comet would hit the Earth. But that
Line was 15 years ago, when I had little appreciation of
(5) geological time. I did not consider then the adage that anything that can happen does happen—given the time. My intuition was right—there is not a chance in a billion years for a big hit—but there have been more than 4 billion years of Earth history. Smaller collisions
(10) have happened frequently, as evidenced by many ancient impact craters. Even during the brief period of human history, there was a very real event at Tunguska.

Tunguska was a quiet hamlet in central Siberia. At
(15) 7:00 a.m. on June 30, 1908, a fireball appeared above the horizon to the southeast. More luminous than the rising Sun, the bright light streaked across the cloudless sky and exploded somewhere to the northwest. The scale of the explosion was unprecedented in recorded
(20) history. When seismographers consulted their instruments and calculated the energy that had been released, they were stunned. In today's terms the explosion had the force of a 10-megaton nuclear detonation.

(25) The brilliant object had been seen for hundreds of kilometers around, and the explosion was heard as far away as 1,000 kilometers.* The shock wave of wind circled the globe twice, and the ejecta from the explosion glowed over Northern Europe through the
(30) next two nights. Vast amounts of fire debris arrived at California two weeks later, noticeably depressing the transparency of the atmosphere over the state.

Fortunately, the object had exploded at a height of 8.5 kilometers above the ground, and the fall region was
(35) very sparsely populated. Hunters who were first to enter the disaster area reported that the whole forest had been flattened and gave accounts of wild forest fires. Systematic investigations did not begin until two decades later. The first team of experts visited the target
(40) area in 1927. They endured hardship to penetrate the devastated forest with horse-drawn wagons to investigate the aftereffect of the blast. Their mapping showed that trees within a radius of 30 to 40 kilometers had been uprooted and blown radially outward from the center of
(45) the blast. Within the blast zone, an area of 2,000 square kilometers had been ravaged by fire.

One kilometer is equal to 0.62 miles. One thousand kilometers equals 620 miles.

Study of the Tunguska site resumed after the Second World War and is still continuing. Although no meteorites have ever been found, soil samples from
(50) Tunguska contain small spherical objects similar to tektites, black glassy objects commonly believed to result from the impact of a meteorite. The material of which tektites are usually composed is only slightly contaminated by extraterrestrial substances from the meteorite
(55) itself. The spherical objects found at Tunguska have been compared to small tektites, or microtektites, which are commonly a fraction of a millimeter in diameter, but the chemical composition of the Tunguska objects resembles cosmic dust. Apparently they were not ejecta thrown
(60) out of an impact crater, but were derived directly from the explosion above the Earth, and descended as extraterrestrial fallout.

What was it that exploded on that sunny morning over Siberia? Astronomers have conjured everything from
(65) black holes to balls of antimatter, but dramatic as the Tunguska event was, it does not seem to require an exotic explanation. The more likely interpretation is conventional: the object was a large meteor.

22 In line 1, the statement "The thought came and went in a flash" refers to the idea that

(A) intuition is important in scientific research
(B) the Earth is immensely old
(C) the speed of Halley's comet is difficult to calculate
(D) the Tunguska event had an extraterrestrial origin
(E) the Earth could experience a collision with a large comet

23 In line 4, the word "appreciation" most nearly means

(A) increase in value
(B) artistic interest
(C) understanding
(D) curiosity
(E) gratitude

GO ON TO THE NEXT PAGE

24 In the third paragraph, the author mentions Northern Europe and California in order to emphasize which point about the Tunguska event?

(A) Although the explosion was locally destructive, the remainder of the world escaped harm.

(B) The magnitude of the explosion was so great that its effects were observable over much of the Northern Hemisphere.

(C) Although the explosion occurred in a remote area, more densely populated areas were also devastated.

(D) No part of the Earth can consider itself secure from the possibility of such an explosion.

(E) The explosion took place in the atmosphere rather than on the ground.

25 The word "depressing" in line 31 most nearly means

(A) reducing
(B) saddening
(C) indenting
(D) constraining
(E) probing

26 Which is most similar to the design of the fallen trees indicated in the 1927 "mapping" mentioned in line 42 ?

(A) The gridlike pattern of a checkerboard
(B) The spokes of a wheel
(C) The parallel lanes of a highway
(D) The spiral of a whirlpool
(E) The steps in a staircase

27 The author uses the evidence of tektite-like objects in the soil (lines 48-62) to establish that

(A) the Tunguska tektites were uncontaminated by extraterrestrial substances

(B) Tunguska had been the site of an earlier meteorite collision

(C) it was an extraterrestrial object that exploded above Tunguska

(D) normal tektites became deformed as a result of the impact of the Tunguska meteorite

(E) the effects of the Tunguska event were widespread

28 The author's conclusion at the end of the passage would be most directly supported by additional information concerning

(A) what quantity of cosmic dust routinely enters the Earth's atmosphere

(B) how an exploding meteor could generate conventional tektites

(C) why experts did not visit the forest until nineteen years after the explosion

(D) where and when the effect of the blast first registered on a seismograph

(E) why a large meteor would explode in the Earth's atmosphere rather than strike the Earth's surface

29 The author uses the example of the Tunguska event primarily to illustrate the

(A) origin and significance of tektites

(B) devastation caused when a meteorite strikes the surface of the Earth

(C) difference between collisions involving comets and those involving meteorites

(D) potential of the Earth's being struck by large extraterrestrial objects

(E) range of scientific theories advanced to explain an uncommon event

30 In maintaining that the Tunguska event was caused by a meteor, the author has assumed all of the following EXCEPT:

(A) The explosion was so destructive that only tiny fragments of the meteor survived.

(B) The altitude of the explosion accounts for the absence of a crater on the ground.

(C) The tektites found in the soil at Tunguska were formed by the 1908 event and not by an earlier event.

(D) The meteor that exploded near Tunguska is the largest one to have come close to the Earth.

(E) The Earth can be involved in collisions with a variety of cosmic objects.

IF YOU FINISH BEFORE TIME IS CALLED, YOU MAY CHECK YOUR WORK ON THIS SECTION ONLY. DO NOT TURN TO ANY OTHER SECTION IN THE TEST.

STOP

Reference Information

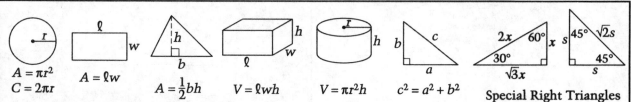

$A = \pi r^2$
$C = 2\pi r$

$A = \ell w$

$A = \frac{1}{2}bh$

$V = \ell wh$

$V = \pi r^2 h$

$c^2 = a^2 + b^2$

Special Right Triangles

The number of degrees of arc in a circle is 360.
The measure in degrees of a straight angle is 180.
The sum of the measures in degrees of the angles of a triangle is 180.

1 Which of the following integers is a divisor of both 36 and 90?

(A) 12
(B) 10
(C) 8
(D) 6
(E) 4

2 Point B is between points A and C on a line. If $AB = 2$ and $BC = 7$, then $AC =$

(A) 2
(B) 3
(C) 5
(D) 7
(E) 9

GO ON TO THE NEXT PAGE

When 3 times a number n is added to 7, the result is 22.

3 Which of the following equations represents the statement above?

(A) $3 + n + 7 = 22$
(B) $n + (3 \times 7) = 22$
(C) $3(n + 7) = 22$
(D) $3 + 7n = 22$
(E) $3n + 7 = 22$

4 If $(y + 2)^2 = (y - 2)^2$, what is the value of y?

(A) 0
(B) 1
(C) 2
(D) 4
(E) 6

5 The sales tax on a \$6.00 meal is \$0.36. At this rate what would be the tax on a \$14.00 meal?

(A) \$0.48
(B) \$0.72
(C) \$0.84
(D) \$0.90
(E) \$0.96

6 Apples are distributed, one at a time, into six baskets. The 1st apple goes into basket one, the 2nd into basket two, the 3rd into basket three, and so on until each basket has one apple. If this pattern is repeated, beginning each time with basket one, into which basket will the 74th apple be placed?

(A) Basket two
(B) Basket three
(C) Basket four
(D) Basket five
(E) Basket six

GO ON TO THE NEXT PAGE

7 If $4(x - 1) - 3x = 12$, then $x =$

(A) 4
(B) 8
(C) 11
(D) 13
(E) 16

9 25 percent of 16 is equivalent to $\frac{1}{2}$ of what number?

(A) 2
(B) 4
(C) 8
(D) 16
(E) 32

$$3, 6, 9, 12, \ldots$$

8 In the sequence above, each term after the first is 3 greater than the preceding term. Which of the following could NOT be a term in the sequence?

(A) 333
(B) 270
(C) 262
(D) 240
(E) 225

10 A car averages 20 miles per gallon of gas in city driving and 30 miles per gallon in highway driving. At these rates, how many gallons of gas will the car use on a 300-mile trip if $\frac{4}{5}$ of the trip is highway driving and the rest is city driving?

(A) 5
(B) 11
(C) 14
(D) 20
(E) 25

GO ON TO THE NEXT PAGE

$$x + 5$$

$$x - 5 \boxed{}$$

11 For which of the following values of x does the rectangle above have an area of 75?

(A) 5
(B) 10
(C) 15
(D) 20
(E) 25

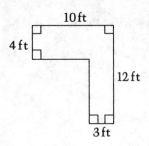

13 What is the perimeter, in feet, of the figure above?

(A) 38
(B) 41
(C) 44
(D) 46
(E) 48

12 To deliver a package, a delivery service charges $0.75 for the first pound, $0.50 per pound or part thereof for the next 5 pounds, and $0.25 per pound or part thereof for each additional pound. If the charge for delivering a package is $4.50, which of the following could be the weight, in pounds, of the package?

(A) 9

(B) 10

(C) $10\frac{1}{2}$

(D) 13

(E) $17\frac{1}{2}$

14 If the product of three consecutive integers written in increasing order equals the middle integer, what is the <u>least</u> of the three integers?

(A)   2
(B)   1
(C)   0
(D) −1
(E) −2

GO ON TO THE NEXT PAGE

15 For all integers x, let

$\boxed{x} = x^2$ when x is an even integer, and

$\boxed{x} = x^2 - 1$ when x is an odd integer.

What is the value of $\boxed{5} - \boxed{4}$?

(A) 10
(B) 9
(C) 8
(D) 1
(E) 0

16 Which of the following is equal to $\dfrac{100 + n}{25}$?

(A) $\dfrac{4 + n}{5}$

(B) $\dfrac{20 + n}{5}$

(C) $4n$

(D) $4 + n$

(E) $4 + \dfrac{n}{25}$

17 Luis earns w dollars an hour for $3x$ hours and then earns y dollars an hour for x more hours. In terms of w, x, and y, how many dollars did he earn altogether?

(A) $x(3w + y)$
(B) $x(w + 3y)$
(C) $4x(3w + y)$
(D) $4x(w + y)$
(E) $4x(w + 3y)$

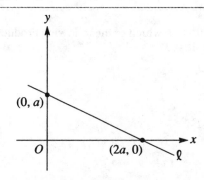

18 In the figure above, what is the slope of line ℓ?

(A) -2

(B) $-\dfrac{1}{2}$

(C) 0

(D) $\dfrac{1}{2}$

(E) 2

GO ON TO THE NEXT PAGE

19 A diagonal of a rectangle forms an angle of measure 60° with each of the two shorter sides of the rectangle. If the length of a shorter side of the rectangle is 2, what is the length of the diagonal?

(A) $2\sqrt{2}$
(B) $2\sqrt{3}$
(C) 3
(D) 4
(E) 5

21 There are 20 students in a class. For a given year, which of the following statements must be true?

I. At least two of these students have their birthdays on a Sunday.
II. At least two of these students have their birthdays on the same day of the week.
III. At least two of these students have their birthdays in the same month.

(A) I only
(B) III only
(C) I and II only
(D) II and III only
(E) I, II, and III

20 If $st^3u^4 > 0$, which of the following products must be positive?

(A) st
(B) su
(C) tu
(D) stu
(E) st^2

$$P = \left(1-\frac{1}{2}\right)\left(1-\frac{1}{3}\right)\left(1-\frac{1}{4}\right)\ldots\left(1-\frac{1}{16}\right)$$

22 The three dots in the product above represent eleven missing factors of the form $\left(1-\frac{1}{n}\right)$, where n represents all of the consecutive integers from 5 to 15, inclusive. Which of the following is equal to P?

(A) $\frac{1}{16}$

(B) $\frac{1}{2}$

(C) $\frac{3}{4}$

(D) $\frac{7}{8}$

(E) $\frac{15}{16}$

GO ON TO THE NEXT PAGE

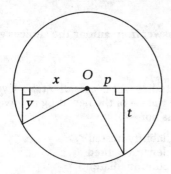

23 In the circle with center O above, the two triangles have legs of lengths x, y, p, and t, as shown. If $x^2 + y^2 + p^2 + t^2 = 72$, what is the circumference of the circle?

(A) 8π
(B) 9π
(C) 12π
(D) 24π
(E) 36π

24 A chemist has a solution consisting of 6 ounces of propanol and 18 ounces of water. She wants to change the solution to 40 percent propanol by adding x ounces of propanol. Which of the following equations could she solve in order to determine the value of x?

(A) $\dfrac{6}{18 + x} = \dfrac{40}{100}$

(B) $\dfrac{6 + x}{18} = \dfrac{40}{100}$

(C) $\dfrac{6 + x}{24} = \dfrac{40}{100}$

(D) $\dfrac{6 + x}{18 + x} = \dfrac{40}{100}$

(E) $\dfrac{6 + x}{24 + x} = \dfrac{40}{100}$

25 Which of the following could be the exact value of n^4, where n is an integer?

(A) 1.6×10^{20}
(B) 1.6×10^{21}
(C) 1.6×10^{22}
(D) 1.6×10^{23}
(E) 1.6×10^{24}

IF YOU FINISH BEFORE TIME IS CALLED, YOU MAY CHECK YOUR WORK ON THIS SECTION ONLY. DO NOT TURN TO ANY OTHER SECTION IN THE TEST.

STOP

Time-30 Minutes — For each question in this section, select the best answer from among the choices given and
35 Questions   fill in the corresponding oval on the answer sheet.

Each sentence below has one or two blanks, each
blank indicating that something has been omitted.
Beneath the sentence are five words or sets of
words labeled A through E. Choose the word or
set of words that, when inserted in the sentence,
best fits the meaning of the sentence as a whole.

Example:

Medieval kingdoms did not become
constitutional republics overnight; on the
contrary, the change was ----.

(A) unpopular
(B) unexpected
(C) advantageous
(D) sufficient
(E) gradual

1   Tarantulas apparently have little sense of ----, for a
hungry one will ignore a loudly chirping cricket
placed in its cage unless the cricket happens to get
in its way.

(A) touch
(B) time
(C) hearing
(D) self-preservation
(E) temperature

2   Though she claimed to be portraying the human
figure, her paintings were entirely ----,
characterized by simple geometric shapes.

(A) lifelike
(B) emotional
(C) naturalistic
(D) formless
(E) abstract

3   Dr. Estella Jiménez believed that the experimental
therapy would create new problems, some of them
predictable but others totally ----.

(A) benign
(B) ineffective
(C) suggestive
(D) unexpected
(E) formal

4   Even more ---- in gesture than in words, the
characters in the movie achieve their greatest ----
in pure silence.

(A) awkward..success
(B) expressive..eloquence
(C) trite..originality
(D) incompetent..performance
(E) skilled..repose

5   These studies will necessarily take several years
because the ---- of the new drug involved in the
project is not ----.

(A) availability..tested
(B) virulence..doubted
(C) effect..immediate
(D) background..practical
(E) value..expendable

6   Although he was ---- by nature, he had to be ---- at
work because of the need to slash costs.

(A) prudent..profligate
(B) ferocious..indefensible
(C) industrious..productive
(D) extravagant..parsimonious
(E) pleasant..amiable

7   Like a martinet, Charles deals with all people in
---- manner that implies they must ---- him.

(A) a haughty..thwart
(B) an imperious..obey
(C) an egalitarian..salute
(D) a timorous..cheat
(E) a cowardly..understand

8   Because of their ---- to expand their share of the
credit card market, banks may be ---- credit to
customers who are poor risks.

(A) reluctance..increasing
(B) rush..decreasing
(C) inability..denying
(D) mandate..limiting
(E) eagerness..extending

9   The Roman soldiers who invaded Britain had little
respect for the Britons, usually referring to them in
---- terms.

(A) pejorative
(B) hypocritical
(C) impressive
(D) irrational
(E) ambiguous

10 Many contemporary novelists have forsaken a
traditional intricacy of plot and detailed depiction
of character for a distinctly ---- presentation of
both.

(A) convoluted
(B) derivative
(C) conventional
(D) conservative
(E) unadorned

GO ON TO THE NEXT PAGE

Each question below consists of a related pair of words or phrases, followed by five pairs of words or phrases labeled A through E. Select the pair that best expresses a relationship similar to that expressed in the original pair.

Example:

CRUMB:BREAD::
(A) ounce:unit
(B) splinter:wood
(C) water:bucket
(D) twine:rope
(E) cream:butter

11 TIPTOE:STEP::

(A) pant:breathe
(B) smooth:wrinkle
(C) whisper:speak
(D) startle:frighten
(E) tickle:giggle

12 MARBLE:STONE::

(A) sand:cement
(B) gold:mine
(C) spoke:wheel
(D) copper:metal
(E) cloud:sky

13 FACTORY:MANUFACTURE::

(A) bookshop:read
(B) office:employ
(C) store:sell
(D) hospital:operate
(E) prison:escape

14 SHOULDER:ROAD::

(A) pane:window
(B) cup:bottle
(C) grain:leather
(D) driveway:garage
(E) margin:page

15 PACT:NATIONS::

(A) compromise:extremes
(B) certificate:qualifications
(C) treaty:hostilities
(D) border:municipalities
(E) contract:parties

16 SECEDE:ORGANIZATION::

(A) promote:job
(B) retreat:position
(C) retire:leisure
(D) bankrupt:wealth
(E) ally:country

17 ASYLUM:PERSECUTION::

(A) building:vandalism
(B) tomb:coffin
(C) refuge:safety
(D) infirmary:diagnosis
(E) shelter:storm

18 NOVICE:SEASONED::

(A) censor:offensive
(B) confidant:trustworthy
(C) ingrate:thankful
(D) tyrant:oppressed
(E) novelist:fictional

19 PARODY:IMITATION::

(A) farce:laughter
(B) caricature:likeness
(C) mask:disguise
(D) deviation:similarity
(E) gem:embellishment

20 MITIGATE:SEVERITY::

(A) weigh:measurement
(B) dissolve:solvent
(C) sterilize:heat
(D) stabilize:fluctuation
(E) examine:outcome

21 CONTROVERSY:DISPUTANT::

(A) stubbornness:pugilist
(B) antagonism:pacifist
(C) imperfection:purist
(D) meditation:hypnotist
(E) indoctrination:propagandist

22 CAREFUL:FASTIDIOUS::

(A) disobedient:mutinous
(B) patronizing:flattering
(C) religious:sacred
(D) mellow:harmonious
(E) fragrant:blooming

23 REPUGNANT:AVERSION::

(A) insatiable:satisfaction
(B) informed:knowledge
(C) bigoted:judgment
(D) shameless:regret
(E) admirable:esteem

GO ON TO THE NEXT PAGE

The passage below is followed by questions based on its content. Answer the questions on the basis of what is stated or implied in the passage and in any introductory material that may be provided.

Questions 24-35 are based on the following passage.

In this passage about language, the author, a Japanese American, recounts an experience he had just after the United States entered the Second World War. In the Midwest, where he lived and taught, hostility toward Japanese Americans at that time was not so severe as it was on the West Coast.

Although language is used to transmit information, the informative functions of language are fused with older and deeper functions so that only a small portion of our everyday utterances can be described as purely
(5) informative. The ability to use language for strictly informative purposes was probably developed relatively late in the course of linguistic evolution. Long before that time, our ancestral species probably made the sorts of cries animals do to express feelings of hunger, fear,
(10) loneliness, and the like. Gradually these noises seem to have become more differentiated, transforming grunts and gibberings into language as we know it today.

Although we have developed language in which accurate reports may be given, we still use language as
(15) vocal equivalents of gestures such as crying in pain or baring the teeth in anger. When words are used as the vocal equivalent of expressive gestures, language is functioning in presymbolic ways. These presymbolic uses of language coexist with our symbolic system, so
(20) that the talking we do in everyday life is a thorough blending of symbolic and presymbolic language.

What we call social conversation is mainly presymbolic in character. When we are at a large social gathering, for example, we all have to talk. It is typical
(25) of these conversations that, except among very good friends, few of the remarks made have any informative value. We talk together about nothing at all and thereby establish rapport.

There is a principle at work in the selection of the
(30) subject matter we deem appropriate for social conversation. Since the purpose of this kind of talk is the establishment of communion, *we are careful to select subjects about which agreement is immediately possible.* Having agreed on the weather, we go on to further
(35) agreements—that the rate of inflation is scandalous, that New York City is an interesting place to visit but that it would be an awful place to live, and so on. With each new agreement, no matter how commonplace, the fear and suspicion of the stranger wears away, and the
(40) possibility of friendship emerges. When further conversation reveals that we have friends or political views or artistic values or hobbies in common, a friend is made, and genuine communication and cooperation can begin.

(45) An incident in my own experience illustrates these points. Early in 1942, a few weeks after war was declared between Japan and the United States and at a time when rumors of Japanese spies were still widely current, I had to wait two or three hours in a small
(50) railroad station in a city in the Midwest. I became aware as time went on that the other people waiting in the station were staring at me suspiciously and feeling uneasy about my presence. One couple with a small child was staring with special uneasiness and whispering to
(55) each other. I therefore took occasion to remark to the husband that it was too bad that the train should be late on so cold a night. He agreed. I went on to remark that it must be especially difficult to travel with a small child in winter when train schedules were so uncertain. Again
(60) the husband agreed. I then asked the child's age and remarked that the child looked very big and strong for his age. Again agreement—this time with a slight smile. The tension was relaxing.

After two or three more exchanges, the man asked, "I
(65) hope you don't mind my asking, but you're Japanese, aren't you? Do you think the Japanese have any chance of winning this war?"

"Well," I replied, "your guess is as good as mine. I don't know any more than I read in the papers. [This
(70) was true.] But I don't see how the Japanese with their lack of coal and steel and oil and their limited industrial capacity, can ever beat a powerful industrialized nation like the United States."

My remark was admittedly neither original nor well
(75) informed. Hundreds of radio commentators and editorial writers were saying exactly the same thing during those weeks. But because they were, the remark *sounded familiar* and was *on the right side*, so that it was easy to agree with. The man agreed at once, with what sounded
(80) like genuine relief. How much the wall of suspicion had broken down was indicated in his next question, "Say, I hope your folks aren't over there while the war is going on?"

"Yes, they are. My father and mother and two
(85) younger sisters are over there."

"Do you ever hear from them?"

"How can I?"

"Do you mean you won't be able to see them or hear from them until after the war is over?" Both he and his
(90) wife looked sympathetic.

There was more to the conversation, but the result was that within ten minutes after it had begun they had invited me to visit them in their city. The other people in the station ceased paying any attention to me and
(95) went back to staring at the ceiling.

GO ON TO THE NEXT PAGE

24 The phrase "older and deeper functions" (line 3) refers to the

(A) grammatical structure of language
(B) expression of emotions through sound
(C) transmission of information
(D) statement of cultural values
(E) original meanings of words

25 The word "differentiated" is used in line 11 to mean

(A) changeable
(B) fused
(C) defined
(D) functional
(E) communicative

26 The author uses the term "presymbolic language" to mean

(A) grunts and cries such as are made by animals
(B) language used between friends
(C) language that lacks an elaborate grammatical structure
(D) nonverbal expressions used in communicating
(E) language that does not convey specific information

27 The primary value of presymbolic language for humans is that it

(A) is easily understood
(B) is common to all languages rather than unique to any one language
(C) permits and aids the smooth functioning of interpersonal relationships
(D) helps us understand and express our emotions
(E) allows for a desirable amount of social mobility

28 Judging from the author's discussion in lines 29-44, the most important function of social conversation is to

(A) dispel suspicion among strangers
(B) discover topics that are interesting to debate
(C) impress others by expressing clever opinions
(D) perfect the use of effective gestures and facial expressions
(E) involve a large number of people in a conversation

29 Which of the following best captures the meaning of the word "communion" in line 32?

(A) Ritual
(B) Initiation
(C) Conversation
(D) Common ground
(E) Social group

30 The comment that New York City "would be an awful place to live" (line 37) is offered by the author as an example of the kind of statement that

(A) might lead to genuine communication
(B) will amuse the reader
(C) shows the author's distrust of New Yorkers
(D) is generally ignored
(E) expresses a basic emotion

31 The most crucial difference between presymbolic and symbolic language lies in the

(A) diversity of topics that can be discussed in each mode
(B) origin and developmental path of each mode in linguistic evolution
(C) degree to which each mode may be accompanied by expressive gestures
(D) purposes served by each mode
(E) clarity each mode makes possible

GO ON TO THE NEXT PAGE

32 The author's remark about Japan's industrial capacity (lines 71-72) helped to relieve the tension because

(A) it showed how much the author knew about Japan
(B) the information was already familiar to the couple
(C) it was not directly related to the war
(D) the author indicated that American newspapers were accurate
(E) the author did not offer the information until the couple asked for it

33 Which of the following best explains why the onlookers in the train station went back to "staring at the ceiling"?

(A) They sympathized with the writer because he was separated from his family.
(B) They did not want to get into conversation with the writer.
(C) They were embarrassed by the fact that the writer was from a country at war with the United States.
(D) The train was late and they had become bored.
(E) They had stopped viewing the author as a suspicious person.

34 The author uses the incident at the train station primarily to illustrate that

(A) distrust between strangers is natural
(B) people react positively to someone who is nice to children
(C) giving people the opportunity to agree with you will make it easier for them to trust you
(D) people of Japanese ancestry living in the United States during the Second World War faced prejudice
(E) it is easy to recognize hostility in strangers

35 Which piece of information about himself would have been most risky for the author to convey at the beginning of the conversation in the train station?

(A) He knows only what he reads in the newspapers.
(B) He believes that Japan lacks vital natural resources.
(C) He does not see how a powerful nation like the United States could be defeated by Japan.
(D) He has close relatives living in Japan.
(E) He does not expect to hear from his family in the near future.

IF YOU FINISH BEFORE TIME IS CALLED, YOU MAY CHECK YOUR WORK ON THIS SECTION ONLY. DO NOT TURN TO ANY OTHER SECTION IN THE TEST. **STOP**

282

Time—30 Minutes
25 Questions

This section contains two types of questions. You have 30 minutes to complete both types. You may use any available space for scratchwork.

Notes:

(1) The use of a calculator is permitted. All numbers used are real numbers.

(2) Figures that accompany problems in this test are intended to provide information useful in solving the problems. They are drawn as accurately as possible EXCEPT when it is stated in a specific problem that the figure is not drawn to scale. All figures lie in a plane unless otherwise indicated.

Reference Information

$A = \pi r^2$
$C = 2\pi r$

$A = \ell w$

$A = \frac{1}{2}bh$

$V = \ell wh$

$V = \pi r^2 h$

$c^2 = a^2 + b^2$

Special Right Triangles

The number of degrees of arc in a circle is 360.
The measure in degrees of a straight angle is 180.
The sum of the measures in degrees of the angles of a triangle is 180.

Directions for Quantitative Comparison Questions

Questions 1-15 each consist of two quantities in boxes, one in Column A and one in Column B. You are to compare the two quantities and on the answer sheet fill in oval

A if the quantity in Column A is greater;
B if the quantity in Column B is greater;
C if the two quantities are equal;
D if the relationship cannot be determined from the information given.

AN E RESPONSE WILL NOT BE SCORED.

Notes:

1. In some questions, information is given about one or both of the quantities to be compared. In such cases, the given information is centered above the two columns and is not boxed.
2. In a given question, a symbol that appears in both columns represents the same thing in Column A as it does in Column B.
3. Letters such as x, n, and k stand for real numbers.

EXAMPLES

Column A	Column B	Answers
E1 5^2	20	● Ⓑ Ⓒ Ⓓ Ⓔ

150° $x°$

| E2 x | 30 | Ⓐ Ⓑ ● Ⓓ Ⓔ |

r and s are integers

| E3 $r + 1$ | $s - 1$ | Ⓐ Ⓑ Ⓒ ● Ⓔ |

GO ON TO THE NEXT PAGE

Column A	Column B

1 | The number of years from the year 1790 to the present | The number of years from the year 1780 to the present

$$x + 3 = 5$$
$$2y + 11 = 15$$

2 | x | y

3 | x | 40

$$\frac{1}{x} = 3$$

4 | x | 3

Page 1 of a book has 50 lines of type.
Page 2 of the same book has 60 lines of type.

Column A	Column B

5 | The number of sentences on page 1 of the book | The number of sentences on page 2 of the book

6 | The remainder when 251,896 is divided by 2 | The remainder when 894,525 is divided by 5

$$3x - 4y = 1$$

7 | $(-1)^{6x - 8y}$ | $(-1)^{9x - 12y}$

• P

_____ ℓ

8 | The number of lines that can be drawn from point P to line ℓ to form a 90° angle with line ℓ | The number of lines that can be drawn from point P to line ℓ to form a 30° angle with line ℓ

GO ON TO THE NEXT PAGE →

SUMMARY DIRECTIONS FOR COMPARISON QUESTIONS

Answer: A if the quantity in Column A is greater;
B if the quantity in Column B is greater;
C if the two quantities are equal;
D if the relationship cannot be determined from the information given.

AN E RESPONSE WILL NOT BE SCORED.

Column A	Column B

Let ★ be an operation defined for any number x by the equation $x ★ x = 2x$.

9

$17\frac{3}{11} ★ 17\frac{3}{11}$ | $17\frac{3}{11} + 17\frac{3}{11}$

---

n percent of 50 is greater than 40.

10

n | 90

The average (arithmetic mean) of x and y is 0.

$x > 0$

11

x | y

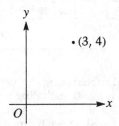

• (3, 4)

12 The distance from the point (3, 4) to the origin | The distance from the point (3, 4) to $(a, 0)$, where $a > 0$

Column A	Column B

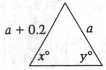

$a + 0.2$ / a

$x°$ $y°$

13

x | y

$2k + 3 < 9$

14

k | 3

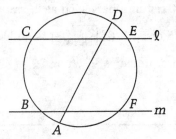

Note: Figure not drawn to scale.

$\ell \parallel m$

AD is a chord of the circle.

15 The length of arc ABC | The length of arc DEF

GO ON TO THE NEXT PAGE

Directions for Student-Produced Response Questions

Each of the remaining 10 questions (16-25) requires you to solve the problem and enter your answer by marking the ovals in the special grid, as shown in the examples below.

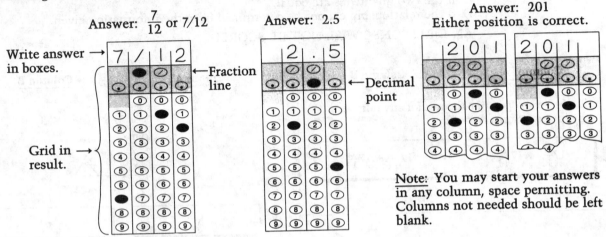

Write answer → in boxes.

← Fraction line

Answer: $\frac{7}{12}$ or 7/12

Answer: 2.5

← Decimal point

Answer: 201
Either position is correct.

Grid in → result.

Note: You may start your answers in any column, space permitting. Columns not needed should be left blank.

- Mark no more than one oval in any column.
- Because the answer sheet will be machine-scored, **you will receive credit only if the ovals are filled in correctly.**
- Although not required, it is suggested that you write your answer in the boxes at the top of the columns to help you fill in the ovals accurately.
- Some problems may have more than one correct answer. In such cases, grid only one answer.
- No question has a negative answer.
- **Mixed numbers** such as $2\frac{1}{2}$ must be gridded as 2.5 or 5/2. (If [2|1|/|2] is gridded, it will be interpreted as $\frac{21}{2}$, not $2\frac{1}{2}$.)

- Decimal Accuracy: If you obtain a decimal answer, **enter the most accurate value the grid will accommodate.** For example, if you obtain an answer such as 0.6666 . . . , you should record the result as .666 or .667. **Less accurate values such as .66 or .67 are not acceptable.**

Acceptable ways to grid $\frac{2}{3}$ = .6666 . . .

16 If $3x = y$ and $y = z + 1$, what is the value of x when $z = 29$?

17 An annual subscription to a certain monthly magazine is \$9.60, including tax and postage. The cost of a single issue of the magazine at a newsstand is \$1.25, including tax. How much money, in dollars, is saved in one year by subscribing to the magazine rather than by purchasing the magazine each month at a newsstand? (Disregard the \$ sign when gridding your answer.)

GO ON TO THE NEXT PAGE →

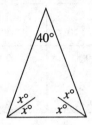

18 In the triangle above, what is the value of x?

19 If $2^n = 8$, what is the value of 3^{n+1}?

20 What is one possible value of x for which $\frac{1}{5} < x < \frac{1}{4}$?

.20 < X < .25

. 21
. 22
. 23
. 24

FAMILIES IN CENTERVILLE—1990

Number of Children	Percent of Families
0	$n\%$
1	18%
2	17%
3	11%
4 or more	10%

21 There were 5,000 families in Centerville in 1990. According to the chart above, how many of the families had no children?

GO ON TO THE NEXT PAGE

22 Two numbers form a "couple" if the sum of their reciprocals equals 2. For example, 8 and $\frac{8}{15}$ form a couple because $\frac{1}{8} + \frac{15}{8} = 2$. If x and y form a couple and $x = \frac{7}{3}$, what is the value of y?

Test Score	Number of Students
90	2
85	1
80	1
60	3

24 The test scores of 7 students are shown above. Let M and m be the median and mean scores, respectively. What is the value of $M - m$?

23 The entire surface of a solid cube with edge of length 6 inches is painted. The cube is then cut into cubes each with edge of length 1 inch. How many of the smaller cubes have paint on exactly 1 face?

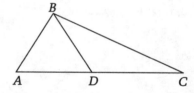

Note: Figure not drawn to scale.

25 In triangle ABC above, $AC = 12$. If the ratio of the area of triangle ABD to the area of triangle CBD is $3 : 5$, what is the length of segment AD?

IF YOU FINISH BEFORE TIME IS CALLED, YOU MAY CHECK YOUR WORK ON THIS SECTION ONLY. DO NOT TURN TO ANY OTHER SECTION IN THE TEST.

STOP

288

Time-15 Minutes — For each question in this section, select the best answer from among the choices given and
13 Questions   fill in the corresponding oval on the answer sheet.

The two passages below are followed by questions based on their content and on the relationship between
the two passages. Answer the questions on the basis of what is stated or implied in the passages and in any
introductory material that may be provided.

Questions 1-13 are based on the following passages.

*The following passages, written in the twentieth century, present two views of the architectural design of cities.
Passage 1 discusses English "garden cities," planned medium-sized cities containing residential, commercial, and
open space. Passage 2 offers a critique of modern cities.*

Passage 1

Attempts have been made by architectural writers
to discredit the garden cities on the ground that they
lack "urbanity." Because the buildings in them are
Line generously spaced and interspersed with gardens, lawns,
(5) and trees, they rarely produce the particular effect of
absolute enclosure or packed picturesqueness not
undeservedly admired by visitors to many ancient cities.
This is true; garden cities exhibit another and a more
popular kind of beauty, as well as a healthier and more
(10) convenient form of layout.
But the garden city is, nonetheless, truly a "city."
The criticism exposes the confusion and aesthetic
narrow-mindedness of the critics. If the word
"urbanity" is used in the accepted sense of "educated
(15) tastefulness," the charge that the garden cities are
without it is an affront to the well-qualified architects
who have taken part in their design. If it is used in the
simple etymological sense of "city-ness," the users
unknowingly expose their crass ignorance of the infinite
(20) diversity that the world's cities display. And if it is used
(illegitimately) as a synonym for high urban density or
crowdedness, it stands for a quality most city dwellers
regard as something to escape from if they can. The
word "urbanity" has been so maltreated that it should
(25) now be eliminated from town planning discussions.
Tastes differ in architectural styles as they do in all the
arts, and the ability to judge is complicated by changes
in fashion, to which critics of the arts seem more
subject than people in general. Persons vary in stability
(30) of taste: for some a thing of beauty is a joy forever, for
others a joy till next month's issue of an architectural
periodical.
The garden cities have been obedient to the prevailing
architectural fashion. Luckily for the profession, average
(35) Britons, though not highly sensitive to architectural
design, do not mind it, so long as the things they really
care about in a house or a town are attended to. They

take great pleasure in grass, trees, and flowers, with
which the garden cities are well endowed. The outlook
(40) from their windows is more important to them than the
look of their dwellings from the street. And though they
would have preferred their dwellings to have some
element of individuality, they accept harmonious
design and grouping without resentment. Thus, given
(45) due respect for their major interest, a pleasing ensemble
is attainable.

Passage 2

To the visually trained person today, the architecture
of the modern city is a remorseless and unremitting
assault on the senses. This kind of urban anarchy is an
(50) outstanding fact of modern life, an expression of
brutalism as harsh and as significant as modern warfare.
Our cities are neither expressions of civilization nor
creators of civilized individuals.
We see this rampant ugliness not only in the
(55) crumbling hearts of older American cities, but in
America's most modern urban areas as well—the tangle
of superhighways that seem to strangle certain West
Coast cities or in suburbs that project the image of a
standardized, anonymous, dehumanized person. Nor
(60) have we escaped this gloomy catalog when we visit cities
that have erected "good taste" into an inoffensive—but
equally repugnant because false—urban "style." Urban
uglification is not limited to any single country: the
posters in the travel agent's office promise famous
(65) monuments and picturesque antiquities, but when you
look through your hotel room window you see smog,
unsanitary streets, and neighborhoods ruined by
rapacious speculation in land and buildings.
Those who do not reject modern cities are condi-
(70) tioned not to see, hear, feel, smell, or sense them as
they are. The greatest obstacle to seemly cities has
become our low expectations, a direct result of our
having become habituated to the present environment

GO ON TO THE NEXT PAGE

and our incapacity to conceive of any better alternative.
(75) Those of us who have made this adjustment are permanently disabled in the use of our senses, brutalized
victims of the modern city.

We can get at what's wrong with a city like
Washington D.C. by considering the question once
(80) asked seriously by a European visitor, "Where can you
take a walk?" He didn't mean an arduous hike, but a
stroll along a city street where you can see the people,
admire the buildings, inspect the goods, and learn about
life in the process.

(85) Perhaps we need a simple litmus-paper test of the
good city. Who lives there? Where is the center? What
do you do when you get there? A successful urban design
involves urbanity, the quality the garden city forgot. It is
found in plazas and squares, in boulevards and prom-
(90) enades. It can be found in Rome's railroad station.
When you find it, never let it go. It is the hardest thing
to create anew.

1 In line 4, the word "generously" most nearly
means

(A) charitably
(B) helpfully
(C) unselfishly
(D) widely
(E) benevolently

2 The author of Passage 1 objects to using the
"simple etymological sense" (line 18) of the word
"urbanity" for which reason?

(A) Different individuals value different aspects of
urban life.
(B) The traditional idea of what is desirable in a
city changes greatly over time.
(C) Discovering the history of a word is often
difficult.
(D) Not all of the world's cities are alike.
(E) It is dangerous to disregard the opinion of
experts.

3 In Passage 1, the reference to "next month's
issue of an architectural periodical" (lines 31-32)
serves to

(A) show that the plans for the garden cities are
well thought of in professional journals
(B) indicate that what seems like a random
process is actually an ordered process
(C) suggest that some people lack their own firm
ideals of beauty
(D) imply that only those who are knowledgeable
about a subject should offer their opinions
(E) emphasize the importance of what the experts
say

4 In lines 34-41, by considering the relative
importance to "average Britons" of the view
from their homes, the author of Passage 1
suggests that

(A) natural light is an important element of urban
design
(B) Britons are not particularly concerned about
the architectural design elements that catch
the attention of critics
(C) the appeal of grass, trees, and flowers has been
overrated by many architectural theorists
(D) the importance of designing buildings that
have a pleasing exterior form needs to be
remembered
(E) Britons often object to being treated like
members of a group rather than like
individuals

5 In the last paragraph of Passage 1, the author
acknowledges which flaw in the design of
the garden city?

(A) The uniformity of the dwellings
(B) The view from many of the windows
(C) The constraint imposed by the landscape
(D) The emphasis placed on plantings
(E) The outmodedness of the architecture

GO ON TO THE NEXT PAGE

6 The references in Passage 2 to "posters" (line 64) and the view from the "hotel room window" (line 66) serve to

(A) give an accurate sense of the two places
(B) highlight the distinction between the ideal and the reality
(C) show what could be, as opposed to what is
(D) criticize those who would say negative things about well-loved places
(E) invoke past splendor in order to point out present flaws

7 In line 68, the phrase "rapacious speculation" refers to

(A) rapid calculations
(B) endless deliberation
(C) immoral thoughts
(D) exploitative investments
(E) illegal gambling

8 If modern cities are so terrible, why, according to Passage 2, do people continue to live in them?

(A) Cities provide more varied employment opportunities than other places.
(B) People see cities for what they are and actually enjoy living in such places.
(C) The cultural opportunities available in cities are more varied than those in rural areas.
(D) Despite their drawbacks, cities have a quality of life that makes them desirable as places to live.
(E) As a consequence of living in cities, people have become unable to think objectively about their environment.

9 The distinction made in Passage 2 between a "walk" and a "hike" (lines 81-84) can best be summarized as which of the following?

(A) The first is primarily a social experience, the second primarily exercise.
(B) The first involves a greater degree of physical exercise than the second.
(C) The first is more likely to be regimented than the second.
(D) The first covers a greater distance than the second.
(E) The first is a popular activity, the second appeals only to a small group.

10 The questions in lines 86-87 chiefly serve to

(A) ask the reader to compare his or her experience with the author's
(B) show that it is easier to point out problems than to find solutions
(C) suggest what the author's definition of urbanity might involve
(D) answer the charges made by the author's critics
(E) outline an area in which further investigation is needed

11 In lines 87-88, the author of Passage 2 is critical of garden cities primarily because

(A) they are too crowded
(B) they lack that quality essential to a good city
(C) their design has not been carried out rationally
(D) people cannot readily accommodate themselves to living in them
(E) they are better places for plants than for people

12 The author of Passage 1 would most likely react to the characterization of garden cities presented in lines 87-88 by pointing out that

(A) recent research has shown the inadequacy of this characterization
(B) the facts of urban life support this characterization
(C) this characterization is dismissed by most authorities
(D) this characterization is neither accurate nor well defined
(E) this characterization expresses poor taste

13 How would the author of Passage 1 respond to the way the author of Passage 2 uses the word "urbanity" to describe the quality found in "Rome's railroad station" (line 90)?

(A) The quality is not to be found in so common a structure as a railroad station.
(B) The word "urbanity" is being used to denigrate an otherwise positive quality.
(C) The word "urbanity" has been so misused as to be no longer meaningful.
(D) "Urbanity" is, in fact, one of the leading characteristics of the garden city.
(E) It is a sign of arrogance to refuse to value this quality.

IF YOU FINISH BEFORE TIME IS CALLED, YOU MAY CHECK YOUR WORK ON THIS SECTION ONLY. DO NOT TURN TO ANY OTHER SECTION IN THE TEST.

STOP

291

Time—15 Minutes
10 Questions

In this section solve each problem, using any available space on the page for scratchwork. Then decide which is the best of the choices given and fill in the corresponding oval on the answer sheet.

Notes:

(1) The use of a calculator is permitted. All numbers used are real numbers.

(2) Figures that accompany problems in this test are intended to provide information useful in solving the problems. They are drawn as accurately as possible EXCEPT when it is stated in a specific problem that the figure is not drawn to scale. All figures lie in a plane unless otherwise indicated.

Reference Information

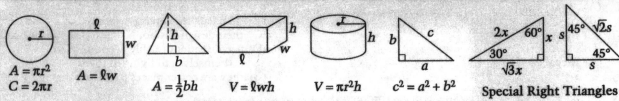

$A = \pi r^2$
$C = 2\pi r$

$A = \ell w$

$A = \frac{1}{2}bh$

$V = \ell wh$

$V = \pi r^2 h$

$c^2 = a^2 + b^2$

Special Right Triangles

The number of degrees of arc in a circle is 360.
The measure in degrees of a straight angle is 180.
The sum of the measures in degrees of the angles of a triangle is 180.

---

1 If x and y are integers, for which of the following ordered pairs (x, y) is $2x + y$ an odd number?

(A) $(0, 2)$
(B) $(1, 2)$
(C) $(2, 1)$
(D) $(2, 4)$
(E) $(3, 0)$

2 If $25 \times 16 \times 9 = r^2 \times 3^2$, then $r^2 =$

(A) 4^2
(B) 5^2
(C) 10^2
(D) 15^2
(E) 20^2

GO ON TO THE NEXT PAGE

DISTRIBUTION OF $10,000 IN
SCHOLARSHIP MONEY

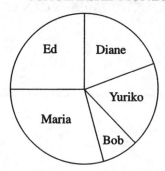

3 The circle graph above shows the distribution of
$10,000 in scholarship money to five students.
Which of the students received an amount closest
to $2,500?

(A) Maria
(B) Bob
(C) Yuriko
(D) Diane
(E) Ed

5 In a sack there are exactly 48 marbles, each
of which is either red, black, or yellow. The
probability of randomly selecting a red marble
from the sack is $\frac{5}{8}$, and the probability of
randomly selecting a black marble from the sack
is $\frac{1}{8}$. How many marbles in the sack are yellow?

(A) 6
(B) 12
(C) 16
(D) 18
(E) 24

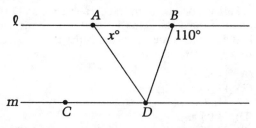

4 In the figure above, lines ℓ and m are parallel and
AD bisects $\angle CDB$. What is the value of x?

(A) 55
(B) 60
(C) 65
(D) 70
(E) 75

6 If the area of rectangle $ABCD$ above is 70 square
units, what is the value of p?

(A) 8
(B) 10
(C) 12
(D) 14
(E) 16

GO ON TO THE NEXT PAGE

7 In a certain basketball league, a player has an average (arithmetic mean) of 22 points per game for 8 games. What is the total number of points this player must score in the next 2 games in order to have an average of 20 points per game for 10 games?

(A) 18
(B) 20
(C) 22
(D) 24
(E) 34

9 Let x and y be positive integers and $n = x^y$.
If $n + \sqrt{n} + \sqrt[3]{n} = 76$, then x CANNOT equal

(A) 64
(B) 16
(C) 8
(D) 4
(E) 2

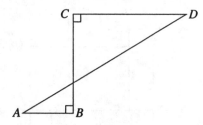

Note: Figure not drawn to scale.

8 In the figure above, $AB = 1$ and $BC = CD = 3$. What is the length of line segment AD?

(A) 5

(B) $2\sqrt{3} + \sqrt{2}$

(C) $3 + \sqrt{2}$

(D) $\sqrt{19}$

(E) 4

10 A faulty clock is set to the correct time at 12:00 noon. If the clock gains 5 minutes per hour, what is the correct time when the faulty clock indicates that 13 hours have passed?

(A) 11:55 p.m.
(B) 12:00 midnight
(C) 1:00 a.m.
(D) 1:05 a.m.
(E) 2:05 a.m.

IF YOU FINISH BEFORE TIME IS CALLED, YOU MAY CHECK YOUR WORK ON THIS SECTION ONLY. DO NOT TURN TO ANY OTHER SECTION IN THE TEST.

STOP

294

SAT I Scoring Worksheet

SAT I Verbal Sections

A. Section 1:

$$\frac{}{\text{no. correct}} - (\frac{}{\text{no. incorrect}} \div 4) = \frac{}{\text{subtotal A}}$$

B. Section 3:

$$\frac{}{\text{no. correct}} - (\frac{}{\text{no. incorrect}} \div 4) = \frac{}{\text{subtotal B}}$$

C. Section 5:

$$\frac{}{\text{no. correct}} - (\frac{}{\text{no. incorrect}} \div 4) = \frac{}{\text{subtotal C}}$$

D. Total unrounded raw score
(Total A + B + C)

$$\frac{}{\text{D}}$$

E. Total rounded raw score
(Rounded to nearest whole number)

$$\frac{}{\text{E}}$$

F. SAT I verbal reported scaled score
(Use the conversion table)

SAT I verbal
score

SAT I Mathematical Sections

A. Section 2:

$$\frac{}{\text{no. correct}} - (\frac{}{\text{no. incorrect}} \div 4) = \frac{}{\text{subtotal A}}$$

B. Section 4:
Questions 1-15 (quantitative comparison)

$$\frac{}{\text{no. correct}} - (\frac{}{\text{no. incorrect}} \div 3) = \frac{}{\text{subtotal B}}$$

C. Section 4:
Questions 16-25 (student-produced response)

$$\frac{}{\text{no. correct}} = \frac{}{\text{subtotal C}}$$

D. Section 6:

$$\frac{}{\text{no. correct}} - (\frac{}{\text{no. incorrect}} \div 4) = \frac{}{\text{subtotal D}}$$

E. Total unrounded raw score
(Total A + B + C + D)

$$\frac{}{\text{E}}$$

F. Total rounded raw score
(Rounded to nearest whole number)

$$\frac{}{\text{F}}$$

G. SAT I mathematical reported scaled score
(Use the conversion table)

SAT I
mathematical
score

Score Conversion Table
SAT I: Reasoning Test
Recentered Scale

SAT I SAMPLE TEST					
Raw Score	Verbal Scaled Score	Math Scaled Score	Raw Score	Verbal Scaled Score	Math Scaled Score
78	800		37	520	560
77	800		36	520	550
76	800		35	510	550
75	800		34	510	540
74	780		33	500	530
73	770		32	490	520
72	760		31	490	520
71	740		30	480	510
70	740		29	470	500
69	730		28	470	500
68	720		27	460	490
67	710		26	460	480
66	700		25	450	470
65	690		24	440	470
64	680		23	440	460
63	670		22	430	450
62	670		21	420	450
61	660		20	410	440
60	650	800	19	410	430
59	650	800	18	400	420
58	640	770	17	390	420
57	640	760	16	390	410
56	630	740	15	380	400
55	620	730	14	370	390
54	620	710	13	360	380
53	610	700	12	350	380
52	610	690	11	350	370
51	600	680	10	340	360
50	600	670	9	330	350
49	590	660	8	320	340
48	580	650	7	310	330
47	580	640	6	300	320
46	570	630	5	290	310
45	570	620	4	280	290
44	560	610	3	270	280
43	560	610	2	250	270
42	550	600	1	240	260
41	550	590	0	230	240
40	540	580	-1	210	230
39	540	570	-2	200	210
38	530	570	-3	200	200
			and below		

This table is for use only with this test.

SAT I: Reasoning Test

Saturday, March 1994

YOUR NAME (PRINT) _____

LAST   FIRST   MI

TEST CENTER _____

NUMBER   NAME OF TEST CENTER   ROOM NUMBER

SAT® I: Reasoning Test

Calculator use is permitted on the mathematics sections only.

You will have three hours to work on the questions in this test book. There are **five 30-minute sections and two 15-minute sections**. The supervisor will tell you when to begin and end each section. If you finish before time is called, you may check your work on that section, but you may <u>not work on any other section</u>.

Do not worry if you are unable to finish a section or if there are some questions you cannot answer. Do not waste time puzzling over a question that seems too difficult for you. Work as rapidly as you can without sacrificing accuracy.

Students often ask whether they should guess when they are uncertain about the answer to a question. Scores on the multiple-choice questions on this test are based on the number of questions answered correctly minus a fraction of the number answered incorrectly. Therefore, it is unlikely that random or haphazard guessing will change your scores significantly. If you have some knowledge of a question, you may be able to eliminate one or more of the answer choices as wrong. It is generally a good idea to guess which of the remaining choices is correct.

Some mathematics questions have no answer choices. Instead, you must solve the problem and record your answer in a special grid on your answer sheet. For these questions, you will receive credit for correct answers, but there will be no deduction for incorrect answers.

Mark all your answers on the separate answer sheet. Mark only one answer for each question. Since the answer sheet will be machine scored, be sure that each mark is dark and that it completely fills the oval. In each section of the answer sheet, there are spaces to answer 40 questions. When there are fewer than 40 questions in a section of your test, use only the spaces that correspond to the question numbers. Do not make stray marks on the answer sheet. If you erase, do so completely, because an incomplete erasure may be scored as an intended response.

You may use the test book for scratchwork, but you will not receive credit for anything written there.

(The passages for this test have been adapted from published material. The ideas contained in them do not necessarily represent the opinions of the College Board or Educational Testing Service.)

DO NOT OPEN THIS BOOK UNTIL THE SUPERVISOR TELLS YOU TO DO SO.

Use a No. 2 pencil only. Be sure each mark is dark and completely fills the intended oval. Completely erase any errors or stray marks.

1. Your Name

First 4 letters of Last Name | First init. | Mid. init.

2.

Your Name: (Print) — Last — First — M.I.

Signature: ___ Date: / /

Home Address: (Print) — Number and Street

City — State — Zip Code

Center: (Print) — City — State — Center Number

IMPORTANT: Please fill in items 8 and 9 exactly as shown on the back cover of your test book.

8. Form Code
(Copy and grid as on back of test book.)

3. Date Of Birth

Month | Day | Year

Jan. Feb. Mar. Apr. May June July Aug. Sept. Oct. Nov. Dec.

4. Social Security Number

5. Sex
Female Male

6. Registration Number
(Copy from your Admission Ticket.)

7. Test Book Serial Number
(Copy from front of test book.)

DO NOT WRITE IN THIS AREA.

FOR ETS USE ONLY

9. Test Form
(Copy from back cover of test book.)

Start with number 1 for each new section. If a section has fewer questions than answer spaces, leave the extra answer spaces blank.

SECTION 1

1–40 (A) (B) (C) (D) (E)

SECTION 2

1–40 (A) (B) (C) (D) (E)

48560 • 09132 • TF23P750e   I.N.207085
1 2 3 4

301

Use a No. 2 pencil only. Be sure each mark is dark and completely fills the intended oval. Completely erase any errors or stray marks.

Start with number 1 for each new section. If a section has fewer questions than answer spaces, leave the extra answer spaces blank.

SECTION 3

1 (A) (B) (C) (D) (E)
2 (A) (B) (C) (D) (E)
3 (A) (B) (C) (D) (E)
4 (A) (B) (C) (D) (E)
5 (A) (B) (C) (D) (E)
6 (A) (B) (C) (D) (E)
7 (A) (B) (C) (D) (E)
8 (A) (B) (C) (D) (E)
9 (A) (B) (C) (D) (E)
10 (A) (B) (C) (D) (E)
11 (A) (B) (C) (D) (E)
12 (A) (B) (C) (D) (E)
13 (A) (B) (C) (D) (E)
14 (A) (B) (C) (D) (E)
15 (A) (B) (C) (D) (E)

16 (A) (B) (C) (D) (E)
17 (A) (B) (C) (D) (E)
18 (A) (B) (C) (D) (E)
19 (A) (B) (C) (D) (E)
20 (A) (B) (C) (D) (E)
21 (A) (B) (C) (D) (E)
22 (A) (B) (C) (D) (E)
23 (A) (B) (C) (D) (E)
24 (A) (B) (C) (D) (E)
25 (A) (B) (C) (D) (E)
26 (A) (B) (C) (D) (E)
27 (A) (B) (C) (D) (E)
28 (A) (B) (C) (D) (E)
29 (A) (B) (C) (D) (E)
30 (A) (B) (C) (D) (E)

31 (A) (B) (C) (D) (E)
32 (A) (B) (C) (D) (E)
33 (A) (B) (C) (D) (E)
34 (A) (B) (C) (D) (E)
35 (A) (B) (C) (D) (E)
36 (A) (B) (C) (D) (E)
37 (A) (B) (C) (D) (E)
38 (A) (B) (C) (D) (E)
39 (A) (B) (C) (D) (E)
40 (A) (B) (C) (D) (E)

If section 3 of your test book contains math questions that are not multiple-choice, continue to item 16 below. Otherwise, continue to item 16 above.

ONLY ANSWERS ENTERED IN THE OVALS IN EACH GRID AREA WILL BE SCORED.
YOU WILL NOT RECEIVE CREDIT FOR ANYTHING WRITTEN IN THE BOXES ABOVE THE OVALS.

16 17 18 19 20

21 22 23 24 25

BE SURE TO ERASE ANY ERRORS OR STRAY MARKS COMPLETELY.

PLEASE PRINT
YOUR INITIALS

First   Middle   Last

Use a No. 2 pencil only. Be sure each mark is dark and completely fills the intended oval. Completely erase any errors or stray marks.

Start with number 1 for each new section. If a section has fewer questions than answer spaces, leave the extra answer spaces blank.

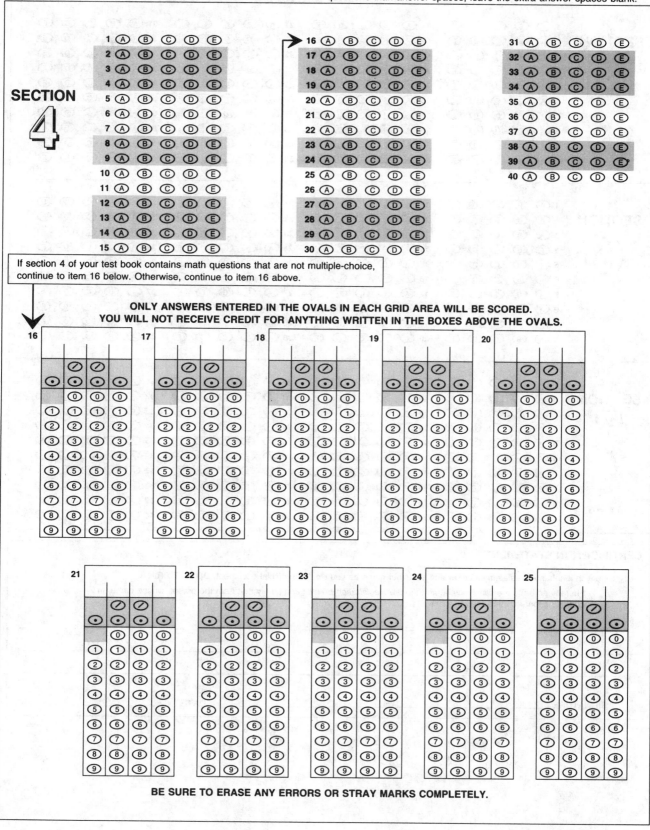

SECTION 4

If section 4 of your test book contains math questions that are not multiple-choice, continue to item 16 below. Otherwise, continue to item 16 above.

ONLY ANSWERS ENTERED IN THE OVALS IN EACH GRID AREA WILL BE SCORED. YOU WILL NOT RECEIVE CREDIT FOR ANYTHING WRITTEN IN THE BOXES ABOVE THE OVALS.

BE SURE TO ERASE ANY ERRORS OR STRAY MARKS COMPLETELY.

PLEASE PRINT YOUR INITIALS

First   Middle   Last

Use a No. 2 pencil only. Be sure each mark is dark and completely fills the intended oval. Completely erase any errors or stray marks.

Start with number 1 for each new section. If a section has fewer questions than answer spaces, leave the extra answer spaces blank.

SECTION 5

1 (A) (B) (C) (D) (E)   11 (A) (B) (C) (D) (E)   21 (A) (B) (C) (D) (E)   31 (A) (B) (C) (D) (E)
2 (A) (B) (C) (D) (E)   12 (A) (B) (C) (D) (E)   22 (A) (B) (C) (D) (E)   32 (A) (B) (C) (D) (E)
3 (A) (B) (C) (D) (E)   13 (A) (B) (C) (D) (E)   23 (A) (B) (C) (D) (E)   33 (A) (B) (C) (D) (E)
4 (A) (B) (C) (D) (E)   14 (A) (B) (C) (D) (E)   24 (A) (B) (C) (D) (E)   34 (A) (B) (C) (D) (E)
5 (A) (B) (C) (D) (E)   15 (A) (B) (C) (D) (E)   25 (A) (B) (C) (D) (E)   35 (A) (B) (C) (D) (E)
6 (A) (B) (C) (D) (E)   16 (A) (B) (C) (D) (E)   26 (A) (B) (C) (D) (E)   36 (A) (B) (C) (D) (E)
7 (A) (B) (C) (D) (E)   17 (A) (B) (C) (D) (E)   27 (A) (B) (C) (D) (E)   37 (A) (B) (C) (D) (E)
8 (A) (B) (C) (D) (E)   18 (A) (B) (C) (D) (E)   28 (A) (B) (C) (D) (E)   38 (A) (B) (C) (D) (E)
9 (A) (B) (C) (D) (E)   19 (A) (B) (C) (D) (E)   29 (A) (B) (C) (D) (E)   39 (A) (B) (C) (D) (E)
10 (A) (B) (C) (D) (E)   20 (A) (B) (C) (D) (E)   30 (A) (B) (C) (D) (E)   40 (A) (B) (C) (D) (E)

SECTION 6

1 (A) (B) (C) (D) (E)   11 (A) (B) (C) (D) (E)   21 (A) (B) (C) (D) (E)   31 (A) (B) (C) (D) (E)
2 (A) (B) (C) (D) (E)   12 (A) (B) (C) (D) (E)   22 (A) (B) (C) (D) (E)   32 (A) (B) (C) (D) (E)
3 (A) (B) (C) (D) (E)   13 (A) (B) (C) (D) (E)   23 (A) (B) (C) (D) (E)   33 (A) (B) (C) (D) (E)
4 (A) (B) (C) (D) (E)   14 (A) (B) (C) (D) (E)   24 (A) (B) (C) (D) (E)   34 (A) (B) (C) (D) (E)
5 (A) (B) (C) (D) (E)   15 (A) (B) (C) (D) (E)   25 (A) (B) (C) (D) (E)   35 (A) (B) (C) (D) (E)
6 (A) (B) (C) (D) (E)   16 (A) (B) (C) (D) (E)   26 (A) (B) (C) (D) (E)   36 (A) (B) (C) (D) (E)
7 (A) (B) (C) (D) (E)   17 (A) (B) (C) (D) (E)   27 (A) (B) (C) (D) (E)   37 (A) (B) (C) (D) (E)
8 (A) (B) (C) (D) (E)   18 (A) (B) (C) (D) (E)   28 (A) (B) (C) (D) (E)   38 (A) (B) (C) (D) (E)
9 (A) (B) (C) (D) (E)   19 (A) (B) (C) (D) (E)   29 (A) (B) (C) (D) (E)   39 (A) (B) (C) (D) (E)
10 (A) (B) (C) (D) (E)   20 (A) (B) (C) (D) (E)   30 (A) (B) (C) (D) (E)   40 (A) (B) (C) (D) (E)

SECTION 7

1 (A) (B) (C) (D) (E)   11 (A) (B) (C) (D) (E)   21 (A) (B) (C) (D) (E)   31 (A) (B) (C) (D) (E)
2 (A) (B) (C) (D) (E)   12 (A) (B) (C) (D) (E)   22 (A) (B) (C) (D) (E)   32 (A) (B) (C) (D) (E)
3 (A) (B) (C) (D) (E)   13 (A) (B) (C) (D) (E)   23 (A) (B) (C) (D) (E)   33 (A) (B) (C) (D) (E)
4 (A) (B) (C) (D) (E)   14 (A) (B) (C) (D) (E)   24 (A) (B) (C) (D) (E)   34 (A) (B) (C) (D) (E)
5 (A) (B) (C) (D) (E)   15 (A) (B) (C) (D) (E)   25 (A) (B) (C) (D) (E)   35 (A) (B) (C) (D) (E)
6 (A) (B) (C) (D) (E)   16 (A) (B) (C) (D) (E)   26 (A) (B) (C) (D) (E)   36 (A) (B) (C) (D) (E)
7 (A) (B) (C) (D) (E)   17 (A) (B) (C) (D) (E)   27 (A) (B) (C) (D) (E)   37 (A) (B) (C) (D) (E)
8 (A) (B) (C) (D) (E)   18 (A) (B) (C) (D) (E)   28 (A) (B) (C) (D) (E)   38 (A) (B) (C) (D) (E)
9 (A) (B) (C) (D) (E)   19 (A) (B) (C) (D) (E)   29 (A) (B) (C) (D) (E)   39 (A) (B) (C) (D) (E)
10 (A) (B) (C) (D) (E)   20 (A) (B) (C) (D) (E)   30 (A) (B) (C) (D) (E)   40 (A) (B) (C) (D) (E)

CERTIFICATION STATEMENT

Copy in longhand the statement below and sign your name as you would an official document. **DO NOT PRINT.**

I hereby agree to the conditions set forth in the *Registration Bulletin* and certify that I am the person whose name and address appear on this answer sheet.

SIGNATURE: _____   DATE: _____

Time—30 Minutes
25 Questions

In this section solve each problem, using any available space on the page for scratchwork. Then decide which is the best of the choices given and fill in the corresponding oval on the answer sheet.

Notes:

1. The use of a calculator is permitted. All numbers used are real numbers.

2. Figures that accompany problems in this test are intended to provide information useful in solving the problems. They are drawn as accurately as possible EXCEPT when it is stated in a specific problem that the figure is not drawn to scale. All figures lie in a plane unless otherwise indicated.

Reference Information

$A = \pi r^2$
$C = 2\pi r$

$A = \ell w$

$A = \frac{1}{2}bh$

$V = \ell w h$

$V = \pi r^2 h$

$c^2 = a^2 + b^2$

Special Right Triangles

The number of degrees of arc in a circle is 360.
The measure in degrees of a straight angle is 180.
The sum of the measures in degrees of the angles of a triangle is 180.

---

1 How many bottles, each holding 8 fluid ounces, are needed to hold 3 quarts of cider? (1 quart = 32 fluid ounces)

(A) 8
(B) 12
(C) 14
(D) 16
(E) 18

2 If $x + 7$ is an even integer, then x could be which of the following?

(A) −2
(B) −1
(C) 0
(D) 2
(E) 4

3 If $(n + 3)(9 - 5) = 16$, then $n =$

(A) 1
(B) 4
(C) 7
(D) 9
(E) 15

GO ON TO THE NEXT PAGE

$$\frac{4}{n}, \frac{5}{n}, \frac{7}{n}$$

4 If each of the fractions above is in its simplest reduced form, which of the following could be the value of n ?

(A) 24
(B) 25
(C) 26
(D) 27
(E) 28

6 A certain building has 2,600 square feet of surface that needs to be painted. If 1 gallon of paint will cover 250 square feet, what is the least whole number of gallons that must be purchased in order to have enough paint to apply one coat to the surface? (Assume that only whole gallons of paint can be purchased.)

(A)   5
(B)   10
(C)   11
(D)   15
(E) 110

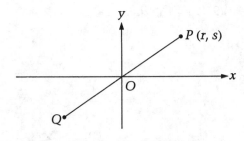

5 In the figure above, if PQ is a line segment and $PO = OQ$, what are the coordinates of point Q ?

(A) (s, r)
(B) $(s, -r)$
(C) $(-s, -r)$
(D) $(-r, s)$
(E) $(-r, -s)$

7 The number p is 4 more than 3 times the number r. The sum of p and r is 10. Which of the following pairs of equations could be used to find the values of p and r ?

(A) $p = 3r + 4$
$p + r = 10$

(B) $p = 3r + 4$
$pr = 10$

(C) $p = 3(r + 4)$
$p + r = 10$

(D) $p + 4 = 3r$
$p + r = 10$

(E) $p + 4 = 3r$
$pr = 10$

GO ON TO THE NEXT PAGE

8 Let a "k-triple" be defined as $(\frac{k}{2},\ k,\ \frac{3}{2}k)$ for some number k. Which of the following is a k-triple?

(A) (0, 5, 10)

(B) $(4\frac{1}{2},\ 5,\ 6\frac{1}{2})$

(C) (25, 50, 75)

(D) (250, 500, 1000)

(E) (450, 500, 650)

9 If the vertices of a square are at $(-3, 4)$, $(3, 4)$, $(3, -2)$, and $(-3, -2)$, what is the area of the square?

(A) 12
(B) 16
(C) 24
(D) 25
(E) 36

10 When a certain rectangle is divided in half, two squares are formed. If each of these squares has perimeter 48, what is the perimeter of the original rectangle?

(A) 96
(B) 72
(C) 36
(D) 24
(E) 12

11 If a ball is thrown straight up at a certain speed, its height h, in feet, after t seconds is given by the formula $h = 40t - 16t^2$. How many feet high will the ball be one second after it is thrown?

(A) 12
(B) 16
(C) 24
(D) 32
(E) 40

12 Which of the following sets of numbers has the property that the product of any two numbers in the set is also a number in the set?

   I. The set of even integers
   II. The set of prime numbers
   III. The set of positive numbers

(A) I only
(B) II only
(C) I and III only
(D) II and III only
(E) I, II, and III

GO ON TO THE NEXT PAGE

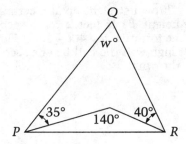

13 In $\triangle PQR$ above, $w =$

(A) 50
(B) 55
(C) 60
(D) 65
(E) 75

14 A class of 30 girls and 40 boys sponsored a hayride. If 60 percent of the girls and 25 percent of the boys went on the ride, what percent of the class went on the ride?

(A) 30%
(B) 35%
(C) 40%
(D) 50%
(E) 70%

15 If $x = yz$, which of the following must be equal to xy ?

(A) yz

(B) yz^2

(C) y^2z

(D) $\dfrac{x}{y}$

(E) $\dfrac{z}{x}$

16 Which of the following operations has the same effect as dividing by $\dfrac{4}{3}$ and then multiplying by $\dfrac{2}{3}$?

(A) Multiplying by $\dfrac{1}{2}$

(B) Multiplying by 2

(C) Dividing by $\dfrac{1}{2}$

(D) Dividing by 3

(E) Dividing by 4

GO ON TO THE NEXT PAGE

17 The average (arithmetic mean) of a, b, s, and t is 6 and the average of s and t is 3. What is the average of a and b?

(A) 3

(B) $\dfrac{9}{2}$

(C) 6

(D) 9

(E) 12

18 During a sale at a music store, if a customer buys one tape at full price, the customer is given a 50 percent discount on a second tape of equal or lesser value. If Linda buys two tapes that have full prices of $15 and $10, by what percent is the total cost of the two tapes reduced during this sale?

(A) 5%
(B) 20%
(C) 25%
(D) 30%
(E) 50%

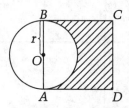

19 In the figure above, AB is a diameter of the circle with center O and $ABCD$ is a square. What is the area of the shaded region in terms of r?

(A) $\pi(r^2 - 4)$

(B) $\pi(4 - \pi)$

(C) $r^2(\pi - 2)$

(D) $r^2(4 - \dfrac{\pi}{2})$

(E) $r^2(2 - \dfrac{\pi}{2})$

20 If the sum of 4 consecutive integers is f, then, in terms of f, what is the least of these integers?

(A) $\dfrac{f}{4}$

(B) $\dfrac{f-2}{4}$

(C) $\dfrac{f-3}{4}$

(D) $\dfrac{f-4}{4}$

(E) $\dfrac{f-6}{4}$

GO ON TO THE NEXT PAGE

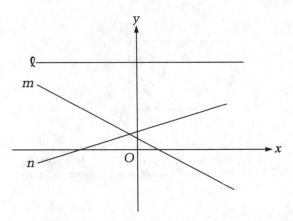

21 In the figure above, lines ℓ, m, and n have slopes r, s, and t, respectively. Which of the following is a correct ordering of these slopes?

(A) $r < s < t$
(B) $r < t < s$
(C) $s < r < t$
(D) $s < t < r$
(E) $t < s < r$

22 In the equation $S = 3\pi r^2$, if the value of r is doubled, then the value of S is multiplied by

(A) $\frac{1}{2}$

(B) 2

(C) 3

(D) 4

(E) 8

23 Excluding rest stops, it took Juanita a total of 10 hours to hike from the base of a mountain to the top and back down again by the same path. If while hiking she averaged 2 kilometers per hour going up and 3 kilometers per hour coming down, how many kilometers was it from the base to the top of the mountain?

(A) 8
(B) 10
(C) 12
(D) 20
(E) 24

24 If $-1 < x < 0$, which of the following statements must be true?

(A) $x < x^2 < x^3$
(B) $x < x^3 < x^2$
(C) $x^2 < x < x^3$
(D) $x^2 < x^3 < x$
(E) $x^3 < x < x^2$

25 One side of a triangle has length 6 and a second side has length 7. Which of the following could be the area of this triangle?

  I. 13
  II. 21
  III. 24

(A) I only
(B) II only
(C) III only
(D) I and II only
(E) I, II, and III

IF YOU FINISH BEFORE TIME IS CALLED, YOU MAY CHECK YOUR WORK ON THIS SECTION ONLY. DO NOT TURN TO ANY OTHER SECTION IN THE TEST.   **STOP**

310

Section 2

**Time—30 Minutes
35 Questions**

For each question in this section, select the best answer from among the choices given and fill in the corresponding oval on the answer sheet.

Each sentence below has one or two blanks, each blank indicating that something has been omitted. Beneath the sentence are five words or sets of words labeled A through E. Choose the word or set of words that, when inserted in the sentence, best fits the meaning of the sentence as a whole.

Example:

Medieval kingdoms did not become constitutional republics overnight; on the contrary, the change was ----.

(A) unpopular
(B) unexpected
(C) advantageous
(D) sufficient
(E) gradual

Ⓐ Ⓑ Ⓒ Ⓓ ●

1 The spacecraft has two ---- sets of electronic components; if one fails, its duplicate will still function.

(A) divergent   (B) identical   (C) simulated
(D) mutual   (E) prohibitive

2 Only if business continues to expand can it ---- enough new jobs to make up for those that will be ---- by automation.

(A) produce. .required
(B) invent. .introduced
(C) create. .eliminated
(D) repeal. .reduced
(E) formulate. .engendered

3 Trinkets intended to have only ---- appeal can exist virtually forever in landfills because of the ---- of some plastics.

(A) arbitrary. .scarcity
(B) theoretical. .resilience
(C) ephemeral. .durability
(D) obsessive. .fragility
(E) impetuous. .cheapness

4 Despite years of poverty and ----, the poet Ruth Pitter produced work that is now ---- by a range of literary critics.

(A) security. .hailed
(B) depression. .criticized
(C) celebrity. .publicized
(D) inactivity. .undermined
(E) adversity. .acclaimed

5 Teachers are, in effect, encouraging ---- when they fail to enforce rules governing the time allowed to students for completion of their assignments.

(A) conformity   (B) procrastination
(C) impartiality   (D) scholarship
(E) plagiarism

6 Although surfing is often ---- as merely a modern pastime, it is actually ---- practice, invented long ago by the Hawaiians to maneuver through the surf.

(A) touted. .a universal
(B) depicted. .an impractical
(C) incorporated. .a leisurely
(D) overestimated. .a high-spirited
(E) dismissed. .a time-honored

7 Fungus beetles are quite ----: they seldom move more than the few yards between fungi, their primary food.

(A) pugnacious   (B) sedentary
(C) gregarious   (D) capricious
(E) carnivorous

8 Many linguists believe that our ability to learn language is at least in part ----, that it is somehow woven into our genetic makeup.

(A) innate   (B) accidental   (C) empirical
(D) transitory   (E) incremental

9 An apparently gratuitous gesture, whether it is spiteful or solicitous, arouses our suspicion, while a gesture recognized to be ---- gives no reason for surprise.

(A) warranted   (B) dubious   (C) affected
(D) benevolent   (E) rancorous

10 The student's feelings about presenting the commencement address were ----; although visibly happy to have been chosen, he was nonetheless ---- about speaking in public.

(A) positive. .insecure
(B) euphoric. .hopeful
(C) unknown. .modest
(D) ambivalent. .anxious
(E) restrained. .confident

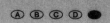

GO ON TO THE NEXT PAGE

Each question below consists of a related pair of words or phrases, followed by five pairs of words or phrases labeled A through E. Select the pair that best expresses a relationship similar to that expressed in the original pair.

Example:

CRUMB : BREAD ::
(A) ounce : unit
(B) splinter : wood
(C) water : bucket
(D) twine : rope
(E) cream : butter

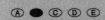

11 RECUPERATE : SURGERY ::
(A) restore : furniture
(B) cleanse : alcohol
(C) cure : illness
(D) revive : faint
(E) hospitalize : patient

12 SKETCH : ARTIST ::
(A) secret : confidant
(B) palette : painter
(C) cell : prisoner
(D) draft : writer
(E) chisel : sculptor

13 YEARN : LONGING ::
(A) beware : danger
(B) rush : patience
(C) enjoy : pleasure
(D) suppress : rage
(E) sleep : insomnia

14 FREIGHT : TRUCK ::
(A) goods : warehouse
(B) customers : store
(C) stevedores : ship
(D) engine : train
(E) passengers : bus

15 CHAT : CONVERSE ::
(A) allege : deny
(B) halt : traverse
(C) purchase : rent
(D) study : learn
(E) browse : read

16 COLLAGE : IMAGES ::
(A) medley : songs
(B) book : volumes
(C) survey : lands
(D) collection : lists
(E) assembly : bills

17 ABASH : EMBARRASSMENT ::
(A) dislike : hypocrisy
(B) pretend : imagination
(C) annoy : irritation
(D) suspect : illegality
(E) demolish : renovation

18 TERRESTRIAL : LAND ::
(A) vegetarian : plants
(B) predatory : animal
(C) nocturnal : day
(D) arid : desert
(E) aquatic : water

19 TRIAL : JURY ::
(A) dispute : arbiter
(B) poll : contestant
(C) championship : spectator
(D) conference : speaker
(E) match : competitor

20 WEDDING : MARRIAGE ::
(A) birthday : cake
(B) coronation : reign
(C) graduation : diploma
(D) promotion : job
(E) decoration : bravery

21 SALVE : WOUND ::
(A) utter : apology
(B) exploit : weakness
(C) mollify : anger
(D) squander : opportunity
(E) emulate : achievement

22 REFUGEE : ASYLUM ::
(A) astronaut : capsule
(B) perfectionist : frustration
(C) consumer : impulse
(D) opportunist : advantage
(E) director : stage

23 MYSTIFY : UNDERSTANDING ::
(A) nip : maturation
(B) insure : disaster
(C) rearrange : order
(D) intensify : endurance
(E) reciprocate : interchange

GO ON TO THE NEXT PAGE →

The passage below is followed by questions based on its content. Answer the questions on the basis of what is <u>stated</u> or <u>implied</u> in the passage and in any introductory material that may be provided.

Questions 24-35 are based on the following passage.

During the 1830's, Parisians began to refer to artistic individuals who pursued unconventional life-styles as Bohemians. The Bohemian world—Bohemia—fascinated members of the bourgeoisie, the conventional and materialistic middle class of French society.

"Bohemia, bordered on the North by hope, work and gaiety; on the South by necessity and courage; on the West and East by slander and the hospital."

Henry Murger (1822-1861)

Line
(5)   For its nineteenth-century discoverers and explorers, Bohemia was an identifiable country with visible inhabitants, but one not marked on any map. To trace its frontiers was to cross constantly back and forth between reality and
(10) fantasy.
      Explorers recognized Bohemia by certain signs: art, youth, socially defiant behavior, the vagabond life-style. To Henry Murger, the most influential mapper, Bohemia was the realm of young artists
(15) struggling to surmount the barriers poverty erected against their vocations, "all those who, driven by an unstinting sense of calling, enter into art with no other means of existence than art itself." They lived in Bohemia because they could not—or not
(20) yet—establish their citizenship anywhere else. Ambitious, dedicated, but without means and unrecognized, they had to turn life itself into an art: "Their everyday existence is a work of genius."
(25)   Yet even Murger admitted that not all Bohemians were future artists. Other reporters did not think even the majority were future artists. To that sharp-eyed social anatomist Balzac*, Bohemia was more simply the country of youth. All the
(30) most talented and promising young people lived in it, those in their twenties who had not yet made their names but who were destined eventually to lead their nation. "In fact all kinds of ability, of talent, are represented there. It is a microcosm. If
(35) the emperor of Russia bought up Bohemia for twenty million—assuming it were willing to take leave of the boulevard pavements—and transferred it to Odessa, in a year Odessa would be Paris." In its genius for life, Balzac's Bohemia resembled
(40) Murger's. "Bohemia has nothing and lives from what it has. Hope is its religion, faith in itself its code, charity is all it has for a budget."
      Artists and the young were not alone in their ability to make more of life than objective condi-

(45) tions seemed to permit. Some who were called Bohemians did so in more murky and mysterious ways, in the darker corners of society. "By Bohemians," a well-known theater owner of the 1840's declared, "I understand that class of individ-
(50) uals whose existence is a problem, social condition a myth, fortune an enigma, who are located nowhere and who one encounters everywhere! Rich today, famished tomorrow, ready to live honestly if they can and some other way if they
(55) can't." The nature of these Bohemians was less easy to specify than either Murger's or Balzac's definitions. They might be unrecognized geniuses or swindlers. The designation "Bohemian" located them in a twilight zone between ingenuity and
(60) criminality.
      These alternative images of Bohemia are ones we still recognize when we use the term: more recent incarnations like the Beat Generation of the 1950's or the hippiedom of the 1960's
(65) contained these real or potential elements, too. Artistic, youthful, unattached, inventive, or suspect, Bohemian styles are recurring features of modern life. Have they not always existed in Western society? In a way, yes: wandering
(70) medieval poets and eighteenth-century literary hacks also exhibited features of Bohemians. But written references to Bohemia as a special, identifiable kind of life appear initially in the nineteenth century. It was in the France of the 1830's and
(75) 1840's that the terms "Bohemia," "*La Bohème*," and "Bohemian" first appeared in this sense. The new vocabulary played on the common French word for gypsy—*bohémien*—which erroneously identified the province of Bohemia, part of old
(80) Czechoslovakia, as the gypsies' place of origin.
      From the start, Bohemianism took shape by contrast with the image with which it was commonly paired: bourgeois life. The opposition is so well established and comes so easily to mind
(85) that it may mislead us, for it implies a form of

GO ON TO THE NEXT PAGE →

313

separation and an intensity of hostility often belied by experience. Bohemia has always exercised a powerful attraction on many solid bourgeois, matched by the deeply bourgeois instincts (90) and aspirations of numerous Bohemians. This mysterious convergence sometimes leads to accusations of insincerity, even dishonesty: "Scratch a Bohemian, find a bourgeois." But the quality revealed by scraping away that false appearance of (95) opposition is seldom hypocrisy. Like positive and negative magnetic poles, Bohemian and bourgeois were—and are—parts of a single field: they imply, require, and attract each other.

*French novelist (1799-1850)

24 The passage is best described as

   (A) a refutation of an ancient misconception
   (B) a definition of a concept
   (C) a discussion of one historical era
   (D) a catalog of nineteenth-century biases
   (E) an example of a class struggle

25 In the quotation at the beginning of the passage (lines 1-3), Bohemia is presented in terms of

   (A) an extended metaphor
   (B) a complex argument
   (C) geographic distances
   (D) a logical paradox
   (E) popular legend

26 Murger's Bohemians would differ most from the bourgeois in that Bohemians

   (A) are motivated by strong artistic impulses
   (B) are primarily political reactionaries
   (C) have higher social status than the bourgeois
   (D) prefer to live off inherited wealth and the generosity of friends
   (E) prefer an anarchic social order to a stable one

27 In line 17, Murger uses the word "unstinting" to emphasize the Bohemians'

   (A) desire for wealth
   (B) power to assimilate bourgeois ideals
   (C) reservations about society
   (D) dedication to their goals
   (E) generous nature

28 The quotation in lines 23-24 ("Their . . . genius") can best be interpreted to mean that the Bohemians

   (A) are lucky to be alive
   (B) are highly successful achievers
   (C) are spirited and creative in spite of meager resources
   (D) live at the expense of the bourgeois
   (E) live chiefly by deceit, theft, and violation of accepted social codes

29 The quotations from Murger suggest that he viewed the Bohemians with

   (A) reserve and suspicion
   (B) benevolence yet perplexity
   (C) amusement and superiority
   (D) timidity and fear
   (E) interest and admiration

30 In contrast to Murger's Bohemia, Balzac's Bohemia was composed of

   (A) young artists struggling in poverty
   (B) young bourgeois playing with a new social role
   (C) the criminal as well as the genuine
   (D) talented artists working together
   (E) talented youths seeking to build their futures

31 In line 44, "objective" most nearly means

   (A) unassuming
   (B) fair
   (C) intentional
   (D) material
   (E) detached

GO ON TO THE NEXT PAGE

32 The quotation in lines 47-55 most probably reflects the point of view of

(A) the gypsies
(B) Murger
(C) Balzac
(D) some Bohemians
(E) some bourgeois

33 Which statement best summarizes the point made in lines 61-71 ?

(A) Bohemians have always been subjected to suspicion and scorn.
(B) The Bohemian is an inescapable feature of urban society.
(C) Bohemianism, as a way of life, is not unique to the nineteenth century.
(D) Eighteenth-century Bohemia was similar to nineteenth-century Bohemia.
(E) The province of Bohemia was home to aspiring young artists.

34 The statement in lines 92-93 ("Scratch . . . bourgeois") is best interpreted as conveying

(A) skepticism about the Bohemians' commitment to their life-style
(B) a desire to study the Bohemian life-style
(C) distrust of both the Bohemian and the bourgeois worlds
(D) a lack of appreciation of the arts
(E) envy of the artist's uncomplicated life-style

35 Which statement best summarizes the author's argument in the last paragraph?

(A) Bohemians were purposely misleading in their actions.
(B) Bohemians received considerable financial support from bourgeois customers.
(C) Bohemians and bourgeois were more similar than is often realized.
(D) Bourgeois were oblivious to the struggles of Bohemians.
(E) Bourgeois and Bohemians inherited the same cultural traditions from their ancestors.

IF YOU FINISH BEFORE TIME IS CALLED, YOU MAY CHECK YOUR WORK ON THIS SECTION ONLY. DO NOT TURN TO ANY OTHER SECTION IN THE TEST. **STOP**

3

Time—30 Minutes
25 Questions

This section contains two types of questions. You have 30 minutes to complete both types. You may use any available space for scratchwork.

Notes:

1. The use of a calculator is permitted. All numbers used are real numbers.

2. Figures that accompany problems in this test are intended to provide information useful in solving the problems. They are drawn as accurately as possible EXCEPT when it is stated in a specific problem that the figure is not drawn to scale. All figures lie in a plane unless otherwise indicated.

Reference Information

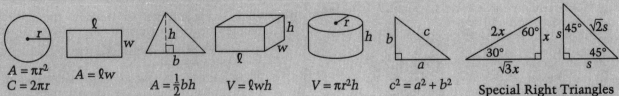

$A = \pi r^2$
$C = 2\pi r$

$A = \ell w$

$A = \frac{1}{2}bh$

$V = \ell wh$

$V = \pi r^2 h$

$c^2 = a^2 + b^2$

Special Right Triangles

The number of degrees of arc in a circle is 360.
The measure in degrees of a straight angle is 180.
The sum of the measures in degrees of the angles of a triangle is 180.

Directions for Quantitative Comparison Questions

Questions 1-15 each consist of two quantities in boxes, one in Column A and one in Column B. You are to compare the two quantities and on the answer sheet fill in oval

A if the quantity in Column A is greater;
B if the quantity in Column B is greater;
C if the two quantities are equal;
D if the relationship cannot be determined from the information given.

AN E RESPONSE WILL NOT BE SCORED.

Notes:

1. In some questions, information is given about one or both of the quantities to be compared. In such cases, the given information is centered above the two columns and is not boxed.
2. In a given question, a symbol that appears in both columns represents the same thing in Column A as it does in Column B.
3. Letters such as x, n, and k stand for real numbers.

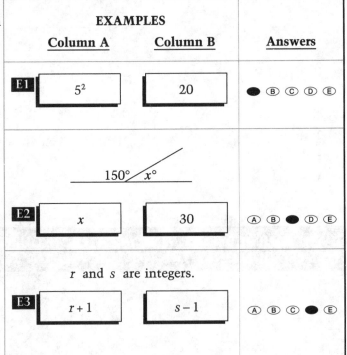

GO ON TO THE NEXT PAGE

<u>Column A</u>	<u>Column B</u>		<u>Column A</u>	<u>Column B</u>

1 $\dfrac{3}{2} - \dfrac{1}{2}$ | $\dfrac{7}{8} - \dfrac{1}{8}$

The average (arithmetic mean) of f and g is greater than the average of f and h.

6 h | g

$rs = 0$

2 r | 0

$$t + v = 76$$
$$t \neq 5$$

7 v | 71

$x^3 = y$

3 x^6 | y^2

For all positive integers a and b, let $\overline{a\rfloor b}$ be defined as $\overline{a\rfloor b} = ab - (a + b)$.

8 $\overline{5\rfloor 2}$ | $\overline{2\rfloor 5}$

4 The circumference of a circle with radius 2 | The sum of the circumferences of two circles, each with radius 1

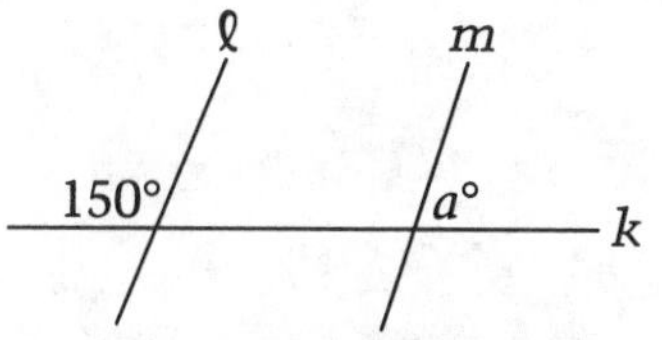

9 The perimeter of a rectangle with area 10 | The perimeter of a rectangle with area 12

150° ... $a°$ ... k ... ℓ ... m

<u>Note:</u> Figure not drawn to scale.

$\ell \parallel m$

5 $5a$ | 150

GO ON TO THE NEXT PAGE →

317

SUMMARY DIRECTIONS FOR COMPARISON QUESTIONS

<u>Answer:</u> A if the quantity in Column A is greater;
B if the quantity in Column B is greater;
C if the two quantities are equal;
D if the relationship cannot be determined from the information given.

Column A	Column B

$r + 3 > 5$

10 $\quad r + 2 \quad\quad\quad\quad\quad 4$

$6x - 2y < 0$

11 $\quad x \quad\quad\quad\quad\quad 0$

Set T consists of all of the 3-digit numbers greater than 450 that contain the digits 2, 4, and 5 with no digit repeated.

12 The number of 3-digit numbers in set T $\quad\quad\quad\quad\quad 4$

Points A and B lie on a circle. Line segment AB does <u>not</u> pass through the center of the circle. The length of line segment AB is 16.

13 The circumference of the circle $\quad\quad\quad\quad\quad 16\pi$

Column A	Column B

$\dfrac{x}{3} = \dfrac{y}{6}$

14 $\quad \dfrac{x+1}{3} \quad\quad\quad\quad\quad \dfrac{y+1}{6}$

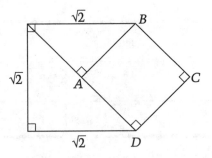

15 The area of square $ABCD$ $\quad\quad\quad\quad\quad \sqrt{2}$

GO ON TO THE NEXT PAGE

Directions for Student-Produced Response Questions

Each of the remaining 10 questions requires you to solve the problem and enter your answer by marking the ovals in the special grid, as shown in the examples below.

Answer: $\frac{7}{12}$ or 7/12

Answer: 2.5

Answer: 201
Either position is correct.

Write answer → in boxes.

← Fraction line

← Decimal point

Grid in → result.

Note: You may start your answers in any column, space permitting. Columns not needed should be left blank.

- Mark no more than one oval in any column.

- Because the answer sheet will be machine-scored, **you will receive credit only if the ovals are filled in correctly.**

- Although not required, it is suggested that you write your answer in the boxes at the top of the columns to help you fill in the ovals accurately.

- Some problems may have more than one correct answer. In such cases, grid only one answer.

- No question has a negative answer.

- **Mixed numbers** such as $2\frac{1}{2}$ must be gridded as 2.5 or 5/2. (If [2 1 / 2] is gridded, it will be interpreted as $\frac{21}{2}$, not $2\frac{1}{2}$.)

- **Decimal Accuracy**: If you obtain a decimal answer, **enter the most accurate value the grid will accommodate.** For example, if you obtain an answer such as 0.6666 . . . , you should record the result as .666 or .667. **Less accurate values such as .66 or .67 are not acceptable.**

Acceptable ways to grid $\frac{2}{3}$ = .6666 . . .

50° 2x° ℓ

16 In the figure above, what is the value of x?

17 If $(x+2)^2 = 25$ and $x > 0$, what is the value of x^2?

GO ON TO THE NEXT PAGE

TRACK MEET AMONG SCHOOLS A, B, AND C

	First Place (5 points)	Second Place (3 points)	Third Place (1 point)
Event I	A		
Event II	A	B	
Event III		C	

18 A partially completed scorecard for a track meet is shown above. Schools A, B, and C each entered one person in each of the three events and there were no ties. What is one possible total score for School C ? (Assume that all points are awarded in each event.)

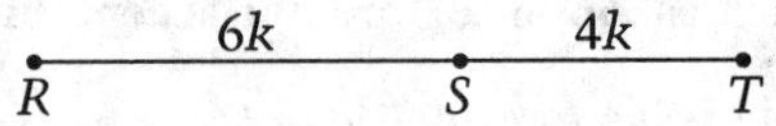

19 If line segment RT above has length 5, what is the value of k ?

$$\begin{array}{r} 7 \\ 4 \\ x \\ y \\ + 5 \\ \hline 32 \end{array} \qquad \begin{array}{r} 7 \\ 4 \\ x \\ z \\ + 5 \\ \hline 52 \end{array}$$

20 In the correctly worked addition problems above, what is the value of $z - y$?

21 Assume that $\frac{1}{4}$ quart of lemonade concentrate is mixed with $1\frac{3}{4}$ quarts of water to make lemonade for 4 people. How many quarts of lemonade concentrate are needed to make lemonade at the same strength for 14 people?

GO ON TO THE NEXT PAGE

22 Let $k \phi j$ be defined as the sum of all integers between k and j. For example, $5 \phi 9 = 6 + 7 + 8 = 21$. What is the value of $(80 \phi 110) - (81 \phi 109)$?

24 A triangle has a base of length 13 and the other two sides are equal in length. If the lengths of the sides of the triangle are integers, what is the shortest possible length of a side?

23 In 1980 the ratio of male students to female students at Frost College was 2 males to 3 females. Since then, the enrollment of male students in the college has increased by 400 and the enrollment of female students has remained the same. The ratio of males to females is currently 1 to 1. How many students are currently enrolled at Frost College?

25 In a stack of six cards, each card is labeled with a different integer 0 through 5. If two cards are selected at random without replacement, what is the probability that their sum will be 3 ?

IF YOU FINISH BEFORE TIME IS CALLED, YOU MAY CHECK YOUR WORK ON THIS SECTION ONLY. DO NOT TURN TO ANY OTHER SECTION IN THE TEST. **STOP**

Section 4 4 4 4 4 4

**Time—30 Minutes
30 Questions**

For each question in this section, select the best answer from among the choices given and fill in the corresponding oval on the answer sheet.

Each sentence below has one or two blanks, each blank indicating that something has been omitted. Beneath the sentence are five words or sets of words labeled A through E. Choose the word or set of words that, when inserted in the sentence, <u>best</u> fits the meaning of the sentence as a whole.

Example:

Medieval kingdoms did not become constitutional republics overnight; on the contrary, the change was ----.

(A) unpopular
(B) unexpected
(C) advantageous
(D) sufficient
(E) gradual

Ⓐ Ⓑ Ⓒ Ⓓ ●

1 Fearing excessive publicity, the patient refused to discuss her situation without a promise of ---- from the interviewer.

(A) empathy   (B) abstinence
(C) attribution   (D) confidentiality
(E) candor

2 Ed's great skills as a basketball player ---- his ---- stature, enabling him to compete successfully against much taller opponents.

(A) reveal. .gargantuan
(B) emphasize. .modest
(C) detract from. .lofty
(D) compensate for. .diminutive
(E) contrast with. .towering

3 The biologist's discovery was truly ----: it occurred not because of any new thinking or diligent effort but because he mistakenly left a few test tubes out of the refrigerator overnight.

(A) assiduous   (B) insightful   (C) fortuitous
(D) exemplary   (E) ominous

4 Alice Walker's *The Temple of My Familiar*, far from being a tight, ---- narrative, is instead ---- novel that roams freely and imaginatively over a half-million years.

(A) traditional. .a chronological
(B) provocative. .an insensitive
(C) forceful. .a concise
(D) focused. .an expansive
(E) circuitous. .a discursive

5 In sharp contrast to the previous night's revelry, the wedding was ---- affair.

(A) a fervent
(B) a dignified
(C) a chaotic
(D) an ingenious
(E) a jubilant

6 The theory of the ---- of cultures argues that all societies with highly developed technologies will evolve similar social institutions.

(A) isolation
(B) aesthetics
(C) convergence
(D) fragmentation
(E) longevity

7 Both by ---- and by gender, American painter Mary Cassatt was an ----, because her artistic peers were French men.

(A) background. .amateur
(B) citizenship. .intellectual
(C) nationality. .anomaly
(D) style. .advocate
(E) skill. .expert

8 She told the conference that, far from having to be ---- subjects of an ---- technology, human beings can actually control the system to improve their collective future.

(A) loyal. .inconsequential
(B) passive. .ungovernable
(C) diligent. .experimental
(D) reluctant. .impeccable
(E) zealous. .incompatible

9 Like a charlatan, Harry tried to ---- the audience with ---- evidence.

(A) confuse. .cogent
(B) persuade. .incontrovertible
(C) dupe. .spurious
(D) educate. .devious
(E) enthrall. .substantiated

GO ON TO THE NEXT PAGE

Each question below consists of a related pair of words or phrases, followed by five pairs of words or phrases labeled A through E. Select the pair that best expresses a relationship similar to that expressed in the original pair.

Example:

CRUMB : BREAD ::
(A) ounce : unit
(B) splinter : wood
(C) water : bucket
(D) twine : rope
(E) cream : butter

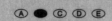

10 ACTOR : CAST ::
(A) musician : orchestra
(B) singer : song
(C) lecturer : class
(D) congregation : church
(E) proofreader : text

11 BORDER : COUNTRY ::
(A) current : river
(B) water : lake
(C) waves : sea
(D) horizon : sunset
(E) shore : ocean

12 CATALOG : SHOPPER ::
(A) contract : lawyer
(B) schedule : worker
(C) menu : diner
(D) article : author
(E) bank : teller

13 VOLATILE : VAPORIZE ::
(A) translucent : illuminate
(B) brittle : bend
(C) frigid : chill
(D) ponderous : lift
(E) soluble : dissolve

14 BUTTRESS : SUPPORT ::
(A) encore : applause
(B) ornament : decoration
(C) choreography : dance
(D) prayer : religion
(E) thesis : evidence

15 ICONOCLAST : ORTHODOXY ::
(A) scientist : theory
(B) impostor : identity
(C) libertarian : tyranny
(D) conformist : expectation
(E) soldier : combat

GO ON TO THE NEXT PAGE

Each passage below is followed by questions based on its content. Answer the questions on the basis of what is <u>stated</u> or <u>implied</u> in the passage and in any introductory material that may be provided.

Questions 16-22 are based on the following passage.

This passage is from a book written by a Chinese American woman about Chinese American women writers.

The question of one's identity is at the same time a simple and very complex issue. Is one to be identified by one's race, nationality, sex, place of
Line birth, place of death, place of longest residence,
(5) occupation, class, relationships to others, personality traits, size, age, interests, religion, astrological sign, salary, by how one perceives oneself, by how one is perceived by others? When born to parents of different races or nationalities, or when born in
(10) one country, reared in another, and finally settled in a third, one cannot give a simple answer to the question of racial or national identity. When one is born female in a world dominated by males of two different races, further complications ensue.
(15) At what point does an immigrant become an American? How does one identify one's nationality if one has moved about the world a great deal? Mai-Mai Sze, for example, was born in China to Chinese parents, taken to England as a young
(20) child, cared for by an Irish nanny, sent to a private high school and college in the United States, to a painting school in France, and now lives in New York City. Another example is Diana Chang, whose mother was Eurasian (of Irish and Chinese
(25) ancestry) and whose father was Chinese; she was born in New York City, taken to China as an infant, reared in the International Sector in Shanghai where she attended American schools, then brought back to the United States for high school
(30) and college. In the early 1970's, scholars included her work in anthologies of Asian American literature but also castigated her for the lack of ethnic pride and themes in her novels.
To complicate further the question of identity,
(35) not only are parentage and geographical factors significant, but external or social factors impinge as well. That recent immigrants feel a sense of alienation and strangeness in a new country is to be expected, but when American-born Chinese
(40) Americans, from families many generations in the United States, are asked where they learned such good English, they too are made to feel foreign and alien. The "double consciousness" with which W. E. B. Du Bois characterized the African Ameri-
(45) can—"this sense of always looking at one's self

through the eyes of others, of measuring one's soul by the tape of a world that looks on in amused contempt and pity"—equally characterizes Chinese Americans. However, if they should go to
(50) the People's Republic of China, they would soon realize, by their unfamiliarity with conditions and customs and by the reactions of the Chinese to them, how American they are. As Lindo Jong tells her daughter in Amy Tan's *The Joy Luck Club*,
(55) "When you go to China . . . you don't even need to open your mouth. They already know you are an outsider. . . . They know just watching the way you walk, the way you carry your face. They know you do not belong."
(60) Thus, the feeling of being between worlds, totally at home nowhere, is at the core of all the writers in this study and, consequently, of the books they write.

16 The passage serves primarily to

(A) inform the reader of the conflicting senses of identity experienced by Chinese American and other multicultural writers
(B) encourage Chinese American writers to write more fully about the variety of cultural experiences they have had
(C) inform Chinese American writers about writers from other cultures who have experienced conflicts similar to theirs
(D) praise the talent and resourcefulness of contemporary Chinese American women writers
(E) refute those who criticize Chinese American literature for its multicultural perspective

17 The author refers to the life of Mai-Mai Sze (lines 18-23) chiefly to illustrate the

(A) difficulty of determining one's identity after many relocations
(B) beneficial effects of a multiethnic heritage
(C) influence of social rank on the perception of ethnic identity
(D) advantages of wide experiences on an author's creativity
(E) disruptive effects on a family caused by extensive travel

GO ON TO THE NEXT PAGE

18 The discussion of Diana Chang's life (lines 23-33) suggests that she was

(A) unfamiliar with the culture of the United States
(B) isolated from other writers
(C) concerned with developing an unusual style
(D) unwilling to identify solely with any one cultural background
(E) trying to influence a small group of specialized readers

19 Which does the author consider the best example of the "external or social factors" mentioned in line 36 ?

(A) The ability to speak several languages
(B) The number of friends one has
(C) The political climate of the country in which one resides
(D) The number of countries one has lived in
(E) The assumptions other people make about one's identity

20 In line 36, "impinge" means

(A) enlarge
(B) contribute
(C) resolve
(D) fall apart
(E) fix firmly

21 The author's views (lines 34-59) about Chinese American identity can best be summarized as which of the following?

(A) Chinese Americans are as curious about their United States heritage as they are about their Chinese heritage.
(B) Chinese Americans have made contributions to both Chinese and United States literature.
(C) Chinese Americans are perceived as foreigners in both the People's Republic of China and the United States.
(D) Chinese Americans are viewed as role models by new immigrants to the United States from the People's Republic of China.
(E) Chinese Americans find their dual heritage an advantage in their writing careers.

22 The quotation (lines 55-59) from *The Joy Luck Club* emphasizes the point that American-born Chinese Americans

(A) would have difficulty understanding the sense of separation felt by their relatives who emigrated
(B) should travel to China to learn about their heritage
(C) would feel alienated in their ancestors' homeland of China
(D) need to communicate with their relatives in China
(E) tend to idealize life in China

GO ON TO THE NEXT PAGE

Questions 23-30 are based on the following passage.

The following passage is from a discussion of various ways that living creatures have been classified over the years.

    The world can be classified in different ways, depending on one's interests and principles of classification. The classifications (also known as
Line taxonomies) in turn determine which comparisons
(5) seem natural or unnatural, which literal or analogical. For example, it has been common to classify living creatures into three distinct groups—plants, animals, and humans. According to this classification, human beings are not a special kind of
(10) animal, nor animals a special kind of plant. Thus any comparisons between the three groups are strictly analogical. Reasoning from inheritance in garden peas to inheritance in fruit flies, and from these two species to inheritance in human beings,
(15) is sheer poetic metaphor.
    Another mode of classifying living creatures is commonly attributed to Aristotle. Instead of treating plants, animals, and humans as distinct groups, they are nested. All living creatures
(20) possess a vegetative soul that enables them to grow and metabolize. Of these, some also have a sensory soul that enables them to sense their environments and move. One species also has a rational soul that is capable of true understanding.
(25) Thus, human beings are a special sort of animal, and animals are a special sort of plant. Given this classification, reasoning from human beings to all other species with respect to the attributes of the vegetative soul is legitimate, reasoning from
(30) human beings to other animals with respect to the attributes of the sensory soul is also legitimate, but reasoning from the rational characteristics of the human species to any other species is merely analogical. According to both classifications, the
(35) human species is unique. In the first, it has a kingdom all to itself; in the second, it stands at the pinnacle of the taxonomic hierarchy.
    Homo sapiens is unique. All species are. But this sort of uniqueness is not enough for many
(40) (probably most) people, philosophers included. For some reason, it is very important that the species to which we belong be uniquely unique. It is of utmost importance that the human species be insulated from all other species with respect to
(45) how we explain certain qualities. Human beings clearly are capable of developing and learning languages. For some reason, it is very important that the waggle dance performed by bees* not count as a genuine language. I have never been
(50) able to understand why. I happen to think that the

waggle dance differs from human languages to such a degree that little is gained by terming them both "languages," but even if "language" is so defined that the waggle dance slips in, bees still
(55) remain bees. It is equally important to some that no other species use tools. No matter how ingenious other species get in the manipulation of objects in their environment, it is absolutely essential that nothing they do count as "tool use."
(60) I, however, fail to see what difference it makes whether any of these devices such as probes and anvils, etc. are really tools. All the species involved remain distinct biological species no matter what decisions are made. Similar observa-
(65) tions hold for rationality and anything a computer might do.

   * After finding food, a bee returns to the hive and indicates, through an elaborate sequence of movements, the location of the food to other members of the hive.

23 According to the author, what is most responsible for influencing our perception of a comparison between species?

   (A) The behavior of the organisms in their natural environment
   (B) The organizational scheme imposed on the living world by researchers and philosophers
   (C) The style of language used by scientists in presenting their research
   (D) The sophistication of the communication between organisms
   (E) The magnitude of hierarchical distance between a species and *Homo sapiens*

24 Which of the following is NOT possible within an Aristotelian classification scheme?

   (A) Two species that are alike in having sensory souls but differ in that one lacks a rational soul
   (B) Two species that are alike in having vegetative souls but differ in that only one has a sensory soul
   (C) A species having a vegetative soul while lacking sensory and rational souls
   (D) A species having vegetative and rational souls while lacking a sensory soul
   (E) A species having vegetative and sensory souls while lacking a rational soul

GO ON TO THE NEXT PAGE

25 Which of the following comparisons would be "legitimate" for all living organisms according to the Aristotelian scheme described in paragraph two?

    I. Comparisons based on the vegetative soul
    II. Comparisons based on the sensory soul
    III. Comparisons based on the rational soul

(A) I only
(B) II only
(C) III only
(D) II and III only
(E) I, II, and III

26 If the author had wished to explain why "most" people (line 40) feel the way they do, the explanation would have probably focused on the

(A) reality of distinct biological species
(B) most recent advances in biological research
(C) behavioral similarities between *Homo sapiens* and other species
(D) role of language in the development of technology
(E) lack of objectivity in the classification of *Homo sapiens*

27 The author uses the words "For some reason" in lines 40-41 to express

(A) rage
(B) disapproval
(C) despair
(D) sympathy
(E) uncertainty

28 Which best summarizes the idea of "uniquely unique" (line 42)?

(A) We are unique in the same way that all other species are unique.
(B) We are defined by attributes that we alone possess and that are qualitatively different from those of other species.
(C) We are, by virtue of our elevated rank, insulated from many of the problems of survival faced by less sophisticated species.
(D) Our awareness of our uniqueness defines us as a rational species.
(E) Our apparently unique status is an unintended by-product of classification systems.

29 In line 44, "insulated from" means

(A) warmed by
(B) covered with
(C) barred from
(D) segregated from
(E) protected from

30 In the third paragraph, the author criticizes those who believe that

(A) the similarities between *Homo sapiens* and other species are more significant than their differences
(B) the differences between *Homo sapiens* and other animals are those of degree, not kind
(C) *Homo sapiens* and animals belong to separate and distinct divisions of the living world
(D) *Homo sapiens* and animals have the ability to control their environment
(E) *Homo sapiens* and other organisms can be arranged in Aristotelian nested groups

IF YOU FINISH BEFORE TIME IS CALLED, YOU MAY CHECK YOUR WORK ON THIS SECTION ONLY. DO NOT TURN TO ANY OTHER SECTION IN THE TEST. STOP

327

Section 5

Time — 15 Minutes
13 Questions

For each question in this section, select the best answer from among the choices given and fill in the corresponding oval on the answer sheet.

The two passages below are followed by questions based on their content and on the relationship between the two passages. Answer the questions on the basis of what is stated or implied in the passages and in any introductory material that may be provided.

Questions 1-13 are based on the following passages.

These passages present two perspectives of the prairie, the grasslands that covered much of the central plains of the United States during the nineteenth century. In Passage 1, a young English journalist writes about his visit to the prairie on a sight-seeing tour in the 1840's. In Passage 2, an American writer describes the area near his childhood home of the early 1870's.

Passage 1

We came upon the Prairie at sunset. It would be difficult to say why, or how—though it was possibly from having heard and read so much about it—
Line but the effect on me was disappointment. Towards
(5) the setting sun, there lay stretched out before my view a vast expanse of level ground, unbroken (save by one thin line of trees, which scarcely amounted to a scratch upon the great blank) until it met the glowing sky, wherein it seemed to dip,
(10) mingling with its rich colors and mellowing in its distant blue. There it lay, a tranquil sea or lake without water, if such a simile be admissible, with the day going down upon it: a few birds wheeling here and there, solitude and silence reigning
(15) paramount around. But the grass was not yet high; there were bare black patches on the ground and the few wild flowers that the eye could see were poor and scanty. Great as the picture was, its very flatness and extent, which left nothing to the
(20) imagination, tamed it down and cramped its interest. I felt little of that sense of freedom and exhilaration that the open landscape of a Scottish moor, or even the rolling hills of our English downlands, inspires. It was lonely and wild, but oppressive in
(25) its barren monotony. I felt that in traversing the Prairies, I could never abandon myself to the scene, forgetful of all else, as I should instinctively were heather moorland beneath my feet. On the Prairie I should often glance towards the distant
(30) and frequently receding line of the horizon, and wish it gained and passed. It is not a scene to be forgotten, but it is scarcely one, I think (at all events, as I saw it), to remember with much pleasure or to covet the looking-on again, in after
(35) years.

Passage 2

In herding the cattle on horseback, we children came to know all the open prairie round about and found it very beautiful. On the uplands a short, light-green grass grew, intermixed with various
(40) resinous weeds, while in the lowland grazing grounds luxuriant patches of blue joint, wild oats, and other tall forage plants waved in the wind. Along the streams, cattails and tiger lilies nodded above thick mats of wide-bladed marsh grass.
(45) Almost without realizing it, I came to know the character of every weed, every flower, every living thing big enough to be seen from the back of a horse.

Nothing could be more generous, more joyous,
(50) than these natural meadows in summer. The flash and ripple and glimmer of the tall sunflowers, the chirp and gurgle of red-winged blackbirds swaying on the willow, the meadowlarks piping from grassy bogs, the peep of the prairie chick and the
(55) wailing call of plover on the flowery green slopes of the uplands made it all an ecstatic world to me. It was a wide world with a big, big sky that gave alluring hints of the still more glorious unknown wilderness beyond.
(60) Sometimes we wandered away to the meadows along the creek, gathering bouquets of pinks, sweet william, tiger lilies, and lady's slippers. The sun flamed across the splendid serial waves of the grasses and the perfumes of a hundred spicy plants
(65) rose in the shimmering midday air. At such times the mere joy of living filled our hearts with wordless satisfaction.

On a long ridge to the north and west, the soil, too wet and cold to cultivate easily, remained

GO ON TO THE NEXT PAGE

(70) unplowed for several years. Scattered over these clay lands stood small wooded groves that we called "tow-heads." They stood out like islands in the waving seas of grasses. Against these dark-green masses, breakers of blue joint radiantly
(75) rolled. To the east ran the river; plum trees and crabapples bloomed along its banks. In June immense crops of wild strawberries appeared in the natural meadows. Their delicious odor rose to us as we rode our way, tempting us to dismount.
(80)   On the bare upland ridges lay huge antlers, bleached and bare, in countless numbers, telling of the herds of elk and bison that had once fed in these vast savannas. On sunny April days the mother fox lay out with her young on southward-
(85) sloping swells. Often we met a prairie wolf, finding in it the spirit of the wilderness. To us it seemed that just over the next long swell toward the sunset the shaggy brown bison still fed in myriads, and in our hearts was a longing to ride
(90) away into the "sunset regions" of our pioneer songs.

1 In creating an impression of the prairie for the reader, the author of Passage 1 makes use of

    (A) reference to geological processes
    (B) description of its inhabitants
    (C) evocation of different but equally attractive areas
    (D) comparison with other landscapes
    (E) contrast to imaginary places

2 In line 13, the author includes the detail of "a few birds" primarily to emphasize the

    (A) loneliness of the scene
    (B) strangeness of the wildlife
    (C) lateness of the evening
    (D) dominance of the sky
    (E) infertility of the land

3 In line 20, "tamed" most nearly means

    (A) composed
    (B) trained
    (C) subdued
    (D) captured
    (E) befriended

4 In line 26, "abandon myself" most nearly means

    (A) dismiss as worthless
    (B) isolate from all others
    (C) overlook unintentionally
    (D) retreat completely
    (E) become absorbed in

5 The author of Passage 1 qualifies his judgment of the prairie by

    (A) pointing out his own subjectivity
    (B) commenting on his lack of imagination
    (C) mentioning his physical fatigue
    (D) apologizing for his prejudices against the landscape
    (E) indicating his psychological agitation

6 In line 66, "mere" most nearly means

    (A) tiny
    (B) trivial
    (C) simple
    (D) direct
    (E) questionable

7 In Passage 2, the author's references to things beyond his direct experience (lines 57-59 and lines 86-91) indicate the

    (A) unexpected dangers of life on the unsettled prairie
    (B) psychological interweaving of imagination and the natural scene
    (C) exaggerated sense of mystery that is natural to children
    (D) predominant influence of sight in experiencing a place
    (E) permanence of the loss of the old life of the prairie

8 In line 74, "masses" metaphorically compares the tow-heads to

    (A) ships on a stormy ocean
    (B) birds on a pond
    (C) reefs submerged by rising waters
    (D) islands amidst the surf
    (E) islands engulfed by a river

GO ON TO THE NEXT PAGE

9 One aspect of Passage 2 that might make it difficult to appreciate is the author's apparent assumption that readers will

(A) have seen nineteenth-century paintings or photographs of the prairie

(B) connect accounts of specific prairie towns with their own experiences of the prairie

(C) be able to visualize the plants and the animals that are named

(D) recognize the references to particular pioneer songs

(E) understand the children's associations with the flowers that they gathered

10 The contrast between the two descriptions of the prairie is essentially one between

(A) misfortune and prosperity

(B) homesickness and anticipation

(C) resignation and joy

(D) bleakness and richness

(E) exhaustion and energy

11 In both passages, the authors liken the prairie to

(A) a desert
(B) an island
(C) a barren wilderness
(D) a large animal
(E) a body of water

12 Both authors indicate that the experience of a beautiful landscape involves

(A) artistic production
(B) detached observation of appearances
(C) emotional turmoil
(D) stimulation of the imagination
(E) fanciful reconstruction of bygone times

13 The contrast between the two passages reflects primarily the biases of a

(A) grown man and a little boy

(B) journalist and a writer of fiction

(C) passing visitor and a local resident

(D) native of Europe and a native of the United States

(E) weary tourist and an energetic farm worker

IF YOU FINISH BEFORE TIME IS CALLED, YOU MAY CHECK YOUR WORK ON THIS SECTION ONLY. DO NOT TURN TO ANY OTHER SECTION IN THE TEST. | STOP

330

Time—15 Minutes
10 Questions

In this section solve each problem, using any available space on the page for scratchwork. Then decide which is the best of the choices given and fill in the corresponding oval on the answer sheet.

Notes:

1. The use of a calculator is permitted. All numbers used are real numbers.

2. Figures that accompany problems in this test are intended to provide information useful in solving the problems. They are drawn as accurately as possible EXCEPT when it is stated in a specific problem that the figure is not drawn to scale. All figures lie in a plane unless otherwise indicated.

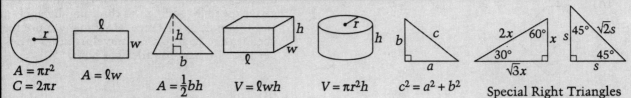
 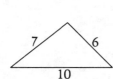

1 If the triangles shown above have the same perimeter, what is the value of x ?

(A) 5
(B) 6
(C) 7
(D) 8
(E) 9

$$\begin{array}{r} \square 5 \\ \square 6 \\ \square 7 \\ + \square 8 \\ \hline 146 \end{array}$$

2 In the correctly worked addition problem above, each $\square$ represents the same digit. What is the value of $\square$?

(A) 3
(B) 4
(C) 6
(D) 8
(E) 10

GO ON TO THE NEXT PAGE

331

Figure I   Figure II

3 A rectangular piece of paper is folded in half as shown in Figure I above. If two opposite corners of the folded paper are cut off as shown in Figure II, which of the following is the design of the paper when unfolded?

(A)

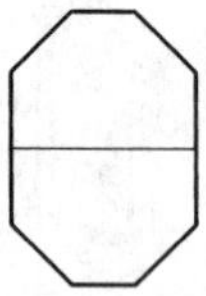

(B)

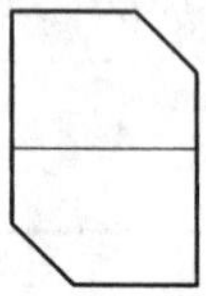

(C)

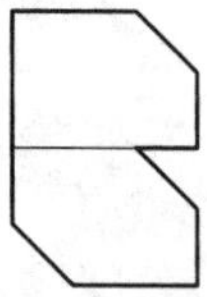

(D)

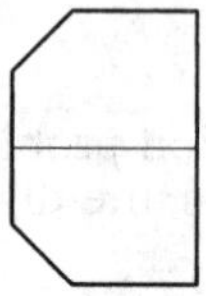

(E)

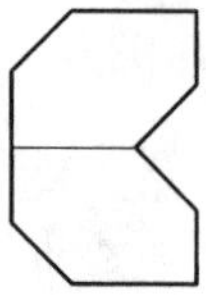

Speed (in miles per hour)	Thinking Distance (in feet)	Braking Distance (in feet)
20	20	20
30	30	45
40	40	80
50	50	125
60	60	180

4 The table above can be used to calculate the distance required to stop a car traveling at a given speed by adding the thinking distance and the braking distance. How many more feet does it take to stop a car traveling at 50 miles per hour than at 20 miles per hour?

(A) 75
(B) 105
(C) 135
(D) 165
(E) 175

GO ON TO THE NEXT PAGE

Note: Figure not drawn to scale.

5 The height of the solid cone above is 18 inches and the radius of the base is 8 inches. A cut parallel to the circular base is made completely through the cone so that one of the two resulting solids is a smaller cone. If the radius of the base of the small cone is 2 inches, what is the height of the small cone, in inches?

(A) 2.5
(B) 4.0
(C) 4.5
(D) 9.0
(E) 12.0

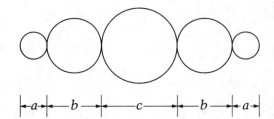

6 The figure above shows a pattern of beads with integer diameter lengths a, b, and c centimeters. This five-bead pattern is to be repeated without variation to make one complete necklace. If $a : b : c = 1 : 2 : 3$, which of the following could be the total length of the beads on the necklace?

(A) 56 cm
(B) 57 cm
(C) 60 cm
(D) 63 cm
(E) 64 cm

NUMBER OF MILES TRAVELED TO
WORK BY EMPLOYEES OF COMPANY X

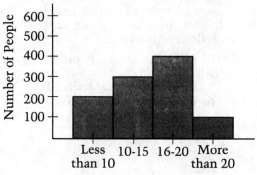

7 According to the graph above, which of the following is the closest approximation to the percent of employees of Company X who travel at least 16 miles to work?

(A) 25%
(B) 30%
(C) 40%
(D) 50%
(E) 60%

GO ON TO THE NEXT PAGE

20, 30, 50, 70, 80, 80, 90

8 Seven students played a game and their scores from least to greatest are given above. Which of the following is true of the scores?

    I. The average (arithmetic mean) is greater than 70.
   II. The median is greater than 70.
  III. The mode is greater than 70.

(A) None
(B) III only
(C) I and II only
(D) II and III only
(E) I, II, and III

9 P is the set of positive factors of 20 and Q is the set of positive factors of 12. If x is a member of set P and y is a member of set Q, what is the greatest possible value of $x - y$?

(A) 4
(B) 8
(C) 14
(D) 19
(E) 20

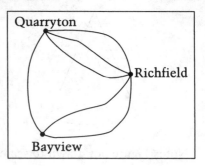

10 The figure above shows all roads between Quarryton, Richfield, and Bayview. Martina is traveling from Quarryton to Bayview <u>and back</u>. How many different ways could she make the round-trip, going through Richfield exactly once on a round-trip and not traveling any section of road more than once on a round-trip?

(A) 5
(B) 6
(C) 10
(D) 12
(E) 16

IF YOU FINISH BEFORE TIME IS CALLED, YOU MAY CHECK YOUR WORK ON THIS SECTION ONLY. DO NOT TURN TO ANY OTHER SECTION IN THE TEST. **STOP**

SAT I Scoring Worksheet

SAT I Verbal Sections

A. Section 2:

_____ − (_____ ÷ 4) = _____
no. correct   no. incorrect   subtotal A

B. Section 4:

_____ − (_____ ÷ 4) = _____
no. correct   no. incorrect   subtotal B

C. Section 5:

_____ − (_____ ÷ 4) = _____
no. correct   no. incorrect   subtotal C

D. Total unrounded raw score
(Total A + B + C)

_____
D

E. Total rounded raw score
(Rounded to nearest whole number)

_____
E

F. SAT I verbal reported scaled score
(Use the appropriate conversion table)

SAT I verbal
score

SAT I Mathematical Sections

A. Section 1:

_____ − (_____ ÷ 4) = _____
no. correct   no. incorrect   subtotal A

B. Section 3:
Questions 1-15 (quantitative comparison)

_____ − (_____ ÷ 3) = _____
no. correct   no. incorrect   subtotal B

C. Section 3:
Questions 16-25 (student-produced response)

_____ = _____
no. correct   subtotal C

D. Section 6:

_____ − (_____ ÷ 4) = _____
no. correct   no. incorrect   subtotal D

E. Total unrounded raw score
(Total A + B + C + D)

_____
E

F. Total rounded raw score
(Rounded to nearest whole number)

_____
F

G. SAT I mathematical reported scaled score
(Use the appropriate conversion table)

SAT I
mathematical
score

Score Conversion Table
SAT I: Reasoning Test
Saturday, March 1994
Recentered Scale

Raw Score	Verbal Scaled Score	Math Scaled Score	Raw Score	Verbal Scaled Score	Math Scaled Score
78	800		36	500	560
77	800		35	500	550
76	800		34	490	540
75	800		33	480	540
74	800		32	480	530
73	780		31	470	520
72	770		30	470	520
71	760		29	460	510
70	740		28	450	510
69	730		27	450	500
68	720		26	440	490
67	710		25	440	490
66	700		24	430	480
65	700		23	420	470
64	690		22	420	470
63	680		21	410	460
62	670		20	400	460
61	660		19	400	450
60	650	800	18	390	440
59	650	800	17	380	440
58	640	780	16	370	430
57	630	760	15	370	420
56	630	740	14	360	420
55	620	720	13	350	410
54	610	710	12	340	400
53	610	700	11	330	390
52	600	690	10	330	380
51	590	680	9	320	380
50	590	670	8	310	370
49	580	660	7	300	360
48	570	650	6	290	350
47	570	640	5	280	330
46	560	630	4	270	320
45	560	620	3	260	310
44	550	610	2	240	300
43	540	610	1	230	280
42	540	600	0	210	260
41	530	590	−1	200	240
40	530	580	−2	200	230
39	520	580	−3	200	200
38	510	570	and		
37	510	560	below		

This table is for use only with this test.

SAT I: Reasoning Test

Saturday, November 1994

SAT® I: Reasoning Test

Calculator use is permitted on the mathematics sections only.

You will have three hours to work on the questions in this test book. There are **five 30-minute sections and two 15-minute sections**. The supervisor will tell you when to begin and end each section. If you finish before time is called, you may check your work on that section, but you may <u>not work on any other section</u>.

Do not worry if you are unable to finish a section or if there are some questions you cannot answer. Do not waste time puzzling over a question that seems too difficult for you. Work as rapidly as you can without sacrificing accuracy.

Students often ask whether they should guess when they are uncertain about the answer to a question. Scores on the multiple-choice questions on this test are based on the number of questions answered correctly minus a fraction of the number answered incorrectly. Therefore, it is unlikely that random or haphazard guessing will change your scores significantly. If you have some knowledge of a question, you may be able to eliminate one or more of the answer choices as wrong. It is generally a good idea to guess which of the remaining choices is correct.

Some mathematics questions have no answer choices. Instead, you must solve the problem and record your answer in a special grid on your answer sheet. For these questions, you will receive credit for correct answers, but there will be no deduction for incorrect answers.

Mark all your answers on the separate answer sheet. Mark only one answer for each question. Since the answer sheet will be machine scored, be sure that each mark is dark and that it completely fills the oval. In each section of the answer sheet, there are spaces to answer 40 questions. When there are fewer than 40 questions in a section of your test, use only the spaces that correspond to the question numbers. Do not make stray marks on the answer sheet. If you erase, do so completely, because an incomplete erasure may be scored as an intended response.

You may use the test book for scratchwork, but you will not receive credit for anything written there.

(The passages for this test have been adapted from published material. The ideas contained in them do not necessarily represent the opinions of the College Board or Educational Testing Service.)

DO NOT OPEN THIS BOOK UNTIL THE SUPERVISOR TELLS YOU TO DO SO.

Use a No. 2 pencil only. Be sure each mark is dark and completely fills the intended oval. Completely erase any errors or stray marks.

1. Your Name

First 4 letters of Last Name				First init.	Mid. init.

2.
Your Name:
(Print)   Last   First   M.I.

Signature: _____   **Date:** ___/___/___

Home Address: _____
(Print)   Number and Street

City   State   Zip Code

Center: _____
(Print)   City   State   Center Number

IMPORTANT: Please fill in items 8 and 9 exactly as shown on the back cover of your test book.

8. Form Code
(Copy and grid as on back of test book.)

3. Date Of Birth

Month	Day	Year
Jan.		
Feb.		
Mar.		
Apr.		
May		
June		
July		
Aug.		
Sept.		
Oct.		
Nov.		
Dec.		

4. Social Security Number

5. Sex
Female   Male

7. Test Book Serial Number
(Copy from front of test book.)

6. Registration Number
(Copy from your Admission Ticket.)

FOR ETS USE ONLY

9. Test Form
(Copy from back cover of test book.)

DO NOT WRITE IN THIS AREA.

Start with number 1 for each new section. If a section has fewer questions than answer spaces, leave the extra answer spaces blank.

SECTION 1

1 A B C D E	11 A B C D E	21 A B C D E	31 A B C D E
2 A B C D E	12 A B C D E	22 A B C D E	32 A B C D E
3 A B C D E	13 A B C D E	23 A B C D E	33 A B C D E
4 A B C D E	14 A B C D E	24 A B C D E	34 A B C D E
5 A B C D E	15 A B C D E	25 A B C D E	35 A B C D E
6 A B C D E	16 A B C D E	26 A B C D E	36 A B C D E
7 A B C D E	17 A B C D E	27 A B C D E	37 A B C D E
8 A B C D E	18 A B C D E	28 A B C D E	38 A B C D E
9 A B C D E	19 A B C D E	29 A B C D E	39 A B C D E
10 A B C D E	20 A B C D E	30 A B C D E	40 A B C D E

SECTION 2

1 A B C D E	11 A B C D E	21 A B C D E	31 A B C D E
2 A B C D E	12 A B C D E	22 A B C D E	32 A B C D E
3 A B C D E	13 A B C D E	23 A B C D E	33 A B C D E
4 A B C D E	14 A B C D E	24 A B C D E	34 A B C D E
5 A B C D E	15 A B C D E	25 A B C D E	35 A B C D E
6 A B C D E	16 A B C D E	26 A B C D E	36 A B C D E
7 A B C D E	17 A B C D E	27 A B C D E	37 A B C D E
8 A B C D E	18 A B C D E	28 A B C D E	38 A B C D E
9 A B C D E	19 A B C D E	29 A B C D E	39 A B C D E
10 A B C D E	20 A B C D E	30 A B C D E	40 A B C D E

Use a No. 2 pencil only. Be sure each mark is dark and completely fills the intended oval. Completely erase any errors or stray marks.

Start with number 1 for each new section. If a section has fewer questions than answer spaces, leave the extra answer spaces blank.

SECTION 3

1 (A) (B) (C) (D) (E)
2 (A) (B) (C) (D) (E)
3 (A) (B) (C) (D) (E)
4 (A) (B) (C) (D) (E)
5 (A) (B) (C) (D) (E)
6 (A) (B) (C) (D) (E)
7 (A) (B) (C) (D) (E)
8 (A) (B) (C) (D) (E)
9 (A) (B) (C) (D) (E)
10 (A) (B) (C) (D) (E)
11 (A) (B) (C) (D) (E)
12 (A) (B) (C) (D) (E)
13 (A) (B) (C) (D) (E)
14 (A) (B) (C) (D) (E)
15 (A) (B) (C) (D) (E)

16 (A) (B) (C) (D) (E)
17 (A) (B) (C) (D) (E)
18 (A) (B) (C) (D) (E)
19 (A) (B) (C) (D) (E)
20 (A) (B) (C) (D) (E)
21 (A) (B) (C) (D) (E)
22 (A) (B) (C) (D) (E)
23 (A) (B) (C) (D) (E)
24 (A) (B) (C) (D) (E)
25 (A) (B) (C) (D) (E)
26 (A) (B) (C) (D) (E)
27 (A) (B) (C) (D) (E)
28 (A) (B) (C) (D) (E)
29 (A) (B) (C) (D) (E)
30 (A) (B) (C) (D) (E)

31 (A) (B) (C) (D) (E)
32 (A) (B) (C) (D) (E)
33 (A) (B) (C) (D) (E)
34 (A) (B) (C) (D) (E)
35 (A) (B) (C) (D) (E)
36 (A) (B) (C) (D) (E)
37 (A) (B) (C) (D) (E)
38 (A) (B) (C) (D) (E)
39 (A) (B) (C) (D) (E)
40 (A) (B) (C) (D) (E)

If section 3 of your test book contains math questions that are not multiple-choice, continue to item 16 below. Otherwise, continue to item 16 above.

ONLY ANSWERS ENTERED IN THE OVALS IN EACH GRID AREA WILL BE SCORED. YOU WILL NOT RECEIVE CREDIT FOR ANYTHING WRITTEN IN THE BOXES ABOVE THE OVALS.

16   17   18   19   20

21   22   23   24   25

BE SURE TO ERASE ANY ERRORS OR STRAY MARKS COMPLETELY.

PLEASE PRINT YOUR INITIALS

First   Middle   Last

342

Start with number 1 for each new section. If a section has fewer questions than answer spaces, leave the extra answer spaces blank.

SECTION 4

1 Ⓐ Ⓑ Ⓒ Ⓓ Ⓔ
2 Ⓐ Ⓑ Ⓒ Ⓓ Ⓔ
3 Ⓐ Ⓑ Ⓒ Ⓓ Ⓔ
4 Ⓐ Ⓑ Ⓒ Ⓓ Ⓔ
5 Ⓐ Ⓑ Ⓒ Ⓓ Ⓔ
6 Ⓐ Ⓑ Ⓒ Ⓓ Ⓔ
7 Ⓐ Ⓑ Ⓒ Ⓓ Ⓔ
8 Ⓐ Ⓑ Ⓒ Ⓓ Ⓔ
9 Ⓐ Ⓑ Ⓒ Ⓓ Ⓔ
10 Ⓐ Ⓑ Ⓒ Ⓓ Ⓔ
11 Ⓐ Ⓑ Ⓒ Ⓓ Ⓔ
12 Ⓐ Ⓑ Ⓒ Ⓓ Ⓔ
13 Ⓐ Ⓑ Ⓒ Ⓓ Ⓔ
14 Ⓐ Ⓑ Ⓒ Ⓓ Ⓔ
15 Ⓐ Ⓑ Ⓒ Ⓓ Ⓔ

16 Ⓐ Ⓑ Ⓒ Ⓓ Ⓔ
17 Ⓐ Ⓑ Ⓒ Ⓓ Ⓔ
18 Ⓐ Ⓑ Ⓒ Ⓓ Ⓔ
19 Ⓐ Ⓑ Ⓒ Ⓓ Ⓔ
20 Ⓐ Ⓑ Ⓒ Ⓓ Ⓔ
21 Ⓐ Ⓑ Ⓒ Ⓓ Ⓔ
22 Ⓐ Ⓑ Ⓒ Ⓓ Ⓔ
23 Ⓐ Ⓑ Ⓒ Ⓓ Ⓔ
24 Ⓐ Ⓑ Ⓒ Ⓓ Ⓔ
25 Ⓐ Ⓑ Ⓒ Ⓓ Ⓔ
26 Ⓐ Ⓑ Ⓒ Ⓓ Ⓔ
27 Ⓐ Ⓑ Ⓒ Ⓓ Ⓔ
28 Ⓐ Ⓑ Ⓒ Ⓓ Ⓔ
29 Ⓐ Ⓑ Ⓒ Ⓓ Ⓔ
30 Ⓐ Ⓑ Ⓒ Ⓓ Ⓔ

31 Ⓐ Ⓑ Ⓒ Ⓓ Ⓔ
32 Ⓐ Ⓑ Ⓒ Ⓓ Ⓔ
33 Ⓐ Ⓑ Ⓒ Ⓓ Ⓔ
34 Ⓐ Ⓑ Ⓒ Ⓓ Ⓔ
35 Ⓐ Ⓑ Ⓒ Ⓓ Ⓔ
36 Ⓐ Ⓑ Ⓒ Ⓓ Ⓔ
37 Ⓐ Ⓑ Ⓒ Ⓓ Ⓔ
38 Ⓐ Ⓑ Ⓒ Ⓓ Ⓔ
39 Ⓐ Ⓑ Ⓒ Ⓓ Ⓔ
40 Ⓐ Ⓑ Ⓒ Ⓓ Ⓔ

If section 4 of your test book contains math questions that are not multiple-choice, continue to item 16 below. Otherwise, continue to item 16 above.

ONLY ANSWERS ENTERED IN THE OVALS IN EACH GRID AREA WILL BE SCORED. YOU WILL NOT RECEIVE CREDIT FOR ANYTHING WRITTEN IN THE BOXES ABOVE THE OVALS.

16   17   18   19   20

21   22   23   24   25

BE SURE TO ERASE ANY ERRORS OR STRAY MARKS COMPLETELY.

PLEASE PRINT YOUR INITIALS

First   Middle   Last

Use a No. 2 pencil only. Be sure each mark is dark and completely fills the intended oval. Completely erase any errors or stray marks.

Start with number 1 for each new section. If a section has fewer questions than answer spaces, leave the extra answer spaces blank.

SECTION 5

1 Ⓐ Ⓑ Ⓒ Ⓓ Ⓔ	11 Ⓐ Ⓑ Ⓒ Ⓓ Ⓔ	21 Ⓐ Ⓑ Ⓒ Ⓓ Ⓔ	31 Ⓐ Ⓑ Ⓒ Ⓓ Ⓔ
2 Ⓐ Ⓑ Ⓒ Ⓓ Ⓔ	12 Ⓐ Ⓑ Ⓒ Ⓓ Ⓔ	22 Ⓐ Ⓑ Ⓒ Ⓓ Ⓔ	32 Ⓐ Ⓑ Ⓒ Ⓓ Ⓔ
3 Ⓐ Ⓑ Ⓒ Ⓓ Ⓔ	13 Ⓐ Ⓑ Ⓒ Ⓓ Ⓔ	23 Ⓐ Ⓑ Ⓒ Ⓓ Ⓔ	33 Ⓐ Ⓑ Ⓒ Ⓓ Ⓔ
4 Ⓐ Ⓑ Ⓒ Ⓓ Ⓔ	14 Ⓐ Ⓑ Ⓒ Ⓓ Ⓔ	24 Ⓐ Ⓑ Ⓒ Ⓓ Ⓔ	34 Ⓐ Ⓑ Ⓒ Ⓓ Ⓔ
5 Ⓐ Ⓑ Ⓒ Ⓓ Ⓔ	15 Ⓐ Ⓑ Ⓒ Ⓓ Ⓔ	25 Ⓐ Ⓑ Ⓒ Ⓓ Ⓔ	35 Ⓐ Ⓑ Ⓒ Ⓓ Ⓔ
6 Ⓐ Ⓑ Ⓒ Ⓓ Ⓔ	16 Ⓐ Ⓑ Ⓒ Ⓓ Ⓔ	26 Ⓐ Ⓑ Ⓒ Ⓓ Ⓔ	36 Ⓐ Ⓑ Ⓒ Ⓓ Ⓔ
7 Ⓐ Ⓑ Ⓒ Ⓓ Ⓔ	17 Ⓐ Ⓑ Ⓒ Ⓓ Ⓔ	27 Ⓐ Ⓑ Ⓒ Ⓓ Ⓔ	37 Ⓐ Ⓑ Ⓒ Ⓓ Ⓔ
8 Ⓐ Ⓑ Ⓒ Ⓓ Ⓔ	18 Ⓐ Ⓑ Ⓒ Ⓓ Ⓔ	28 Ⓐ Ⓑ Ⓒ Ⓓ Ⓔ	38 Ⓐ Ⓑ Ⓒ Ⓓ Ⓔ
9 Ⓐ Ⓑ Ⓒ Ⓓ Ⓔ	19 Ⓐ Ⓑ Ⓒ Ⓓ Ⓔ	29 Ⓐ Ⓑ Ⓒ Ⓓ Ⓔ	39 Ⓐ Ⓑ Ⓒ Ⓓ Ⓔ
10 Ⓐ Ⓑ Ⓒ Ⓓ Ⓔ	20 Ⓐ Ⓑ Ⓒ Ⓓ Ⓔ	30 Ⓐ Ⓑ Ⓒ Ⓓ Ⓔ	40 Ⓐ Ⓑ Ⓒ Ⓓ Ⓔ

SECTION 6

1 Ⓐ Ⓑ Ⓒ Ⓓ Ⓔ	11 Ⓐ Ⓑ Ⓒ Ⓓ Ⓔ	21 Ⓐ Ⓑ Ⓒ Ⓓ Ⓔ	31 Ⓐ Ⓑ Ⓒ Ⓓ Ⓔ
2 Ⓐ Ⓑ Ⓒ Ⓓ Ⓔ	12 Ⓐ Ⓑ Ⓒ Ⓓ Ⓔ	22 Ⓐ Ⓑ Ⓒ Ⓓ Ⓔ	32 Ⓐ Ⓑ Ⓒ Ⓓ Ⓔ
3 Ⓐ Ⓑ Ⓒ Ⓓ Ⓔ	13 Ⓐ Ⓑ Ⓒ Ⓓ Ⓔ	23 Ⓐ Ⓑ Ⓒ Ⓓ Ⓔ	33 Ⓐ Ⓑ Ⓒ Ⓓ Ⓔ
4 Ⓐ Ⓑ Ⓒ Ⓓ Ⓔ	14 Ⓐ Ⓑ Ⓒ Ⓓ Ⓔ	24 Ⓐ Ⓑ Ⓒ Ⓓ Ⓔ	34 Ⓐ Ⓑ Ⓒ Ⓓ Ⓔ
5 Ⓐ Ⓑ Ⓒ Ⓓ Ⓔ	15 Ⓐ Ⓑ Ⓒ Ⓓ Ⓔ	25 Ⓐ Ⓑ Ⓒ Ⓓ Ⓔ	35 Ⓐ Ⓑ Ⓒ Ⓓ Ⓔ
6 Ⓐ Ⓑ Ⓒ Ⓓ Ⓔ	16 Ⓐ Ⓑ Ⓒ Ⓓ Ⓔ	26 Ⓐ Ⓑ Ⓒ Ⓓ Ⓔ	36 Ⓐ Ⓑ Ⓒ Ⓓ Ⓔ
7 Ⓐ Ⓑ Ⓒ Ⓓ Ⓔ	17 Ⓐ Ⓑ Ⓒ Ⓓ Ⓔ	27 Ⓐ Ⓑ Ⓒ Ⓓ Ⓔ	37 Ⓐ Ⓑ Ⓒ Ⓓ Ⓔ
8 Ⓐ Ⓑ Ⓒ Ⓓ Ⓔ	18 Ⓐ Ⓑ Ⓒ Ⓓ Ⓔ	28 Ⓐ Ⓑ Ⓒ Ⓓ Ⓔ	38 Ⓐ Ⓑ Ⓒ Ⓓ Ⓔ
9 Ⓐ Ⓑ Ⓒ Ⓓ Ⓔ	19 Ⓐ Ⓑ Ⓒ Ⓓ Ⓔ	29 Ⓐ Ⓑ Ⓒ Ⓓ Ⓔ	39 Ⓐ Ⓑ Ⓒ Ⓓ Ⓔ
10 Ⓐ Ⓑ Ⓒ Ⓓ Ⓔ	20 Ⓐ Ⓑ Ⓒ Ⓓ Ⓔ	30 Ⓐ Ⓑ Ⓒ Ⓓ Ⓔ	40 Ⓐ Ⓑ Ⓒ Ⓓ Ⓔ

SECTION 7

1 Ⓐ Ⓑ Ⓒ Ⓓ Ⓔ	11 Ⓐ Ⓑ Ⓒ Ⓓ Ⓔ	21 Ⓐ Ⓑ Ⓒ Ⓓ Ⓔ	31 Ⓐ Ⓑ Ⓒ Ⓓ Ⓔ
2 Ⓐ Ⓑ Ⓒ Ⓓ Ⓔ	12 Ⓐ Ⓑ Ⓒ Ⓓ Ⓔ	22 Ⓐ Ⓑ Ⓒ Ⓓ Ⓔ	32 Ⓐ Ⓑ Ⓒ Ⓓ Ⓔ
3 Ⓐ Ⓑ Ⓒ Ⓓ Ⓔ	13 Ⓐ Ⓑ Ⓒ Ⓓ Ⓔ	23 Ⓐ Ⓑ Ⓒ Ⓓ Ⓔ	33 Ⓐ Ⓑ Ⓒ Ⓓ Ⓔ
4 Ⓐ Ⓑ Ⓒ Ⓓ Ⓔ	14 Ⓐ Ⓑ Ⓒ Ⓓ Ⓔ	24 Ⓐ Ⓑ Ⓒ Ⓓ Ⓔ	34 Ⓐ Ⓑ Ⓒ Ⓓ Ⓔ
5 Ⓐ Ⓑ Ⓒ Ⓓ Ⓔ	15 Ⓐ Ⓑ Ⓒ Ⓓ Ⓔ	25 Ⓐ Ⓑ Ⓒ Ⓓ Ⓔ	35 Ⓐ Ⓑ Ⓒ Ⓓ Ⓔ
6 Ⓐ Ⓑ Ⓒ Ⓓ Ⓔ	16 Ⓐ Ⓑ Ⓒ Ⓓ Ⓔ	26 Ⓐ Ⓑ Ⓒ Ⓓ Ⓔ	36 Ⓐ Ⓑ Ⓒ Ⓓ Ⓔ
7 Ⓐ Ⓑ Ⓒ Ⓓ Ⓔ	17 Ⓐ Ⓑ Ⓒ Ⓓ Ⓔ	27 Ⓐ Ⓑ Ⓒ Ⓓ Ⓔ	37 Ⓐ Ⓑ Ⓒ Ⓓ Ⓔ
8 Ⓐ Ⓑ Ⓒ Ⓓ Ⓔ	18 Ⓐ Ⓑ Ⓒ Ⓓ Ⓔ	28 Ⓐ Ⓑ Ⓒ Ⓓ Ⓔ	38 Ⓐ Ⓑ Ⓒ Ⓓ Ⓔ
9 Ⓐ Ⓑ Ⓒ Ⓓ Ⓔ	19 Ⓐ Ⓑ Ⓒ Ⓓ Ⓔ	29 Ⓐ Ⓑ Ⓒ Ⓓ Ⓔ	39 Ⓐ Ⓑ Ⓒ Ⓓ Ⓔ
10 Ⓐ Ⓑ Ⓒ Ⓓ Ⓔ	20 Ⓐ Ⓑ Ⓒ Ⓓ Ⓔ	30 Ⓐ Ⓑ Ⓒ Ⓓ Ⓔ	40 Ⓐ Ⓑ Ⓒ Ⓓ Ⓔ

CERTIFICATION STATEMENT

Copy in longhand the statement below and sign your name as you would an official document. **DO NOT PRINT.**

I hereby agree to the conditions set forth in the *Registration Bulletin* and certify that I am the person whose name and address appear on this answer sheet.

_____

_____

_____

SIGNATURE: _____ DATE: _____

Time—30 Minutes 25 Questions	In this section solve each problem, using any available space on the page for scratchwork. Then decide which is the best of the choices given and fill in the corresponding oval on the answer sheet.

Notes:

1. The use of a calculator is permitted. All numbers used are real numbers.

2. Figures that accompany problems in this test are intended to provide information useful in solving the problems. They are drawn as accurately as possible EXCEPT when it is stated in a specific problem that the figure is not drawn to scale. All figures lie in a plane unless otherwise indicated.

Reference Information

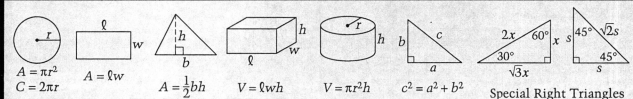

$A = \pi r^2$
$C = 2\pi r$
$A = \ell w$
$A = \frac{1}{2}bh$
$V = \ell w h$
$V = \pi r^2 h$
$c^2 = a^2 + b^2$
Special Right Triangles

The number of degrees of arc in a circle is 360.
The measure in degrees of a straight angle is 180.
The sum of the measures in degrees of the angles of a triangle is 180.

---

1 If $(x - 5) + 5 = 12$, what is the value of x?

(A) 2
(B) 7
(C) 12
(D) 17
(E) 22

2 Which of the following numbers has the digit 8 in the hundredths place?

(A) 0.008
(B) 0.080
(C) 0.800
(D) 80.0
(E) 800.0

3 If $2x + y = 5$, what is the value of $4x + 2y$?

(A) 5
(B) 8
(C) 10
(D) 15
(E) 20

4 Gene and JoAnn each bought some Ink-O pens and an ink eraser. Gene paid $1.75 for 3 pens and 1 eraser. JoAnn paid $1.25 for 2 pens and 1 eraser. What is the price of one of the pens?

(A) $0.10
(B) $0.15
(C) $0.25
(D) $0.50
(E) $0.60

GO ON TO THE NEXT PAGE

NUMBER OF COLLEGES AND UNIVERSITIES
IN NEW ENGLAND BY STATE

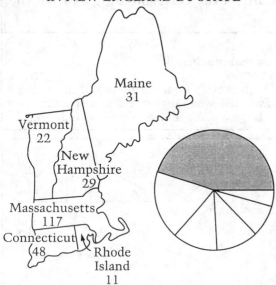

Maine
31

Vermont
22

New
Hampshire
29

Massachusetts
117

Connecticut
48

Rhode
Island
11

5 If the data in the map above were represented in the unlabeled circle graph, which of the following states would be represented by the shaded sector?

(A) Connecticut
(B) Massachusetts
(C) Vermont
(D) New Hampshire
(E) Maine

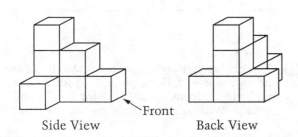

Side View   Back View

Front

6 The figure above shows two views of a solid that is constructed from cubes of the same size. How many cubes are needed to construct the solid?

(A) Eleven
(B) Ten
(C) Nine
(D) Eight
(E) Seven

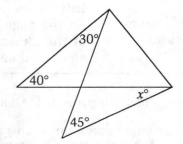

30°
40°
45°
x°

7 In the figure above, what is the value of x ?

(A) 65
(B) 45
(C) 40
(D) 30
(E) 25

8 If $4^{x+1} = 64$, what is the value of x ?

(A) 2
(B) 3
(C) 4
(D) 5
(E) 6

9 Of the students in a certain homeroom, 9 are in the school play, 12 are in the orchestra, and 15 are in the choral group. If 5 students participate in exactly 2 of the 3 activities and all other students participate in only 1 activity, how many students are in the homeroom?

(A) 31
(B) 30
(C) 26
(D) 25
(E) 21

GO ON TO THE NEXT PAGE

10 If $y = \dfrac{x^2}{z}$ and $x \neq 0$, then $\dfrac{1}{x^2} =$

(A) yz

(B) $\dfrac{y}{z}$

(C) $\dfrac{z}{y}$

(D) $y - \dfrac{1}{z}$

(E) $\dfrac{1}{yz}$

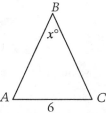

Note: Figure not drawn to scale.

11 In the figure above, $AB = BC$. If $x = 60$, then $AB =$

(A) 3

(B) 6

(C) $3\sqrt{2}$

(D) $3\sqrt{3}$

(E) $6\sqrt{3}$

12 What percent of 4 is 5 ?

(A) 75%
(B) 80%
(C) 125%
(D) 150%
(E) 180%

13 Through how many degrees does the minute hand of a clock turn from 3:10 p.m. to 3:25 p.m. of the same day?

(A) 15°
(B) 30°
(C) 45°
(D) 60°
(E) 90°

14 The length of a rectangle is 4 times the width. If the perimeter of the rectangle is 60, what is the width?

(A) 6
(B) 7.5
(C) 10
(D) 12
(E) 15

GO ON TO THE NEXT PAGE

15 If n is divided by 9, the remainder is 5. What is the remainder if $3n$ is divided by 9 ?

(A) 4
(B) 5
(C) 6
(D) 7
(E) 8

16 If $a \times b \times c = 72$, where a, b, and c are integers and $a > b > c > 1$, what is the greatest possible value of a ?

(A) 12
(B) 18
(C) 24
(D) 36
(E) 72

17 What is the slope of a line that passes through the origin and the point $(-2, -1)$?

(A) 2
(B) $\frac{1}{2}$
(C) 0
(D) $-\frac{1}{2}$
(E) -2

18 Julie has cats, fish, and frogs for pets. The number of frogs she has is 1 more than the number of cats, and the number of fish is 3 times the number of frogs. Of the following, which could be the total number of these pets?

(A) 15
(B) 16
(C) 17
(D) 18
(E) 19

19 If x is an integer, which of the following could NOT equal x^3 ?

(A) -8
(B) 0
(C) 1
(D) 16
(E) 27

20 If $x = 7 + y$ and $4x = 6 - 2y$, what is the value of x ?

(A) -4
(B) $-\frac{4}{3}$
(C) $-\frac{1}{6}$
(D) $\frac{10}{3}$
(E) 10

GO ON TO THE NEXT PAGE

CHESS CLUB MEMBERSHIP

Status	Number of Members Under 20 Years Old	Number of Members 20 Years or Older	Total
Number of Amateurs	4		9
Number of Professionals		8	11
Total	7	13	20

21 The incomplete table above categorizes the members of a chess club according to their age and status. During a tournament, each member of the club plays exactly one game with each of the other members. How many games of chess are played between amateurs 20 years or older and professionals under 20 years old during the tournament?

(A) 8
(B) 12
(C) 15
(D) 16
(E) 30

22 A bag contains a number of pieces of candy of which 78 are red, 24 are brown, and the remainder are yellow. If the probability of selecting a yellow piece of candy from this bag at random is $\frac{1}{3}$, how many yellow pieces of candy are in the bag?

(A) 34
(B) 51
(C) 54
(D) 102
(E) 306

GO ON TO THE NEXT PAGE

23 If $p = 4\left(\dfrac{x + y + z}{3}\right)$, then, in terms of p, what is the average (arithmetic mean) of x, y, and z ?

(A) $4p$

(B) $3p$

(C) $\dfrac{p}{3}$

(D) $\dfrac{p}{4}$

(E) $\dfrac{p}{12}$

24 If $n > 0$ and $9x^2 + kx + 36 = (3x + n)^2$ for all values of x, what is the value of $k - n$?

(A) 0
(B) 6
(C) 12
(D) 30
(E) 36

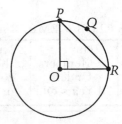

25 The circle in the figure above has center O. Which of the following measures for the figure would be sufficient by itself to determine the radius of the circle?

   I.   The length of arc PQR
  II. The perimeter of $\triangle OPR$
 III. The length of chord PR

(A) None
(B) I only
(C) II only
(D) III only
(E) I, II, and III

IF YOU FINISH BEFORE TIME IS CALLED, YOU MAY CHECK YOUR WORK ON THIS SECTION ONLY. DO NOT TURN TO ANY OTHER SECTION IN THE TEST. **STOP**

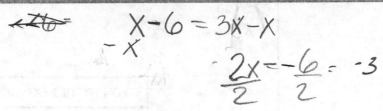

**Time—30 Minutes
36 Questions**

For each question in this section, select the best answer from among the choices given and fill in the corresponding oval on the answer sheet.

Each sentence below has one or two blanks, each blank indicating that something has been omitted. Beneath the sentence are five words or sets of words labeled A through E. Choose the word or set of words that, when inserted in the sentence, <u>best</u> fits the meaning of the sentence as a whole.

Example:

Medieval kingdoms did not become constitutional republics overnight; on the contrary, the change was ----.

(A) unpopular
(B) unexpected
(C) advantageous
(D) sufficient
(E) gradual   Ⓐ Ⓑ Ⓒ Ⓓ ●

1 Because his paintings represented the Midwest of the mid-1800's as a serene and settled landscape, Robert Duncanson ---- Easterners hesitant about moving westward that relocation was indeed ----.

(A) convinced. .ridiculous
(B) contradicted. .necessary
(C) reminded. .rash
(D) assured. .safe
(E) persuaded. .risky

2 Rachel Carson's book *Silent Spring*, which described a world made lifeless by the accumulation of hazardous pesticides, ---- a grass-roots campaign to ---- the indiscriminate use of such substances.

(A) catalyzed. .propagate
(B) protested. .limit
(C) conceived. .encourage
(D) inspired. .control
(E) allowed. .recommend

3 Florida Congresswoman Ileana Ros-Lehtinen chose to focus on how national issues affect her own ----, those voters she represents.

(A) opponents   (B) constituents —  voters that live in
(C) successors   (D) mentors   (E) colleagues that area

4 In a society that abhors ----, the nonconformist is persistently ----.

(A) creativity. .glorified
(B) rebelliousness. .suppressed
(C) insurgency. .heeded
(D) smugness. .persecuted
(E) stagnation. .denigrated

5 Instead of presenting a balanced view of both sides of the issue, the speaker became increasingly ----, insisting on the correctness of his position.

(A) inarticulate   (B) dogmatic   (C) elliptical
(D) tactful   (E) ambiguous

6 Astronomers who suspected that the sunspot cycle is not eleven years long have been ---- by studies ---- their belief that the entire cycle is actually twice that long.

(A) vindicated. .confirming
(B) exonerated. .refuting
(C) discredited. .substantiating
(D) encouraged. .rejecting
(E) humiliated. .proving

7 He ---- the practices of aggressive autograph seekers, arguing that anyone distinguished enough to merit such ---- also deserved to be treated courteously.

(A) decried. .adulation
(B) defended. .adoration
(C) endorsed. .brusqueness
(D) ignored. .effrontery
(E) vilified. .disdain

8 Andrew has enrolled in a specialized culinary arts program as a way of indulging his ---- French cuisine.

(A) abstinence from   (B) tenacity over
(C) distaste for   (D) acquisition of
(E) predilection for

9 Someday technology may make door-to-door mail delivery seem ----, that is, as incongruous as pony express delivery would seem now.

(A) recursive   (B) contemporaneous
(C) predictable   (D) anachronistic
(E) revered

10 The novelist brings out the ---- of human beings time and time again by ---- their lives to the permanence of the vast landscape.

(A) absurdity. .relating
(B) transience. .likening
(C) evanescence. .contrasting
(D) complexity. .comparing
(E) uniqueness. .opposing

GO ON TO THE NEXT PAGE

Each question below consists of a related pair of words or phrases, followed by five pairs of words or phrases labeled A through E. Select the pair that best expresses a relationship similar to that expressed in the original pair.

Example:

CRUMB : BREAD ::
(A) ounce : unit
(B) splinter : wood
(C) water : bucket
(D) twine : rope
(E) cream : butter

Ⓐ ● Ⓒ Ⓓ Ⓔ

11 ERASER : PAGE ::
(A) mop : floor
(B) sponge : soap
(C) pen : ink
(D) nail : wall
(E) bleach : stain

12 GOGGLES : EYES ::
(A) belt : waist
(B) earrings : ears
(C) razor : hair
(D) gloves : cold
(E) helmet : head

13 PORTFOLIO : DOCUMENTS ::
(A) album : photographs
(B) government : policies
(C) drama : acts
(D) excavation : artifacts
(E) rhythm : drums

14 TENTACLES : OCTOPUS ::
(A) petals : flower
(B) tadpoles : frog
(C) claws : crab
(D) algae : seaweed
(E) quills : porcupine

15 TICKET : ADMISSION ::
(A) letter : salutation
(B) coupon : discount
(C) receipt : payment
(D) license : travel
(E) application : interview

16 PROFICIENCY : EXPERT ::
(A) recognition : winner
(B) victory : athlete
(C) passion : enthusiast
(D) appointment : official
(E) medicine : doctor

17 COSMETICS : EMBELLISH ::
(A) calculation : assess
(B) ornament : adorn
(C) painting : hang
(D) posture : improve
(E) dish : garnish

18 CARPING : CRITICIZE ::
(A) vain : admire
(B) obliging : help
(C) retiring : boast
(D) jealous : possess
(E) wary : surprise

19 RECLUSIVE : COMPANIONSHIP ::
(A) frugal : extravagance
(B) organized : structure
(C) pitiful : compassion
(D) provocative : anger
(E) moody : unhappiness

20 TACTILE : TOUCH ::
(A) musical : hearing
(B) audible : volume
(C) nasal : smell
(D) sensitive : feeling
(E) visible : sight

21 SORT : CRITERION ::
(A) shuffle : order
(B) train : competence
(C) rank : value
(D) divide : quantity
(E) poll : opinion

22 FORENSICS : ARGUMENTATION ::
(A) autopsy : death
(B) syntax : grammar
(C) jurisprudence : law
(D) archaeology : site
(E) etymology : dictionary

23 INTRANSIGENT : COMPROMISE ::
(A) permanent : stability
(B) dogged : surrender
(C) disorganized : chaos
(D) lonesome : friendship
(E) strenuous : exercise

GO ON TO THE NEXT PAGE

352

The passage below is followed by questions based on its content. Answer the questions on the basis of what is stated or implied in the passage and in any introductory material that may be provided.

Questions 24-36 are based on the following passage.

recollective.

This excerpt is the beginning of a memoir, published in 1989, by a woman who emigrated with her family from Poland to Canada when she was a teenager.

It is April 1959, I'm standing at the railing of the Batory's upper deck, and I feel that my life is ending. I'm looking out at the crowd that has gath-

Line
(5) ered on the shore to see the ship's departure from Gdynia—a crowd that, all of a sudden, is irrevocably on the other side—and I want to break out, run back, run toward the familiar excitement, the waving hands, the exclamations. We can't be leaving all this behind—but we are. I am thirteen

(10) years old, and we are emigrating. It's a notion of such crushing, definitive finality that to me it might as well mean the end of the world.

My sister, four years younger than I, is clutching my hand wordlessly; she hardly understands

(15) where we are, or what is happening to us. My parents are highly agitated; they had just been put through a body search by the customs police. Still, the officials weren't clever enough, or suspicious enough, to check my sister and me—lucky for us,

(20) since we are both carrying some silverware we were not allowed to take out of Poland in large pockets sewn onto our skirts especially for this purpose, and hidden under capacious sweaters.

When the brass band on the shore strikes up the

(25) jaunty mazurka rhythms of the Polish anthem, I am pierced by a youthful sorrow so powerful that I suddenly stop crying and try to hold still against the pain. I desperately want time to stop, to hold the ship still with the force of my will. I am suf-

(30) fering my first, severe attack of nostalgia, or *tesknota*—a word that adds to nostalgia the tonalities of sadness and longing. It is a feeling whose shades and degrees I'm destined to know intimately, but at this hovering moment, it comes

(35) upon me like a visitation from a whole new geography of emotions, an annunciation of how much an absence can hurt. Or a premonition of absence, because at this divide, I'm filled to the brim with what I'm about to lose—images of Cracow, which

(40) I loved as one loves a person, of the sunbaked villages where we had taken summer vacations, of the hours I spent poring over passages of music with my piano teacher, of conversations and escapades with friends. Looking ahead, I come across

(45) an enormous, cold blankness—a darkening, and erasure, of the imagination, as if a camera eye has snapped shut, or as if a heavy curtain has been pulled over the future. Of the place where we're going—Canada—I know nothing. There are vague

(50) outlines of half a continent, a sense of vast spaces and little habitation. When my parents were hiding in a branch-covered forest bunker during the war, my father had a book with him called *Canada Fragrant with Resin* which, in his horrible confine-

(55) ment, spoke to him of majestic wilderness, of animals roaming without being pursued, of freedom. That is partly why we are going there, rather than to Israel, where most of our Jewish friends have gone. But to me, the word "Canada" has

(60) ominous echoes of the "Sahara." No, my mind rejects the idea of being taken there, I don't want to be pried out of my childhood, my pleasures, my safety, my hopes for becoming a pianist. The Batory pulls away, the foghorn emits its lowing, shofar[1]

(65) sound, but my being is engaged in a stubborn refusal to move. My parents put their hands on my shoulders consolingly; for a moment, they allow themselves to acknowledge that there's pain in this departure, much as they wanted it.

(70) Many years later, at a stylish party in New York, I met a woman who told me that she had an enchanted childhood. Her father was a highly positioned diplomat in an Asian country, and she had lived surrounded by sumptuous elegance. . . . No

(75) wonder, she said, that when this part of her life came to an end, at age thirteen, she felt she had been exiled from paradise, and had been searching for it ever since.

No wonder. But the wonder is what you can

(80) make a paradise out of. I told her that I grew up in a lumpen[2] apartment in Cracow, squeezed into three rudimentary rooms with four other people, surrounded by squabbles, dark political rumblings, memories of wartime suffering, and daily struggle

(85) for existence. And yet, when it came time to leave, I, too, felt I was being pushed out of the happy, safe enclosures of Eden.

---

[1] A trumpet made from a ram's horn and sounded in the synagogue on the Jewish High Holy Days

[2] Pertaining to dispossessed, often displaced, individuals who have been cut off from the socioeconomic class with which they would ordinarily have been identified

GO ON TO THE NEXT PAGE →

24 This passage serves mainly to

(A) provide a detailed description of what the author loved most about her life in Poland

(B) recount the author's experience of leaving Cracow

(C) explain why the author's family chose to emigrate

(D) convey the author's resilience during times of great upheaval

(E) create a factual account of the author's family history

25 In lines 2-3, "I feel that my life is ending" most nearly reflects the author's

(A) overwhelming sense of the desperate life that she and her family have led

(B) sad realization that she is leaving a familiar life

(C) unsettling premonition that she will not survive the voyage to Canada

(D) severe state of depression that may lead her to seek professional help

(E) irrational fear that she will be permanently separated from her family

26 In lines 5-6, the author's description of the crowd on the shore suggests that

(A) her family does not expect to find a warm welcome in Canada

(B) her relatives will not be able to visit her in Canada

(C) her family's friends have now turned against them

(D) she will find it difficult to communicate with her Polish friends

(E) the step she is taking is irreversible

27 The passage as a whole suggests that the author differs from her parents in that she

(A) has happier memories of Poland than her parents do

(B) is more sociable than they are

(C) feels no response to the rhythms of the Polish anthem

(D) has no desire to wave to the crowd on the shore

(E) is not old enough to comprehend what she is leaving behind

28 For the author, the experience of leaving Cracow can best be described as

(A) enlightening

(B) exhilarating

(C) annoying

(D) wrenching

(E) ennobling

29 In lines 17-19, the author's description of the customs police suggests that the author views them with

(A) alarm

(B) skepticism

(C) disrespect

(D) caution

(E) paranoia

30 In lines 29-37, the author indicates that "nostalgia" differs from "tesknota" in that

(A) tesknota cannot be explained in English

(B) tesknota denotes a gloomy, bittersweet yearning

(C) tesknota is a feeling that never ends

(D) nostalgia is a more painful emotion than tesknota

(E) nostalgia connotes a greater degree of desire than tesknota

31 By describing her feelings as having "shades and degrees" (line 33), the author suggests that

(A) she is allowing herself to grieve only a little at a time

(B) she is numb to the pain of her grief

(C) she is overwhelmed by her emotions

(D) her sadness is greatest at night

(E) her emotional state is multifaceted

GO ON TO THE NEXT PAGE

32 In lines 33-34, the phrase "I'm destined to know intimately" implies that the author

(A) cannot escape the path her father has chosen for the family
(B) believes that the future will bring many new emotional experiences
(C) will be deeply affected by the experience of emigrating
(D) must carefully analyze her conflicting emotional reactions
(E) has much to learn about the experience of emigrating

33 The author refers to the "camera eye" (line 46) and the "heavy curtain" (line 47) in order to suggest

(A) the difference between reality and art
(B) the importance of images to the human mind
(C) the difference between Poland and Canada
(D) her inability to overcome her fear of death
(E) her inability to imagine her future life

34 The description of the author as "engaged in a stubborn refusal to move" (lines 65-66) suggests her

(A) determination to claim her space on the crowded deck of the ship
(B) refusal to accept the change in her life
(C) wish to strike back at her parents for taking her away from Poland
(D) resolve not to become a Canadian citizen
(E) need to stay in close proximity to her family

35 In lines 66-69, the author suggests that her parents' comforting gesture indicates

(A) a recognition of feelings of distress over their departure
(B) their exhilaration and relief at the thought of personal freedom
(C) a great deal of ambivalence regarding their decision
(D) pain so great that they can feel no joy in their departure
(E) a complete loss of feeling due to the stressful events

36 The author mentions the anecdote about the person she met at a "stylish party in New York" (line 70) in order to

(A) prove that the author had become less childlike and more sophisticated
(B) demonstrate that the author's parents had become affluent in Canada
(C) describe how wealthy children are raised in Asian countries
(D) make an important point about childhood happiness
(E) show that the author had ultimately lived in the United States as well as in Canada

IF YOU FINISH BEFORE TIME IS CALLED, YOU MAY CHECK YOUR WORK ON THIS SECTION ONLY. DO NOT TURN TO ANY OTHER SECTION IN THE TEST. **STOP**

355

Time—30 Minutes 25 Questions	This section contains two types of questions. You have 30 minutes to complete both types. You may use any available space for scratchwork.

Notes:

1. The use of a calculator is permitted. All numbers used are real numbers.

2. Figures that accompany problems in this test are intended to provide information useful in solving the problems. They are drawn as accurately as possible EXCEPT when it is stated in a specific problem that the figure is not drawn to scale. All figures lie in a plane unless otherwise indicated.

Reference Information

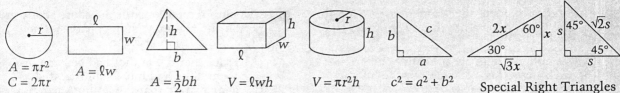

$A = \pi r^2$
$C = 2\pi r$

$A = \ell w$

$A = \frac{1}{2}bh$

$V = \ell wh$

$V = \pi r^2 h$

$c^2 = a^2 + b^2$

Special Right Triangles

The number of degrees of arc in a circle is 360.
The measure in degrees of a straight angle is 180.
The sum of the measures in degrees of the angles of a triangle is 180.

Directions for Quantitative Comparison Questions

Questions 1-15 each consist of two quantities in boxes, one in Column A and one in Column B. You are to compare the two quantities and on the answer sheet fill in oval

    A if the quantity in Column A is greater;
    B if the quantity in Column B is greater;
    C if the two quantities are equal;
    D if the relationship cannot be determined from the information given.

AN E RESPONSE WILL NOT BE SCORED.

Notes:

1. In some questions, information is given about one or both of the quantities to be compared. In such cases, the given information is centered above the two columns and is not boxed.
2. In a given question, a symbol that appears in both columns represents the same thing in Column A as it does in Column B.
3. Letters such as x, n, and k stand for real numbers.

EXAMPLES

	Column A	Column B	Answers
E1	5^2	20	● Ⓑ Ⓒ Ⓓ Ⓔ

$150° \diagup x°$

E2	x	30	∞Ⓐ Ⓑ ● Ⓓ Ⓔ

r and s are integers.

E3	$r + 1$	$s - 1$	Ⓐ Ⓑ Ⓒ ● Ⓔ

GO ON TO THE NEXT PAGE

SUMMARY DIRECTIONS FOR COMPARISON QUESTIONS

Answer: A if the quantity in Column A is greater;
B if the quantity in Column B is greater;
C if the two quantities are equal;
D if the relationship cannot be determined from the information given.

Column A	Column B

1 The average (arithmetic mean) of –3, 1, and 3 | The average (arithmetic mean) of –3, 2, and 3

$$x > y$$
$$y = z$$

2 x | z

The vertices of equilateral polygon $ABCDE$ lie on a circle.

3 The length of arc ABC | The length of arc CDE

r and s are positive integers.

4 $\dfrac{r}{r+s}$ | $\dfrac{r+s}{r}$

Point P, with coordinates (x, y), is exactly 5 units from the origin.

5 x | y

Column A	Column B

6 The area of $PQRS$ | 30

Eggs cost x cents per dozen.
$(x > 0)$

7 The cost of 60 eggs | $6x$ cents

$$A = \{1, 2, 3\}$$
$$B = \{4, 5, 6, 7\}$$

8 The total number of ordered pairs (a, b) that can be formed where a is from set A and b is from set B | The total number of ordered pairs (b, a) that can be formed where b is from set B and a from set A

GO ON TO THE NEXT PAGE

357

SUMMARY DIRECTIONS FOR COMPARISON QUESTIONS

Answer: A if the quantity in Column A is greater;
         B if the quantity in Column B is greater;
         C if the two quantities are equal;
         D if the relationship cannot be determined from the information given.

Column A	Column B

$$z = \frac{x}{y}$$

9

z	y

Square S and equilateral triangle T have equal areas.

10

The length of a side of S	The length of a side of T

The first number in a sequence of 10 numbers is 3.

11

The sum of the 10 numbers in the sequence	30

Column A	Column B

Machine M produces 27 cans in h hours.
$$0 < h < \frac{1}{2}$$

12

The number of cans machine M produces in 2 hours at this rate	54

$x > 3$

13

$3(3 - x)$	$x(3 - x)$

$$x + \frac{1}{7} = y$$

14

$y - 1$	$x - 1$

$w > 0$

15

w increased by 400 percent of w	$5w$

GO ON TO THE NEXT PAGE

Directions for Student-Produced Response Questions

Each of the remaining 10 questions requires you to solve the problem and enter your answer by marking the ovals in the special grid, as shown in the examples below.

Answer: $\frac{7}{12}$ or 7/12

Write answer → in boxes.

←Fraction line

Grid in → result.

Answer: 2.5

←Decimal point

Answer: 201
Either position is correct.

Note: You may start your answers in any column, space permitting. Columns not needed should be left blank.

- Mark no more than one oval in any column.

- Because the answer sheet will be machine-scored, **you will receive credit only if the ovals are filled in correctly.**

- Although not required, it is suggested that you write your answer in the boxes at the top of the columns to help you fill in the ovals accurately.

- Some problems may have more than one correct answer. In such cases, grid only one answer.

- No question has a negative answer.

- **Mixed numbers** such as $2\frac{1}{2}$ must be gridded as 2.5 or 5/2. (If ⟨2 1 / 2⟩ is gridded, it will be interpreted as $\frac{21}{2}$, not $2\frac{1}{2}$.)

- **Decimal Accuracy**: If you obtain a decimal answer, **enter the most accurate value the grid will accommodate.** For example, if you obtain an answer such as 0.6666 . . . , you should record the result as .666 or .667. **Less accurate values such as .66 or .67 are not acceptable.**

Acceptable ways to grid $\frac{2}{3}$ = .6666 . . .

16 Raul packed 144 bottles of soft drink in cartons of 6 bottles each and Julio packed 144 bottles of soft drink in cartons of 24 bottles each. How many <u>more</u> cartons did Raul use than Julio used?

17 On a certain map, a distance of 25 miles is represented by 1.0 centimeter. How many miles are represented by 3.3 centimeters on the map?

GO ON TO THE NEXT PAGE

359

18 The sum of k and $k + 1$ is greater than 9 but less than 17. If k is an integer, what is one possible value of k ?

19
$$\begin{array}{r} 0.XY \\ + 0.YX \\ \hline 0.XX \end{array}$$

In the correctly worked addition problem above, X and Y are digits. What must the digit Y be?

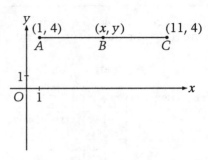

20 If $AB = BC$ in the figure above, what is the x-coordinate of point B ?

21 For all nonnegative numbers a, let $\boxed{a}$ be defined by $\boxed{a} = \dfrac{\sqrt{a}}{3}$. If $\boxed{a} = 2$, what is the value of a ?

GO ON TO THE NEXT PAGE

360

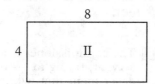

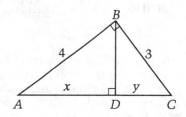

22 A rectangular solid has two faces the same size and shape as figure I above and four faces the same size and shape as figure II above. What is the volume of the solid?

24 In right $\triangle ABC$ above, $\dfrac{y}{3} = \dfrac{3}{x+y}$. What is the value of y ?

23 How many of the first one hundred positive integers contain the digit 9 ?

25 For the numbers r, s, and t, the average (arithmetic mean) is twice the median. If $r < s < t$, $r = 0$, and $t = ns$, what is the value of n ?

IF YOU FINISH BEFORE TIME IS CALLED, YOU MAY CHECK YOUR WORK ON THIS SECTION ONLY. DO NOT TURN TO ANY OTHER SECTION IN THE TEST.

Time—30 Minutes
31 Questions

For each question in this section, select the best answer from among the choices given and fill in the corresponding oval on the answer sheet.

Each sentence below has one or two blanks, each blank indicating that something has been omitted. Beneath the sentence are five words or sets of words labeled A through E. Choose the word or set of words that, when inserted in the sentence, best fits the meaning of the sentence as a whole.

Example:

Medieval kingdoms did not become constitutional republics overnight; on the contrary, the change was ----.

(A) unpopular
(B) unexpected
(C) advantageous
(D) sufficient
(E) gradual

(A) (B) (C) (D) ●

1 Some lizards display the characteristic of ----: if their tails are broken off during predatory encounters, the tails will eventually grow back.

(A) adaptation   (B) mimicry
(C) regeneration   (D) aggression
(E) mutability

2 The two travelers may have chosen ---- routes across the continent, but the starting point was the same for each.

(A) coinciding   (B) direct   (C) charted
(D) divergent   (E) intersecting

3 The author's use of copious detail, though intended to ---- the reader's appreciation of a tumultuous era, was instead regarded by many as a barrage of ---- information.

(A) excite..illuminating
(B) reverse..accurate
(C) curtail..boring
(D) deepen..trivial
(E) deter..historical

4 Seemingly permeated by natural light, Rufino Tamayo's painting looks as if it had been created with ---- hues.

(A) luminous   (B) florid   (C) ominous
(D) varnished   (E) fading

5 The commissioner is an irreproachable public servant, trying to ---- integrity and honor to a department that, while not totally corrupt, has nonetheless been ---- by greed and corruption.

(A) deny..overrun
(B) impute..tainted
(C) attribute..purified
(D) entrust..invigorated
(E) restore..undermined

6 Emily Dickinson was ---- poet, making few concessions to ordinary grammar or to conventions of meter and rhyme.

(A) a sensitive   (B) an imitative
(C) an idiosyncratic   (D) a realistic
(E) a decorous

7 Conflicting standards for allowable radiation levels in foods made ---- appraisals of the damage to crops following the reactor meltdown extremely difficult.

(A) reliable   (B) private   (C) intrusive
(D) conscious   (E) inflated

8 In earlier ages, a dilettante was someone who delighted in the arts; the term had none of the ---- connotations of superficiality that it has today and, in fact, was considered ----.

(A) implicit..disreputable
(B) romantic..threatening
(C) patronizing..complimentary
(D) irritating..presumptuous
(E) entertaining..prestigious

9 The historian noted irony in the fact that developments considered ---- by people of that era are now viewed as having been ----.

(A) inspirational..impetuous
(B) bizarre..irrational
(C) intuitive..uncertain
(D) actual..grandiose
(E) improbable..inevitable

GO ON TO THE NEXT PAGE

362

Each question below consists of a related pair of words or phrases, followed by five pairs of words or phrases labeled A through E. Select the pair that best expresses a relationship similar to that expressed in the original pair.

Example:

CRUMB : BREAD ::
(A) ounce : unit
(B) splinter : wood
(C) water : bucket
(D) twine : rope
(E) cream : butter

Ⓐ ● Ⓒ Ⓓ Ⓔ

10 CURRENT : ELECTRICITY ::
(A) gauge : measurement
(B) forge : metal
(C) beam : light
(D) ripple : lake
(E) curve : circle

11 EMBROIDERY : CLOTH ::
(A) bracelet : jewelry
(B) mural : wall
(C) tattoo : design
(D) paint : color
(E) flower : vase

12 WAITER : DINER ::
(A) ballerina : dancer
(B) clerk : customer
(C) nurse : orderly
(D) juror : judge
(E) captain : teammate

13 KERNEL : NUT ::
(A) yolk : egg
(B) grape : raisin
(C) flour : bread
(D) soil : seed
(E) thorn : stem

14 NIGHTMARE : DREAM ::
(A) semaphore : signal
(B) dread : expectation
(C) lure : trap
(D) fear : victim
(E) frustration : confusion

15 COGENT : PERSUASIVENESS ::
(A) pardoned : blame
(B) staid : manner
(C) tactful : awkwardness
(D) conceited : reputation
(E) lucid : clarity

GO ON TO THE NEXT PAGE →

Each passage below is followed by questions based on its content. Answer the questions on the basis of what is <u>stated</u> or <u>implied</u> in each passage and in any introductory material that may be provided.

Questions 16-20 are based on the following passage.

This excerpt discusses the relationship between plants and their environments.

Why do some desert plants grow tall and thin like organ pipes? Why do most trees in the tropics keep their leaves year round? Why in the Arctic
Line tundra are there no trees at all? After many years
(5) without convincing general answers, we now know much about what sets the fashion in plant design.

Using terminology more characteristic of a ther-
mal engineer than of a botanist, we can think of
(10) plants as mechanisms that must balance their heat budgets. A plant by day is staked out under the Sun with no way of sheltering itself. All day long it absorbs heat. If it did not lose as much heat as it gained, then eventually it would die. Plants get rid
(15) of their heat by warming the air around them, by evaporating water, and by radiating heat to the atmosphere and the cold, black reaches of space. Each plant must balance its heat budget so that its temperature is tolerable for the processes of life.
(20) Plants in the Arctic tundra lie close to the ground in the thin layer of still air that clings there. A foot or two above the ground are the winds of Arctic cold. Tundra plants absorb heat from the Sun and tend to warm up; they probably
(25) balance most of their heat budgets by radiating heat to space, but also by warming the still air that is trapped among them. As long as Arctic plants are close to the ground, they can balance their heat budgets. But if they should stretch up as
(30) a tree does, they would lift their working parts, their leaves, into the streaming Arctic winds. Then it is likely that the plants could not absorb enough heat from the Sun to avoid being cooled below a critical temperature. Your heat budget
(35) does not balance if you stand tall in the Arctic.

Such thinking also helps explain other charac-
teristics of plant design. A desert plant faces the opposite problem from that of an Arctic plant — the danger of overheating. It is short of water and
(40) so cannot cool itself by evaporation without dehy-
drating. The familiar sticklike shape of desert plants represents one of the solutions to this problem: the shape exposes the smallest possible surface to incoming solar radiation and provides
(45) the largest possible surface from which the plant

can radiate heat. In tropical rain forests, by way of contrast, the scorching Sun is not a problem for plants because there is sufficient water.

This working model allows us to connect the
(50) general characteristics of the forms of plants in different habitats with factors such as temperature, availability of water, and presence or absence of seasonal differences. Our Earth is covered with a patchwork quilt of meteorological conditions, and
(55) the patterns of this patchwork are faithfully reflected by the plants.

16 The passage primarily focuses on which of the following characteristics of plants?

(A) Their ability to grow equally well in all environments
(B) Their effects on the Earth's atmosphere
(C) Their ability to store water for dry periods
(D) Their fundamental similarity of shape
(E) Their ability to balance heat intake and output

17 Which of the following could best be substi-
tuted for the words "sets the fashion in" (line 6) without changing the intended meaning?

(A) improves the appearance of
(B) accounts for the uniformity of
(C) defines acceptable standards for
(D) determines the general characteristics of
(E) reduces the heat budgets of

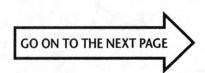
GO ON TO THE NEXT PAGE

18 According to the passage, which of the following is most responsible for preventing trees from growing tall in the Arctic?

(A) The hard, frozen ground
(B) The small amount of available sunshine
(C) The cold, destructive winds
(D) The large amount of snow that falls each year
(E) The absence of seasonal differences in temperature

19 The author suggests that the "sticklike shape of desert plants" (lines 41-42) can be attributed to the

(A) inability of the plants to radiate heat to the air around them
(B) presence of irregular seasonal differences in the desert
(C) large surface area that the plants must expose to the Sun
(D) absence of winds strong enough to knock down tall, thin plants
(E) extreme heat and aridity of the habitat

20 The contrast mentioned in lines 46-48 specifically concerns the

(A) availability of moisture
(B) scorching heat of the Sun
(C) seasonal differences in temperature
(D) variety of plant species
(E) heat radiated by plants to the atmosphere

GO ON TO THE NEXT PAGE

Questions 21-31 are based on the following passage.

This passage is from a book by an African American woman who is a law professor. opinion

This semester I have been teaching a course entitled Women and Notions of Property. I have been focusing on the ways in which gender affects
Line individuals' perspectives—gender in this instance
(5) having less to do with the biology of male and female than with the language of power relations, of dominance and submission, of assertion and deference, of big and little. An example of the stories we discuss is the following, used to illus-
(10) trate the rhetoric of power relations, whose examination, I tell my students, is at the heart of the course.

Walking down Fifth Avenue in New York not long ago, I came up behind a couple and their
(15) young son. The child, about four or five years old, had evidently been complaining about big dogs. The mother was saying, "But why are you afraid of big dogs?" "Because they're big," he responded with eminent good sense. "But what's the differ-
(20) ence between a big dog and a little dog?" the father persisted. "They're *big*," said the child. "But there's really no difference," said the mother, pointing to a large, slavering wolfhound with narrow eyes and the calculated amble of a gang-
(25) ster, and then to a beribboned Pekingese the size of a roller skate, who was flouncing along just ahead of us all, in that little fox-trotty step that keeps Pekingeses from ever being taken seriously. "See?" said the father. "If you look really closely
(30) you'll see there's no difference at all. They're all just dogs."

And I thought: Talk about a static, unyielding, totally uncompromising point of reference. These people must be lawyers. Where else do people
(35) learn so well the idiocies of High Objectivity? How else do people learn to capitulate so uncritically to a norm that refuses to allow for difference? How else do grown-ups sink so deeply into the authoritarianism of their own world view that
(40) they can universalize their relative bigness so completely as to obliterate the viewpoint of their child's relative smallness? (To say nothing of the viewpoint of the slavering wolfhound, from whose own narrow perspective I dare say the little
(45) boy must have looked exactly like a lamb chop.)

I use this story in my class because I think it illustrates a paradigm of thought by which children are taught not to see what they see; by which African Americans are reassured that there is no
(50) real inequality in the world, just their own bad dreams; and by which women are taught not to experience what they experience, in deference to men's ways of knowing. The story also illustrates the possibility of a collective perspective or social
(55) positioning that would give rise to a claim for the legal interests of groups. In a historical moment when individual rights have become the basis for any remedy, too often group interests are defeated by, for example, finding the one four year old who
(60) has wrestled whole packs of wolfhounds fearlessly to the ground; using that individual experience to attack the validity of there ever being any generalizable fear of wolfhounds by four year olds; and then recasting the general group experience as a
(65) fragmented series of specific, isolated events rather than a pervasive social phenomenon ("You have every right to think that that wolfhound has the ability to bite off your head, but that's just your point of view").

(70) My students, most of whom signed up expecting to experience that crisp, refreshing, clear-headed sensation that "thinking like a lawyer" purportedly endows, are confused by this and all the stories I tell them in my class on
(75) Women and Notions of Property. They are confused enough by the idea of property alone, overwhelmed by the thought of dogs and women as academic subjects, and paralyzed by the idea that property, ownership, and rights might have a
(80) gender and that gender might be a matter of words.

21 In lines 2-8, the author describes "gender" primarily in terms of

(A) early childhood experience
(B) genetics and hormonal chemistry
(C) the distribution of power in relationships
(D) the influence of role models on personality formation
(E) the varying social conventions in different cultures

22 In line 19, "eminent" most nearly means

(A) famed
(B) exalted
(C) protruding
(D) influential
(E) obvious

GO ON TO THE NEXT PAGE

23 The description of the two dogs in lines 23-28 serves primarily to

(A) defuse a tense situation with humor
(B) discredit what the parents are saying
(C) emphasize the dogs' resemblance to their owners
(D) suggest that dogs are more sensible than humans
(E) illustrate a legal concept regarding pet ownership

24 In line 24, "calculated" most nearly means

(A) scheming
(B) predetermined
(C) deliberate
(D) predictable
(E) estimated

25 The author uses the term "authoritarianism" in line 39 in order to

(A) link habits of thought with political repression
(B) ridicule the parents in the story by using comically exaggerated terms
(C) criticize the harsh teaching methods used in law schools
(D) show that the attitude represented by the parents is unconstitutional
(E) allude to parental roles in societies of the past

26 The author describes the wolfhound's viewpoint (lines 42-45) in order to

(A) refute those who disapprove of storytelling as a teaching tool
(B) introduce an example of desirable objectivity
(C) suggest that it is similar to the parents' viewpoint
(D) show that viewpoints are not always predictable
(E) lend credence to the child's point of view

27 The "paradigm of thought" in lines 46-53 may be described as one that disposes people toward

(A) cooperating with one another for the common good
(B) discussing family problems frankly and openly
(C) resorting to violence when thwarted
(D) discounting their own experiences
(E) suing others over trivial matters

28 The process of defeating group interests described in lines 56-69 is one in which

(A) an exception is made to look like a general rule
(B) a logical flaw in the group's arguments is attacked
(C) a crucial legal term is used in a misleading way
(D) statistical evidence is distorted to the opposition's advantage
(E) personal arguments are used to discredit group leaders

29 The author presents the idea of wrestling "whole packs of wolfhounds" (line 60) as an example of

(A) an argument that no lawyer would find plausible
(B) an event so unusual as to be irrelevant
(C) something that only a child would attempt
(D) a morally reprehensible act
(E) an easier task than studying law

30 In lines 66-69, the "right" is characterized as

(A) central to the concept of democracy
(B) probably not attainable without a constitutional amendment
(C) something that is hardly worth having
(D) something that powerful groups are reluctant to give up
(E) something that most people are not aware that they have

31 The final paragraph suggests that the author probably believes that a law professor's main duty is to

(A) make a highly technical subject exciting to students
(B) jar students out of unexamined assumptions about the study of law
(C) emphasize the importance of clear legal writing
(D) encourage more students from disadvantaged groups to become lawyers
(E) train students in the practical skills they will need in the courtroom

IF YOU FINISH BEFORE TIME IS CALLED, YOU MAY CHECK YOUR WORK ON THIS SECTION ONLY. DO NOT TURN TO ANY OTHER SECTION IN THE TEST. **STOP**

367

Reference Information

        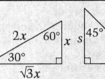

$A = \pi r^2$
$C = 2\pi r$ $A = \ell w$ $A = \frac{1}{2}bh$ $V = \ell wh$ $V = \pi r^2 h$ $c^2 = a^2 + b^2$ Special Right Triangles

The number of degrees of arc in a circle is 360.
The measure in degrees of a straight angle is 180.
The sum of the measures in degrees of the angles of a triangle is 180.

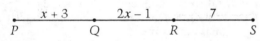

1 In the figure above, what is the length of PS in terms of x ?

(A) $x + 2$
(B) $x + 9$
(C) $2x + 2$
(D) $3x + 9$
(E) $3x + 11$

2 Brenda received pledges from 30 people for a 50-mile bike-a-thon. If Brenda rode 50 miles and each person gave $0.10 for each mile she rode, which of the following gives the total dollar amount of money Brenda collected?

(A) $30 \times 50 \times 0.10$
(B) $30 \times 50 + 0.10$
(C) $50 \times 0.10 + 30$
(D) $50 + 30 \times 0.10$
(E) $30 + 50 + 0.10$

GO ON TO THE NEXT PAGE

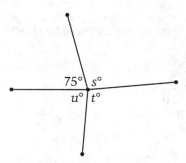

3 In the figure above, what is the value of $s + t + u$?

(A) 105
(B) 115
(C) 225
(D) 285
(E) 295

4 On a report, the typing begins $\frac{3}{4}$ inch from the left edge of the paper and ends $1\frac{1}{2}$ inches from the right edge. If the width of the paper is $8\frac{1}{2}$ inches, how many inches per line is used for typing?

(A) $7\frac{3}{4}$

(B) $7\frac{1}{2}$

(C) 7

(D) $6\frac{1}{2}$

(E) $6\frac{1}{4}$

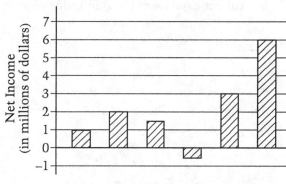

NET INCOME OF COMPANY X, 1985-1990

5 According to the graph above, Company X showed the greatest change in net income between which two consecutive years?

(A) 1985 and 1986
(B) 1986 and 1987
(C) 1987 and 1988
(D) 1988 and 1989
(E) 1989 and 1990

GO ON TO THE NEXT PAGE

6 If $r = as^4$ and $s = bt^3$, which of the following is a correct expression for r in terms of a, b, and t?

(A) abt^{12}

(B) ab^4t^7

(C) ab^4t^{12}

(D) $a^4b^4t^7$

(E) $a^4b^4t^{12}$

8 If p and r are integers, $p \neq 0$, and $p = -r$, which of the following must be true?

(A) $p < r$
(B) $p > r$
(C) $p + r < 0$
(D) $p - r < 0$
(E) $pr < 0$

7 What is the area of a right triangle whose perimeter is 36 and whose sides are x, $x + 3$, and $x + 6$?

(A) 27
(B) 54
(C) 81
(D) 108
(E) 135

GO ON TO THE NEXT PAGE

9 One number is 3 times another number, and their sum is −10. What is the lesser of the two numbers?

(A) −2.5
(B) −3.0
(C) −5.5
(D) −7.0
(E) −7.5

Digit of N	Digit of ⓃN
0	1
1	2
2	3
3	4
4	5
5	6
6	7
7	8
8	9
9	0

10 For any positive integer N, the symbol Ⓝ represents the number obtained when every digit of N, <u>except</u> the leftmost digit, is replaced by its corresponding digit in the second column of the table above. For which of the following is Ⓝ less than N?

(A) $N = 349$
(B) $N = 394$
(C) $N = 487$
(D) $N = 934$
(E) $N = 984$

IF YOU FINISH BEFORE TIME IS CALLED, YOU MAY CHECK YOUR WORK ON THIS SECTION ONLY. DO NOT TURN TO ANY OTHER SECTION IN THE TEST. **STOP**

371

Time — 15 Minutes
11 Questions

For each question in this section, select the best answer
from among the choices given and fill in the corresponding
oval on the answer sheet.

The two passages below are followed by questions based on their content and on the relationship between
the two passages. Answer the questions on the basis of what is stated or implied in the passages and in
any introductory material that may be provided.

Questions 1-11 are based on the following pair of passages.

Robinson Crusoe, *a novel first published in
England in 1719, was written by Daniel Defoe. It
relates the story of Crusoe's successful efforts to
make a tolerable existence for himself after being
shipwrecked alone on an apparently uninhabited
island. The passages below are adapted from two
twentieth-century commentaries by Ian Watt and
James Sutherland on the novel's main character.*

opinion

Passage 1—Ian Watt (1957)

That Robinson Crusoe is an embodiment of
economic individualism hardly needs demonstration. All of Defoe's heroes and heroines pursue
money, and they pursue it very methodically.
(5) Crusoe's bookkeeping conscience, indeed, has
established an effective priority over all of his
other thoughts and emotions. The various forms of
traditional group relationship—family, village, a
sense of nationality—all are weakened, as are the
(10) competing claims of noneconomic individual
achievement and enjoyment, ranging from spiritual salvation to the pleasures of recreation. For
the most part, the main characters in Defoe's
works either have no family or, like Crusoe, leave
(15) it at an early age never to return. Not too much
importance can be attached to this fact, since
adventure stories demand the absence of conventional social ties. Still, Robinson Crusoe does have
a home and family, and he leaves them for the
(20) classic reason of economic individualism—that it
is necessary to better his condition. "Something
fatal in that propension of nature" calls him to the
sea and adventure, and against "settling to business" in the station to which he is born—and this
(25) despite the elaborate praise that his father heaps
upon that condition. Leaving home, improving the
lot one was born to, is a vital feature of the indi-
vidualist pattern of life.
    Crusoe is not a mere footloose adventurer, and
(30) his travels, like his freedom from social ties, are

merely somewhat extreme cases of tendencies that
are normal in modern society as a whole since, by
making the pursuit of gain a primary motive,
economic individualism has much increased the
(35) mobility of the individual. More specifically, the
story of Robinson Crusoe is based on some of the
many volumes recounting the exploits of those
voyagers who in the sixteenth and seventeenth
centuries had assisted the development of capital-
(40) ism. Defoe's story, then, expresses some of the
most important tendencies of the life of his time,
and it is this that sets his hero apart from most
other travelers in literature. Robinson Crusoe is
not, like Ulysses, an unwilling voyager trying to
(45) get back to his family and his native land: profit
is Crusoe's only vocation, and the whole world is
his territory.

Passage 2—James Sutherland (1971)

To Ian Watt, Robinson Crusoe is a characteristic
embodiment of economic individualism. "Profit,"
(50) he assures us, "is Crusoe's only vocation," and
"only money—fortune in its modern sense—is a
proper cause of deep feeling." Watt therefore
claims that Crusoe's motive for disobeying his
father and leaving home was to better his economic
(55) condition, and that the argument between Crusoe
and his parents in the early pages of the book is
really a debate "not about filial duty or religion,
but about whether going or staying is likely to be
the most advantageous course materially: both
(60) sides accept the economic motive as primary." We
certainly cannot afford to ignore those passages in
which Crusoe attributes his misfortunes to an evil
influence that drove him into "projects and under-
takings beyond my reach, such as are indeed often
(65) the ruin of the best heads in business." But

GO ON TO THE NEXT PAGE

surely the emphasis is not on the economic motive as such, but on the willingness to gamble and seek for quick profits beyond what "the nature of the thing permitted." Crusoe's father wished
(70) him to take up the law as a profession, and if Crusoe had done so, he would likely have become a very wealthy man indeed. Crusoe's failure to accept his father's choice for him illustrates not economic individualism so much as Crusoe's lack
(75) of economic prudence, indifference to a calm and normal bourgeois life, and love of travel.
    Unless we are to say—and we have no right to say it—that Crusoe did not know himself, profit hardly seems to have been his "only vocation."
(80) Instead, we are presented with a man who was driven (like so many contemporary Englishmen whom Defoe either admired or was fascinated by) by a kind of compulsion to wander footloose about the world. As if to leave no doubt about his rest-
(85) less desire to travel, Crusoe contrasts himself with his business partner, the very pattern of the economic motive and of what a merchant ought to be, who would have been quite happy "to have gone like a carrier's horse, always to the same inn,
(90) backward and forward, provided he could, as he called it, find his account in it." Crusoe, on the other hand, was like a rambling boy who never wanted to see again what he had already seen. "My eye," he tells us, "was never satisfied with
(95) seeing, was still more desirous of wand'ring and seeing."

1 The first paragraph of Passage 1 (lines 1-28) primarily explores the contrast between

(A) economics and religion
(B) business and adventure
(C) family responsibilities and service to one's country
(D) Crusoe's sense of duty and his desire for pleasure
(E) economic individualism and group-oriented behavior

2 Watt refers to "spiritual salvation" (lines 11-12) as an example of

(A) something in which Crusoe seemed to show relatively little interest
(B) the ultimate goal in life for most of Defoe's contemporaries
(C) an important difference in priorities between Crusoe and his father
(D) something that Defoe believed was incompatible with the pursuit of pleasure
(E) a crucial value that Crusoe's family failed to pass on to him

3 Which statement about Crusoe is most consistent with the information in Passage 1 ?

(A) He left home because his father forced him to do so.
(B) He single-mindedly pursued financial gain.
(C) He was driven to seek pleasure through world travel.
(D) He had a highly developed sense of morality.
(E) He was economically imprudent to a fault.

4 In line 86, "pattern" most nearly means

(A) configuration
(B) duplicate
(C) decoration
(D) perfection
(E) model

5 It can be inferred that Crusoe's business partner was "like a carrier's horse" (line 89) in that the partner was

(A) satisfied with a life of routine
(B) descended from ancestors who were both noble and strong
(C) strong enough to bear any burden
(D) stubborn in refusing to change
(E) loyal to Crusoe to a degree of near servility

6 In context, the phrase "find his account in it" (line 91) can best be interpreted to mean

(A) be exposed to new experiences
(B) make a reasonable profit
(C) seek adventure around the world
(D) become popular and well known
(E) acquire great power and responsibility

GO ON TO THE NEXT PAGE →

7 Crusoe's self-assessment quoted at the end of Passage 2 (lines 94-96) serves primarily to

(A) reveal that Crusoe did not know himself as well as he thought he did
(B) suggest that vision entails more than merely seeing
(C) suggest that, though boylike, Crusoe was more like Ulysses than Watt acknowledges
(D) provide support for Sutherland's view of Crusoe
(E) introduce one of Crusoe's traits

8 Both passages indicate that Crusoe's father was

(A) similar to the parents of main characters in other works by Defoe
(B) confident that his son would succeed in whatever field he chose
(C) in favor of more prudent behavior by his son
(D) opposed to the business partners chosen by his son
(E) proud of his son's ability to survive comfortably after being shipwrecked

9 In both passages, Crusoe's attitude toward the idea of "settling to business" (lines 23-24) like his father is described as

(A) eager anticipation
(B) conventional acceptance
(C) confused uncertainty
(D) moral suspicion
(E) innate opposition

10 The authors of the two passages would apparently agree that Crusoe was

(A) motivated only by personal financial gain
(B) profoundly unaware of his basic nature and calling in life
(C) commendable in his devotion to his family and his business partners
(D) willing to take risks while traveling
(E) responsible for whatever misfortunes befell him in life

11 The primary focus of this pair of passages is

(A) earlier commentaries on Defoe's *Robinson Crusoe*
(B) the exact nature of the flaws in Crusoe's character
(C) the style and structure of *Robinson Crusoe*
(D) Defoe's positive portrayal of greed
(E) Crusoe's motivation for leaving home and traveling abroad

IF YOU FINISH BEFORE TIME IS CALLED, YOU MAY CHECK YOUR WORK ON THIS SECTION ONLY. DO NOT TURN TO ANY OTHER SECTION IN THE TEST. STOP

374

SAT I Scoring Worksheet

SAT I Verbal Sections

A. Section 2:

_____ − (_____ ÷ 4) = _____
no. correct   no. incorrect   subtotal A

B. Section 4:

_____ − (_____ ÷ 4) = _____
no. correct   no. incorrect   subtotal B

C. Section 7:

_____ − (_____ ÷ 4) = _____
no. correct   no. incorrect   subtotal C

D. Total unrounded raw score
(Total A + B + C)

_____
D

E. Total rounded raw score
(Rounded to nearest whole number)

_____
E

F. SAT I verbal reported scaled score
(Use the conversion table)

SAT I verbal
score

SAT I Mathematical Sections

A. Section 1:

_____ − (_____ ÷ 4) = _____
no. correct   no. incorrect   subtotal A

B. Section 3:
Questions 1-15 (quantitative comparison)

_____ − (_____ ÷ 3) = _____
no. correct   no. incorrect   subtotal B

C. Section 3:
Questions 16-25 (student-produced response)

_____ = _____
no. correct   subtotal C

D. Section 6:

_____ − (_____ ÷ 4) = _____
no. correct   no. incorrect   subtotal D

E. Total unrounded raw score
(Total A + B + C + D)

_____
E

F. Total rounded raw score
(Rounded to nearest whole number)

_____
F

G. SAT I mathematical reported scaled score
(Use the conversion table)

SAT I
mathematical
score

Score Conversion Table
SAT I: Reasoning Test
Saturday, November 1994
Recentered Scale

Raw Score	Verbal Scaled Score	Math Scaled Score	Raw Score	Verbal Scaled Score	Math Scaled Score
78	800		37	510	560
77	800		36	510	550
76	800		35	500	540
75	800		34	500	540
74	790		33	490	530
73	780		32	480	520
72	760		31	480	520
71	750		30	470	510
70	740		29	470	500
69	730		28	460	500
68	720		27	460	490
67	710		26	450	480
66	700		25	440	480
65	690		24	440	470
64	680		23	430	460
63	670		22	430	460
62	660		21	420	450
61	660		20	410	440
60	650	800	19	410	430
59	640	790	18	400	430
58	630	770	17	390	420
57	630	750	16	390	410
56	620	730	15	380	410
55	610	720	14	370	400
54	610	700	13	360	390
53	600	690	12	360	380
52	600	680	11	350	370
51	590	670	10	340	370
50	580	660	9	330	360
49	580	650	8	320	350
48	570	640	7	310	340
47	570	640	6	300	320
46	560	630	5	290	310
45	560	620	4	280	300
44	550	610	3	270	280
43	540	600	2	260	270
42	540	600	1	240	250
41	530	590	0	230	230
40	530	580	-1	220	210
39	520	570	-2	200	200
38	520	570	and below		

This table is for use only with this test.

| Time—30 Minutes 25 Questions | In this section solve each problem, using any available space on the page for scratchwork. Then decide which is the best of the choices given and fill in the corresponding oval on the answer sheet. |

Notes:

(1) The use of a calculator is permitted. All numbers used are real numbers.

(2) Figures that accompany problems in this test are intended to provide information useful in solving the problems. They are drawn as accurately as possible EXCEPT when it is stated in a specific problem that the figure is not drawn to scale. All figures lie in a plane unless otherwise indicated.

Reference Information

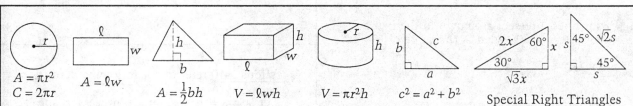

$A = \pi r^2$
$C = 2\pi r$

$A = \ell w$

$A = \frac{1}{2}bh$

$V = \ell wh$

$V = \pi r^2 h$

$c^2 = a^2 + b^2$

Special Right Triangles

The number of degrees of arc in a circle is 360.
The measure in degrees of a straight angle is 180.
The sum of the measures in degrees of the angles of a triangle is 180.

---

1 If $e + f = -1$, then $(e + f)^2 =$

(A) 1

(B) $\frac{1}{4}$

(C) 0

(D) $-\frac{1}{2}$

(E) -1

2 If x is a positive number, then 50 percent of $10x$ equals

(A) $2x$
(B) $4x$
(C) $5x$
(D) $20x$
(E) $50x$

3 If $\frac{m + 5}{15} = \frac{5}{3}$, then $m =$

(A) 4
(B) 8
(C) 10
(D) 12
(E) 20

4 What is the <u>least</u> of three consecutive integers whose sum is 18 ?

(A) 2
(B) 3
(C) 4
(D) 5
(E) 6

GO ON TO THE NEXT PAGE →

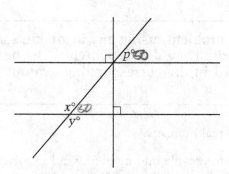

Note: Figure not drawn to scale.

5 Four lines intersect as shown in the figure above. If $p = 50$, what is the value of $x + y$?

(A) 230
(B) 240
(C) 260
(D) 270
(E) 300

6 If $\frac{5}{6}n = 60$, then $\frac{1}{6}n =$

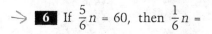

(A) 8
(B) 10
(C) 12
(D) 50
(E) 72

7 If $y = \dfrac{x + 1}{x - 3}$ and y is a real number, then

x CANNOT equal which of the following?

(A) 1
(B) 2
(C) 3
(D) 4
(E) 5

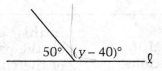

8 In the figure above, $y =$

(A) 90
(B) 140
(C) 150
(D) 160
(E) 170

Questions 9-10 refer to the following definition.

Let $r \blacktriangle s = rs + s$ for all integers r and s.

9 What is the value of $4 \blacktriangle 5$?

(A) 18
(B) 20
(C) 24
(D) 25
(E) 40

10 If $r \blacktriangle s = 0$ and $s \neq 0$, what must r equal?

(A) −2
(B) −1
(C) 0
(D) 1
(E) 2

GO ON TO THE NEXT PAGE

11 Points P, Q, R, and S lie on a line, in that order. If $PQ < QR < RS$ and the length of RS is 4, which of the following could be the length of PS ?

(A) 16
(B) 15
(C) 14
(D) 12
(E) 10

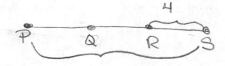

12 Each of three vases contains 12 flowers. Some flowers are to be removed from one vase and placed in another vase to make the ratio of flowers in the three vases $3 : 2 : 1$. What is the least number of flowers that need to be moved to accomplish this?

18:12:6

(A) 18
(B) 12
(C) 10
(D) 8
(E) 6

$3x + 2x + 1x = 36$

$6x = 36 = x=6$

13 If $10x + y = 8$ and $7x - y = 9$, what is the value of $3x + 2y$?

(A) −2
(B) −1
(C) $\frac{8}{9}$
(D) 1
(E) 17

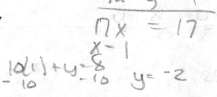

$3(1) + 2(-2) = -1$

$10x + y = 8$
$7x - y = 9$
$17x = 17$
$x = 1$
$10(1) + y = 8$
$y = -2$

14 At a certain school, 160 seniors out of the total senior class of 200 students attended the last football game of the season. If 180 juniors also attended that game, and if the fraction of juniors who attended was equal to the fraction of seniors who attended, what was the total number of students in the junior class?

(A) 144
(B) 177
(C) 180
(D) 220
(E) 225

$\frac{160}{200} = \frac{180}{x}$
$x = 225$

GO ON TO THE NEXT PAGE

387

Questions 15-16 refer to the following table, which shows the amounts collected from the first 25 donors in a charity drive.

CHARITY-DRIVE DONATIONS

10   30   30   80

Amount of Donation	$1	$5	$10	$20	$25
Number of Donors	10	6	3	4	2

200

15 What is the mode of the amounts collected from the first 25 donors?

(A) $1
(B) $5
(C) $8
(D) $20
(E) $25

70
-80
150
25

16 The goal of the charity drive was to collect $500 in donations. What percent of the goal was reached with the amounts collected from the first 25 donors?

(A)   2.5%
(B)   4%
(C)   20%
(D)   25%
(E)   40%

= $500

$\frac{200}{500}$

17 Five different line segments are to be drawn so that each of the segments has an endpoint at point P. What is the greatest number of these line segments that could be intersected by some other line not drawn through P?

(A) 5
(B) 4
(C) 3
(D) 2
(E) 1

$$x(x - 1)(x + 2)$$

18 For which of the following values of x is the value of the expression above negative?

(A) -2

(B) $-\frac{1}{2}$

(C) 0

(D) $\frac{1}{2}$

(E) 2

GO ON TO THE NEXT PAGE

19 The product of two positive integers is less than 50, and the sum of the two integers is greater than 20. Which of the following could be one of the integers?

(A) 5
(B) 10
(C) 15
(D) 20
(E) 50

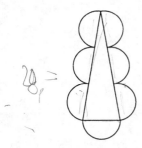

20 The figure above consists of an isosceles triangle and 7 semicircles, each having the same diameter. If the perimeter of the triangle is 28, what is the <u>radius</u> of one of the semicircles?

, (A) 1
(B) 2
(C) 4
(D) 6
(E) 7

21 A certain set of disks contains only red disks, blue disks, and green disks. If the probability of randomly choosing a red disk is $\frac{1}{5}$ and the probability of randomly choosing a blue disk is $\frac{1}{3}$, what is the probability of randomly choosing a green disk?

(A) $\frac{2}{15}$

(B) $\frac{1}{3}$

(C) $\frac{7}{15}$

(D) $\frac{8}{15}$

(E) It varies with the number of disks in a set.

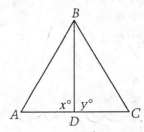

Note: Figure not drawn to scale.

22 In $\triangle ABC$ above, $AD = DC$. Which of the following must be true?

(A) $AB = BC$
(B) $x = y = 90$
(C) Area of $\triangle ABD =$ area of $\triangle CBD$
(D) Perimeter of $\triangle ABD =$ perimeter of $\triangle CBD$
(E) Measure of $\angle BAD =$ measure of $\angle BCD$

GO ON TO THE NEXT PAGE

23 If $\dfrac{r \cdot r \cdot r}{r + r + r} \times \dfrac{1}{k} = 1$ for all nonzero r, then $k =$

(A) $\dfrac{r^2}{3}$

(B) $\dfrac{3}{r^2}$

(C) $\dfrac{1}{3r^3}$

(D) $3r^2$

(E) $\dfrac{3}{r}$

25 A school newspaper enlarged both the length and width of a rectangular photograph by 60 percent. The new photograph was too large for the space available, so its length and width were then reduced by 25 percent. The area of the final photograph was what percent greater than the area of the original?

(A) 20%
(B) 35%
(C) 44%
(D) 82%
(E) 85%

24 If Jim receives m marbles in addition to the number of marbles he had originally, he will have t times as many as he had originally. In terms of m and t, how many marbles did Jim have originally?

(A) $t - m$

(B) $\dfrac{t + 1}{m}$

(C) $\dfrac{m}{t + 1}$

(D) $\dfrac{m}{t}$

(E) $\dfrac{m}{t - 1}$

IF YOU FINISH BEFORE TIME IS CALLED, YOU MAY CHECK YOUR WORK ON THIS SECTION ONLY. DO NOT TURN TO ANY OTHER SECTION IN THE TEST. **STOP**

Section 2   2

Time—30 Minutes
30 Questions

For each question in this section, select the best answer from among the choices given and fill in the corresponding oval on the answer sheet.

Each sentence below has one or two blanks, each blank indicating that something has been omitted. Beneath the sentence are five words or sets of words labeled A through E. Choose the word or set of words that, when inserted in the sentence, best fits the meaning of the sentence as a whole.

Example:

Medieval kingdoms did not become constitutional republics overnight; on the contrary, the change was ----.

(A) unpopular
(B) unexpected
(C) advantageous
(D) sufficient
(E) gradual

Ⓐ Ⓑ Ⓒ Ⓓ ●

1 Some potatoes of the Andes contain ---- known as glycoalkaloids, poisons that induce stomach pains, vomiting, and even death.

(A) nutrients   (B) secretions   (C) inversions
(D) toxins   (E) preservatives

2 The chamber orchestra refuses to identify its members; it is this insistence on ---- that sets this ensemble apart.

(A) longevity   (B) disparity   (C) anonymity
(D) mediocrity   (E) dissonance

3 Gwendolyn Brooks's character Maud Martha appears ---- but feels great rage: she ---- her emotions with a mask of compliance.

(A) responsive..echoes
(B) nonchalant..exposes
(C) docile..camouflages
(D) uncontrolled..belies
(E) invincible..catapults

4 He maintains that ethnic and cultural ---- are generalizations no more related to what an individual is actually like than are the ---- representations of constellations to the actual nature of a star.

(A) traditions..chemical
(B) stereotypes..pictorial
(C) details..figurative
(D) heritages..prophetic
(E) specimens..graphic

5 Her naturally optimistic outlook rapidly restored her ----, but he, because of his ---- disposition, continued to foresee nothing but a series of pains and regrets.

(A) humor..adventurous
(B) bitterness..cheerful
(C) confidence..resilient
(D) contentiousness..callous
(E) exuberance..gloomy

6 Due to complexities in the life cycle of malaria parasites, scientists have been consistently ---- in their attempts to develop an effective vaccine.

(A) thwarted   (B) prepared   (C) conditional
(D) secretive   (E) encouraged

7 Understandably, it is the ---- among theater critics who become most incensed when producers insist on ---- celebrated classic plays.

(A) strategists..discussing
(B) mediators..staging
(C) conformists..praising
(D) traditionalists..recognizing
(E) purists..reinterpreting

8 A ---- person, he found the training almost unbearably monotonous, but he resolved to check his ---- and perform the basic tasks required.

(A) bitter..submissiveness
(B) reclusive..reserve
(C) dynamic..restlessness
(D) mercurial..constancy
(E) vivacious..ambition

9 Well-publicized disagreements in the scientific community have so ---- many laypersons that they now ---- new warnings about the health effects of popular foods.

(A) inundated..regulate
(B) exasperated..discount
(C) bedazzled..ridicule
(D) vindicated..exaggerate
(E) disqualified..minimize

GO ON TO THE NEXT PAGE

Each question below consists of a related pair of words or phrases, followed by five pairs of words or phrases labeled A through E. Select the pair that best expresses a relationship similar to that expressed in the original pair.

Example:

CRUMB : BREAD ::
(A) ounce : unit
(B) splinter : wood
(C) water : bucket
(D) twine : rope
(E) cream : butter

Ⓐ ● Ⓒ Ⓓ Ⓔ

10 BERET : CAP ::
(A) tie : shirt
(B) hem : skirt
(C) ring : finger
(D) sneaker : shoe
(E) zipper : jacket

11 APPRENTICE : ARTISAN ::
(A) minister : congregation
(B) actor : script
(C) amateur : hobby
(D) statue : sculptor
(E) cadet : officer

e

12 ANECDOTE : STORY ::
(A) laughter : joke
(B) quotation : footnote
(C) melody : tune
(D) limerick : poem
(E) column : newspaper

13 FRACTIOUS : OBEDIENCE ::
(A) rigid : adaptability
(B) notorious : infamy
(C) decisive : authority
(D) merciful : justice
(E) deliberate : action

a

14 FRUGALITY : STINGY ::
(A) warmth : generous
(B) resolution : whimsical
(C) reflection : thoughtful
(D) pride : haughty
(E) jauntiness : morose

15 TYRANT : GOVERN ::
(A) inspector : examine
(B) inquisitor : question
(C) cynic : believe
(D) fugitive : escape
(E) volunteer : work

b

GO ON TO THE NEXT PAGE

Each passage below is followed by questions based on its content. Answer the questions on the basis of what is <u>stated</u> or <u>implied</u> in each passage and in any introductory material that may be provided.

Questions 16-24 are based on the following passage.

In this passage, the narrator describes her mother, Kathleen Godwin.

Several years ago, my mother began giving me unusual birthday presents. Wrapped in conventional gift paper, they pose as innocent surprises,
Line but every one of them is capable of detonating.
(5) One recent birthday she must have been feeling especially . . . What's the word to describe someone who both stirs things up and plays a deep game? Inciter? Igniter? Evocateur? Evocatrix? "Elusive presence" isn't a bad description:
(10) always there, but never completely grasped.

Anyway, one recent birthday she presented me with a whole box of these time bombs from the past. Included was the December 1945 issue of *LOVE Short Stories*. Turning to the table of
(15) contents, I saw a story by Kathleen Godwin and another by Charlotte Ashe. Beside the name Charlotte Ashe had been penciled in "Kathleen," as if I might not remember who Charlotte Ashe was. When this issue of the magazine came out, we
(20) were living on Charlotte Street, in Asheville. My mother was the most glamorous person I knew. I was not completely sure of her, the way I was sure of my grandmother, who in our household performed the tasks associated with motherhood
(25) while Kathleen Godwin went out in all weather to breadwin for us, and her alter ego Charlotte Ashe concocted the extra romance for two cents a word on the weekends. (One story per author to an issue was the magazine's policy.)
(30) She was more like a magical older sister, my mother, in those impressionable days when the soft clay of my personality was being sculpted. She came and she went (mostly went, it seemed). She dashed off to her various jobs each day, returning
(35) after dark in elated exhaustion. She was long since divorced by then, but was playing her cards close to her chest. "When people ask, I say your father's in the service. It's true, he's in the navy. The rest is nobody's business." Many years later, she told
(40) me they were also more likely to give jobs to wives of servicemen.

Or widows. After the war ended, she was obliged to kill him off. Once he came up from Florida to visit us, and she made us say he was
(45) my uncle. I obeyed, my grandmother obeyed, *he* obeyed—he was very good-natured about it. I was

sorry not to be able to claim him to my friends, because he was so handsome and amusing. But Kathleen was running the show.
(50) His navy letters to her were in that same birthday box of explosives that included the *LOVE Short Stories* and her master's thesis on masques.*

These selected birthday offerings, I have begun to understand, are not just a way of cleaning out
(55) her closets, or even of doling out to me artifacts from our shared past; they are also an art form. They are cunning little stage sets through which someone who recognizes the "pieces" can then reenter the past and watch reruns of the old
(60) masques being played out in those days. Only now, the same someone would have grown out of the emotional dependencies of her childhood (one would hope!) and is therefore ready to appreciate the masques artistically, as interesting embodi-
(65) ments of the human drama . . . could enter the masques, if she likes, and play the parts of the other actors. And begin to make all sorts of connections about who these people were, and who she is, and what they all had in common.

*Short dramatic entertainments in which performers are in disguise

16 The narrator most likely mentions the "gift paper" (line 3) to suggest

(A) her poignant memories of special occasions
(B) the anticipation she feels when receiving these gifts
(C) the contrast between the appearance and the contents of the packages
(D) that gift paper is often more interesting than the gifts
(E) the carelessness with which her mother prepares the gifts

17 The series of one-word questions in line 8 primarily reflects

(A) a child's confusion
(B) a child's amusement over a game
(C) the mother's changeable personality
(D) an adult's resentment at being tricked
(E) an adult's attempt to find a fitting label

GO ON TO THE NEXT PAGE

18 In the third paragraph (lines 19-29), the narrator emphasizes Kathleen's

(A) sentimentality
(B) gullibility
(C) unconventionality
(D) dependability
(E) generosity

19 The parenthetical comment in lines 28-29 is most likely included to

(A) provide insight into how fame affected the mother
(B) indicate why the mother used two names
(C) indicate that the narrator had a sudden afterthought
(D) indicate the difficulties in finding subjects to write about
(E) help the narrator refocus on how her mother became a writer

20 The reference to "soft clay" (line 32) serves to

(A) show what a lasting impression the narrator made on others
(B) suggest the versatility of Kathleen's creative talents
(C) suggest Kathleen's unpretentious nature
(D) express the unreliable nature of the narrator's memories
(E) emphasize Kathleen's influence over the narrator

21 The phrase "(one would hope!)" in lines 62-63 expresses the narrator's

(A) need for reassurance about her own talents
(B) optimism about the wisdom of human beings
(C) surprise at her mother's thoughtfulness
(D) uncertainty about having achieved full maturity
(E) confusion over her mother's intentions

22 The primary motive behind Kathleen's gift giving is to

(A) prove that all members of the family had shared in its survival
(B) provide her daughter with a vehicle for experiencing past dramas
(C) help the narrator to understand the challenges a writer faces
(D) set the stage for her future relationship with her daughter
(E) establish a link to the plots of her old stories

23 With which of the following statements would Kathleen Godwin most likely agree?

(A) Sometimes it is necessary to be less than entirely forthright.
(B) Being too innovative jeopardizes personal growth.
(C) Obstacles prevent individuals from achieving their goals.
(D) Individuals should consult others before making career choices.
(E) Traditional social practices should be rigorously respected.

24 The narrator primarily conveys which of the following regarding her mother?

(A) Amused wonderment
(B) Reluctant gratitude
(C) Unresolved insecurity
(D) Casual acceptance
(E) Suppressed resentment

GO ON TO THE NEXT PAGE

Questions 25-30 are based on the following passage.

The following excerpt is from a 1970 book dealing with the philosophy of science.

In popular misconception, science is believed to be omnipotent: what it has not yet achieved, it will ultimately achieve. It is believed to be infal-
Line lible; to say of anything that it is scientific is
(5) thought to give it the impress of truth, the certainty that brooks no shadow of doubt. Even the packets of breakfast cereals bear witness to this; advertising owes much of its power to the weight carried by a so-called scientific statement;
(10) to attribute scientific qualities to some process or other is to stifle criticism. Naturally, the adver-
tiser allows no hint of uncertainty to mar claims dubbed scientific; hence they become indisputable, eternally true, profoundly significant—at least
(15) they do in the eyes of those susceptible to the wiles of advertising. The television screen and the loudspeaker are as blatant and even more clam-
orous. Popular journalism preaches the same gospel: science is certainty; the findings of a
(20) research team must be true; mistakes are never made; progress is uninterrupted.
  — A result of this clamor is the unquestioning acceptance of the belief that science has proven such and such statements to be true; that the find-
(25) ings of science correspond to reality, and are there-
fore inevitable, indisputable, and final—claims that no scientist would make, claims that no philosopher could admit. There has been another influence at work that bolsters this belief. This is
(30) the view that even some scientists themselves profess to have of their subject, a view that owes its origin to the immense influence of the philosopher Ernst Mach (1838-1916), who developed a conception of science as a convenient summary of
(35) experience. The purpose of science, he said, was to save time and trouble in recording observations. Science was the most economical adaptation of thought to facts and was as external to the facts as is a map, a timetable, or a telephone directory. It
(40) must not go beyond experience by affirming anything that cannot be tested by experience; above all, scientists must be immediately prepared to drop a theory the moment an observation turns up to conflict with it. Scientists must have an
(45) absolute respect for observations; they must hold scientific theories in judicial detachment. Scien-

tists must be passionless observers, unbiased by emotion, intellectually cold.
(50) The facts are otherwise. The history of science shows us, again and again, great discoveries made by passionate adherence to ideas forged in the white heat of imagination. It shows us slow construction, brick by patient brick, of a scientific edifice, often in complete disregard of apparently
(55) conflicting evidence. And it shows us bold imagi-
native leaps made in the dark, in unjustified antic-
ipation of success, only later to receive astonishing experimental confirmation.

25 In line 6, the phrase "certainty . . . doubt" refers to which property popularly ascribed to science?

(A) Provable tenets
(B) Healthy exchange of ideas
(C) Widely held beliefs
(D) Absolute authority
(E) Unswerving dedication

26 As used in line 5, "impress" most nearly means

(A) depth
(B) influence
(C) sensitivity
(D) pressure
(E) stamp

GO ON TO THE NEXT PAGE

27 The breakfast cereal example (lines 6-11) is used to support the view that

(A) responsible manufacturers ensure the quality of their products through scientific research

(B) children increasingly have become the targets of advertising

(C) scientific claims are used to enhance the appeal of certain products

(D) more scientific research is needed in the area of nutrition

(E) the effects of advertising have so far been minimal

28 The word "clamor" (line 22) is used to

(A) characterize the promulgation by the media of a certain image of science

(B) emphasize the author's view that scientific findings can seem confusing

(C) indicate the excitement in the scientific community over a dramatic breakthrough

(D) exaggerate the differences of opinion between advertising and journalism

(E) represent the debate that exists about the role of science in everyday matters

29 The sentence beginning "The history" (lines 49-52) indicates that scientific discoveries

(A) do not always depend on ploddingly rational, organized thinking

(B) rarely hold up when they are arrived at frivolously

(C) usually reflect the personality of the scientists who made them

(D) are approached so illogically that scientists work best alone

(E) are made in such states of emotion that researchers overlook important data

30 Which example most accurately illustrates what is being described in lines 55-57 ("And it shows . . . success")?

(A) The excavation of the ruins of an ancient city to search for clay writing tablets

(B) A voyage across an ocean in search of a hypothesized new continent

(C) The microscopic inspection of muscle tissue in order to discover its anatomy

(D) The accidental discovery of a new galaxy while scanning the sky for comets

(E) An experiment in which one group of people is given a drug and another group a placebo

IF YOU FINISH BEFORE TIME IS CALLED, YOU MAY CHECK YOUR WORK ON THIS SECTION ONLY. DO NOT TURN TO ANY OTHER SECTION IN THE TEST. **STOP**

396

| Time—30 Minutes 25 Questions | This section contains two types of questions. You have 30 minutes to complete both types. You may use any available space for scratchwork. |

Notes:

1. The use of a calculator is permitted. All numbers used are real numbers.

2. Figures that accompany problems in this test are intended to provide information useful in solving the problems. They are drawn as accurately as possible EXCEPT when it is stated in a specific problem that the figure is not drawn to scale. All figures lie in a plane unless otherwise indicated.

Reference Information

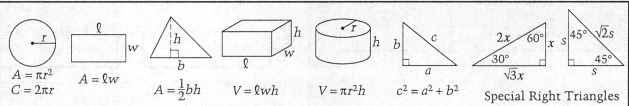

$A = \pi r^2$
$C = 2\pi r$

$A = \ell w$

$A = \frac{1}{2}bh$

$V = \ell wh$

$V = \pi r^2 h$

$c^2 = a^2 + b^2$

Special Right Triangles

The number of degrees of arc in a circle is 360.
The measure in degrees of a straight angle is 180.
The sum of the measures in degrees of the angles of a triangle is 180.

Directions for Quantitative Comparison Questions

Questions 1-15 each consist of two quantities in boxes, one in Column A and one in Column B. You are to compare the two quantities and on the answer sheet fill in oval

    A if the quantity in Column A is greater;
    B if the quantity in Column B is greater;
    C if the two quantities are equal;
    D if the relationship cannot be determined from the information given.

AN E RESPONSE WILL NOT BE SCORED.

Notes:

1. In some questions, information is given about one or both of the quantities to be compared. In such cases, the given information is centered above the two columns and is not boxed.

2. In a given question, a symbol that appears in both columns represents the same thing in Column A as it does in Column B.

3. Letters such as x, n, and k stand for real numbers.

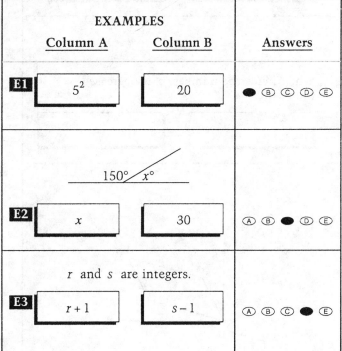

EXAMPLES

| Column A | Column B | Answers |

E1 5^2 20   ● Ⓑ Ⓒ Ⓓ Ⓔ

$150° \quad x°$

E2 x 30   Ⓐ Ⓑ ● Ⓓ Ⓔ

r and s are integers.

E3 $r + 1$ $s - 1$ Ⓐ Ⓑ Ⓒ ● Ⓔ

GO ON TO THE NEXT PAGE

SUMMARY DIRECTIONS FOR COMPARISON QUESTIONS

Answer: A if the quantity in Column A is greater;
B if the quantity in Column B is greater;
C if the two quantities are equal;
D if the relationship cannot be determined from the information given.

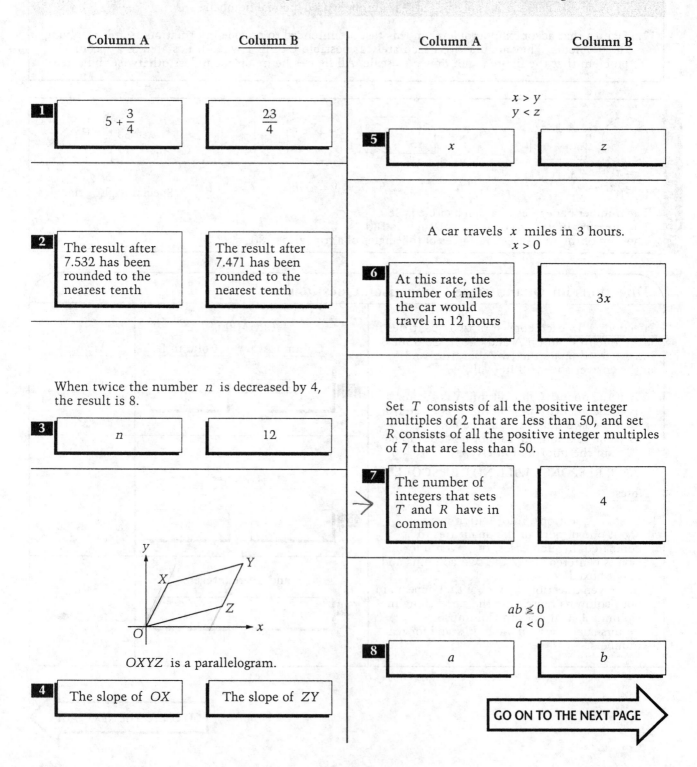

Column A	Column B

1 $5 + \dfrac{3}{4}$ | $\dfrac{23}{4}$

2 The result after 7.532 has been rounded to the nearest tenth | The result after 7.471 has been rounded to the nearest tenth

When twice the number n is decreased by 4, the result is 8.

3 n | 12

OXYZ is a parallelogram.

4 The slope of *OX* | The slope of *ZY*

Column A	Column B

$x > y$
$y < z$

5 x | z

A car travels x miles in 3 hours.
$x > 0$

6 At this rate, the number of miles the car would travel in 12 hours | $3x$

Set T consists of all the positive integer multiples of 2 that are less than 50, and set R consists of all the positive integer multiples of 7 that are less than 50.

7 The number of integers that sets T and R have in common | 4

$ab \lessgtr 0$
$a < 0$

8 a | b

GO ON TO THE NEXT PAGE

SUMMARY DIRECTIONS FOR COMPARISON QUESTIONS

<u>Answer:</u> A if the quantity in Column A is greater;
B if the quantity in Column B is greater;
C if the two quantities are equal;
D if the relationship cannot be determined from the information given.

Column A	Column B

$x°$, $y°$, and $z°$ are the measures of three of the four angles of a parallelogram.

9

$x + y$	$2z$

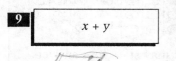

$$\begin{array}{r} 4R \\ S6 \\ + 6S \\ \hline 144 \end{array}$$

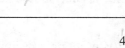

R and S represent different digits in the correctly worked addition problem.

10

R	S

11

The number of different prime factors of 28 that are greater than 2	The number of different prime factors of 24 that are greater than 2

The product of two consecutive positive integers equals 6 times the smaller integer.

12

The sum of the two integers	10

Column A	Column B

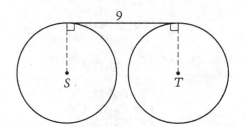

9

The circle with center S has the same area as the circle with center T.

13

The radius of the circle with center S	5

a is a positive integer.

14

The remainder when a is divided by 7	The remainder when a^2 is divided by 7

A square piece of paper with sides of length s is cut into exactly five pieces with areas 9, 9, 10, 10, and 11.

15

s	8

GO ON TO THE NEXT PAGE ➡

Directions for Student-Produced Response Questions

Each of the remaining 10 questions requires you to solve the problem and enter your answer by marking the ovals in the special grid, as shown in the examples below.

Answer: $\frac{7}{12}$ or 7/12   Answer: 2.5

Write answer → in boxes.

←Fraction line

←Decimal point

Answer: 201
Either position is correct.

Grid in → result.

Note: You may start your answers in any column, space permitting. Columns not needed should be left blank.

- Mark no more than one oval in any column.
- Because the answer sheet will be machine-scored, **you will receive credit only if the ovals are filled in correctly.**
- Although not required, it is suggested that you write your answer in the boxes at the top of the columns to help you fill in the ovals accurately.
- Some problems may have more than one correct answer. In such cases, grid only one answer.
- No question has a negative answer.
- **Mixed numbers** such as $2\frac{1}{2}$ must be gridded as 2.5 or 5/2. (If $2\ 1\ /\ 2$ is gridded, it will be interpreted as $\frac{21}{2}$, not $2\frac{1}{2}$.)

- **Decimal Accuracy**: If you obtain a decimal answer, **enter the most accurate value the grid will accommodate.** For example, if you obtain an answer such as 0.6666 . . . , you should record the result as .666 or .667. **Less accurate values such as .66 or .67 are not acceptable.**

Acceptable ways to grid $\frac{2}{3}$ = .6666 . . .

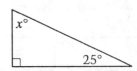

16 In the right triangle above, what is the value of x?

17 If $x + y + z = 1,450$ and $x = -250$, what is the value of $y + z$?

$-250 + y + z = 1,450$

GO ON TO THE NEXT PAGE

18 The product of 5 and n is a multiple of 10. If the product is greater than 0 and less than 50, what is one possible value of n ?

20 The "digital root" of a positive integer is found by adding its digits, adding the digits of the resulting number, and so on, until the result is a single digit. For example, the digital root of 876 is 3 because $8 + 7 + 6 = 21$ and $2 + 1 = 3$. What is the least integer greater than 500 with a digital root of 1 ?

19 Typically, 4 apples of a certain variety weigh 1 pound. Ten pounds of these apples cost $8.00. At this rate, what is the cost, in dollars, of a dozen apples? (Disregard the dollar sign when gridding your answer. If, for example, your answer is $1.37, grid 1.37)

21 If $3x^2 = 15$, what is the value of $3x^4$?

$4 = 1 lbs$

$10 lbs = \$8$

$\dfrac{4}{1} = \dfrac{12}{3 lbs}$

$\dfrac{10}{8} = 3$

$8 = 40 apple = 10 lbs$

GO ON TO THE NEXT PAGE

401

22 For $x > 0$, let x be defined as $2x - 1$.

What is the value of $\dfrac{6}{3}$?

24 The time T, in hours, needed to produce X units of a product is given by the formula $T = pX + s$, where p and s are constants. If it takes 265 hours to produce 100 units and 390 hours to produce 150 units, what is the value of s ?

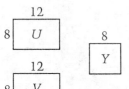

23 In the figure above, Y and Z are squares and U, V, W, and X are rectangles. If the six quadrilaterals were attached at their edges to form a rectangular box, what would be the volume of this box?

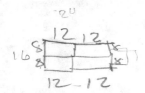

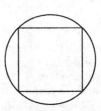

25 In the figure above, a square with side of length $\sqrt{2}$ is inscribed in a circle. If the area of the circle is $k\pi$, what is the exact value of k ?

IF YOU FINISH BEFORE TIME IS CALLED, YOU MAY CHECK YOUR WORK ON THIS SECTION ONLY. DO NOT TURN TO ANY OTHER SECTION IN THE TEST. **STOP**

402

Time—30 Minutes
35 Questions

For each question in this section, select the best answer from among the choices given and fill in the corresponding oval on the answer sheet.

Each sentence below has one or two blanks, each blank indicating that something has been omitted. Beneath the sentence are five words or sets of words labeled A through E. Choose the word or set of words that, when inserted in the sentence, best fits the meaning of the sentence as a whole.

Example:

Medieval kingdoms did not become constitutional republics overnight; on the contrary, the change was ----.

(A) unpopular
(B) unexpected
(C) advantageous
(D) sufficient
(E) gradual

Ⓐ Ⓑ Ⓒ Ⓓ ●

1 Unlike the politician, who must spend his or her energy in public show or endless meetings, the artist needs ---- for significant efforts.

(A) approval   (B) prudence   (C) motivation
(D) solitude   (E) perseverance

2 The fact that MTV, the cable channel devoted primarily to music, provided extensive coverage of the 1992 presidential race demonstrates how ---- politics and popular music culture have become.

(A) obscured   (B) contradictory
(C) interrelated   (D) enclosed
(E) permeated

3 Rod monochromasy, a type of color blindness that renders a person's vision strongest when light is weakest, is so rarely ---- that it is often ----.

(A) encountered. .misdiagnosed
(B) remedied. .contaminated
(C) reported. .publicized
(D) discerned. .transmuted
(E) calibrated. .unappreciated

4 Renowned for maintaining her ---- even in the most chaotic situations, Frances was utterly ----.

(A) dignity. .incorrigible
(B) composure. .imperturbable
(C) prosperity. .blunt
(D) equanimity. .clairvoyant
(E) control. .insignificant

5 Always ready to ---- achievement, Miller was as eager to praise a new production as the more mean-spirited critics were to ---- it.

(A) reward. .review
(B) impede. .ignore
(C) recognize. .deride
(D) expose. .study
(E) embrace. .promote

6 Eduardo Galeano's novel consists of discrete vignettes, so the reader must supply the invisible ---- binding such apparently ---- parts.

(A) emotions. .impersonal
(B) interpretations. .somber
(C) descriptions. .related
(D) connections. .independent
(E) categories. .cohesive

7 The ---- of Queen Elizabeth I impressed her contemporaries: she seemed to know what dignitaries and foreign leaders were thinking.

(A) symbiosis   (B) malevolence
(C) punctiliousness   (D) consternation
(E) perspicacity

8 Unable to attend the reunion, Marlene could enjoy it only in a ---- fashion, through the photographs taken there.

(A) gratuitous   (B) vigorous   (C) vicarious
(D) lethargic   (E) sullen

9 Many of today's physicians and patients are ---- high technology, captivated by computer-designed drugs and laser surgery.

(A) nervous about   (B) defensive about
(C) tolerant of   (D) enamored of
(E) overwhelmed by

10 Joe Louis was ---- fighter: he inspired fear in many of his opponents.

(A) a serene   (B) an impetuous   (C) an insipid
(D) a malleable   (E) a redoubtable

GO ON TO THE NEXT PAGE

403

Each question below consists of a related pair of words or phrases, followed by five pairs of words or phrases labeled A through E. Select the pair that <u>best</u> expresses a relationship similar to that expressed in the original pair.

Example:

CRUMB : BREAD ::
(A) ounce : unit
(B) splinter : wood
(C) water : bucket
(D) twine : rope
(E) cream : butter

11 MONEY : BANK ::
(A) food : basket
(B) park : city
(C) cash : store
(D) book : library
(E) article : magazine

12 STEAMROLLER : FLATTEN ::
(A) cafeteria : dine
(B) automobile : refuel
(C) television : repair
(D) umbrella : fold
(E) refrigerator : chill

13 DESIGN : BUILD ::
(A) compose : perform
(B) rehearse : improvise
(C) erase : write
(D) repair : overhaul
(E) pose : paint

14 CHEESE : MILK ::
(A) cookie : crumb
(B) jam : fruit
(C) bread : crust
(D) wheat : grain
(E) pasta : sauce

15 FACE : EXPRESSION ::
(A) mask : identity
(B) portrait : frame
(C) eyes : vision
(D) voice : tone
(E) nose : profile

16 ABDUCTION : PERSON ::
(A) duress : threat
(B) robbery : property
(C) deception : credulity
(D) larceny : victim
(E) battery : weapon

17 BILLBOARD : ADVERTISEMENT ::
(A) wall : mural
(B) purchase : price
(C) menu : restaurant
(D) aisle : supermarket
(E) monument : unveiling

18 IMPLAUSIBLE : ABSURD ::
(A) shadowy : illuminated
(B) flamboyant : public
(C) surprising : shocking
(D) superfluous : truncated
(E) latent : potential

19 CREST : HILL ::
(A) fathom : sea
(B) plateau : valley
(C) curtain : window
(D) trunk : tree
(E) roof : house

20 ANALGESIC : PAIN ::
(A) antiseptic : cleanliness
(B) tranquilizer : anxiety
(C) sedative : sleep
(D) antibiotic : medicine
(E) pathology : disease

21 BOMBASTIC : SPEECH ::
(A) fashionable : taste
(B) ostentatious : display
(C) durable : fabric
(D) penetrating : analysis
(E) scrumptious : confection

22 FRATERNIZE : AMIABLE ::
(A) expiate : reprehensible
(B) respect : honored
(C) collaborate : cooperative
(D) persist : successful
(E) compliment : impolite

23 NUANCE : SUBTLE ::
(A) pun : sarcastic
(B) fib : honest
(C) inquiry : discreet
(D) hint : indirect
(E) clue : mysterious

GO ON TO THE NEXT PAGE

404

The two passages below are followed by questions based on their content and on the relationship between the two passages. Answer the questions on the basis of what is <u>stated</u> or <u>implied</u> in the passages and in any introductory material that may be provided.

Questions 24-35 are based on the following passages.

In the fifth century B.C., most of the Greek world was divided into two powerful alliances, that of the Athenians and that of the Peloponnesians. In 433 B.C. an incident occurred that seemed to doom the shaky truce between the two sides. A nonallied city, Corcyra, appealed to the Athenians for military help against Corinth, a rival city in the Peloponnesian alliance. The following passages are taken from an account by a Greek historian presenting the speeches given by the Corcyraeans and the Corinthians in the Athenian assembly.

Passage 1 (Corcyra)

Athenians, in this situation, it is right and proper that certain points should be made clear. We have come to ask for help, but we cannot

Line claim that this help is due us because of any great
(5) services we have done to you in the past or on the basis of any existing alliance. We must therefore convince you first that by giving us this help you will be acting in your own interests, or certainly not against your own interests; and then we must
(10) show that our gratitude can be depended on. If on all these points you find our arguments unconvincing, we must not be surprised if our mission ends in failure.

What has happened is that our policy in the
(15) past appears to have been against our own present interests and at the same time makes it look inconsistent of us to be asking help from you. We used to think that our neutrality was a wise thing, since it prevented us from being dragged into
(20) danger by other peoples' policies; now we see it clearly as a lack of foresight and as a source of weakness. We recognize that if we have nothing but our own national resources, it is impossible for us to survive. It should not be held against us that
(25) now we have faced the facts and are reversing our old policy of keeping ourselves to ourselves. There is nothing sinister in our action; we merely recognize that we made a mistake.

If you grant our request, you will find that in
(30) many ways it was a good thing that we made it at this particular time. First of all, you will not be helping aggressors, but people who are the victims of aggression. Secondly, we are now in extreme peril, and if you welcome our alliance at this
(35) moment you will win our undying gratitude. And then, we are, after you, the greatest naval power in Greece. You would have paid a lot of money and still have been very grateful to have us on your side. Is it not, then, an extraordinary stroke
(40) of good luck for you (and one that will cause pain among your enemies) to have us coming over voluntarily into your camp, giving ourselves up to you without involving you in any dangers or any expense? It is a situation where we, whom you
(45) are helping, will be grateful to you, the world in general will admire you for your generosity, and yourselves will be stronger than you were before. There is scarcely a case in history where all these advantages have been available at the same time,
(50) nor has it often happened before that a power looking for an alliance can say to those whose help it asks that it can give as much honor and as much security as it will receive.

Passage 2 (Corinth)

"Wisdom" and "moderation" are the words
(55) used by the Corcyraeans in describing their old policy of avoiding alliances. In fact the motives were entirely evil, and there was nothing good about them at all. They wanted no allies because their actions were wrong, and they were ashamed
(60) of calling others to witness their own misdoings. The geographical situation of Corcyra gives its inhabitants a certain independence. The ships of other states are forced to put in to their harbors much more often than Corcyraean ships visit
(65) the harbors of other states. So, in cases where a Corcyraean has been guilty of injuring some other national, the Corcyraeans are themselves their own judges, and there is no question of having the case tried by independent judges appointed by
(70) treaty. So this neutrality of theirs, which sounds so innocent, was in fact a disguise adopted not to preserve them from having to share in the wrongdoings of others, but in order to give them a perfectly free hand to do wrong themselves, making
(75) away with other people's property by force when they are strong enough, cheating them whenever they can manage to do so, and so enjoying their gains without any vestige of shame. Yet if they really were the honorable people they pretend to
(80) be, this very independence of theirs would have given them the best possible opportunity for showing their good qualities in the relations of common justice.

The right course, surely, is either for you to pre-
(85) serve a strict neutrality or else to join us against them. At least you have treaty obligations toward Corinth, whereas you have never even had a peace treaty with Corcyra.

GO ON TO THE NEXT PAGE

405

24 Which of the following best describes the two appeals to the Athenians?

(A) Passage 1 cites historical reasons, while Passage 2 refers to economic ones.
(B) Passage 1 focuses on the Athenians' obligations to neighboring states, while Passage 2 focuses on the dangers to the Athenians if they remain neutral.
(C) Passage 1 stresses the advantages of the alliance to Athens, while Passage 2 stresses Corcyra's untrustworthiness.
(D) Both Passage 1 and Passage 2 appeal to the Athenians' sense of pride.
(E) Both Passage 1 and Passage 2 emphasize a desperate need for assistance.

25 The word "mission" (line 12) most nearly means

(A) religious enterprise
(B) vocation
(C) conversion
(D) diplomatic effort
(E) group sent to a foreign country

26 The argumentative strategy used by the Corcyraeans in the first paragraph of Passage 1 can best be described as

(A) ridiculing the opposing claims of the Corinthians
(B) professing to be frank about Corcyra's own past behavior
(C) appealing to the Athenians' sympathy for a city with shared cultural ties
(D) attempting to frighten the Athenians with the consequences of not allying
(E) attempting to make the Athenians feel guilty

27 The word "sinister" (line 27) most nearly means

(A) ill-omened
(B) ill-intentioned
(C) unfavorable
(D) gruesome
(E) deadly

28 The word "camp" (line 42) most nearly means a

(A) recreational facility
(B) military base
(C) temporary dwelling
(D) newly built settlement
(E) group with common interests

29 The Corinthians argue that the Corcyraeans are able to steal from others because

(A) their political neutrality enables them to avoid legal sanctions
(B) their alliance with the Athenians shields them from other states
(C) their navy is strong enough to intimidate other states
(D) there is no system of justice to regulate relations among the states
(E) there are no trade agreements among neighboring states

30 The Corinthians' recommendations to the Athenians in Passage 2 include all of the following EXCEPT to

(A) do what is right and proper
(B) remain neutral
(C) unite with the Corinthians against the Corcyraeans
(D) punish a state that has behaved badly
(E) promote isolationism

31 Lines 61-65 ("The geographical . . . other states") indirectly establish that Corcyra

(A) contained major shipping ports
(B) was located close to its enemies
(C) often experienced harsh weather
(D) was very prone to violence
(E) supplied most of Athens' ships

GO ON TO THE NEXT PAGE

32 In comparison to the tone of Passage 1, the tone of Passage 2 is more

(A) detached
(B) condemnatory
(C) humble
(D) condescending
(E) sympathetic

33 Which event, had it occurred, would have been most likely to persuade the Athenians to take sides?

(A) The Corcyraeans initiated an attack on the Corinthians.
(B) The Corcyraeans provided proof of a planned Corinthian attack on the Athenians.
(C) The Corcyraeans more fully explained their earlier wish to remain unallied.
(D) The Corinthians solicited the aid of their other allies.
(E) The Corinthians demonstrated their skill in argumentation more effectively.

34 Both passages discuss the

(A) Corcyraeans' neutrality
(B) Corcyraeans' desire to dominate the waterways
(C) Corinthians' alliance with the Athenians
(D) Athenians' sense of fairness
(E) Athenians' naval power

35 Which pairing best describes what the Corcyraeans and the Corinthians, respectively, believe will motivate the Athenians to act?

(A) Greed *versus* desire for solidarity
(B) Honor *versus* desire for vengeance
(C) Self-interest *versus* sense of duty
(D) Survival *versus* desire for domination
(E) Power *versus* fear of regional threat

Time—15 Minutes 10 Questions	In this section solve each problem, using any available space on the page for scratchwork. Then decide which is the best of the choices given and fill in the corresponding oval on the answer sheet.

Notes:

(1) The use of a calculator is permitted. All numbers used are real numbers.

(2) Figures that accompany problems in this test are intended to provide information useful in solving the problems. They are drawn as accurately as possible EXCEPT when it is stated in a specific problem that the figure is not drawn to scale. All figures lie in a plane unless otherwise indicated.

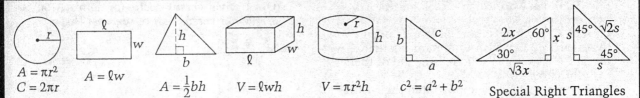

$A = \pi r^2$
$C = 2\pi r$
$A = \ell w$
$A = \frac{1}{2}bh$
$V = \ell w h$
$V = \pi r^2 h$
$c^2 = a^2 + b^2$
Special Right Triangles

The number of degrees of arc in a circle is 360.
The measure in degrees of a straight angle is 180.
The sum of the measures in degrees of the angles of a triangle is 180.

---

1 If $a = 6$ and $b = 5$, what is the value of $2a - 3b$?

(A) −9
(B) −3
(C) 1
(D) 3
(E) 27

---

2 If 1 "hexaminute" is equivalent to 6 minutes of time, how many hexaminutes are equivalent to 3 hours of time?

(A) 1,080
(B) 540
(C) 180
(D) 60
(E) 30

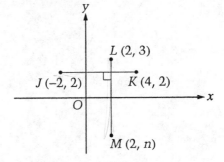

3 In the figure above, the length of JK is equal to the length of LM. What is the value of n ?

(A) −4
(B) −3
(C) −2
(D) 2
(E) 3

GO ON TO THE NEXT PAGE

4 If the average (arithmetic mean) of 5 and k is equal to the average of 2, 6, and k, what is the value of k?

(A) 1
(B) 2
(C) 5
(D) 6
(E) 8

5 A rectangle with length 12 and width 5 has an area that is 4 times the area of a triangle with base 3. What is the height of the triangle?

(A) 5
(B) 10
(C) 15
(D) 20
(E) 25

6 Tina sells 8-ounce glasses of lemonade in her snack shop. It costs her $3.20 to make 64 of the 8-ounce glasses of lemonade. If each glass has additional overhead costs of $0.25 and Tina wants to make a profit of $0.35 per glass, how much should she charge for a glass of lemonade?

(A) $0.50
(B) $0.55
(C) $0.60
(D) $0.65
(E) $0.75

3.20 ÷ 64

GO ON TO THE NEXT PAGE

409

x-scale ——— 20 ——————— 60 ———

y-scale ——— 50 ——————— 100 ———

7 On the linear scales above, 20 and 60 on the x-scale correspond to 50 and 100, respectively, on the y-scale. Which of the following linear equations could be used to convert an x-scale value to a y-scale value?

(A) $y = x + 30$
(B) $y = x + 40$
(C) $y = 1.25x + 25$
(D) $y = 1.25x + 30$
(E) $y = 0.8x + 34$

8 The first term of a sequence of integers is 100. Every term after the first is equal to $\frac{1}{2}$ of the immediately preceding term if that preceding term is even, or is equal to $\frac{1}{2}$ of the immediately preceding term plus $\frac{1}{2}$ if that preceding term is odd. What is the fifth term of the sequence?

(A) 13
(B) 12
(C) 7
(D) 6
(E) 4

GO ON TO THE NEXT PAGE

9 A word-processing operator typed 44 words per minute. After practice, the operator's speed increased to 55 words per minute. By what percent did the operator's speed increase?

(A) 10%
(B) 11%
(C) 20%
(D) 25%
(E) 28%

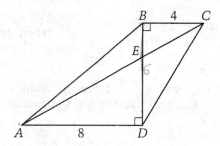

Note: Figure not drawn to scale.

10 In the figure above, if $BD = 6$, what is the area of $\triangle ABE$?

(A) 8
(B) 10
(C) 12
(D) 14
(E) 16

IF YOU FINISH BEFORE TIME IS CALLED, YOU MAY CHECK YOUR WORK ON THIS SECTION ONLY. DO NOT TURN TO ANY OTHER SECTION IN THE TEST. **STOP**

411

Time—15 Minutes
13 Questions

For each question in this section, select the best answer from among the choices given and fill in the corresponding oval on the answer sheet.

The passage below is followed by questions based on its content. Answer the questions on the basis of what is <u>stated</u> or <u>implied</u> in the passage and in any introductory material that may be provided.

Questions 1-13 are based on the following passage.

The following passage is taken from a chapter in a history of jazz. It discusses the genius of Louis Armstrong (1900-1971), a trumpeter of great inventiveness.

Louis Armstrong happened to be a genius. That particular word has probably been misused more regularly by writers on jazz than by those on any
Line of the other arts, with the exception, of course, of
(5) film. Virtually every jazz musician able to hold an instrument properly has at one time or another been described as a genius; patently, the description is usually unwarranted.

But if the term means anything at all, it
(10) describes Armstrong. I take the word to mean somebody whose accomplishments are beyond analysis. An artist makes relationships; a great artist makes new and surprising ones, showing us how apparently disparate shapes can be fitted
(15) together. With ordinary artists, we can discover in their background and character where they drew their material from; with geniuses, we often are unable to determine how they arrived at their startling conclusions. Armstrong's melodic gift
(20) was simply astonishing, and there is no explaining where it came from or how it worked its magic. Consider this: Armstrong did not begin to play the cornet until he was <u>fourteen</u>, a relatively late age for a musician to start. Within months, despite
(25) the fact that he could not read music, he was leader of his school band. Four years later he was cornetist with the leading jazz band in New Orleans. In another four years, when he was not yet twenty-three, he was acknowledged by his
(30) peers to be the best jazz musician alive. By the time he was twenty-eight, he had made a series of records that not only changed the course of jazz history, and therefore the history of Western music as well, but also remains one of the greatest
(35) achievements in jazz.

What makes Armstrong's playing so remarkable? First, there is his mastery of his instrument. His tone is warm and full, like honey, in all registers. The way he begins a musical phrase is one of
(40) the strongest and cleanest of any jazz trumpeter. Where many jazz brass players employ a smooth

—and continuous style replete with slurs and half-tonguings, Armstrong always introduced a note with a razor-sharp front edge. His vibrato* is
(45) broad, but slower than the slightly nervous vibrato of Joe Oliver and other New Orleans players. Although his command of the high register would not be considered remarkable today, he was far ahead of his peers in this respect; in fact,
(50) Armstrong brought high-register playing into jazz. In sum, there is no other sound in jazz like Armstrong's. It is immediately identifiable—rich and welcoming. (It should also be noted that Armstrong habitually hits held notes just fraction-
(55) ally flat, and pulls up to true pitch, a procedure, we remember, that Milton Metfessel's phonophotography machine showed to be customary with Black folksingers.)

But ultimately it is his melodic conception that
(60) dazzles us. Melody is one of those things in music that is difficult to talk about. Harmony has its theory, which is based on reasoned assumptions; rhythm can be approached almost mathematically; and form has analogues in architecture, drama, and
(65) geometry. Yet why is it that a particular fragment of melody moves us? Jazz musicians have often spoken of a player's "telling his story"; drummer Jo Jones claimed that he could hear actual words and indeed whole sentences in Lester Young's
(70) saxophone playing. Too, critics of classical music have spoken of the conversational element in melody. It is difficult to know how much to make of this, but in the best music we do catch the feeling that the composer or improvising musician is
(75) talking to us, telling us a story, or making an important point about something we can almost, but not quite, put into words. This effect is no doubt created in part by the resemblances that exist between music and speech. A story or lecture
(80) is coherent. It proceeds from here to there in logical fashion, and if it is to move us it will contain certain common dramatic devices—that is, it will elaborate on an initial statement; it will contain climaxes, asides and detours, tensions and resolu-
(85) tions; and it will round off with a final statement. The best music behaves in the same way, and it may be these formal similarities that give music the effect of speech.

GO ON TO THE NEXT PAGE →

This conversational element is abundantly
(90) present in Louis Armstrong's music. He had a
greater sense of form than any other player in
the history of jazz. His solos are not made of
sequences of melodic fragments related only in
mood; they consist of parts contributing to a
(95) whole. They have unity—a beginning, middle,
and end. Not all the time, of course; Armstrong,
like any player, had his weak moments, and there
were times when he was simply showing off. But
in his best work, that dramatic form is always
present.

*A slightly tremulous tonal effect achieved by slight and rapid
variations in pitch

1 The author implies that, like writers on jazz,
film critics

(A) confer undeserved praise on artists
(B) place too much emphasis on an artist's
background
(C) are usually more impressed by reputation
than by quality
(D) have too little experience of the art they
analyze
(E) have a tendency to be intolerant of minor
flaws

2 In lines 10-12 ("I take . . . beyond analysis"),
the author is doing which of the following?

(A) Providing a concrete example
(B) Defining an important term
(C) Proving an assertion
(D) Seeking support from other authorities
(E) Stating a fact

3 In lines 12-19 ("An artist . . . conclusions"),
the author differentiates between

(A) a musician who is trained and one who is
not
(B) Armstrong and other great artists
(C) what promotes and what holds back true
creativity
(D) an ordinary artist and a genius
(E) social background and personal character

4 The accomplishments listed in lines 22-35
reinforce which of the following ideas?

(A) Help from his peers served to promote
Armstrong's career.
(B) Armstrong's hard work and perseverance
ultimately earned him great rewards.
(C) Armstrong was only one of the great inno-
vators who changed the course of jazz.
(D) Armstrong's enormous talent fueled his
meteoric rise.
(E) Armstrong built on a foundation laid by
earlier musicians.

5 According to the passage, which of the following is an innovation of Armstrong's?

(A) A smooth style of playing
(B) A lack of vibrato
(C) Playing jazz in the high register
(D) Playing notes forcefully
(E) A warm-sounding tone

6 In line 42, "replete with" means

(A) complicated by
(B) marred by
(C) replaced by
(D) in addition to
(E) containing many

7 In the third paragraph, the author emphasizes
that Armstrong's style of playing was

(A) rhythmic and precise
(B) spare yet memorable
(C) emotionally draining
(D) highly traditional
(E) unmistakably characteristic

8 The sentence in parentheses (lines 53-58)
serves primarily to

(A) describe one aspect of Armstrong's playing
that the speaker regrets
(B) link Armstrong's playing to another musi-
cal form
(C) satirize the use of scientific machinery for
making aesthetic judgments
(D) offer a reason for Armstrong's early success
(E) provide an example of the result of
Armstrong's lack of musical training

GO ON TO THE NEXT PAGE

9 The author states that listeners are most moved by Armstrong's

(A) harmonic complexity
(B) melodic sensibility
(C) rhythmic precision
(D) well-honed technique
(E) startling inventiveness

10 In the fourth paragraph, the idea of telling a story is used as

(A) support for the view that jazz is more emotional than is classical music
(B) an alternative to more scientific theories of harmony
(C) an analogy to explain melodic form
(D) an example of a technique used mainly by Lester Young
(E) an example of a technique that prevents excess emotional expression

11 One element that the author particularly values in the construction of a melody is

(A) logical coherence
(B) elaborate ornamentation
(C) compelling rhythm
(D) implied harmonies
(E) true pitch

12 The sentence "Not all . . . off" (lines 96-98) is unique in the passage in that it

(A) makes no use of concrete detail
(B) is not focused on Armstrong's playing
(C) is not concerned with a theoretical aspect of music
(D) presents a criticism of Armstrong
(E) offers a personal assessment of Armstrong

13 In the final paragraph, the author emphasizes which of the following characteristics of Armstrong's music?

(A) Its emotional impact
(B) Its purity of tone
(C) Its innovativeness
(D) Its structure
(E) Its origins

IF YOU FINISH BEFORE TIME IS CALLED, YOU MAY CHECK YOUR WORK ON THIS SECTION ONLY. DO NOT TURN TO ANY OTHER SECTION IN THE TEST. **STOP**

414

SAT I Scoring Worksheet

SAT I Verbal Sections

A. Section 2:
$$\underline{\hspace{3cm}} - (\underline{\hspace{3cm}} \div 4) = \underline{\hspace{3cm}}$$
no. correct   no. incorrect   subtotal A

B. Section 4:
$$\underline{\hspace{3cm}} - (\underline{\hspace{3cm}} \div 4) = \underline{\hspace{3cm}}$$
no. correct   no. incorrect   subtotal B

C. Section 7:
$$\underline{\hspace{3cm}} - (\underline{\hspace{3cm}} \div 4) = \underline{\hspace{3cm}}$$
no. correct   no. incorrect   subtotal C

D. Total unrounded raw score
(Total A + B + C)
$$\underline{\hspace{3cm}}$$
D

E. Total rounded raw score
(Rounded to nearest whole number)
$$\underline{\hspace{3cm}}$$
E

F. SAT I verbal reported scaled score
(See the appropriate conversion table on back cover)

SAT I verbal
score

SAT I Mathematical Sections

A. Section 1:
$$\underline{\hspace{3cm}} - (\underline{\hspace{3cm}} \div 4) = \underline{\hspace{3cm}}$$
no. correct   no. incorrect   subtotal A

B. Section 3:
Questions 1-15 (quantitative comparison)
$$\underline{\hspace{3cm}} - (\underline{\hspace{3cm}} \div 3) = \underline{\hspace{3cm}}$$
no. correct   no. incorrect   subtotal B

C. Section 3:
Questions 16-25 (student-produced response)
$$\underline{\hspace{3cm}} = \underline{\hspace{3cm}}$$
no. correct   subtotal C

D. Section 6:
$$\underline{\hspace{3cm}} - (\underline{\hspace{3cm}} \div 4) = \underline{\hspace{3cm}}$$
no. correct   no. incorrect   subtotal D

E. Total unrounded raw score
(Total A + B + C + D)
$$\underline{\hspace{3cm}}$$
E

F. Total rounded raw score
(Rounded to nearest whole number)
$$\underline{\hspace{3cm}}$$
F

G. SAT I mathematical reported scaled score
(See the appropriate conversion table on back cover)

SAT I
mathematical
score

417

Score Conversion Table
SAT I: Reasoning Test
Saturday, May 1995
Recentered Scale

Raw Score	Verbal Scaled Score	Math Scaled Score	Raw Score	Verbal Scaled Score	Math Scaled Score
78	800		37	510	560
77	800		36	500	560
76	800		35	500	550
75	800		34	490	540
74	790		33	490	540
73	770		32	480	530
72	750		31	480	520
71	740		30	470	520
70	730		29	470	510
69	720		28	460	500
68	700		27	450	500
67	690		26	450	490
66	690		25	440	480
65	680		24	440	480
64	670		23	430	470
63	660		22	430	470
62	650		21	420	460
61	650		20	410	450
60	640	800	19	410	450
59	630	780	18	400	440
58	630	760	17	400	430
57	620	740	16	390	430
56	610	720	15	380	420
55	610	710	14	380	420
54	600	700	13	370	410
53	600	690	12	370	400
52	590	680	11	360	390
51	580	670	10	350	390
50	580	660	9	340	380
49	570	650	8	330	370
48	570	650	7	330	360
47	560	640	6	320	350
46	560	630	5	310	340
45	550	620	4	300	330
44	550	610	3	290	310
43	540	610	2	270	300
42	540	600	1	260	280
41	530	590	0	240	260
40	520	580	-1	230	240
39	520	580	-2	210	210
38	510	570	-3 and below	200	200

This table is for use only with this test.

SAT I: Reasoning Test

Sunday, May 1995

419

SAT® I: Reasoning Test

Calculator use is permitted on the mathematics sections only.

You will have three hours to work on the questions in this test book. There are **five 30-minute sections and two 15-minute sections**. The supervisor will tell you when to begin and end each section. If you finish before time is called, you may check your work on that section, but you may <u>not work on any other section</u>.

Do not worry if you are unable to finish a section or if there are some questions you cannot answer. Do not waste time puzzling over a question that seems too difficult for you. Work as rapidly as you can without sacrificing accuracy.

Students often ask whether they should guess when they are uncertain about the answer to a question. Scores on the multiple-choice questions on this test are based on the number of questions answered correctly minus a fraction of the number answered incorrectly. Therefore, it is unlikely that random or haphazard guessing will change your scores significantly. If you have some knowledge of a question, you may be able to eliminate one or more of the answer choices as wrong. It is generally a good idea to guess which of the remaining choices is correct.

Some mathematics questions have no answer choices. Instead, you must solve the problem and record your answer in a special grid on your answer sheet. For these questions, you will receive credit for correct answers, but there will be no deduction for incorrect answers.

Mark all your answers on the separate answer sheet. Mark only one answer for each question. Since the answer sheet will be machine scored, be sure that each mark is dark and that it completely fills the oval. In each section of the answer sheet, there are spaces to answer 40 questions. When there are fewer than 40 questions in a section of your test, use only the spaces that correspond to the question numbers. Do not make stray marks on the answer sheet. If you erase, do so completely, because an incomplete erasure may be scored as an intended response.

You may use the test book for scratchwork, but you will not receive credit for anything written there.

(The passages for this test have been adapted from published material. The ideas contained in them do not necessarily represent the opinions of the College Board or Educational Testing Service.)

DO NOT OPEN THIS BOOK UNTIL THE SUPERVISOR TELLS YOU TO DO SO.

420

Use a No. 2 pencil only. Be sure each mark is dark and completely fills the intended oval. Completely erase any errors or stray marks.

1. Your Name

First 4 letters of Last Name				First init.	Mid. init.

(grid of bubbles A–Z for each column)

2.

Your Name: _____
(Print) Last   First   M.I.

Signature: _____ Date: __/__/__

Home Address: _____
(Print) Number and Street

City   State   Zip Code

Center: _____
(Print) City   State   Center Number

IMPORTANT: Please fill in items 8 and 9 exactly as shown on the back cover of your test book.

8. Form Code
(Copy and grid as on back of test book.)

(grid: A–Z columns and 0–9 columns)

FOR ETS USE ONLY

3. Date Of Birth

Month	Day	Year
Jan. ○		
Feb. ○		
Mar. ○	0 0	0 0
Apr. ○	1 1	1 1
May ○	2 2	2 2
June ○	3 3	3 3
July ○	4 4	4
Aug. ○	5 5	5
Sept. ○	6 6	6
Oct. ○	7 7	7
Nov. ○	8 8	8
Dec. ○	9	9

4. Social Security Number

(grid of bubbles 0–9)

5. Sex
Female ○   Male ○

6. Registration Number
(Copy from your Admission Ticket.)

(grid of bubbles 0–9)

7. Test Book Serial Number
(Copy from front of test book.)

9. Test Form
(Copy from back cover of test book.)

DO NOT WRITE IN THIS AREA.

Start with number 1 for each new section. If a section has fewer questions than answer spaces, leave the extra answer spaces blank.

SECTION 1

1 Ⓐ Ⓑ Ⓒ Ⓓ Ⓔ 11 Ⓐ Ⓑ Ⓒ Ⓓ Ⓔ 21 Ⓐ Ⓑ Ⓒ Ⓓ Ⓔ 31 Ⓐ Ⓑ Ⓒ Ⓓ Ⓔ
2 Ⓐ Ⓑ Ⓒ Ⓓ Ⓔ 12 Ⓐ Ⓑ Ⓒ Ⓓ Ⓔ 22 Ⓐ Ⓑ Ⓒ Ⓓ Ⓔ 32 Ⓐ Ⓑ Ⓒ Ⓓ Ⓔ
3 Ⓐ Ⓑ Ⓒ Ⓓ Ⓔ 13 Ⓐ Ⓑ Ⓒ Ⓓ Ⓔ 23 Ⓐ Ⓑ Ⓒ Ⓓ Ⓔ 33 Ⓐ Ⓑ Ⓒ Ⓓ Ⓔ
4 Ⓐ Ⓑ Ⓒ Ⓓ Ⓔ 14 Ⓐ Ⓑ Ⓒ Ⓓ Ⓔ 24 Ⓐ Ⓑ Ⓒ Ⓓ Ⓔ 34 Ⓐ Ⓑ Ⓒ Ⓓ Ⓔ
5 Ⓐ Ⓑ Ⓒ Ⓓ Ⓔ 15 Ⓐ Ⓑ Ⓒ Ⓓ Ⓔ 25 Ⓐ Ⓑ Ⓒ Ⓓ Ⓔ 35 Ⓐ Ⓑ Ⓒ Ⓓ Ⓔ
6 Ⓐ Ⓑ Ⓒ Ⓓ Ⓔ 16 Ⓐ Ⓑ Ⓒ Ⓓ Ⓔ 26 Ⓐ Ⓑ Ⓒ Ⓓ Ⓔ 36 Ⓐ Ⓑ Ⓒ Ⓓ Ⓔ
7 Ⓐ Ⓑ Ⓒ Ⓓ Ⓔ 17 Ⓐ Ⓑ Ⓒ Ⓓ Ⓔ 27 Ⓐ Ⓑ Ⓒ Ⓓ Ⓔ 37 Ⓐ Ⓑ Ⓒ Ⓓ Ⓔ
8 Ⓐ Ⓑ Ⓒ Ⓓ Ⓔ 18 Ⓐ Ⓑ Ⓒ Ⓓ Ⓔ 28 Ⓐ Ⓑ Ⓒ Ⓓ Ⓔ 38 Ⓐ Ⓑ Ⓒ Ⓓ Ⓔ
9 Ⓐ Ⓑ Ⓒ Ⓓ Ⓔ 19 Ⓐ Ⓑ Ⓒ Ⓓ Ⓔ 29 Ⓐ Ⓑ Ⓒ Ⓓ Ⓔ 39 Ⓐ Ⓑ Ⓒ Ⓓ Ⓔ
10 Ⓐ Ⓑ Ⓒ Ⓓ Ⓔ 20 Ⓐ Ⓑ Ⓒ Ⓓ Ⓔ 30 Ⓐ Ⓑ Ⓒ Ⓓ Ⓔ 40 Ⓐ Ⓑ Ⓒ Ⓓ Ⓔ

SECTION 2

1 Ⓐ Ⓑ Ⓒ Ⓓ Ⓔ 11 Ⓐ Ⓑ Ⓒ Ⓓ Ⓔ 21 Ⓐ Ⓑ Ⓒ Ⓓ Ⓔ 31 Ⓐ Ⓑ Ⓒ Ⓓ Ⓔ
2 Ⓐ Ⓑ Ⓒ Ⓓ Ⓔ 12 Ⓐ Ⓑ Ⓒ Ⓓ Ⓔ 22 Ⓐ Ⓑ Ⓒ Ⓓ Ⓔ 32 Ⓐ Ⓑ Ⓒ Ⓓ Ⓔ
3 Ⓐ Ⓑ Ⓒ Ⓓ Ⓔ 13 Ⓐ Ⓑ Ⓒ Ⓓ Ⓔ 23 Ⓐ Ⓑ Ⓒ Ⓓ Ⓔ 33 Ⓐ Ⓑ Ⓒ Ⓓ Ⓔ
4 Ⓐ Ⓑ Ⓒ Ⓓ Ⓔ 14 Ⓐ Ⓑ Ⓒ Ⓓ Ⓔ 24 Ⓐ Ⓑ Ⓒ Ⓓ Ⓔ 34 Ⓐ Ⓑ Ⓒ Ⓓ Ⓔ
5 Ⓐ Ⓑ Ⓒ Ⓓ Ⓔ 15 Ⓐ Ⓑ Ⓒ Ⓓ Ⓔ 25 Ⓐ Ⓑ Ⓒ Ⓓ Ⓔ 35 Ⓐ Ⓑ Ⓒ Ⓓ Ⓔ
6 Ⓐ Ⓑ Ⓒ Ⓓ Ⓔ 16 Ⓐ Ⓑ Ⓒ Ⓓ Ⓔ 26 Ⓐ Ⓑ Ⓒ Ⓓ Ⓔ 36 Ⓐ Ⓑ Ⓒ Ⓓ Ⓔ
7 Ⓐ Ⓑ Ⓒ Ⓓ Ⓔ 17 Ⓐ Ⓑ Ⓒ Ⓓ Ⓔ 27 Ⓐ Ⓑ Ⓒ Ⓓ Ⓔ 37 Ⓐ Ⓑ Ⓒ Ⓓ Ⓔ
8 Ⓐ Ⓑ Ⓒ Ⓓ Ⓔ 18 Ⓐ Ⓑ Ⓒ Ⓓ Ⓔ 28 Ⓐ Ⓑ Ⓒ Ⓓ Ⓔ 38 Ⓐ Ⓑ Ⓒ Ⓓ Ⓔ
9 Ⓐ Ⓑ Ⓒ Ⓓ Ⓔ 19 Ⓐ Ⓑ Ⓒ Ⓓ Ⓔ 29 Ⓐ Ⓑ Ⓒ Ⓓ Ⓔ 39 Ⓐ Ⓑ Ⓒ Ⓓ Ⓔ
10 Ⓐ Ⓑ Ⓒ Ⓓ Ⓔ 20 Ⓐ Ⓑ Ⓒ Ⓓ Ⓔ 30 Ⓐ Ⓑ Ⓒ Ⓓ Ⓔ 40 Ⓐ Ⓑ Ⓒ Ⓓ Ⓔ

421

Use a No. 2 pencil only. Be sure each mark is dark and completely fills the intended oval. Completely erase any errors or stray marks.

Start with number 1 for each new section. If a section has fewer questions than answer spaces, leave the extra answer spaces blank.

SECTION 3

1 Ⓐ Ⓑ Ⓒ Ⓓ Ⓔ	16 Ⓐ Ⓑ Ⓒ Ⓓ Ⓔ	31 Ⓐ Ⓑ Ⓒ Ⓓ Ⓔ
2 Ⓐ Ⓑ Ⓒ Ⓓ Ⓔ	17 Ⓐ Ⓑ Ⓒ Ⓓ Ⓔ	32 Ⓐ Ⓑ Ⓒ Ⓓ Ⓔ
3 Ⓐ Ⓑ Ⓒ Ⓓ Ⓔ	18 Ⓐ Ⓑ Ⓒ Ⓓ Ⓔ	33 Ⓐ Ⓑ Ⓒ Ⓓ Ⓔ
4 Ⓐ Ⓑ Ⓒ Ⓓ Ⓔ	19 Ⓐ Ⓑ Ⓒ Ⓓ Ⓔ	34 Ⓐ Ⓑ Ⓒ Ⓓ Ⓔ
5 Ⓐ Ⓑ Ⓒ Ⓓ Ⓔ	20 Ⓐ Ⓑ Ⓒ Ⓓ Ⓔ	35 Ⓐ Ⓑ Ⓒ Ⓓ Ⓔ
6 Ⓐ Ⓑ Ⓒ Ⓓ Ⓔ	21 Ⓐ Ⓑ Ⓒ Ⓓ Ⓔ	36 Ⓐ Ⓑ Ⓒ Ⓓ Ⓔ
7 Ⓐ Ⓑ Ⓒ Ⓓ Ⓔ	22 Ⓐ Ⓑ Ⓒ Ⓓ Ⓔ	37 Ⓐ Ⓑ Ⓒ Ⓓ Ⓔ
8 Ⓐ Ⓑ Ⓒ Ⓓ Ⓔ	23 Ⓐ Ⓑ Ⓒ Ⓓ Ⓔ	38 Ⓐ Ⓑ Ⓒ Ⓓ Ⓔ
9 Ⓐ Ⓑ Ⓒ Ⓓ Ⓔ	24 Ⓐ Ⓑ Ⓒ Ⓓ Ⓔ	39 Ⓐ Ⓑ Ⓒ Ⓓ Ⓔ
10 Ⓐ Ⓑ Ⓒ Ⓓ Ⓔ	25 Ⓐ Ⓑ Ⓒ Ⓓ Ⓔ	40 Ⓐ Ⓑ Ⓒ Ⓓ Ⓔ
11 Ⓐ Ⓑ Ⓒ Ⓓ Ⓔ	26 Ⓐ Ⓑ Ⓒ Ⓓ Ⓔ	
12 Ⓐ Ⓑ Ⓒ Ⓓ Ⓔ	27 Ⓐ Ⓑ Ⓒ Ⓓ Ⓔ	
13 Ⓐ Ⓑ Ⓒ Ⓓ Ⓔ	28 Ⓐ Ⓑ Ⓒ Ⓓ Ⓔ	
14 Ⓐ Ⓑ Ⓒ Ⓓ Ⓔ	29 Ⓐ Ⓑ Ⓒ Ⓓ Ⓔ	
15 Ⓐ Ⓑ Ⓒ Ⓓ Ⓔ	30 Ⓐ Ⓑ Ⓒ Ⓓ Ⓔ	

If section 3 of your test book contains math questions that are not multiple-choice, continue to item 16 below. Otherwise, continue to item 16 above.

ONLY ANSWERS ENTERED IN THE OVALS IN EACH GRID AREA WILL BE SCORED.
YOU WILL NOT RECEIVE CREDIT FOR ANYTHING WRITTEN IN THE BOXES ABOVE THE OVALS.

16 17 18 19 20

21 22 23 24 25

(Each grid contains ⊘ . 0 1 2 3 4 5 6 7 8 9 ovals)

BE SURE TO ERASE ANY ERRORS OR STRAY MARKS COMPLETELY.

PLEASE PRINT
YOUR INITIALS

First Middle Last

Use a No. 2 pencil only. Be sure each mark is dark and completely fills the intended oval. Completely erase any errors or stray marks.

Start with number 1 for each new section. If a section has fewer questions than answer spaces, leave the extra answer spaces blank.

SECTION 4

1 (A) (B) (C) (D) (E)
2 (A) (B) (C) (D) (E)
3 (A) (B) (C) (D) (E)
4 (A) (B) (C) (D) (E)
5 (A) (B) (C) (D) (E)
6 (A) (B) (C) (D) (E)
7 (A) (B) (C) (D) (E)
8 (A) (B) (C) (D) (E)
9 (A) (B) (C) (D) (E)
10 (A) (B) (C) (D) (E)
11 (A) (B) (C) (D) (E)
12 (A) (B) (C) (D) (E)
13 (A) (B) (C) (D) (E)
14 (A) (B) (C) (D) (E)
15 (A) (B) (C) (D) (E)

16 (A) (B) (C) (D) (E)
17 (A) (B) (C) (D) (E)
18 (A) (B) (C) (D) (E)
19 (A) (B) (C) (D) (E)
20 (A) (B) (C) (D) (E)
21 (A) (B) (C) (D) (E)
22 (A) (B) (C) (D) (E)
23 (A) (B) (C) (D) (E)
24 (A) (B) (C) (D) (E)
25 (A) (B) (C) (D) (E)
26 (A) (B) (C) (D) (E)
27 (A) (B) (C) (D) (E)
28 (A) (B) (C) (D) (E)
29 (A) (B) (C) (D) (E)
30 (A) (B) (C) (D) (E)

31 (A) (B) (C) (D) (E)
32 (A) (B) (C) (D) (E)
33 (A) (B) (C) (D) (E)
34 (A) (B) (C) (D) (E)
35 (A) (B) (C) (D) (E)
36 (A) (B) (C) (D) (E)
37 (A) (B) (C) (D) (E)
38 (A) (B) (C) (D) (E)
39 (A) (B) (C) (D) (E)
40 (A) (B) (C) (D) (E)

If section 4 of your test book contains math questions that are not multiple-choice, continue to item 16 below. Otherwise, continue to item 16 above.

ONLY ANSWERS ENTERED IN THE OVALS IN EACH GRID AREA WILL BE SCORED.
YOU WILL NOT RECEIVE CREDIT FOR ANYTHING WRITTEN IN THE BOXES ABOVE THE OVALS.

16 17 18 19 20

21 22 23 24 25

BE SURE TO ERASE ANY ERRORS OR STRAY MARKS COMPLETELY.

PLEASE PRINT
YOUR INITIALS

First   Middle   Last

Start with number 1 for each new section. If a section has fewer questions than answer spaces, leave the extra answer spaces blank.

SECTION 5

SECTION 6

SECTION 7

CERTIFICATION STATEMENT

Copy in longhand the statement below and sign your name as you would an official document. **DO NOT PRINT.**

I hereby agree to the conditions set forth in the *Registration Bulletin* and certify that I am the person whose name and address appear on this answer sheet.

SIGNATURE: _____   DATE: _____

424

1 1 1 1 1 1 1

**Time—30 Minutes
25 Questions**

In this section solve each problem, using any available space on the page for scratchwork. Then decide which is the best of the choices given and fill in the corresponding oval on the answer sheet.

Notes:

1. The use of a calculator is permitted. All numbers used are real numbers.

2. Figures that accompany problems in this test are intended to provide information useful in solving the problems. They are drawn as accurately as possible EXCEPT when it is stated in a specific problem that the figure is not drawn to scale. All figures lie in a plane unless otherwise indicated.

Reference Information

$A = \pi r^2$
$C = 2\pi r$

$A = \ell w$

$A = \frac{1}{2}bh$

$V = \ell wh$

$V = \pi r^2 h$

$c^2 = a^2 + b^2$

Special Right Triangles

The number of degrees of arc in a circle is 360.
The measure in degrees of a straight angle is 180.
The sum of the measures in degrees of the angles of a triangle is 180.

---

1 When 19 is divided by an integer n, the remainder is 1. Which of the following could NOT be the value of n?

(A) 2
(B) 3
(C) 4
(D) 6
(E) 9

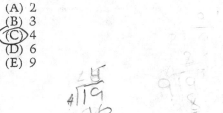

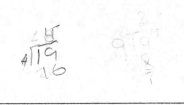

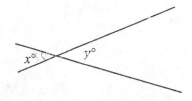

2 In the figure above, if $x = 38$, what is the value of y?

(A) 38
(B) 52
(C) 76
(D) 128
(E) 142

$w < t > x < y < z$

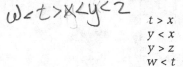

$t > x$
$y < x$
$y > z$
$w < t$

3 Which of the five quantities in the inequalities above is greatest?

(A) t
(B) w
(C) x
(D) y
(E) z

GO ON TO THE NEXT PAGE

4 When printing a book, a printing company charges $70,000 for setting up the presses plus $6 for each book printed. Which of the following gives the total charge C, in dollars, when n books are printed?

(A) $C = 70{,}000 + 6n$

(B) $C = 70{,}000 \times 6n$

(C) $C = 70{,}006 + n$

(D) $C = 70{,}006n$

(E) $C = \dfrac{70{,}000}{6}n$

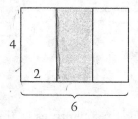

4

2

6

5 In the figure above, two squares with sides of length 4 overlap to form a 4-by-6 rectangle. What is the area of the shaded region?

(A) 4
(B) 8
(C) 12
(D) 14
(E) 16

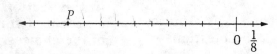

P

0 $\frac{1}{8}$

6 On the number line above, the marks are equally spaced. What is the coordinate of point P?

(A) $-\dfrac{3}{2}$

(B) $-\dfrac{11}{8}$

(C) $-\dfrac{5}{4}$

(D) -1

(E) $-\dfrac{1}{4}$

7 Which of the following would become the square of an integer if its digits were reversed?

(A) 21
(B) 31
(C) 41
(D) 51
(E) 61

GO ON TO THE NEXT PAGE

426

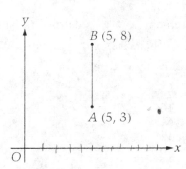

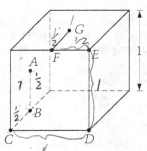

8 In the figure above, point C (not shown) is located to the right of segment AB so that segment AC is parallel to the x-axis. If the length of AC is 7, what are the coordinates of point C?

(A) (3, 10)
(B) (5, 10)
(C) (5, 15)
(D) (12, 3)
(E) (12, 8)

11 On the cube with edge of length 1 shown above, points A and G are the centers of the left and top faces, respectively. Points B and F are midpoints of the edges. What is the length of the path
$A \rightarrow B \rightarrow C \rightarrow D \rightarrow E \rightarrow F \rightarrow G$?

(A) $3\frac{1}{2}$

(B) $3\frac{3}{4}$

(C) 4

(D) $4\frac{1}{2}$

(E) $4\frac{3}{4}$

9 When 126.39 is rounded to the nearest hundred, which digit does not change?

(A) 1
(B) 2
(C) 6
(D) 3
(E) 9

12 If $(2^t)^t = 2^{16}$ and $t > 0$, what is the value of t?

(A) 1
(B) 2
(C) 4
(D) 8
(E) 16

10 There were n tropical fish in a pet-shop tank on a Saturday. By the following Saturday, exactly half the fish had been purchased. Similarly, by each of the next two consecutive Saturdays, half as many fish were left as on the previous Saturday. Which of the following could have been the value of n?

(A) 10
(B) 21
(C) 26
(D) 56
(E) 60

GO ON TO THE NEXT PAGE

13 Only three of the four points A, B, C, and D are on the same line. How many different lines containing only two of the points can be drawn?

(A) Two
(B) Three
(C) Four
(D) Five
(E) Six

15 The statement $x \Rightarrow y$ is defined to be true if $\frac{x}{3} > \frac{y}{2}$; otherwise, $x \Rightarrow y$ is false. Which of the following is true?

(A) $3 \Rightarrow 2$
(B) $9 \Rightarrow 10$
(C) $12 \Rightarrow 6$
(D) $15 \Rightarrow 12$
(E) $16 \Rightarrow 16$

GYMNASIUM USE DURING 1986

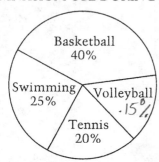

100% corresponds to 300 days

14 According to the graph above, if the gymnasium was used for no more than one sport on any given day, for how many of the 300 days was the gymnasium used for volleyball in 1986 ?

(A) 15 days
(B) 20 days
(C) 30 days
(D) 45 days
(E) 60 days

16 Joe can buy a pair of canvas shoes for $7 or a pair of leather shoes for $35. At these prices, what is the ratio of the cost of 6 pairs of canvas shoes to the cost of 3 pairs of leather shoes?

(A) 1 to 10
(B) 1 to 5
(C) 2 to 5
(D) 2 to 15
(E) 3 to 10

$$s = 5 + 5^2 + 5^3 + \ldots + 5^n$$

17 If s is formed by adding consecutive positive integer powers of 5 as shown above, for which of the following values of n will s be divisible by 10 ?

(A) 3
(B) 5
(C) 9
(D) 15
(E) 20

GO ON TO THE NEXT PAGE

18 If p and r are different prime numbers greater than 9, which of the following must be true?

    I. $\frac{p}{r}$ is less than 1.

    II. $p + r$ is not prime.

    III. $p \times r$ has three different positive integer factors greater than 1.

(A) None
(B) III only
(C) I and II
(D) I and III
(E) II and III

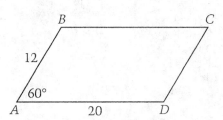

19 In parallelogram $ABCD$ above, if sides AB and AD have lengths as shown, what is the length of the altitude to side AD ?

(A)   10
(B) $6\sqrt{3}$ (approximately 10.39)
(C) 12
(D) $10\sqrt{2}$ (approximately 14.14)
(E) $12\sqrt{3}$ (approximately 20.78)

20 If $y = 3$ and $\frac{x}{y} = x - y$, what is the value of x ?

(A) $-\frac{9}{2}$

(B) $-\frac{3}{2}$

(C) 0

(D) $\frac{3}{2}$

(E) $\frac{9}{2}$

21 If $\dfrac{\sqrt{5}}{m} = \dfrac{m}{\sqrt{20}}$, which of the following could be a value of m ?

(A) $\sqrt{10}$
(B)   5
(C) $2\sqrt{10}$
(D)   10
(E)   100

GO ON TO THE NEXT PAGE

22 A certain 90-mile trip took 2 hours. Exactly $\frac{1}{3}$ of the distance traveled was by rail, and this part of the trip took $\frac{1}{5}$ of the travel time. What was the average rate, in miles per hour, of the rail portion of the trip?

(A) 12 mph
(B) 30 mph
(C) 45 mph
(D) 60 mph
(E) 75 mph

30 ml in 24 min

23 For all positive integers x, let be defined as the sum of the integers from 1 to x, inclusive. Which of the following equals ⑥ – ⑤ ?

(A) ①
(B) ②
(C) ③
(D) ⑤
(E) ⑥

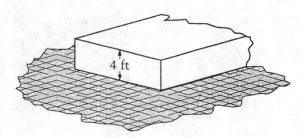

24 Sanchez' Warehouse wants to install a 3-foot-wide ramp from the level floor to the top of the 4-foot-high platform shown above. A regulation states that for every 2 feet that such a ramp rises vertically, the bottom of the ramp must be placed 5 feet farther from the bottom of the platform. If the material for the top surface of the ramp comes in 3-foot widths and whole-foot lengths, what is the minimum length of this material that must be purchased?

(A) 5 ft
(B) 8 ft
(C) 10 ft
(D) 11 ft
(E) 20 ft

25 Which of the following equations have (has) only one integer solution?

I. $x + 9x = 0$
II. $x^2 + 9x = 0$
III. $x^3 + 9x = 0$

(A) I only
(B) II only
(C) III only
(D) I and III only
(E) I, II, and III

IF YOU FINISH BEFORE TIME IS CALLED, YOU MAY CHECK YOUR WORK ON THIS SECTION ONLY. DO NOT TURN TO ANY OTHER SECTION IN THE TEST. **STOP**

Section 2

2   2   2   2   2

Time—30 Minutes
30 Questions

For each question in this section, select the best answer from among the choices given and fill in the corresponding oval on the answer sheet.

Each sentence below has one or two blanks, each blank indicating that something has been omitted. Beneath the sentence are five words or sets of words labeled A through E. Choose the word or set of words that, when inserted in the sentence, best fits the meaning of the sentence as a whole.

Example:

Medieval kingdoms did not become constitutional republics overnight; on the contrary, the change was ----.

(A) unpopular
(B) unexpected
(C) advantageous
(D) sufficient
(E) gradual

(A) (B) (C) (D) ●

1   As ---- as she is ----, Lourdes Lopez has combined hard work with natural talent to succeed as a ballerina.

(A) diligent. .gifted
(B) conciliatory. .effusive
(C) stringent. .demanding
(D) accomplished. .dilatory
(E) restrained. .conditioned

2   When an already ---- machine is modified to correct existing problems, there is always a chance that the modifications will ---- more problems than they solve.

(A) perfected. .promote
(B) imposing. .curtail
(C) complex. .create
(D) intricate. .eliminate
(E) flawed. .alleviate

3   Although some political analysts do predict legislative events with ---- degree of accuracy, most analysts are ---- only 50 percent of the time, a figure that could be produced by guessing alone.

(A) a studied. .logical
(B) a slight. .unfavorable
(C) an exacting. .unknown
(D) an impressive. .correct
(E) an incalculable. .right

4   In this production the king is portrayed as an initially ---- leader utterly transformed by his overwhelming thirst for power into a ---- tyrant.

(A) benevolent. .vicious
(B) heartless. .devious
(C) devoted. .reluctant
(D) prominent. .secluded
(E) notorious. .masterful

5   No one was hurt in the ----, but the fire marshals are busy searching for evidence of arson.

(A) inundation   (B) conflagration
(C) provocation   (D) confrontation
(E) substitution

6   Many experts agree that global warming is a crisis born of one ---- reality: modern societies ---- and indeed are sustained by combustible fossil fuels.

(A) indisputable. .expunge
(B) trivial. .foster
(C) irrefutable. .require
(D) discreditable. .invoke
(E) ineffable. .devastate

7   This new study of Sojourner Truth focuses primarily on her ----, on her speeches rather than her actions.

(A) reform   (B) militancy   (C) strategy
(D) principle   (E) rhetoric

8   She was a woman of contrasts: periods of ---- alternated with periods of frenetic activity.

(A) animation   (B) torpor   (C) invincibility
(D) profundity   (E) ebullience

9   Though difficult, it is ---- to study shearwaters in their land-based breeding colonies; studying these birds at sea, however, poses an almost ---- problem.

(A) enterprising. .inventive
(B) helpful. .salutary
(C) necessary. .facile
(D) feasible. .insuperable
(E) possible. .implausible

GO ON TO THE NEXT PAGE

431

Each question below consists of a related pair of words or phrases, followed by five pairs of words or phrases labeled A through E. Select the pair that best expresses a relationship similar to that expressed in the original pair.

Example:

CRUMB : BREAD ::
(A) ounce : unit
(B) splinter : wood
(C) water : bucket
(D) twine : rope
(E) cream : butter

Ⓐ ● Ⓒ Ⓓ Ⓔ

10 FLY : AIR ::
(A) ignite : fire
(B) run : race
(C) travel : road
(D) plant : earth
(E) swim : water

11 PIN : CLOTH ::
(A) bell : door
(B) needle : syringe
(C) ladle : pot
(D) nail : wood
(E) chisel : stone

12 CLIP : FILM ::
(A) photograph : negative
(B) sequel : program
(C) excerpt : book
(D) fabric : garment
(E) marble : sculpture

13 PHARMACY : MEDICINE ::
(A) school : student
(B) confectionery : candy
(C) orchard : farm
(D) oven : bread
(E) field : grain

14 ABSOLVE : OBLIGATION ::
(A) confer : privilege
(B) confess : penitence
(C) offend : propriety
(D) exempt : rule
(E) regulate : statute

15 ELUCIDATE : CLARIFICATION ::
(A) substantiate : evidence
(B) postulate : verification
(C) propitiate : wrath
(D) reveal : obscurity
(E) overwhelm : quantity

GO ON TO THE NEXT PAGE →

Each passage below is followed by questions based on its content. Answer the questions on the basis of what is stated or implied in each passage and in any introductory material that may be provided.

Questions 16-21 are based on the following passage. Opinion

The passage below reflects one author's controversial opinion about the one-term presidency of John Quincy Adams.

The education of John Quincy Adams (1767-1848) was the most superb of any of the United States Presidents, and consequently absolutely
Line crippling. He was too brilliant; he knew too many
(5) languages, books, nations, and political and philosophical systems (having spent many years abroad as United States minister to several European nations) to be able to preside with any grace or tolerance over the dingy republic of his day.
(10) James Monroe, who was President from 1817 to 1825, had appointed Adams as his secretary of state, at that time the country's second most important office and the surest way to the presidency. Although Adams was generally admired—
(15) certainly he was our best secretary of state—he was not much liked. He was often bored by the politicians he had to deal with. And he himself liked neither political party: "Between both, I see the impossibility of pursuing the dictates of my
(20) own conscience."
During this period General Andrew Jackson, who had become a national hero at the Battle of New Orleans in 1815, was on the rampage in Spanish Florida. Jackson had interpreted the
(25) government's orders to punish some Seminole tribes as a license for invasion of foreign territory,
— conquest, and military executions. These capers appealed hugely to the electorate and, in the presidential election of 1824, Jackson received 99 elec-
(30) toral college* votes; Adams received 84; William H. Crawford, 41; Speaker of the House Henry Clay, 37. Since no candidate had the required majority, the election went to the House of Representatives for decision. Unable to win himself, Clay gave his
(35) support to Adams, who became President in February 1825. Adams then appointed Clay as secretary of state.
Jackson and his allies were rightly indignant at losing an election in which Jackson had, after all,
(40) received the most votes; they regarded as corrupt the alliance between Adams and Clay.
Adams' administration proved to be a disaster. He was hopeless when it came to the greasy art of survival in United States politics. He had great
(45) plans to foster education, science, commerce, and

civil service reform; but his projects were too rigorous and too unpolitical to be accepted. For instance, the United States had not one astronomical station, while in Europe there were 130
(50) "lighthouses of the sky." This happy phrase of
— Adams was received with perfect derision by the mob. It was plain that Adams was not suited to lead a democracy. He was too intelligent, too unyielding, too tactless. Needless to say, Jackson
(55) swamped him in the 1828 election. The Jackson slogan was prophetic of the era: "Jackson who can fight, and Adams who can write."
But Adams saw things more clearly than did most of the mob-pleasing politicians. In 1837, after
(60) President Jackson's brutal treatment of the Creeks and Cherokees, Adams wrote: "We have done more harm to the Indians since our Revolution than had been done to them by the French and English. . . . These are crying sins for which we are answerable before a higher Jurisdiction."

*The electoral college is an institution created by the Constitution which allocates the population's votes to representatives—a certain number per state—who then officially elect the President.

16 The author most likely believes that Adams would have been a more popular President if he had

(A) deferred to Clay's judgement
(B) been more openly loyal to his party
(C) been better informed about the living conditions of ordinary Americans
(D) implemented projects to aid Native Americans
(E) sacrificed his integrity to political expediency

17 The author uses "capers" (line 27) to refer to

(A) unsuccessful escapades
(B) immoral military acts
(C) government orders
(D) legislative compromises
(E) voter reactions

GO ON TO THE NEXT PAGE

18 It can be inferred from the passage that Adams agreed to appoint Clay to the post of secretary of state in order to

(A) avoid having to appoint Jackson to the post
(B) satisfy the indignant electorate
(C) repay Clay for helping him obtain the necessary House votes
(D) win back the favor of his party after a divisive campaign
(E) counteract his reputation for inaction by making a decisive move

19 Which of the following best expresses the author's opinion of the voters during the time of the Adams presidency?

(A) They were easily misled by high-sounding speeches.
(B) They were easily fooled by corrupt politicians.
(C) They were shrewd in judgment despite a lack of sophistication.
(D) They were enthusiastic about new technologies and innovative ideas.
(E) They were easily impressed by military success.

20 The word "perfect" (line 51) most nearly means

(A) excellent
(B) complete
(C) blameless
(D) mature
(E) pristine

21 The quotation of Jackson's 1828 campaign slogan (lines 56-57) serves mainly to

(A) illustrate how well Jackson suited the national mood
(B) foreshadow the vital role of the military later in the century
(C) ridicule the conventional wisdom that the pen is mightier than the sword
(D) show how an effective slogan can win an election
(E) reveal the expressiveness of Jackson's simple writing style

GO ON TO THE NEXT PAGE

Questions 22-30 are based on the following passage.

I returned, and saw under the sun that the race is not to the swift nor the battle to the strong, neither yet bread to the wise, nor yet riches to
Line *men of understanding, nor yet favor to men of*
(5) *skill; but time and chance happeneth to them all.*
— *Ecclesiastes 9 : 11*

Widely condemned as a false or pseudo sport, televised professional wrestling constantly challenges the ideal of free and open competition. In a sport without statistics, the win-loss percentage of
(10) a wrestling star is not relevant knowledge. In wrestling, it's how one plays the game that truly counts: a hero in defeat is still heroic; a villain triumphant is still to be despised. And in this privileging of character at the expense of authenticity,
(15) professional wrestling lampoons naïve ideals associated with the winner-take-all justice of the competition ethic. Professional wrestling champions a much richer brand of justice—a justice derived from character, not conquest.
(20) People don't bet on the outcome of professional wrestling matches, obviously, because wrestling requires the suspension of disbelief of a moviegoer, not a gambler. However, in the United States, the wrestling fan is typically ridiculed as a gullible and
(25) stupid creature, while the gambler is frequently honored as daring and clever. Assuming that some wrestling fans actually believe matches are authentic (and there is reason to believe most do not), one wonders who is the more deceived: the
(30) wrestling fan who believes in the spectacle of good versus evil, or the gambler who trusts the arbitrary amoral order of legitimate spectator sports.
A subversive sport form, professional wrestling completely calls into question assumptions about
(35) rules and rule enforcement attached to the ideal of competition. In professional wrestling, the rules are obviously and painfully arbitrary and unevenly enforced; they generally work in favor of the villain and against the hero. The referee, though
(40) usually sincere and well intentioned, is frequently distracted and often blind to villainous violations the partisan crowd can easily spot. Typically, the hero respects the rules until it becomes obvious to all that obedience will ultimately result in defeat;
(45) then, in a wonderful eruption of chaos, the hero takes the law into his own hands—and, sometimes, justice emerges from the fray. In professional wrestling, justice isn't handed down from above. Instead, justice results from individual
(50) action and an eventual disregard of arbitrary rules

impeding vindication. In wrestling as in life, law and order do not equal justice and equality.
Although now located on television's fringes, professional wrestling was a prime-time spectacle
(55) during the 1950's. In those early years of broadcast television, a wrestler named Gorgeous George became a pivotal figure in television's world of sports. George's performance emphasized character more than athletic excellence. His success did not
(60) go unnoticed by performers in more legitimate sports. Indeed, George provided inspiration to one of the greatest sports stars of modern times— professional heavyweight-boxing champion Muhammad Ali.
(65) According to Ali, a performance by Gorgeous George was an epiphanic experience for him—one that illuminated the subtle dynamics of hype:

Gorgeous George came into the television studio. He made his entrance combing his
(70) long blond hair like a movie idol. "Look at my velvet skin," he purred. "Look at my pretty hair. If that bum messes up my hair tomorrow night, I'll annihilate him! I want all of you out there to come to the
(75) Sports Palace early because I'm gonna mop the floor with this bum. If he beats me, I'll cut off my golden hair and throw the hair out in the audience and go bald." The next night instead of resting for my fight,
(80) I was at the Sports Palace along with a standing-room-only crowd, wanting to see what would happen to George. I saw how this strategy had worked.

By observing George, Ali arrived at a key
(85) element of television stardom: personality, character, and flamboyance are as interesting to audiences and as crucial to media stardom as competitive superiority.

22 The author uses the quotation at the beginning of the passage to emphasize which of the following?

(A) Religious insights are an important means of arriving at the truth.
(B) Skill and ability are not always rewarded.
(C) Time is on the side of those who wait patiently for change.
(D) Trickery and guile are important to achieving success.
(E) The values represented by so-called heroes need to be examined carefully.

GO ON TO THE NEXT PAGE

23 In lines 17-18, the word "champions" most nearly means

(A) triumphs (B) overpowers (C) rescues
(D) engages (E) espouses

24 The author considers professional wrestling a "subversive sport" (line 33) because

(A) it is extremely popular, even though many critics question its validity
(B) it seems to question the underlying assumptions of most sports
(C) it offers an escape from the dreary world of day-to-day living
(D) the villain occasionally prospers, even though the fans are cheering for the hero
(E) the athletic skills of professional wrestlers are actually much greater than most people realize

25 The hero's initial respect for the rules and subsequent disregard of them (referred to in lines 42-47) most nearly suggests that

(A) the rules have no emotional, psychological, or practical relevance
(B) by breaking the rules all contestants can make certain that justice will be done
(C) the rules apply only to the villain, whereas the hero is free to disregard them
(D) rules should be enforced so the spectator can enjoy an orderly match
(E) obeying the rules does not guarantee that justice will be done

26 At the end of the third paragraph of the passage, the comparison between professional wrestling and life states that

(A) wrestling is often more realistic than life
(B) wrestling is amusing, whereas life is a serious matter
(C) life is not always fair
(D) the so-called rules prevent the individual from acting
(E) the so-called rules aid only the powerful

27 According to the author, professional wrestling most nearly resembles

(A) professional boxing (B) college football
(C) military service (D) theater
(E) gambling

28 In line 83, "this strategy" refers to

(A) the techniques Gorgeous George used to defeat his opponent
(B) the way in which Gorgeous George used his television appearance to draw a crowd to his match
(C) Gorgeous George's personal invitation to Muhammad Ali to attend the match at the Sports Palace
(D) Gorgeous George's frank admission that he might lose the match at the Sports Palace
(E) Gorgeous George's delight in portraying himself as a monstrous villain

29 The author uses the example of Gorgeous George primarily to

(A) add humor to the piece
(B) mock old-style professional wrestling matches
(C) contrast his career with Muhammad Ali's career
(D) emphasize the significance of showmanship
(E) suggest that the hero and villain are sometimes indistinguishable in professional wrestling

30 What did Muhammad Ali learn from Gorgeous George?

(A) The ability to dominate one's opponents is important.
(B) It is not necessary to rest before an important match.
(C) Outrageous behavior attracts the attention of fans and the media.
(D) Personal vanity can tarnish one's public image.
(E) Only demonstrations of athletic ability can rouse an audience.

Time—30 Minutes
25 Questions

This section contains two types of questions. You have 30 minutes to complete both types. You may use any available space for scratchwork.

Notes:

1. The use of a calculator is permitted. All numbers used are real numbers.

2. Figures that accompany problems in this test are intended to provide information useful in solving the problems. They are drawn as accurately as possible EXCEPT when it is stated in a specific problem that the figure is not drawn to scale. All figures lie in a plane unless otherwise indicated.

Reference Information

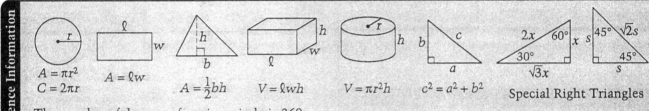

$A = \pi r^2$
$C = 2\pi r$

$A = \ell w$

$A = \frac{1}{2}bh$

$V = \ell wh$

$V = \pi r^2 h$

$c^2 = a^2 + b^2$

Special Right Triangles

The number of degrees of arc in a circle is 360.
The measure in degrees of a straight angle is 180.
The sum of the measures in degrees of the angles of a triangle is 180.

Directions for Quantitative Comparison Questions

Questions 1-15 each consist of two quantities in boxes, one in Column A and one in Column B. You are to compare the two quantities and on the answer sheet fill in oval

   A if the quantity in Column A is greater;
   B if the quantity in Column B is greater;
   C if the two quantities are equal;
   D if the relationship cannot be determined from the information given.

AN E RESPONSE WILL NOT BE SCORED.

Notes:

1. In some questions, information is given about one or both of the quantities to be compared. In such cases, the given information is centered above the two columns and is not boxed.
2. In a given question, a symbol that appears in both columns represents the same thing in Column A as it does in Column B.
3. Letters such as x, n, and k stand for real numbers.

EXAMPLES

Column A	Column B	Answers
E1 5^2	20	● Ⓑ Ⓒ Ⓓ Ⓔ

150° $x°$

Column A	Column B	Answers
E2 x	30	Ⓐ Ⓑ ● Ⓓ Ⓔ

r and s are integers.

Column A	Column B	Answers
E3 $r + 1$	$s - 1$	Ⓐ Ⓑ Ⓒ ● Ⓔ

GO ON TO THE NEXT PAGE →

SUMMARY DIRECTIONS FOR COMPARISON QUESTIONS

<u>Answer:</u> A if the quantity in Column A is greater;
B if the quantity in Column B is greater;
C if the two quantities are equal;
D if the relationship cannot be determined from the information given.

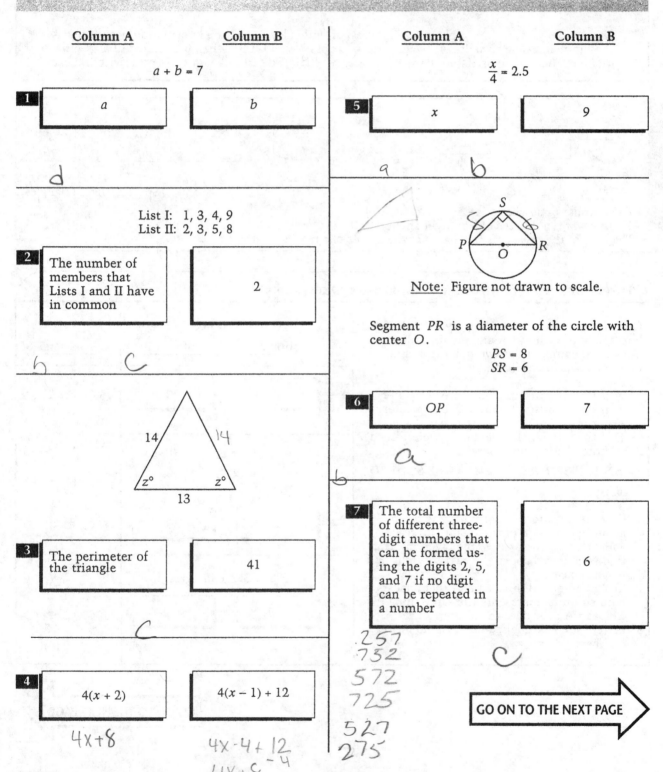

Column A	Column B

$a + b = 7$

1 | a | b

d

List I: 1, 3, 4, 9
List II: 2, 3, 5, 8

2 | The number of members that Lists I and II have in common | 2

b   C

14 14
$z°$ $z°$
13

3 | The perimeter of the triangle | 41

C

4 | $4(x + 2)$ | $4(x - 1) + 12$

4x+8   4x-4+12
4x+8
C

Column A	Column B

$\frac{x}{4} = 2.5$

5 | x | 9

a   b

Note: Figure not drawn to scale.

Segment PR is a diameter of the circle with center O.

$PS = 8$
$SR = 6$

6 | OP | 7

a
b

7 | The total number of different three-digit numbers that can be formed using the digits 2, 5, and 7 if no digit can be repeated in a number | 6

257
732
572
725
527
275

C

GO ON TO THE NEXT PAGE →

438

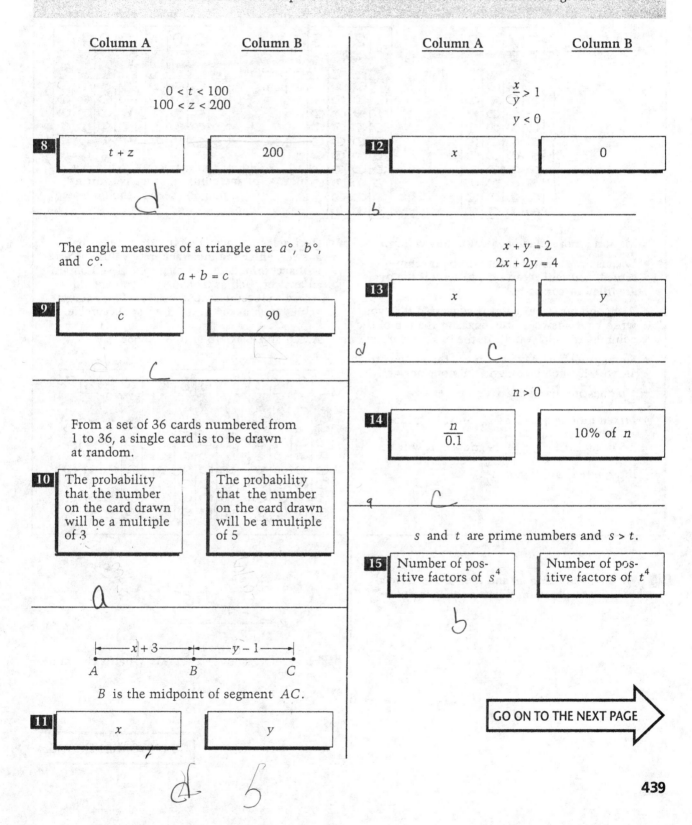

SUMMARY DIRECTIONS FOR COMPARISON QUESTIONS

Answer: A if the quantity in Column A is greater;
B if the quantity in Column B is greater;
C if the two quantities are equal;
D if the relationship cannot be determined from the information given.

Column A	Column B

$0 < t < 100$
$100 < z < 200$

8 $t + z$ | 200

d

The angle measures of a triangle are $a°$, $b°$, and $c°$.

$a + b = c$

9 c | 90

c

From a set of 36 cards numbered from 1 to 36, a single card is to be drawn at random.

10 The probability that the number on the card drawn will be a multiple of 3 | The probability that the number on the card drawn will be a multiple of 5

a

$\vdash\!\!-x + 3-\!\!\dashv\!\!-y - 1-\!\!\dashv$
$A \qquad\quad B \qquad\quad C$

B is the midpoint of segment AC.

11 x | y

Column A	Column B

$\dfrac{x}{y} > 1$
$y < 0$

12 x | 0

b

$x + y = 2$
$2x + 2y = 4$

13 x | y

d   *c*

$n > 0$

14 $\dfrac{n}{0.1}$ | 10% of n

c

s and t are prime numbers and $s > t$.

15 Number of positive factors of s^4 | Number of positive factors of t^4

b

GO ON TO THE NEXT PAGE →

Directions for Student-Produced Response Questions

Each of the remaining 10 questions requires you to solve the problem and enter your answer by marking the ovals in the special grid, as shown in the examples below.

Answer: $\frac{7}{12}$ or 7/12

Answer: 2.5

Answer: 201
Either position is correct.

Write answer → in boxes.

← Fraction line

← Decimal point

Grid in → result.

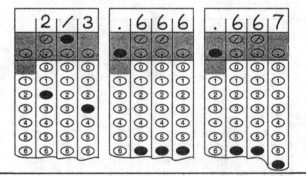

Note: You may start your answers in any column, space permitting. Columns not needed should be left blank.

- Mark no more than one oval in any column.

- Because the answer sheet will be machine-scored, **you will receive credit only if the ovals are filled in correctly.**

- Although not required, it is suggested that you write your answer in the boxes at the top of the columns to help you fill in the ovals accurately.

- Some problems may have more than one correct answer. In such cases, grid only one answer.

- No question has a negative answer.

- **Mixed numbers** such as $2\frac{1}{2}$ must be gridded as 2.5 or 5/2. (If ⬚2⬚1⬚/⬚2 is gridded, it will be interpreted as $\frac{21}{2}$, not $2\frac{1}{2}$.)

- **Decimal Accuracy:** If you obtain a decimal answer, **enter the most accurate value the grid will accommodate.** For example, if you obtain an answer such as 0.6666 . . . , you should record the result as .666 or .667. **Less accurate values such as .66 or .67 are not acceptable.**

Acceptable ways to grid $\frac{2}{3}$ = .6666 . . .

16 When 8 is added to n and the sum is divided by 2, the result is 16. What is the value of n?

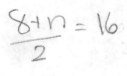

$$\frac{8+n}{2} = 16$$

24

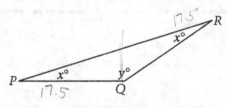

17 In $\triangle PQR$ above, $x = 17.5$. What is the value of y?

$145°$

GO ON TO THE NEXT PAGE →

440

18 If $10x = 1$ and $20y = 1$, what is the value of $x + y$?

.15

$\frac{3}{20}$

19 A shipping container holds 15 blocks of cheese. If each block of cheese weighs $1\frac{1}{4}$ pounds, how many containers are needed to package an order of 600 pounds of cheese?

1.25 lbs

15×18.75 lbs

1 con = 15 blk

18.75 lbs   1.25 lbs

$\frac{1\,con}{18.75} = \frac{32}{600\,lbs}$

32 containers

20 The average (arithmetic mean) of 6 integers is exactly 6. If a seventh integer is added to the 6 integers, the average of the 7 integers is exactly 13. What is the seventh integer?

55

21 Let $\lozenge$ be defined for all nonzero numbers a and b by $a \lozenge b = \frac{10a}{b}$. If $x \lozenge 7 = 200$, what is the value of x?

140

GO ON TO THE NEXT PAGE

22 The sum of three positive integers is 30. If one of the integers is 7, what is the greatest possible value of the product of the other two integers?

~~7~~   132

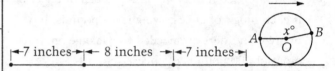

1/3   1/2   2/3   3/1

A   B C D E   F
0   x   1   3

4/9

23 On the number line above, points B and E divide segment AF into three equal segments and points C and D divide segment BE into three equal segments. If x is the number that corresponds to point C, what is the value of x ?

.444

.6

24 What is the least positive integer k for which $120 \times k$ is the square of an integer?

|←7 inches→|←   8 inches   →|←7 inches→|

25 In the figure above, a wheel with center O rolls, without slipping, in a straight line across a level floor. Two spots of wet paint at points A and B on the rim of the wheel leave marks on the floor, as indicated by the dots on the floor. What is the value of x ?

IF YOU FINISH BEFORE TIME IS CALLED, YOU MAY CHECK YOUR WORK ON THIS SECTION ONLY. DO NOT TURN TO ANY OTHER SECTION IN THE TEST. **STOP**

442

Section 5

5

For each question in this section, select the best answer from among the choices given and fill in the corresponding oval on the answer sheet.

Each sentence below has one or two blanks, each blank indicating that something has been omitted. Beneath the sentence are five words or sets of words labeled A through E. Choose the word or set of words that, when inserted in the sentence, best fits the meaning of the sentence as a whole.

Example:

Medieval kingdoms did not become constitutional republics overnight; on the contrary, the change was ----.

(A) unpopular
(B) unexpected
(C) advantageous
(D) sufficient
(E) gradual

Ⓐ Ⓑ Ⓒ Ⓓ ●

1 Compared with the excitement of London, the ---- that prevails in this sleepy English village is quite remarkable.

(A) ingenuity   (B) impermanence
(C) ambivalence   (D) tranquillity
(E) aestheticism

2 At that time theories concerning the type of life that might exist on other planets were still ---- because they rested on crude and ---- information about planetary atmospheres.

(A) inaccurate..substantial
(B) nebulous..specific
(C) authoritative..factual
(D) speculative..incomplete
(E) misleading..definitive

3 To ---- Mexico's rich cultural legacy in the United States, scholars from both countries collaborated to ---- the impressive exhibit of Mexican artifacts.

(A) celebrate..circumvent
(B) validate..mediate
(C) commemorate..launch
(D) hoard..differentiate
(E) disperse..disrupt

4 The author's habit of indulging in obvious generalizations ---- his credibility as an expert on the details of job management.

(A) relates   (B) enhances   (C) dictates
(D) undermines   (E) cancels

5 Lately there has been a ---- of interest in Patel's writing, and it has become difficult to buy her books even in specialized secondhand bookstores.

(A) retention   (B) concealment
(C) moderation   (D) suppression
(E) resurgence

6 Contrary to what may be expected, most people are not generally ---- being asked for help but tend to welcome the chance to assist others.

(A) exasperated by
(B) condemned for
(C) agreeable to
(D) experienced in
(E) naïve about

7 They sought to oust their party chair because her proposal seemed ----; it contradicted their fundamental economic policies.

(A) garrulous   (B) remedial   (C) formulaic
(D) heretical   (E) cursory

8 Those Renaissance scholars who reproduced almost verbatim the accounts written a century earlier were essentially ----, not genuine authorities on the events they recorded.

(A) historians   (B) translators
(C) researchers   (D) participants
(E) transcribers

9 Shy and timid by nature, Martin became even more ---- when in the presence of his supervisor.

(A) boisterous   (B) retiring   (C) oblivious
(D) perturbed   (E) gallant

10 Because Alexander the Great was an omnipotent ruler, his death was a ----, marking the end of the old order and the beginning of chaos.

(A) tribute   (B) watershed   (C) verdict
(D) reparation   (E) connotation

GO ON TO THE NEXT PAGE

Each question below consists of a related pair of words or phrases, followed by five pairs of words or phrases labeled A through E. Select the pair that best expresses a relationship similar to that expressed in the original pair.

Example:

CRUMB : BREAD ::
(A) ounce : unit
(B) splinter : wood
(C) water : bucket
(D) twine : rope
(E) cream : butter

Ⓐ ● Ⓒ Ⓓ Ⓔ

11 DETECTIVE : CLUES ::
(A) student : school
(B) deer : trail
(C) bloodhound : scent
(D) merchant : receipt
(E) sleuth : mystery

12 RESOLE : SHOE ::
(A) refine : chemicals
(B) rescue : emergency
(C) repair : damage
(D) rerun : television
(E) restring : guitar

13 GLOSSARY : DEFINITION ::
(A) authorship : manuscript
(B) handbook : instruction
(C) copyright : publication
(D) dilemma : resolution
(E) headline : newspaper

14 LOGO : COMPANY ::
(A) seed : fruit
(B) money : bank
(C) flag : country
(D) cloud : rain
(E) cover : book

15 CONCERN : ANXIETY ::
(A) fear : panic
(B) delay : hurry
(C) apology : regret
(D) observation : secrecy
(E) safety : terror

16 LAW : REPEAL ::
(A) apartment : renovate
(B) license : revoke
(C) conviction : arrest
(D) amendment : propose
(E) motion : veto

17 MURMUR : VOICES ::
(A) outline : shadows
(B) echo : sound
(C) rustle : leaves
(D) uproar : silence
(E) blink : eye

18 EBB : TIDE ::
(A) receive : radio
(B) splash : wave
(C) blossom : flower
(D) wane : moon
(E) hibernate : bear

19 FLAGRANT : DISCRETION ::
(A) emphatic : delivery
(B) furtive : discovery
(C) renowned : celebrity
(D) depraved : purity
(E) vengeful : retribution

20 NOMAD : ITINERANT ::
(A) judge : influenced
(B) performer : public
(C) prude : shocked
(D) soldier : brave
(E) sage : wise

21 CENSURE : REPREHENSIBLE ::
(A) prize : valuable
(B) provide : supportive
(C) applaud : enthusiastic
(D) inquire : informed
(E) continue : initial

22 DECEPTIVE : RUSE ::
(A) grasping : greed
(B) intense : passion
(C) imperious : command
(D) cynical : belief
(E) crass : blunder

23 VACUOUS : INSIGHT ::
(A) reticent : stillness
(B) merciful : forgiveness
(C) gullible : shrewdness
(D) capricious : impulse
(E) brusque : offense

GO ON TO THE NEXT PAGE

The two passages below are followed by questions based on their content and on the relationship between the two passages. Answer the questions on the basis of what is <u>stated</u> or <u>implied</u> in the passages and in any introductory material that may be provided.

Questions 24-35 are based on the following passages.

Both of the following excerpts discuss significant influences during the authors' formative years. The author of Passage 1 is a White historian from Australia, and the author of Passage 2 is an African American novelist.

Passage 1

The curriculum in our all-girls' high school was inherited from Great Britain, and consequently it was utterly untouched by progressive notions in
Line education. We read British poetry, novels, and
(5) short stories. We might have been in the English countryside for all the attention we paid to Australian literature. It did not count. We, for our part, dutifully learned Shakespeare's imagery drawn from the English landscape. We memorized
(10) Keats's "Ode to Autumn" or Shelley's "To a Skylark" without ever having seen the progression of seasons and the natural world they referred to. This gave us the impression that great poetry and fiction were written by and about people and
(15) places far distant from Australia. As for landscape, we learned by implication that ours was ugly, because it deviated totally from the landscape of Britain.

Much about our way of life symbolized the
(20) colonial mentality. Its signs were visible in the maps on our classroom walls, extended depictions of the globe with much of Africa, all of the Indian subcontinent, parts of Southeast Asia, and half of North America colored the bright red of the
(25) British Empire. Our uniforms, copies of those of English schools, indicated that we were only partially at home in our environment. We wore tunics, blouses, flannel blazers, cotton stockings, hats, and gloves. No one paused to think that
(30) gloves and blazers had a function in damp English springs that they lacked entirely in our blazing summers.

This kind of education can have interesting effects, even years later, on a student's perception
(35) of reality. At college, when I read Engels' *The Origin of the Family, Private Property and the State*, I treated its discussion of women's roles in modern society as though it were about some distant and different species rather than my own
(40) sex. I had unthinkingly taken on the identity of the male writer and intellect present in everything that I read and did not take in emotionally that the subordination Engels wrote about applied to me.

Passage 2

As a child, I didn't know that African American
(45) people wrote books. I did not read for pleasure. When I was sixteen I got a job shelving books for the public library. One day when I went to put a book away, I saw James Baldwin's[1] face staring up at me. "Who in the world is this?" I wondered. I
(50) remember feeling embarrassed and did not read Baldwin's book because I was too afraid. I couldn't imagine that he'd have anything better or different to say than Henry Thoreau, Ernest Hemingway, William Faulkner, and a horde of other mostly
(55) White male writers that I had been introduced to in Literature 101 in high school. Not only had there not been any African American authors included in any of those textbooks, but I'd never been given a clue that if we did have anything
(60) important to say, somebody would actually publish it. Needless to say, I was not just naïve, but had not yet acquired an ounce of Black pride.

And then things changed.

It wasn't until after Malcolm X[2] had been assas-
(65) sinated that I found out who he was. I know I should be embarrassed, but I'm not. I read his autobiography and it literally changed my life. First and foremost, I realized that it was ridiculous to be ashamed of being Black, that we had a
(70) history and much to be proud of. I began to appreciate our strength as a people. I started thinking about my role in the world and not just on my street. I started *thinking*—thinking about things I'd never thought about before—and the thinking
(75) turned into questions. But I had more questions than answers.

So I went to college. When I looked through the catalog and saw a class called Afro-American Liter-ature, I signed up and couldn't wait for the first
(80) day of class. Did we really have enough writers to warrant an entire class? I couldn't believe the rush I felt once I discovered Langston Hughes, Zora Neale Hurston, Ralph Ellison, Jean Toomer, Richard Wright, and Ann Petry. I'm surprised that
(85) I didn't need glasses by the end of the semester. My world opened up. I accumulated and gained a

GO ON TO THE NEXT PAGE →

totally new insight about, and perception of, our
lives as Black people, as if I had been an outsider
and was finally let in. To discover that our lives
(90) held as much significance and importance as those
of our White counterparts was more than gratify-
ing, it was exhilarating. Not only had we lived
diverse, interesting, provocative, and relentless
lives, but during, through, and as a result of all
(95) these painful experiences, some folks had taken
the time to write it down.

[1] James Baldwin (1924-1987) was a prominent African American
writer.
[2] Malcom X (1925-1965) was a prominent Black Muslim leader.

24 In Passage 1, what is the author's main point
about the attention given to the English landscape in her high school?

(A) It concentrated too much on a literary
rather than a scientific approach.
(B) It implied that the students' own environment was less inspiring.
(C) Like the rest of the course content, it
failed to interest the students.
(D) It developed in the students a permanent
appreciation for English ideas of beauty.
(E) It encouraged students to appreciate
English literature through English landscape paintings.

25 In line 17, "deviated" most nearly means

(A) rebelled   (B) changed   (C) erred
(D) swerved   (E) differed

26 In Passage 1, the "colonial mentality" (line 20)
is characterized as

(A) a necessary evil
(B) an inescapable presence
(C) a source of enlightenment
(D) a means to social advantage
(E) a welcome unifier of diverse peoples

27 The phrase "interesting effects" (lines 33-34)
most directly refers to

(A) psychological depression
(B) social snobbery
(C) a lack of self-knowledge
(D) a distrust of new ideas
(E) an opposition to injustice

28 The author of Passage 2 recounts her discovery
at age sixteen of James Baldwin's book
(lines 47-49) primarily to

(A) convey her pleasure in encountering a new
African American author
(B) reveal her annoyance at the library's short-
age of good books
(C) indicate her lack of familiarity with
African American literature
(D) demonstrate that she was not interested in
African American writers
(E) suggest that she was not prepared to read
adult literature

29 In Passage 2, the author's initial reaction to
Baldwin's picture (lines 47-56) indicates that

(A) people read with more attention when
interested in the subject matter
(B) young people are more sophisticated than
many adults think
(C) confronting new information can shake a
person's sense of security
(D) adolescents are often rebellious against
their elders' ideas
(E) adolescents generally exhibit little fear of
the unknown

30 The author of Passage 2 refers to Thoreau,
Hemingway, and Faulkner (lines 53-54) in
making the point that

(A) she was interested in going to college
(B) she enjoyed literature more than other
subjects
(C) the American literary tradition was not
inferior to other literary traditions
(D) she thought everything of significance had
already been said by White authors
(E) it was difficult for African American
authors to get published

GO ON TO THE NEXT PAGE

31 In the sentence beginning "I know I should . . ." (lines 65-66), the author indicates that she might once have been criticized for her

(A) lack of awareness of contemporary political issues
(B) failure to read novels by African American authors
(C) dismissal of authors studied in high school
(D) inability to take pleasure in reading
(E) preoccupation with ideas rather than experiences

32 Both passages recount educational experiences that are characterized by

(A) a discovery of the joys of reading
(B) a rebellion against obsolete ideas
(C) the study of complex but neglected literatures
(D) teachers who had no regard for students' physical comfort
(E) curricula that contained significant omissions

33 A significant difference between the two passages is that Passage 1

(A) describes the effects of an upbringing, while Passage 2 describes the effects as well as a significant change
(B) focuses on an individual transformation, while Passage 2 focuses on relationships between groups of people
(C) emphasizes the strengths of a classical education, while Passage 2 criticizes its shortcomings
(D) examines curricular inadequacies, while Passage 2 traces their causes through history
(E) discusses a problem in high school education, while Passage 2 discusses a problem at the college level

34 Both passages make the point that a good education is one that

(A) provides students with both political and literary works to read
(B) stresses real-world experience over reading
(C) incorporates a diversity of viewpoints
(D) allows a student to discover reading material independently
(E) makes use of natural imagery

35 Unlike the author of Passage 2, as a college student the author of Passage 1

(A) stayed emotionally detached from her coursework
(B) viewed the dominant culture with skepticism
(C) considered reading a recreational pastime
(D) disagreed with her classmates' political opinions
(E) grew to appreciate the education she had received

IF YOU FINISH BEFORE TIME IS CALLED, YOU MAY CHECK YOUR WORK ON THIS SECTION ONLY. DO NOT TURN TO ANY OTHER SECTION IN THE TEST. **STOP**

Time—15 Minutes 10 Questions	In this section solve each problem, using any available space on the page for scratchwork. Then decide which is the best of the choices given and fill in the corresponding oval on the answer sheet.

Notes:

1. The use of a calculator is permitted. All numbers used are real numbers.

2. Figures that accompany problems in this test are intended to provide information useful in solving the problems. They are drawn as accurately as possible EXCEPT when it is stated in a specific problem that the figure is not drawn to scale. All figures lie in a plane unless otherwise indicated.

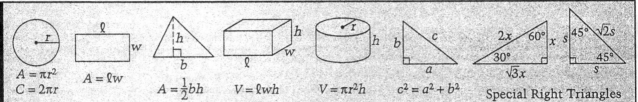

$A = \pi r^2$
$C = 2\pi r$

$A = \ell w$

$A = \frac{1}{2}bh$

$V = \ell wh$

$V = \pi r^2 h$

$c^2 = a^2 + b^2$

Special Right Triangles

The number of degrees of arc in a circle is 360.
The measure in degrees of a straight angle is 180.
The sum of the measures in degrees of the angles of a triangle is 180.

---

1 At a certain store, 3 apples and 3 bananas cost $1.26 and 2 apples and 2 bananas cost $0.84. How much will 5 apples and 5 bananas cost at these prices?

(A) $3.30
(B) $3.15
(C) $2.52
(D) $2.10
(E) $1.89

1, 1, 2, 4, 8, 16, 32, .(64) 128 256

2 In the sequence above, each term after the first is obtained by finding the sum of <u>all</u> terms preceding the given term. If this pattern continues indefinitely, 256 will be which term of the sequence?

(A) 8th
(B) 9th
(C) 10th
(D) 11th
(E) 12th

---

3 On a certain day, 20 percent of the students in a class were absent. Of those who were present, 20 percent went on a field trip. What percent of all the students in the class went on this trip?

(A) 4%
(B) 16%
(C) 20%
(D) 40%
(E) 80%

GO ON TO THE NEXT PAGE

4 Andrea lives 1.5 miles from her school. On a particular day, she walked 0.5 mile, stopped for 1 minute to tie her shoelaces, then walked 0.25 mile, stopped for 3 minutes to talk to friends, then ran the remaining distance to school. Which of the following graphs could correctly represent her journey to school on this day ?

(A)

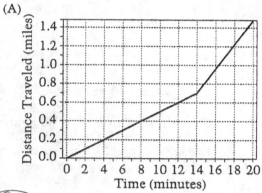

(B)

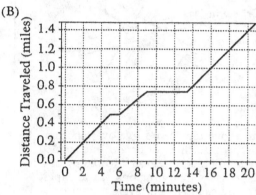

(C)

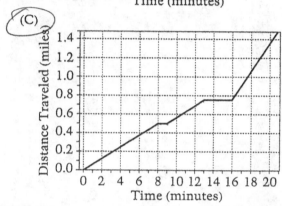

(D)

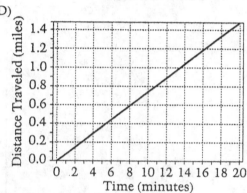

(E)

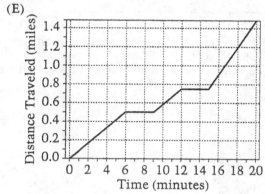

 GO ON TO THE NEXT PAGE

449

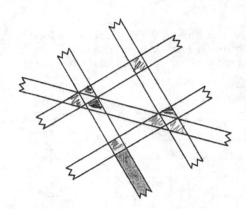

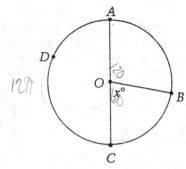

Note: Figure not drawn to scale.

5 The figure above represents five overlapping pieces of tape on a sheet of paper. The shaded area is an example of a region covered by one layer of tape. How many regions of the paper are covered by exactly two layers of tape?

(A) Two
(B) Four
(C) Five
(D) Six
(E) Eight

7 In the circle shown above, O is the center and AC is a diameter. If the length of arc CDA is 12π and $x = 60$, what is the length of arc BC?

(A) 2π
(B) 3π
(C) 4π
(D) 5π
(E) 6π

6 If $\dfrac{x}{3} + \dfrac{y}{7} = \dfrac{29}{21}$, where x and y are positive integers, what is the value of $x + y$?

(A) 3
(B) 7
(C) 8
(D) 10
(E) 17

8 If a "strone" and a "bennet" are each units of length such that 5 strones is equivalent to 2 bennets, how many cubic strones are there in 1 cubic bennet?

(A) $\dfrac{125}{2}$

(B) $\dfrac{125}{8}$

(C) $\dfrac{25}{4}$

(D) $\dfrac{5}{8}$

(E) $\dfrac{4}{25}$

GO ON TO THE NEXT PAGE

9 A cardboard cube of volume 64 cubic inches is disassembled. Its 6 faces are placed side by side in one horizontal row without overlap. What is the area of the rectangle formed by the 6 faces?

(A) 96 sq in
(B) 72 sq in
(C) 64 sq in
(D) 48 sq in
(E) 24 sq in

10 Last year the chess team won $\frac{7}{9}$ of its matches. If the team won 16 of its first 32 matches, what was the least number of matches it could have played last year?

(A) 40
(B) 54
(C) 56
(D) 63
(E) 72

$7/9 = .77$

IF YOU FINISH BEFORE TIME IS CALLED, YOU MAY CHECK YOUR WORK ON THIS SECTION ONLY. DO NOT TURN TO ANY OTHER SECTION IN THE TEST. **STOP**

Time—15 Minutes
13 Questions

For each question in this section, select the best answer from among the choices given and fill in the corresponding oval on the answer sheet.

The passage below is followed by questions based on its content. Answer the questions on the basis of what is <u>stated</u> or <u>implied</u> in the passage and in any introductory material that may be provided.

Questions 1-13 are based on the following passage.

The passage below is from a book by a journalist who has studied the Arctic and traveled there extensively.   recollection

It may be that as many as 38,000 Greenland right whales were killed in the Davis Strait fishery during the early part of the nineteenth century, largely by the British fleet. A sound estimate of
(5) the size of that population today is 200. What happened in the heyday of Arctic whaling represents in microcosm the large-scale advance of nonindigenous cultures into the Arctic. It is a disquieting reminder that the modern Arctic
(10) industries—oil, gas, and mineral extraction— might be embarked on a course as disastrously short-lived as that of the whaling industry. Our natural histories of this region 150 years later are still cursory and unintegrated. This time around,
(15) however, the element at greatest risk is not the whale but the coherent vision of the indigenous people. Only indigenous groups such as the Inuit, the Yupik, the Inupiat, and others can provide a sustained narrative of human relationships with
(20) the Arctic landscape independent of the desire to control or possess. Most nonindigenous views lack historical depth and are still largely innocent of what is obscure and subtle there.

Conceptions of the Arctic vary markedly. Its
(25) future disposition is not viewed in the same way by a Montreal attorney working on the settlement of Inuit land claims, by a Swedish naval architect designing an ice-breaking tanker, by an *inuk* pulling on his fishnets at the mouth of the Hayes
(30) River, by a biologist watching a caribou herd encounter the trans-Alaska pipeline, or by a tourist bound for a caviar-and-champagne luncheon at the North Pole. Such a variety of human views and interests in one particular part of the planet is not
(35) new; what is new, and troubling for people who, like me, live in the Temperate Zone, is a difference in the land itself, which changes the very nature of these considerations. In the Temperate Zone we are accustomed to dealing with land-
(40) scapes that can easily accommodate opposing

views; the long growing seasons, mild temperatures, great variety of creatures, and moderate rainfall make up for much human abuse. Arctic ecosystems are different—they are far more
(45) vulnerable ecologically to attempts to "accommodate both sides." Of concern in the North, then, is the impatience with which reconciliation and compromise are now being sought.

As Temperate Zone people, we have long been
(50) ill-disposed toward deserts and expanses of tundra and ice. They have been wastelands for us; historically we have not cared at all what happened in them or to them. I am inclined to think, however, that their value will one day prove to be ines-
(55) timable to us. Because the regimes of light and time in the Arctic are so different from what we are used to, this landscape is able to expose in startling ways the complacency of our thoughts about land in general. The unfamiliar rhythms of
(60) the Arctic, the fundamental strangeness of a land in which the sun does not set on a summer evening, point up the narrow impetuosity of the schedules of industrialized nations. The periodically frozen Arctic Ocean is at present an insur-
(65) mountable impediment to timely shipping. This land, for some, is irritatingly and uncharacteristically uncooperative. If an enlightened plan for increased human activity in the Arctic is to be devised, we will need a more particularized under-
(70) standing of the land itself—not a more refined mathematical knowledge but a deeper understanding of its essential characteristics, as if it were, itself, another sort of civilization with which we had to reach some accord.
(75) Once in winter I was far out on the sea ice north of Melville Island in the high Arctic observing a crew drilling for oil. I saw a seal surface at some hourless moment of the day in a moon pool, the open water directly underneath the drilling
(80) platform. The seal and I regarded each other in

GO ON TO THE NEXT PAGE →

absolute stillness, I in my parka, arrested in the middle of an errand, the seal in the motionless water, its dark brown eyes glistening in its gray, catlike head. Curiosity held it. What held me
(85) was: how far out on the edge of the world I am. A movement of my head shifted the hood of my parka slightly, and the seal was gone in an explosion of water. Its eyes had been enormous. I walked to the edge of the moon pool and stared
(90) into the dark ocean. To contemplate what people are doing out here and ignore the universe of the seal, to consider human quest and plight and not know the land, I thought, seemed fatal—not perhaps for tomorrow, or next year, but inevitably
(95) at some point in the future of our relationship with the Arctic.

1 In the first paragraph, the author refers to events in the Davis Strait fishery in order to provide

(A) details about the daily operations of the British whaling fleet
(B) an example of the ability of some species to survive human predation
(C) a reason why whales should not be hunted or killed
(D) an illustration of shortsighted human activity in the Arctic
(E) estimates of Arctic whale populations whose accuracy should be challenged

2 The author discusses the nineteenth-century Arctic whaling industry in order to

(A) correct a misconception
(B) provide a warning
(C) reconcile two points of view
(D) introduce an appealing model from history
(E) furnish a contrast to twentieth-century Arctic industries

3 The author suggests that "modern Arctic industries" (lines 9-10) seem likely to

(A) employ large numbers of indigenous Arctic peoples
(B) be less successful economically than was the whaling industry
(C) do harm regardless of their intentions
(D) insist that unique features of the Arctic be recorded and studied
(E) cause international conflicts

4 The reference to "Our natural histories" of the Arctic (lines 12-13) suggests that

(A) current versions are superior to those of the preceding century
(B) collaborations between indigenous people and nonindigenous people have resulted in comprehensive studies of the region
(C) modern Arctic industries are not likely to repeat mistakes made in earlier times
(D) sustained narratives of indigenous Arctic dwellers have successfully substituted for more formal studies
(E) the region has not yet been investigated enough to allow nonindigenous people to understand it

5 In line 22, "innocent of" most nearly means

(A) not harmful to
(B) not guilty of
(C) uncorrupted by
(D) optimistic about
(E) oblivious to

6 Why is the Arctic unable to "accommodate opposing views" (lines 40-41) as easily as does the Temperate Zone?

(A) Indigenous people and nonindigenous people have competing land claims in the Arctic.
(B) There are fewer people and more desertlike expanses of land in the Arctic.
(C) Industrialized nations have widely differing ideas of how to develop the Arctic.
(D) Arctic ecosystems are more fragile than those of the Temperate Zone.
(E) The Arctic has been subjected to more human abuse than the Temperate Zone has.

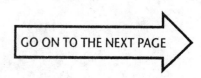

GO ON TO THE NEXT PAGE

7 Which of the following would the author most likely believe about the process of "reconciliation and compromise" (lines 47-48) in the Arctic?

(A) It will probably be too expensive to be practical.
(B) It is undesirable if pursued according to Temperate Zone customs.
(C) It has been the direct cause of past environmental problems.
(D) It will be effective only if implemented immediately.
(E) It provides an opportunity to avoid mistakes made in the Temperate Zone.

8 The author states that Temperate Zone people view the uses made of "expanses of tundra and ice" (lines 50-51) with

(A) complete indifference
(B) uncertainty and confusion
(C) aesthetic appreciation
(D) a sense of personal entitlement
(E) an eye toward the future

9 The author mentions that "the sun does not set on a summer evening" (lines 61-62) in order to

(A) provide a contrast with bitterly cold Arctic nights
(B) allude to an important symbol in indigenous Arctic cultures
(C) illustrate differences between the Arctic and other geographic regions
(D) explain why Temperate Zone people become complacent when visiting the Arctic
(E) suggest why the Arctic Ocean remains frozen during the winter

10 The author mentions "another sort of civilization" (line 73) in order to suggest the

(A) way in which technology has changed indigenous Arctic cultures
(B) way in which the land should be treated by people
(C) way outsiders are perceived by indigenous people
(D) extent to which the Arctic transforms visitors
(E) extent of the conflict between industry and science

11 The encounter with the seal (lines 75-90) makes the author keenly aware of the

(A) helplessness of sea creatures
(B) human appetite for destruction
(C) scenic beauty of the Arctic sea ice
(D) mysterious unfamiliarity of the Arctic environment
(E) financial value of natural resources in the Arctic

12 The description of what occurred on the oil-drilling platform (lines 75-90) serves chiefly to provide

(A) an example of the role of modern industry in the Arctic
(B) an illustration of an undesirable confrontation in the Arctic
(C) a personal and concrete example of the author's argument
(D) a solution to the problems discussed previously by the author
(E) a rebuttal to the views summarized previously by the author

13 In lines 91-92, the phrase "universe of the seal" refers to the

(A) natural world of the Arctic
(B) area north of Melville Island
(C) contradictory nature of aquatic mammals
(D) moon pool beneath the Arctic drilling platform
(E) interrelated ecosystems of the Earth as a whole

SAT I Scoring Worksheet

SAT I Verbal Sections

A. Section 2:

_____ − (_____ ÷ 4) = _____
no. correct   no. incorrect   subtotal A

B. Section 5:

_____ − (_____ ÷ 4) = _____
no. correct   no. incorrect   subtotal B

C. Section 7:

_____ − (_____ ÷ 4) = _____
no. correct   no. incorrect   subtotal C

D. Total unrounded raw score
(Total A + B + C)

_____
D

E. Total rounded raw score
(Rounded to nearest whole number)

_____
E

F. SAT I verbal reported scaled score
(See the appropriate conversion table on back cover)

SAT I verbal
score

SAT I Mathematical Sections

A. Section 1:

_____ − (_____ ÷ 4) = _____
no. correct   no. incorrect   subtotal A

B. Section 3:
Questions 1-15 (quantitative comparison)

_____ − (_____ ÷ 3) = _____
no. correct   no. incorrect   subtotal B

C. Section 3
Questions 16-25 (student-produced response)

_____ = _____
no. correct   subtotal C

D. Section 6:

_____ − (_____ ÷ 4) = _____
no. correct   no. incorrect   subtotal D

E. Total unrounded raw score
(Total A + B + C + D)

_____
E

F. Total rounded raw score
(Rounded to nearest whole number)

_____
F

G. SAT I mathematical reported scaled score
(See the appropriate conversion table on back cover)

SAT I
mathematical
score

Score Conversion Table
SAT I: Reasoning Test
Sunday, May 1995
Recentered Scale

Raw Score	Verbal Scaled Score	Math Scaled Score	Raw Score	Verbal Scaled Score	Math Scaled Score
78	800		36	500	550
77	800		35	500	550
76	800		34	490	540
75	800		33	490	530
74	800		32	480	520
73	790		31	480	520
72	770		30	470	510
71	760		29	460	500
70	750		28	460	500
69	730		27	450	490
68	720		26	450	480
67	710		25	440	480
66	700		24	440	470
65	700		23	430	460
64	690		22	420	460
63	680		21	420	450
62	670		20	410	440
61	660		19	400	440
60	650	800	18	400	430
59	650	800	17	390	420
58	640	790	16	380	420
57	630	770	15	380	410
56	630	750	14	370	410
55	620	730	13	360	400
54	610	720	12	350	390
53	610	710	11	340	380
52	600	690	10	340	380
51	590	680	9	330	370
50	590	670	8	320	360
49	580	660	7	310	350
48	570	650	6	300	340
47	570	640	5	290	340
46	560	640	4	280	330
45	560	630	3	270	320
44	550	620	2	250	300
43	540	610	1	240	290
42	540	600	0	220	280
41	530	590	-1	210	260
40	530	580	-2	200	250
39	520	580	-3	200	230
38	520	570	-4	200	210
37	510	560	-5 and below	200	200

This table is for use only with this test.

**Time—30 Minutes
35 Questions**

For each question in this section, select the best answer from among the choices given and fill in the corresponding oval on the answer sheet.

Each sentence below has one or two blanks, each blank indicating that something has been omitted. Beneath the sentence are five words or sets of words labeled A through E. Choose the word or set of words that, when inserted in the sentence, best fits the meaning of the sentence as a whole.

Example:

Medieval kingdoms did not become constitutional republics overnight; on the contrary, the change was ----.

(A) unpopular
(B) unexpected
(C) advantageous
(D) sufficient
(E) gradual

Ⓐ Ⓑ Ⓒ Ⓓ ●

1 Although Christa Wolf was one of East Germany's most famous authors, her works were often ---- and, therefore, often unavailable.

(A) suppressed   (B) revised   (C) imitated
 (D) tolerated   (E) analyzed

2 A few of the people on the island may n̶ but most have no hope of ---- even the basic amenities of life.

(A) poorly..enjoying
(B) pretentiously..yielding
(C) responsibly..acquiring
(D) lavishly..attaining
(E) simply..missing

3 The new pluralism in art ---- a great variety of styles and points of view while denying ---- to any single approach.

(A) ignores..originality
(B) distorts..probability
(C) espouses..embellishment
(D) undermines..secrecy
(E) accommodates..dominance

4 Interest in the origin of life is ----; all cultures and societies have narratives about creation.

(A) distant   (B) mythical   (C) universal
 (D) debatable   (E) superficial

5 The number of African American inventors from the 1600's to the late 1800's will never be ----, since their work was often ---- by others.

(A) seen..reintegrated
(B) determined..expropriated
(C) withheld..trivialized
(D) disclosed..uncensored
(E) archived..marketed

6 Housewares and bookbindings by designer Josef Hoffmann exemplify a range of styles, from simple and austere to ---- and opulent.

(A) basic   (B) efficient   (C) severe
 (D) florid   (E) straightforward

7 Although the personality that emerges from May Sarton's autobiography seems unmistakably ----, the journals for which she became famous described her ---- life in a sparsely populated area.

(A) complex..intricate
(B) celebrated..humorous
(C) affable..solitary
(D) stoic..isolated
(E) scholarly..intellectual

8  ...ly end to the strike, but the ...ers were ---- because both sides refused to compromise.

(A) cordial   (B) dubious   (C) benevolent
 (D) biased   (E) prophetic

9 He was always ---- in performing his tasks, waiting until the last moment to finish them.

(A) dilatory   (B) incompetent
 (C) extroverted   (D) surreptitious
 (E) obtrusive

10 In effect, the Voting Rights Act of 1965 ---- African Americans in the southern United States by outlawing restrictions that had barred them from voting.

(A) inspired   (B) promulgated
 (C) enfranchised   (D) preserved
 (E) proliferated

GO ON TO THE NEXT PAGE

Each question below consists of a related pair of words or phrases, followed by five pairs of words or phrases labeled A through E. Select the pair that best expresses a relationship similar to that expressed in the original pair.

Example:

CRUMB : BREAD ::
(A) ounce : unit
(B) splinter : wood
(C) water : bucket
(D) twine : rope
(E) cream : butter

(A) ● (C) (D) (E)

11 DROUGHT : RAIN ::
(A) desert : sun
(B) hurricane : wind
(C) epidemic : disease
(D) volcano : lava
(E) famine : nourishment

12 ANTIBIOTIC : INFECTION ::
(A) thermometer : fever
(B) anesthesia : surgery
(C) vaccine : inoculation
(D) antiseptic : alcohol
(E) antidote : poisoning

13 HUMIDIFIER : MOISTURE ::
(A) iron : wrinkle
(B) candle : wax
(C) tub : liquid
(D) furnace : heat
(E) chimney : smoke

14 CONDOLENCE : MOURNER ::
(A) secret : stranger
(B) loan : borrower
(C) rescue : knight
(D) congratulation : victor
(E) record : athlete

15 PETAL : FLOWER ::
(A) oak : tree
(B) staple : paper
(C) sprout : seed
(D) tooth : comb
(E) tide : beach

16 RUTHLESS : COMPASSION ::
(A) theatrical : emotion
(B) naïve : sophistication
(C) scrupulous : propriety
(D) self-righteous : indignation
(E) formidable : awe

17 EMOLLIENT : SOFTEN ::
(A) oil : lubricate
(B) disinfectant : contaminate
(C) concrete : harden
(D) storm : thunder
(E) steam : evaporate

18 CAPTION : CARTOON ::
(A) byline : newspaper
(B) laughter : comedy
(C) subtitle : film
(D) translation : paraphrase
(E) billboard : road

19 BERATE : CRITICIZE ::
(A) goad : urge
(B) accuse : apologize
(C) regret : remember
(D) betray : follow
(E) evaluate : praise

20 PERCEPTIVE : DISCERN ::
(A) determined : hesitate
(B) authoritarian : heed
(C) persistent : persevere
(D) abandoned : neglect
(E) restrained : rebel

21 EMULATE : PERSON ::
(A) admire : reputation
(B) obey : leader
(C) cooperate : partner
(D) mimic : gesture
(E) mock : sarcasm

22 INCUMBENT : OFFICE ::
(A) politician : campaign
(B) tenant : dwelling
(C) jailer : cell
(D) secretary : desk
(E) retiree : service

23 CONUNDRUM : PERPLEX ::
(A) theory : refute
(B) explanation : suffice
(C) blueprint : construct
(D) entertainment : divert
(E) expedition : discover

GO ON TO THE NEXT PAGE

The passage below is followed by questions based on its content. Answer the questions on the basis of what is stated or implied in the passage and in any introductory material that may be provided.

Questions 24-35 are based on the following passage.

recollection

The following selection is taken from the auto-biography of a Hispanic American writer.

In fourth grade I embarked upon a grandiose reading program. "Give me the names of impor-tant books," I would say to startled teachers. They
Line soon found out that I had in mind "adult books."
(5) I ignored their suggestion of anything I suspected was written for children. And whatever I read, I read for extra credit. Each time I finished a book, I reported the achievement to a teacher and basked in the praise my effort earned. Despite my best
(10) efforts, however, there seemed to be more and more books I needed to read. At the library I would literally tremble as I came upon whole shelves of books I hadn't read. So I read and I read and I read. Librarians who initially frowned when
(15) I checked out the maximum ten books at a time started saving books they thought I might like. Teachers would say to the rest of the class, "I only wish that the rest of you took reading as seri-ously as Richard obviously does."
(20) But at home I would hear my mother, who was not an educated woman, wondering, "What do you see in your books?" (Was reading a hobby like her knitting? Was so much reading even healthy for a boy? Was it a sign of "brains"? Or was it just a
(25) convenient excuse for not helping around the house on Saturday mornings?) Always, "What do you see?"

What did I see in my books? I had the idea that they were crucial for my academic success, though
(30) I couldn't have said exactly how or why. In the sixth grade I simply concluded that what gave a book its value was some major idea or theme it contained. If that core essence could be mined and memorized, I would become learned like my
(35) teachers. I decided to record in a notebook the themes of the books that I read. After reading *Robinson Crusoe*, I wrote that its theme was "the value of learning to live by oneself." When I com-pleted *Wuthering Heights*, I noted the danger of
(40) "letting emotions get out of control." Rereading these brief moralistic appraisals usually left me disheartened. I couldn't believe that they were really the source of reading's value. But for many more years, they constituted the only means I had
(45) of describing to myself the educational value of books.

In spite of my earnestness, I found reading a pleasurable activity. I came to enjoy the lonely good company of books. Early on weekday morn-
(50) ings, I'd read in my bed. I'd feel a mysterious com-fort then, reading in the dawn quiet. On weekends I'd go to the public library to read, surrounded by old men and women. Or, if the weather was fine, I would take my books to the park and read in the
(55) shade of a tree.

I also had favorite writers. But often those writers I enjoyed most I was least able to value. When I read William Saroyan's *The Human Comedy*, I was immediately pleased by the narra-
(60) tor's warmth and the charm of his story. But as quickly I became suspicious. A book so enjoyable to read couldn't be very "important." Another summer I determined to read all the novels of Dickens. Reading his fat novels, I loved the feeling
(65) I got—after the first hundred pages—of being at home in a fictional world where I knew the names of the characters and cared about what was going to happen to them. And it bothered me that I was forced away at the conclusion, when the fiction
(70) closed tight, like a fortune-teller's fist—the futures of all the major characters neatly resolved. I never knew how to take such feelings seriously, however. Nor did I suspect that these experiences could be part of a novel's meaning. Still, there were plea-
(75) sures to sustain me after I'd finished my books. Carrying a volume back to the library, I would be pleased by its weight. I'd run my fingers along the edges of the pages and marvel at the breadth of my achievement. Around my room, growing stacks of
(80) paperback books reinforced my assurance.

I entered high school having read hundreds of books. My habit of reading made me a confident speaker and writer of English and in various ways, books brought me academic success as I hoped
(85) they would. But I was not a good reader. Merely bookish, I lacked a point of view when I read. Rather, I read in order to acquire a point of view. I vacuumed books for epigrams, scraps of informa-tion, ideas, themes—anything to fill the hollow
(90) within me and make me feel educated. When one of my teachers suggested to his drowsy tenth-grade English class that a person could not have a "complicated idea" until that person had read at least two thousand books, I heard the remark
(95) without detecting either its irony or its very com-plicated truth.

GO ON TO THE NEXT PAGE

24 The author uses the phrase "embarked upon" (line 1) to emphasize which of the following?

(A) The transient nature of the fictional world
(B) His commitment to an exploration of the world of books
(C) His realization that literature can change one's outlook
(D) The fear he feels about leaving the familiar world of his parents
(E) His sense of isolation from his classmates

25 The author initially believed "important books" (lines 2-3) to be books that

(A) did not contain any references to children
(B) had been praised by critics
(C) were recommended by his mother
(D) were directed toward a mature audience
(E) were written by renowned authors

26 The author would "literally tremble" (line 12) at the library because he

(A) did not know which books were important
(B) was intimidated by the librarians
(C) felt a personal connection to all the authors represented there
(D) was worried that he would never be able to read all the books
(E) was excited by the idea of being allowed to borrow books

27 The author's purpose in mentioning that some of the librarians "frowned" (line 14) is most likely to

(A) indicate that his reading project was met with some skepticism at first
(B) imply that they thought children should not check out books written for adults
(C) suggest that what he was doing was wrong
(D) explain why he was so frightened at the library
(E) characterize librarians who favor intellectual children

28 The mother's attitude toward the boy's interest in reading (lines 20-27) can be best described as

(A) exasperation
(B) indignation
(C) perplexity
(D) sympathy
(E) admiration

29 In line 33, "mined" most nearly means

(A) followed
(B) dug out
(C) entrenched
(D) tunneled
(E) blown up

30 The author states that he was "disheartened" (line 42) because

(A) he was unable to find books that were of lasting value
(B) the tragic themes of the books he was reading were depressing to him
(C) his ability to write descriptions was lagging behind his reading ability
(D) his teachers were not giving him as much encouragement as he needed
(E) his desire for meaning was not being met by the themes that he wrote down

31 The fourth paragraph (lines 47-55) describes the author as

(A) comfortable only in the company of fellow scholars
(B) dissatisfied with the rate at which his reading progressed
(C) happy with his books despite his isolation from others
(D) lonely because he often had no other children around him
(E) determined to get outside and enjoy nature

GO ON TO THE NEXT PAGE

468

32 The author uses the phrase "the fiction closed tight" (lines 69-70) in order to

(A) demonstrate that the endings of the novels were not believable
(B) blur the distinction between fictional works and real life
(C) indicate how impenetrable some of the novels were
(D) criticize the artificiality of Dickens' characters
(E) show his unhappiness at having to part with a fictional world

33 In line 75 "sustain" most nearly means

(A) defend
(B) support
(C) endure
(D) prolong
(E) ratify

34 The author uses the phrase "the breadth of my achievement" (lines 78-79) primarily in order to suggest that

(A) he was confusing quantity with quality
(B) the books he had read varied widely in difficulty
(C) he should have been prouder of himself than he was
(D) he believes every child should read as much as possible
(E) no one else knew how much he was reading

35 The author implies that "a good reader" (line 85) is one who

(A) engages in a structured reading program
(B) reads constantly and widely
(C) reads with a critical perspective
(D) makes lists of books to be read
(E) can summarize a book's theme simply and concisely

IF YOU FINISH BEFORE TIME IS CALLED, YOU MAY CHECK YOUR WORK ON THIS SECTION ONLY. DO NOT TURN TO ANY OTHER SECTION IN THE TEST. **STOP**

469

Time—30 Minutes
25 Questions

In this section solve each problem, using any available space on the page for scratchwork. Then decide which is the best of the choices given and fill in the corresponding oval on the answer sheet.

Notes:

1. The use of a calculator is permitted. All numbers used are real numbers.

2. Figures that accompany problems in this test are intended to provide information useful in solving the problems. They are drawn as accurately as possible EXCEPT when it is stated in a specific problem that the figure is not drawn to scale. All figures lie in a plane unless otherwise indicated.

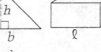

1. If $2x + y = 7$ and $y = 5x$, then $x =$

$y = 7 - 2x$
$y = 5x$

(A) $\frac{1}{7}$

(B) $\frac{5}{7}$

(C) 1

(D) $\frac{7}{5}$

(E) 7

---

2. If it takes Sam 6 hours working at a constant rate to complete his science project, what part of the project is completed in 2 hours?

$\frac{6}{100} = \frac{2}{?}$

(A) $\frac{1}{12}$

(B) $\frac{1}{8}$

(C) $\frac{1}{6}$

(D) $\frac{1}{4}$

(E) $\frac{1}{3}$

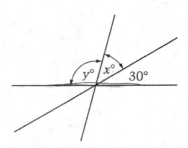

3. Three lines intersect in the figure above. What is the value of $x + y$?

(A) 170
(B) 160
(C) 150
(D) 140
(E) 120

GO ON TO THE NEXT PAGE

470

4 If $2p + 5 = 20$, then $2p - 5 =$

$-5 \quad -5$
$2p \quad 15$

(A) 0
(B) 5
(C) 10
(D) 15
(E) 25

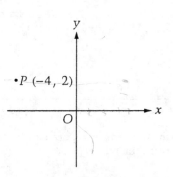

5 In the figure above, a line is to be drawn through point P so that it never crosses the x-axis. Through which of the following points must the line pass?

(A) (4, 2)
(B) (4, −2)
(C) (2, 4)
(D) (2, −4)
(E) (−4, −2)

6 The ratio of 8 to 3 is equal to the ratio of 24 to what number?

(A) 8
(B) 9
(C) 19
(D) 29
(E) 64

$8x + 3x = 24x + 19x$

7 What number decreased by 6 equals 3 times the number?

(A) −3

(B) −1

(C) $-\dfrac{2}{3}$

(D) $\dfrac{2}{3}$

(E) 3

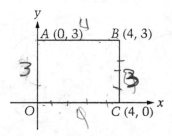

8 What is the area of rectangle $OABC$ in the figure above?

(A) 7
(B) 9
(C) 12
(D) 14
(E) 16

9 The distance from Town A to Town B is 5 miles and the distance from Town B to Town C is 4 miles. Which of the following could NOT be the distance, in miles, from Town A to Town C ?

(A) 1
(B) 4
(C) 8
(D) 9
(E) 10

GO ON TO THE NEXT PAGE

Questions 10-12 refer to the following information.

    Alissa makes a number wheel to represent the integers from 0 through 99, inclusive. The short hand points to the tens digit, and the long hand points to the units digit.

    For example, the number wheel above shows 07, which we would write as 7.

10   Which of the following represents the sum of the two integers represented on the two number wheels above?

(A)

(B)
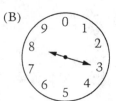

(C)
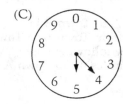

(D)
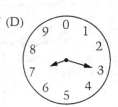

(E)
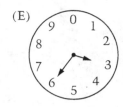

11   Which of the following is the next greater prime number after the prime number represented above?

(A) 15
(B) 17
(C) 33
(D) 37
(E) 41

12   Exactly how many integers can be represented on this number wheel?

(A)   91
(B)   98
(C)   99
(D) 100
(E) 101

13   Exactly $\frac{1}{2}$ yard of ribbon is needed to make a certain bow. Which of the following lengths of ribbon could be used to make the bow with the least amount remaining?

(A) $\frac{2}{5}$ yd

(B) $\frac{3}{5}$ yd

(C) $\frac{3}{4}$ yd

(D) $\frac{1}{3}$ yd

(E) $\frac{2}{3}$ yd

GO ON TO THE NEXT PAGE →

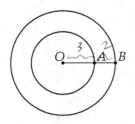

14 In the figure above, both circles have their centers at point O, and point A lies on segment OB. If $OA = 3$ and $AB = 2$, what is the ratio of the circumference of the smaller circle to the circumference of the larger circle?

(A) $\dfrac{2}{3}$

(B) $\dfrac{3}{5}$

(C) $\dfrac{9}{16}$

(D) $\dfrac{1}{2}$

(E) $\dfrac{4}{9}$

15 The total weight of Bill and his son Tommy is 250 pounds. If Bill's weight is 10 pounds more than 3 times Tommy's, what is Tommy's weight in pounds?

(A) 40
(B) 50
(C) 60
(D) 80
(E) 90

16 Set I contains six consecutive integers. Set J contains all integers that result from adding 3 to each of the integers in set I and also contains all integers that result from subtracting 3 from each of the integers in set I. How many more integers are there in set J than in set I?

(A) 0
(B) 2
(C) 3
(D) 6
(E) 9

17 If $s \neq 0$, then $\dfrac{\frac{1}{6}}{\frac{2s}{}} =$

(A) $\dfrac{1}{3s}$

(B) $\dfrac{3}{s}$

(C) $\dfrac{s}{3}$

(D) $\dfrac{3s}{2}$

(E) $3s$

GO ON TO THE NEXT PAGE

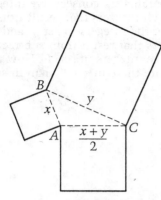

18 In the figure above, triangle ABC has sides of lengths x, y, and $\dfrac{x+y}{2}$. On each side, a square is constructed as shown. What is the sum of the lengths of the sides of the resulting 9-sided figure, in terms of x and y?

(A) $\dfrac{9x + 9y}{2}$

(B) $\dfrac{7x + 7y}{2}$

(C) $\dfrac{3x + 3y}{2}$

(D) $5x + 5y$

(E) $4x + 4y$

19 If x is an integer and $\dfrac{x+7}{2}$ is an integer, which of the following must be true?

  I. x is odd.

  II. x is a multiple of 7.

  III. $\dfrac{x+5}{2}$ is an integer.

(A) I only
(B) II only
(C) III only
(D) I and II
(E) I and III

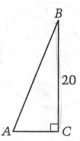

Note: Figure not drawn to scale.

20 If the area of the triangle in the figure above is 100, what is the length of side AB?

(A) $10\sqrt{3}$ (approximately 17.32)

(B) $10\sqrt{5}$ (approximately 22.36)

(C) 20

(D) 24

(E) 25

21 If $(x + 3)(x + 5) - (x - 4)(x - 2) = 0$, then $x =$

(A) -2

(B) $-\dfrac{1}{2}$

(C) 0

(D) $\dfrac{1}{2}$

(E) 2

GO ON TO THE NEXT PAGE

474

22 If $x < y$, which of the following must be true?

(A) $x^2 < y^2$

(B) $-y < -x$

(C) $x^2 < xy$

(D) $xy < y^2$

(E) $2x < y$

24 In a certain club, the median age of the members is 11. Which of the following must be true?

   I. The oldest member in the club is at least 1 year older than the youngest.

  II. If there is a 10 year old in the club, there is also a 12 year old.

 III. The mode of the members' ages is 11.

(A) None

(B) I only

(C) II only

(D) III only

(E) II and III

23 The first term of a sequence is -3 and every term after the first is 5 more than the term immediately preceding it. What is the value of the 101st term?

(A) 505

(B) 502

(C) 500

(D) 497

(E) 492

25 In a certain shop, items were put in a showcase and assigned prices for January. Each month after that, the price was 10 percent less than the price for the previous month. If the price of an item was p dollars for January, what was the price for April?

(A) $0.4p$

(B) $0.6p$

(C) $0.6561p$

(D) $0.7p$

(E) $0.729p$

IF YOU FINISH BEFORE TIME IS CALLED, YOU MAY CHECK YOUR WORK ON THIS SECTION ONLY. DO NOT TURN TO ANY OTHER SECTION IN THE TEST. **STOP**

**Time — 30 Minutes
30 Questions**

For each question in this section, select the best answer from among the choices given and fill in the corresponding oval on the answer sheet.

Each sentence below has one or two blanks, each blank indicating that something has been omitted. Beneath the sentence are five words or sets of words labeled A through E. Choose the word or set of words that, when inserted in the sentence, best fits the meaning of the sentence as a whole.

Example:

Medieval kingdoms did not become constitutional republics overnight; on the contrary, the change was ----.

(A) unpopular
(B) unexpected
(C) advantageous
(D) sufficient
(E) gradual

(A) (B) (C) (D) ●

1 The usually ---- Mr. Henderson shocked his associates by reacting violently to the insignificant and moderate comments of his critic.

(A) demanding   (B) inarticulate   (C) aggressive
(D) persuasive   (E) composed

2 Disappointingly, the researchers' failure was a direct result of their ----; we had not expected that their focus would be so indistinct.

(A) egoism   (B) irreverence   (C) relevance
(D) vagueness   (E) hindsight

3 Although her restaurant already has a large and devoted following, Magda tries to expand her ---- by offering special promotions.

(A) clientele   (B) investments   (C) coverage
(D) staffing   (E) liability

4 By showing such a large shaded area, this map of wildlife distribution encourages the ---- that certain species living in isolated spots are actually ----.

(A) misconception. .widespread
(B) impression. .remote
(C) illusion. .extant
(D) notion. .carnivorous
(E) sense. .feral

5 The author portrays research psychologists not as disruptive ---- in the field of psychotherapy, but as effective ---- working ultimately toward the same ends as the psychotherapists.

(A) proponents. .opponents
(B) antagonists. .pundits
(C) interlocutors. .surrogates
(D) meddlers. .usurpers
(E) intruders. .collaborators

6 Despite their ---- backgrounds, those who fought for women's right to vote successfully overcame their differences in a ---- effort.

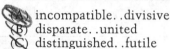

(A) incompatible. .divisive
(B) disparate. .united
(C) distinguished. .futile
(D) eccentric. .prosaic
(E) comparable. .joint

7 The candidate recognized that his attempt to build a broad base of support had been ----, but he was still ---- by the magnitude of his defeat.

(A) obstinate. .elated
(B) insightful. .impenitent
(C) persuasive. .exultant
(D) thwarted. .discomfited
(E) successful. .satisfied

8 Although it is not ----, Clara Rodriguez' book on Puerto Rican life is especially useful because the supply of books on the subject is so ----.

(A) intense. .vast
(B) obsolete. .outdated
(C) ostentatious. .varied
(D) comprehensive. .meager
(E) contemporary. .plentiful

9 Wave direction, apparently the primary ---- used by young turtles to navigate in water, is later ---- by their orientation to magnetic fields.

(A) mechanism. .confused
(B) vestige. .propagated
(C) restraint. .complemented
(D) agent. .propelled
(E) cue. .supplanted

GO ON TO THE NEXT PAGE

Each question below consists of a related pair of words or phrases, followed by five pairs of words or phrases labeled A through E. Select the pair that best expresses a relationship similar to that expressed in the original pair.

Example:

CRUMB : BREAD ::
(A) ounce : unit
(B) splinter : wood
(C) water : bucket
(D) twine : rope
(E) cream : butter

Ⓐ ● Ⓒ Ⓓ Ⓔ

10 MUSEUM : EXHIBIT ::
(A) studio : painter
(B) library : research
(C) theater : performance
(D) picture : frame
(E) orchestra : conductor

11 LENS : GLASS ::
(A) well : water
(B) saw : wood
(C) sweater : wool
(D) fuel : fire
(E) ink : paper

12 ARENA : CONFLICT ::
(A) mirage : reality
(B) forum : discussion
(C) asylum : pursuit
(D) utopia : place
(E) amphitheater : stage

13 ARABLE : CULTIVATION ::
(A) exploited : protection
(B) healthy : medication
(C) insular : discovery
(D) productive : surplus
(E) navigable : sailing

14 REFURBISH : WORN ::
(A) revive : exhausted
(B) reward : outstanding
(C) resume : interrupted
(D) replace : stolen
(E) repaint : glossy

15 DEFEND : UNTENABLE ::
(A) escape : unfettered
(B) judge : punitive
(C) modify : invariable
(D) flourish : vigorous
(E) protect : dangerous

GO ON TO THE NEXT PAGE ➡

Each passage below is followed by questions based on its content. Answer the questions on the basis of what is stated or implied in each passage and in any introductory material that may be provided.

Questions 16-20 are based on the following passage.

opinion

The following passage is adapted from an essay on women and writing by a noted contemporary American poet.

As I tried to understand my dual roles of writer and mother, I realized that most, if not all, human lives are full of fantasy—passive daydreaming that
Line need not be acted on. But to write poetry or fiction,
(5) or even to think well, is not to fantasize, or even to put fantasies on paper. For a poem to coalesce, for a character or an action to take shape, there has to be an imaginative transformation of reality that is in no way passive. And a certain freedom of
(10) the mind is needed—freedom to press on, to enter the currents of your thought like a glider pilot, knowing that your motion can be sustained, that the buoyancy of your attention will not be suddenly snatched away. Moreover, if the imagination
(15) is to transcend and transform experience, it has to question, to challenge, to conceive of alternatives, perhaps to the very life you are living at that moment. You have to be free to play around with the notion that day might be night, love might be
(20) hate; nothing can be too sacred for the imagination to turn into its opposite or to call experimentally by another name. For writing is renaming. Now, to be maternally with small children all day in the old way, to be with a man in the old way of
(25) marriage, requires a holding back, a putting aside of that imaginative activity, and demands instead a kind of conservatism. I want to make it clear that I am not saying that in order to write well, or think well, it is necessary to become unavailable
(30) to others, or to become a devouring ego. This has been the myth of the masculine artist and thinker, and I do not accept it. But to be a female human being trying to fulfill traditional female functions in a traditional way is in direct conflict with the
(35) subversive function of the imagination. The word "traditional" is important here. There must be ways, and we will be finding out more and more about them, in which the energy of creation and the energy of relation can be united. But in those
(40) years I always felt the conflict as a failure of love in myself. I had thought I was choosing a full life: the life available to most men, in which sexuality, work, and parenthood could coexist. But I felt, at twenty-nine, guilt toward the people clos-
(45) est to me, and guilty toward my own being. I wanted, then, more than anything, the one thing of which there was never enough: time to think, time to write.

16 The passage is primarily concerned with the

(A) different ways a writer uses imagination
(B) variety of roles a woman has during her lifetime
(C) contrasting theories of writing that are held today
(D) tendency for authors to confuse the real and the imaginary
(E) tension between traditional female roles and a writer's needs

17 The author's statement that "writing is renaming" (line 22) suggests a conviction that writing involves

(A) gaining a large vocabulary of traditional definitions
(B) safeguarding language from change through misuse
(C) realizing that definitions are more important than perceptions
(D) transforming ideas in an active and creative manner
(E) overcoming the desire to use contradictory examples

18 The author's attitude toward those who believe a writer must become a "devouring ego" (line 30) in order to write well is one of

(A) reluctant agreement
(B) confused ambivalence
(C) casual indifference
(D) emphatic disapproval
(E) personal abhorrence

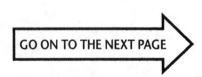
GO ON TO THE NEXT PAGE

19 The author suggests that, in the future, women writers who are caring for small children will have the opportunity to

(A) join two tasks into a single effort that requires little attention
(B) integrate two pursuits in a way that enhances both experiences
(C) identify two roles as a means of choosing one role over the other
(D) articulate two impulses that have become indistinguishable
(E) obtain the formal training necessary to accomplish two goals

20 According to the passage, which of the following is a necessary prerequisite to writing well?

(A) Opportunities for the imagination to function actively
(B) Freedom to read widely among great writers of the past
(C) Shaping thoughts through disciplined study
(D) Complete withdrawal into the self
(E) Desire for literary continuity

GO ON TO THE NEXT PAGE

Questions 21-30 are based on the following passage.   ~fact~

The following passage was adapted from an account by two scientists about the emergence of genetics, the science of inherited traits.

You have seen them in movies: scientists who are infallible and coldly objective—little more than animated computers in white lab coats. They
Line take measurements and record results as if the
(5) collection of data were the sole object of their lives. The assumption: If one gathers enough facts about something, the relationships between those facts will spontaneously reveal themselves.
Nonsense!
(10) The myth of the infallible scientist evaporates when one thinks of the number of great ideas in science whose originators were correct in general but wrong in detail. The English physicist John Dalton (1766-1844) gets credit for modern atomic
(15) theory, but his mathematical formulas for calculating atomic weights were incorrect. The Polish astronomer Copernicus, who corrected Ptolemy's ancient concept of an Earth-centered universe, nevertheless was mistaken in the particulars of the
(20) planets' orbits.
Luck, too, has played a determining role in scientific discovery. The French chemist Pasteur demonstrated that life does not arise spontaneously from air. But it may have been luck that he
(25) happened to use an easy-to-kill yeast and not the hay bacillus that another, long-forgotten, investigator had chosen for the same experiment. We now know that hay bacillus is heat-resistant and grows even after the boiling that killed Pasteur's yeast. If
(30) Pasteur had used the hay bacillus, his "proof" would not have materialized.
Gregor Mendel, the founder of modern genetics, epitomizes the humanness of the scientist. Plant hybridization intrigued and puzzled Mendel, an
(35) Augustinian monk with some training in mathematics and the natural sciences. He had read in the professional literature that crosses between certain species regularly yielded many hybrids with identical traits; but when hybrids were
(40) crossed, all kinds of strange new combinations of traits cropped up. The principle of inheritance, if there was one, was elusive.
Mendel had the basic idea that there might be simple mathematical relationships among plants
(45) in different generations. To pursue this hypothesis, he decided to establish experimental plots in the monastery garden at Brünn, raise a number of varieties of peas, interbreed them, count and classify the offspring of each generation, and see whether
(50) any reliable mathematical ratios could be deduced.
After many years of meticulously growing, harvesting, and counting pea plants, Mendel thought

he had something worth talking about. So, in 1865, he appeared before the Brünn Society for the Study
(55) of Natural Science, reported on his research, and postulated what have since come to be called the Mendelian laws. Society members listened politely but, insofar as anybody knows, asked few questions and engaged in little discussion. It may even be
(60) that, as he proceeded, a certain suspicion emerged out of the embarrassed silence. After all, Mendel lacked a degree and had published no research. Now, if Pasteur had advanced this idea . . .
Mendel's assertion that separate and distinct
(65) "elements" of inheritance must exist, despite the fact that he couldn't produce any, was close to asking the society to accept something on faith. There was no evidence for Mendel's hypothesis other than his computations; and his wildly uncon-
(70) ventional application of algebra to botany made it difficult for his listeners to understand that those computations *were* the evidence.
Mendel undoubtedly died without knowing that his findings on peas had indeed illuminated a well-
(75) nigh universal pattern. Luck had been with him in his choice of which particular traits to study. We now know that groups of genes do not always act independently. Often they are linked, their effect being to transmit a "package" of traits. Knowing
(80) nothing about genes, let alone the phenomenon of linkage, Mendel was spared failure because the traits that he chose to follow were each controlled separately.* The probability of making such a happy choice in random picks is only about 1 in 163!

*Some scientists believe that Mendel actually did have some idea of linkage and did choose traits purposefully.

21 The word "Nonsense!" (line 9) conveys the extent to which the authors

(A) object to the tendency of scientists to rely on existing data
(B) reject the way in which scientists are portrayed in the media
(C) are amused at the accidental nature of some scientific findings
(D) oppose the glorification of certain scientists at the expense of others
(E) realize the necessity of objectivity in research

GO ON TO THE NEXT PAGE

22 The authors cite the example of Copernicus (lines 16-20) to substantiate which of the following claims?

(A) The achievements of scientists are not always recognized.
(B) Scientific progress depends on a variety of factors.
(C) Scientists often suffer from professional jealousy and competition.
(D) Noted scientists are not always wholly accurate in their theories.
(E) A scientist may stumble on an important truth accidentally.

23 The term "humanness" (line 33) as it is applied to Mendel refers to

(A) the tendency to rely excessively on emotion
(B) an interest in improving the human condition through scientific research
(C) an attitude of forgiveness toward those who underrated him
(D) a combination of intellect, intuition, and good fortune
(E) a talent for persevering in the face of opposition

24 In the passage, Pasteur's use of a certain yeast is comparable to

(A) a previous investigator's use of the hay bacillus
(B) Dalton's discovery of atomic weights
(C) Mendel's choice of traits to study
(D) Copernicus' study of the universe
(E) Mendel's use of mathematical ratios

25 In lines 61-63, the authors imply that in comparison to Mendel, Pasteur

(A) was a more proficient researcher
(B) based his theories on more extensive investigations
(C) possessed a more impressive professional reputation
(D) was more meticulous in his observations
(E) devoted more energy to promoting his scientific ideas

26 The "universal pattern" (line 75) refers to

(A) the initial skepticism with which new ideas are received
(B) a tendency of botanists to resist purely theoretical proof
(C) the way peas tend to exhibit the quality of linked traits
(D) the way traits usually reappear in succeeding generations
(E) a similarity between Mendel's experiments and those of succeeding geneticists

27 The word "happy" (line 84) most nearly means

(A) joyful
(B) fortunate
(C) willing
(D) dazed
(E) pleasing

28 The passage suggests that Mendel's contemporaries assumed that valid biological theories

(A) are often proposed by inexperienced researchers
(B) cannot be based on mathematical proof alone
(C) must be supported by years of careful research
(D) often represent a departure from established practice
(E) must be circulated to a wide audience

29 The passage suggests that Mendel's experiments succeeded because

(A) Mendel was able to convince his colleagues to support his research
(B) Mendel discovered flaws in his research design and corrected them
(C) Mendel had a thorough understanding of the concept of linked traits
(D) the scientific community finally understood the connection between mathematical computations and heredity
(E) the traits in peas happen to reappear in a distinct and predictable way

30 As described in the passage, the experiences of Mendel are most like those of

(A) Albert Einstein, who fled Nazi Germany to become the most famous physicist of this century
(B) Pierre Curie, whose career as a chemist was cut short by a tragic accident
(C) Barbara McClintock, whose theories about inherited traits in corn were not understood or accepted until long after she had advanced them
(D) Leonardo da Vinci, whose numerous attempts to make a successful flying machine resulted in failure
(E) James Watson and Francis Crick, who competed with other teams of scientists in the race to unravel the genetic code

IF YOU FINISH BEFORE TIME IS CALLED, YOU MAY CHECK YOUR WORK ON THIS SECTION ONLY. DO NOT TURN TO ANY OTHER SECTION IN THE TEST. **STOP**

481

Section 4 4 4 4 4

Time—30 Minutes
25 Questions

This section contains two types of questions. You have 30 minutes to complete both types. You may use any available space for scratchwork.

Notes:

1. The use of a calculator is permitted. All numbers used are real numbers.

2. Figures that accompany problems in this test are intended to provide information useful in solving the problems. They are drawn as accurately as possible EXCEPT when it is stated in a specific problem that the figure is not drawn to scale. All figures lie in a plane unless otherwise indicated.

Reference Information

$A = \pi r^2$
$C = 2\pi r$

$A = \ell w$

$A = \frac{1}{2}bh$

$V = \ell w h$

$V = \pi r^2 h$

$c^2 = a^2 + b^2$

Special Right Triangles

The number of degrees of arc in a circle is 360.
The measure in degrees of a straight angle is 180.
The sum of the measures in degrees of the angles of a triangle is 180.

Directions for Quantitative Comparison Questions

Questions 1-15 each consist of two quantities in boxes, one in Column A and one in Column B. You are to compare the two quantities and on the answer sheet fill in oval

  A if the quantity in Column A is greater;
  B if the quantity in Column B is greater;
  C if the two quantities are equal;
  D if the relationship cannot be determined
     from the information given.

AN E RESPONSE WILL NOT BE SCORED.

Notes:

1. In some questions, information is given about one or both of the quantities to be compared. In such cases, the given information is centered above the two columns and is not boxed.
2. In a given question, a symbol that appears in both columns represents the same thing in Column A as it does in Column B.
3. Letters such as x, n, and k stand for real numbers.

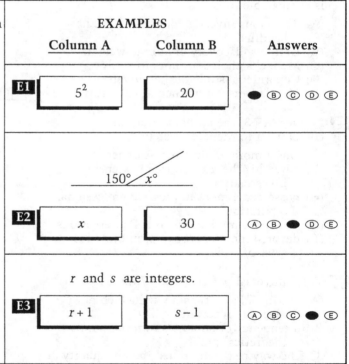

EXAMPLES

Column A	Column B	Answers
E1 5^2	20	● Ⓑ Ⓒ Ⓓ Ⓔ

150° $x°$

Column A	Column B	Answers
E2 x	30	Ⓐ Ⓑ ● Ⓓ Ⓔ

r and s are integers.

Column A	Column B	Answers
E3 $r+1$	$s-1$	Ⓐ Ⓑ Ⓒ ● Ⓔ

GO ON TO THE NEXT PAGE →

SUMMARY DIRECTIONS FOR COMPARISON QUESTIONS

<u>Answer:</u> A if the quantity in Column A is greater;
B if the quantity in Column B is greater;
C if the two quantities are equal;
D if the relationship cannot be determined from the information given.

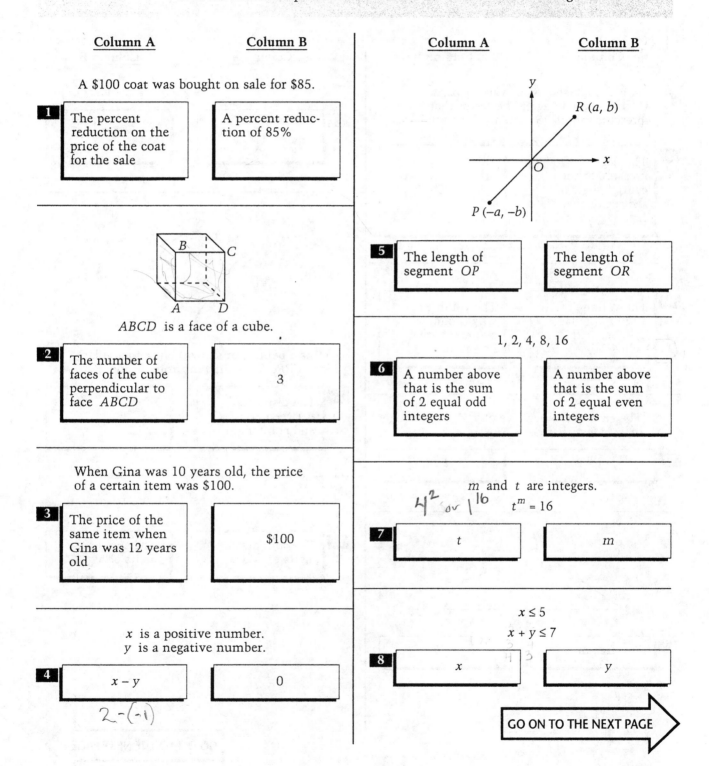

Column A	Column B

A $100 coat was bought on sale for $85.

1 | The percent reduction on the price of the coat for the sale | A percent reduction of 85%

ABCD is a face of a cube.

2 | The number of faces of the cube perpendicular to face *ABCD* | 3

When Gina was 10 years old, the price of a certain item was $100.

3 | The price of the same item when Gina was 12 years old | $100

x is a positive number.
y is a negative number.

4 | $x - y$ | 0

$2 - (-1)$

Column A	Column B

$R\,(a, b)$

$P\,(-a, -b)$

5 | The length of segment *OP* | The length of segment *OR*

1, 2, 4, 8, 16

6 | A number above that is the sum of 2 equal odd integers | A number above that is the sum of 2 equal even integers

m and *t* are integers.
4^2 or 16 $t^m = 16$

7 | t | m

$x \le 5$
$x + y \le 7$

8 | x | y

GO ON TO THE NEXT PAGE

4 4 4 4 4 4

SUMMARY DIRECTIONS FOR COMPARISON QUESTIONS

Answer: A if the quantity in Column A is greater;
B if the quantity in Column B is greater;
C if the two quantities are equal;
D if the relationship cannot be determined from the information given.

Column A	Column B

rent

A circle graph shows the various parts of a household budget. The sector that represents rent is 25 percent of the total area.

9 | The degree measure of the central angle of the sector that represents rent | 90°

10 | The volume of a right circular cylinder with radius 3 | The volume of a right circular cylinder with height 3

The sum of the negative of t and the square of s is less than 2.

11 | $t + 2$ | s^2

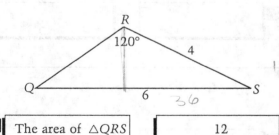

12 | The area of $\triangle QRS$ | 12

Column A	Column B

$f > g > 0$

13 | $\dfrac{f+1}{f}$ | $\dfrac{g+1}{g}$

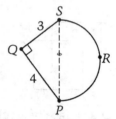

T is a point (not shown) on semicircular arc SRP. T is different from S and P.

14 | The distance between point Q and point T | 3

k is a positive integer.
$v = 10 \times k$

15 | The sum of the digits of k | The sum of the digits of v

GO ON TO THE NEXT PAGE

484

Directions for Student-Produced Response Questions

Each of the remaining 10 questions requires you to solve the problem and enter your answer by marking the ovals in the special grid, as shown in the examples below.

Answer: $\frac{7}{12}$ or 7/12

Answer: 2.5

Answer: 201
Either position is correct.

Write answer in boxes. →

←Fraction line

←Decimal point

Grid in result. →

Note: You may start your answers in any column, space permitting. Columns not needed should be left blank.

- Mark no more than one oval in any column.

- Because the answer sheet will be machine-scored, **you will receive credit only if the ovals are filled in correctly.**

- Although not required, it is suggested that you write your answer in the boxes at the top of the columns to help you fill in the ovals accurately.

- Some problems may have more than one correct answer. In such cases, grid only one answer.

- No question has a negative answer.

- **Mixed numbers** such as $2\frac{1}{2}$ must be gridded as 2.5 or 5/2. (If $\boxed{2\,|\,1\,/\,2}$ is gridded, it will be interpreted as $\frac{21}{2}$, not $2\frac{1}{2}$.)

- **Decimal Accuracy**: If you obtain a decimal answer, **enter the most accurate value the grid will accommodate.** For example, if you obtain an answer such as 0.6666 . . . , you should record the result as .666 or .667. **Less accurate values such as .66 or .67 are not acceptable.**

Acceptable ways to grid $\frac{2}{3}$ = .6666 . . .

16 If $\diamond\!\!\!\!\begin{smallmatrix} a & b \\ c & d \end{smallmatrix}\!\!\!\!\diamond$ is defined by $\diamond\!\!\!\!\begin{smallmatrix} a & b \\ c & d \end{smallmatrix}\!\!\!\!\diamond = ad + bc$, what is the value of $\diamond\!\!\!\!\begin{smallmatrix} 2 & 3 \\ 6 & 4 \end{smallmatrix}\!\!\!\!\diamond$?

2(4) + 3(6) =
8 + 18

17 A recipe calls for $7\frac{1}{3}$ tablespoons of milk. This amount is equivalent to how many teaspoons of milk? (3 teaspoons = 1 tablespoon)

7.33 - milk

21

GO ON TO THE NEXT PAGE

18 If $0.92x = 9.2$, what is the value of $\frac{1}{x}$?

$x = 10$

$\dfrac{1}{10}$

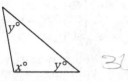

Note: Figure not drawn to scale.

$36, 37$

19 In the triangle above, x and y are integers.
If $35 < y < 40$, what is one possible value of x ?

108
106

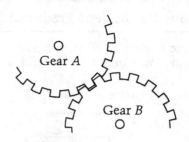

Note: Figure not drawn to scale.

20 The figure above shows parts of two circular gears whose teeth interlock when the gears turn. Gear A has 72 teeth and gear B has 48 teeth. How many complete revolutions does gear A make when gear B makes 9 complete revolutions?

21 If the sum of two numbers is 2 and their difference is 1, what is their product?

2

$1 + 1$

GO ON TO THE NEXT PAGE

486

22 If $27^{15} = 3^y$, what is the value of y ?

23 If the perimeter of a rectangle is 10 times the width of the rectangle, then the length of the rectangle is how many times the width?

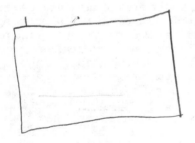

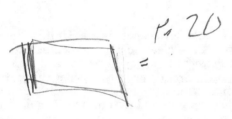

24 There are 120 red marbles and 80 blue marbles in a bag that contains 200 marbles. If only blue marbles are to be added to the bag so that the probability of randomly drawing a blue marble from the bag becomes $\frac{2}{3}$, how many blue marbles must be added to the bag?

$$120x + 80x = 200$$

25 The average (arithmetic mean) of 5 positive integers is 350. Two of the integers are 99 and 102 and the other integers are greater than 102. If all 5 integers are different, what is the greatest possible value for any of the 5 integers?

IF YOU FINISH BEFORE TIME IS CALLED, YOU MAY CHECK YOUR WORK ON THIS SECTION ONLY. DO NOT TURN TO ANY OTHER SECTION IN THE TEST. **STOP**

For each question in this section, select the best answer from among the choices given and fill in the corresponding oval on the answer sheet.

The two passages below are followed by questions based on their content and on the relationship between the two passages. Answer the questions on the basis of what is stated or implied in the passages and in any introductory material that may be provided.

Questions 1-13 refer to the following passages.

These two passages reflect two different views of the values and integrity of journalism. Passage 1 is from a 1990 account of the origins of investigative journalism and "muckraking." Passage 2 was written in the 1920's by a noted satirist famous for voicing strong opinions. recollective

Passage 1

Since the lineage of investigative journalism is most directly traceable to the Progressive era of the early 1900's, it is not surprising that the
Line President of the United States at the time was
(5) among the first to articulate its political dimensions. Theodore Roosevelt called investigative reporters "muckrakers," after a character from John Bunyan's *Pilgrim's Progress* who humbly cleaned "the filth off the floor." Despite the mis-
(10) givings implied by the comparison, Roosevelt saw the muckrakers as "often indispensable to the well-being of society":

> There are in the body politic, economic and
> social, many and grave evils, and there is
(15) > urgent necessity for the sternest war upon
> them. There should be relentless exposure
> of and attack upon every evil man, whether
> politician or businessman.

Roosevelt recognized the value-laden character
(20) of investigative journalism. He perceived correctly that investigative reporters are committed to unearthing *wrongdoing*. For these journalists, disclosures of morally outrageous conduct maximize the opportunity for the forces of "good" to recog-
(25) nize and do battle with the forces of "evil."
—So, the current folklore surrounding investigative reporting closely resembles the American ideal of popular democracy. Vigilant journalists bring wrongdoing to public attention. An informed
(30) citizenry responds by demanding reforms from their elected representatives. Policymakers respond in turn by taking corrective action. Partly a product of its muckraking roots, this idealized perspective is also an outgrowth of the commonly perceived
(35) effects of exposés published in the early 1970's. The most celebrated of these exposés were the news stories that linked top White House officials to Watergate crimes.* These stories were widely held responsible for the public's loss of confidence
(40) in the Nixon administration, ultimately forcing the President's resignation.
—Investigative journalists *intend* to provoke outrage in their reports of malfeasance. Their work is validated when citizens respond by demanding
(45) change from their leaders. By bringing problems to public attention, the "journalists of outrage" attempt to alter societal agendas.

*The burglarizing of the Democratic party headquarters at the Watergate complex and other crimes committed during the 1972 presidential elections

Passage 2

What ails newspapers in the United States is the fact that their gigantic commercial development
(50) compels them to appeal to larger and larger masses of undifferentiated people and that the truth is the commodity that the masses of undifferentiated people cannot be induced to buy. The dominant citizen of democratic society, despite a superficial
(55) appearance of intelligence, is really quite incapable of anything resembling reasoning.
So, the problem before a modern newspaper, hard pressed by the need of carrying on a thoroughly wholesome business, is that of enlisting the interest
(60) of these masses of people, and by interest, of course, I do not mean their mere listless attention, but their active emotional cooperation. Unless a newspaper can manage to arouse these people's *feelings* it might just as well not have at them at all, for their feelings
(65) are the essential part of them, and it is out of their feelings that they dredge up their obscure loyalties and aversions. Well, and how are their feelings to be stirred up? At bottom, the business is quite simple. First scare them—and then reassure them.
(70) First get people into a panic with a bugaboo—and then go to the rescue, gallantly and uproariously, with a stuffed club to lay it. First fake 'em—and then fake 'em again.

GO ON TO THE NEXT PAGE →

(75) Insofar as our public gazettes have any serious business at all, it is the business of snouting out and exhibiting new and startling horrors, atrocities, impending calamities, tyrannies, villainies, enormities, mortal perils, jeopardies, outrages, catastrophes—first snouting out and exhibiting
(80) them, and then magnificently circumventing and disposing of them. The first part is easy. It is almost unheard of for the mob to disbelieve in a new bugaboo. As soon as the hideous form is unveiled it begins to quake and cry out: the reser-
(85) voir of its primary fears is always ready to run over. And the second part is not much more difficult. The one thing demanded of the remedy is that it be simple, more or less familiar, easy to comprehend, that it make no draft upon the higher
(90) cerebral centers—that it avoid leading the shy and delicate intelligence of the mob into strange and hence painful fields of speculation. All healthy journalism in America—healthy in the sense that it flourishes spontaneously and needs no outside
(95) aid—is based firmly upon just such an invention and scotching of bugaboos. And so is all politics. Whatever stands above that fundamental imposture is an artificiality. Intelligent and honest journalism and politics—these things, in a democratic
(100) society, have no legitimate place. They are, when they are encountered, exotic curiosities, pale and clammy orchids, half-fabulous beasts in cages.

1 Passage 1 suggests that Roosevelt's choice of name for investigative reporters reflects his belief that

(A) they were irresponsible about checking the accuracy of their reporting
(B) their writing style was unrefined and colloquial
(C) they were motivated by greed and desire for fame
(D) they were unsung and underpaid
(E) they did unpleasant but necessary work

2 The terms "folklore" (line 26) and "idealized perspective" (line 33) suggest that the author of Passage 1 would agree with which statement?

(A) Democracy and journalism are incompatible.
(B) Investigative journalism depends on creating a false villain.
(C) Many people have a romanticized conception of the role of journalists.
(D) Readers are easily swayed by appeals to their patriotism.
(E) People seldom believe what they read in newspapers.

3 The author of Passage 1 refers to the report on the "Watergate crimes" (line 38) primarily as an example of

(A) a story covered better by television than by print media
(B) editorial pandering to an ignorant public
(C) journalism that had a tangible effect on politics
(D) a flagrant abuse of the freedom of the press
(E) the subversion of legitimate political power

4 In the last paragraph of Passage 1 (lines 42-47), the author is

(A) showing how investigative reporting has broken with its past tradition
(B) acknowledging that reporters are not merely trying to impart information
(C) disparaging those who believe that meaningful reform is possible
(D) expressing sympathy for victims of overzealous reportage
(E) citing an exception to the generalization mentioned by Roosevelt

5 The brand of journalism discussed in Passage 1 is based on the assumption that

(A) public awareness of injustice is necessary for change to occur
(B) newspapers are read chiefly for information that will help people to get ahead
(C) most people take for granted that politicians are corrupt
(D) most people are suspicious of whistle-blowers
(E) most people's beliefs are inconsistent with their actions

6 In line 53, "dominant" most nearly means

(A) compelling
(B) influential
(C) headstrong
(D) typical
(E) superior

GO ON TO THE NEXT PAGE

7 The tactics described in lines 69-73 convey the

(A) main difference between reporters' and editors' attitudes toward the public
(B) immense difficulty involved in solving society's problems
(C) physical danger that occasionally awaits reporters
(D) extent to which journalism relies on manipulation
(E) reason why newspapers are so seldom profitable

8 In the last sentence of Passage 2, the author mentions orchids and beasts in order to

(A) give an example of sensationalism in newspaper reporting
(B) suggest something so unusual as to be bizarre
(C) indicate a preference for fiction over news
(D) chide newspapers for dealing with excessively morbid subjects
(E) cite exceptions that disprove the previous sentence

9 Both passages indicate that a fundamental ingredient in the success of a newspaper is

(A) financial assistance from the government
(B) a thirst for truth
(C) commercial development
(D) reporters of great integrity
(E) an engaged readership

10 The author of Passage 2 would most likely respond to the journalists' view in Passage 1 of the battle between the forces of "good" and "evil" (lines 24-25) by

(A) praising the journalists' idealism
(B) mocking the journalists' naïveté
(C) admiring the journalists' wit
(D) arguing that good and evil are not easily defined
(E) offering exceptions to the general rule

11 Unlike Passage 2, Passage 1 assumes that newspapers generally

(A) cater to a thoughtful, responsible citizenry
(B) rely on an obedient and docile public for assent
(C) are compromised by the advertising that supports them
(D) are read by only an elite minority of subscribers
(E) require close supervision by government censors

12 Both authors' discussions assume that the public

(A) ignores the press more often than not
(B) will react when prompted by the press
(C) is indifferent to corruption
(D) has a higher degree of literacy than is found in most other countries
(E) is well-informed and astute in its political choices

13 The two authors would most likely agree with which statement?

(A) Newspapers are a powerful means of getting the public's attention.
(B) Journalism is an important force for good.
(C) Competition between newspapers tends to improve the coverage of news.
(D) Most investigative journalism is actually driven by the profit motive.
(E) A knowledge of history is more important to a journalist than is a talent for writing.

IF YOU FINISH BEFORE TIME IS CALLED, YOU MAY CHECK YOUR WORK ON THIS SECTION ONLY. DO NOT TURN TO ANY OTHER SECTION IN THE TEST. **STOP**

Section 7

7

Time—15 Minutes
10 Questions

In this section solve each problem, using any available space on the page for scratchwork. Then decide which is the best of the choices given and fill in the corresponding oval on the answer sheet.

Notes:

1. The use of a calculator is permitted. All numbers used are real numbers.

2. Figures that accompany problems in this test are intended to provide information useful in solving the problems. They are drawn as accurately as possible EXCEPT when it is stated in a specific problem that the figure is not drawn to scale. All figures lie in a plane unless otherwise indicated.

Reference Information

$A = \pi r^2$
$C = 2\pi r$

$A = \ell w$

$A = \frac{1}{2}bh$

$V = \ell wh$

$V = \pi r^2 h$

$c^2 = a^2 + b^2$

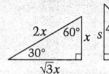
Special Right Triangles

The number of degrees of arc in a circle is 360.
The measure in degrees of a straight angle is 180.
The sum of the measures in degrees of the angles of a triangle is 180.

---

1 If $x^2 = y^3$ and $x = 8$, what is the value of y ?

(A) 2
(B) 4
(C) 5
(D) 6
(E) 12

$8^2 = 64$

---

2 Stickers are 4 for \$0.80 (including tax) and trading cards are 3 for \$1.05 (including tax). What is Kim's change from \$5.00 if she buys 8 stickers and 6 trading cards at these prices?

(A) \$0.30
(B) \$1.00
(C) \$1.30
(D) \$3.70
(E) \$4.00

6.40

6.35

GO ON TO THE NEXT PAGE

3 C is the midpoint of line segment AB, and D and E are the midpoints of line segments AC and CB, respectively. If the length of DE is 8, what is the length of AB ?

(A)　4
(B)　8
(C)　12
(D)　16
(E)　32

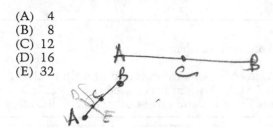

4 Carla has 2 more than 3 times the number of cassette tapes that Jules has. If C represents the number of Carla's tapes and if J represents the number of Jules's tapes, which of the following is a correct expression relating C and J ?

(A)　$C = 2J + 3$
(B)　$C = 2(J + 3)$
(C)　$C = 3J - 2$
(D)　$C = 3J + 2$
(E)　$C = 3(J + 2)$

C

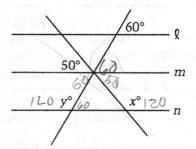

5 In the figure above, five lines intersect as shown. If lines ℓ, m, and n are parallel, what is the value of $x + y$?

(A)　210
(B)　220
(C)　230
(D)　240
(E)　250

GO ON TO THE NEXT PAGE

Questions 6-7 refer to the following table.

PROJECTED SALES FOR GAME Q

Price of Game Q	Projected Number of Games Sold
$50	50,000
$30	100,000
$10	150,000

6 Based on the projections, how much more money would be received from sales of game Q when the price is $30 than when the price is $50?

(A) $50,000
(B) $100,000
(C) $500,000
(D) $1,000,000
(E) $2,750,000

---

7 Which of the following graphs best represents the relationship between the price of game Q and the projected number of games sold, as indicated by the table?

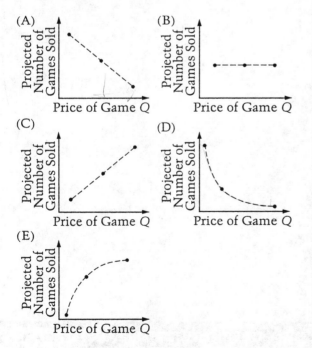

8 In the repeating decimal
$$0.\overline{12468} = 0.1246812468\ldots,$$
where the digits 12468 repeat, which digit is in the 4,000th place to the right of the decimal point?

(A) 1
(B) 2
(C) 4
(D) 6
(E) 8

GO ON TO THE NEXT PAGE

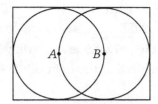

9 In the figure above, A and B are the centers of the two circles. If each circle has area 10, what is the area of the rectangle?

(A) 20

(B) $20 - \dfrac{10}{\pi}$

(C) $\dfrac{40}{\pi}$

(D) $\dfrac{50}{\pi}$

(E) $\dfrac{60}{\pi}$

10 There are 3 roads from Plattsville to Ocean Heights and 4 roads from Ocean Heights to Bay Cove. If Martina drives from Plattsville to Bay Cove and back, passes through Ocean Heights in both directions, and does not travel any road twice, how many different routes for the trip are possible?

(A) 72
(B) 36
(C) 24
(D) 18
(E) 12

SAT I Scoring Worksheet

SAT I Verbal Sections

A. Section 1:

$$\underline{\hspace{3cm}} - (\underline{\hspace{3cm}} \div 4) = \underline{\hspace{3cm}}$$
no. correct — no. incorrect — subtotal A

B. Section 3:

$$\underline{\hspace{3cm}} - (\underline{\hspace{3cm}} \div 4) = \underline{\hspace{3cm}}$$
no. correct — no. incorrect — subtotal B

C. Section 6:

$$\underline{\hspace{3cm}} - (\underline{\hspace{3cm}} \div 4) = \underline{\hspace{3cm}}$$
no. correct — no. incorrect — subtotal C

D. Total unrounded raw score
(Total A + B + C)

$$\underline{\hspace{3cm}}$$
D

E. Total rounded raw score
(Rounded to nearest whole number)

$$\underline{\hspace{3cm}}$$
E

F. SAT I verbal reported scaled score
(See the appropriate conversion table on back cover)

SAT I verbal
score

SAT I Mathematical Sections

A. Section 2:

$$\underline{\hspace{3cm}} - (\underline{\hspace{3cm}} \div 4) = \underline{\hspace{3cm}}$$
no. correct — no. incorrect — subtotal A

B. Section 4:
Questions 1-15 (quantitative comparison)

$$\underline{\hspace{3cm}} - (\underline{\hspace{3cm}} \div 3) = \underline{\hspace{3cm}}$$
no. correct — no. incorrect — subtotal B

C. Section 4:
Questions 16-25 (student-produced response)

$$\underline{\hspace{3cm}} = \underline{\hspace{3cm}}$$
no. correct — subtotal C

D. Section 7:

$$\underline{\hspace{3cm}} - (\underline{\hspace{3cm}} \div 4) = \underline{\hspace{3cm}}$$
no. correct — no. incorrect — subtotal D

E. Total unrounded raw score
(Total A + B + C + D)

$$\underline{\hspace{3cm}}$$
E

F. Total rounded raw score
(Rounded to nearest whole number)

$$\underline{\hspace{3cm}}$$
F

G. SAT I mathematical reported scaled score
(See the appropriate conversion table on back cover)

SAT I
mathematical
score

Score Conversion Table
SAT I: Reasoning Test
Saturday, November 1995
Recentered Scale

Raw Score	Verbal Scaled Score	Math Scaled Score	Raw Score	Verbal Scaled Score	Math Scaled Score
78	800		37	510	560
77	800		36	510	560
76	800		35	500	550
75	780		34	490	540
74	770		33	490	530
73	750		32	480	530
72	740		31	480	520
71	730		30	470	510
70	720		29	470	510
69	710		28	460	500
68	700		27	450	490
67	690		26	450	490
66	680		25	440	480
65	680		24	440	470
64	670		23	430	470
63	660		22	420	460
62	660		21	420	460
61	650		20	410	450
60	640	800	19	410	440
59	640	790	18	400	440
58	630	770	17	390	430
57	620	750	16	390	420
56	620	730	15	380	420
55	610	720	14	370	410
54	610	710	13	370	400
53	600	700	12	360	400
52	600	690	11	350	390
51	590	680	10	340	380
50	580	670	9	340	370
49	580	660	8	330	360
48	570	650	7	320	350
47	570	640	6	310	340
46	560	630	5	300	330
45	560	630	4	290	320
44	550	620	3	280	300
43	540	610	2	270	290
42	540	600	1	260	270
41	530	590	0	240	260
40	530	590	-1	230	240
39	520	580	-2	210	220
38	520	570	-3 and below	200	200

This table is for use only with this test.

SAT I: Reasoning Test

Saturday, May 1996

SAT® I: Reasoning Test

Calculator use is permitted on the mathematics sections only.

You will have three hours to work on the questions in this test book. There are **five 30-minute sections and two 15-minute sections**. The supervisor will tell you when to begin and end each section. If you finish before time is called, you may check your work on that section, but you may <u>not work on any other section</u>.

Do not worry if you are unable to finish a section or if there are some questions you cannot answer. Do not waste time puzzling over a question that seems too difficult for you. Work as rapidly as you can without sacrificing accuracy.

Students often ask whether they should guess when they are uncertain about the answer to a question. Scores on the multiple-choice questions on this test are based on the number of questions answered correctly minus a fraction of the number answered incorrectly. Therefore, it is unlikely that random or haphazard guessing will change your scores significantly. If you have some knowledge of a question, you may be able to eliminate one or more of the answer choices as wrong. It is generally a good idea to guess which of the remaining choices is correct.

Some mathematics questions have no answer choices. Instead, you must solve the problem and record your answer in a special grid on your answer sheet. For these questions, you will receive credit for correct answers, but there will be no deduction for incorrect answers.

Mark all your answers on the separate answer sheet. Mark only one answer for each question. Since the answer sheet will be machine scored, be sure that each mark is dark and that it completely fills the oval. In each section of the answer sheet, there are spaces to answer 40 questions. When there are fewer than 40 questions in a section of your test, use only the spaces that correspond to the question numbers. Do not make stray marks on the answer sheet. If you erase, do so completely, because an incomplete erasure may be scored as an intended response.

You may use the test book for scratchwork, but you will not receive credit for anything written there.

(The passages for this test have been adapted from published material. The ideas contained in them do not necessarily represent the opinions of the College Board or Educational Testing Service.)

DO NOT OPEN THIS BOOK UNTIL THE SUPERVISOR TELLS YOU TO DO SO.

Use a No. 2 pencil only. Be sure each mark is dark and completely fills the intended oval. Completely erase any errors or stray marks.

1. Your Name

First 4 letters of Last Name | First init. | Mid. init.

(A) (B) (C) (D) (E) (F) (G) (H) (I) (J) (K) (L) (M) (N) (O) (P) (Q) (R) (S) (T) (U) (V) (W) (X) (Y) (Z)

2.

Your Name: _____
(Print)
Last   First   M.I.

Signature: _____   Date: __/__/__

Home Address: _____
(Print)
Number and Street

City   State   Zip Code

Center: _____
(Print)
City   State   Center Number

IMPORTANT: Please fill in items 8 and 9 exactly as shown on the back cover of your test book.

8. Form Code

(Copy and grid as on back of test book.)

(A) (B) (C) (D) (E) (F) (G) (H) (I) (J) (K) (L) (M) (N) (O) (P) (Q) (R) (S) (T) (U) (V) (W) (X) (Y) (Z)
0 1 2 3 4 5 6 7 8 9

3. Date Of Birth

Month	Day	Year
Jan.		
Feb.		
Mar.	0 0	0 0
Apr.	1 1	1 1
May	2 2	2 2
June	3 3	3 3
July	4	4 4
Aug.	5	5 5
Sept.	6	6 6
Oct.	7	7 7
Nov.	8	8 8
Dec.	9	9

4. Social Security Number

0 1 2 3 4 5 6 7 8 9 (across all columns)

5. Sex

Female ○   Male ○

7. Test Book Serial Number
(Copy from front of test book.)

6. Registration Number

(Copy from your Admission Ticket.)

0 1 2 3 4 5 6 7 8 9 (across all columns)

FOR ETS USE ONLY

9. Test Form
(Copy from back cover of test book.)

DO NOT WRITE IN THIS AREA.

Start with number 1 for each new section. If a section has fewer questions than answer spaces, leave the extra answer spaces blank.

SECTION 1

1–40 (A) (B) (C) (D) (E)

SECTION 2

1–40 (A) (B) (C) (D) (E)

Q2564-06/1   CHW93050
48560 • 09132 • TF23P750e
1   2   3   4
I.N.207085

501

Use a No. 2 pencil only. Be sure each mark is dark and completely fills the intended oval. Completely erase any errors or stray marks.

Start with number 1 for each new section. If a section has fewer questions than answer spaces, leave the extra answer spaces blank.

SECTION 3

1 (A) (B) (C) (D) (E)
2 (A) (B) (C) (D) (E)
3 (A) (B) (C) (D) (E)
4 (A) (B) (C) (D) (E)
5 (A) (B) (C) (D) (E)
6 (A) (B) (C) (D) (E)
7 (A) (B) (C) (D) (E)
8 (A) (B) (C) (D) (E)
9 (A) (B) (C) (D) (E)
10 (A) (B) (C) (D) (E)
11 (A) (B) (C) (D) (E)
12 (A) (B) (C) (D) (E)
13 (A) (B) (C) (D) (E)
14 (A) (B) (C) (D) (E)
15 (A) (B) (C) (D) (E)

16 (A) (B) (C) (D) (E)
17 (A) (B) (C) (D) (E)
18 (A) (B) (C) (D) (E)
19 (A) (B) (C) (D) (E)
20 (A) (B) (C) (D) (E)
21 (A) (B) (C) (D) (E)
22 (A) (B) (C) (D) (E)
23 (A) (B) (C) (D) (E)
24 (A) (B) (C) (D) (E)
25 (A) (B) (C) (D) (E)
26 (A) (B) (C) (D) (E)
27 (A) (B) (C) (D) (E)
28 (A) (B) (C) (D) (E)
29 (A) (B) (C) (D) (E)
30 (A) (B) (C) (D) (E)

31 (A) (B) (C) (D) (E)
32 (A) (B) (C) (D) (E)
33 (A) (B) (C) (D) (E)
34 (A) (B) (C) (D) (E)
35 (A) (B) (C) (D) (E)
36 (A) (B) (C) (D) (E)
37 (A) (B) (C) (D) (E)
38 (A) (B) (C) (D) (E)
39 (A) (B) (C) (D) (E)
40 (A) (B) (C) (D) (E)

If section 3 of your test book contains math questions that are not multiple-choice, continue to item 16 below. Otherwise, continue to item 16 above.

ONLY ANSWERS ENTERED IN THE OVALS IN EACH GRID AREA WILL BE SCORED.
YOU WILL NOT RECEIVE CREDIT FOR ANYTHING WRITTEN IN THE BOXES ABOVE THE OVALS.

16 17 18 19 20

21 22 23 24 25

BE SURE TO ERASE ANY ERRORS OR STRAY MARKS COMPLETELY.

PLEASE PRINT YOUR INITIALS

First   Middle   Last

THE COLLEGE BOARD — SAT I

Use a No. 2 pencil only. Be sure each mark is dark and completely fills the intended oval. Completely erase any errors or stray marks.

Start with number 1 for each new section. If a section has fewer questions than answer spaces, leave the extra answer spaces blank.

SECTION 4

1 (A) (B) (C) (D) (E)
2 (A) (B) (C) (D) (E)
3 (A) (B) (C) (D) (E)
4 (A) (B) (C) (D) (E)
5 (A) (B) (C) (D) (E)
6 (A) (B) (C) (D) (E)
7 (A) (B) (C) (D) (E)
8 (A) (B) (C) (D) (E)
9 (A) (B) (C) (D) (E)
10 (A) (B) (C) (D) (E)
11 (A) (B) (C) (D) (E)
12 (A) (B) (C) (D) (E)
13 (A) (B) (C) (D) (E)
14 (A) (B) (C) (D) (E)
15 (A) (B) (C) (D) (E)

16 (A) (B) (C) (D) (E)
17 (A) (B) (C) (D) (E)
18 (A) (B) (C) (D) (E)
19 (A) (B) (C) (D) (E)
20 (A) (B) (C) (D) (E)
21 (A) (B) (C) (D) (E)
22 (A) (B) (C) (D) (E)
23 (A) (B) (C) (D) (E)
24 (A) (B) (C) (D) (E)
25 (A) (B) (C) (D) (E)
26 (A) (B) (C) (D) (E)
27 (A) (B) (C) (D) (E)
28 (A) (B) (C) (D) (E)
29 (A) (B) (C) (D) (E)
30 (A) (B) (C) (D) (E)

31 (A) (B) (C) (D) (E)
32 (A) (B) (C) (D) (E)
33 (A) (B) (C) (D) (E)
34 (A) (B) (C) (D) (E)
35 (A) (B) (C) (D) (E)
36 (A) (B) (C) (D) (E)
37 (A) (B) (C) (D) (E)
38 (A) (B) (C) (D) (E)
39 (A) (B) (C) (D) (E)
40 (A) (B) (C) (D) (E)

If section 4 of your test book contains math questions that are not multiple-choice, continue to item 16 below. Otherwise, continue to item 16 above.

ONLY ANSWERS ENTERED IN THE OVALS IN EACH GRID AREA WILL BE SCORED.
YOU WILL NOT RECEIVE CREDIT FOR ANYTHING WRITTEN IN THE BOXES ABOVE THE OVALS.

16 17 18 19 20

21 22 23 24 25

BE SURE TO ERASE ANY ERRORS OR STRAY MARKS COMPLETELY.

PLEASE PRINT YOUR INITIALS

First   Middle   Last

503

Use a No. 2 pencil only. Be sure each mark is dark and completely fills the intended oval. Completely erase any errors or stray marks.

Start with number 1 for each new section. If a section has fewer questions than answer spaces, leave the extra answer spaces blank.

SECTION 5

1 A B C D E	11 A B C D E	21 A B C D E	31 A B C D E
2 A B C D E	12 A B C D E	22 A B C D E	32 A B C D E
3 A B C D E	13 A B C D E	23 A B C D E	33 A B C D E
4 A B C D E	14 A B C D E	24 A B C D E	34 A B C D E
5 A B C D E	15 A B C D E	25 A B C D E	35 A B C D E
6 A B C D E	16 A B C D E	26 A B C D E	36 A B C D E
7 A B C D E	17 A B C D E	27 A B C D E	37 A B C D E
8 A B C D E	18 A B C D E	28 A B C D E	38 A B C D E
9 A B C D E	19 A B C D E	29 A B C D E	39 A B C D E
10 A B C D E	20 A B C D E	30 A B C D E	40 A B C D E

SECTION 6

1 A B C D E	11 A B C D E	21 A B C D E	31 A B C D E
2 A B C D E	12 A B C D E	22 A B C D E	32 A B C D E
3 A B C D E	13 A B C D E	23 A B C D E	33 A B C D E
4 A B C D E	14 A B C D E	24 A B C D E	34 A B C D E
5 A B C D E	15 A B C D E	25 A B C D E	35 A B C D E
6 A B C D E	16 A B C D E	26 A B C D E	36 A B C D E
7 A B C D E	17 A B C D E	27 A B C D E	37 A B C D E
8 A B C D E	18 A B C D E	28 A B C D E	38 A B C D E
9 A B C D E	19 A B C D E	29 A B C D E	39 A B C D E
10 A B C D E	20 A B C D E	30 A B C D E	40 A B C D E

SECTION 7

1 A B C D E	11 A B C D E	21 A B C D E	31 A B C D E
2 A B C D E	12 A B C D E	22 A B C D E	32 A B C D E
3 A B C D E	13 A B C D E	23 A B C D E	33 A B C D E
4 A B C D E	14 A B C D E	24 A B C D E	34 A B C D E
5 A B C D E	15 A B C D E	25 A B C D E	35 A B C D E
6 A B C D E	16 A B C D E	26 A B C D E	36 A B C D E
7 A B C D E	17 A B C D E	27 A B C D E	37 A B C D E
8 A B C D E	18 A B C D E	28 A B C D E	38 A B C D E
9 A B C D E	19 A B C D E	29 A B C D E	39 A B C D E
10 A B C D E	20 A B C D E	30 A B C D E	40 A B C D E

CERTIFICATION STATEMENT

Copy in longhand the statement below and sign your name as you would an official document. **DO NOT PRINT.**

I hereby agree to the conditions set forth in the *Registration Bulletin* and certify that I am the person whose name and address appear on this answer sheet.

_____

_____

_____

SIGNATURE: _____   DATE: _____

Section 1   1 1 1 1 1 1   1

For each question in this section, select the best answer from among the choices given and fill in the corresponding oval on the answer sheet.

Each sentence below has one or two blanks, each blank indicating that something has been omitted. Beneath the sentence are five words or sets of words labeled A through E. Choose the word or set of words that, when inserted in the sentence, best fits the meaning of the sentence as a whole.

Example:

Medieval kingdoms did not become constitutional republics overnight; on the contrary, the change was ----.

(A) unpopular
(B) unexpected
(C) advantageous
(D) sufficient
(E) gradual

(A) (B) (C) (D) ●

1 The Uzbeks are a people of Central Asia who are chiefly ----, deriving their livelihood from growing grains and cotton.

(A) nomads   (B) industrialists
(C) technologists   (D) pillagers
(E) agriculturalists

2 The ---- of animated films on college campuses is evident from the ---- books analyzing cartoon classics that have been sold in college bookstores.

(A) availability . . limited
(B) predominance . . incidental
(C) suppression . . overdue
(D) reduction . . scholarly
(E) popularity . . numerous

3 Once a ---- issue, the idea that complex organic molecules may be present in interstellar space no longer sparks debate.

(A) laudatory   (B) rare   (C) controversial
(D) plausible   (E) defunct

4 Although his methods of composition have had a ---- and ---- influence on jazz, Thelonious Monk is unique among great jazz artists in not having attracted a legion of slavish imitators.

(A) superb . . untimely
(B) profound . . lasting
(C) pervasive . . unaccounted
(D) dubious . . universal
(E) severe . . unfavorable

5 Because scholarship in that field is still in its nascent stage, many researchers have argued that to develop ---- model would be ----, but to demonstrate progress toward a model is essential at this time.

(A) a tentative . . decisive
(B) a definitive . . premature
(C) a superfluous . . inadvisable
(D) an impressive . . vital
(E) an irrelevant . . necessary

6 The psychic claimed to know what the signs ----, but no one trusted her ability as a prophet.

(A) disfigured   (B) deterred   (C) repudiated
(D) portended   (E) circumvented

7 From classic fiction to the latest journalism, the theme of the typical plague story is one of ----: whenever a writer describes an epidemic as a plague, an extremely fatalistic view is implied.

(A) eccentricity   (B) tedium   (C) inevitability
(D) mystery   (E) excitement

8 Unlike her brother Henry, who extolled the merits of the English, Alice James lost no opportunity to ---- them.

(A) tolerate   (B) restrict   (C) abide
(D) disparage   (E) glorify

9 During the 1960's, attorneys who ---- court orders that declared various kinds of racial segregation unconstitutional often did so at the risk of retaliation from civil rights ----.

(A) filed . . victims
(B) questioned . . skeptics
(C) defied . . opponents
(D) obtained . . foes
(E) demanded . . leaders

GO ON TO THE NEXT PAGE

Each question below consists of a related pair of words or phrases, followed by five pairs of words or phrases labeled A through E. Select the pair that best expresses a relationship similar to that expressed in the original pair.

Example:

CRUMB : BREAD ::
(A) ounce : unit
(B) splinter : wood
(C) water : bucket
(D) twine : rope
(E) cream : butter Ⓐ ● Ⓒ Ⓓ Ⓔ

10 DRAFT : POEM ::
(A) proof : photograph
(B) reproduction : painting
(C) index : catalog
(D) verse : refrain
(E) review : film

11 SIGNAL : TRANSMITTED ::
(A) message : garbled
(B) disease : immunized
(C) letter : sent
(D) number : added
(E) sound : amplified

12 GLIMMER : LIGHT ::
(A) catastrophe : event
(B) link : chain
(C) stench : smell
(D) trace : substance
(E) product : process

13 RANT : SPEECH ::
(A) swagger : conduct
(B) relax : leisure
(C) pronounce : dialect
(D) riot : control
(E) disdain : respect

14 RUSE : DECEIVE ::
(A) altercation : reconcile
(B) apology : transgress
(C) diversion : amuse
(D) incentive : perform
(E) coup : govern

15 FRENETIC : ACTIVITY ::
(A) effusive : sentiment
(B) didactic : speaker
(C) mirthful : melancholy
(D) precocious : youth
(E) subtle : expression

GO ON TO THE NEXT PAGE ➡

Each passage below is followed by questions based on its content. Answer the questions on the basis of what is <u>stated</u> or <u>implied</u> in each passage and in any introductory material that may be provided.

Questions 16-24 are based on the following passage.

In this autobiographical excerpt, the author recounts memories of early childhood. Her father had joined the United States Navy; he found an apartment and moved the family from Puerto Rico to New Jersey in 1955. Recollection

My mother was only twenty years old, I was not quite three, and my brother was a toddler when we arrived at El Building, as the place had been chris-
Line tened by its residents.
(5) I remember the way the heater pipes banged and rattled, startling all of us out of sleep until we got so used to the sound that we automatically either shut it out or raised our voices above the racket. The hiss from the valve punctuated my sleep,
(10) which has always been fitful, like a nonhuman presence in the room — the dragon sleeping at the entrance of my childhood. But the pipes were a connection with all the other lives being lived around us. Having come from a house made for a
(15) single family back in Puerto Rico — my mother's extended-family home — it was curious to me to know that strangers lived under our floor and above our heads, and that the heater pipe went through everyone's apartment. (My first punishment in El
(20) Building came as a result of playing tunes on the pipes in my room to see if there would be an answer.) My mother was as new to this concept of beehive life as I was, but had been given strict orders by my father to keep the doors locked, the
(25) noise down, ourselves to ourselves.
It became my father's obsession to get out of the barrio,[1] and thus we were never permitted to form bonds with the place or with the people who lived there. Yet the building was also a comfort to my
(30) mother, who never got over yearning for *la isla* (Puerto Rico). She felt surrounded by her language: the walls were thin, and voices speaking and arguing in Spanish could be heard all day. Salsa music blasted out of radios turned on early in the
(35) morning and left on for company.
Though Father preferred that we do our grocery shopping at the supermarket when he came home on weekend leaves, my mother insisted that she could only cook with products whose labels she
(40) could read, and so, during the week, I accompanied her and my little brother to La Bodega — a hole-in-the-wall grocery store across the street from El Building. There we squeezed down three narrow aisles jammed with various products. We would
(45) linger at La Bodega, for it was there that my mother breathed best, taking in the familiar aromas of foods she knew from Mamá's kitchen, and it was also there that she got to speak to the other women of

El Building without violating outright Father's
(50) dictates about fraternizing with our neighbors.
But he did his best to make our "assimilation" painless. I can still see him carrying a Christmas tree up several flights of stairs to our apartment, leaving a trail of aromatic pine. We were the only
(55) ones in El Building that I knew of who got presents both on Christmas Day and on *Día de Reyes*,[2] the day when the Three Kings brought gifts to Hispanic children.
Our greatest luxury in El Building was having
(60) our own television set. My brother quickly became an avid watcher of Captain Kangaroo. I loved all the family series, and by the time I started first grade in school, I could have drawn a map of middle America as exemplified by the lives of characters in "Father
(65) Knows Best," "Leave It to Beaver," and "My Three Sons." Compared to our neighbors in El Building, we were rich. My father's navy check provided us with financial security and a standard of living that the factory workers envied. The only thing his
(70) money could not buy us was a place to live away from the barrio — his greatest wish and Mother's greatest fear.

[1] A neighborhood where most of the residents are Spanish-speaking

[2] "Day of Kings," January 6, a holiday that celebrates the visit of the Three Kings to the infant Jesus

16 The details about the family members in lines 1-4 introduce which element of the overall portrait?

(A) Their cautious curiosity
(B) Their lack of experience
(C) Their capacity to bear hardship
(D) Their suspicion of authority
(E) Their desire to learn

GO ON TO THE NEXT PAGE

Excerpts from Silent Dancing by Judith Ortiz-Cofer are reprinted with permission from the publisher of Silent Dancing: A Partial Remembrance of a Puerto Rican Childhood (Houston: Arte Publico Press-Univerity of Houston, 1990.)

17 The author's reference to a beehive (line 23) contributes to her depiction of the apartment by

(A) describing trivial but vivid details unnoticed by the adults
(B) evoking unexpected surprises in daily life
(C) revealing unconscious fears about the large city
(D) emphasizing the liveliness inside the building
(E) demonstrating the fantasies of the family

18 The author's observations about the walls in lines 31-33 help illustrate her claim that

(A) life in the barrio was confusing to her mother
(B) the environment evoked memories of her mother's cultural heritage
(C) El Building was similar to other buildings in the neighborhood
(D) the lack of privacy distressed her parents
(E) the apartment lacked adequate heat in the winter

19 The discussion of grocery shopping in lines 36-50 highlights the

(A) parents' differing attitudes toward their neighborhood
(B) parents' ambition to achieve financial success
(C) tensions between the more traditional mother and her "Americanized" daughter
(D) children's sense of isolation from potential playmates
(E) family's carefully nurtured loyalty to Puerto Rican culture

20 By stating that "he did his best" (line 51), the author acknowledges that the father

(A) understood that adjusting to new surroundings would pose a challenge to his family
(B) felt that the best way for the family to adjust to new surroundings was to continue living as they had in Puerto Rico
(C) insisted that the family adopt new traditions right away because an abrupt change is less painful than a gradual one
(D) wanted his family to get along with its neighbors
(E) wanted his children's religious and moral education to be pleasant and enjoyable

21 In lines 51-58, the author's discussion of the Christmas season most directly suggests that

(A) Christmas trees were a part of the holiday traditions of most people in the building
(B) the author was alarmed at her father's weariness after carrying the heavy tree up many flights of stairs
(C) the family observed the holiday traditions of both the continental United States and Puerto Rico
(D) the author was impressed that her father purchased the tree, because the family did not have much money
(E) Puerto Rican families traditionally exchanged gifts on two winter holidays

22 When the author states "I could have drawn a map" (line 63), she implies that as a child she

(A) preferred to watch educational programming
(B) judged United States society by the high quality of television programs
(C) believed that television depicted typical family life in the United States
(D) watched television programs that reflected the reality of her own childhood
(E) paid more attention to television than did most children her age

23 The final sentence (lines 69-72) encourages the reader to view the family's prosperity as ultimately

(A) disastrous in its consequences
(B) limited in its benefits
(C) discouraging in its cultural demands
(D) disturbing in its exclusion of relatives
(E) bewildering in its suddenness

24 Which best characterizes the overall impression of the father conveyed in the passage?

(A) He was the single most dominant influence in the children's daily life.
(B) He feared losing touch with the traditions of his native land.
(C) He represented the best aspects of both cultures for his daughter.
(D) He wanted his family to adopt a new life and culture.
(E) He wanted the children to respect only their adopted culture's traditions.

GO ON TO THE NEXT PAGE

Questions 25-30 are based on the following passage.

This passage is an excerpt from a book written by a historian and published in 1972. fact

During the latter part of the nineteenth century, the proportion of women in the United States working for wages rose steadily, and most of these
Line women entered paid employment out of economic
(5) necessity. Daughters, wives, unmarried women, and widows had always worked—in the home or on the farm; they now worked also in the factory or shop. "Work" was always the content of most women's lives, but this fact was at odds with the prevailing
(10) myth of "true womanhood," according to which the domestic role was a part of woman's nature—her way of being, rather than a way of life that could be chosen or rejected. Women's paid work outside the home, though it was undertaken to support their
(15) families, made a mockery of the domestic ideal of wife and mother. The social status of the employed woman would remain low so long as the image of the woman at home gracing her hearth, unsullied by the affairs of the world, remained the ideal.
(20) Nevertheless, in the late nineteenth century increasing numbers of women sought employment outside the home at some time in their lives. Young unmarried women were predominant in the female work force, which suggests that with marriage and
(25) motherhood most women reverted to the traditional role of economic dependence—unless their husbands were unable to earn a living wage. Widows and married women whose husbands were disabled or absent constituted the second major group of
(30) working women. Only among Black Americans, and among immigrants whose children worked in industry with them, were there substantial numbers of mothers who held jobs when their husbands were also employed.
(35) All women who sought work outside the home suffered repercussions from the idea that women's earning function was secondary, that women ought to be supported by someone rather than support themselves. Women were rarely paid at the same
(40) rate as men. In factories at the end of the century, women workers earned on the average only about half as much as men did, yet need drove women to accept these low-paying jobs. Women workers often were accused of undercutting wages and unsettling
(45) the labor market. Young women living with their parents were assumed to be earning "pin money" and thus not to be dependent on their salaries.

Women workers were treated as casual laborers who had no urge for advancement and no future in an
(50) organization because home and family comprised their natural interests. Women employed outside the home were seen as an anomaly by nineteenth-century standards, which rigidly prescribed separate spheres of activity for men and women, but of course they were not an anomaly at all.

25 The author's view of the treatment of nineteenth-century working women is best described as

(A) shock and amazement
(B) amused contempt
(C) disapproval
(D) anger
(E) disbelief

26 The two things that are "at odds" (line 9) can best be described as the

(A) kinds of jobs women could actually get and the work they aspired to do
(B) harsh conditions in working women's homes and the gracious homes that women were supposed to create
(C) actual living standards of working women and the image of the successful career woman
(D) reasons why most women entered the work force and the high ambitions some had to improve the world
(E) reality of women's working lives and the idealization of women's domestic role

27 In line 27, the word "living" is best interpreted to mean

(A) active
(B) vivid
(C) animated
(D) genuine
(E) sufficient

GO ON TO THE NEXT PAGE

28 Which statement can be inferred from the discussion of nineteenth-century Black Americans and immigrants in lines 30-34 ?

(A) Members of these two groups constituted a majority of the industrial work force.

(B) Men in these two groups were frequently not paid enough to support their families.

(C) Men in these two groups were more likely than White, nonimmigrant men to be responsible for child care.

(D) Women in these two groups were subjected to more gender stereotyping than White, nonimmigrant women were.

(E) Women in these two groups were more likely than White, nonimmigrant women to be economically dependent on men.

29 Which quotation best illustrates the opinion about women in the labor market mentioned in lines 43-45 ?

(A) "[Men] have only to consider [women] as human beings, and to ensure them the fair and thorough development of all the faculties."

(B) "Women are rendered more useful than they otherwise would be. The husband would experience a new source of profit and support from the increased activity of his wife."

(C) "Women and children who perform a great part of the work can be hired nearly as cheaply here as in England."

(D) "This state of affairs cannot be altered; it is better to unite [with women] than strike against them."

(E) "Women have moved into the labor force and their presence has rendered many a good breadwinner jobless."

30 Which question about nineteenth-century women is NOT answered in the passage?

(A) Why was it generally believed in the nineteenth century that the domestic role was natural to women?

(B) Why did even the women who were supporting families work in jobs that paid poorly?

(C) How were women workers often viewed by employers and men in the workplace?

(D) What economic consequences did women face because they were considered secondary wage earners?

(E) Why were single women more likely to work than married women?

IF YOU FINISH BEFORE TIME IS CALLED, YOU MAY CHECK YOUR WORK ON THIS SECTION ONLY. DO NOT TURN TO ANY OTHER SECTION IN THE TEST.  STOP

Section 2

**Time—30 Minutes
25 Questions**

In this section solve each problem, using any available space on the page for scratchwork. Then decide which is the best of the choices given and fill in the corresponding oval on the answer sheet.

Notes:

1. The use of a calculator is permitted. All numbers used are real numbers.

2. Figures that accompany problems in this test are intended to provide information useful in solving the problems. They are drawn as accurately as possible EXCEPT when it is stated in a specific problem that the figure is not drawn to scale. All figures lie in a plane unless otherwise indicated.

Reference Information

$A = \pi r^2$
$C = 2\pi r$

$A = \ell w$

$A = \frac{1}{2}bh$

$V = \ell wh$

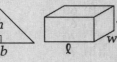
$V = \pi r^2 h$

$c^2 = a^2 + b^2$

Special Right Triangles

The number of degrees of arc in a circle is 360.
The measure in degrees of a straight angle is 180.
The sum of the measures in degrees of the angles of a triangle is 180.

---

1 Of a set of 36 pencils, $\frac{1}{3}$ are blue. If exactly 8 of the blue pencils do not have erasers, then how many of the blue pencils have erasers?

(A) 4
(B) 8
(C) 12
(D) 20
(E) 28

2 If $x \neq 0$, then $(x^2)^2 \div x^2 =$

(A) 1
(B) x
(C) x^2
(D) x^3
(E) x^6

3 If $r \cdot s \cdot t \cdot u = 0$ and $s \cdot t \cdot u \cdot v = 1$, which of the following must be equal to zero?

(A) r
(B) s
(C) t
(D) u
(E) v

GO ON TO THE NEXT PAGE

511

$x + 10$

$3x$

4 In the square above, what is the value of x ?

(A) 3
(B) 5
(C) 10
(D) 15
(E) 20

5 When 25 is divided by 7, the remainder is the same as when 49 is divided by which of the following numbers?

(A) 3
(B) 4
(C) 5
(D) 6
(E) 7

6 If $t = 3$, then $2t^3 + (2t)^3 =$

(A) 36
(B) 108
(C) 234
(D) 270
(E) 432

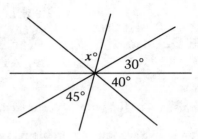

7 In the figure above, four lines intersect at a point. What is the value of x ?

(A) 55
(B) 60
(C) 65
(D) 70
(E) 75

8 A palindrome is a number that is unchanged when the order of the digits is reversed; for example, 979 is a palindrome. Which of the following numbers is 1 less than a palindrome?

(A) 454
(B) 455
(C) 4545
(D) 4553
(E) 4555

GO ON TO THE NEXT PAGE

9 In a class of 28 college students, half are women and 20 are sophomores. If 3 of the women are not sophomores, how many sophomores in the class are men?

(A) 3
(B) 6
(C) 9
(D) 11
(E) 14

10 If $(x - 1)^2 = 2x + 1$ and $x \neq 0$, what is the value of x ?

(A) 1
(B) 2
(C) 3
(D) 4
(E) 5

11   1, 3, 4, 5, 11

From the list of numbers above, two different numbers will be chosen. Of the following, which could be the average (arithmetic mean) of the two numbers?

  I. 3
 II. 4
III. 6

(A) I only
(B) II only
(C) III only
(D) I and II only
(E) I, II, and III

12 Which of the following statements must be true concerning the result obtained by squaring a positive fraction that is less than 1 ?

(A) It is less than the original fraction.

(B) It is less than 0.

(C) It is greater than the original fraction.

(D) It is greater than 1.

(E) It is between 0 and $\frac{1}{2}$.

13 If p is r more than twice s, what is r in terms of p and s ?

(A) $p + \frac{1}{2}s$

(B) $p + 2s$

(C) $p - \frac{1}{2}s$

(D) $p - 2s$

(E) $\frac{p - s}{2}$

GO ON TO THE NEXT PAGE

14 If $\dfrac{2x}{x} + \dfrac{1}{x} = 4$, then $x =$

(A) $-\dfrac{1}{8}$

(B) $\dfrac{1}{8}$

(C) $\dfrac{1}{2}$

(D) $\dfrac{3}{2}$

(E) 2

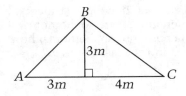

16 In the figure above, what is the perimeter of $\triangle ABC$ in terms of m ?

(A) $10m$

(B) $15m$

(C) $17m$

(D) $7m + 3\sqrt{2}\,m$

(E) $12m + 3\sqrt{2}\,m$

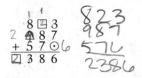

15 In the correctly worked addition problem above, □ , △ , and ⊙ represent digits. What is the sum of □ , △ , and ⊙ ?

(A) 17
(B) 18
(C) 19
(D) 20
(E) 21

17 If k is an integer and $r = k^2 + 3k + 9$, which of the following statements about r must be true for all values of k ?

(A) r is even.
(B) r is odd.
(C) r is divisible by 3.
(D) r is not divisible by 3.
(E) r is the square of an integer.

GO ON TO THE NEXT PAGE

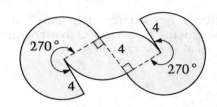

18 The figure above is partitioned into sectors of circles with radius 4. What is the area of the shaded region?

(A) 16π
(B) 24π
(C) 28π
(D) 32π
(E) 40π

20 Don intended to place a mark $2\frac{1}{4}$ inches from one end of a narrow rod $9\frac{1}{4}$ inches long, but he mistakenly placed the mark $2\frac{1}{4}$ inches from the other end. How far, in inches, is his mark from the location where he intended to place it?

(A) $4\frac{1}{4}$

(B) $4\frac{3}{4}$

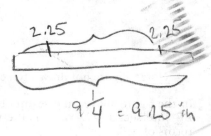

(C) $5\frac{1}{4}$

(D) $5\frac{3}{4}$

(E) 7

19 If $y - x = 5$ and $2y + z = 11$, what is the value of $x + y + z$?

(A) 3
(B) 6
(C) 8
(D) 16
(E) 55

21 If $-1 < x < y < 0$, then of the following, which has the greatest value?

(A) $y - x$
(B) $x + y$
(C) $x - y$
(D) $2x - y$
(E) $2y - x$

GO ON TO THE NEXT PAGE

515

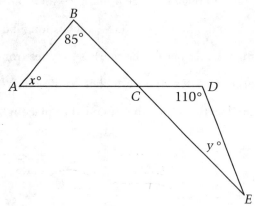

Note: Figure not drawn to scale.

22 In the figure above, line segments *AD* and *BE* intersect at *C*. What is the value of *x* in terms of *y*?

(A) 85 − y
(B) 90 − y
(C) y + 15
(D) y + 25
(E) y + 35

23 After Jenny deposited *s* dollars into her savings account, she had *d* dollars in the account. If she then withdrew (*s* − 70) dollars from this account, how many dollars did she have left in the account?

200−10+70

(A) d − s − 70
(B) d − s + 70
(C) d + s − 70
(D) d − s
(E) d − 70

24 The slope of line segment *PQ* is 2. If *P* has coordinates (2, *r*) and *Q* has coordinates (5, *t*), what is the value of *t* − *r* ?

(A) $\frac{2}{3}$

(B) $\frac{3}{2}$

(C) 2

(D) 3

(E) 6

m = 2

$\frac{y_1 - y_2}{x_1 - x_2}$ $\overline{2-5}$ = $\overline{-3}$

25 If *a*, *b*, and *c* represent three numbers where *b* = *a* + 3 and *c* = *b* + 6, what is the result when the median of the three numbers is subtracted from the average (arithmetic mean) of the numbers?

(A) 0
(B) 1
(C) 1.5
(D) 2
(E) 2.5

IF YOU FINISH BEFORE TIME IS CALLED, YOU MAY CHECK YOUR WORK ON THIS SECTION ONLY. DO NOT TURN TO ANY OTHER SECTION IN THE TEST. **STOP**

516

Time—30 Minutes
35 Questions

For each question in this section, select the best answer from among the choices given and fill in the corresponding oval on the answer sheet.

Each sentence below has one or two blanks, each blank indicating that something has been omitted. Beneath the sentence are five words or sets of words labeled A through E. Choose the word or set of words that, when inserted in the sentence, <u>best</u> fits the meaning of the sentence as a whole.

Example:

Medieval kingdoms did not become constitutional republics overnight; on the contrary, the change was ----.

(A) unpopular
(B) unexpected
(C) advantageous
(D) sufficient
(E) gradual
Ⓐ Ⓑ Ⓒ Ⓓ ●

1 Sports can be ---- because they demonstrate the value of teamwork, fair play, and discipline.

(A) entertaining   (B) enervating
(C) individualistic   (D) educational
(E) disruptive

2 In a survey, many parents who wish to ---- virtues such as family togetherness reported that they prefer television shows about the daily lives of closely knit families to those ---- violent conflicts and adventures.

(A) discredit..portraying
(B) identify..criticizing
(C) promote..depicting
(D) foster..rejecting
(E) dispute..satirizing

3 Despite the critics' ---- of the actress's performance in her most recent film, their acclaim seems to have done little to further her career.

(A) perusal   (B) parody   (C) commendation
(D) extenuation   (E) ignorance

4 The ---- waters of the shallow lake made the fish clearly visible to Dr. Muraoka and his survey team.

(A) turbulent   (B) treacherous
(C) serpentine   (D) pellucid   (E) putrid

5 Dagmar did not enjoy the dessert; there was so much sugar in it that it was ----.

(A) unpalatable   (B) subtle   (C) caustic
(D) convoluted   (E) invigorating

6 The constriction of small blood vessels can be ---- when it leads to ---- of the blood flow; however, a reduced blood flow is sometimes actually beneficial.

(A) advantageous..an interruption
(B) deleterious..a stoppage
(C) healthful..a resumption
(D) innocuous..a coagulation
(E) injurious..a progression

7 A study of Berthe Morisot's painting technique reveals that her apparent ---- and ---- execution were never as casual as they seemed but actually resulted from years of practice and concentration.

(A) craft..studied
(B) improvisation..diligent
(C) spontaneity..rapid
(D) deception..flawless
(E) accomplishment..laborious

8 Jones believes that since extrasensory experiences are by their very nature subjective, they are not ---- and cannot, therefore, be ---- scientifically.

(A) intrepid..perceived
(B) transitory..validated
(C) extrinsic..accepted
(D) uncanny..increased
(E) observable..substantiated

9 For the parade, the tailor designed an elaborate outfit too ---- for even the most foolish dandy.

(A) rustic   (B) subdued   (C) demure
(D) foppish   (E) trite

10 Once an occasional liar, Jessica has become ---- one in that she lies habitually.

(A) a perfidious   (B) a rancorous
(C) a selective   (D) an arcane
(E) an inveterate

GO ON TO THE NEXT PAGE

Each question below consists of a related pair of words or phrases, followed by five pairs of words or phrases labeled A through E. Select the pair that best expresses a relationship similar to that expressed in the original pair.

Example:

CRUMB : BREAD ::
(A) ounce : unit
(B) splinter : wood
(C) water : bucket
(D) twine : rope
(E) cream : butter

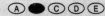

11 DATABASE : INFORMATION ::
(A) volume : index
(B) incinerator : trash
(C) safe : lock
(D) library : books
(E) store : purchases

12 PLUCK : BIRD ::
(A) hibernate : bear
(B) shampoo : dog
(C) shear : sheep
(D) shave : whiskers
(E) brush : hair

13 SNORE : ASLEEP ::
(A) hiss : sharp
(B) frown : happy
(C) echo : repetitive
(D) gasp : shocked
(E) shrug : indifferent

14 TENT : CIRCUS ::
(A) concert : orchestra
(B) screen : movie
(C) stage : lecturer
(D) theater : play
(E) cage : animal

15 DEODORIZE : SMELL ::
(A) imprison : cell
(B) invest : gain
(C) dispatch : message
(D) defraud : income
(E) fumigate : pest

16 COBBLER : SHOE ::
(A) cyclist : bicycle
(B) farmer : field
(C) pilot : runway
(D) baker : wheat
(E) mechanic : machine

17 FORT : ATTACK ::
(A) vault : theft
(B) spice : flavor
(C) fence : house
(D) army : battle
(E) jail : conviction

18 MAGNETIC : ATTRACT ::
(A) transparent : see
(B) toxic : poison
(C) electric : insulate
(D) ill : inoculate
(E) massive : lift

19 ELEGY : SADNESS ::
(A) lullaby : baby
(B) limerick : humor
(C) ballad : story
(D) serenade : night
(E) medley : series

20 RECLAMATION : LAND ::
(A) annexation : territory
(B) evaluation : condition
(C) restitution : injury
(D) restoration : structure
(E) resuscitation : rescue

21 HIERARCHY : RANKED ::
(A) equation : solved
(B) critique : biased
(C) chronology : sequential
(D) infinity : fixed
(E) rationale : intuitive

22 BEACON : GUIDANCE ::
(A) cave : exploration
(B) trail : forest
(C) well : thirst
(D) shroud : concealment
(E) jar : liquid

23 BIBLIOGRAPHY : PUBLICATIONS ::
(A) palette : brushes
(B) menu : dishes
(C) manuscript : editions
(D) sculpture : figures
(E) gallery : exhibits

GO ON TO THE NEXT PAGE

The two passages below are followed by questions based on their content and on the relationship between the two passages. Answer the questions on the basis of what is <u>stated</u> or <u>implied</u> in the passages and in any introductory material that may be provided.

Questions 24-35 are based on the following passages.

Henry David Thoreau (1817-1862) is among the most famous advocates of a "simple" life of meditation and close contact with nature, unhampered by materialistic concerns. Passage 1 is adapted from his description of the years when he lived alone in a cabin in the woods in Massachusetts, observing nature and engaging in literary work. Passage 2, by a twentieth-century English writer, comments on Thoreau's life in the woods.

Passage 1 opinion

For more than five years I maintained myself thus solely by the labor of my hands, and I found that, by working about six weeks in a year, I could
Line meet all the expenses of living. The whole of my
(5) winters, as well as most of my summers, I had free and clear for study.

As I preferred some things to others, and especially valued my freedom, as I could live roughly and yet succeed well, I did not wish to spend my
(10) time in earning rich carpets or fine furniture, or a house in the Grecian or the Gothic style. If there are any to whom it is no interruption to acquire these things, and who know how to use them when acquired, I relinquish to them the pursuit. Some are
(15) "industrious," and appear to love labor for its own sake, or perhaps because it keeps them out of worse mischief; to such I have at present nothing to say. For myself I found that the occupation of a day laborer* was the most independent of any,
(20) especially as it required only thirty or forty days in a year to support one.

In short, I am convinced both by faith and experience, that to maintain one's self on this earth is not a hardship but a pastime, so long as we live simply
(25) and wisely. It is not necessary that a man earn his living by the sweat of his brow, unless he sweats easier than I do.

One young man of my acquaintance, who has inherited some acres, told me that he thought he
(30) should live as I did, *if he had the means.* I would not have any one adopt *my* mode of living on any account, for I desire that there may be as many different persons in the world as possible. I would have each young man be very careful to find out
(35) and pursue *his own* way, and not his father's or his mother's or his neighbor's instead. The youth may build or plant or sail, only let him not be hindered from doing that which he tells me he would like to do.

Passage 2 opinion

(40) Now, the one thing that is entirely fatal to leading the simple life is the desire to stimulate the curiosity of others in the matter. Thoreau, who is by many regarded as the apostle of the simple life, is the most conspicuous example of this. Thoreau
(45) was a man of extremely simple tastes, it is true. He ate pulse, whatever that may be, and drank water; he was deeply interested in the contemplation of nature, and he loved to disembarrass himself of all the apparatus of life. It was really that he hated
(50) trouble more than anything in the world; he found that by working six weeks in the year, he could earn enough to enable him to live in a hut in a wood for the rest of the year; he did his household work himself, and his little stock of money sufficed
(55) to buy his food and clothes, and to meet his small expenses. But Thoreau was indolent rather than simple; and what spoiled his simplicity was that he was forever hoping that he would be observed and admired; he was forever peeping out of the corner of
(60) his eye, to see if inquisitive strangers were hovering about to observe the hermit at his contemplation.

And then, too, it was easier for Thoreau to make money than it would be for a more ordinary youth. When Thoreau wrote his famous maxim, "To main-
(65) tain oneself on this earth is not a hardship but a pastime," he did not add that he was himself a man of remarkable mechanical gifts; he made, when he was disposed, admirable pencils, he was an excellent land surveyor, and an author as well. Moreover,
(70) he was a celibate by nature. He would no doubt have found if he had had a wife and children, and no aptitude for skilled labor, that he would have had to work as hard as any one else.

He thought and talked too much about simpli-
(75) city; and the fact is that simplicity, like humility, cannot exist side by side with self-consciousness. You cannot become simple by doing elaborately, and making a parade of doing, the things that the truly simple person would do without thinking about them.

* A day laborer works for daily wages and is often an unskilled worker.

GO ON TO THE NEXT PAGE

519

24 The "pursuit" referred to in line 14 has as its object

(A) intellectual freedom
(B) financial independence
(C) aesthetic superiority
(D) social accolades
(E) luxurious possessions

25 In line 24, "simply" most nearly means

(A) guilelessly
(B) ordinarily
(C) foolishly
(D) clearly
(E) modestly

26 In the context of Passage 2, "trouble" (line 50) most likely refers to

(A) unnecessary exertion
(B) civil unrest
(C) financial hardship
(D) emotional distress
(E) personal conflict

27 The depiction of Thoreau in lines 56-61 ("But Thoreau . . . contemplation") creates the impression of a man who

(A) plays a complex, mysterious role
(B) lies about his deepest beliefs
(C) follows a demanding ideal
(D) enjoys the company of others
(E) strikes a self-conscious pose

28 Which statement, if true, would most effectively challenge the view of Thoreau presented in lines 70-73 of Passage 2 ("He would . . . any one else") ?

(A) Thoreau anonymously supported relatives in financial distress.
(B) Thoreau isolated himself because he craved notoriety.
(C) Thoreau earned a small income by writing about life in the woods.
(D) Thoreau lived sparingly in anticipation of owning a more comfortable house.
(E) Thoreau found lasting peace of mind in the contemplation of nature.

29 Overall, the author of Passage 2 characterizes Thoreau as an

(A) unreliable adviser with a limited view of social realities
(B) avaricious guide with less-than-honorable intentions
(C) immoral philosopher who rejects essential standards
(D) immature youth with insufficient knowledge of the world
(E) unscrupulous popularizer who deliberately deceives others

30 The author of Passage 2 would consider which advice most important for a young person seeking the simple life?

(A) You cannot achieve it by a deliberate attempt.
(B) You should have great respect for nature.
(C) You must have a sincere dedication to your task.
(D) You will not succeed unless you are already wealthy.
(E) You must first become a recluse.

31 Which statement is a logical extension of the argument made by the author of Passage 2 ?

(A) No individual leading the simple life can be as convincing as Thoreau was.
(B) No one who is living a truly simple life can write a book about simple living.
(C) The conditions of our century make it impossible to lead the simple life.
(D) Living a simple lifestyle is unnatural.
(E) None of the advocates of the simple life has been a pragmatic person.

GO ON TO THE NEXT PAGE

520

32 Both passages assert that the simple life is

(A) not suitable for all people
(B) not acceptable in conventional societies
(C) not easy to find for one's self
(D) essential to one's peace of mind
(E) crucial for creative people

33 What information in Passage 1 provides the most direct evidence of the "simple tastes" (line 45) referred to by the author of Passage 2 ?

(A) Thoreau's appreciation of freedom (lines 4-6)
(B) Thoreau's commentary on the list of items (lines 7-14)
(C) Thoreau's reliance on "faith" (line 22)
(D) Thoreau's comment on "hardship" (line 24)
(E) Thoreau's discussion of an inheritance (lines 28-30)

34 Which statement about self-awareness in the simple life most accurately represents the ideas expressed in the two passages?

(A) Passage 1 says it must be taught; Passage 2 believes it must be avoided.
(B) Passage 1 urges all readers to cultivate it; Passage 2 believes it is appropriate only for some.
(C) Passage 1 assumes it is important; Passage 2 considers it self-defeating.
(D) Passage 1 praises examples of it; Passage 2 mandates it.
(E) Passage 1 celebrates it; Passage 2 ignores it.

35 Which point made in Passage 1 does the author of Passage 2 fail to address?

(A) Living the simple life matters less than finding the right way of life for one's self.
(B) The simple life is an appropriate choice for a person with simple tastes.
(C) Earning one's living is not a difficult or tiresome task.
(D) An individual who lives simply can exist for months without earning money.
(E) Pursuing the simple life necessarily involves rejecting many options.

IF YOU FINISH BEFORE TIME IS CALLED, YOU MAY CHECK YOUR WORK ON THIS SECTION ONLY. DO NOT TURN TO ANY OTHER SECTION IN THE TEST.  STOP

521

Section 4 4 4 4 4

Time—30 Minutes	This section contains two types of questions. You have
25 Questions	30 minutes to complete both types. You may use any available space for scratchwork.

Notes:

1. The use of a calculator is permitted. All numbers used are real numbers.

2. Figures that accompany problems in this test are intended to provide information useful in solving the problems. They are drawn as accurately as possible EXCEPT when it is stated in a specific problem that the figure is not drawn to scale. All figures lie in a plane unless otherwise indicated.

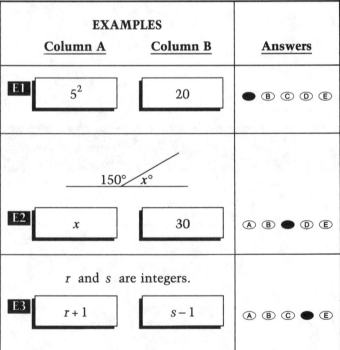

$A = \pi r^2$
$C = 2\pi r$
$A = \ell w$
$A = \frac{1}{2}bh$
$V = \ell wh$
$V = \pi r^2 h$
$c^2 = a^2 + b^2$
Special Right Triangles

The number of degrees of arc in a circle is 360.
The measure in degrees of a straight angle is 180.
The sum of the measures in degrees of the angles of a triangle is 180.

Directions for Quantitative Comparison Questions

Questions 1-15 each consist of two quantities in boxes, one in Column A and one in Column B. You are to compare the two quantities and on the answer sheet fill in oval

 A if the quantity in Column A is greater;
 B if the quantity in Column B is greater;
 C if the two quantities are equal;
 D if the relationship cannot be determined from the information given.

AN E RESPONSE WILL NOT BE SCORED.

Notes:

1. In some questions, information is given about one or both of the quantities to be compared. In such cases, the given information is centered above the two columns and is not boxed.
2. In a given question, a symbol that appears in both columns represents the same thing in Column A as it does in Column B.
3. Letters such as x, n, and k stand for real numbers.

EXAMPLES

	Column A	Column B	Answers
E1	5^2	20	● Ⓑ Ⓒ Ⓓ Ⓔ
E2	x (150°/x°)	30	Ⓐ Ⓑ ● Ⓓ Ⓔ
E3	$r+1$ (r and s are integers.)	$s-1$	Ⓐ Ⓑ Ⓒ ● Ⓔ

GO ON TO THE NEXT PAGE

522

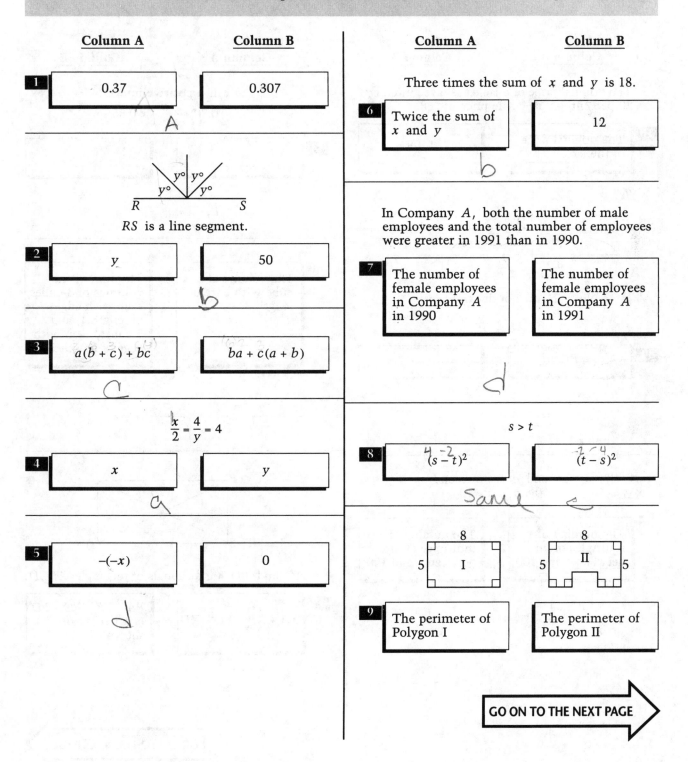

Column A	Column B

1 0.37 — 0.307

A

RS is a line segment.

2 y — 50

b

3 $a(b + c) + bc$ — $ba + c(a + b)$

C

$$\frac{x}{2} = \frac{4}{y} = 4$$

4 x — y

a

5 $-(-x)$ — 0

d

Column A	Column B

Three times the sum of x and y is 18.

6 Twice the sum of x and y — 12

b

In Company A, both the number of male employees and the total number of employees were greater in 1991 than in 1990.

7 The number of female employees in Company A in 1990 — The number of female employees in Company A in 1991

d

$s > t$

8 $(s - t)^2$ — $(t - s)^2$

Same

9 The perimeter of Polygon I — The perimeter of Polygon II

GO ON TO THE NEXT PAGE →

523

4 4 4 4 4 4

Column A	**Column B**

The original price of a jacket is discounted by 20 percent, giving a sale price of $88.

10 | The original price of the jacket | $108

20% .20

b

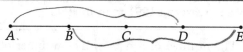

Note: Figure not drawn to scale.

$$AD = BE$$

11 | BC | CD

c

m and *n* are integers.
$$0 < m < n < 10$$

12 | The number of multiples of *m* between 1 and 100 | The number of multiples of *n* between 1 and 100

Column A	**Column B**

x is a positive integer.
$$0.80 < \frac{x}{x+1} < 0.85$$

13 | *x* | 4

4

14 | The volume of a cube with edge of length 3 | The sum of the volumes of 3 cubes, each with edge of length 1, and 3 cubes, each with edge of length 2

AC and BD are diagonals of rectangle $ABCD$.

15 | $XA + XB + XC + XD$ | $PA + PB + PC + PD$ (segments not shown)

C

GO ON TO THE NEXT PAGE ➡

524

Directions for Student-Produced Response Questions

Each of the remaining 10 questions requires you to solve the problem and enter your answer by marking the ovals in the special grid, as shown in the examples below.

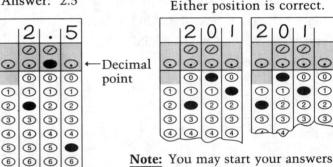

Answer: $\frac{7}{12}$ or 7/12   Answer: 2.5   Answer: 201
Either position is correct.

Write answer in boxes. ←   ← Fraction line   ← Decimal point

Grid in result.

Note: You may start your answers in any column, space permitting. Columns not needed should be left blank.

- Mark no more than one oval in any column.

- Because the answer sheet will be machine-scored, **you will receive credit only if the ovals are filled in correctly.**

- Although not required, it is suggested that you write your answer in the boxes at the top of the columns to help you fill in the ovals accurately.

- Some problems may have more than one correct answer. In such cases, grid only one answer.

- No question has a negative answer.

- **Mixed numbers** such as $2\frac{1}{2}$ must be gridded as 2.5 or 5/2. (If $\boxed{2 1 / 2}$ is gridded, it will be interpreted as $\frac{21}{2}$, not $2\frac{1}{2}$.)

- **Decimal Accuracy**: If you obtain a decimal answer, **enter the most accurate value the grid will accommodate.** For example, if you obtain an answer such as 0.6666 . . . , you should record the result as .666 or .667. **Less accurate values such as .66 or .67 are not acceptable.**

Acceptable ways to grid $\frac{2}{3}$ = .6666 . . .

---

16 If $r = 2s$ and $s = 2t$, what is the value of t when $r = 500$?

$$500 = 2(2t)$$
$$\frac{500 = 4t}{4}$$

125

17 Let $x \circledast y$ be defined as $x + \dfrac{1}{y}$, where $y \neq 0$. What is the value of $5 \circledast 4$?

GO ON TO THE NEXT PAGE →

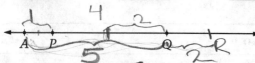

18 A, P, and Q are located on a line in the order shown above. A fourth point, R, not shown, lies on the same line so that the distance between Q and R is $\frac{1}{2}PQ$. If $AP = 1$ and $AQ = 5$, what is one possible value of the distance between A and R ?

7

20 In an election a total of 5,000 votes were cast for the three candidates, X, Y, and Z. Candidate Z received 900 votes. If candidate Y received more votes than candidate Z and candidate X received more votes than candidate Y, what is the <u>least</u> number of votes that candidate X could have received?

$Z = 900 < Y = 1 < X = 4099$

$X + Y = 4100$

4099

150

19 An orchard contains 75 peach trees, 75 apple trees, and no other trees. If 20 of the peach trees and 40 of the apple trees were pruned, what fraction of the total number of trees were pruned?

$75\ P - 20 = 55$ arent pruned
$75\ a - 40$ 35
60 90

$70\% = $ Peaches
$00\% = $ apples $\dfrac{60}{150} = \dfrac{6}{15}$

$\dfrac{6}{15}$

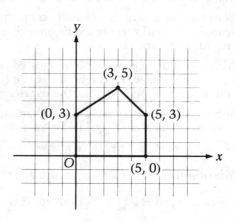

21 What is the area of the region bounded by the five darkened line segments in the figure above?

GO ON TO THE NEXT PAGE →

22 If 20 percent of 100 is equal to 500 percent of n, then n is equal to what number?

24 Jason remembers only the first five digits of a seven-digit phone number, but he is sure that neither of the last two digits is zero. If he dials the first five digits, then dials two more digits, each chosen at random from the nonzero digits, what is the probability that he will dial the correct number?

AVERAGE ANNUAL PURCHASING POWER OF THE DOLLAR AS MEASURED BY CONSUMER PRICES	
Year	Purchasing Power
1940	2.38
1950	1.39
1960	1.13
1970	0.86
1980	0.41

23 According to the data in the table above, the purchasing power of the 1940 dollar was approximately what multiple, rounded to the nearest integer, of the purchasing power of the 1980 dollar?

14, 17, 32, 50, 83, 134, . . .

25 Starting with the third number in the sequence of numbers above, each number is 1 more than the sum of the two numbers just before it. For example, $32 = 1 + (14 + 17)$. Of the first 100 numbers in this sequence, how many are even numbers?

IF YOU FINISH BEFORE TIME IS CALLED, YOU MAY CHECK YOUR WORK ON THIS SECTION ONLY. DO NOT TURN TO ANY OTHER SECTION IN THE TEST. STOP

Time—15 Minutes
13 Questions

For each question in this section, select the best answer from among the choices given and fill in the corresponding oval on the answer sheet.

The passage below is followed by questions based on its content. Answer the questions on the basis of what is <u>stated</u> or <u>implied</u> in the passage and in any introductory material that may be provided.

Questions 1-13 are based on the following passage.

Is the human preference for one place over another determined by genetics? Do we unconsciously yearn for the geographical environment in which our species developed? These questions are explored in the following passage. opinion

The archaeological evidence seems clear on the question of our original environment. For most of two million years, hominids lived on the savannas
Line of Africa—vast, park-like lands dotted by groves
(5) and scattered trees. They appear to have avoided the equatorial rain forests on one side and the deserts on the other. There was nothing inevitable about this choice. The two extreme habitats have no special qualities that deny them to primates. Most
(10) monkeys and apes flourish in the rain forest, and two species of baboons are specialized for life in the relatively barren grasslands and semideserts of Africa. The prehistoric species of *Homo* can be viewed both as the ancestors of modern human
(15) beings and as one more product among many in the development of primates. In the latter role they belong to the minority of species that hit upon an intermediate topography, the tropical savanna. Most students of early human evolution agree that the
(20) bipedal locomotion and free-swinging arms fitted these ancestral forms very well to the open land, where they were able to exploit an abundance of fruits, tubers, and game.
The body is predisposed to life on the savanna.
(25) But is the mind? The scientist Gordon Orians has suggested that this is indeed the case. He points out that people today work hard to create a savanna-like environment in such improbable sites as formal gardens, cemeteries, and suburban shopping malls. They
(30) hunger for open spaces but not for a barren landscape, for some amount of order in the surrounding vegetation but less than geometric perfection. According to his formulation, the ancestral environment contained three key features.
(35) First, the savanna by itself, with nothing more added, offered an abundance of animal and plant food to which the omnivorous hominids were well adapted, as well as the clear view needed to detect animals and rival bands at long distances. Second,
(40) some topographic relief was desirable. Cliffs, hillocks, and ridges were the vantage points from which to make a still more distant surveillance,
while their overhangs and caves served as natural shelters at night. During longer marches, the scat-
(45) tered clumps of trees provided auxiliary retreats, often sheltering bodies of drinking water. Finally, lakes and rivers offered fish, mollusks, and new kinds of edible plants. Because few natural enemies of humans can cross deep water, the shorelines
(50) became natural perimeters of defense.
People tend to put these three elements together: it seems that whenever people are given a free choice, they move to open, tree-studded land on prominences overlooking water. This worldwide
(55) tendency is no longer dictated by the hard necessities of hunter-gatherer life. It has become largely aesthetic. Those who exercise the greatest degree of free choice, the rich and powerful, congregate on high land and above lakes and rivers and along
(60) ocean bluffs. On such sites they build palaces, villas, temples, and corporate retreats. Psychologists have noticed that people entering unfamiliar places tend to move toward towers and other large objects breaking the skyline. Given leisure time, they stroll
(65) along shores and riverbanks.
I will grant at once the strangeness of the comparison and the possibility that the convergence is merely a coincidence. But entertain for a while longer the idea that landscape architects and gar-
(70) deners, and we who enjoy their creations without special instruction or persuasion, are responding to a deep genetic memory of humanity's optimal environment. That statistically, given a completely free choice, people gravitate toward a savanna-like envi-
(75) ronment. The theory accommodates a great many seemingly disconnected facts from other parts of the world.
Not long ago I joined a group of Brazilian scientists on a tour of the upland savanna around the
(80) capital city of Brasília. We went straight to one of the highest elevations as if following an unspoken command. We looked out across the rippled terrain

GO ON TO THE NEXT PAGE

528

of high grass, parkland, and forest enclaves and
watched birds circling in the sky. We scanned the
(85) cumulus clouds that tower like high mountains
above the plains during the wet season. We traced
gallery forests, groves of trees that wind along the
banks of the widely spaced streambeds. It was, all
agreed, very beautiful.

(90)　　The practical-minded will argue that certain environments are just "nice" and there's an end to it. So
why dilate on the obvious? The answer is that the
obvious is usually profoundly significant. Some
environments are indeed pleasant for the same gen-
(95) eral reason that sugar is sweet and team sports
exhilarating. Each response has its peculiar meaning
rooted in the distant genetic past. To understand
why we have one particular set of ingrained preferences and not another, out of the vast number of
(100) possible preferences, remains a central question in
the study of human nature.

1 In the sentence beginning "There was nothing"
(lines 7-8), the author does which of the following?

(A) Shows that reasons for habitat choices are
best understood in terms of evolution.
(B) Suggests that early hominids were equipped
to survive in other habitats.
(C) Claims that the views of those who seek
religious explanations are without merit.
(D) Underlines the fact that the archaeological
evidence about the early hominids is
clear.
(E) Emphasizes the decisive ways in which
apes and baboons differ from early
hominids.

2 The author mentions the "extreme habitats"
(line 8) in order to

(A) show that all habitats have certain advantages
(B) show that climates that are suitable for
one species are not suitable for another
species
(C) make the case that primates can live in a
variety of environments
(D) point out the difference between baboons
and other primates
(E) question the validity of archaeological
evidence

3 According to the author, Gordon Orians
(line 25) has suggested that people have the
tendency to

(A) congregate on high land to feel secure
(B) conceal themselves behind large objects as
a means of protection
(C) seek subconsciously to re-create their
ancestral environment
(D) hunger for spaces that resemble shopping
malls
(E) enjoy leisure time in unfamiliar places

4 As used in line 40, "relief" most nearly means

(A) comfort
(B) elevation
(C) reduction
(D) pause
(E) subsidy

5 The author mentions "Cliffs, hillocks, and
ridges" (lines 40-41) to give examples of
topographic features that

(A) became early sites of religious ceremonies
(B) provided a wide variety of food sources for
early hominids
(C) are characteristic of the extreme habitats
avoided by early hominids
(D) are in contrast with shopping malls and
formal gardens
(E) enabled early hominids to see approaching
prey and enemies

6 In line 55, "hard" most nearly means

(A) brittle
(B) strong
(C) complex
(D) technical
(E) harsh

GO ON TO THE NEXT PAGE

7 By including corporate retreats in the list in lines 60-61, the author

   (A) rebukes corporate executives for their arrogance
   (B) implies that power has always tended to corrupt
   (C) makes the case that the corporate elite are not sensitive to the environment
   (D) suggests that the rich and powerful include corporate executives
   (E) argues against the human instinct to seek protection against enemies

8 In line 69, "idea" most nearly means

   (A) proposition
   (B) discovery
   (C) misconception
   (D) scheme
   (E) estimate

9 The author likens the action of the group on the outskirts of Brasília to a response to "an unspoken command" (lines 81-82) in order to

   (A) show how people in groups lose their individuality
   (B) illustrate that even scientists respect intuition
   (C) indicate the distance between modern humans and early hominids
   (D) underline the importance of language in human development
   (E) suggest that the power of inherited preferences is still strong

10 The author describes the trip to Brazil in order to

   (A) illustrate a major difference between Africa and Brazil
   (B) give an example of an environment that would have been hostile to hominids
   (C) illustrate the author's appreciation of beauty
   (D) support an argument with an example from personal experience
   (E) show the importance of coincidence to the argument that has been developed

11 The author suggests which of the following about the "practical-minded" (line 90) ?

   (A) They fail to appreciate the profound beauty of the savanna.
   (B) They value economic considerations over philosophical considerations.
   (C) They are in agreement with many theorists.
   (D) They fail to appreciate the beauty of the natural world.
   (E) They are unwilling to ask probing questions about human nature.

12 In the last paragraph (lines 90-101), the author assumes that our responses to such things as sugar and team sports are

   (A) influenced by the genetic history of our species
   (B) largely a reflection of local culture
   (C) shared with other primates
   (D) different for different individuals
   (E) influenced by the geography in which human beings developed

13 Which statement, if true, would most directly weaken the author's argument regarding people's feelings about environments?

   (A) Mountainous regions generally are more sparsely populated than plains are.
   (B) Many national parks have characteristics of the savannas.
   (C) Most urban planners agree that it is important, even though expensive, to set aside land for parks.
   (D) Few people feel comfortable standing on cliffs, hillocks, and ridges.
   (E) Successful landscape architects are those who create settings that are reminiscent of savannas.

IF YOU FINISH BEFORE TIME IS CALLED, YOU MAY CHECK YOUR WORK ON THIS SECTION ONLY. DO NOT TURN TO ANY OTHER SECTION IN THE TEST.

Section 7

Time—15 Minutes
10 Questions

In this section solve each problem, using any available space on the page for scratchwork. Then decide which is the best of the choices given and fill in the corresponding oval on the answer sheet.

Notes:

1. The use of a calculator is permitted. All numbers used are real numbers.

2. Figures that accompany problems in this test are intended to provide information useful in solving the problems. They are drawn as accurately as possible EXCEPT when it is stated in a specific problem that the figure is not drawn to scale. All figures lie in a plane unless otherwise indicated.

Reference Information

$A = \pi r^2$
$C = 2\pi r$ $A = \ell w$ $A = \frac{1}{2}bh$ $V = \ell wh$ $V = \pi r^2 h$ $c^2 = a^2 + b^2$ Special Right Triangles

The number of degrees of arc in a circle is 360.
The measure in degrees of a straight angle is 180.
The sum of the measures in degrees of the angles of a triangle is 180.

1 If $\dfrac{30}{48} = \dfrac{5}{p}$ what is the value of p ?

(A) 6
(B) 8
(C) 15
(D) 16
(E) 24

2 Which of the following CANNOT be the average (arithmetic mean) of four positive even integers?

(A) 1
(B) 2
(C) 6
(D) 9
(E) 12

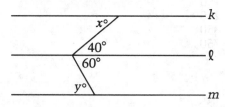

3 In the figure above, lines k, ℓ, and m are parallel. What is the sum of x and y ?

(A) 40
(B) 60
(C) 80
(D) 90
(E) 100

GO ON TO THE NEXT PAGE

531

Questions 4-5 refer to the following graph.

LAND CLASSIFICATION IN A CERTAIN REGION

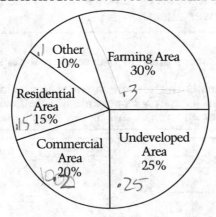

4 In this region, for every 1,000 acres classified as commercial area, how many acres are classified as residential area?

(A)   5
(B)   150
(C)   250
(D)   350
(E)   750

5 Based on the graph, which of the following statements must be true?

   I. In this region, 30 percent of the residents live on farms.
   II. Farming is the greatest source of income in this region.
   III. If 10 percent of the undeveloped area is reclassified as commercial area, there will be as much commercial area as farming area.

(A) None
(B) I only
(C) III only
(D) I and II only
(E) I, II, and III

GO ON TO THE NEXT PAGE

Row A	2	3	4	5	6
Row B	4	6	8	18	32
Row C	2	6	9	12	16
Row D	1	4	9	18	36
Row E	3	4	6	18	32

6 Which row shown above contains both the square of an integer and the square of twice the same integer?

(A) A
(B) B
(C) C
(D) D
(E) E

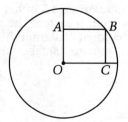

8 In the figure above, O is the center of the circle and B is a point on the circle. In rectangle $OABC$, if $OA = 4$ and $OC = 5$, what is the area of the circle?

(A) 9π
(B) 16π
(C) 25π
(D) 41π
(E) 64π

7 P, Q, R, and S are four towns. P is farther north than Q and R; S is farther south than P; and Q is farther south than R. Which town is farthest south?

(A) P
(B) Q
(C) R
(D) S
(E) It cannot be determined from the information given.

GO ON TO THE NEXT PAGE

9 Carol wants to arrange 3 of her 4 plants in a row on a shelf. If each of the plants is in a different-colored container, how many different arrangements can she make?

(A) 7
(B) 12
(C) 24
(D) 28
(E) 36

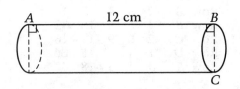

10 The figure above represents a right circular cylindrical tube made out of paper. The circumference of each circular base is 10 centimeters, the length of AB is 12 centimeters, and BC is a diameter of a base. If the tube is cut along AB, opened, and flattened, what is the length of AC, in centimeters?

(A) 13
(B) 17
(C) 22
(D) $2\sqrt{61}$
(E) $\sqrt{146.5}$

IF YOU FINISH BEFORE TIME IS CALLED, YOU MAY CHECK YOUR WORK ON THIS SECTION ONLY. DO NOT TURN TO ANY OTHER SECTION IN THE TEST.　STOP

SAT I Scoring Worksheet

SAT I Verbal Sections

A. Section 1:

$$\underline{\hspace{3cm}} - (\underline{\hspace{3cm}} \div 4) = \underline{\hspace{3cm}}$$
no. correct — no. incorrect — subtotal A

B. Section 3:

$$\underline{\hspace{3cm}} - (\underline{\hspace{3cm}} \div 4) = \underline{\hspace{3cm}}$$
no. correct — no. incorrect — subtotal B

C. Section 6:

$$\underline{\hspace{3cm}} - (\underline{\hspace{3cm}} \div 4) = \underline{\hspace{3cm}}$$
no. correct — no. incorrect — subtotal C

D. Total unrounded raw score
(Total A + B + C)

_____
D

E. Total rounded raw score
(Rounded to nearest whole number)

_____
E

F. SAT I verbal reported scaled score
(Use the conversion table)

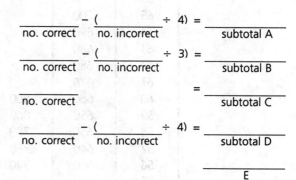

SAT I verbal
score

SAT I Mathematical Sections

A. Section 2:

$$\underline{\hspace{3cm}} - (\underline{\hspace{3cm}} \div 4) = \underline{\hspace{3cm}}$$
no. correct — no. incorrect — subtotal A

B. Section 4:
Questions 1-15 (quantitative comparison)

$$\underline{\hspace{3cm}} - (\underline{\hspace{3cm}} \div 3) = \underline{\hspace{3cm}}$$
no. correct — no. incorrect — subtotal B

C. Section 4:
Questions 16-25 (student-produced response)

$$\underline{\hspace{3cm}} = \underline{\hspace{3cm}}$$
no. correct — subtotal C

D. Section 7:

$$\underline{\hspace{3cm}} - (\underline{\hspace{3cm}} \div 4) = \underline{\hspace{3cm}}$$
no. correct — no. incorrect — subtotal D

E. Total unrounded raw score
(Total A + B + C + D)

_____
E

F. Total rounded raw score
(Rounded to nearest whole number)

_____
F

G. SAT I mathematical reported scaled score
(Use the conversion table)

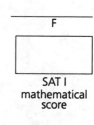

SAT I
mathematical
score

Score Conversion Table
SAT I: Reasoning Test
Saturday, May 1996
Recentered Scale

Raw Score	Verbal Scaled Score	Math Scaled Score	Raw Score	Verbal Scaled Score	Math Scaled Score
78	800		37	510	570
77	800		36	510	560
76	800		35	500	550
75	800		34	500	550
74	800		33	490	540
73	790		32	480	530
72	770		31	480	530
71	760		30	470	520
70	750		29	470	510
69	740		28	460	510
68	730		27	450	500
67	720		26	450	500
66	710		25	440	490
65	700		24	430	480
64	690		23	430	480
63	680		22	420	470
62	680		21	410	460
61	670		20	410	460
60	660	800	19	400	450
59	650	800	18	390	440
58	650	780	17	380	440
57	640	760	16	370	430
56	630	740	15	370	420
55	620	730	14	360	420
54	620	710	13	350	410
53	610	700	12	340	400
52	600	690	11	330	400
51	600	680	10	320	390
50	590	670	9	310	380
49	590	660	8	300	370
48	580	650	7	290	360
47	570	640	6	280	350
46	570	630	5	260	340
45	560	630	4	250	330
44	560	620	3	240	320
43	550	610	2	220	300
42	540	600	1	210	290
41	540	600	0	200	270
40	530	590	-1	200	250
39	530	580	-2	200	230
38	520	570	-3 and below	200	200

This table is for use only with this test.

SAT I: Reasoning Test

Sunday, May 1996

SAT® I: Reasoning Test

Calculator use is permitted on the mathematics sections only.

You will have three hours to work on the questions in this test book. There are **five 30-minute sections and two 15-minute sections**. The supervisor will tell you when to begin and end each section. If you finish before time is called, you may check your work on that section, but you may <u>not work on any other section</u>.

Do not worry if you are unable to finish a section or if there are some questions you cannot answer. Do not waste time puzzling over a question that seems too difficult for you. Work as rapidly as you can without sacrificing accuracy.

Students often ask whether they should guess when they are uncertain about the answer to a question. Scores on the multiple-choice questions on this test are based on the number of questions answered correctly minus a fraction of the number answered incorrectly. Therefore, it is unlikely that random or haphazard guessing will change your scores significantly. If you have some knowledge of a question, you may be able to eliminate one or more of the answer choices as wrong. It is generally a good idea to guess which of the remaining·choices is correct.

Some mathematics questions have no answer choices. Instead, you must solve the problem and record your answer in a special grid on your answer sheet. For these questions, you will receive credit for correct answers, but there will be no deduction for incorrect answers.

Mark all your answers on the separate answer sheet. Mark only one answer for each question. Since the answer sheet will be machine scored, be sure that each mark is dark and that it completely fills the oval. In each section of the answer sheet, there are spaces to answer 40 questions. When there are fewer than 40 questions in a section of your test, use only the spaces that correspond to the question numbers. Do not make stray marks on the answer sheet. If you erase, do so completely, because an incomplete erasure may be scored as an intended response.

You may use the test book for scratchwork, but you will not receive credit for anything written there.

(The passages for this test have been adapted from published material. The ideas contained in them do not necessarily represent the opinions of the College Board or Educational Testing Service.)

DO NOT OPEN THIS BOOK UNTIL THE SUPERVISOR TELLS YOU TO DO SO.

Use a No. 2 pencil only. Be sure each mark is dark and completely fills the intended oval. Completely erase any errors or stray marks.

1. Your Name

First 4 letters of Last Name | First init. | Mid. init.

(A)(B)(C)(D)(E)(F)(G)(H)(I)(J)(K)(L)(M)(N)(O)(P)(Q)(R)(S)(T)(U)(V)(W)(X)(Y)(Z)

2.

Your Name:
(Print)
Last — First — M.I.

Signature: _____ **Date:** __/__/__

Home Address: _____
(Print)
Number and Street

City — State — Zip Code

Center: _____
(Print)
City — State — Center Number

IMPORTANT: Please fill in items 8 and 9 exactly as shown on the back cover of your test book.

8. Form Code
(Copy and grid as on back of test book.)

3. Date Of Birth

Month	Day	Year
Jan.		
Feb.		
Mar.		
Apr.		
May		
June		
July		
Aug.		
Sept.		
Oct.		
Nov.		
Dec.		

4. Social Security Number

5. Sex
Female ○ Male ○

7. Test Book Serial Number
(Copy from front of test book.)

6. Registration Number
(Copy from your Admission Ticket.)

9. Test Form
(Copy from back cover of test book.)

FOR ETS USE ONLY

DO NOT WRITE IN THIS AREA.

Start with number 1 for each new section. If a section has fewer questions than answer spaces, leave the extra answer spaces blank.

SECTION 1

1–40 (A)(B)(C)(D)(E)

SECTION 2

1–40 (A)(B)(C)(D)(E)

541

Start with number 1 for each new section. If a section has fewer questions than answer spaces, leave the extra answer spaces blank.

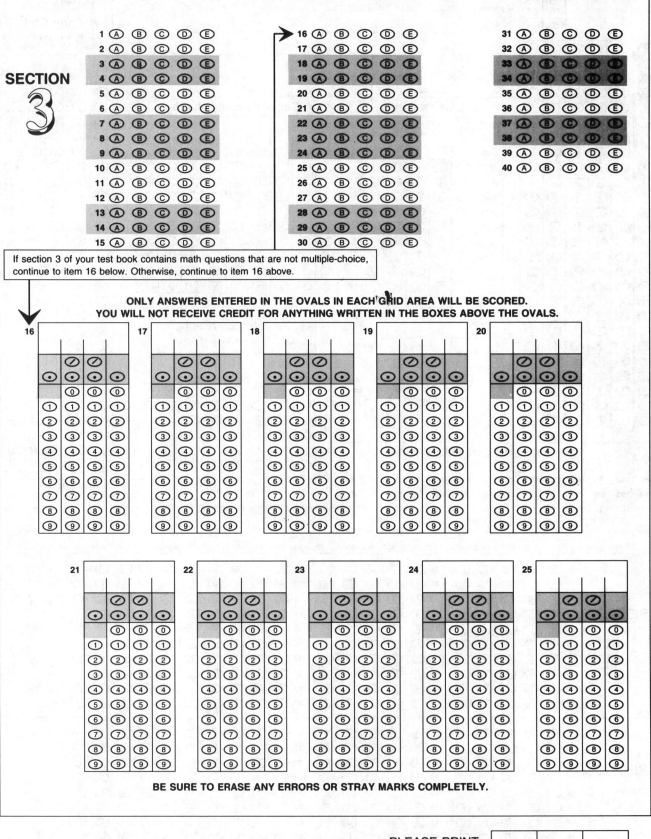

SECTION 3

If section 3 of your test book contains math questions that are not multiple-choice, continue to item 16 below. Otherwise, continue to item 16 above.

ONLY ANSWERS ENTERED IN THE OVALS IN EACH GRID AREA WILL BE SCORED.
YOU WILL NOT RECEIVE CREDIT FOR ANYTHING WRITTEN IN THE BOXES ABOVE THE OVALS.

BE SURE TO ERASE ANY ERRORS OR STRAY MARKS COMPLETELY.

PLEASE PRINT
YOUR INITIALS

First   Middle   Last

Start with number 1 for each new section. If a section has fewer questions than answer spaces, leave the extra answer spaces blank.

SECTION 4

1 (A) (B) (C) (D) (E)
2 (A) (B) (C) (D) (E)
3 (A) (B) (C) (D) (E)
4 (A) (B) (C) (D) (E)
5 (A) (B) (C) (D) (E)
6 (A) (B) (C) (D) (E)
7 (A) (B) (C) (D) (E)
8 (A) (B) (C) (D) (E)
9 (A) (B) (C) (D) (E)
10 (A) (B) (C) (D) (E)
11 (A) (B) (C) (D) (E)
12 (A) (B) (C) (D) (E)
13 (A) (B) (C) (D) (E)
14 (A) (B) (C) (D) (E)
15 (A) (B) (C) (D) (E)

16 (A) (B) (C) (D) (E)
17 (A) (B) (C) (D) (E)
18 (A) (B) (C) (D) (E)
19 (A) (B) (C) (D) (E)
20 (A) (B) (C) (D) (E)
21 (A) (B) (C) (D) (E)
22 (A) (B) (C) (D) (E)
23 (A) (B) (C) (D) (E)
24 (A) (B) (C) (D) (E)
25 (A) (B) (C) (D) (E)
26 (A) (B) (C) (D) (E)
27 (A) (B) (C) (D) (E)
28 (A) (B) (C) (D) (E)
29 (A) (B) (C) (D) (E)
30 (A) (B) (C) (D) (E)

31 (A) (B) (C) (D) (E)
32 (A) (B) (C) (D) (E)
33 (A) (B) (C) (D) (E)
34 (A) (B) (C) (D) (E)
35 (A) (B) (C) (D) (E)
36 (A) (B) (C) (D) (E)
37 (A) (B) (C) (D) (E)
38 (A) (B) (C) (D) (E)
39 (A) (B) (C) (D) (E)
40 (A) (B) (C) (D) (E)

If section 4 of your test book contains math questions that are not multiple-choice, continue to item 16 below. Otherwise, continue to item 16 above.

ONLY ANSWERS ENTERED IN THE OVALS IN EACH GRID AREA WILL BE SCORED. YOU WILL NOT RECEIVE CREDIT FOR ANYTHING WRITTEN IN THE BOXES ABOVE THE OVALS.

16   17   18   19   20

21   22   23   24   25

BE SURE TO ERASE ANY ERRORS OR STRAY MARKS COMPLETELY.

PLEASE PRINT
YOUR INITIALS

First   Middle   Last

543

Use a No. 2 pencil only. Be sure each mark is dark and completely fills the intended oval. Completely erase any errors or stray marks.

Start with number 1 for each new section. If a section has fewer questions than answer spaces, leave the extra answer spaces blank.

SECTION 5

1 Ⓐ Ⓑ Ⓒ Ⓓ Ⓔ	11 Ⓐ Ⓑ Ⓒ Ⓓ Ⓔ	21 Ⓐ Ⓑ Ⓒ Ⓓ Ⓔ	31 Ⓐ Ⓑ Ⓒ Ⓓ Ⓔ
2 Ⓐ Ⓑ Ⓒ Ⓓ Ⓔ	12 Ⓐ Ⓑ Ⓒ Ⓓ Ⓔ	22 Ⓐ Ⓑ Ⓒ Ⓓ Ⓔ	32 Ⓐ Ⓑ Ⓒ Ⓓ Ⓔ
3 Ⓐ Ⓑ Ⓒ Ⓓ Ⓔ	13 Ⓐ Ⓑ Ⓒ Ⓓ Ⓔ	23 Ⓐ Ⓑ Ⓒ Ⓓ Ⓔ	33 Ⓐ Ⓑ Ⓒ Ⓓ Ⓔ
4 Ⓐ Ⓑ Ⓒ Ⓓ Ⓔ	14 Ⓐ Ⓑ Ⓒ Ⓓ Ⓔ	24 Ⓐ Ⓑ Ⓒ Ⓓ Ⓔ	34 Ⓐ Ⓑ Ⓒ Ⓓ Ⓔ
5 Ⓐ Ⓑ Ⓒ Ⓓ Ⓔ	15 Ⓐ Ⓑ Ⓒ Ⓓ Ⓔ	25 Ⓐ Ⓑ Ⓒ Ⓓ Ⓔ	35 Ⓐ Ⓑ Ⓒ Ⓓ Ⓔ
6 Ⓐ Ⓑ Ⓒ Ⓓ Ⓔ	16 Ⓐ Ⓑ Ⓒ Ⓓ Ⓔ	26 Ⓐ Ⓑ Ⓒ Ⓓ Ⓔ	36 Ⓐ Ⓑ Ⓒ Ⓓ Ⓔ
7 Ⓐ Ⓑ Ⓒ Ⓓ Ⓔ	17 Ⓐ Ⓑ Ⓒ Ⓓ Ⓔ	27 Ⓐ Ⓑ Ⓒ Ⓓ Ⓔ	37 Ⓐ Ⓑ Ⓒ Ⓓ Ⓔ
8 Ⓐ Ⓑ Ⓒ Ⓓ Ⓔ	18 Ⓐ Ⓑ Ⓒ Ⓓ Ⓔ	28 Ⓐ Ⓑ Ⓒ Ⓓ Ⓔ	38 Ⓐ Ⓑ Ⓒ Ⓓ Ⓔ
9 Ⓐ Ⓑ Ⓒ Ⓓ Ⓔ	19 Ⓐ Ⓑ Ⓒ Ⓓ Ⓔ	29 Ⓐ Ⓑ Ⓒ Ⓓ Ⓔ	39 Ⓐ Ⓑ Ⓒ Ⓓ Ⓔ
10 Ⓐ Ⓑ Ⓒ Ⓓ Ⓔ	20 Ⓐ Ⓑ Ⓒ Ⓓ Ⓔ	30 Ⓐ Ⓑ Ⓒ Ⓓ Ⓔ	40 Ⓐ Ⓑ Ⓒ Ⓓ Ⓔ

SECTION 6

1 Ⓐ Ⓑ Ⓒ Ⓓ Ⓔ	11 Ⓐ Ⓑ Ⓒ Ⓓ Ⓔ	21 Ⓐ Ⓑ Ⓒ Ⓓ Ⓔ	31 Ⓐ Ⓑ Ⓒ Ⓓ Ⓔ
2 Ⓐ Ⓑ Ⓒ Ⓓ Ⓔ	12 Ⓐ Ⓑ Ⓒ Ⓓ Ⓔ	22 Ⓐ Ⓑ Ⓒ Ⓓ Ⓔ	32 Ⓐ Ⓑ Ⓒ Ⓓ Ⓔ
3 Ⓐ Ⓑ Ⓒ Ⓓ Ⓔ	13 Ⓐ Ⓑ Ⓒ Ⓓ Ⓔ	23 Ⓐ Ⓑ Ⓒ Ⓓ Ⓔ	33 Ⓐ Ⓑ Ⓒ Ⓓ Ⓔ
4 Ⓐ Ⓑ Ⓒ Ⓓ Ⓔ	14 Ⓐ Ⓑ Ⓒ Ⓓ Ⓔ	24 Ⓐ Ⓑ Ⓒ Ⓓ Ⓔ	34 Ⓐ Ⓑ Ⓒ Ⓓ Ⓔ
5 Ⓐ Ⓑ Ⓒ Ⓓ Ⓔ	15 Ⓐ Ⓑ Ⓒ Ⓓ Ⓔ	25 Ⓐ Ⓑ Ⓒ Ⓓ Ⓔ	35 Ⓐ Ⓑ Ⓒ Ⓓ Ⓔ
6 Ⓐ Ⓑ Ⓒ Ⓓ Ⓔ	16 Ⓐ Ⓑ Ⓒ Ⓓ Ⓔ	26 Ⓐ Ⓑ Ⓒ Ⓓ Ⓔ	36 Ⓐ Ⓑ Ⓒ Ⓓ Ⓔ
7 Ⓐ Ⓑ Ⓒ Ⓓ Ⓔ	17 Ⓐ Ⓑ Ⓒ Ⓓ Ⓔ	27 Ⓐ Ⓑ Ⓒ Ⓓ Ⓔ	37 Ⓐ Ⓑ Ⓒ Ⓓ Ⓔ
8 Ⓐ Ⓑ Ⓒ Ⓓ Ⓔ	18 Ⓐ Ⓑ Ⓒ Ⓓ Ⓔ	28 Ⓐ Ⓑ Ⓒ Ⓓ Ⓔ	38 Ⓐ Ⓑ Ⓒ Ⓓ Ⓔ
9 Ⓐ Ⓑ Ⓒ Ⓓ Ⓔ	19 Ⓐ Ⓑ Ⓒ Ⓓ Ⓔ	29 Ⓐ Ⓑ Ⓒ Ⓓ Ⓔ	39 Ⓐ Ⓑ Ⓒ Ⓓ Ⓔ
10 Ⓐ Ⓑ Ⓒ Ⓓ Ⓔ	20 Ⓐ Ⓑ Ⓒ Ⓓ Ⓔ	30 Ⓐ Ⓑ Ⓒ Ⓓ Ⓔ	40 Ⓐ Ⓑ Ⓒ Ⓓ Ⓔ

SECTION 7

1 Ⓐ Ⓑ Ⓒ Ⓓ Ⓔ	11 Ⓐ Ⓑ Ⓒ Ⓓ Ⓔ	21 Ⓐ Ⓑ Ⓒ Ⓓ Ⓔ	31 Ⓐ Ⓑ Ⓒ Ⓓ Ⓔ
2 Ⓐ Ⓑ Ⓒ Ⓓ Ⓔ	12 Ⓐ Ⓑ Ⓒ Ⓓ Ⓔ	22 Ⓐ Ⓑ Ⓒ Ⓓ Ⓔ	32 Ⓐ Ⓑ Ⓒ Ⓓ Ⓔ
3 Ⓐ Ⓑ Ⓒ Ⓓ Ⓔ	13 Ⓐ Ⓑ Ⓒ Ⓓ Ⓔ	23 Ⓐ Ⓑ Ⓒ Ⓓ Ⓔ	33 Ⓐ Ⓑ Ⓒ Ⓓ Ⓔ
4 Ⓐ Ⓑ Ⓒ Ⓓ Ⓔ	14 Ⓐ Ⓑ Ⓒ Ⓓ Ⓔ	24 Ⓐ Ⓑ Ⓒ Ⓓ Ⓔ	34 Ⓐ Ⓑ Ⓒ Ⓓ Ⓔ
5 Ⓐ Ⓑ Ⓒ Ⓓ Ⓔ	15 Ⓐ Ⓑ Ⓒ Ⓓ Ⓔ	25 Ⓐ Ⓑ Ⓒ Ⓓ Ⓔ	35 Ⓐ Ⓑ Ⓒ Ⓓ Ⓔ
6 Ⓐ Ⓑ Ⓒ Ⓓ Ⓔ	16 Ⓐ Ⓑ Ⓒ Ⓓ Ⓔ	26 Ⓐ Ⓑ Ⓒ Ⓓ Ⓔ	36 Ⓐ Ⓑ Ⓒ Ⓓ Ⓔ
7 Ⓐ Ⓑ Ⓒ Ⓓ Ⓔ	17 Ⓐ Ⓑ Ⓒ Ⓓ Ⓔ	27 Ⓐ Ⓑ Ⓒ Ⓓ Ⓔ	37 Ⓐ Ⓑ Ⓒ Ⓓ Ⓔ
8 Ⓐ Ⓑ Ⓒ Ⓓ Ⓔ	18 Ⓐ Ⓑ Ⓒ Ⓓ Ⓔ	28 Ⓐ Ⓑ Ⓒ Ⓓ Ⓔ	38 Ⓐ Ⓑ Ⓒ Ⓓ Ⓔ
9 Ⓐ Ⓑ Ⓒ Ⓓ Ⓔ	19 Ⓐ Ⓑ Ⓒ Ⓓ Ⓔ	29 Ⓐ Ⓑ Ⓒ Ⓓ Ⓔ	39 Ⓐ Ⓑ Ⓒ Ⓓ Ⓔ
10 Ⓐ Ⓑ Ⓒ Ⓓ Ⓔ	20 Ⓐ Ⓑ Ⓒ Ⓓ Ⓔ	30 Ⓐ Ⓑ Ⓒ Ⓓ Ⓔ	40 Ⓐ Ⓑ Ⓒ Ⓓ Ⓔ

CERTIFICATION STATEMENT

Copy in longhand the statement below and sign your name as you would an official document. **DO NOT PRINT.**

I hereby agree to the conditions set forth in the *Registration Bulletin* and certify that I am the person whose name and address appear on this answer sheet.

_____

_____

_____

SIGNATURE: _____ DATE: _____

Section 1 ¹ 1 1 1 1 1 1

| Time—30 Minutes
25 Questions | In this section solve each problem, using any available space on the page for scratchwork. Then decide which is the best of the choices given and fill in the corresponding oval on the answer sheet. |

Notes:

1. The use of a calculator is permitted. All numbers used are real numbers.

2. Figures that accompany problems in this test are intended to provide information useful in solving the problems. They are drawn as accurately as possible EXCEPT when it is stated in a specific problem that the figure is not drawn to scale. All figures lie in a plane unless otherwise indicated.

$A = \pi r^2$
$C = 2\pi r$

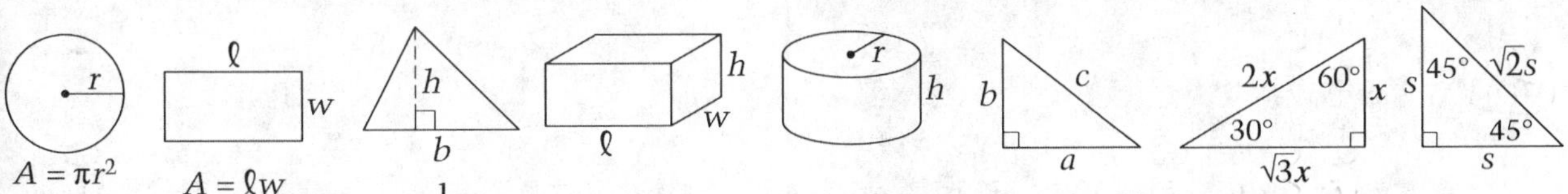

$A = \ell w$

$A = \frac{1}{2}bh$

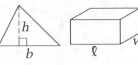
$V = \ell w h$

$V = \pi r^2 h$

$c^2 = a^2 + b^2$

Special Right Triangles

The number of degrees of arc in a circle is 360.
The measure in degrees of a straight angle is 180.
The sum of the measures in degrees of the angles of a triangle is 180.

1 If an object travels at 2 feet per minute, how many feet does it travel in a half hour?

(A) 1
(B) $2\frac{1}{2}$
(C) 10
(D) 30
(E) 60 ⟵ *(circled)*

handwritten: 2ft = 1 mn
? = 30 min

3 Ben spends $1.95 for lunch at school each day. He wants to estimate the amount he will spend for lunch during the month of May, which has 22 school days. Which of the following will give him the best estimate?

(A) $1.00 × 20
(B) $1.50 × 20
(C) $2.00 × 20 ⟵ *(circled)*
(D) $1.50 × 25
(E) $2.00 × 30

2 Mona just bought a book from a bookstore that sells only biographies and novels. Which of the following must be true?

(A) The book is a novel.
(B) The book is a biography.
(C) The book is not a dictionary.
(D) The book is not a humorous novel.
(E) The book is not a biography of John Adams.

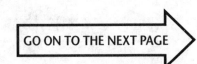
GO ON TO THE NEXT PAGE

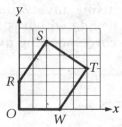

4 In the figure above, which two sides of polygon *ORSTW* have the same slope?

(A) *OR* and *OW*
(B) *OW* and *ST*
(C) *RS* and *ST*
(D) *RS* and *WT*
(E) *ST* and *WT*

5 If *n* is an even integer greater than 2, what is the next greater even integer in terms of *n* ?

(A) *n* + 1
(B) *n* + 2
(C) *n* + 3
(D) 2*n*
(E) *n*²

 2, 4, 6, 8, 10
n

6 A piece of wire *x* feet in length is cut into exactly 6 pieces, each 2 feet 4 inches in length. What is the value of *x* ? (1 foot = 12 inches)

(A) $12\frac{1}{3}$ 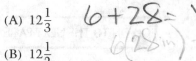 6 + 28 = X
6(28 in) = X

(B) $12\frac{1}{2}$

(C) 13

(D) $13\frac{1}{2}$

(E) 14

7 Of the following numbers, which is least?

(A) $1 + \frac{1}{3}$ 1.3

(B) $1 - \frac{1}{3}$ .66

(C) $\frac{1}{3} - 1$

(D) $1 \times \frac{1}{3}$ .33

(E) $1 \div \frac{1}{3}$

{2, 5, 6, 7, 10}

8 How many different pairs of unequal numbers can be chosen from the set above so that their sum is greater than 10 ? (Do not consider a pair such as 5, 2 to be different from 2, 5.)

(A) 7
(B) 10
(C) 14
(D) 32
(E) 60

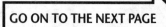
GO ON TO THE NEXT PAGE

9 In the figure above, the three diameters divide the circle into six equal regions. If the circle is rotated 120° in a clockwise direction in its plane, which of the following represents the resulting circle?

(A)

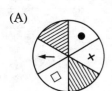

(B)

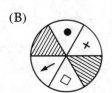

(C)

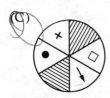

(D)

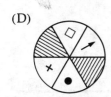

(E)

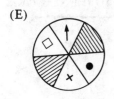

10 From 1 p.m. to 5 p.m. on Monday, a group of photographers will be taking individual pictures of 600 students. If it takes 2 minutes to take each student's picture, how many photographers are needed?

(A) Two
(B) Three
(C) Four
(D) Five
(E) Fifteen

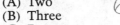

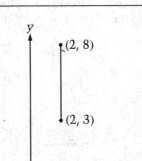

11 In the figure above, the line segment joining the points (2, 3) and (2, 8) forms one side of a square. Which of the following could be the coordinates of another vertex of that square?

(A) (–2, 5)
(B) (–2, 3)
(C) (5, 2)
(D) (7, 2)
(E) (7, 8)

GO ON TO THE NEXT PAGE

12 Three business partners are to share profits of $24,000 in the ratio 5 : 4 : 3. What is the amount of the <u>least</u> share?

(A) $1,200
(B) $3,000
(C) $6,000
(D) $8,000
(E) $10,000

13 If p is a prime number greater than 3, which of the following is NOT a factor of $6p$?

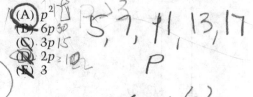

(A) p^2
(B) $6p$
(C) $3p$
(D) $2p$
(E) 3

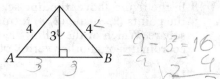

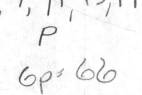

14 In the figure above, what is the length of AB ?

(A) 5
(B) 7
(C) $2\sqrt{7}$ (approximately 5.29)
(D) $4\sqrt{2}$ (approximately 5.66)
(E) $4\sqrt{3}$ (approximately 6.93)

15 What is the least possible integer for which 20 percent of that integer is greater than 1.2 ?

(A) 2
(B) 3
(C) 4
(D) 6
(E) 7

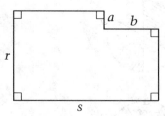

16 Which of the following is equal to the perimeter of the figure above?

(A) $r + s + a + b$
(B) $2r + s + (a + b)$
(C) $2(r + s) - (a + b)$
(D) $2(r + s) + (a + b)$
(E) $2(r + s)$

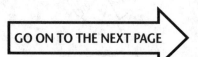

GO ON TO THE NEXT PAGE

548

17 If $y = 1 + \dfrac{1}{x}$ and $x > 1$, then y could equal

(A) $\dfrac{1}{7}$

(B) $\dfrac{5}{7}$

(C) $\dfrac{9}{7}$

(D) $\dfrac{15}{7}$

(E) $\dfrac{19}{7}$

18 Five distinct points lie in a plane such that 3 of the points are on line ℓ and 3 of the points are on a different line, m. What is the total number of lines that can be drawn so that each line passes through exactly 2 of these 5 points?

(A) Two
(B) Four
(C) Five
(D) Six
(E) Ten

Add 3 to x.
Divide this sum by 4.
Subtract 2 from this quotient.

19 Which of the following is the result obtained by performing the operations described above?

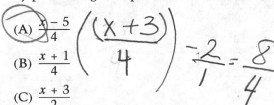

(A) $\dfrac{x-5}{4}$

(B) $\dfrac{x+1}{4}$

(C) $\dfrac{x+3}{2}$

(D) $\dfrac{3x-8}{4}$

(E) $\dfrac{x+1}{2}$

20 If the ratio of q to r is 4 to 5, which of the following could be true?

(A) $q = 0$, $r = \dfrac{4}{5}$

(B) $q = 2$, $r = \dfrac{5}{2}$

(C) $q = 5$, $r = 6$

(D) $q = 15$, $r = 12$

(E) $q = 16$, $r = 25$

GO ON TO THE NEXT PAGE

21 Which of the following gives the number of revolutions that a tire with diameter x meters will make in traveling a distance of y kilometers without slipping? (1 kilometer = 1,000 meters)

(A) $\dfrac{1,000y}{\pi x}$

(B) $\dfrac{1,000}{\pi xy}$

(C) $\dfrac{500}{\pi x}$

(D) $\dfrac{y}{1,000\pi x}$

(E) $\dfrac{\pi x}{1,000y}$

1, 2, 1, −1, −2, −1, 1, 0   2−1=1

22 The first five terms of a sequence are shown above. After the second term, each term can be obtained by subtracting from the previous term the term before that. For example, the third term can be obtained by subtracting the first term from the second term. What is the sum of the first 36 terms of the sequence?

(A) 0
(B) 4
(C) 12
(D) 24
(E) 30

−1 −1 = 2

−2 +1 = −1

23 If $n > 1$ and each of the three integers n, $n + 2$, and $n + 4$ is a prime number, then the set of three such numbers is called a "prime triple." There are how many different prime triples?

(A) None
(B) One
(C) Two
(D) Three
(E) More than three

24 If j and k are integers and $j + k = 2j + 4$, which of the following must be true?

I. j is even.
II. k is even.
III. $k - j$ is even.

(A) None
(B) I only
(C) II only
(D) III only
(E) I, II, and III

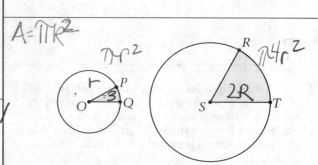

$A = \pi R^2$

25 In the figure above, the radius of the circle with center S is twice the radius of the circle with center O and the measure of $\angle RST$ is twice that of $\angle POQ$. If the area of the shaded region of circle O is 3, what is the area of the shaded region of circle S?

(A) 24

(B) 12

(C) 6

(D) 3

(E) $\dfrac{3}{2}$

Section 2 2 2 2 2

Time—30 Minutes
30 Questions

For each question in this section, select the best answer from among the choices given and fill in the corresponding oval on the answer sheet.

Each sentence below has one or two blanks, each blank indicating that something has been omitted. Beneath the sentence are five words or sets of words labeled A through E. Choose the word or set of words that, when inserted in the sentence, <u>best</u> fits the meaning of the sentence as a whole.

Example:

Medieval kingdoms did not become constitutional republics overnight; on the contrary, the change was ----.

(A) unpopular
(B) unexpected
(C) advantageous
(D) sufficient
(E) gradual

Ⓐ Ⓑ Ⓒ Ⓓ ●

1 The unification of Upper and Lower Egypt around 3000 B.C. acted as a catalyst, ---- a flowering of Egyptian culture.

(A) triggering (B) describing (C) suspending
(D) polarizing (E) symbolizing

2 If his works had been regarded merely as those of a fool, he might have met with only ---- , not with violent enmity and strict censorship.

(A) brutality (B) loathing (C) rebellion
(D) ridicule (E) execution

3 Recent evidence that a special brain cell is critical to memory is so ---- that scientists are ---- their theories of how the brain stores information to include the role of this cell.

(A) pervasive..reproducing
(B) perplexing..formulating
(C) obscure..confirming
(D) extreme..restoring
(E) compelling..revising

4 The ---- act was ---- even to the perpetrator, who regretted his deed to the end of his life.

(A) vulgar..unaffected
(B) heinous..appalling
(C) vengeful..acceptable
(D) timorous..intrepid
(E) forgettable..offensive

5 The observation that nurses treating patients with pellagra did not ---- the disease led epidemiologists to question the theory that pellagra is ----.

(A) risk..deadly
(B) fear..curable
(C) acknowledge..common
(D) contract..contagious
(E) battle..preventable

6 The general view of gorillas as menacing, ferocious King Kongs was not successfully ---- until Dian Fossey's field studies in the 1960's showed gorillas to be peaceable, rather fainthearted creatures, unlikely to ---- humans.

(A) counteracted..please
(B) enhanced..murder
(C) verified..attack
(D) dispelled..captivate
(E) challenged..threaten

7 The quotation attributing to the mayor the view that funds for police services should be cut was ----: it completely ---- the mayor's position that more police should be hired.

(A) inflammatory..justified
(B) abbreviated..curtailed
(C) meticulous..misstated
(D) egregious..underscored
(E) spurious..misrepresented

8 A ---- is concerned not with whether a political program is liberal or conservative but with whether it will work.

(A) radical (B) utopian (C) pragmatist
(D) partisan (E) reactionary

9 Thomas Jefferson's decision not to ---- lotteries was sanctioned by classical wisdom, which held that, far from being a ---- game, lots were a way of divining the future and of involving the gods in everyday affairs.

(A) expand..sacred
(B) publicize..vile
(C) condemn..debased
(D) legalize..standardized
(E) restrict..useful

GO ON TO THE NEXT PAGE →

551

Each question below consists of a related pair of words or phrases, followed by five pairs of words or phrases labeled A through E. Select the pair that best expresses a relationship similar to that expressed in the original pair.

Example:

CRUMB : BREAD ::
(A) ounce : unit
(B) splinter : wood
(C) water : bucket
(D) twine : rope
(E) cream : butter

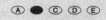

10 FLAP : WING ::
(A) speak : sound
(B) wave : hand
(C) whisper : word
(D) stub : toe
(E) sing : bird

11 POISON : TOXIC ::
(A) mixture : soluble
(B) sugar : sweet
(C) medicine : prescribed
(D) milk : bottled
(E) solid : liquid

12 DEDUCTION : RATIONAL ::
(A) hunch : intuitive
(B) ploy : spontaneous
(C) maxim : hackneyed
(D) hypothesis : tested
(E) daydream : bored

13 BEAUTY : AESTHETE ::
(A) pleasure : hedonist
(B) emotion : demagogue
(C) opinion : sympathizer
(D) seance : medium
(E) luxury : ascetic

14 FLIPPANCY : JOLLITY ::
(A) recognition : achievement
(B) practice : expertise
(C) camaraderie : combativeness
(D) insolence : pride
(E) politeness : behavior

15 INCANTATION : WORDS ::
(A) malediction : harm
(B) oration : formality
(C) talisman : object
(D) enchantment : happiness
(E) divination : future

GO ON TO THE NEXT PAGE

Each passage below is followed by questions based on its content. Answer the questions on the basis of what is stated or implied in each passage and in any introductory material that may be provided.

Questions 16-20 are based on the following passage.

The following passage is about Black American fiction and the Romantic literary tradition. The Romance novel is a literary form that took shape during the eighteenth and nineteenth centuries. Different from the sentimental, escapist writing often described as romantic, Romance novels focus on the heroic dimensions of life, using symbolism to express abstract ideas.

During the nineteenth century, the traditional Romance became an important mode of expression for many Black American writers. A frequent char-
Line acteristic of Romantic writing is the use of histori-
(5) cal material; Black writers have used this genre to transform an often harsh historical reality into an imagined world ruled by their own ethical vision. In transforming history into fiction, Romantic writers have given their work a mythic quality
(10) that deepens the significance of plot, character, and historical event.
Clotel, a novel written in 1853 by William Wells Brown, is an early example from this roman-tic tradition. *Clotel*'s heroes are idealized, fighting
(15) slavery through superhuman action, and are used to convey a complex political message. For Brown, the Black man or woman was destined to move toward spiritual perfection, but was being blocked by the dehumanizing effects of slavery. The conflict
(20) in *Clotel* is both an ongoing political one, between slaves and their owners, and a wider moral conflict between good and evil; the story is placed in both a historical context and the larger context of human ethical progress. The resolution is satisfyingly hope-
(25) ful—a victory over obstacles.
More than a hundred years after Brown wrote, Black writers like Toni Morrison and David Bradley work in a very different historical context. Yet one of the major themes for these two writers, the inves-
(30) tigation of relationships between North American and African culture, is as deeply historical as Brown's concern with slavery. Both Morrison and Bradley address the close relationships between myth and history by writing of people who undertake the
(35) archetypal quest for selfhood. Their characters are compelled to confront not only their own personal histories, but their cultural histories as well. Both of these writers also explore this cultural history stylistically, by experimenting with rhetorical
(40) devices traditionally identified with both African and Western experience, including the oral narra-
tive and the mythological theme of the journey to the home of one's ancestors.
Reaching into the past has meant that spiritual-
(45) ity, religion, and the supernatural play an important role in the work of both of these writers. Yet rather than mythologizing history, as some of their prede-cessors had done, these writers chose to explore the mythical aspects already present in African American
(50) culture. Both emphasize that religion for many con-temporary Black Americans can be at the same time a reclamation of African philosophy and a reenvi-sioning of the Judeo-Christian tradition; religion is for these writers the source of a conviction that
(55) knowledge of one's ancestors is crucial to self-knowledge. By developing these ancient themes, Morrison and Bradley have considerably expanded the boundaries of the Romantic tradition in which they have worked.

16 Which of the following titles best summarizes the content of the passage?

(A) A Return to Romance: The Contemporary Revival of a Nineteenth-Century Tradition
(B) The Role of Plot and Character in the Black American Literary Tradition
(C) Oral Narrative and Religion in the Romantic Fiction of Black American Novelists
(D) Moral Conflict in Literature: Slavery and the Black American Novelist
(E) History and the Romantic Tradition in Black American Fiction

17 It can be inferred from the passage that by describing the characters in Brown's *Clotel* as "idealized" (line 14), the author means that they

(A) believe themselves to be more virtuous than they actually are
(B) are not particularly realistic but represent attitudes admired by Brown
(C) represent the kind of person Brown would have liked to be
(D) are as close to being perfectly described as fictional characters can be
(E) are blind to the real problems that prevent them from succeeding

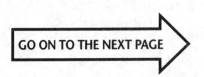
GO ON TO THE NEXT PAGE

18 The "quest for selfhood" (line 35) undertaken by Morrison's and Bradley's characters is best described as an effort to

(A) come closer to the spiritual perfection described in Romantic fiction
(B) learn to describe their personal experiences through traditional storytelling
(C) understand themselves in terms of both their personal and their cultural pasts
(D) investigate the mythical and spiritual characteristics of their predecessors
(E) assert their own attitudes and ideas, especially when they differ from those of their ancestors

19 By stating that Morrison and Bradley explore history "stylistically" (line 39), the author means that they

(A) believe that style is the most important element in their fiction
(B) use a variety of fashionable techniques
(C) researched their own families before writing about their characters' ancestors
(D) use traditional forms of expression in writing current fiction
(E) use words and phrases from ancient languages to make their novels more authentic

20 Which of the following best describes the structure of the author's discussion in this passage?

(A) Examination of the aspects of Brown's work that led to important later developments in Black Romantic literature
(B) Description of first the advantages and then the disadvantages of the use of Romance in Black fiction
(C) Use of early and recent examples to demonstrate both change and continuity in Black Romantic fiction
(D) Use of comparison to demonstrate that contemporary Black Romantic fiction is superior to that of the nineteenth century
(E) Discussion of the work of three authors in order to develop a general definition of the Romantic literary genre

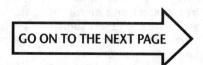
GO ON TO THE NEXT PAGE

Questions 21-30 are based on the following passage.

The following excerpt from a novel focuses on a single photograph of a father and son taken in 1942 by a family friend.

Even without the shadow that partially obscures the child's face, it would be difficult to read much into its full anonymous curves. The sun is directly
Line overhead, so that the cap's brim shadows most of
(5) his face. Only the eyebrows, cheeks, and nose catch the sun directly, making them appear touched with the dead white of clown's paint. This, in turn, may lead us to see more sadness in the eyes than is really there, as though they have been baffled wit-
(10) nesses to some violent tableau. The chin is tucked downward so that the eyes must glance up to greet the camera, giving to the entire figure a quality of uncertainty, of barely contained fear. Even the timorous lip-trembling half-smile contributes to
(15) this effect. But perhaps he is only uncomfortable. The folds in his plaid jacket and trousers suggest they are made of wool, and the cap is certainly of camel's hair. Yet the full-leafed trees and shrub-bery visible in the photograph suggest midsum-
(20) mer, and with the sun overhead, the wincing look on the child's round face may be the result of coarse wool chafing his skin. At any rate, he seems uncomfortable and shy, with feet pigeon-toed awkwardly together. The single detail that
(25) argues against this impression is that he has hooked his thumbs into the pockets of his jacket, and his surprisingly long, lean fingers lend the gesture a note of adult confidence, even of swagger. These hands, which will later be much admired,
(30) are thus unconsciously arranged in a posture that will become habitual. There is another photograph, taken a quarter-century later, in which the hands are identically arranged, thumbs hooked into the pockets of a midnight-blue tuxedo jacket. And yet,
(35) taken in its entirety, there is little enough visible in the child's picture to provoke narration. Indeed, the cap, the chubby, boyish face, the sagging jacket, the wrinkled trousers are assembled into an almost anonymous image of a well-fed, modestly well-
(40) dressed little boy. Those who knew his son at the same age would have seen an astonishing similar-ity to the child who poses here, but the son is not born until nearly two decades after this photograph is made.

(45) "Stand just there, by your father," Juanita says. The boy moves stiffly to the left, never taking his eyes from the camera in her hands. "Closer, now." He inches his left foot out, and brings his right up to join it. Then he ducks his head to avoid the
(50) stabbing rays of the sun, but still keeps his eyes firmly fixed on the camera, as though it is the only presence here besides himself, its twinkling eye his trusty guardian. Suddenly his slight body stiffens as a large hand is placed firmly between
(55) his shoulders. It feels immense, and he thinks it could crush his back as easily as it crumples an empty package of cigarettes. And now his own hands, which had hung loosely at his sides, feel weak and threatened. They will never possess the
(60) strength of the densely muscled, tightly tendoned hand that rests sinisterly on his back. He fears that as he grows they will remain weak and small, never capable of seizing with carefully aligned thumbs the leather-wrapped handle of a golf club,
(65) of grasping the butts of revolvers, the ivory steer-ing wheel of an automobile, the wooden T of lawnmower handles. Yet he cannot be ashamed of them, for they are sturdy enough, capable of hold-ing open the pages of a book, of guiding pencils
(70) and crayons into recognizable approximations of houses and horses and dump trucks. Unsure though he is of their ultimate abilities, the child nonethe-less takes premature joy in the work of hands, and cannot be ashamed of his own. Therefore, he brings
(75) them slightly forward, hooking his thumbs into his jacket pocket, and lightly curling his fingers down against the plaid of the fabric. The trembling that began in them when the man's large hand was placed between his shoulders is stilled now.

21 The opening two sentences (lines 1-5) introduce a sense of

(A) mystery
(B) malice
(C) intense emotion
(D) disillusionment
(E) youthful innocence

GO ON TO THE NEXT PAGE

22 The effect of the sentence beginning "But perhaps" (line 15) is to

(A) introduce the author's change of attitude from criticism of the boy to sympathy
(B) lighten the tone by revealing the humor in the situation
(C) suggest that the boy's expression is open to interpretation
(D) express an opinion that is not supported by the photograph
(E) furnish a clue to the author's identity and relationship to the boy

23 The description of the clothing in lines 16-22 contributes to a sense of the

(A) comical nature of the scene
(B) family's eccentricity
(C) family's extreme poverty
(D) boy's independent spirit
(E) boy's overall unease

24 As used in line 28, "a note" most nearly means

(A) an observation
(B) a brief record
(C) an element
(D) a message
(E) a comment

25 In the second paragraph, the father is portrayed as exemplifying

(A) virile competence
(B) sophisticated intellect
(C) courageous perseverance
(D) unpredictable irrationality
(E) paternal generosity

26 How does the second paragraph function in relation to the first paragraph?

(A) It reiterates comments in the first paragraph.
(B) It provides clarification of ambiguities in the first paragraph.
(C) It functions as an extension of an analogy begun in the first paragraph.
(D) It uses information from the first paragraph to make predictions.
(E) It provides a more abstract argument than does the first paragraph.

27 The author's reference to "his trusty guardian" (line 53) suggests that the

(A) child is obliged to find comfort in an inanimate object
(B) child is fascinated by sparkling images
(C) child respects Juanita more than he respects his father
(D) father is more reliable than he appears to be
(E) father has always considered his child's happiness before his own

28 Which aspect of the author's description emphasizes a major contrast in the passage?

(A) The boy's face
(B) The boy's cap
(C) The photographer
(D) The characters' hands
(E) The sun

29 The second paragraph suggests that the boy in the photograph apparently regards his father with

(A) embittered resentment
(B) indifferent dismissal
(C) cynical suspicion
(D) fearful respect
(E) proud possessiveness

30 Throughout the passage, the primary focus is on

(A) the implications of the boy's pose in the photograph
(B) reasons for the photograph's existence
(C) mysteries solved by evidence in the photograph
(D) the valuable memories evoked by old photographs
(E) speculations about the age of the boy in the photograph

IF YOU FINISH BEFORE TIME IS CALLED, YOU MAY CHECK YOUR WORK ON THIS SECTION ONLY. DO NOT TURN TO ANY OTHER SECTION IN THE TEST. **STOP**

Time—30 Minutes 25 Questions	This section contains two types of questions. You have 30 minutes to complete both types. You may use any available space for scratchwork.

Notes:

1. The use of a calculator is permitted. All numbers used are real numbers.

2. Figures that accompany problems in this test are intended to provide information useful in solving the problems. They are drawn as accurately as possible EXCEPT when it is stated in a specific problem that the figure is not drawn to scale. All figures lie in a plane unless otherwise indicated.

Reference Information

$A = \pi r^2$
$C = 2\pi r$

$A = \ell w$

$A = \frac{1}{2}bh$

$V = \ell w h$

$V = \pi r^2 h$

$c^2 = a^2 + b^2$

Special Right Triangles

The number of degrees of arc in a circle is 360.
The measure in degrees of a straight angle is 180.
The sum of the measures in degrees of the angles of a triangle is 180.

Directions for Quantitative Comparison Questions

Questions 1-15 each consist of two quantities in boxes, one in Column A and one in Column B. You are to compare the two quantities and on the answer sheet fill in oval

  A if the quantity in Column A is greater;
  B if the quantity in Column B is greater;
  C if the two quantities are equal;
  D if the relationship cannot be determined from the information given.

AN E RESPONSE WILL NOT BE SCORED.

Notes:

1. In some questions, information is given about one or both of the quantities to be compared. In such cases, the given information is centered above the two columns and is not boxed.
2. In a given question, a symbol that appears in both columns represents the same thing in Column A as it does in Column B.
3. Letters such as x, n, and k stand for real numbers.

	EXAMPLES		
	Column A	**Column B**	**Answers**
E1	5^2	20	● Ⓑ Ⓒ Ⓓ Ⓔ
	$150° \; x°$		
E2	x	30	Ⓐ Ⓑ ● Ⓓ Ⓔ
	r and s are integers.		
E3	$r + 1$	$s - 1$	Ⓐ Ⓑ Ⓒ ● Ⓔ

GO ON TO THE NEXT PAGE

557

SUMMARY DIRECTIONS FOR COMPARISON QUESTIONS

<u>Answer</u>: A if the quantity in Column A is greater;
B if the quantity in Column B is greater;
C if the two quantities are equal;
D if the relationship cannot be determined from the information given.

Column A	Column B

1 | 10 percent of 500 | 5 |

The number 34,759 is to be rounded to the nearest thousand.

2 | The digit in the thousands place of the rounded number | The digit in the hundreds place of the rounded number |

A club sold a total of 200 candy bars, some at $0.50 each and the rest at $1.00 each.

3 | The total amount collected from the sale of the $0.50 candy bars | The total amount collected from the sale of the $1.00 candy bars |

$$a = 2$$
$$c = 3$$

4 | $ab + 5$ | $a(b + c)$ |

$$x < 6 + y$$

5 | x | y |

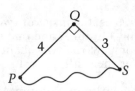

Column A — 280   Column B
90 + 90 + 100 + n   360
280 + n = 360

The angles of a quadrilateral have measures 90°, 90°, 100°, and $n°$.

6 | 80 ~~n~~ | 90 |

b

$$d > 1$$

7 | $\dfrac{d}{d - 1}$ | 1 |

Q
4   3
P   S

8 | The length of the curved path from point P to point S | 5 |

Two sets of vertical angles are formed by two intersecting lines. The sum of the measures of one set of vertical angles is $2x$ and the sum of the measures of the other set is $2y$.

9 | x | y |

GO ON TO THE NEXT PAGE

SUMMARY DIRECTIONS FOR COMPARISON QUESTIONS

<u>Answer:</u> A if the quantity in Column A is greater;
B if the quantity in Column B is greater;
C if the two quantities are equal;
D if the relationship cannot be determined from the information given.

Column A   **Column B**

<u>Questions 10-11</u> refer to the following definition.

Let $\langle m, n \rangle$ be defined as the set of all integers between m and n, excluding m and n. For example, $\langle 0, 3.5 \rangle = \{1, 2, 3\}$.

x is in $\langle 2, 6 \rangle$.
y is in $\langle 6, 9 \rangle$.

10 | x | y

z is in $\langle \sqrt{5}, \pi \rangle$

11 | z | 3

All of the members of Club M also belong to Club P. Club P has exactly 20 members.

12 | The number of members in Club M | 15

$s = a - b$
$t = b - c$
$u = c - a$

13 | $s + t + u$ | 0

Column A   **Column B**

x represents the sum of the first 20 positive integers.

y represents the sum of the first 10 positive integers.

14 | $x - y$ | 100

SOYBEAN PRODUCTION IN STATE Z

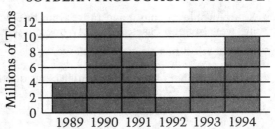

Soybean production decreased by x percent from 1990 to 1991 and increased by y percent from 1993 to 1994 in State Z.

15 | x | y

GO ON TO THE NEXT PAGE

559

Directions for Student-Produced Response Questions

Each of the remaining 10 questions requires you to solve the problem and enter your answer by marking the ovals in the special grid, as shown in the examples below.

Answer: $\frac{7}{12}$ or 7/12

Answer: 2.5

Answer: 201
Either position is correct.

Write answer → in boxes.

←Fraction line

←Decimal point

Grid in → result.

Note: You may start your answers in any column, space permitting. Columns not needed should be left blank.

- Mark no more than one oval in any column.

- Because the answer sheet will be machine-scored, **you will receive credit only if the ovals are filled in correctly.**

- Although not required, it is suggested that you write your answer in the boxes at the top of the columns to help you fill in the ovals accurately.

- Some problems may have more than one correct answer. In such cases, grid only one answer.

- No question has a negative answer.

- **Mixed numbers** such as $2\frac{1}{2}$ must be gridded as 2.5 or 5/2. (If 2 1 / 2 is gridded, it will be interpreted as $\frac{21}{2}$, not $2\frac{1}{2}$.)

- **Decimal Accuracy**: If you obtain a decimal answer, **enter the most accurate value the grid will accommodate.** For example, if you obtain an answer such as 0.6666 . . . , you should record the result as .666 or .667. **Less accurate values such as .66 or .67 are not acceptable.**

Acceptable ways to grid $\frac{2}{3}$ = .6666 . . .

16 If $a > 1$ and $a^b a^4 = a^{12}$, what is the value of b ?

17 If $s = \frac{1}{x}$ and $q = \frac{1}{y}$ and if $x = 2$ and $y = 3$, what is the value of $\frac{1}{s} + \frac{1}{q}$?

GO ON TO THE NEXT PAGE

18 The grand prize for winning a contest is $10,000. After 28 percent of the prize is deducted for taxes, the winner receives the balance of the prize in annual payouts of equal amounts over a 3-year period. How many dollars will the prizewinner receive each year of the 3 years? (Disregard the $ sign when gridding your answer.)

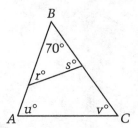

19 In $\triangle ABC$ above, what is the value of $r + s + u + v$?

20 If $x^2 > x^4$ and $x > 0$, what is one possible value for x ?

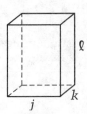

21 In the figure above, the area of the base of the rectangular box is 21 and the area of one of the faces is 30. Each of the dimensions j, k, and ℓ is an integer greater than 1. What is the volume of the rectangular box?

GO ON TO THE NEXT PAGE

$$\begin{array}{r} AB \\ + BA \\ \hline CD4 \end{array}$$

22 In the correctly worked addition problem above, each letter represents a different nonzero digit. What is one possible value of the two-digit number represented above as AB ?

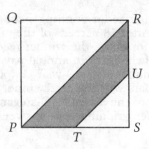

24 In square $PQRS$ above, $QR = 1$, $RU = US$, and $PT = TS$. What is the area of the shaded region?

23 If x and y are positive integers, $x + y < 15$, and $x > 5$, what is the greatest possible value of $x - y$?

25 A barrel contains only apples and oranges. There are twice as many apples as oranges. The apples are either red or yellow, and 4 times as many apples are red as are yellow. If one piece of fruit is to be drawn at random from the barrel, what is the probability that the piece drawn will be a yellow apple?

IF YOU FINISH BEFORE TIME IS CALLED, YOU MAY CHECK YOUR WORK ON THIS SECTION ONLY. DO NOT TURN TO ANY OTHER SECTION IN THE TEST. STOP

Time — 30 Minutes
36 Questions

For each question in this section, select the best answer from among the choices given and fill in the corresponding oval on the answer sheet.

Each sentence below has one or two blanks, each blank indicating that something has been omitted. Beneath the sentence are five words or sets of words labeled A through E. Choose the word or set of words that, when inserted in the sentence, best fits the meaning of the sentence as a whole.

Example:

Medieval kingdoms did not become constitutional republics overnight; on the contrary, the change was ----.

(A) unpopular
(B) unexpected
(C) advantageous
(D) sufficient
(E) gradual
     Ⓐ Ⓑ Ⓒ Ⓓ ●

1 The visitor was of an ---- age: white-haired, but baby-faced, he might have been twenty-five or fifty.

(A) assiduous   (B) unalterable   (C) indecorous
    (D) indeterminate   (E) extenuating

2 Unfortunately, for North American Indians the arrival of European settlers often meant ---- their lands, their ways of life, and even their very existence.

(A) a renewal of
(B) a respect for
(C) an assault on
(D) a retention of
(E) an idea of

3 Different species of mosquito conduct the essential activities of eating, growing, and reproducing in so many ways that no rule of mosquito behavior is without some ----.

(A) result   (B) objectivity   (C) exception
    (D) clarity   (E) enforcement

4 Even more interesting than the completed masterpiece can be the ---- work of the artist: the first-draft manuscript, the initial pencil sketches, the symphony rehearsal.

(A) rough   (B) intense   (C) varied
    (D) thoughtless   (E) atypical

5 Oceanographic research has shown that ridges on the ocean floor are not ---- features, but part of a 4,000-mile-long mountain range.

(A) conditional   (B) unchanging
  (C) observable   (D) definable
    (E) isolated

6 Although Jack and Mary Lynch are often ---- to strangers, they show only ---- to a pack of nearly extinct buffalo wolves, working seven days a week to help save the endangered species.

(A) gracious. .disdain
(B) rude. .exasperation
(C) gruff. .kindness
(D) agreeable. .gentleness
(E) condescending. .hostility

7 We need not be ---- about our performance thus far, but neither should we be ----: there is ample room for improvement.

(A) haughty. .generous
(B) lazy. .industrious
(C) apologetic. .smug
(D) opulent. .showy
(E) sympathetic. .crude

8 The art collection of the children's museum is quite ----, ranging from furniture to sculpture to finger painting.

(A) imaginary   (B) repetitive   (C) elusive
    (D) eclectic   (E) circumscribed

9 By subsidizing small farms, the new government is hoping to ---- the flow of people into the cities and ---- farming.

(A) reverse. .incorporate
(B) arrest. .encourage
(C) boost. .initiate
(D) enhance. .regulate
(E) diminish. .prohibit

10 Despite Atlanta's large Black community, African American theater companies in that city are anything but ----; in fact, in 1993 there was only one, Jomandi Productions.

(A) legion   (B) advantageous   (C) bourgeois
    (D) nondescript   (E) wily

GO ON TO THE NEXT PAGE

Each question below consists of a related pair of words or phrases, followed by five pairs of words or phrases labeled A through E. Select the pair that best expresses a relationship similar to that expressed in the original pair.

Example:

CRUMB : BREAD ::
(A) ounce : unit
(B) splinter : wood
(C) water : bucket
(D) twine : rope
(E) cream : butter

Ⓐ ● Ⓒ Ⓓ Ⓔ

11 CAMERA : PHOTOGRAPHER ::
(A) house : architect
(B) sink : plumber
(C) studio : painter
(D) meat : butcher
(E) drill : dentist

12 FORMAT : NEWSPAPER ::
(A) binding : book
(B) design : building
(C) direction : sign
(D) market : commodity
(E) catalogue : library

13 DECIBEL : SOUND ::
(A) ingredient : food
(B) ruler : length
(C) calories : menu
(D) degree : temperature
(E) headphones : music

14 ARID : DRY ::
(A) glacial : cold
(B) coastal : tidal
(C) damp : muddy
(D) snowbound : polar
(E) shallow : deep

15 FISSION : ENERGY ::
(A) reaction : response
(B) distortion : image
(C) nutrient : growth
(D) evaporation : liquid
(E) combustion : heat

16 LOBBYIST : CAUSE ::
(A) legislator : voter
(B) clergy : congregation
(C) advertiser : product
(D) defendant : verdict
(E) consumer : goods

17 JOURNAL : ARTICLE ::
(A) dance : ballet
(B) magazine : cover
(C) set : scenery
(D) anthology : poem
(E) concert : orchestra

18 EMISSARY : REPRESENT ::
(A) draftee : enroll
(B) novice : train
(C) president : elect
(D) guard : protect
(E) comedian : laugh

19 POTENTATE : POWER ::
(A) broadcaster : news
(B) virtuoso : skill
(C) protégé : sponsorship
(D) maverick : group
(E) colleague : camaraderie

20 POSTSCRIPT : LETTER ::
(A) preamble : document
(B) footnote : reference
(C) epilogue : play
(D) signature : name
(E) index : page

21 IMPIOUS : REVERENCE ::
(A) profane : behavior
(B) paranoid : persecution
(C) contrite : offense
(D) superficial : depth
(E) contemptuous : scorn

22 DISINGENUOUS : CRAFTINESS ::
(A) ecstatic : contentment
(B) idolatrous : doubt
(C) narcissistic : appearance
(D) penitent : wrongdoing
(E) surreptitious : stealth

23 EXCULPATE : BLAME ::
(A) extricate : difficulty
(B) exemplify : illustration
(C) expedite : process
(D) divulge : secret
(E) bewilder : confusion

GO ON TO THE NEXT PAGE →

The passage below is followed by questions based on its content. Answer the questions on the basis of what is <u>stated</u> or <u>implied</u> in the passage and in any introductory material that may be provided.

Questions 24-36 are based on the following passage.

The following passage is adapted from a book published in 1990. It is about unusual scientific enterprises that to some seemed impossible.

Gerald Feinberg, the Columbia University physicist, once went so far as to declare that "everything possible will eventually be accomplished." He
Line didn't even think it would take very long for this
(5) to happen: "I am inclined to put two hundred years as an upper limit for the accomplishment of any possibility that we can imagine today."

Well, that of course left only the impossible as the one thing remaining for daring intellectual
(10) adventurers to whittle away at. Feinberg, for one, thought that they'd succeed even here. "Everything will be accomplished that does not violate known fundamental laws of science," he said, "as well as many things that do violate those laws."

(15) So in no small numbers scientists tried to do the impossible. And how understandable this was. For what does the independent and inquiring mind hate more than being told that something just can't be done, pure and simple, by any agency at all, at any
(20) time, no matter what. Indeed, the whole concept of the impossible was something of an affront to creativity and advanced intelligence, which was why being told that something was impossible was an unparalleled stimulus for getting all sorts of
(25) people to try to accomplish it anyway, as witness all the attempts to build perpetual motion machines, antigravity generators, time-travel vehicles, and all the rest.

Besides, there was always the residual possi-
(30) bility that the naysayers would turn out to be wrong and the yeasayers right, and that one day the latter would reappear to laugh in your face. As one cryonicist* put it, "When you die, you're dead. When I die, I might come back. So who's
(35) the dummy?"

It was a point worth considering. How many times in the past had certain things been said to be impossible, only to have it turn out shortly thereafter that the item in question had already
(40) been done or soon would be. What greater cliché was there in the history of science than the comic litany of false it-couldn't-be-dones; the infamous case of Auguste Comte saying in 1844 that it would never be known what the stars were made

(45) of, followed in a few years by the spectroscope being applied to starlight to reveal the stars' chemical composition; or the case of Lord Rutherford, the man who discovered the structure of the atom, saying in 1933 that dreams of controlled nuclear
(50) fission were "moonshine."

And those weren't even the worst examples. No, the huffiest of all it-couldn't-be-done claims centered on the notion that human beings could actually fly, either at all, or across long distances,
(55) or to the moon, the stars, or wherever else. It was as if for unstated reasons human flight was something that couldn't be allowed to happen. "The demonstration that no possible combination of known substances, known forms of machinery and
(60) known forms of force, can be united in a practical machine by which man shall fly long distances through the air, seems to the writer as complete as it is possible for the demonstration of any physical fact to be." That was Simon Newcomb, the Johns
(65) Hopkins University mathematician and astronomer in 1906, three years after the Wright brothers actually flew.

There had been so many embarrassments of this type that about midcentury Arthur C. Clarke came
(70) out with a guideline for avoiding them, which he termed Clarke's Law: "When a distinguished but elderly scientist states that something is possible, he is almost certainly right. When he states that something is impossible, he is very probably wrong."

(75) Still, one had to admit there were lots of things left that were really and truly impossible, even if it took some ingenuity in coming up with a proper list of examples. Such as: "A camel cannot pass through the eye of a needle." (Well, unless of course
(80) it was a very large needle.) Or: "It is impossible for a door to be simultaneously open and closed." (Well, unless of course it was a revolving door.)

Indeed, watertight examples of the really and truly impossible were so exceptionally hard to
(85) come by that paradigm cases turned out to be either trivial or absurd. "I know I will never play the piano like Vladimir Horowitz," offered Milton Rothman, a physicist, "no matter how hard I try." Or, from Scott Lankford, a mountaineer: "Everest
(90) on roller skates."

No one would bother trying to overcome those impossibilities, but off in the distance loomed some other, more metaphysically profound specimens. They beckoned like the Mount Everests of

GO ON TO THE NEXT PAGE

(95) science: antigravity generators, faster-than-light travel, antimatter propulsion, space warps, time machines. There were physicists aplenty who took a look at these peaks and decided they had to climb them.

*Someone who believes in the possibility of freezing the dead and reanimating them at some later date when it is technically feasible to do so.

24 As used in line 5, the word "inclined" most nearly means

(A) headed upward
(B) deviated
(C) oblique
(D) prejudiced
(E) disposed

25 If the claim made by Feinberg in lines 11-14 should turn out to be true, which of the following must also be true?

(A) Science works by great leaps, not little steps.
(B) Scientists will work harder than they do today.
(C) Scientists' knowledge of fundamental laws is incomplete.
(D) The rate of scientific discovery will decrease.
(E) The definition of the impossible will remain constant.

26 The motivation ascribed to "no small numbers" (line 15) of scientists is most nearly analogous to that of

(A) treasure hunters who have recently found a map indicating the exact location of an extremely valuable treasure
(B) underdogs who have been told that they do not have a chance of beating the defending champions
(C) a police detective who works night and day to bring a dangerous criminal to justice
(D) a project director who oversees a project carefully to see that it comes in under budget
(E) a scientist who performs experiments to show that a rival's theory is not supported by the evidence

27 In what sense was the concept of the impossible an "affront" (line 21)?

(A) It implied that previous scientific achievements were not very impressive.
(B) It suggested that the creativity of scientists was limited.
(C) It called into question the value of scientific research.
(D) It implied that scientists work for personal glory rather than for practical advantages.
(E) It blurred the distinction between science and religious belief.

28 The devices mentioned in lines 26-28 are cited as examples of

(A) projects that will be completed in the near future
(B) the kinds of things that can be considered only in science fiction
(C) devices that will enhance the well-being of humanity
(D) proof of the irresponsibility of leading scientists
(E) impossible projects that have generated much interest

29 The cryonicist's remarks (lines 33-35) depend on the notion that the cryonicist has

(A) everything to gain and nothing to lose
(B) a reasonable chance of remaining healthy for several years
(C) only one chance in life
(D) total confidence in technological progress
(E) greater intellectual powers than others

30 The author cites Lord Rutherford's accomplishment (lines 47-48) in order to show that

(A) even the most knowledgeable scientists are often too pessimistic
(B) many failed to see the negative aspects of nuclear technology
(C) Rutherford predicted future events more reliably than did Comte
(D) only those with technical expertise can predict future developments
(E) experts in one field should do research in that field only

GO ON TO THE NEXT PAGE

31 It can be inferred from the passage that the author considers Newcomb's comments (lines 57-64) more irresponsible than Comte's (lines 42-45) for which of the following reasons?

(A) Newcomb spoke on a subject in which he had almost no expertise.
(B) Newcomb made his assertions after the basic principle that suggested the contrary had been demonstrated.
(C) Newcomb was too willing to listen to those whose point of view was not sufficiently rigorous.
(D) Newcomb was disappointed not to be the first to announce the accomplishment of a feat previously thought impossible.
(E) Newcomb disagreed with those who had supported his views in the past.

32 The assumption in Clarke's Law (lines 71-74) is that

(A) if an experiment is repeated often enough it will prove or disprove a hypothesis to the extent that the results are identical in every case
(B) it is unlikely that those who have devoted their lives to the study of a particular science can imagine possibilities that run counter to their experience
(C) scientific discoveries grow not so much out of the lives and careers of individual scientists as out of the spirit of the age
(D) scientists who are embroiled in a controversy are less likely to make valid deductions than an impartial observer would be
(E) works of science fiction are often useful in predicting the future course of scientific progress

33 The parenthetical remarks in lines 79-82 serve to

(A) indicate why those who disagree with the author are in error
(B) support the author's position by citing authorities
(C) distance the author from controversial opinions
(D) point out problems with certain examples of the impossible
(E) prove that many arguments advanced earlier are sound

34 The implication of the author's comments in lines 83-86 is that

(A) scientists who focus on the impossible do not pay enough attention to details
(B) a scientist's notions of the impossible reveal the biases of the scientist's particular field
(C) in the past, things thought to be impossible have often turned out to be the next major scientific breakthrough
(D) the difficulty of finding examples supports the idea that most things thought to be impossible might be achieved
(E) people define as impossible things that they themselves find too difficult to be worth attempting

35 The reference to Mount Everest in lines 89-90 differs from that in lines 94-95 in that the first reference is an example of

(A) something easy to do, whereas the second reference is an example of something difficult
(B) goals that have been achieved in the past, whereas the second reference is an example of goals to be considered
(C) a tall mountain, whereas the second reference is an example of the tallest mountain
(D) an old-fashioned goal, whereas the second reference is an example of spiritual inspiration
(E) something outlandish, whereas the second reference is an example of a goal worth pursuing

36 Unlike the impossibilities mentioned in lines 86-90, those mentioned in lines 95-97 are

(A) considered worth attempting by some scientists
(B) now considered possible by most scientists
(C) absurd examples found only in science fiction
(D) without practical applications
(E) not really impossible, just prohibitively expensive

IF YOU FINISH BEFORE TIME IS CALLED, YOU MAY CHECK YOUR WORK ON THIS SECTION ONLY. DO NOT TURN TO ANY OTHER SECTION IN THE TEST. STOP

567

Section 6   6   6   6

<table>
<tr><td>Time—15 Minutes
10 Questions</td><td>In this section solve each problem, using any available space on the page for scratchwork. Then decide which is the best of the choices given and fill in the corresponding oval on the answer sheet.</td></tr>
</table>

Notes:

1. The use of a calculator is permitted. All numbers used are real numbers.

2. Figures that accompany problems in this test are intended to provide information useful in solving the problems. They are drawn as accurately as possible EXCEPT when it is stated in a specific problem that the figure is not drawn to scale. All figures lie in a plane unless otherwise indicated.

Reference Information

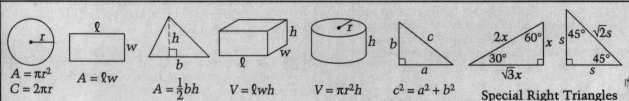

$A = \pi r^2$
$C = 2\pi r$

$A = \ell w$

$A = \frac{1}{2}bh$

$V = \ell w h$

$V = \pi r^2 h$

$c^2 = a^2 + b^2$

Special Right Triangles

The number of degrees of arc in a circle is 360.
The measure in degrees of a straight angle is 180.
The sum of the measures in degrees of the angles of a triangle is 180.

---

1 If $a + 2a + 3a = 3b - 3$ and if $b = 1$, what is the value of a ?

(A) 0
(B) $\frac{1}{6}$
(C) 1
(D) 3
(E) 6

3 The product of two integers is between 102 and 115. Which of the following CANNOT be one of the integers?

(A) 5
(B) 10
(C) 12
(D) 15
(E) 20

TABLE OF APPROXIMATE CONVERSIONS

Number of Inches	5	10	x
Number of Centimeters	12.7	25.4	50.8

2 What is the value of x in the table above?

(A) 15
(B) 18
(C) 20
(D) 22
(E) 25

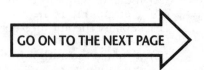

GO ON TO THE NEXT PAGE

Questions 4-5 refer to the following information.

Two companies charge different rates for painting lines on a road.

• Company *X* charges $0.50 per foot of line painted and no base price.

• Company *Y* charges a base price of $100.00 plus $0.30 per foot of line painted.

4 Which of the following expressions gives the charge, in dollars, for painting *f* feet of line if Company *X* does the job?

(A) 0.20*f*

(B) 0.50*f*

(C) *f* + 0.50

(D) 0.20*f* + 100

(E) $\dfrac{f}{0.50}$

5 Which of the following graphs could show the relation between the length of line painted and the charge if Company *Y* does the job?

(A)
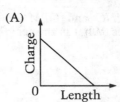

(B)
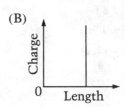

(C)
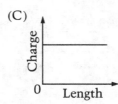

(D)
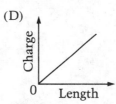

(E)
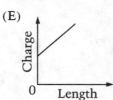

GO ON TO THE NEXT PAGE

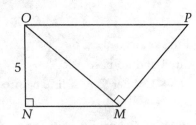

Note: Figure not drawn to scale.

6 In the figure above, *MNO* and *OPM* are isosceles right triangles. What is the length of *OP* ?

(A) 8

(B) 10

(C) $5\sqrt{3}$ (approximately 8.66)

(D) $7\sqrt{2}$ (approximately 9.90)

(E) $5\sqrt{5}$ (approximately 11.18)

7 If the average (arithmetic mean) of 5 consecutive even integers is n, what is the median of these 5 integers?

(A) 0
(B) 2
(C) n
(D) $n - 2$
(E) $n - 4$

8 If a and b are different positive integers and $5a + b = 32$, what is the sum of all possible values of a ?

(A) 6
(B) 11
(C) 15
(D) 18
(E) 21

GO ON TO THE NEXT PAGE

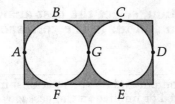

9   In the figure above, the circles touch each other and touch the sides of the rectangle at the lettered points shown. The radius of each circle is 1. Of the following, which is the best approximation of the area of the shaded region?

(A) 6
(B) 4
(C) 3
(D) 2
(E) 1

P   T   ℓ

10   In the figure above, points P and T lie on line ℓ. How many different points on ℓ are twice as far from point T as from point P?

(A) None
(B) One
(C) Two
(D) Four
(E) More than four

IF YOU FINISH BEFORE TIME IS CALLED, YOU MAY CHECK YOUR WORK ON THIS SECTION ONLY. DO NOT TURN TO ANY OTHER SECTION IN THE TEST. **STOP**

571

For each question in this section, select the best answer from among the choices given and fill in the corresponding oval on the answer sheet.

The two passages below are followed by questions based on their content and on the relationship between the two passages. Answer the questions on the basis of what is <u>stated</u> or <u>implied</u> in the passages and in any introductory material that may be provided.

Questions 1-12 are based on the following passages.

These passages, adapted from works by prominent twentieth-century British authors, are about Joan of Arc (c. 1412-1431), a young Frenchwoman who played a major role in the Hundred Years' War between France and England. She came to prominence when English forces occupied much of French territory.

Passage 1

The report of a supernatural visitant sent by God to save France, which inspired the French, clouded the minds and froze the energies of the English. The sense of awe, and even of fear, robbed them of
(5) their assurance. Upon Joan's invocation the spirit of victory changed sides, and the French began an offensive that never rested until the English invaders were driven out of France. She called for an immediate onslaught upon the besiegers, and herself led
(10) the storming parties against them. Wounded by an arrow, she plucked it out and returned to the charge. She mounted the scaling-ladders and was hurled half-stunned into the ditch. Prostrate on the ground, she commanded new efforts. "Forward, fellow coun-
(15) trymen!" she cried. "God has delivered them into our hands." One by one the English forts fell and their garrisons were slain. The siege was broken, and Orléans was saved. The English retired in good order, and the Maid[1] prudently restrained the citi-
(20) zens from pursuing them into the open country.

Despite her victories and her services to Charles VII, King of France, the attitude of both the Court and the Church toward Joan eventually began changing. It became clear that she served God
(25) rather than the Church,[2] and France rather than one particular political interest. Indeed, the whole conception of France seems to have sprung and radiated from her. Thus, the powerful particularist interests which had hitherto supported her were
(30) estranged.

Joan was captured by the Burgundians, a rival French faction of Orléans, and sold to the rejoicing English for a moderate sum. For a whole year her fate hung in the balance, while careless, ungrateful
(35) Charles lifted not a finger to save her. There is no record of any ransom being offered. History, however, has recorded the comment of an English soldier who witnessed her death at the stake. "We are lost," he said. "We have burnt a saint." All this proved true.
(40) Joan of Arc perished on May 29, 1431, and thereafter the tides of war flowed remorselessly against England.

Joan was a being so uplifted from the ordinary run of humankind that she finds no equal in a
(45) thousand years. The records of her trial present us with facts alive today through all the mists of time. Out of her own mouth can she be judged in each generation. She embodied the natural goodness and valour of the human race in unexampled
(50) perfection. Unconquerable courage, infinite compassion, the virtue of the simple, the wisdom of the just, shone forth in her. She glorifies as she freed the soil from which she sprang. All soldiers should read her story and ponder on the words and deeds
(55) of the true warrior, who in one single year, though untaught in technical arts, reveals in every situation the key of victory.

[1] Joan of Arc was known as the Maid of Orléans.
[2] The Roman Catholic church prior to the Reformation of the sixteenth century

Passage 2

Joan of Arc, a village girl from the Vosges, was born about 1412; burnt for heresy, witchcraft, and
(60) sorcery in 1431; but finally declared a saint by the Roman Catholic church in 1920. She is the most notable Warrior Saint in the Christian calendar, and the most unusual fish among the eccentric worthies of the Middle Ages. She was the pioneer
(65) of rational dressing for women, and dressed and fought and lived as men did.

Because she contrived to assert herself in all

GO ON TO THE NEXT PAGE

these ways with such force that she was famous
throughout western Europe before she was out of
(70) her teens (indeed she never got out of them), it is
hardly surprising that she was judicially burnt,
ostensibly for a number of capital crimes that we
no longer punish as such, but essentially for what
we call unwomanly and insufferable presumption.
(75) At eighteen Joan's pretensions were beyond those
of the proudest pope or the haughtiest emperor.
She claimed to be the ambassador and plenipoten-
tiary[3] of God. She patronized her own king and
summoned the English king to repentance and
(80) obedience to her commands. She lectured, talked
down, and overruled statesmen and prelates. She
pooh-poohed the plans of generals, leading their
troops to victory on plans of her own. She had an
unbounded and quite unconcealed contempt for
(85) official opinion, judgment, and authority. Had she
been a sage and monarch, her pretensions and
proceedings would have been trying to the official
mind. As her actual condition was pure upstart,
there were only two opinions about her. One was
(90) that she was miraculous: the other, that she was
unbearable.

[3] One who is given full power to act

1 Lines 10-16 portray Joan as

(A) rebellious
(B) courageous
(C) compassionate
(D) desperate
(E) fair

2 The word "retired" in line 18 most nearly means

(A) discarded
(B) recalled
(C) retreated
(D) slept peacefully
(E) ceased working

3 The sentence beginning "It became clear"
(lines 24-26) indicates that Joan

(A) was more interested in military affairs
than in religious or political ones
(B) preferred fighting for the underdog and
lost interest once her side was winning
(C) had no particular loyalties, only vague
and abstract ideas
(D) was devoted to God and country rather
than to any religious or political
institutions
(E) fought for religious reasons that had
nothing to do with her allegiance to
Charles VII

4 The statement by the English soldier in
lines 38-39 serves primarily to

(A) explain the valorous behavior of the
English in battle
(B) exemplify the awe Joan inspired in the
English soldiers
(C) illustrate the affection the English really
felt for Joan
(D) indicate the religious conviction behind
the English cause
(E) provide the justification of Joan's later
sainthood

5 The phrase "technical arts" (line 56) refers to

(A) military craft
(B) mechanical skills
(C) formal schooling
(D) practical affairs
(E) scientific knowledge

6 Which of the following best describes the
approach of Passage 1?

(A) Straightforward, factual narration
(B) Analysis of a historical theory
(C) Comparison and contrast
(D) Colorful, dramatic description
(E) Criticism couched in sarcasm

7 Passage 2 views Joan's victories as stemming
from her

(A) saintly behavior toward friend and foe alike
(B) natural goodness and essential simplicity
(C) threats to resort to witchcraft to frighten
the enemy
(D) ability to command the respect of kings
(E) strength of personality and determination

8 The phrase "her actual condition was pure
upstart" in line 88 indicates that Joan

(A) behaved spontaneously and optimistically
(B) defied conventional strategies of warfare
(C) was unaware of what was expected of her
(D) was not a member of the elite
(E) used illegal means to achieve her ends

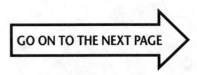
GO ON TO THE NEXT PAGE

9 Both passages discuss which of the following regarding Joan?

(A) Her moral and ethical philosophy
(B) Her military background and training
(C) Her relationship to the Church and to the state
(D) The effect of her death on the outcome of the war
(E) The views that English subjects had of her

10 Which of the following questions is NOT explicitly answered by either passage?

(A) What was Joan charged with?
(B) Why did it take so long for Joan to be honored with sainthood?
(C) Where did Joan come from?
(D) What part did Joan personally play in the battle between the English and the French?
(E) How valuable was Joan to her country?

11 Both passages agree that Joan met with resistance primarily because of her

(A) attempt to undermine the Church and its teachings
(B) headstrong behavior and unwillingness to compromise
(C) petty squabbling with officials
(D) inability to continue to win military victories
(E) refusal to accept the typical female role of her time

12 Both passages suggest which of the following about the French and English monarchies?

(A) Both monarchies felt threatened by the power that Joan was able to command.
(B) The two monarchies were unable to settle their differences because of Joan's influence.
(C) Both monarchies were torn by internal strife.
(D) The English monarchy was more intent on waging war than was the French monarchy.
(E) Religion played a more significant role in the French monarchy than in that of the English.

SAT I Scoring Worksheet

SAT I Verbal Sections

A. Section 2:

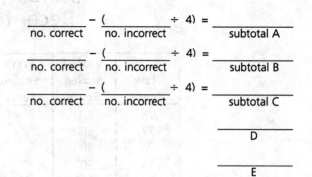

$$\underline{}_{\text{no. correct}} - (\underline{}_{\text{no. incorrect}} \div 4) = \underline{}_{\text{subtotal A}}$$

B. Section 5:

$$\underline{}_{\text{no. correct}} - (\underline{}_{\text{no. incorrect}} \div 4) = \underline{}_{\text{subtotal B}}$$

C. Section 7:

$$\underline{}_{\text{no. correct}} - (\underline{}_{\text{no. incorrect}} \div 4) = \underline{}_{\text{subtotal C}}$$

D. Total unrounded raw score
(Total A + B + C)

$$\underline{}_{\text{D}}$$

E. Total rounded raw score
(Rounded to nearest whole number)

$$\underline{}_{\text{E}}$$

F. SAT I verbal reported scaled score
(Use the conversion table)

SAT I verbal
score

SAT I Mathematical Sections

A. Section 1:

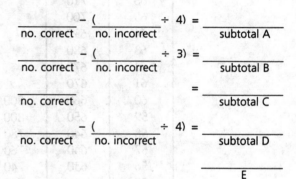

$$\underline{}_{\text{no. correct}} - (\underline{}_{\text{no. incorrect}} \div 4) = \underline{}_{\text{subtotal A}}$$

B. Section 3:
Questions 1-15 (quantitative comparison)

$$\underline{}_{\text{no. correct}} - (\underline{}_{\text{no. incorrect}} \div 3) = \underline{}_{\text{subtotal B}}$$

C. Section 3:
Questions 16-25 (student-produced response)

$$\underline{}_{\text{no. correct}} = \underline{}_{\text{subtotal C}}$$

D. Section 6:

$$\underline{}_{\text{no. correct}} - (\underline{}_{\text{no. incorrect}} \div 4) = \underline{}_{\text{subtotal D}}$$

E. Total unrounded raw score
(Total A + B + C + D)

$$\underline{}_{\text{E}}$$

F. Total rounded raw score
(Rounded to nearest whole number)

$$\underline{}_{\text{F}}$$

G. SAT I mathematical reported scaled score
(Use the conversion table)

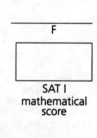

SAT I
mathematical
score

Score Conversion Table
SAT I: Reasoning Test
Sunday, May 1996
Recentered Scale

Raw Score	Verbal Scaled Score	Math Scaled Score	Raw Score	Verbal Scaled Score	Math Scaled Score
78	800		37	520	580
77	800		36	510	570
76	800		35	510	560
75	800		34	500	550
74	800		33	490	550
73	800		32	490	540
72	780		31	480	530
71	770		30	480	530
70	750		29	470	520
69	740		28	460	510
68	730		27	460	510
67	720		26	450	500
66	710		25	450	490
65	700		24	440	490
64	690		23	430	480
63	680		22	430	470
62	670		21	420	460
61	670		20	410	460
60	660	800	19	410	450
59	650	800	18	400	440
58	640	780	17	390	430
57	640	760	16	390	430
56	630	740	15	380	420
55	620	730	14	370	410
54	620	720	13	360	400
53	610	710	12	360	390
52	600	700	11	350	380
51	600	690	10	340	370
50	590	680	9	330	360
49	590	670	8	320	350
48	580	660	7	310	340
47	570	650	6	300	330
46	570	640	5	290	320
45	560	640	4	280	310
44	560	630	3	270	290
43	550	620	2	250	280
42	550	610	1	240	270
41	540	600	0	220	250
40	530	600	-1	200	240
39	530	590	-2	200	220
38	520	580	-3 and below	200	200

This table is for use only with this test.

One-on-One with the SAT®

TEST PREP FROM THE TEST MAKERS

Now you can prepare for the SAT the fun and easy way with software from the experts at the College Board!

Check out the unique features that make *One-on-One* your best choice:
Try out the enclosed free demo disk and see for yourself how *One-on-One with the SAT* can help your students do their best on the SAT.

System Requirements:
Windows 3.1 or higher; IBM PC or compatible (386 or higher); 4 Mb RAM; 10 Mb hard disk space; VGA monitor; optional sound card

- **To place an order by phone, call 1-800-323-7155, M-F, 8 a.m.–11 p.m. ET (credit card only)**
- **For information, call (212) 713-8165**

The College Board
Educational Excellence for All Students